Modernity and Crises of Identity

Modernity and Crises of Identity

Culture and Society in Fin-de-Siècle Vienna

Jacques Le Rider

Translated by Rosemary Morris

CONTINUUM · NEW YORK

1993

The Continuum Publishing Company
370 Lexington Avenue, New York, NY 10017

Printed in Great Britain

Library of Congress Cataloging-in-Publication Data
Le Rider, Jacques.
    [Modernité viennoise et crises d l'identité. English]
    Modernity and crises of identity : culture and society in fin-de-
siècle Vienna / Jacques Le Rider; translated by Rosemary Morris.
        p.   cm.
    Includes bibliographical references and index.
    ISBN 0-8264-0631-9
    1. Identity (Psychology)—History—20th century.   2. Gender
identity—History—20th century.   3. Jews—Identity—History—20th
century.   4. Vienna (Austria)—Intellectual life.   5. Civilization,
Modern—20th century—Psychological aspects.   I. Title.
BF697.L3913   1993
155.2′09436′13—dc20   93-20689
                                                             CIP

Contents

Introduction

After completing an earlier study of the works of Otto Weininger (with particular reference to the outstandingly influential *Sex and Character*), I progressed naturally towards a more wide-ranging consideration of three themes: the modernist identity crisis and the attempts to overcome it; challenges to the traditional polarization of male and female, the apparently natural foundation on which a vital part of our cultural tradition has been constructed; and finally the crisis of Jewish identity towards the close of the nineteenth century, marked in Central Europe by the final achievement of emancipation and by progressive assimilation, but also by the emergence of antisemitism and its contemporary, nationalism. These three apparently distinct themes turned out to be closely linked. If my conclusions are accepted, the three themes will in fact seem inseparable, determining the character of that period of cultural history commonly called 'Viennese modernism', which I shall define more closely in my first chapter.

The political and social emancipation of the individual, which is accepted as being part of late eighteenth-century and early nineteenth-century modernism, went hand in hand with a confident and haughty affirmation of individuality in the realms of the ethical and the aesthetic. But Schopenhauer and Nietzsche turned their attention to the ills and illusions of individualism, and their critical analysis was extended into turn-of-the-century psychology and sociology: the autonomy and isolation of the individual began to look like one of the most ambivalent manifestations of modernism. The crisis of the individual, experienced as an identity crisis, is at the heart of all the questionings we find in literature and the humane sciences, in Hugo von Hofmannsthal as much as in Freud (see chapter 2).

Some creative writers of the 1900s, reacting against feelings of isolation, the fragility of the subjective self and the instability of inner and of superficial identity, explored the possibility of rebuilding identity through what might be called radicalized individualism. Three types, the mystic (in Hofmannsthal, for example), the genius (as conceived by Otto Weininger) and Narcissus (as reinterpreted by Lou Andreas-Salomé) stand out as leading affirmations of the self-sufficiency of the individual cut off from any or all human communities: the self forced back on itself and seeing the reality of the world face to face. Here the affirmation of self-identity is reached by reformulating a philosophy which identifies spirit and being, and sees the subject and the object as one.

These types (the mystic, the genius and Narcissus) turn out in fact to be under particular threat, always bound to fleeting moments of supreme happiness or the fast-fading intoxication of omnipotence. Their inevitable collapse pitches the subject back into an even more painful feeling of discontinuity, of loss of identity. Utopian mysticism, genius and narcissism, as ways of being, share the same aspiration to transcend the limits laid down by life: they gloss over the male–female divide and incline towards an ideal of androgyny; they aspire to the self-destruction of an ego pained by its inability to accept the gifts of chance (sex, race . . .), and to the refashioning of an ego more perfect (chapters 3 and 4).

In this context we might reread the extraordinary memoirs of President Daniel Paul Schreber, or the theoretical constructs of Otto Weininger – or, again, some of the writings of the young Hofmannsthal, such as his stories of mystical experiences or of narcissistic psychoneurosis linked with the confusion of sexual identity. The failure of masculine identity was the theme which led me to compare those three authors (chapter 5). Schreber's lurking desire for femininity and Weininger's anguished rejection of it conjured from these two 'sublime madmen' bitter attacks on contemporary decadence and plans for the regeneration of the modern world. These latter characteristics proved to be typical of a certain critique of modernism found widely from Friedrich Nietzsche to Walter Benjamin, and found especially in Viennese circles, from Karl Kraus to Robert Musil (chapter 6).

The case of Otto Gross merits particular attention in this context, as representing the exact opposite of Weininger's: while *Sex and Character* pushes antifeminism to its uttermost extreme as a reaction against the feminization Weininger detected in modern culture, the works of the 'untamed' psychologist Gross end with a call to matriarchal revolution and the abolition of the Law of the Father (chapter 7).

In Freud and Hofmannsthal, and also in the paintings of Gustav Klimt, the questions, impossible yearnings and agonies which spring from reflection on the modern redistribution of masculine and feminine roles are expressed through a metaphor drawn from archaeology: the archaic Creto-Mycenaean civilization which preceded classical Greek culture. Nietzsche anticipated these themes when he introduced Ariadne, mistress of the Cretan labyrinth, alongside Dionysos. But the modernism of 1900 was no longer the modernism of the early Romantics. Whereas Hölderlin's Antigone revolts against the powerful dictatorship of Creon's patriarchal rule, Hofmannsthal's Elektra faces a chaotic world in which masculine authority has become unstable, leaving the field clear for a bloody war between mother and daughter. In 1905 the Viennese intellectual Rosa Mayreder boldly wrote that the problem of contemporary feminism was no longer the despotism of men, but their inability to keep order in the world they had put together (chapter 8).

In the *Kulturkritik* debates of the first years of the twentieth century there is another figure as omnipresent as the categories of masculine and feminine: the Jew. Alongside visions of a culture becoming dominated by the female, we find visions of a culture becoming dominated by the Jew; the antifeminism of certain critics of modernism is expressed through a logic analogous to that of antisemitism. This analogy in fact points to a deep-rooted dimension of culture in the 1900s: the emerging relationship between the masculine identity crisis – the redistribution of male and female roles – on the one hand, and the confrontation between Jews and non-Jews, on the other. The historical and sociological approach shows that the two movements – female emancipation and the emancipation of the Jews – had similar successes, similar contradictions, similar failures. Freudian theory traces antifeminism and antisemitism back to a common root in the unconscious. In the work of Arthur Schnitzler, the woman and the Jew share the difficult and sometimes tragic role of hero and victim of modernity (chapter 9).

The historical circumstances of the Jewish intellectuals who settled in Vienna helps us to understand why they in particular were predestined to experience the modern crisis of identity. The Jewish students who attended the University of Vienna during the last thirty years of the nineteenth century (from the generation of Sigmund Freud, who entered the university in 1873, to that of Karl Kraus, who entered in 1892) all suffered the shock of antisemitism. The liberal ideology, a bequest of 1848, which had favoured the assimilation of Jews into Viennese culture and society, was abruptly called into question. The shock to most of these Jewish intellectuals was particularly painful, and they surmounted it as best they could. Their milieu denied them the identity which they would have chosen and desired if left to themselves – German nationality. But their education had very largely cut them off from traditional Judaism. For most of them it meant no more than a half-forgotten family heirloom. Finding that their enemies were constantly reminding them of their Jewish identity, as did the numerous Jewish movements which developed in Vienna in the last quarter of the nineteenth century, they had to redefine for themselves the word 'Jew' and their own sense of Jewishness (chapter 10).

As against the false judgements of antisemites, who knew a Jew when they saw one (or thought they did), these intellectuals rebuilt their Jewish identity from a combination of elements which they drew from their own private history, which they rediscovered in the history of their 'people' (designated more and more as their 'race') and which they found imposed on them by contemporary events. Freud's case turns out to be particularly interesting: though determined to assume his own 'Jewishness', he rejected the essentials of Jewish religious traditions and had no comfortable illusions about the contemporary predicament of the Jews. The Jewish element in *The Interpretation of Dreams* seems rooted in the author's unconscious, but is most often connected with memories of past humiliations and injustices (chapter 11).

It was by a long and complicated route that Freud arrived at his last word on Jewish identity, in *Moses and Monotheism*. This final work shows no return to the religious sources of Judaism, but the reverse: an astonishingly free and sometimes provocative invention of a Jewish identity which has been completely and utterly redefined. Freud's Jewishness was first expressed in his self-analysis; its final reformulation is found in this 'historical novel', with a hero, Moses, who could well be an autobiographical projection – the last self-identification – of Sigmund Freud the man. Another Viennese Jew, Theodor Herzl, dreamed of becoming the latter-day Moses of the Jewish people. The two destinies – Freud's and Herzl's – could be paralleled: this makes it easier to understand all that separates them, why Freud meets Herzl in one of the dreams of his *Interpretation*, and why Freud followed the progress of Zionism with sympathetic attention, but without ever giving it his full allegiance (chapter 12).

Paradoxically, it could be said that Karl Kraus, who had come to be regarded by his admirers as the very symbol of the critical spirit free from all allegiance, usually knuckled under when his Jewish identity was involved. Concerned as he was to assert his distinctiveness within Viennese intellectual circles by every possible means, he yet retained a lifelong lingering desire to lose himself in German culture, and above all, in the German language. Anything which threw doubt on this identification drew from Kraus an impassioned and (it must be said) frequently unconvincing response: he joined the anti-Dreyfus faction, and when commenting on the proceedings of ritual murder which were exposing a Jew to the worst of antisemitic prejudice, he was chiefly concerned to dissociate himself from any kind of 'Jewish solidarity'. In his literary journal he welcomed Houston Stewart Chamberlain and sang his praises, while he never lost a chance of displaying his contempt for Heinrich Heine. In a narrowly redefined sense of the term, we might be justified in accusing Kraus of 'Jewish self-hatred' (*jüdischer Selbsthass*) (chapter 13).

Among the representatives of 'Young Vienna' literature, Richard Beer-Hofman was alone in taking up the defence and illustration of Jewish identity. His novel *Der Tod Georgs* ('George's Death') begins by attacking forgetfulness of Judaism and the 'Jewish spirit', which had gone astray in individualistic aestheticism. His 'cultural Zionism' did not please Hugo von Hofmannsthal and was at opposite poles to the scepticism of Arthur Schnitzler. Following a schema reminiscent of the trilogy of novels by his French contemporary Maurice Barrès, his 'cult of the self' led to the rediscovery of 'national energy'. All interpretations of *Der Tod Georgs* since Lukács's have emphasized the supposed discontinuity between the narcissism of the protagonist at the beginning of the story and his realization of collective responsibility in the closing pages. In fact, Beer-Hofmann's originality lies in presenting the affirmation of Jewish identity as an extension of the character's narcissism, the prettiest trinket on the aesthete's bosom. The author seems to be suggesting that (to paraphrase Nietzsche) Jewishness can be justified only as an aesthetic phenomenon. It is in the context of the 'Young Jewish movement' (*jungjüdische Bewegung*) and of the 'cultural Zionism' which was developing immediately after 1900 in Martin Buber's circle that this unorthodox reconstruction of Jewish identity within modernism can be fully understood (chapter 14).

The common element in the careers of Freud, Herzl, Kraus and Beer-Hofmann is the astonishing freedom of their attempts at defining 'the Jew' in an age of assimilation, antisemitism and Zionism. The disquieting variety of their responses suggests that in the historical and cultural context of Viennese modernism, the only Jew we can allude to is an 'imagined' one. For each individual, Jewish identity was formulated as a fiction, a long 'story' in which one's own experiences and one's own subconscious were as important as the history of the Jewish people and their traditional religious texts. The painful feeling of 'emptiness' which hit these Jewish intellectuals when they realized the failure of their attempts at assimilation according to liberal principles, and found themselves thrown back on a Jewish identity which remained to them unattainable, led them in the next few decades to find some rather original answers to the 'Jewish question'.

The redistribution of the cultural roles of masculinity and femininity triggered individual crises of disturbed, and subsequently redefined, sexual identity, while literature and *Kulturkritik* contrasted antifeminist terrors with utopias of feminism, homosexuality and androgyny. The challenge presented by antisemitism to the assimilation of Jews into German culture shattered Jewish identity into an astonishing variety of individual self-identifications with myths and role models both personal and collective. These two series of phenomena give a particularly spectacular illustration of the theme of identity crisis which is the distinctive mark of Viennese modernism – and which also explains the ambivalence of that period, when Vienna was at one and the same time the home of modernism and the 'testing ground for apocalypse', to quote Kraus. For the generalized identity crisis paved the way for some of the greatest ills of the twentieth century, such as political antisemitism and the rebirth of nationalism, as much as for the setting up of a new type of person, which Musil dubbed the 'man without qualities'.

Three authors have been my guides and points of reference throughout this study: Nietzsche, Freud and Musil. Nietzsche's critique of contemporary decadence and his call for the regeneration of modern man left a deep impression on all the Viennese writers and intellectuals we shall be discussing. The moment *Thoughts Out of Season* was published, Nietzsche's message, though only in outline, made its first converts in Vienna. Some, like Freud, rejected it, though they were still indelibly marked by this intellectual encounter; for most Viennese modernists, Nietzsche was the common starting point of their own individual journeys.

Freudian psychoanalysis is one of the theories which give an account of the human condition in the age of chronic identity crisis. Strictly speaking, as we shall see, the notion of identity fades under analysis into a more or less stable series of identifications. The present study owes some of its essential ideas to psychoanalysis, but it is not intended to be strictly or exclusively psychoanalytical. Freud the man appears in it as frequently as Freudian theory. The temptation to apply to Freud himself a process inspired by psychoanalysis was indeed irresistible, given the abundant material for interpretation made available by his biographers. I have attempted to do this in relation to his very personal approach to Jewish identity.

It could be said that all Robert Musil's works, fictional and theoretical, put the theme of identity crisis at the centre of his preoccupations. Musil lived through Viennese modernism and also, in the 1920s and 1930s, became the historian and a critical (and detached) analyst of that period. In *The Man Without Qualities* he gathered together observations and reflections which are fundamental to our purpose. Above all, Musil revealed one of the interpretive horizons of the identity crisis. While showing mercilessly how most individuals are in a hurry to avoid this crisis by plunging into the first involvement (however irrational) that becomes available, he also suggested that this loss of identity could turn out to be highly productive: it allowed a salutary deconstruction of the conventions whose sterile constraints weigh so heavy on society. It creates a clean slate on which to inscribe the rules of a new ethics.

It was in France that the subject of Viennese modernism in all its aspects – artistic, literary, philosophical and political – first became popular. The interest in it there can be dated from the special issue of the review *Critique* entitled 'Vienne, début d'un siècle' which appeared in 1975 (nos 339–40), and it culminated in the 1986 exhibition *Vienne, 1880–1938: L'apocalypse joyeuse* at the Pompidou Centre in Paris. It has given rise to a goodly number of publications. The same upsurge of interest is detectable in neighbouring countries and in the United States. We have only to recall the principal exhibitions and their voluminous accompanying catalogues, which remain as works of reference: *Experiment Weltuntergang: Wien um 1900* (Hamburg, Kunsthalle, 1981); *Arti a Vienna: Dalla Secessione alla caduta dell'Impero Absburgico* (Venice, Biennale, 1984); *Wien, 1870–1930: Traum und Wirklichkeit* (Vienna, Künstlerhaus, 1985); *Vienna 1900: Art, Architecture, Design* (New York, Museum of Modern Art, 1986). Each of these exhibitions foregrounded the visual arts, but also presented wide-ranging information on every important aspect of Viennese culture.

The popularity of Viennese themes in the 1970s and 1980s leads one to ask why it is that Viennese modernism seems so relevant. Recent discussions of the notion of 'postmodernism' may help to provide a partial answer. Out of all the artistic and intellectual output of turn-of-the-century Vienna, what appeals to us above all is the evidence of a critical approach to modernity, centring on aesthetic, ethical or psychological priorities and questioning certain modernist ideas, such as the idea of progress guided by scientific and technological rationality, or the programme of emancipation envisaged by individuals inspired by Enlightenment optimism. Viennese modernism can be interpreted as an anticipation of certain important 'postmodern' themes.

My method in the present study has been influenced in a decisive way by the work of Carl E. Schorske collected in *Fin-de-Siècle Vienna: Politics and Culture* (London, 1979; Cambridge, 1981), by William M. Johnston's monumental and encyclopedic *The Austrian Mind: An Intellectual and Social History* (University of California Press, 1972) and also (with reservations on some points of detail) by Allan Janik and Stephen Toulmin's essay *Wittgenstein's Vienna* (New York, 1973). These three works, with their exemplary multidisciplinary approach, attempt to portray the intellectual face of the Viennese golden age by applying similar analyses to the literary works of Hofmannsthal, Freud's psychoanalysis, Herzl's political essays and the scientific and philosophical works of Ernst Mach. At the same time they are ready to refer to the paintings of Gustav Klimt, the architectural and urbanist manifestos of Otto Wagner or the musical ideas of Gustav Mahler – to name but a few. Gotthart Wunberg's collection *Die Wiener Moderne: Literatur, Kunst und Musik zwischen 1890 und 1910* (Stuttgart, 1981) takes a similar line, but sets stricter limits on the time-frame and the corpus of texts and other documents associated with Viennese modernism. It seemed natural that the theme of identity crisis should lead me to venture into various domains of cultural history, although literature, philosophy and psychoanalysis were my point of departure and constant frame of reference.

The literary works (by Hofmannsthal, Schnitzler, Beer-Hofmann, Kraus and others) to which I have given particular attention were chosen to fit the overall theme of my inquiry. My choice, and the interpretation which emerges from my general approach, may surprise those who specialize in a particular author. But this is precisely the advantage of a multidisciplinary approach: hypotheses inspired by philosophy, psychoanalysis and culture may throw a new and revealing light on certain literary works, giving a new coherence to characteristics long recognized by literary critics. I have not attempted to fit them into an interpretive schema, but I have tried to draw the maximum advantage from the self-evident fact that the meaning of a text changes according to the context in which it is placed.

Part I

Destruction and Reconstruction of Identity

1

Reflections on Viennese Modernity

Definition and specific traits

The years between 1890 and 1910 saw the development and emergence in Vienna of what historians of literature and ideas have agreed to call 'Viennese modernism' or 'modernity', a translation of the German *Wiener Moderne*. Those twenty years, which were the logical outcome of political, cultural and social changes initiated in 1848 (and whose repercussions were still perceptible in Vienna up to 1938), were marked by the simultaneous emergence of new movements in several domains: philosophy (positivism and epistemology in Ernst Mach's circle, phemonenology and the philosophy of language in Franz Brentano's); the humane sciences (Sigmund Freud's psychoanalysis, the art history of Alois Riegl, Franz Wickhoff and their followers); social sciences (the renewal of political economy by Carl Menger and his school, and of the study of law by Hans Kelsen); literature (Hugo von Hofmannsthal, Hermann Bahr and 'Young Vienna'); the visual arts (Gustav Klimt and the Secession, decorative arts and the Wiener Werkstätte, the brusque emergence of Expressionism with Oskar Kokoschka and Egon Schiele); architecture (from Otto Wagner to Adolf Loos); music (from Gustav Mahler to Arnold Schönberg); and finally in politics (the birth of modern antisemitism and Zionism, and the formation of Austro-Marxism).

Certain specific traits of this 'Viennese modernity' are explicable in terms of the sociocultural position of the Austro-Hungarian monarchy, which was simultaneously behind and in advance of the rest of Europe. Compared with the other great European capitals – London, Paris, Berlin – late nineteenth-century Vienna looked socially, economically and politically out of date. There was a similar lag in the cultural sphere, for the persistence of some uniquely Austrian traditions had long kept Vienna apart from some of the main currents. Austrian philosophy, for example, failed to follow the post-Kantian controversies, while artistic and literary naturalism found no foothold in Vienna.

Rudolf Haller, and more recently Alberto Coffa, have highlighted the exceptional nature of the Austrian philosophical tradition (Coffa calls it a 'semantic tradition') as the key to the dominant tendencies of 'Viennese modernity'.[1] According to Haller, the two masters who decided the direction to be taken by nineteenth-century Austrian philosophy were Johann Friedrich Herbart (1776–1841) and Bernard Bolzano (1781–1848). Roger Bauer also emphasized the influence of Jacobi (1743–1819).[2] Like Herbart, Bolzano – dubbed by one of his disciples 'the new anti-Kant' (in allusion to Benedikt Stattler's treatise *Anti-Kant*, published in Munich in 1788)[3] – defended empiricism, realism, linguistic criticism and the philosophy of science (in the tradition of Liebniz, Locke and Hume) against 'German' Idealism, and especially against Hegel and the Hegelians.

Franz Brentano (1853–1917) took up this heritage and extended it, setting the seal on a specifically 'Austrian' philosophy closer to 'English' thinking than to anything post-Kantian. This is why in 1900 John Stuart Mill seemed to be exercising a greater influence on Viennese modernity than Kant (in 1879–80 Freud had assisted with the translation of Mill's complete works). This genealogy of the 'Austrian mind' was reinforced by the positivism of Ernst Mach (Brentano's notes on Mach's *Erkenntnis und Irrtum* show a profound convergence of viewpoints, despite the criticisms of detail);[4] it leads to Ludwig Wittgenstein, the Viennese Circle and the *Gestaltpsychologie* founded by Christian von Ehrenfels (1850–1922), a disciple of Brentano via Alexius Meinong (1853–1920). Thus, as far as philosophy is concerned, the Austrian 'lag' behind the development of German thought seems to have given rise to a valuable and profound originality.

The feelings of the younger generation in 1890 were expressed retrospectively by the literary critic Hermann Bahr in 1901: 'Let me remind you of the situation we were still in ten years ago, during that sad time in the 1880s when we were cut off from the artistic life of Europe.'[5] When Viennese intellectuals looked towards Berlin it was with a certain envy: 'They had Sedan, Bismarck and Wagner. And what did we have?' exclaimed Bahr in his memoirs of 1923.[6] The Austrian artist or writer had to compensate for Germany's 'outward' success as a great power – her military victories, the evident solidity of her *Reich* and the prestige of her *Kultur* – by turning inwards. While naturalism busied itself with the states of things (*Sachenstände*, Bahr's pun on the French *états des choses*), the Viennese would turn to 'states of mind'. Individuality and subjectivity were to be cultivated and explored at the expense of social ideas and realistic styles.[7]

Here we must mention Carl E. Schorske's masterly analysis of the progressions of Sigmund Freud. The genesis of the founding studies of psychoanalysis, in particular *The Interpretation of Dreams*, goes hand in hand with a social and intellectual withdrawal. Freud's difficulties in his university and scientific career were added to by political disappointment. After the victory of the antisemitic Christian Socialist Karl Lueger in the 1895 Viennese municipal elections, the Liberal Party, with which Freud instinctively sympathized, seemed to have been excluded from political power. Cruelly disappointed by politics, he assigned himself an intellectual task, 'to neutralize politics by reducing it to psychological categories'.[8]

The Interpretation of Dreams bears a Latin epigraph 'Flectere si nequeo superos, Acheronta movebo' ('If I cannot bend the gods above, I shall stir up Hell') which is the key to Freud's strategy of withdrawal to the inner self. Ernst Simon, in his now classic essay on 'Sigmund Freud the Jew',[9] has shown that this epigraph, from the *Aeneid*, had previously been chosen by the Social Democrat Ferdinand Lassalle for his 1859 pamphlet 'The Italian War and the Task of Prussia'. A letter written to Wilhelm Fliess on 17 July 1899 confirms that at that time Freud was taking 'the Lassalle' with him as holiday reading. As Schorske puts it, 'Lassalle thus threatened "those above" with the latent forces of national revolution . . . Freud transferred the hint of subversion through the return of the repressed from the realm of politics to that of the psyche.'[10]

Prussia after Sadowa and Sedan was clearly on the up-and-up, whereas the Habsburg monarchy seemed to be in irremediable decline. The theme of decadence which dominates fin-de-siècle literature may seem far removed from the social and political reality of France, Britain or Germany, but in Vienna it carried a particular weight of truth. On 13 May 1894 Hugo von Hofmannsthal, returning from a walk through Vienna in company with his friend Richard Beer-Hofmann, wrote in his diary:

> What a desperate (or exasperated) generation of artists we are, swimming through the noisy and confused tempest of the times with 'the crown of art between our teeth'. Those who come after us will be greater than we, but all the same we are the *first complete artists* since Sturm und Drang. How surprising it is that we should be perhaps the last thinking men in Vienna, the last complete men, with a soul, while after us there will perhaps come a great barbarism, a Slav and Jewish world, a sensual world. Think of Vienna destroyed, her walls all fallen, the inside of her body laid bare, her wounds covered by rampant vegetation, everywhere bright green foliage, silence, lapping water, all life extinct: what a splendid outlook, a splendid vision! Imagine being on watch in one of the Trajan's columns still standing before the Karlskirche, and walking through the ruins with thoughts that no one can understand any more.[11]

Hofmannsthal's vision of the ruined city prefigures that of Alfred Kubin in his fantasy novel *Die andere Seite* ('The Other Side', 1909). The theme is closely linked to the theme of decadence which pervades a large part of Austrian literature and was to inspire the novels of Joseph Roth. The Vienna of Hofmannsthal's vision was to take its place as one of the highlights of European decadence, one of the cities which symbolized art and death, alongside Venice and 'dead Bruges'.[12]

Between myth and reality

There were many who even went so far as to doubt that there was such a thing as Viennese culture. In his essay 'The Union with Germany' (*Der Anschluss an Deutschland*), written in 1919, Robert Musil looked back:

> Austrian culture was a false Viennese perspective . . . While acknowledging that Austria had a singularly rich personal culture, we must admit that she was

singularly poor in culture in the true, that is intellectual, sense. If we compare the resources of Austrian and German universities, the number and importance of their libraries and museums, the opportunities of discovering art from other countries, the number and importance of learned journals, the intensity and breadth of public debates over intellectual problems, the quality of dramatic performances – let us recall that almost all Austrian books are made in Germany, that almost all Austrian writers owe their living to German publishers . . . The myth of Austrian culture, which is supposed to be prospering within the composite state better than elsewhere . . . is only a theory which has never been proved.[13]

Musil himself, drawing the logical conclusion from this piece of reasoning, had lived for several years in Berlin. However, other Viennese intellectuals, chief among them Hofmannsthal, were to try to consolidate and illustrate the notion of a specific Viennese and Austrian cultural identity. From the 1890s onwards Hermann Bahr made himself the spokesman of the Austrian revival. In 1908, to celebrate the sixtieth anniversary of the accession of Franz Josef I (then aged seventy-eight), the Klimt group organized an exhibition, the *Kunstschau*, which was intended to 'demonstrate the willpower of Austrian art'.[14] It can safely be said that Viennese artists and intellectuals of the 1900s, almost without exception, were concerned about their national identity within the German cultural orbit.

Those of Vienna's inhabitants who loved her most had occasional attacks of genuine despair which Bahr dubbed *Wiener Selbsthass*, Viennese self-hatred.[15] Part of it was the difficulty of being an innovator, a 'modernist', within a culture notoriously conservative and hostile to the smallest signs of independence. Freud found Vienna impossible to live in, yet he had to live there.[16] In his letters to Wilhelm Fliess, of Berlin, he was constantly making comparisons between the two capitals, such as: 'The whole atmosphere of Vienna is such that it does little to steel one's will or to foster that confidence of success which is characteristic of you Berliners' (29 August 1898).[17] Ernest Jones tells how when he first met Freud, before learning of his aversion for Vienna, he once innocently said to him that it must be exciting to live in a city so full of new ideas. To Jones's great surprise, Freud sprang up and protested tartly: 'I have lived here for fifty years and have never come across a new idea here.'[18]

The feeling was common to almost all the representatives of Viennese modernism. On 10 May 1896 Hofmannsthal wrote to Beer-Hofmann: 'The life we lead in Vienna is a misery. We really must intersperse it from time to time with unambitious little trips, stays in unattractive small towns or in the country. Intellectually we are living like tarts who eat nothing but French salad and sorbet.'[19] By contrast, Hofmannsthal found life in Berlin a positive liberation, and distance made him only the more aware of the drawbacks of life in Vienna, as he shows in this letter to his father written in 1909: 'The atmosphere of jealousy, nit-picking and stagnation in Vienna can only be savoured in moderation and with interruptions, and what has happened to Grillparzer must surely be connected with the deathly silliness which pervades life there.'[20]

Thus it is only in retrospect that certain historians of Viennese modernity – creating an updated version of the 'Habsburg myth' – are able to wonder at the exceptional fertility of that cultural milieu, as if it had been a kind of 'Silicon Valley of the mind' (the expression is Allan Janik's).[21] Freud, Hofmannsthal and their contemporaries felt shackled, almost exiled, by their life in Vienna, and never ceased to envy the cultural, intellectual and academic life of other great European cities. They would never have dreamed of vaunting their city as a centre of modernism. They would have been readier to describe it as a bastion of everything that was archaic.

Claudio Magris's *Il mito absburgico nella letteratura austriaca moderna*, first published in 1963, marked the early beginning of the rediscovery of 'Viennese modernity'. In the thirty or so years since then a fundamental misunderstanding has arisen. Who in 1963 still believed in the 'Habsburg myth' of a beautiful and harmonious lost *ordo*? Magris himself exposed the myth the better to pour scorn on it, while treating it with affectionate irony. But today everybody really believes in the 'Vienna myth' of a golden age of European culture, and Magris's thesis-cum-pamphlet is in danger of being taken as a defence and illustration of the Viennese heritage.

The real Magris had the biting irony of a Lukács coupled with the critical vigour of an inhabitant of Trieste for whom the Habsburg empire had always been the strangler of democratic liberties. For him the *mito absburgico* was an 'ideological falsification', a glossy product of official propaganda which had miraculously become an 'authentic and positive idea and force' for a whole gallery of noted writers, from Franz Grillparzer to Joseph Roth.

> The old Austria, engaged in discovering that it was built on sand, as was all reality, appeared in public in the seductive guise of order and harmonious wholeness; it gave rise to a literature which, with disillusioned lucidity, unmasked the vacuum of civilization and the nihilism of modern learning ... The history of the Habsburg myth is the history of a civilization which, in the name of its love for order, discovered the disorder of the world.

After the First World War and the collapse of the Danube monarchy, after the black years of hyperinflation and the rise of Nazism, that myth, intended to bolster the cohesion of an ever more anachronistic state, began to speak of a lost golden age of harmony between peoples and of general good living. Faced with unbridled nationalism and racism in Central Europe, many a writer and intellectual of what had been Austria-Hungary reinvoked the political mystery of *sacrificium nationis* which could turn a German or Czech individual into an 'Austrian'. This nostalgia inspired one contemporary form of reactionary rhetoric[22] which was quite distinct from the German tradition. The 'Habsburg myth' exalted the paternalism of the old Franz Josef speaking to 'my peoples', like the father in Kafka who runs through his eleven sons.

Since the dawn of the twentieth century the myth has been perpetuated by serious historical scholars, beginning with Heinrich von Sbrik, who contrasted its 'lyrical and sentimental *oikumene*' with the voluntarist principle of the Prussian state – as well as with such theorists of the Habsburg *ordo* as

Leopold von Andrian. One might add that the changes at present sweeping Central Europe under the combined effect of the reunification of Germany and the dislocation of the Soviet empire have restored the Habsburg myth to some sort of importance as a utopian vision of a harmonious community of peoples in the Danube basin, from Vienna to the Black Sea and the Adriatic.[23]

The spirit of the myth turns immobility into a 'wise and grandiose stasis with a masterly ability to postpone solutions and leave conflicts to fritter themselves into nonexistence', since 'any step, even the smallest, would be a step towards the abyss' (in the words of Franz Werfel). Political immobility thus becomes a model of human behaviour, an ethics of the extinction of all passions, a striving after an ordered, not to say bureaucratic, exteriority; while any kind of individualism is taken to be exhibitionist and anarchic – in fact, a deadly sin. The aspiration towards order in both animate and inanimate things makes disorder both perceptible and intolerable: every little fragmentation, every existence apart is a measurable loss to the whole, a shattering of the hierarchy. And the hold of the Habsburg myth on the Austrian soul was all the more insidious in that (as Magris suggests) it is possible to speak of a 'negative adherence' to it by authors who set out to demolish it, from Kafka's *Castle* to Thomas Bernhard's *Perturbation*. Magris never speaks of Bernhard and seldom speaks of Freud, but one could suggest that the Habsburg myth found its way into psychoanalysis via the hierarchization of the unconscious and the highly disenchanted and resigned Freudian model for squaring the individual equation with the sociopolitical order.

The unbridled individualism of Romanticism was less congenial to the Habsburg myth than the discreet, somewhat melancholy and sceptical hedonism of popular comedy and operetta, from the puppet theatre *Hanswurst* to the *Fledermaus*. The model Austrian citizen of the first part of the nineteenth century (from 1815 to 1848, from Biedermeier to the *Vormarz*) exhibits the 'heroism of impotence', made up of cautious circumspection and a marked preference for home comforts – qualities which distinguished the perfect subject of the Metternich regime, founded on 'absolutism tempered by inefficiency'. Magris shows very clearly that the new Austrian patriotism which gradually arose after the Napoleonic wars focused on heroes such as the Tyrolean Andreas Hofer, in whom Baron Hormayr saw 'the enemy of all hastiness and innovation'.

Magris devotes one of his most engaging chapters to the great dramatist and writer Franz Grillparzer who, after 1848, was to become the poet laureate of Austrian liberal conservatism. The anti-titanic Grillparzer taught that every man must conform to a higher order and cultivate the virtues of fidelity, piety, courage, moderation and self-sacrifice. The suspicion of action we find from Grillparzer to Stifter goes naturally with the cult of nature as a store of immutable laws and a remedy for the illusions of promethean individualism. Condemnation of the collective sinfulness of 1848 was accompanied by a fascination with the Slav and Hungarian world, with its wide open spaces and its legends, the very stuff the Habsburg dream was made on.

According to the Habsburg myth, the state was founded not on rights but on duties. The Emperor himself felt that he fulfilled a responsible task as the chief official of his own administration. Individual power and responsibility weighed heavily, and the hierarchy offered reassuring protection. The poet never for an instant thought of himself as the guide of his people: Grillparzer sees him as a poor musician, symbol of a modest and dignified resignation, while in Stifter his meticulous descriptions are a remedy for neurasthenia. It was an unhappy conservatism: all progress was a concealed regression, a march towards barbarism.

By around 1900, the Habsburg myth was being sapped by the destructive forces which were to drag Habsburg Europe into a world war. It was then, according to Magris, that the theme of decadence became omnipresent. For Hofmannsthal and Rilke, that past age no longer signified wisdom and dignity, but decay: they were the 'heirs of an extinct civilization'. In *Törless* Musil analysed the confusions of a 'collapsing, rotten society'. The sole refuges were the artificial paradise of the Viennese café, the dispersal of impressionism, the aesthetics of fragmentation, the nonchalance of Schnitzler's Anatole. Hofmannsthal, says Magris, was to end up 'in the half-sleep of his tower of anachronism'; Kraus proclaimed the apocalypse of Viennese culture, while Schnitzler pitilessly dissected its corpse.

Now, thirty years later, Magris's remarks on this period of 'Viennese modernism' of about 1900 have become commonplaces, doubtless prestigious but highly schematized. All my efforts in the present book are directed the other way, towards showing the great vitality of Viennese culture at that time, together with the utopian outlook and theoretical fecundity of the 'identity crisis' which is the common denominator of the Viennese moderns. Vienna was *not* a heavily ornamented neo-baroque morgue containing the grandiose catafalque of the Habsburg myth. If we accept that somewhat unilateral vision, we will be passing a pejorative judgement on all present-day reception of 'fin-de-siècle Vienna'. Magris himself, since that first book, has published so many stimulating studies and documents on that exceptional moment in European cultural history that all his later work reads like a kind of refutation of the 'burial certificate' he drew up in 1963. In fact, Magris would have us add a new chapter to the *Mito absburgico*, showing that in the 1980s and later the Austrian mind from 1848 to 1938 has become a particularly 'living' myth. But that myth cannot be reduced to the 'Habsburg myth'. It is an integral part of the archaeology of our own postmodernity as we approach the end of the twentieth century.

II

Economic and social modernization

In spite of the restlessness of Freud, Hofmannsthal and others, the relative backwardness of Vienna and the Austrian part of the monarchy had been partially alleviated by spectacular advances after 1870. Between 1830 and 1870, the annual growth rate in the area corresponding to post-1919 Austria was 0.72 per cent (as against 1.27 per cent in France and 1.17 per cent in

Germany); from 1870 to 1913, the rate rose to 1.46 per cent (1.06 per cent in France and 1.51 per cent in Germany). The disparity would, of course, look much more striking if we considered the whole territory of the Habsburg monarchy, because development in the east was slower and less consistent. If we calculate the gross national product per head of the population on a base of 100 for the area covered by Austria after 1919, the figure for France emerges as 120 per head in 1870 and 101 in 1913, suggesting that the national wealth of Austria in proportion to the number of inhabitants had almost completely caught up with that of France by 1913. If we are to believe such economic analyses,[24] the economic modernization of the Austrian territory of the monarchy happened later than in France or Germany, but was faster after 1870, and reached the same level as in other major European countries by 1913.

In the nineteenth century, various factors had slowed the growth of the Austrian (and Viennese) economy. The transport cost of raw materials (iron ore) and energy sources (coal) kept the production costs of steel products higher in Vienna than in Berlin even in 1900. For a long time the shortage of skilled workers hampered the progress of modern industries: it was a long time before liberal laws on public education were introduced (the Reichsvolksschulgesetz dates from 1869), and in 1890 27 per cent of the inhabitants of Cisleithania (on the Austrian side of the empire) were illiterate (15 per cent in 1910). This did not prevent a permanent seepage, at the other end of the social scale, of qualified personnel into Germany, where career prospects were brighter. A further handicap was the lack of liquid capital for industrial investment: much Austrian wealth was tied up in land, and banks preferred to lend to the state (which had a structural indebtedness) or to the great aristocratic families. The power of the banks, which is no guarantee of dynamism, seems to have been especially great in Austria: it is no coincidence that it was Austria which inspired the Austro-Marxist Rudolf Hilferding to write his treatise on capital, *Das Finanzcapital* (1910).

The Habsburg monarchy was short of leading capitalists and industrial entrepreneurs: the aristocracy was suspicious of industrial investment and would only engage in it under the protection of monopolies guaranteed by the administration on a mercantilist basis. This lack of a native lead was partially compensated by an influx of German capital and German industrial managers, but also by the important role played by Protestants and Jews. The more prosperous regions of the monarchy took an almost colonialist attitude towards the eastern provinces, which meant that Austrian heavy industry did not really benefit from the 'large market' offered by its vast territories, the last internal customs barriers having fallen with the Zollverein of 1850.[25] The Habsburg monarchy was a jigsaw of differing economic interests which partially coincided with nationalistic disputes. Austria proper looked to Germany rather than to other areas of the monarchy.[26]

We may observe in passing that in the beginning Vienna's cultural modernism, like its economic modernization, was dependent on foreign imports. *Wiener Moderne* started with a wholesale importation of ideals and models from Germany, France, Italy, Scandinavia and even America. Adolf Loos was profoundly and lastingly influenced by his stay in the United States, especially Chicago and New York, from 1893 to 1896. Hermann Bahr acted as a kind of intellectual import–export agent, defending the new Austrian talent abroad in Berlin and Paris, and introducing Vienna to the latest literary fashions from France and Germany.

The purely economic factors in Austria's 'backwardness' which accumulated through the nineteenth century were aggravated by some of the specific characteristics of her society. Agriculture was still by far the principal industry: in Cisleithania in 1910, 53 per cent of those in employment worked in agriculture, while in Hungary the figure was 69 per cent. The bureaucracy, with its pervasive dirigiste and protectionist outlook, seemed to be one of the strongest unifying factors in bourgeois society: it helps to explain the absence of real conflict between the ruling house, the aristocracy and the bourgeoisie, and also the attachment of small artisans and traders to an order governed by corporations and cartels. (Liberal reforms in economic life were never really to be accepted; especially in the aftermath of the crash of 1873, they led to the Christian Socialist reaction and the spread of antisemitism among the masses.) In general it seems that anti-capitalist forces were still dominant in the Austria of 1900, perhaps as a long-term consequence of the Counter-Reformation, which had deprived the monarchy of the Protestant elite described by Max Weber as instrumental in bringing modernization to Germany.

On the other hand, state capitalism was undoubtedly popular. Lueger practised it systematically in Viennese local government from the end of the century onwards: in 1880 the Viennese railways were nationalized, and most public service companies – gas, water, electricity – were in public ownership before 1914. The persistence of the aristocratic social ideal, especially in Vienna, is striking. Close study of the architecture and living conditions of the Ringstrasse[27] shows that the lifestyle aspired to (in vain) by the high and middle ranks of the bourgeoisie was still that of a stately home. This no doubt explains the remarkable prosperity of craftsmen and minor luxury industries in Vienna, along with the flourishing field of 'decorative arts' which proved the most fertile ground for the Viennese Jugendstil.

The economic progress of Vienna was cut short by the stock-market crash of 1873, which also put a premature stop to the era of liberalism. The crisis affected two of the most prosperous interests in Vienna, building and public works (including the important brickworks), and railway engineering. It eventually spread to all sectors, and its repercussions were still being felt in the early 1880s. The most dynamic sector up to the First World War was the electrical industry, in which German interests were predominant. Siemens had made one attempt to establish itself in Vienna between 1858 and 1864; it gained a definite foothold in 1879. In 1898 it was AEG's turn to settle. By 1902 these two firms controlled half the market. If we add other foreign firms such as Westinghouse and Brown-Boveri, two-thirds of the Viennese electrical industry was dependent on foreign capital by 1914.

Other leading Viennese industries were agricultural machinery (Clayton and Shuttleworth) and armaments, which alone were employing 12,000 people just before the war. Food and brewing were also of great importance.[28]

Between 1890 and 1913 the Viennese economy grew steadily. As an indication of the rate of modernization, in 1902 44.8 per cent of firms and 50.8 per cent of workers were not working directly for clients, but sold through intermediaries.[29] The larger firms were an exception to this, however: 87 per cent of firms registered in 1902 were employing one to five workers; only eight, out of a total of 133,870, employed more than a thousand people.[30] Thus economic modernization was still only relative.

The most spectacular change in Vienna was surely the growth in its population. The total population of greater Vienna (centre and suburbs) rose from 842,951 in 1869 to 1,927,606 in 1910: an increase of 80.3 per cent in the central areas and 253.3 per cent in the suburbs.[31] During the same period, large cities grew at a similar rate in most countries. Between 1860 and 1910 the population of Berlin rose from 496,000 to 2,071,257; that of Paris from 1,696,141 to 2,888,119; and that of London from 2,800,000 to 4,522,961.[32] As with other capital cities, there was considerable immigration into Vienna during this time: the two ethnic groups which contributed the most to this immigrant population were the Czechs and the Jews. Poles, and to a lesser extent Hungarians, made up other easily recognizable minorities.

It is a self-evident fact, which nonetheless deserves some stress, that this massive immigration from the eastern territories of the monarchy not only served to renew the population and the popular cultures of Vienna, but also explains why Vienna (like Paris and London) became home to some of the brightest talents of the whole empire. Freud was three years old when his family settled in Vienna in 1859. Theodor Herzl came to study at the University of Vienna in 1878, after completing his school education in Budapest.

Labour statistics help to give a clearer picture of the population of Vienna. In 1900 there were 120,960 people working in government or in offices (including 26,622 in the armed forces and 36,795 in local government or the liberal professions); 101,866 were domestic servants, 432,483 manual workers and 17,500 casual workers.[33] In 1900 Vienna, like most European metropolises, was a city of contrasts, with a wretched proletariat living in inhuman conditions. The hard life led by women in the sewing and tailoring workshops, or by workmen in the brickfields and on the building sites, was described by eye-witnesses such as Alfons Petzold and Max Winter,[34] and in the memoirs of militant workers like Johann Böhm,[35] as well as in reports by works inspectors and social researchers,[36] and finally in publications by Social Democrats (not forgetting a few photographic records).[37] All these help to reveal a merciless world which, for all Hofmannsthal and his friends had to say about it, might never have existed.

Under the Liberal administration, and the Christian Socialist one which followed, the city of Vienna was to a great extent modernized. The great public works which were inaugurated by the building of the Ringstrasse went alongside an equally spectacular renewal of the infrastructure. The Danube and Wien rivers were canalized, the water supply renewed, an urban railway network built, gas and electricity laid on – a series of important services which compared favourably with other European capitals,[38] even if some problems (working-class housing and public hospitals, for example) had still not been solved.[39] In 1890, the administrative map was redrawn and the former suburbs were turned into new urban districts. 'So no special significance should be attached to the name of the city. Like all big cities, it consisted of irregularity, change, sliding forward, keeping in step, collisions of things and affairs . . .'[40]

Intellectuals in a political vacuum

This very real economic and social modernization of Austria and its capital is a reminder to us to add a pinch of salt to the pessimistic pronouncements of contemporaries, which are still sometimes taken as evidence of the 'decadence' of the Habsburg monarchy between 1848 and 1914. Economic history confirms that Vienna was slightly behind Budapest and Berlin in its economic modernization in the 1850s and 1860s, but that in the two decades prior to the First World war economic growth was equally rapid in all three Central European capitals, provoking very similar changes in lifestyle and similar social problems.[41]

The clichés about Viennese decadence are evidently inspired chiefly by the problems of political life in Vienna and the monarchy generally. There is indeed a striking contrast between the neo-absolutist style of government, encumbered with archaic survivals, and the largely modern society. Emperor Franz Josef's personal antipathy towards every manifestation of 'modern' life, including telephones, cars, lifts, bathrooms and electric light – not to mention contemporary art and architecture – is legendary, and symbolizes the contradictions within a state that seemed vulnerable to the slightest change. According to Jean-Paul Bled, 'while Franz Josef's character became more rigid with age, in opposition to the progress to which society was committed, the unvarying order of his daily life settled him into what Franz Werfel calls a "magnificent stasis".'[42]

By the beginning of the twentieth century the major democratic advances of 1848 had largely lost their meaning. The great mass parties which had dominated Austrian politics since the Liberal decline, the Christian Socialists and the Social Democrats, had failed on two vital points: they had proved unable to take control of the central bureaucracy, and they had found no strategy for dealing with the nationalist problem.[43] The utopian dream of emancipation and national harmony and equality which the Liberals had harboured in 1848 had remained out of reach. Nationalist factional interests had ousted party intentions in the Viennese parliament and paralysed the activity of political institutions. Even in Vienna, the keystone of the 'Habsburg myth' as described by Claudio Magris[44] – that is, the supranational ideology which ought to have brought different nationalities together – seemed to have dangerous cracks. The pan-Germanist demonstrations of German nationalists, the xenophobia shown towards the large Czech community (whose bitterness was expressed by the poet Josef Svatopluk Machar in his collection *Tristium Vindobana*, I–XX, 1889–92, published in 1893) and the active spread of political antisemitism made Vienna more of a battleground of different nationalities than a multinational melting-pot.

This negative view of the situation should not blind us to certain successes, acknowledged by most historians. The public services were efficient and the state bureaucracy did its work well, despite its top-heaviness and occasional inadequacy. Joseph Roth has not been the only one to commend the sense of duty shown by minor officials representing the state in the provinces. Adam Wandruszka, general editor of the monumental history of the Habsburg monarchy from 1948 to 1918 being published under the auspices of the Austrian Academy of Sciences has entitled his foreword to the volume on law and administration 'Ein vorbildlicher Rechtsstaat?' ('A state of exemplary legality?').[45] Despite the linguistic caution implied by the question mark, the historian himself seems to have been influenced by the 'Habsburg myth'. Should we conclude that in spite of its archaisms and its nationalistic squabbles the Habsburg state was, after all, 'modern'?[46] Or should we rather look for the truth in the works of Franz Kafka and Karl Kraus?

After a long contemplation of the virtues and vices of the modern Habsburg state, the historian Robert A. Kann suggests *a contrario* that the overall failure of the monarchy to subject the infinitely complex conglomeration of societies under its aegis to a unitary and rational concept of the state was merely the obverse of its leading virtue: moderation and respect for difference. For – Kann observes – the only effective solution to the nationalism problem would have been a totalitarian regime, whereas the logic of the Habsburg monarchy led rather to an organic pluralism.[47] With political institutions paralysed, the emperor and his court locked behind an unyielding facade, and a despotic (though avowedly neutral and impartial) bureaucracy, Austria was in what Hermann Broch calls a 'political vacuum'. This was the ultimate outcome of a 'last attempt to save the Austrian state system by a radical depoliticization' which (according to Broch) had been undertaken at the time of the Counter-Reformation.[48]

No way out into political life, so look for a substitute: this, in sum, was the peculiar political situation of a good many Viennese intellectuals at the turn of the century. The young Bahr and Otto Weininger turned to pan-Germanist Wagnerianism, seeking the answer to Viennese 'decadence' in a cultural and ideological attachment to the German Reich. The Zionist movement was a reaction to the rise in antisemitism, while young intellectuals and artists, disappointed by the collapse of liberalism, fell back on individualism and aestheticism (as demonstrated by Carl E. Schorske).[49] All these new tendencies had one thing in common: they drew their inspiration from history and ancestral tradition, or looked for regeneration in art, unconsciously following the natural inclination of the ruling power, which was tending to eliminate politics and replace it with mythology.

The myth of the ruling house was the Habsburg myth, addressed to its peoples (*Völker*) the better to suppress their national feelings and propagate the image of a supranational dynasty based on a dynamic directly opposed to that of Prussia. Set against it were the new Germanic, biblical or aesthetic mythologies of intellectuals; they were busy rediscovering – or inventing – a place for themselves in one or other of the ancestral *Völker* to fill the void left by the unattainable 'Austro-Hungarian' national identity. We shall see, in particular, how for 'assimilated' Jews in Vienna this lack of, and search for, a national identity sometimes led them along paths of astonishing creativity.

III

Modernists respect their predecessors

Viennese modernism, as the result of a recent and still incomplete modernization, had two distinguishing characteristics. First, the modernist 'front' was less aggressive there than in other cultural centres. Viennese modernists recognized the authority of their predecessors. They were much given to 'secession', by which they did not mean a total break with orthodoxy: Klimt's 'Secession' was an institution as official as the Salon of the Academy, and enjoyed the same kind of state support. Indeed, Klimt had begun his career by decorating the official palaces in the Ringstrasse – the frescoes in the Burgtheater. On the celebrated facade of the Michaelerplatz Adolf Loos paid dutiful tribute to the classicism of 1800: this 'conservative revolutionary' was a great admirer of Karl Friedrich Schinkel.[50] Karl Kraus wrote in praise of Nestroy; Schönberg was not above the occasional pastiche of Johann Strauss.

Hofmannsthal and his friends defined themselves as continuers of the great classical tradition as readily as they claimed to be modernists. In 1902, Rudolf Borchardt made a speech about Hofmannsthal in Göttingen, pausing to fulminate against the perpetrators of 'modern art', calling them enemies of strict form and lovers of vagueness – which they called 'nuance' – and of sloppiness – which they called 'sketching'. They were, he said, guilty of 'bastardizing' poetry and reducing it to impressions and atmospheres, abandoning themselves to a moral anarchy which they disguised as snobbery.[51] This philippic (which must have embarrassed Hofmannsthal, who was not given to linguistic excess) shows that in that circle the adjective 'modernist' could be exceedingly pejorative.

Viennese modernism was by no means triumphal or sure of itself. It kept a strong awareness of loss, of a decadence which must be fought, of a world in a state of collapse and a still undefined future. The Viennese modernists trod their chosen path with the consciousness of a necessity which seemed to them almost like fate. They seldom thought of reducing this malaise to a political problem: to them, modernism was part of aesthetics, ethics, psychology or philosophy, and always an individual question. Nietzsche's scorn for 'modern ideas' (pity for the weak and mediocre which allowed them to triumph, the confusions of historicism, blind worship of science) made a profound impression on his admirers. In *Ecce Homo* Nietzsche gave this definition of the meaning of his *Beyond Good and Evil*: 'This book (1886) is a criticism of *modernity* [*Modernität*], embracing the modern sciences, arts, even politics, together with certain indications as to a type which would be the reverse of modern man, or as little like him as possible, a noble yea-saying type.'[52]

Most Viennese 'modernists' shared Hofmannsthal's gloomy persuasion that, as he said in 1906, 'The characteristics of our era are ambiguity and indeterminacy. It can rest only on unsafe ground, never forgetting that every ground which former generations thought was solid is now unsafe.'[53] Werner Hofmann and Carl Schorske have shown the cultural pessimism which dominates Klimt's design for the university frescoes: 'Klimt's vision can be explained in the following way: it is not philosophy *ex cathedra* which will bring enlightenment to mankind, nor the progress of medicine which will free it from suffering, nor jurisprudence, locked up in imposing institutions, which will protect it against the arbitrary will of the goddesses of vengeance.'[54] In the years leading up to 1914, Kraus's loathing for 'modern times', which inspired his series of pamphlets and satires, led him (after a few excursions into something approaching social democracy) to a violently reactionary position governed by the nostalgia for an age of innocence (the *Vormärz*), during which ethical, aesthetic and social hierarchies supposedly remained undisturbed. And he ended up by declaring, in *Die Fackel* in 1913, 'I hate all kinds of regression only because they let progress drag them in the opposite direction,' emphasizing that his 'political concepts, if indeed I have any, stop short of the French Revolution'.[55]

Many more examples could be given of this lack of confidence in modernity, which Roth and Musil were to identify retrospectively as a distinguishing mark of the Viennese cultural milieu (though it is true that Musil was to consider the idea of decadence with as much suspicion as that of progress, as can be seen in his critical essay on Spengler). Even genuine aesthetic innovation was rarely accompanied by any kind of triumphalism. When Schönberg looked back on his reform of music, it was with a sort of stoic resignation: 'I am being forced in this direction . . . I am obeying an inner compulsion which is stronger than any upbringing'; or 'No one else wanted the job, so I had to take it on.'[56]

There has been a misunderstanding in the case of Adolf Loos, which hinges on the word 'functionalist'. In a 1965 lecture entitled 'Functionalism Today', Theodor Adorno began by quoting Loos before fulminating against the errors of architecture in the 1950s and 1960s. Without explictly connecting cause and effect, he suggested a direct descendance from Loos's ideas to post-war architecture.[57] The very word 'functionalism' has unpleasant connotations of the rule of a narrowly economic and technocratic reality. In fact, Loos always rejected any modernism which was prepared to countenance industrial mass production. He sang the praises of craftsmanship and called himself a master builder (*Baumeister*) rather than architect. His 'functionalism' was a humanism: man, as he was, at any moment in the history of culture, with his needs, his traditions and his tastes, was the measure of all things. The master builder acknowledged no other norm, whether administrative, economic or political.

Loos rejected the hegemony of art as firmly as the tyranny of the normal. Adorno, in the same lecture, quoted Loos's dictum that 'A house must please everybody, unlike a work of art, which need not please anybody,' to underline the risk of aesthetic decline in modern architecture. In fact, Loos was only saying that a culture does not need artists to shape its living space, only good craftsmen and builders – because an artist is no more capable of creating livable-with architecture than a biologist is or (to all appearances) ever will be capable of designing higher forms of life. If Europe really had a culture of her own, she would not need to agonize over her architecture. The bareness of the Michaelerplatz facade was not the product of a would-be modernism of a functionalist type. It was not 'ahead of its time'; one might rather be tempted to define it as architecture in suspense, awaiting a new, spontaneous dialect of architectural language, rejecting ornaments and historical references intended to mask an absence of style. Was Vienna ever to have a 'modern' culture worthy of the name? That was probably the question which Loos was asking on his Michaelerplatz facade.

The modernists: Otto Wagner and Hermann Bahr

Some of the leaders of Viennese modernity adopted a more enthusiastic and optimistic tone. Thus spoke the architect Otto Wagner in his 1895 treatise *Moderne Architektur*,[58] announcing that the time of eclectic historicism which had produced all that 'neo' style building along the Ringstrasse – neo-Hellenistic, neo-Roman, neo-Renaissance, neo-Flemish, neo-Gothic, neo-Baroque – was now past. But Wagner was content to proclaim the new and reject the old. He had no precise plan of action, except the need for architecture to keep pace with technical progress. His path from decorative Jugendstil to a barer style is evidence not of certainty, but of a never-ending search for transcendance. The powers that be in Austria never gave him the chance to realize his most grandiose ambitions. Successive refusals of his designs for a Museum of the City of Vienna in the first decade of the twentieth century symbolized (according to Peter Haiko) 'the defeat of architectural modernism' in the capital.[59] Similarly, his grand plans for urban development never got beyond futuristic visions and utopian dreams.[60]

Transcendence (*Überwindung*) was the favourite word of the literary critic Hermann Bahr, but his influence over his Viennese 'protegés' must not be exaggerated: from a very early stage Hofmannsthal and Schnitzler were poking covert fun at this self-styled mouthpiece of Viennese modernity. But his development still serves as an interesting example and symptom of the 'modern condition' whereby today's moderns are tomorrow's ancients, and all modernity is doomed to be almost instantly outdated. For Bahr, the Darwinian imperative of evolution (*Entwicklung*) was reinforced by a naively Marxist aspiration towards transcendance. 'Above all, don't get stuck, don't hold on, don't remain the same as you were, for any sort of novelty is better, if only because it is more recent than the old,' he wrote in 1886.[61]

Bahr himself is a dazzling example of Protean modernity: at one time or another he was a Wagnerian, an admirer of Bismarck, a Marxist, a naturalist, a symbolist, a secessionist, an expressionist, and finally (from 1912 onwards) a Catholic – not counting a number of transitional stages. What is most striking – and seems most characteristically Viennese – about this critic, with his enthusiasm for being in the vanguard of every passing 'ism', is the fact that the real content of modernism for him was nothing other than the reign of the individual. The 'modern' creator trusted no particular school, rule or tradition, and knew only one law, that of his own nerves, senses, instinct and subjectivity. Bahr saw in Hofmannsthal the perfection of this modernity: he was new, but in the tradition of his forebears (to paraphrase Chénier, he made old verses on new thoughts), but he was nonetheless entirely modern because, as Bahr saw it, he followed only the spontaneous and natural promptings of his own sensibility, 'nerves' and ideas.

Aesthetic individualism and the cult of the 'genius'

This approach to the modern, which defines it as the self-assertion of the individual, explains why so many Viennese modernists, from Hofmannsthal to Klimt, seem retrospectively to have lagged behind other artists (German, French, Russian) of the period, who were more experimental, more innovative, more revolutionary. Baudelaire, perturbed by the relativism inherent in ever-changing 'modernisms', observed that to define the modern as transitory 'too easily robs the beautiful of its aristocratic character',[62] and went on to say that 'Modernity is transitory, fleeting, contingent, one half of art; the other half is eternal and immutable.'[63] Hermann Bahr tempered this anxiety born of the transitoriness of the modern by proclaiming the individuality of the creative 'genius' who, beyond every metamorphosis, guaranteed the coherence and legitimacy of the project of the modern.

René Huyghe, in an essay on Delacroix and Baudelaire, notes that 'aesthetic individualism could be consummated only through the modern concept of the genius.'[64] And indeed most representatives of Viennese modernity shared in this cult of the genius. Otto Weininger even made it the subject of a detailed psychological study. Klimt, Loos, Kraus and Schönberg all believed in the 'genius', beginning with their own personal genius: the final claim to legitimacy of a self-proclaimed creator, and a citadel in which modernism could dwell safe from its academic or philistine detractors. The theme of 'genius' fascinated the sharpest critical minds – Freud, Musil, Wittgenstein. Perhaps it ought to be considered inseparable from the notion of modernity itself. Once traditions, schools, canons and standards of taste had been subjected to radical criticism, and the legitimacy of art had been rooted exclusively in the force of creative individuality, the 'genius' was bound to reappear.

Modernity or postmodernity?

Vienna has a special place in current arguments over the notions of modernity and postmodernity. The Viennese modernists may indeed have prefigured some of the great postmodern themes: the triumph and crisis of individualism (in the sense given to it by Louis Dumont and Gilles Lipovetsky);[65] the nostalgia for a mythology capable of regenerating society (the 'total work of art' dreamed of by the secessionist artists who, guided by a few important figures such as Klimt in his supervision of the conception of the Stoclet palace, subjected every aspect of life, from architecture to the details of interior decoration, to the 'new style'; but also Zionism and nationalisms which set their utopian visions in the distant past, where history fades into myth); distrust of scientific and technological rationalism (expressed through linguistic criticism or in the striving of architects to reconcile the decorative with the functional); the questioning of the status of modern art, somewhere between elitism and democratization.

As Jean Baudrillard puts it, 'in every cultural context, there is a significant interaction of the old and the new. But this does not mean that "modernity", meaning a historical and polemical condition of change and crisis, is everywhere present.'[66] Consciousness of modernity often goes hand in hand with a feeling of decadence. Jacques le Goff recently reminded us that the word 'modern', in the sense that we use it today, was widespread in the fifth and sixth centuries, during the fall of the Roman empire. In the twelfth century, during one of the first quarrels between ancients and moderns, Walter Map spoke of *modernitas*, by which he meant the critical assessment of an evolution which had already lasted for centuries.[67]

Nineteenth-century modernization was characterized by an extension of central government, scientific and technical progress leading to social change and the disappearance of certain cultural traditions, population growth and economic growth, urbanization and the development of new means of communication and information. These changes meant that the terms of the debate had to be redefined; we must now make clear what they were. Modernization, as an economic, social and political process, cast doubt on collective cultural identities, and also on individual subjective identity. Modernism meant that 'modern ideas' hardened into a doctrine: first of all, the idea of progress, including progress in art and religion. Finally, modernity meant a way of living, thinking and creating which was not afraid of change and innovation, but still kept a critical awareness of modernization; it expressed itself in aesthetic or theoretical language, and kept its distance from 'modernism'. Baudelaire's virulent denunciations of the present-day world went alongside his exaltation of the modern. Similarly, Viennese modernity was in many respects antimodern.

If we define modernity as an awareness of the crises which emerged from modernization, we can interpret the postmodernity of the 1970s and 1980s as a radical reformulation of modernity. The notion of postmodernity was first applied to a historical period beginning towards the end of the 1960s and defined in economic, sociological and political terms – Alain Touraine in 1969 and Daniel Bell in 1973 were speaking of 'postindustrial' societies[68] – but also in aesthetic terms. The avant-garde – abstract painting, serial music, functionalist architecture – had become the conformist norm and so could be contested, permitting any kind of innovative combination.[69]

For postmodernists it was an open question whether the *Aufklärung* – the Enlightenment – had remained unfinished, or had simply failed. They were ready to cast doubt on reason and its 'reasonable' individuals. They identified with the psychological approach which, from Nietzsche to Freud, found an Other apart from reason to explain the fragility of the autonomous individual. They took up the critiques of an instrumental and classifying reason which Adorno and Horkheimer had used to unmask the violence inherent in subject–object relations. They drew on Wittgenstein's philosophy of language which deconstructs the subject as author and judge of his own semantic intentions. Finally, aesthetic postmodernity contested the tyranny of the avant-garde and the idea that every age has a state of artistic advancement which is the basis for deciding what is aesthetically acceptable. Postmodernity, so defined, renewed and radicalized the activities of modernity, and did not shrink from contesting the very foundations of the modern. It did not necessarily imply a return to eclecticism or historicism, as was claimed by its false prophets and detractors, but it rewrote modernity in such as way as to criticize the modern and so pave the way for its reconstruction.[70]

Successive waves of modernism show certain affinities beyond their differences: for example, similarities can be found between the modernity of the early Romantics and Viennese modernity, or between the latter and the Weimar modernity of the 1920s and 1930s. Some important events in modernity carry a potential for the postmodern which has been realized in present-day postmodernity. Jürgen Habermas suggests that it was Nietzsche's thought which marked the advent of postmodernity in philosophy.[71] But it is also possible to see Friedrich Schlegel as a precursor of postmodernity, as Ernst Behler did.[72] From this viewpoint we could see the living heritage of Viennese modernity as a prefiguration of our own postmodernity.

In a socioeconomic and political context which long remained premodern or incompletely modernized in comparison with Germany, France and England, the Viennese artists and intellectuals of our present study were particularly sensitive to the upsets caused in all aspects of life by the ever more rapid modernization of the late nineteenth century and after. Their unique situation probably explains why Vienna is repeatedly evoked in the present-day debate on postmodernity. For example, Jean-François Lyotard, in his chapter on 'Delegitimation' in *La condition postmoderne*, argues that 'in postmodern culture, the problem of the legitimation of power presents itself in a different way. Long disquisitions have lost credibility, whatever the method used to unify them: disquisitions of speculation, disquisitions on emancipation . . .'[73] This pessimism, he claims, nourished the Viennese modernists at the dawn of the twentieth century: the artists – Musil, Kraus, Hofmannsthal, Loos, Schönberg and Broch – but also the philosophers, Mach and Wittgenstein: 'They probably took the theoretical and artistic awareness of delegitimation and responsibility for it as far as they would go.'[74]

The exhibition at the Pompidou Centre in 1986 was devised by Jean Clair, author of *Considérations sur l'état des beaux-arts: Critique de la modernité*, a decisive contribution to the debate on postmodernity.[75] The preface to the catalogue, called 'A Sceptical Modernity', attacked the dogmatism of the avant-garde and emphasized that the history of art remains to be written, but not until we have cast off the conformism which measures all early twentieth-century works along the yardstick of progress towards abstraction. After that, Viennese modernity may become a favourite site for the archaeologists of the postmodern.

For myself, I have laid stress on the crisis of the individual in modernity[76] and its corollary, the identity crisis, and in a way I have reconnected with the analyses of Georg Simmel. Simmel showed how modern man, solely responsible for himself in the face of whatever values he may meet with, is in a state of permanent anxiety, 'because the essence of the modern is psychologism, the experience and interpretation of the world according to the reactions of our inner selves, as if in an inner world; it is the dissolving of all stability in subjectivity.'[77]

2

Individualism, Solitude and Identity Crisis

I

Individualism as a modern virtue and malady: Schopenhauer, Nietzsche, Simmel, Dilthey

The numerous manifestos of the literary critic Hermann Bahr give us the idea of a modernism grounded in the exaltation of individualism and subjectivity. But Bahr was merely varying one of the fundamental themes of the 1900s, the irresistible rise of individualism. What the Enlightenment had seen as the condition for progress, early Romantics had turned into a central tenet of *Kulturkritik*. 'Enlightened' modernism had enrolled itself under the banner of subjective freedom, guaranteed within the social order by private law, within the state by demands for political equality, and in private life by moral autonomy and *Bildung*, through whose mediation the individual participated in collective *Kultur*. The spirit of subjectivity had challenged the attitudes to life hallowed by religion or tradition. But soon emancipation became a threat of alienation, a threat to social integration.[1] Individualism, a modern victory, seemed an ambivalent one to most critics of modernity: it was an inescapable ethical, logical and aesthetic demand, but they found it necessary to distinguish between individualism proper and its narrowing or deforming manifestations.

To explain how man brought evil into the world, Schopenhauer showed that he was

a prisoner of the *principium individuationis*, and clings fiercely to the total separation it places between himself and others, so that he seeks only his own well-being, indifferent to that of others whose being is completely alien to him, separated from his own by a deep abyss; and that he even considers others as mere ghosts bereft of reality... Now, this violence of the will is already, in itself and immediately, a source of continual suffering. Firstly because all will is born of a lack, that is, of suffering. Secondly because the causal chain of being necessarily forbids the accomplishment of most of his desires.[2]

Human individuation cuts the individual off from the great 'chain' of the world; it creates the illusion of egocentricity and individualism which poisons human and social relations, as well as the split between subject and object which condemns the individual to misery. That was the great lesson which the 1900 generation learned from Schopenhauer: it informs, for example, the climax of Thomas Mann's *Buddenbrooks* (1901). Thomas Buddenbrook, deep in *The World as Will and Representation*, suddenly finds that his own individuality is 'poor, grey, inadequate, wearisome', and stops him improving himself: 'prison, bonds and limitations everywhere.'[3] In Schopenhauer it is through aesthetic intuition that the individual breaks free from his individuation and appeases his individual will.

Nietzsche developed this theme in *The Birth of Tragedy*: 'The artist has already surrendered his subjectivity in the Dionysian process ... The "I" of the lyrist sounds therefore from the abyss of being ... in so far as the subject is the artist, however, he has already been released from his individual will ... for only as an *aesthetic phenomenon* is existence and the world eternally justified.'[4] Through his writings and fragments, Nietzsche deepens the essential difference between the despicable individualism of modern society and the noble individualism of the will to power. On the one side he notes: 'Apparently contrary, the two characteristics of modern Europeans: individualism [*das Individualistische*] and the demand for equal rights: at last I understand.'[5] And in *Human, All Too Human* he wrote that 'To have a philosophical mind' was 'to participate, by knowledge, in the life and being of many by not treating oneself as a fixed individual, one and unchanging.'[6]

But on the other hand, the affirmation of the individual could be a prerequisite for the renewal of culture. For Nietzsche, the condemnation of individualism was one of the last echoes of Christian morality: everyone seemed to be savouring the idea that the individual had to adapt to the needs of society, and must find his happiness in thinking of himself as a useful member of the community. What people really wanted, said Nietzsche, was nothing less than to weaken and suppress the individual.[7] Tyrants and anarchists, each in their own way, were the first stirrings of resistance to this levelling: 'It is when "morals decay" that those beings whom one calls tyrants first make their appearance; they are the forerunners of the *individual*, and as it were early matured *firstlings*.'[8] In a fragment from the 1880s, Nietzsche defined individualism as 'a modest and still unconscious form of the will to power'. From this viewpoint 'socialism is simply a stirring of individualism,' and 'anarchism, in its turn, is simply a stirring of socialism.'[9]

The opposition between the contradictory duo of individual and society and the still utopian vision of accord between individuality and social conscience dominated most of the characteristic theories of post-Nietzschean *Lebensphilosophie*. Georg Simmel put the problem of modern individualism at the heart of sociological thinking. He distinguished between the 'quantitative' individualism inherited from the eighteenth century and the 'qualitative' individualism of the nineteenth. According to the first, 'There dwells in every individual, as an essence, universal man, just as every piece of matter, whatever its individual structure, represents in its essence the regular laws of matter in general. From this one could also draw the right to make a direct link between liberty and equality.'[10] According to the second, 'It is normally no longer a question of being a free individual, but of being such and such a determinable and non-interchangeable individual. . . . This tendency pervades the whole of modern life: the individual in search of himself, as if he did not yet possess himself, with no certain foothold except within himself.'[11] Simmel's concept of social relations did not challenge the contemporary rule of individualism; he saw the interaction of the individual with society as a creative dynamic. But this left an irreducible tension, because the subjective sensibility of modern man prevented him from belonging to traditional structures or submitting to constraints which paid no respect to his own tastes and sensitivities.[12] Historians of private life, whose conclusions bear out Simmel's observations, find that in the course of the nineteenth century the modern individual succeeded in freeing more and more of his secret and intimate private life from the grip of society. Reality outstripped theory: more and more people were rebelling against collective and familial discipline, and declaring their need for their own time or space.[13] Individualism was a disruptive force which could not be turned back into a unifying social dynamic until society had succeeded in 'desubjectivizing the individual'.[14]

Wilhelm Dilthey had the idea, not unrelated to some of Simmel's, that the course of history depended on the interaction of individuals. It led him to ground the work of the historian in psychological method, with autobiography as its model product. 'Autobiography is the highest and most instructive way we have to understand life . . . And it brings us to the roots of all understanding of history.'[15] But here again the individual has acquired a 'trans-subjective' significance: the unity seen in all the works of the *Aufklärung* and of Romanticism depended on the fact that it was one and the same man, one and the same soul, which was expressed, whether in poetry, in a philosophical system, or in music.[16]

Agonies and ecstasies of solitude

After Nietzsche, individualism was felt to be an ambivalent phenomenon; turn-of-the-century attitudes oscillated between diagnosing and criticizing it as a modern cultural malady, and exalting the individual as the ultimate foundation of all true culture. As for the way of life which this individualism seemed to foster, it was the feeling of *solitude*. It could be proudly assumed or painfully endured. Nietzsche illustrates the position: 'Lonesomeness! Too long have I lived wildly in wild remoteness, to return to thee without tears! . . . One thing is forsakenness, another matter is lonesomeness: *that* hast thou now learned! And that amongst men thou wilt ever be wild and strange – wild and strange even when they love thee: for above all they want to be *treated indulgently!*'[17] Sometimes this solitude is an icy one, as in the chapter of *Zarathustra* entitled 'On the olive mount': 'This is the wise waggish-will and good-will of my soul, that it *concealeth not* its winters and glacial storms; it concealeth not its chilblains either. To one man, lonesomeness is the flight of the sick one; to the other, it is the flight *from* the sick ones.'[18] Sometimes it is challenging and triumphant:

> May I be allowed to hazard a suggestion concerning one last trait in my charac-
> ter, which in my intercourse with other men has led me into some difficulties?
> ... My humanity is a perpetual process of self-mastery. But I need solitude: that
> is to say, recovery, return to myself, the breathing of free, crisp, bracing air ...
> the whole of my *Zarathustra* is a dithyramb in honour of solitude, or, if I have
> been understood, in honour of purity.[19]

Solitude seems to be the price of a declared individualism.

Nietzsche brought into philosophy a theme already present in the literary tradition: the 'hapless genius', the 'misunderstood visionary' of the Roman-tics.[20] He laid claim to a way of life which his acquaintances sometimes took as a joke: 'He was a lot less solitary than he pretended,' declared Franz Overbeck, 'he enjoyed being so, he insisted on being solitary.'[21] In reality, for Nietzsche the theme was not a mere passing fancy, or a pose. It decided the contour of his thought, which could justly be called 'monologic'.[22] Doubtless the inescapable solitude of the modern individual was one consequence of the 'death of God'.

Almost all the representative artists and intellectuals of 1900s modernism were to share in this theme of solitude: it could be a challenge and a curse, as with Zarathustra, or it could be the distinctive mark of the 'hero of modern life' – Baudelaire's dandy, strolling lonely amid the crowds. In Nietzsche's fragments from the years 1887–8 there are several quotations from Baudelaire on the theme of solitude: 'The man of genius wants to be one, therefore solitary ... glory is to remain one, and prostitute oneself in one's own way.'[23] While staying in Nice in the autumn and winter of 1887–8, Nietzsche had read Crépet's edition of Baudelaire's posthumous works and unpublished correspondence, which had just come out (1887).[24] Baudelaire had what Georges Blin calls a 'superstition of difference': 'His solitude is a passionate conquest, yet he suffers from it and detests it, albeit half-heartedly ... Like Julien Sorel, Baudelaire makes a categorical imperative out of an unlikeness that ordinary people look on as a sin.'[25] Nietzsche, reading Baudelaire, was both fascinated and horrified by this 'decadent' feeling of solitude which culminates in the masochistic *Heautontimoroumenos* ('The Self-Tormentor') and in self-detestation. But Sartre's comment on Baudelaire could be applied to Nietzsche as well: 'He called on solitude so that it would at least come to him from himself – so that he would not have it inflicted on him.'[26]

Rilke, in his *Florentine Journal*, speaks in Nietzschean terms about the artist's 'will to solitude',[27] and Rudolf Kassner summed up this view of life in 1928: 'This solitude means for the modern personality what the golden halo of the saints meant to the early painters.'[28] But the glory of solitude could also be felt as a malediction. Rilke's Maltese, Laurids Brigge, describes the solitude which weighs on him in his 'chambers of chance':

My last hope then was always the window. I would imagine that out there there might still be something which belonged to me, even now, in this hour of the sudden poverty of death. But scarcely had I looked in that direction than I wished that the window had been barricaded as firmly as the wall. For then I knew that everything out there was going on with the same indifference, that nothing existed out there except my solitude. The solitude I had made all around me, whose grandeur was not in proportion to my heart.[29]

The literature of the 1900s gives numerous examples of solitary characters sitting or standing by a window, particularly and almost universally in works by Viennese authors. 'Alone, sitting by the window' is the first stage direction Hofmannsthal uses to indroduce Claudio, hero of his lyrical play 'Death and the Fool' (*Der Tor und der Tod*, 1893). In Schnitzler's novella 'Dying' (*Sterben*, 1892), Felix, the sick man, is rapidly deserted by everyone and places his bed near the window through which he observes the living. In Beer-Hofmann's 'George's Death' (*Der Tod Georgs*, 1900), Paul, left lonely by the death of his friend George, is seen at the beginning of the story near a window: 'Those shapes on the wall were the black shadow of the window-frame . . . Like a fence of black hearts, the leaves of the lime tree showed in front of the window.'[30] The extremest manifestation is in Hofmannsthal's essay on Swinburne, in which the artist's isolation is symbolized by the covered windows: 'The windows are hidden under tapestries, behind which can be imagined a garden à la Watteau, with nymphs, fountains and golden swings, or a park at dusk with copses of dark poplars. But in reality, what is going on out there is life, noisy, rowdy, ruthless and inchoate.'[31]

Later, Ulrich, the 'man without qualities', who bears the hereditary mark of this 'Viennese modernity', was also to be introduced to the reader standing alone at a window: 'He was standing at one of the windows, looking through the delicate green filter of the garden's green air into the brownish street, and for the last ten minutes, watch in hand, he had been counting the cars, carriages, and trams, and the pedestrians' faces.'[32] In the last chapter, before the coming of the 'empire of the millennium', Ulrich feels a sort of dislocation in the surrounding reality:

'It's a difference of attitude. I am becoming different and so whatever is connected with me is becoming different too,' Ulrich thought, sure that he was observing himself clearly.

But it might also have been said that his solitude – a condition that existed, after all, not only within him but also around him, thus connecting both – it might have been said, and he himself felt it, that this solitude was becoming ever denser or ever larger. It passed through the walls. It grew out into the town. Without actually expanding, it grew out into the world. 'What world?' he thought. 'There isn't any!' It seemed to him that this concept no longer had any meaning.[33]

This passage is central to our argument, since I intend to show that the identity crisis of the self cut off from the world goes with symptoms of a loss of reality which express the problematics of subject-object Identity.

The feeling of solitude was so strong among the writers of 'Young Vienna' that it made all human contacts seem superficial and illusory. 'What does all that matter to us, and all those games, / we who are so greatly and eternally alone, / forever wandering without ever seeking a goal?', cries Hofmannsthal in his poem 'Ballad of External Life' (1895). And although Beer-Hofmann's poem 'Lullaby for Myriam' (1897) is a celebration of newborn life and the joys of fatherhood, it contains the lines, 'Blind – thus we walk in solitude, / And no one in this world can be a companion to anyone any more – / Sleep, my baby, sleep!'[34]

Felix Salten, who was closely associated with the 'Young Vienna' group, speaks in his literary memoirs of the restrained cordiality of personal relations among these young writers, which gave the impression of lukewarmness or even coldness. He says that Arthur Schnitzler hated any physical contact, and recoiled brusquely if someone laid a friendly hand on his shoulder. Beer-Hofmann seems always to have kept himself at a distance which deterred most people. Apparently he once said to Salten, referring to the Young Vienna group: 'Friends? At bottom we are not friends – but we can just about endure one another's company.'[35] Hofmannsthal confided to his private diary:

> Solitude. As I was writing to Rudolf Borchardt, I decided to tell him about the solitude I feel all around me and my works. This might sound like hypocrisy; but at the same time I realized that there really are different sorts of solitude, and even that, with each friend, a new solitude makes itself felt, its dark waters lit up by this new lighthouse.[36]

For Hofmannsthal, this feeling of solitude accompanied a refusal to let literary critics fit him into any literary movement; as early as 1898 he was accusing Bahr of espousing a never-ending series of trends, although (said Hofmannsthal) 'what really matters is what the individual is and does – productive individuality.'[37]

Private writings and the eros of estrangement

One of the characteristics of Viennese literary modernism is that it produced few manifestoes or collective programmes – except Bahr's, which were always provisional and about to be 'transcended'. Each individual preferred to deepen his own singularity, his own genius, independently – or in private: they were fascinated by private diaries. Schnitzler kept his with impressive minuteness and regularity, as its recent publication shows.[38] Hofmannsthal, too, regularly kept up his private 'notes', and in 1891 he wrote an enthusiastic review of Amiel's *Journal*.

The irremediable solitude of the individual cast doubt on language as a suitable instrument of communication. This deep-rooted scepticism is one aspect of the 'crisis of language' so often described as a characteristic phenomenon of the crisis of modernity around 1900. In his 'Contributions to a Critique of Language', which first came out in 1901, Fritz Mauthner (whose thinking was profoundly influenced by Nietzsche)[39] included a paragraph headed 'Solitude' and declared that:

> People are always churning out the old cliché that language creates links
> between people. But no one has yet thought of deploring the fact that all the
> misery of solitude is solely due to language . . . Like the ocean between the
> continents, language tosses about between individuals. They say that the ocean
> links countries together, because from time to time a boat docks, or sails, and
> anchors – if it has not sunk in the interim. The sea is a separation, and only tidal
> waves, aroused by unknown forces, strike now here, now there, against unknown
> shores, depositing weeds and pebbles. Similarly, language only conveys the
> lowliest things from one person to another. And in between, amidst the surge
> and tempest, in the empty foam that dashes against heaven, far from all inhabited
> lands, poetry and seasickness exist side by side.[40]

The symbolist theatre, after Maeterlinck, was to place silence at the very heart
of drama, taking the incapacity of language to express subjective feelings
and the overflowing of the unsaid which suffocates human relations as its
dominant themes.

Even love had lost its power to bring individuals together. In 1922 Ludwig
Klages, in his treatise on 'The Cosmogonic Eros', was to sum up the concept
of life which pervaded the aesthetics of 1900. There is an excellent analysis of
it in Musil's 'Journals'.[41] Klages emphasized that erotic passion did not create
any bond of sympathy: it actually needed a certain distance between the
partners. The lover's experience was not addressed to the other person, but to
his or her *image* plucked from the instability of the world. 'Eros, in its supreme
realization, remains an *eros of estrangement*, and the individual in its throes
looks on his partner as an Other of unfathomable depth who is never allied to
him, like an eye of the great All observing him from the purple depths of
night.'[42] Human love, said Klages, hid more than it revealed of the 'secrets of
the world'. In 1900 Lou Andreas-Salomé, in her 'Reflections on the Problem
of Love', decided that only the person who holds himself aloof can be loved
for long, because he alone, in his living self-sufficiency, can symbolize for the
Other the power of Life. 'Everyone must take root in his own soil so as to
become a World in the eyes of his beloved.'[43] In 1910, in her treatise on
'Eroticism', she denounced, quoting Schopenhauer, the 'duplicities of love',
and suggested that it was better for lovers not to know each other too well, but
to remain strangers to each other.[44] Similarly, Rilke wrote:

> Loving, for a long time ahead and far on into life, is – solitude, enhanced and
> deepened loneness for him who loves. Love is at first not anything that means
> unfolding, surrendering, and uniting with another: it is a high inducement to the
> individual to open, to become something in himself, to become world, to become
> world to himself for another's sake.[45]

Love, in Rilke, often seems very close to the 'cosmogonic eros' in which
the self, freed from the scourge of subjective consciousness, is pure soul,
capable of uniting instantly with 'images' – but the beloved is too much with
it, and becomes an obstacle: 'Lovers, without the other who masks their sight,
/ would be close to it, and astonished . . . / Sometimes, as if by mistake, an
opening appears behind the other . . . / but no one ever overtakes the other.'[46]

Monologue and dialogue: Weininger and Ebner

With the grandiloquence that runs through *Sex and Character* (1903), Otto Weininger gives his metaphysical formulation of the solitude theme:

> Man is alone in the world, in tremendous eternal isolation.
>
> He has no object outside himself; lives for nothing else . . . he is far removed from being the slave of his wishes, of his abilities, of his necessities; he stands far above social ethics; he is alone. . . . Nothing is superior to him, to the isolated absolute unity. But there are no alternatives for him; he must respond to his own categorical imperatives, absolutely, impartially. 'Freedom,' he cries . . . 'rest, peace from the enemy; peace, not this endless striving . . .' What is the use of it all, he cries to the universe . . . To acquiesce in his loneliness is the splendid supremacy of the Kantian.[47]

In this passage, Weininger tries to restore to the individualism and solitude so characteristic of modernity the 'superhuman' heroism of Nietzsche's Zarathustra. Indeed, Weininger himself, like all the Viennese modernists, felt this solitude (as his suicide in 1903 at the age of twenty-three shows). The solitude was both willed and suffered like a sort of chronic sickness: a 'metaphysical' illness in the Kierkegaardian sense as much as a psychological disturbance. It was the philosopher Ferdinand Ebner, in his book 'The Word and Spiritual Realities' (published in 1921), who gave the most emphatic interpretation of this 'existentialist' element in Weininger, showing that *Sex and Character* is one of the most striking manifestations of the *Icheinsamkeit* (ego-loneliness) which afflicted the modern individual and which, according to Ebner, could only be cured by experience of a Thou accessible through words.[48] The dialogue with another, passing through dialogue with God, is opposed to the poetic or philosophical model of the genius driven back on his own subjectivity.

II

Depersonalization and 'nerves'

The subjectivity into which the individual recoils seems to be a fragile, threatened kernel. 'The author', said Hofmannsthal, referring to Amiel, 'witnesses his own disintegration,' and he concludes his review by citing the Genoese author's 'Depression, langour of flesh and spirit . . . How hard it is to live, oh my weary heart!'[49] Speaking of the work of the young Hofmannsthal, one critic has gone so far as to speak of 'schizophrenia as a poetical structure' and of 'depersonalization syndrome'.[50] This approach to literary criticism is an attempt to avoid falling back into the applied psychopathology of literature and art so frequently practised at the turn of the century: for example, by Max Nordau, in 'Degeneration' (1892–3), in which all the resources of psychiatric diagnosis, from simple neurasthenia to hysteria and psychosis, are exploited so as to analyse – and in Nordau's case to condemn – modernism in literature.

The Viennese modernists were fond of using the suggestively vague term 'nervous complaints' to describe their inner state. Some encouragement for this idea came from the 'Essays in Contemporary Psychology' by Paul Bourget, who was well known to the Viennese, both Bahr and Hofmannsthal having written long articles about him in 1891.[51] In the first chapter of the 'Essays', on Baudelaire, Bourget described the *taedium vitae* and ennui which was manifest in modernity: 'A universal nausea for the inadequacies of this world is afflicting Slavs, Germans and Latins. In the first it is manifested through nihilism, in the second through pessimism, and in ourselves through bizarre and solitary neuroses.'[52]

In a letter to Schnitzler in 1891 Beer-Hofmann complained of a nervous complaint which was disturbing his sleep and getting in the way of his work;[53] in 1899 we find Schnitzler confiding his anxieties about his own nerves to his private diary.[54] In August 1897, Hofmannsthal advised Leopold von Andrian to consult a doctor – Arthur Schnitzler – about his 'neurasthenia'.[55] In his personal journal for 1889, Hofmannsthal (then aged fifteen) noted 'nervous relaxation ... dangerous game, risk of intellectual over-excitement (acquired books by Lombroso, Krafft-Ebing; interest in psychiatry)'.[56] In 1896, Peter Altenberg described a woman suffering from 'hypertrophy of the self': 'It's a nervous illness, or rather it makes the nerves ill.'[57]

Nietzsche, who read the 'Essays in Contemporary Psychology' in 1883,[58] was one of the first to suggest that 'modernity' and 'nervous complaints' were virtually synonymous. In *Human, All Too Human* he wrote:

> In the vicinity of madness: the sum total of sensations, knowledge and experience, i.e. the whole burden of culture, has become so great that there is a general danger of over-stimulation of the nervous and thinking capacity, so much so that the cultured classes in the European countries are completely neurotic and almost all of their great families have a relative on the brink of madness.[59]

Here we recognize one of Nietzsche's favourite themes: the analysis of decadence. 'Nerve trouble' was becoming the modern malady *par excellence*, a necessary stage on the way to a possible renaissance.

With his habitual naivety and exaggeration, Hermann Bahr put 'nervous complaints' at the centre of his manifesto 'The Transcendence of Naturalism' (1891). It can even be said that he put it at the centre of his new 'art of poetry':

> The new idealism expresses the new humanity. It is made of nerves; the rest is dead, withered, dried up. It now lives entirely on nerves, it reacts only as its nerves dictate. Everything which happens to it is to do with nerves, its effects are all obtained from nerves. But words come from reason or the senses, so it can only use them as a sort of language of flowers: its language is all parables and symbols. It can change languages frequently, because they are always approximate and unconstraining; and all in all that is a mere disguise. The content of the new idealism is nerves, nerves, nerves, and – a costume: decadence is taking over from rococo and the Gothic masquerade.[60]

These declarations are patently ridiculous, and Karl Kraus, in his 1899 pamphlet 'Demolished Literature', had great sport with the 'collections of new nerves' that were wont to assemble at the Café Griensteidl.

In his 1908 article on '"Civilized" Sexual Morality and Modern Nervous Illness', Freud began by summarizing the theories of W. Erb (author of a book entitled 'The Growing Nervous Troubles of our Times'), Binswanger and Krafft-Ebing, then introduced some ideas which presage *Civilization and its Discontents*; he emphasized that most contemporary theories of 'nerves' were ignoring the most important causative factors of such disturbances. If we set aside the vaguer types of 'nervous' states, said Freud, and concentrate on actual nervous illnesses, the malign influence of civilization boils down to a harmful repression of sexual life (particularly among certain social classes) by civilized 'morality'.[61] The idea of linking nerve trouble and sexuality had nothing original about it at the time. But, as Peter Gay has pointed out, all novelists and psychologists were making the link between debauchery and nerves. Freud was the first to stand the notion on its head and make excessive sexual repression into the major cause of nervous illness.[62]

It will be seen, then, that everyone at the turn of the century was talking about 'nerves'. Their obsessive recurrence in the language of contemporaries of Viennese modernism gives some indication of that awareness of cultural crisis which Schorske calls the emergence of 'psychological man', unhappy and unstable, who was rising from the ashes of the 'classical liberal view of man' cherished by *Bildung*.[63] When Bahr hailed the advent of the 'art of nerves' he was making a positive element of modern consciousness out of what most Viennese artists had already felt or described as a permanent state of anxiety within modernity. The individual had been challenged to overcome, with nothing but his own subjective resources, problems which were far beyond his capacity: a crisis of the social and political subject faced with the consequences – and sometimes even the failure – of the great strategies of emancipation, and with the slackening of the old bonds of cultural integration (Viennese aestheticism being considered as a consequence of a loss of political opportunity); a crisis of the psychological subject whose 'libidinal economy' (to borrow a phrase from Jean-François Lyotard) was attempting to control conflicts which remained insoluble within social reality. The attempt could end in pathological upset.

From the deconstruction of identity to the fiction of the self

All these crises together constituted the identity crisis – if we allow that 'identity' can be defined along the lines proposed by Paul Ricoeur in an essay inspired by his thoughts on the *Essais sur l'individualisme* of Louis Dumont. How do we go from the notion of the individual to the notion of identity? The first step is purely epistemological and concerns *any* individual in its relation to the species. Ricoeur speaks here of *individuation*. The ensuing transition comes from the same problem approached along pragmatical lines: speech distinguishes the *human* individual from individuals in general by reason of the 'I say that', 'I declare that'. The second stage means more or less extracting the *I* from the *I say that* to produce a *say 'I'*. For Ricoeur that moment relates no longer to individuation in the epistemological sense, but to *identification*, and shows how a person identifies himself by saying *I*. The second transition involves a reflexion on narrative identity: the operation of narrative leads from pragmatics, which takes no account of time or of changes which take time, to the ethical implications of speech acts. This posits a responsible or 'imputable' subject. At this stage we are genuinely dealing with an *ipse*, '*I myself*'.[64]

Ricoeur's definitions let us understand identity as a continual process of construction via successive stages (individuation, identification, imputation) corresponding to fresh definitions of the correlation between 'I' and 'not-I' (the world, others, other people). We can then understand the identity crisis as a doubt of the 'self' which makes the individual regress through previous stages in the construction of his personal identity, leading to the questioning of individuation – and this, in a word, was the mystic obsession of most Viennese modernists. The questioning also bore on identification, and what answer there was came from an imaginary field drawn from personal history and cultural discourse: for someone designated as a Jew, for example, it might be Jewish identity; but it could also be sexual identity.

The identity crisis was the deconstructive process whereby a new and more or less stable identity was (re)constructed – unless it turned out to be impossible to reconstitute a solid identity, in which case the subject had to learn to live with a more or less permanent crisis. This very process of crisis and restabilization of identity led to a reformulation of the modern condition which, from this viewpoint, might be seen as *postmodernity*. Indeed, it could be said that criticism of the whole notion of the subject is an essential theme of postmodernist deconstruction, in that the latter, according to Manfred Frank, postulates that 'the fully developed idea of subjectivity is the last expression to date of the triumph of rationalism over the "will to power" (Nietzsche), the "being" (Heidegger), "*différance*" (Derrida), "non-identity" (Adorno) and "alterity" (Levinas, Foucault).'[65]

Ricoeur's analyses in *Temps et récit*[66] describe the constitution of identity as a narrative operation. The individual identifies with what he tells about himself and what other people tell about him. He is, to quote Wilhelm Schapp (a disciple of Husserl), 'in Geschichten verstrickt', 'ensnared in stories', and 'the self itself has no qualities: all the qualities reside in the stories.'[67] Autobiography[68] and the private diary[69] are the two major literary forms of identity building through narrative, the 'fiction of the self' which is also at work in curative psychoanalysis.

As we have seen, all the principal representatives of Viennese modernism cultivated private writing as a genre. Hofmannsthal, Schnitzler and Musil ruminated in their diaries on the theme of identity crisis which they were putting at the heart of their work. The ground work of psychological analysis, *The Interpretation of Dreams*, comes over partly as a combination of a private notebook (accounts of dreams noted down day by day) and an autobiography. All the time he was 'inventing' political Zionism, Theodor Herzl was confiding to his diary the anguished fumblings which accompanied his reconstruction of Jewish identity. The self-narrating, self-fictionalizing elements which each brought to bear on his personal identity crisis are, beyond all differences of genre, a common element in most of the texts which we shall be examining in this book: it is one of the unifying elements in our sources.

And yet the rejection of 'qualities' and identifications can take the individual to the brink of suicide. For, as Gunther Anders wrote in 1936, 'If men lingered perpetually over the impossibility of self-identification, they would, to put it brutally, have no other way out than suicide – the only way out for the Stoics; no other way of abolishing what one is in a state of non-liberty, or of doing away with contingency.'[70]

The man without qualities: Mach, Freud, Nietzsche, Musil

As the unity of the person and the 'classical subject' broke down, Robert Musil's 'man without qualities' stood out as the man who refused all hasty identifications and remained in suspense, perennially receptive. One cannot say that he is in search of his identity, like the hero of the traditional *Bildungsroman*; his attitude is rather one of waiting. This was no caprice of the author: the choice of the 'man without qualities' was in fact dictated by a certain historical situation, that of Vienna at the dawn of the twentieth century, in 1913, on the brink of the First World War. The disintegration of the individual is described through the disintegration of the world.[71] The characters who surround the man without qualities each represent an attempt at founding a stable identity: Leinsdorf, the statesman, who stakes everything on political power; the sentimental Diotima and the calculating Arnheim, who invoke the strength of the soul against the dessication of rationalism; the derisory general Stumm von Bordwehr who knows only one order, that of military discipline; the sectarian Hans Sepp, supporter of the antisemitic and pan-Germanist *Blut und Boden*. One could cite many other examples of characters who shore up their tottering equilibrium by identifying with social roles or ideological causes.

As opposed to these characters with their delusions of solidity, there are other pathological 'cases' who illustrate the sickness of a culture which has thrown individuals back on themselves and lost the power to 'give each of its members a place' (Wittgenstein):[72] Moosbrugger, the sex murderer, whose destiny is an accusation against society, as is that of Büchner's Woyzeck, or the hysterical Clarissa. The third, unfinished part of *The Man Without Qualities* describes a mystical experience through an incestuous affair between brother and sister. Should we interpret this refusal to make particular identifications, this renunciation of the unattainable self, this loss of self in being, as Musil's final answer? His vigilant irony would surely not have let him stop short at this stage in Ulrich's career. But the ending remains conjectural. Perhaps, indeed, there is no possible ending.

The 'identity crisis' really does seem to be the distinguishing mark of Viennese modernity. Two master thinkers of the generation which created this modernity, Mach and Freud, set the theme at the heart of their theories. Mach, a physician who gave the Viennese public a new formulation of the monist doctrine of positivism, talks of the 'unsavable ego' (*das unrettbare Ich*) in his 'Analysis of Sensations' (first published in 1885), the metapsychological crown of his philosophy. He systematically reduces the ego and the world to 'complexes of sensations' which can be analysed as elementary biophysical processes. For Young Vienna this 'integral phenomenalism'[73] was the cruellest possible demystification of all their certainties about identity. It was the inspiration for Hofmannsthal's *The Lord Chandos Letter*; Weininger felt obliged to 'refute' Mach so as to save Culture; and Musil, as is well known, was to be profoundly influenced by the doctrine to which he devoted his doctoral dissertation, completed in 1908. The combined influence of Mach and Nietzsche suggested to these authors that behind all the substantialist masks and illusions of language there was nothing but an aching void of subjectivity. In 1904, rather later than Young Vienna, Bahr seized on the 'unsavable ego' as a slogan for his latest conversion, this time to expressionism.

Freud, no less than Mach, threw into turmoil the notions of permanence, continuity and cohesion traditionally connected with the idea of individual identity. André Green summarizes: 'for Freud the individual is not a concept. Secondly: the Ego is not the subject; thirdly and finally, the subject cannot define itself in psychoanalysis except by its relation to its progenitors.'[74] After Freud there was not much point in pursuing the identity of the subject, except to confirm its illusory nature. Or rather, it was better thereafter to substitute for the idea of identity the idea of *identification*, *Identifizierung* – or even better, of identification*s*. The subject gains consistency only to the extent that it identifies with unconscious images – father, mother, ego, etc. Identifications can be successful, but they can also be competitive or even conflicting, like the 'ego visitors' who strive among themselves to dominate the subject.[75] Each is unstable and can be manipulated. In the favourable sense this can mean that curative analysis progressively substitutes an identification more tolerable to the subject for one which threatens its stability; in the negative sense it means that the Freudian subject is apt to dissolve into a horde, a mass or a mob.

Psychoanalysis can elucidate the structure and development of the psychic personality only in terms of pathological processes (because 'it is strictly impossible to have direct access to any representation whatever of the "normal"')[76] or in terms of dreams, because there are such things as dream-identifications, sometimes only in a few features, sometimes in snatches of other people's conversation. The first stage of Freud's theory of identifications is connected with his study of neurosis and hysteria: the neurotic identification is 'fictional' in type and obeys a style of unconscious thought which modifies the ego. The latter suffers the effects of sexual desire represented by the characters of the hysterical 'fiction':

> The ego falls apart and seems malleable and taxable, a passion of the other, of multiplicity, of the unconscious libido, a puppet in a play whose real motivation cannot be guessed at except by following the interaction of identifications. These observations force us to acknowledge the fissured structure (strata, traces, layer

upon layer of infantile loves) and also the fictional structure (novel, identification) of the ego.[77]

The essay 'A Childhood Memory of Leonardo da Vinci' (1910) emphasizes identification as a genetic and structural function. Leonardo's homosexuality was the result of identification with his mother, precociously seductive and abandoned by his father. Identification with the mother allowed him to forget her as an object of incest, while retaining her eternally in every love relationship and every homosexual impulse. This identification was narcissistic, turning the object libido into a narcissistic libido whose object was the ego.[78] In *Totem and Taboo* (1912), Freud shows how the individual acquires an identity, after repressing incest and cannibalism, by identifying with the totem. Thereafter brothers' relation to the ideal (the dead Father) leads to the mutual identification of subjects as members of a community governed by the paternal law.

In chapter 7 of *Group Psychology and the Analysis of the Ego* (1920), on 'Identification', Freud distinguishes three kinds of identifications: the primary identification with the father, which prepares the Oedipus conflict; neurotic identifications, which can be detected from symptoms which psychoanalysts must patiently track down; and finally identification with someone who is admired – a *Führer*, a master, an exemplary friend, etc. This process leads Jean Florence to conclude that psychoanalysis is an attempt to 'give a rigorous account of what is non-identical to the self. Freud chose identification to express the non-accomplishment of identity.'[79]

In *The Ego and the Id* (1923), Freud asked what, in those conditions, could still be presented as the 'nucleus of the ego'.[80] A solid nucleus? It is better imagined as an atomic nucleus which can be split. This is the image suggested by Ibsen in *Peer Gynt* (1867, first performed in 1876), which could be defined as a dramatized search for an undiscoverable identity. Towards the end of Act V, Peer Gynt reflects on his own existence, and strips off a series of onion skins, each of which represents one of his metamorphoses, observing 'What a terrible lot of layers there are! Surely I'll soon get down to the heart? No – there isn't one!'[81] In Weininger's posthumously published *Über die letzten Dinge* ('Last Things', 1904) there is an essay on *Peer Gynt* written the day after its première in Vienna in May 1902.[82] Weininger thought that the character 'was totally bereft of ego . . . he has no white soul, and not even a black one.'[83]

In the light of psychoanalysis, the feeling every subject has of its own identity becomes an endless, unpredictable interplay of conscious and unconscious identities: identity projected into the future and identity fed on remembrance; identity of family, group or national membership and identity of rejected memberships; identity of 'normality' and identity conferred by life (sex, race, age, etc.); and the aspiration to negate and transcend all these limitations.[84] The psychoanalytical approach also confirms that as regards the destiny of the subject, identification fantasies can supplant 'real' identity to such an extent that the opposition between reality and fantasy is meaningless in any attempts to understand a personality.

This might well be an essential aspect of Viennese (post)modernism:

radical contesting of the classical subject and quasi-permanent identity crisis. But before that we must emphasize the other characteristic of that modernism: its appeal to individualism as a foundation of creativity, the only thing capable of taking over from styles and academies which had become history, the conviction that modern culture had to be a 'culture of the ego'. It is a strange paradox: the 'cult of the ego' went hand in hand with the discovery of the vacuity or fragility of that very ego. To understand this apparent contradiction we ought probably to return to Schopenhauer and Nietzsche, and distinguish between two meanings of 'ego': ego as individuation and ego as totality. Because the Young Vienna generation was returning, quite deliberately, to the paths first traced by Nietzsche.[85]

In *The Twilight of Idols* Nietzsche denounced 'the error of false causality': 'And as for the ego! It has become legendary, fictional, a play on words: it has ceased utterly and completely from thinking, feeling, and willing! . . . What is the result of it all? There are no such things as spiritual causes. The whole of popular experience on this subject went to the devil! That is the result of it all.'[86] But slightly later in the same book, he gave a positive example of someone who had triumphed over an identity crisis: Goethe.

> There was no greater event in his life than that *ens realissimum*, surnamed Napoleon. Goethe conceived a strong, highly-cultured man . . . Such a spirit, *become free*, appears in the middle of the universe with a feeling of joyous and confident fatalism; he believes that only individual things are bad, and that as a whole the universe justifies and affirms itself. – *He no longer denies*. . . . But such a faith is the highest of all faiths: I christened it with the name of *Dionysos*.[87]

If Gottfried Benn is right in saying that 'Nietzsche marks the loss of the ego in the biographical sense,'[88] the 'strong' man will be the man who can construct his own identity by integrating his *whole* past into his present ego. The law of the eternal return applies to the ego before becoming a theory of the world,[89] and autobiography, if it is to succeed, must (as indicated by the subtitle of *Ecce Homo*) show 'how one becomes what one is'.[90] The fictional ego discovers its identity when it convinces itself, as in fragment 341 of the *Joyful Wisdom*, that

> This life, as thou livest it at present, and hast lived it, thou must live it once more, and also innumerable times, and there will be nothing new in it, but every pain and every joy and every thought and every sigh, and all the unspeakably small and great in thy life must come to thee again, and all in the same series and sequence.[91]

This will give rise to a new feeling of identity, the one attained by Zarathustra when he cries, 'It returneth only, it cometh back to me at last: my own self, and such of it as hath been long abroad, and scattered among things and accidents.'[92]

Some such 'dionysian' solution was aspired to by those who had suffered the shock of the 'unsavable ego' which, according to Mach and Freud, was characteristic of modernity. They were seeking what Musil's hero calls 'the other state', which puts the ego in communication with the Whole, progressing from the realization of the irretrievable frailty of the 'individual' to the attempt at 'reconciliation in totality'. This meant first and foremost the totality of *oneself*: a 'reconciliation' which was really the very same thing as radical individualism. To be more precise, there were three figures which obsessed the Viennese of the dawning twentieth century: the mystic, Narcissus, and the genius. Three attempts to rebuild identity on the ruins of the subject.

3

The Mystic and the Genius

I

The neo-empiricism of Mach and the 'vacuum of values'

According to Georges Gusdorf's definition, which applies equally well to the 'neo-Romanticism' within Viennese modernism, the Romantic movement puts the ego in a place of honour.[1] Romanticism was a reaction against the rationalist and empiricist outlook of the eighteenth century, which tended to reduce the ego to a 'point of application for a prefabricated truth', the grammatical subject of a universal discourse, or a receptacle for sensations. The statue of Condillac was an illustration of this quasi-annihilation of the ego.[2] Rousseau and Kant paved the way for the Romantic reaction: the first rediscovered the irreplaceable ego of autobiography and the inner life of the solitary thinker, while the other restored the transcendental I in the teeth of empiricism. But this I had nothing in common with personal identity: 'This "I", "he" or other thinking thing does not represent anything more than a transcendental subject of thoughts = X, and it is only through the thoughts which are its predicates that we can know this subject, of which separately we can never have the slightest conception.'[3]

Schelling breaks through the barriers of transcendental idealism so that the ego can move towards the thing-in-itself. The philosophy of identity confronts the error of taking the mind for the subject and nature for the object: mind and nature are both subject/object, the former inclining rather too far towards subjectivity and the latter towards objectivity. To combat the dualist mentality and the divorce of mind from matter, the philosophy of identity disputes the difference, and proclaims the oneness of apparently opposing realities. What in Schelling appears to be an immediate (but concealed) datum of consciousness can be defined as a sort of universal monism, though Schelling himself does not use that notion. The scientific monism of the 1900s, as formulated by Haeckel, Ostwald and also Mach,[4] spurred writers and philosophers to new attempts at restoring the subject-object identity, reacting to the modern ego-identity crisis as well as to a feeling of lost reality.

In the philosophical section of *Sex and Character*, Otto Weininger emphasizes the importance of the 'inaugural event' found in so many Romantic autobiographies, and which he calls 'das Ich-Ereignis',[5] with illustrations from Jean-Paul, Schelling and Novalis. This overtly neo-Romantic chapter in *Sex and Character* follows immediately after Weininger's refutation of Mach's doctrine. Weininger considered that Mach, like Hume and Lichtenberg, conceived the universe as a coherent mass and the ego as a point where this coherent mass had a denser consistency. Nothing was real except the sensations which constituted a strongly cohesive whole within the individual. Thus the ego was not a real unity, but merely a practical one which was unsavable (*unrettbar*), so that there was small regret in giving up the idea of individual immortality. 'Mach's idea of the ego', concludes Weininger, 'is a mere waiting room for sensations.'[6]

In Mach's treatise 'The Analysis of Sensations', first published in Prague in 1885, he relates his own 'inaugural event', whose revelatory character was analogous to the Romantic *Ich-Ereignis*, but whose content was utterly different. The author tells how at a very early age (about fifteen) he had the luck to come across Kant's *Prolegomena to All Future Metaphysics* in his father's library. It made a disturbing and unforgettable impression on him. He continues: 'Some two or three years later I suddenly felt the superfluity of "things in themselves". One joyous summer day in the country, the world, including my own selfhood, suddenly appeared to me as a coherent mass of sensations, in which my sense of self was only and simply a stronger cohesion.'[7]

The importance of Mach's psychology for Viennese modernism has often been studied.[8] But most studies have suggested Mach's psychophysical reductionism as one of the sources of literary impressionism.[9] I shall rather be emphasizing the *reaction* to Mach, not only in Weininger (who most clearly shows the need to outdo Mach), but also in Hofmannsthal, and later in Musil. For the intellectuals of Young Vienna (who also studied at the Vienna University, where Mach taught from 1895 to 1898), Mach's neo-empiricism was a symptom of the cultural crisis which Hermann Broch summed up in his great essay on 'Hofmannsthal and his Times': 'Vienna was the centre of the vacuum of European values.'[10]

By 'vacuum of values' (*Wert-Vakuum*), Broch meant the reign of sceptical rationalism which set scientific and technical research at the pinnacle of cultural values. It was a depressingly banal insistence on the primacy of scientific knowledge, as Musil remarked in his 1908 thesis on Mach: 'Mach's viewpoint is the one which mostly prevails today ... for the time being the situation is so favourable to it that we must confine ourselves to establishing the facts.'[11] Which is to say that Mach sums up the modern *doxa*. *Wert-Vakuum* also meant the reduction of ethics to utilitarian socialism. In Mach, the most down-to-earth notion of usefulness is elevated into the keystone of epistemology under the name of 'the principle of economy': 'Science itself can be considered as a minimalist problem, which consists of setting out the facts as perfectly as possible with the least possible intellectual outlay.'[12]

The *Wert-Vakuum* meant the enmeshing of personal creativity in eclecticism and historicism. Even in Mach the two tendencies are clearly discernible: the eclecticism of a philosopher whose thought had moved steadily away from Kant towards Berkeley;[13] and the historicism of a scholar who submitted the discipline of research to a 'historico-critical' principle according to which – by reference to history – one could understand how the confusion of a priori with experience had created non-problems: 'How many obscure problems become clear when one studies their historical development!' he exclaimed.[14]

Finally, the *Wert-Vakuum* was the triumph of an individualism devoid of all pretence to individuality. At the end of Mach's attempt to deconstruct metaphysics the ego becomes 'unsavable' by a psychology anxious to proceed with rigour, as it is unsavable by the ethics of the metaphysician. Nothing is left but 'elements': sensations and complexes of sensations (colours, sounds, pressures, spaces, lengths of time). The great idols of metaphysics have been cast down; but, as Musil pointed out in his critique of Mach, this did not prevent substances from creeping back into the scattered mass of elements . . .

Mach brings us back to Gusdorf's 'statue of Condillac'. Locke compares the human mind to an unwritten page. And Hume, who defines the philosophical position to which Mach's conceptions lead, confines himself to an anthropology of impersonality, or depersonalization:

> For my part, when I enter most intimately into what I call *myself*, I always stumble on some particular perception or other, of heat or cold, light or shade, love or hatred, pain or pleasure. I never can catch *myself* at any time without a perception, and never can observe any thing but the perception. When my perceptions are remov'd for any time, as by sound-sleep; so long am I insensible of *myself*, and may truly be said not to exist.[15]

The mystical conversion of Lord Chandos

Mach has it that the dissolution of metaphysical substance can lead to the calm and happy smile of the disillusioned sage. For the Viennese the idea of the *unrettbares Ich* was an unmitigated catastrophe. Bahr, writing his essay on Mach in 1899–1900 ('discovering' yet again what Hofmannsthal and his friends had known for ages), tells us that he arrived at 'The Analysis of Sensations' via Théodule Ribot's 'Diseases of the Personality' (1885). Ribot 'shows us people who have suffered a sudden loss of ego and are beginning, like newborn beings, a new existence, which at times they find taken from them again, quite suddenly and mysteriously, to fall back into their old life; some have a triple or even a quadruple ego.'[16]

Hofmannsthal, whose private diaries contain passages which might have been written directly under Mach's influence,[17] analyses the disease of personality in *The Lord Chandos Letter*. Written in 1902, it purports to be a letter from Philip, Lord Chandos, youngest son of the Marquis of Bath, to Francis Bacon, apologizing for having given up all interest in literature.[18] It seems likely that Hofmannsthal is using his fictional alter ego, Chandos, to retrace his own adolescent crisis. In 1902 he was twenty-eight, and his poetical work, begun ten years earlier and animated by a 'genius' so strong that Bahr called him 'a Goethe still sitting on the school bench', seemed substantially finished. The infant prodigy had grown up. This is Chandos's description of the ensuing crisis: before, all existence had come to him 'in a sort of continual intoxication, like one great unity'; now he has the painful impression that all coherence has been lost, both from his thoughts and from his vision of the world. At nineteen he could write the most perfect works without difficulty, thought about composing an encyclopaedia, and trusted in the power of words and well-wrought language to understand and order the cosmos; now he feels 'an unaccountable discomfort whenever I simply tried to pronounce the words "spirit", "soul", or "body". . . . the abstract words that the tongue necessarily shapes when passing any kind of judgment simply fell to dust in my mouth like decaying mushrooms.'[19] This mistrust of language makes Chandos incapable of espousing any ideas he finds in books: 'Among them I was overcome by a feeling of awful solitude; I felt like someone shut up in a garden with nothing but unseeing statues, and I soon fled into the open once more.'[20]

Hofmannsthal makes Chandos send this letter to Francis Bacon, founder of English empiricism and thus the philosophical forebear of Locke, Hume and Mach. Gotthart Wunberg[21] has demonstrated Bacon's influence on Hofmannsthal, as shown, for example, in these notes written in his diary in 1894−5:

> Words are the locked and bolted prisons of the divine *pneuma* and of truth. Idolatry − adoration of an *eidolon*, a symbol which at some time has been a living thing to some human being, worked miracles, been the dazzling revelation of the divine mystery of the world: linguistic concepts are such *eidola*. Usually they are no more sacred than actual idols, nor more truly rich than a buried urn, nor more genuinely 'strong' than a buried sword. Everything which is, is; being and meaning are the same thing; consequently, all being is symbol.[22]

The word *eidola* is probably borrowed from Bacon: in his *Novum Organon* (1620) he mentions various forms which may obscure human knowledge and judgement: *idola tribus, idola specus, idola fori, idola theatri*. Hofmannsthal had become familiar with Bacon through the lectures of the philosopher Franz Brentano, who is often called the father of the Austrian tradition which ends in Wittgenstein and the Viennese Circle. In his first semester at the university in 1892−3, Hofmannsthal had followed Brentano's course in 'practical philosophy', and it is well known that Brentano often claimed to draw inspiration from Bacon.

From this viewpoint the 'crisis of poetic language', often seen as the central theme of the Chandos letter, seems rather to be subordinate to the more general theme of the crisis of identity in an ego undermined by an empiricist-type critique which reduced subjectivity to a series of perceptions. Hofmannsthal's originality (like Weininger he sought to 'transcend' Mach's conclusions) lies in the surprising conversion which allows the 'deconstructed' ego, broken down into complexes of sensations, to reconstitute itself in a mystical impulse by reconstructing a world made available to the ego as symbol.

Returning to the *Letter*, we discover that the life led by Chandos after this depersonalization 'crisis' takes place 'outside the mind, without thought'. He knows moments of new and very intense happiness:

> A watering can, a harrow left standing in a field, a dog in the sun, a run-down churchyard, a cripple, a small farmhouse, any of these can become the vessel for my revelation. Each of them, or for that matter any of a thousand others like them that the eye glides over with understandable indifference can all at once, at some altogether unpredictable instant, assume for me an aspect so sublime and moving that it beggars all words.[23]

The detachment of the ego from the external world, originally felt as a loss and a catastrophe because it went against all preconceived notions, actually dissipates the substantialist illusions of language which make an artificial separation between the ego and the world, whereas, deep down, subject and object are indivisible.

Mysticism and life: Kassner, Rilke, Hofmannsthal

Here, from a different direction, we again approach the monism characteristic of Mach's thinking. Lord Chandos's experience is of a necessary conversion of the subject to a better apprehension of reality. Hofmannsthal calls it a 'mysticism without God',[24] through which the subject attains the bliss of true sensation, which puts the ego in unison with the world and abolishes the bogus division between subject and object which is accredited by language. The best comments on this singular form of 'aesthetic mysticism' are given indirectly by Rudolf Kassner in his first book, published in 1900 and entitled *Die Mystik, die Künstler und das Leben, über englische Dichter und Maler im 19. Jahrhundert: Accorde* ('The Mystic, Artists and Life: On English Poets and Painters of the Nineteenth Century: Agreements').

In his chapter on William Blake, Kassner says that 'The wisdom of the mystic is the power of the poet. If originally all was harmony, poets, those "metaphysical comforters", can restore it in various ways.'[25] According to Kassner, art and poetry unveil the total unity (*All-Einheit*) of things in the world, especially that of subjects and objects, and of internal and external reality – but also the unity of soul and body, life and death. By the power of their imagination they create a world close to magic, archaic belief, marvels or dreams. In 1930 Kassner was to say of his first book: 'It does not mention Hofmannsthal, but there is no lack of allusions to him.'[26] Hofmannsthal wrote to tell him that he had read the book 'as a book, but sometimes even as a letter addressed to me ... Never, when following the thought of Schopenhauer, Nietzsche and other authors, have I felt such happiness, such an illumination of the depths of my own being.'[27] According to this viewpoint, Hofmannsthal amalgamated Mach's empiricism with the heritage of Nietzsche so as to rejoin the mainstream of German sensibility around 1900: *Leben*, life itself.[28] For what this great mystical experience of immanence unveils to

Chandos is simply the great oneness of life, which he thereafter recognizes in all things, from the least to the greatest. His crisis takes him away from book learning and the false community of science towards real life, both individualist and in harmony with reality. As every object of reality becomes for him an epiphany, Chandos begins to resemble Rilke's Rodin: 'He has learned to embrace this life with a still more confiding love. It reveals itself to him as to an initiate, hiding nothing, without mistrust in him. He recognizes it in the least thing as much as in the greatest; in what is scarcely visible and in what is immense.'[29]

States of such felicity are experienced only intermittently. Chandos says:

> I have the feeling that my body is made up of nothing but ciphers, and that all things are therefore accessible to me. Or that we all might enter into a new communication with the whole of existence if only we began to think with our hearts. Yet once the strange enchantment leaves me, I find I am left with nothing to say about it . . . Aside from these rare occurrences, which, moreover, I hardly know whether to attribute to my mind or my body, I live a life of almost unimaginable emptiness, and find it difficult to mask my inner numbness from my wife; or from my staff the indifference I feel regarding the affairs of my estates.[30]

Mystic ecstasy is an essentially unstable state whose peaks and troughs are like the unpredictable rhythms of poetic inspiration. The fleeting restoration of the identity of subject and object is not enough for a continuous feeling of personal identity to be regained.

Chandos's example shows how the figure of the mystic demonstrates the reversal of negative into positive: individualism, which to the young Hofmannsthal was a state of moral crisis, solitude (alone-ness/*Allein-heit*) and uncertainty, is radicalized and transformed into a positive value of individuality in harmony with the world and with life (all-one-ness/*All-ein-heit*). As Georg Simmel wrote, 'The deepest concentration within ourselves, transcending all the multiplicity of the world, brings us to the utter oneness of all things.'[31] The individual ceases to be a mere individuation, a disintegrating atom, and becomes once more a totality; he regains his rightful place at the very centre of the world and of life.

Hermann Bahr, always quick to perceive contemporary tendencies, noted in his diary for 1889 that 'Everywhere we desire the synthesis of the external and the internal, the world and the ego, the most savage (brutal, unconfined) force˙ and the most tender and hypersensitive refinement.'[32] The conclusions of experimental psychology and psychophysical positivism, which had almost reached the point of leaving the individual on the stricken field of the *unrettbares Ich*, took on a new meaning as the deconstruction of the illusions of identity and superficial certainties which endowed the ego with a certain consistency; they created a clean slate on which to inscribe the new, founding perceptions which could recreate a world in harmony with subjectivity. Thanks to the uncompromising lessons in humility which it administered to the subject, reductionist psychology had acted as a sort of school of poverty and self-deprivation through which one could graduate to the mystic revelation.

Scepticism, logic and mysticism: Mauthner, Wittgenstein, Musil

In 1903, under the influence of Fritz Mauthner, Gustav Landauer acknowledged the contemporary rebirth of mysticism in his book *Skepsis und Mystik. Versuche im Anschluss an Mauthners Sprachkritik* ('Scepticism and Mysticism: Essays Inspired by Mauthner's Critique of Language').[33] He summarized Mauthner's theory as the opposition between the sphere of *ratio*, which united the ego to the world through the medium of words (although words could not transpose the world as it was lived into language) and the sphere of mysticism, in which world and ego were fused together in unmediated unity. Landauer observed that where traditional mysticism spoke of the union of the here and now with transcendency, the union of the self with God, the mysticism of the 1900s sought only the union of the world with *life*, the fusion of the ego with the *deeper self*. Mauthner himself gave a memorable description of his reasoning: 'The critique of language was my first and last word. Looking back, the critique of language appears as a universally destructive scepticism; but looking forward, playing with illusions, it is an aspiration to unity, it is mysticism.'[34] By 'unity' in this context, Mauthner meant the unity of the word and the reality it was describing – in fact, the unity of subject and object.

Mauthner's philosophical voyage deserves a mention here, since in many ways it resembles Hofmannsthal's. In his own study of the derivation of his thought, Mauthner said he had been influenced by Shakespeare's aesthetic treatment of language (as described in Otto Ludwig's *Shakespeare-Studien*); by the example of Bismarck, who proclaimed that speeches carried no weight and nothing counted except blood and iron – action, in fact; and finally and especially by Nietzsche and Mach.[35] Fritz Mauthner (1849–1923) had attended Mach's lectures when the latter was teaching at the University of Prague between 1869 and 1873. This same combined influence of Nietzsche and Mach can be observed in Hofmannsthal.

Mauthner said that

> Our only images of the world are those of language; we know nothing of the world, either for ourselves, or to tell it to others, except what can be said in one or other of the human languages. Nature has no superhuman language of its own; nature is silent, and only men can say something about themselves and the world.[36]

Like Hofmannsthal in his private diary quoted above, Mauthner takes from Plato the concept of the *eidola* which make up language.[37] He distinguishes three worlds corresponding to three forms of life: the 'adjectivized' world (*die adjektivische Welt*), which is more or less synonymous with the 'perceptible' world, incommunicable by language but accessible in the best instances through art; the 'substantive' world (*die substantivische Welt*), which is that of being, belief in the reality of things in space, mythology and also mysticism; and the 'verbal' world (*die verbale Welt*), which is, on the higher level, that of science, and is always *docta ignorantia* precisely because of the insufficiency of human language.[38]

Mauthner's 'godless mysticism' acknowledged two authorities: Magister Eckhart (whose most important works had been published in 1903, in a modernized German version by Gustav Landauer)[39] and Agrippa of Nettesheim (1486–1535), author of the treatise 'On the Vanity and Uncertainty of the Arts and Sciences, and the Excellence of the Word of God' (*De incertitudine et vanitate scientiarum et artium et de excellentia verbi Dei*), which Mauthner himself edited in 1913,[40] not to mention the influence of Buddhism.[41] Mauthner, invoking the authority of Hume and Mach, reaches the climax of his metaphysical scepticism: 'Without doubt the representation of a permanent self cannot now be saved [ist nicht mehr zu retten]. The agnostic mysticism at which I have now arrived, and which really has nothing to do with any confession . . . can assuredly dispense with God.'[42]

Finally, Mauthner's mysticism became tinged with aestheticism: a genius, he averred, can understand the world without concepts and without language. There may also be in true thought, in what we call philosophy, such blessed moments of unspoken understanding:

> Hours of dawn, hours of wakefulness, then suddenly the veil of day falls aside and, as on a moonlight night, the path to the mystery of the Great Unity lies open before us. Then the way is closed again, as soon as the discoverer sets his first tentative foot upon the path. The light becomes dark again as soon as he opens his eyes. His understanding is shattered as soon as he tries to capture it in concepts or words, for himself or for others. The Great Unity could keep its cohesion only within the silent self; at the first word, all unity is dislocated and disappears, even the unity of the self. Nothing more can be said [Nichts lässt sich mehr sagen].[43]

Mauthner's theory makes it easier to understand the scope of Lord Chandos's 'crisis'. It will be recalled that scepticism *vis-à-vis* all human knowledge was at the root of his conversion: it was to apologize for interrupting his scientific labours that he wrote to his master, Francis Bacon. We can also see that Chandos is, at bottom, only a manifestation of the Artist according to Nietzsche's early philosophy, a mind which has risen to an aesthetic contemplation which abolishes the *principium individuationis* and the disturbing disjunction between the subject and the world.

In his *Tractatus Logico-Philosophicus*, Wittgenstein refers to Mauthner in order to distance himself from him: '4-0031: All philosophy is a "critique of language" (though not in Mauthner's sense).' If Wittgenstein was trying to avoid Mauthner's universal scepticism and his contradictions, particularly that of using language to show up the limitations of language,[44] we may ask if the mystical tendencies of the final propositions in the *Tractatus* do not proceed from an attitude very similar to those of Chandos/Hofmannsthal and Mauthner:[45]

> 6-52: We feel that even when *all possible* scientific questions have been answered, the problems of life remain completely untouched. . . . 6-522: There are, indeed, things which cannot be put into words. They *make themselves manifest*. 7: What we cannot speak about we must pass over in silence [Wovon man nicht sprechen kann, darüber muss man schweigen].

Proposition 7, the last sentence of the *Tractatus*, can easily be misunderstood. It is probably better to give the expression 'darüber muss man schweigen' a pre-eminently active meaning: keeping silent does not simply mean not speaking, but means taking up an attitude of waiting, of openness, of wordless seeking, all probably necessary conditions for something to be *made manifest*, as said in proposition 6.522. In Wittgenstein, as in Chandos, the preoccupation with mysticism is linked with a grave crisis of identity, which he went through just before the outbreak of the First World War, during the war and through the early 1920s (which were indeed years of silence, if we except the delayed publication of the *Tractatus*). Wittgenstein's letters to Bertrand Russell in this period have the same tone as Chandos's fictional letter to Bacon. A brilliant pupil explains to his master that his inner crisis is forcing him to put off his academic labours to a more favourable hour. Just before the outbreak of war he wrote to Russell: 'I cannot write anything to do with logic today. Perhaps you think I am wasting my time thinking about myself; but how could I be a logician if I cannot yet be human? Before anything else I must put myself in order.'[46] At the time Wittgenstein was reading Tolstoy and his commentaries on the Gospels, which brought him back to the mysticism of primitive Christianity, along with Saint Augustine, Kierkegaard, Dostoievsky . . .

The notion of 'creative silence' which concludes the *Tractatus* was to be a point of departure for Robert Musil, who in 1906 headed his *Törless* with an epigraph from the chapter entitled 'Mystic morality' in Maeterlinck's *Poor Man's Treasury*: 'As soon as we express something, we strangely diminish it. We think we have plunged to the bottom of the abyss, and when we come to the surface again, the drop of water glittering at the end of our pale fingers is nothing like the sea whence it came . . .' Later, Musil was to revise his opinion of Maeterlinck, and say hard things about this 'salon philosopher'.[47] For Musil was to become anxious to distinguish his own search from the mysticism which was becoming more and more fashionable in the first two decades of the twentieth century (for example, in Walter Rathenau). Bahr had already alluded to a 'mania for mysticism' (*Sucht nach dem Mystischen*) which was unsurprising in 'fin de siècle' decadents;[48] even before him, Paul Bourget had noted à propos of Baudelaire that 'Faith will depart, but mysticism, even if expelled from the intelligence, will remain as a feeling.'[49] In 1930, Hermann Broch spoke of the 'sterile recourse to mysticism' which he found at work in contemporary philosophy.[50] In *Törless*, the originality of Musil's quest is clear. Törless's schoolboy meditations on the square root of minus one prefigure the alliance between mathematical rationality and mystical knowledge which Ulrich desires in *The Man Without Qualities*. Musil had transcended Landauer's opposition between scientific *ratio* and mystical *unio*.

The double meaning of Musil's chosen title, *The Man Without Qualities*, well illustrates this astonishing fusion of scientific rationality and mystic morality. 'Without qualities' is a notion deriving in part from his study of Mach, who reduced all reality (including the self) to its qualities alone: Musil started from Mach and took the additional step of dissolving the qualities of reality. That was the object of the novel's opening chapters: to show that 'copious description cannot reveal anything more than a "qualifiable" world . . . In it one can then situate a particular ensemble which 'can be designated as a "man without qualities" ... then you have a reality which is literally unqualifiable'.[51] This dissolving of the world and the subject into qualities sets free the 'sense of the possible'.

'Without qualities': the notion is borrowed directly from the vocabulary of Magister Eckhart. The mystical union with God requires an effort of divestment – subjectivity and divinity laid bare to each other. The soul must die to its terrestrial existence in order to be reborn in contact with God. Similarly, all the images and attributes with which mankind has clothed God must be set aside to open the path which leads to the Unnameable, to God 'Ohne Eigenschaften', as Eckhart expressed it.[52] For the mystic, qualities belong to the world of terrestrial works, of the non-immediate. (Here we see the ultimate outcome of the mystical tradition which opposes *paupertas* to *proprietas*.) The mystical state, 'without qualities', is the ultimate outcome of the 'Entwerden' which Ulrich speaks of at the beginning of the novel's second volume.[53] The word is virtually untranslatable: it means literally 'cessation of becoming', 'un-living'.

Is there a solution to the identity crisis of the subject opened up by the dominant neo-positivism of the end of the century – a doctrine summed up in Mach's 'unrettbares Ich', the irrecoverable, unsavable self? For Hofmannsthal, Mauthner and later Musil, and perhaps for Wittgenstein also, the solution was to be sought in the systematic deconstruction of the subject, beginning with its language, which allows it to receive enlightenment from 'another state'. For Weininger, a similar function of help and salvation for the self, wrecked by the assaults of neo-empiricism and experimental psychology, lay in the figure of the genius.

II

Weininger and the categorical imperative of genius

In March 1902 Weininger, who had begun (like most students of his age) by respecting the authority of Mach, wrote to his friend Hermann Swoboda: 'I have done with Mach's and Avenarius' theory of science.'[54] The first chapter of the second part of *Sex and Character* attacks Mach's 'dogmatic scepticism', the atomism of Weismann, Wundt and Petzoldt, and the experimental psychology of William Stern: 'Psychology becomes platitude when it attempts to do without philosophy ... Positivism is revealed as a veritable nihilism.'[55] Weininger then devotes several chapters to the theory of the genius, who is characterized in the first place by his exceptionally developed memory. Genius is omnireminiscence, and the genius can recall his past life better than the common run of mortals and write an exhaustive autobiography. Weininger's arguments here are grounded in Schopenhauer (chapter 31 of *The World as Will and Representation*).

One of Weininger's most striking ideas is his theory of the genius as microcosm:

The ego of the genius ... is simply itself universal comprehension ... the great man contains the whole universe within himself; genius is the living micro-cosm ... he is everything ... he constructs from everything his ego that holds the universe ... and so, for him, all things have significance, all things are sym-bolical. ... and all this is possible for him because the outer world is as fully and strongly connected as the inner in him ... the universe and the ego have become one in him.[56]

Not only does the soul of the genius contain the entire universe: it is also a summary of humanity. The personality of the genius contains every human type, from the criminal to the saint, and it enjoys unlimited understanding of human passions. In 'Concerning the Ultimate Outcome' and in the post-humous 'Fragments and Aphorisms',[57] Weininger makes the theory of the microcosm into the foundations of a universal symbolism.

Weininger's microcosmic genius has an obvious neo-Romantic dimension which at times seems to echo Novalis.[58] But Weininger (like Musil) appeals over the heads of the Romantics to the classics of mysticism, especially Jacob Böhme. The state of universal apperception achieved by the genius is related to the state of mystical union. Hermann Bahr's diary for 1894 contains this reflection, which establishes a clear link between the idea of genius and the aesthetic Nietzscheanism of the 1900s: 'Bearded Dionysos. Serene ecstasy – ecstasy as a state, not just a fugitive instant – genius seems to me to be the duration of ecstasy. Anyone can rise for a moment to an integral feeling, that is, an intuition of God. Anyone can become the All for an instant. But to remain so always – that is genius.'[59]

The genius is centred on himself, but Weininger denies that this radical individualism can be taxed with egocentricity and declares that the peak of individualism is the same as the peak of universalism. Mach, who denied the subject, was sadly mistaken, in Weininger's view, when he thought that the renunciation of one's own self could produce an ethical attitude which excluded scorn of others and personal arrogance. For the ego is the pre-requisite of all social morality.[60] Genius, the highest potential quality of individuality, is in fact a categorical imperative applicable to the whole of humanity: 'Genius is, in its essence, nothing but the full completion of the idea of a man, and, therefore, every man ought to have some quality of it, and it should be regarded as a possible principle for everyone.'[61] Weininger's utopia renews the inspiration in Schlegel's fragment: 'Genius is not arbitrary: it comes of freedom, like *Witz*, love and faith, which will one day become arts and sciences. You must ask genius of everyone, but do not count on getting it. A Kantian would call this the categorical imperative of genius.'[62]

Thus the universal moral law is integrated with the individual, and genius as seen by Weininger illustrates the principle which Georg Simmel said was characteristic of modernity. Only the law of the individual can govern every aspect of life, wrote Simmel, for it is nothing less than totality transmuted into duty, the very centrality of this life – and he concluded, 'The morality of rational and universal law yields to that of individual law.'[63] The subject, reaching the peak of individuality, becomes endowed with the universal. The same formula could be applied to Musil's mystic.[64] He noted, in a review of Walter Rathenau's *Mechanics of the Mind*:

> The fundamental experience of the mystic is born . . . of an aspiration analagous to the force of love, an anonymous power of concentration, a gathering together and inner regrouping of intuitive forces. What must be overcome is no longer a contrary force, inertia or suffering, but a paralysis . . . The will is loosed, we are no longer ourselves – and yet, for the first time, we are ourselves. The soul which awakens at such a moment wills nothing, promises nothing, but none the less remains active. It has nothing to do with the law: its ethical principle is an awakening, a soaring to the heights. There is no more ethical activity, but a simple state which leaves no room for any immoral act or being.[65]

'The other state' and moral creativity in Musil

The mystical state allows the self to escape the laws of social morality, which have ceased to be more than conventions or sterile constraints, and to reunite itself with the ethical law which is granted to its inner creativity. 'Until now, morality has been static. Stable character, established law, ideals. But now, dynamic morality.' These notes by Musil[66] show us the deeper meaning of 'the other state'. The 'irrecoverable self' of the modern condition described by Mach had fallen in ruins, and dragged traditional moral codes down with it. For one who refused any hasty identification with current ideas and shifting fashions ('People can no longer find their own souls and they adopt the first group soul [*Gruppenseele*] which comes along and which they least dislike'),[67] there was no option but to seek deep in his own self for the answer to questions left in suspense by the 'irrecoverable self'.

For a morality become sterile and dusty it was necessary to substitute an individualist ethic, whose maxims would be found by the 'new men without qualities' within themselves. The influence of Nietzsche on this utopia of Musil's is apparent. But we can also see the risk of misunderstanding inherent in this recourse to mysticism. Musil himself was well aware of it. The promise of spiritual renewal in the 'other state' was caricatured by the spirit of the irrationalist *Weltanschauung* which could be seen at work in the 'baffled Europe' of the 1920s:

> Malaise. Swarms of sects in Germany. Anxious looks towards Russia, the Far East, India. We blame economics, civilization, rationalism, nationalism; we imagine a decline, a slackening of the race . . . There are people who make out that we have lost all morality. Others make out that we lost our innocence when we swallowed forever, along with the apple, the demon of intellectualism. Still others, that we ought to transcend civilization and get back to culture as the Greeks knew it. And so on.[68]

Musil suggested no direct answer to this cultural crisis. His position remained apolitical. His notion of 'the other state' remained difficult to transmit, wholly personal and indeed asocial (Ulrich and his sister Agatha defy civil and moral law and choose to situate themselves on the margin of society):

all in all, unattainable. But Musil's contemporaries strove to attain Musil's utopia by caricaturing it, confusing Ulrich with the minor characters who attend him in the novel (like the buffoons, monkeys, dwarfs and demons who go with Zarathustra as the incarnation of the permanent threat of treason to his doctrine): Hans Sepp, the pan-Germanist antisemite; Arnheim, who reduces the great themes of mysticism to pontifical commonplaces; Lindner, the rigid, militant petty bourgeois. It has been pointed out that the vocabulary Musil uses to describe 'the other state' has some disturbing similiarities with the vocabulary of other writers who rallied to the cause of 'the other State' – Austrian clerico-fascism or Nazism.[69] Such comparisons cast no aspersions on Musil, but they force us to consider the ambiguities of the 'mystical' response to the identity crisis of the subject.

III

From individualism to the restoration of communities

There was another representative of Viennese modernism who never managed to linger for long in an unstable state of aesthetic mystical contemplation: Hofmannsthal eventually yielded to the need for an identification which could permanently 'save' the threatened ego of his double, Chandos. Alongside the individual (individualist) reconciliation with the whole, Hofmannsthal was soon to lay a 'ceremony of wholeness', a ritualized politics from which nobody need feel excluded, to harmonize the conflicting impulses born of individuals. He would try to restore the *ordo* of an 'ancien régime' anterior to the French Revolution through the theatre and the civilizing influence he attributed to the Salzburg Festival, and would end by invoking 'that isolated Self, with no recourse but itself, the titanic seeker [who] reveals himself to reach the highest communality by closing in himself the thousand fissures fragmenting a people which for centuries has been without a single link to bind it into one culture' – and by speaking of 'a conservative revolution on a scale unparalleled in European history'.[70]

The genius of the Weininger kind, more even than 'the other state', is open to criticism. Weininger's own journey through *Sex and Character* shows the direction which the cult of the genius was likely to take in this early part of the century: the last chapters sink into an antisemitic and overtly pan-Germanist Wagnerianism. Weininger's constant oscillation between the notions of genius and of 'great man' or of 'hero' à la Carlyle finally led him to affirm a sort of *Führerprinzip*. He always remained viscerally anti-political and denied that the head of state could possibly be a 'great man': that *epitheton ornans* could apply only to founders of religions or (in modern times) of *Weltanschauungen*, or to great artists – the model, evidently, being Richard Wagner.

In Nietzsche, the idea of genius was a way out of the situation of contemporary nihilism: the genius, with his anarchic individuality, could substitute for an outdated morality a 'decisionism' capable of generating new values.[71] The genius had the look of an aristocrat who despised the democratic levelling of the masses, and identified himself with the superman animated by the dionysiac lust for life. The ideal was incarnated by Wagner at the time of the *Birth of Tragedy* and by Nietzsche in his *Thoughts Out of Season*. After a critical phase in *Human, All Too Human*, in which the genius is unmasked by the philosopher of disillusionment, Nietzsche reactivated the idea in an altered form. Genius was now to be an imperative rather than an accomplishment: transcendence, contestation, seeking; laughter, dancing and play; will to power, transvaluation of values, eternal return.

It is this final Nietzsche who has the closest links with Musil's search for 'the other state'. But the turn-of-the-century mind was still attached to the earlier, Wagnerian Nietzsche. Symptomatic of the cult of the genius was 'Rembrandt the Educator', by Julius Langbehn, who lived in Vienna from 1892 to 1894.[72] It was published in 1890 and became a bestseller. Langbehn saw individualism as 'the original motive force of all Germanness'.[73] Everything depended on the great individuals who combined aristocratic authority and imperial grandeur against the mediocrity of modern democracy. The words which flow most frequently from Langbehn's pen are *Individualität*, *Persönlichkeit* and *Seele*, accompanying *Rasse*, *Blut* and *Volk*. One of his chapters is entitled 'Mysticism', which it designates as one of the fundamental tendencies of the German genius.

It would take too long to explain Langbehn's doctrine in detail; its only merit is the strikingly clear way it condenses many clichés of the pan-Germanist *Weltanschauung* of the time.[74] But it must be recalled that the identity crisis and its mystical outcome in Hofmannsthal, Weininger or Musil has its counterpart in German and Austrian society; there was a collective identity crisis which was linked with the modernization of everyday life, and which culminated in an ideology whose slogans have a distant and caricatural, but troubling, resemblance to the literary figures we have analysed in this chapter.

4

Narcissus

I

Narcissus, hero of modern life

Our own 'fin de siècle' has found one of its favourite labels in the title
of a book by Christopher Lasch, published in 1979: we live in the 'age of
narcissism'.[1] The most remarkable echo of these ideas in France is *L'ère du
vide: Essais sur l'individualisme contemporain*, by the 'postmodern' theorist Gilles
Lipovetsky:

> It is from the widespread desertion of social aims and values, instigated by the
> progress of personalization, that narcissism arises. Disaffection from the great
> systems of meaning and overinvestment in the self go hand in hand . . . everything
> is conducive to a pure individualism, also called 'psi', free from the framework
> of the masses and tending towards a generalized valuation of the subject.[2]

Earlier on, the sociologist Richard Sennett had seen a connection between the
'fall of public man' and 'the rise of private man'. Just as after the death of
Augustus the decline in Roman public life had led to a quest for religious
transcendence, so in our own era, loss of interest in public affairs had
reinforced the tendency to fall back on one's own resources.[3]

The *Kulturkritik* of the previous 'fin de siècle' prefigured these themes in
its judgement on artistic and intellectual milieux. In *Entartung* ('Degeneration',
1892–3), Max Nordau accused the founders of modernism – Baudelaire,
Wilde and Nietzsche – of 'egomania'. *Ego Narcissus*: such is the formula
used by Leopold von Andrian as an epigraph to his novella *Der Garten der
Erkenntnis* ('The Garden of Knowledge', 1895), which is a digest of the
modernist aesthetic of Young Vienna.

However, the word 'narcissism' meant something quite different to
Andrian's generation than it does to the sociologists of contemporary postmodernism. It had a utopian dimension, whereas nowadays it refers only to
the psychopathology of a culture and ethics in a state of crisis. Narcissism, like

the quest of the mystic or the imperative of genius, embodied the hope for a radicalization of modern *individualism* as a reaction and response to the process of *individuation* which appeared to be afflicting civilization. For the disciples of the young Maurice Barrès, heirs to Baudelaire's dandy, 'self-worship' (*culte du moi*) served as a fertile provocation. The gentle Narcissus had become a 'hero of modern life', forever in search of his 'artificial paradise'. That is what made him subversive. In a world peopled with 'imbecilic Narcissuses who saw the common herd as a mirror reflecting their own image',[4] the poet cultivated his individuality like a kind of hashish which, 'like all solitary joys, makes the individual useless to humankind and society superfluous to the individual, making him admire himself incessantly and pushing him daily closer to the luminous abyss in which, Narcissus-like, he admires his own face'.[5]

The double direction of Narcissism: Lou Andreas-Salomé

'Narcissism as a Double Direction' was the title of a psychoanalytical essay by Lou Andreas-Salomé which appeared in 1921 in the magazine *Imago*.[6] It condenses, twenty years after the event, the aesthetic and moral programme of the years around 1900. It may seem paradoxical to cite an essay published just after the First World War as representative evidence of the mind of that earlier epoch. But a reading of 'Private Notebooks of the Last Years (1934–6)'[7] confirms that Andreas-Salomé never, to her dying day, renounced her fidelity to the ideas she had conceived in dialogue with Nietzsche and Rilke and then confirmed and developed in the school of Freud. The background and horizon of her thought was always a *Lebensphilosophie* of Nietzschean inspiration. In her 1894 essay on Nietzsche, she wrote:

> Nietzsche, in his philosophy of the future, no longer believes that superhumanity comes ready made: man must first create it himself, and for that his only resources are the elementary forces given him by nature. Thus it is not a case of preferring, to this world, a world beyond which transcends it, but of conjuring from the heart of this world a beyond of unsurpassable plenitude and richness. In *Thus Spake Zarathustra*, which might be called the greatest hymn of modern individualism, Nietzsche celebrated the liberation of the vital forces of individualism in accents of incomparable beauty.[8]

The feeling expressed in nearly all Andreas-Salomé's writings is nostalgia for a great lost unity which once bound together the individual and the world, the unity which must be regained if the lost equilibrium of existence is to be restored. She projects this concern on to the thought of Nietzsche, whose final conclusion she sums up as follows: 'Man feels mystically aggrandized until he coincides with the whole of the universe and of life . . . God, the world and the "self" thus merge into a single concept which gives the individual his rule of conduct in the same way as any other metaphysical, moral or religious system.'[9] Her autobiography begins with this sentence: 'A moment before, we

were an indivisible whole, all being was inseparable from us; and now we have
been hurled into birth, we have become a little fragment . . .'[10] At the end of
the process of individuation, having attained full self-awareness, we are not
only enlarged and enriched, we have also suffered a loss – or so she states in
her 1931 essay, 'Open Letter to Freud'.[11] This feeling of a loss of oneness
seeks compensation in the 'cosmogonic eros' (here Lou is quoting Klages),[12]
in art, or in the maxims of Goethe and oriental wisdom.

It is surprising to see that in Andreas-Salomé psychoanalysis itself can
reinforce the same line of thought, subject to a certain amount of reinterpretation. In her 'Open Letter to Freud' she defines successful analysis as an
act of love, a return to oneself which is also a return to a feeling of oneness
with the whole;[13] instincts are links between the 'universal being' and 'the
being of the self'.[14] This vision found philosophical and scientific confirmation
in the doctrine of monism. The affirmation of a matter–soul continuum, a
necessary continuity between the theory of the elements and the doctrine of
the soul, founded a curious synthesis of positivism and *Naturphilosophie*,
invoking the great cohesion of the universe to support a feeling of belonging
to a macrocosmic whole.[15] Hofmannsthal, for example, wrote under the
influence of Ernst Haeckel and Ernst Mach (doyen of the Viennese branch of
monism): 'We are one with everything that is, and everything that ever was;
we are not cut off from anything, we are not a thing apart.'[16]

Although the epistemology of psychoanalysis owes a good deal to certain
aspects of the monist doctrine,[17] Freud never overtly acknowledged any debt
to it. When he spoke of 'monism' it was always in pejorative allusion to the
'confusionism' of Carl Gustav Jung.[18] Freud had no sympathy with the monist
Weltanschauung, and while he encouraged Andreas-Salomé in her psychoanalytic researches, he commented ironically on his disciple's taste for grand
synthesis:

> Every time I read one of your letters of appraisal I am amazed at your talent for
> going beyond what has been said, completing it and making it converge at some
> distant point. Naturally, I do not always agree with you. I so rarely feel the need
> for synthesis. The unity of this world seems to me so self-evident as not to need
> emphasis. What interests me is the separation and breaking up into its com-
> ponent parts of what would otherwise revert to an inchoate mass.[19]

However, this grand unity was the theme of a fragment, supposedly by
Goethe, to whose influence Freud, in his memoirs, attributed his decision to
study medicine: 'Nature! We are surrounded and embraced by her – incapable
of escaping her and unable to penetrate deeper into her.'[20] But at the time
when Andreas-Salomé was in dialogue with him, Freud had long since
renounced the *Schwärmerei* of his student years.

It was in the opening pages of *Civilization and its Discontents* that Freud
gave the clearest expression of his scepticism *vis-à-vis* every form of what,
borrowing an expression from Romain Rolland, he called 'oceanic feeling'.[21]
To Rolland, this caution, this reluctance to grant any positive status to
mystical religious experience, showed a surprising and regrettable limitation in

Freud's thinking, just as disconcerting as his lack of interest in music.[22] Similarly, Freud always had an antipathy to the 'mystical inclinations' he found in Carl Gustav Jung.[23] And yet in Andreas-Salomé, to whom Freud showed every mark of confidence and esteem, the mystical note sounds on every page. While she was always attracted by the universal, by synthesis, by clarification, by the fringes of mysticism, Freud insisted on the investigation of the single fact, on the requirement that ensembles should be broken down into their component parts, and on a provisional acceptance of obscurity when he came across a problem that could not yet be solved.[24]

The theory of narcissism was the essential meeting point between Lou and Freud. He said as much in his letter of July 1917:

> It is quite evident . . . how you anticipate and complement me each time, how you strive prophetically to unite my fragments into a structural whole. I am under the impression that this is true to a special degree since I began employing the concept of the narcissistic libido. Without this, I feel, you too might have slipped away from me to the system-builders, to Jung or even more to Adler.[25]

Narcissism as a *double direction* is the guiding notion of Andreas-Salomé's 1921 essay, which is the best evidence of her original contribution – or should we say her happy infidelity? – to psychoanalytical theory. She says that the concept of narcissism should be widened: it is not merely that the libido is invested in the ego, essentially ego-centric, it also means 'our own rooting in the original state of which we are still part, though we are in process of detaching ourselves from it, just as a plant remains attached to the ground, though it grows away from it towards the light.'[26] This is what Andreas-Salomé means by the 'second direction' of narcissism: 'a sustained intuitive identification with the whole, reunion with the whole as the fundamental positive goal of the libido';[27] 'the pleasure of going beyond oneself, ceasing to be an obstacle to oneself as ego in a happy reunion with the original state before the ego existed'.[28] It is through narcissism that the reconciliation of ego and sexuality, which society tends to set at odds, is effected.[29]

In the mirror stage in early childhood (a recent commentator has suggested a parallel with Jacques Lacan's theory here,[30] but this comparison risks obscuring the essential point, the macrocosmic dimension of narcissism in Lou's theory), and in the disintegration of the ego in the psychotic, Andreas-Salomé saw a reappearance of the fundamental conflict between the conscious self and the aspiration to soften the outlines of individuality – between the clear distinction of ego and non-ego and a state of fusion. The human types which she calls 'the religious man' and 'the philosopher' would then represent stabilized forms of an original feeling of identification with the 'whole': 'the great religious man, the great philosopher . . . have retained their most ardent instincts, drawn from the original force of narcissism.'[31]

This view leads to a reinterpretation of the myth of Narcissus. Andreas-Salomé argues that too much attention has been paid to its auto-erotism, and not enough to the fact that Narcissus in the legend does not see himself in an artificial mirror, but in a mirror of nature: perhaps he did see nothing but himself in the water, but did he see himself as an integral part of a whole?[32] Thus the narcissistic feeling combines 'sadness and happiness, what escapes itself, what closes in on itself, self-giving and self-assertion',[33] and here Lou quotes (in a slightly abridged form)[34] the poem 'Narziss' (1913) by Rainer Maria Rilke, which ends as follows:

> What takes shape there and resembles me
> and, trembling, arises in signs full of tears
> has perhaps been in a woman
> reborn, but remained out of reach,
>
> however far I pursue it in her.
> But it is resting on the ruffled
> indifferent water, and under my crown of roses
> I, astonished, can behold it long.
>
> There, it is not loved. Down there is
> nothing but impassible, downfallen stones,
> and I can well see how sorrowful I am.
> Was that my image, there in her eyes?[35]

Rilke's masculine Narcissus is distressed by the separation of his self from the reflection. He cannot reach the state of perfect circularity which, for the angel in the Second Duino Elegy (1912), represented the oneness of self, reflection and mirror.[36] He does not know the bliss of satisfied narcissism, which is exemplified by the swan, the rose and the fountain,[37] and which seems to be enjoyed by the woman in the mirror.[38]

Ambiguities of the notion of 'primary narcissism'

Andreas-Salomé's originality was to extend 'the notion of primary narcissism', a notion which, as Jean Laplanche and Jean-Bertrand Pontalis point out in their *Vocabulaire de la psychanalyse*, remains debatable in Freud and varies extremely from one author to another.[39] Developing the second notion, Freud uses the term 'primary narcissism' to mean a preliminary stage of life, previous even to the development of the ego, of which life in the womb would be the archetype. Whether the notion be accepted or rejected, the term is always used for a rigorously 'non-object' or at least 'undifferentiated' state, with no gap between the subject and the external world. Laplanche and Pontalis point out two possible objections to this concept of narcissism. Terminologically, it loses sight of any reference to self-image; factually, the existence of such a stage is very problematic. Some authors believe that object relations exist in the newborn child from the outset – what Balint calls the 'primary love object' – and therefore reject as mythical the notion of primary narcissism as a first, non-object state of life outside the womb.[40]

This reminder shows how far Lou had ventured on to dangerous ground. Freud's writings remain allusive, and apparently contradictory, when they attempt to define primary narcissism as a stage in the development of the subject.[41] The school of Sandor Ferenczi has pushed the theory along one of the directions indicated by Freud, contrasting narcissism with object eroticism.

This would locate the roots of narcissism in prenatal life, and the memory (or reconstructed myth) of a state of felicity, free from conflicts and excitements ('lost paradise', 'golden age'), would nourish a nostalgia common to all individuals.[42] But this approach is ambiguous, if we consider that aspiring to a state of total unexcitability is a constant in Freud's thinking, connected with the death wish. The largely speculative notion of primary non-object narcissism thus sends us back to the fundamental alternative suggested by André Green in *Narcissisme de vie, narcissisme de mort*.[43]

Freud is much more explicit, however, when he applies narcissism theory to anthropology. In *Totem and Taboo* (1912–13), which came shortly before *Narcissism: An Introduction* (1914), he detailed a model of evolution in three main stages. The first phase, characteristic of primitive humanity and, in individual history, of the young child, is marked by a belief in the 'omnipotence of thoughts' and the 'magical power of language'. Freud calls this stage, which can be compared to a dream state, the animistic stage, in which the unity of the ego has not yet appeared in the individual – which does not deter Freud from calling it 'egoistic'.

This is one example of the ambiguities already mentioned which so often attend the theme of primary narcissism in Freud.[44] There is a similar contradiction, for example, between this passage from *The Ego and the Id*:

> At the very beginning, all the libido is accumulated in the id, while the ego is still in process of formation or is still feeble. The id sends part of this libido out into erotic object-cathexes, whereupon the ego, now grown stronger, tries to get hold of this object-libido and force itself on the id as a love-object. The narcissism of the ego is thus a secondary one, which has been withdrawn from objects[45]

and this from *An Outline of Psychoanalysis* (published in 1940):

> the ego, in which at first the whole available quota of libido is stored up. We call this state absolute, primary *narcissism*. It lasts until the ego begins to cathect the ideas of objects with libido, to transform narcissistic libido into object-libido.[46]

Must we keep up the distinction laid down in *Narcissism: An Introduction* between 'auto-erotism' and narcissism?

> I may point out that we are bound to suppose that a unity comparable to the ego cannot exist in the individual from the start; the ego has to be developed. The auto-erotic instincts, however, are there from the very first; so there must be something added to auto-erotism – a new psychical action – in order to bring about narcissism.[47]

Or can we consider the early, auto-erotic stage *as* primary narcissism? Andreas-Salomé implicitly says 'yes' to the second question and exploits the ambiguities to give a Freudian justification to her theory of the 'double direction' of narcissism.

In *Totem and Taboo*, Freud pursues his study of the evolution of civilization, saying that the 'omnipotence of thought' in primitives is a proof of their narcissism; then he makes a comparison between the phases in the development of the human world view (*Weltanschauung*) and the stages in the libidinal development of the individual. Chronologically and in its content, the animist phase corresponds to narcissism, the religious phase to a choice of object characterized by the relationship with the parents, and the scientific phase is equivalent to the maturity of the individual who has renounced the pleasure principle and seeks his object in the external world by coming to terms with reality.[48]

The first of these phases in the evolution of civilization is immediately subjected to a value judgement: to Freud it seems egoistic and culturally inferior, for 'It may be said that in primitive men the process of thinking is still to a great extent sexualized. This is the origin of their belief in the omnipotence of thoughts.'[49] The affirmation of a serious claim to culture assumes an objective and non-emotional way of thinking, an investment of the object in the 'scientific' mode. The age of narcissism *must* be left behind. Only the dreamer and the artist can fall back into the primitive stage in which the world is erotic and enchanted.

Similarly, the individual is socialized by sacrificing his narcissism, his megalomania, and by the abdication of 'that dark despot, the ego'.[50] In society, the effects of narcissism are entirely pernicious: it either makes the individual asocial or predestines him to be a tyrant. (Freud wrote in *Group Psychology and the Analysis of the Ego* that the *Führer* loved no one but himself, he was 'absolutely narcissistic'.)[51] More generally, narcissism, in so far as it impoverished relationships with other people, disturbed the subject's relationship to reality. It was no doubt his reflections on psychosis that decided Freud to introduce narcissism into his theory.[52] The analysis of the Dr Schreber case of paranoia showed how the breaking of social bonds and the retreat into narcissism could make someone lose his grip on reality. On all these points, Andreas-Salomé adopted a completely different view, suggesting that on the contrary narcissism created most favourable conditions for a harmonious and creative relationship between the subject and other people, and between the subject and reality.

Andreas-Salomé's 'heresy' lies firstly in completing and reinterpreting Freud's scattered pronouncements on primary narcissism, to make it into a complete 'second direction'; and secondly in a re-evaluation of narcissism, not as a morally inferior stage, but as an asset which became lost in the process of individual and collective development, as a necessary element in personal equilibrium and the progress of civilization. This essential difference between the concepts of Freud and of Lou gave rise to other, not insignificant disagreements: for example, concerning their theories of femininity.

The narcissistic woman

In *Narcissism: An Introduction* Freud explains how

> With the onset of puberty the maturing of the female sexual organs . . . seems to bring about an intensification of the original narcissism, and this is unfavourable

to the development of a true object choice with its accompanying sexual over-valuation. Women, especially if they grow up with good looks, develop a certain self-contentment which compensates them for the social restrictions that are imposed upon them in their choice of object.[53]

This narcissistic self-sufficiency makes women enigmatic in men's eyes and comparable to children, the great predatory animals, Dostoievsky's arch-criminal, and the humorist.

Freud feels called upon to insist at the end of the passage just quoted that there is no 'tendentious desire on my part to depreciate women'.[54] A contemporary woman critic comments on this apology: 'For what reason should the narcissism of woman be supposed to depreciate her? Why, if not because of a certain ethics which identifies narcissism with an egoism which "must be overcome"?'[55] In Andreas-Salomé, female narcissism acquires a completely different meaning.[56] It means the deeper rooting of women in original whole-ness, which protects them against making too sharp a division between subject and object, soul and body. Lou does not see this specificity as being in any way a drawback. On the contrary, it shows the superiority of woman over man, whose modern condition has accentuated his rootlessness and intellec-tualization to a pathological degree.

Andreas-Salomé was expressing these ideas in her own way long before she met with Freud and psychoanalysis.[57] The theory of narcissism gave her a chance to set them out once again. Lou, when re-evaluating the 'second direction' of narcissism, was also outlining a critique of scientific and tech-nical rationality as defined by Freudian psychoanalysis. In *Instincts and Their Vicissitudes* (1915), Freud declared that the opposition ego/non-ego, subject/object, is forced on the individual at an early stage by his experience of his power to dominate certain external stimuli by muscular action, whereas he remains powerless to control his instinctual drives. Intellectual activity may seem to him an area in which he is still sovereign, and this feeling stimulates an inquiring mind.[58] Mastery of desire (*Reizbewältigung*), which is also at the roots of hatred, masochism and sadism, is to Freud a necessary precondition for a scientific world view. The inquirer, armed with his power of discrimi-nation, sallies forth as a 'knight of hatred'. Love, with its tendency to super-abundance, represents that tentacular power which theory attempts to cut down to size.[59] The spirit of objectivity is, in the end, no more than a special case of aggression: 'The external, the objective and the hate object seem to be identical from the beginning,' Freud wrote.[60]

Freud thought that in the state of narcissism, on the other hand, the external world excites in the subject not interest, but indifference: thus narcissism is incompatible with the scientific outlook. For the rest, Freud admits that the aggressive attitude to nature implicit in scientific rationality may be one of the 'discontents' of civilization.[61] Andreas-Salomé suggests that there are other ways of acquiring knowledge of nature than this aggressive approach by the scientific mind. Narcissism allows her to renew the Orphic myth of an intimate and intuitive knowledge of the world whose model is artistic creation.

For Freud, art is merely a narcissistic child's game,[62] even, in epistemological terms, a regression,[63] which may indeed offer a comfort and a pleasant
illusion capable of soothing the 'discontents' of civilization, but cannot claim
to any knowledge of reality, or even make a serious contribution to the
progress of culture. Only genius (which psychoanalysis does not undertake to
'explain') deserves rather more indulgence and consideration. But the normal
and preferable way to adulthood is not to become an artist, but to embrace
what Freud calls the scientific mind. Andreas-Salomé, by contrast, saw the
Artist as a prefiguration of the Superman, and thought the truth of art was as
deep as that of science. In this, she remained faithful to the ideas of the young
Nietzsche and of Rilke.

For Andreas-Salomé, the artistic genius had certain things in common with
women. Genius, she thought, attached itself to a still incompletely differ-
entiated being: like women, the genius was not so master of his capabilities
and states of mind; he was more sensitive, and more influenced by the
obscure forces which drew him on, unbeknown to his conscious thought and
will.[64] Her essay on narcissism ends in a grandiose parallel between the state
of creative genius and Godhead:

> It is in the creative element that we find the colours and images by which the
> near-divine becomes earthly. And if man imagines a God creating the world, it
> is so as to explain not only the world, but also the nature – the narcissistic nature
> – of that God: even if this world does contain a substantial amount of evil and
> ill-will, religious faith will only vanish in the presence of a God who did not dare
> to become a work, to become a world.[65]

The poet finds himself on an equal footing with this artistic and supremely
narcissistic God. 'What will you do, God, if I die?' asks the monk in Rilke's
1905 poem 'The Book of Hours':

> With me you will lose all meaning.
> After me you will have no dwelling-place
> Where words, close and warm, can welcome you.
> What will you do, my God? I am full of fear.[66]

In Hermann Bahr's journal for 1894 we find this reflection: 'It is absurd to
imagine God in a state of completeness, immobility, petrifaction. He is in
perpetual flux. Tirelessly he creates corrections to himself, that is to say, his
works. The organs of these corrections, through which he reflects, deliberates
and makes decisions, are the artists.'[67] Individualism and the cult of the
genius are united under the aegis of narcissism: a utopia which shows yet
again that it is possible to create, using only the powers of cosmogonic
subjectivity, true values capable of giving meaning to life, in defiance of mass
society, the disenchantment of the world by science and technology, and the
rootlessness of the modern condition.[68]

II

The dionysian narcissism of the poets of 'Young Vienna'

It could be said of most of the Young Vienna writers – Hofmannsthal, Andrian, Beer-Hofmann – that their subject identity crisis begins with an experience of death narcissism and seeks a solution in life narcissism. However, no such solution will be granted to the hero of Andrian's story *Der Garten der Erkenntnis* ('The Garden of Knowledge', 1895), which ends: 'Thus the prince died without having known.'[69] From the beginning, this prince had displayed some typical symptoms of narcissistic personality. At the age of twelve, wrote Andrian,

> Erwin was lonelier and more introverted than he was ever later to be; his soul and body lived mysteriously one within the other, almost a double life; things in the external world had for him the value they have in dreams; they were the words of a language which happened to be his own, but only his own will endowed them with meaning, place, or colour.[70]

Prince Erwin, when he reaches his author's age (Andrian wrote the story when he was nineteen), has become a melancholic and a hypochondriac, obsessed by a malady he acquired young (the consumption which will eventually kill him), and his sex life seems to be more or less platonic: though attracted to young men (as Andrian was in real life), he marries a woman who 'was beautiful, with the beauty of those late portrait busts which make us wonder momentarily whether they represent a young Asian sovereign or an ageing Roman empress'.[71] This hermaphrodite being expresses the fantasy of the neuter gender which manifests the rejection of sexual difference, and which André Green situates at the heart of 'death narcissism': 'the final end of narcissism is to efface all trace of the Other in the Desire of the One. What primary narcissism aims to accomplish by the abolition of tensions is either death or immortality – it comes to the same thing.'[72]

One day, Erwin, between sleeping and waking, has a hallucination: he sees a face grimacing at him from behind a window; when he lights the lamp in his room he finds before him not a window, but a mirror reflecting his own image, and 'trembling with desire he leaned against the wall and his soul delighted in the memory of the trouble felt by his body'.[73] All in all, Andrian's story is a precocious exemplification of Otto Rank's 1914 article on the *doppelgänger*, which in his analysis is closely connected with narcissism.[74] Several times, Prince Erwin meets a strange personage who resembles him and causes him anxiety; after the third encounter, he dies.

Claudio, the hero of Hofmannsthal's poetic drama *Der Tor und der Tod* ('Death and the Fool', 1893), is also a type of narcissism:

> What do I know of the life of men?
> Yes, I have been immersed in it,
> But at most I have understood it,

> I could never merge with it,
> I have never abandoned myself to it.
> I have stayed to one side, born inwardly dumb.
> (Tableau I)[75]

A little later, looking back over his sentimental life, he throws away a bundle of love letters and cries:

> Look there, I can show you: letters, look!
> full of oaths and loving words and complaints;
> Do you think I ever felt what they . . .
> Felt what my replies seemed to say?
> There, you see my whole love life,
> In which I spoke of nothing but myself, myself alone.[76]

Claudio longs endlessly for the lost paradise of primary narcissism:

> As a child I dwelt thus in the radiance of spring,
> and thought I hovered in the Whole,
> An infinite nostalgia beyond all confines
> Filled me with whirlwind presentiments;
> Then came the times of travel, bathed in intoxication,
> Where sometimes glittered the whole world.[77]

But it is finally death that brings the dionysian intoxication to Claudio, greeting him with these words:

> Arise! Cast off this instinctive fear!
> I am fearful no more, I am no skeleton!
> Of the lineage of Dionysos and Venus
> A great god of the soul is before you.[78]

It is the same dionysian personage who came, like a *doppelgänger*, to greet Prince Erwin.[79] Claudio sinks into the euphoria of utter Nirvana, the extreme relapse into narcissism, into death: 'Since dead was my life, oh life, be my death!'[80]

This conversion from death narcissism to life narcissism takes place in the *Chandos Letter*. The previous existence of that disciple of Francis Bacon had been consoled by the awareness of belonging to a great cosmic whole: 'I perceived nature in all things . . . And in all of nature I perceived my own self.'[81] The encyclopaedia of nature and the mind which Chandos planned to write 'was to be called simply *Nosce te ipsum*'.[82] Through his ordeal Chandos experiences the death of his superficial self, a death in the same sense as Prince Erwin's or Claudio's, but which allows the rebirth of a deeper self. Thus Chandos turns to life narcissism along the 'religious' lines described by Andreas-Salomé in her essay on the 'other direction' of narcissism.

Beer-Hofmann's story *Der Tod Georgs* ('George's Death', 1900) tells of a conversion similar to Chandos's, leading from a self-destructive narcissism to one which is borne up by the individual's own life-force. Beer-Hofmann's originality was to put a discovery of Jewish identity and the choice of what could be called 'aesthetic Zionism' just where Hofmannsthal's Chandos put his pantheistic mysticism. The conversion of Paul, hero of *Der Tod Georgs*, will be more solid and lasting than that of Chandos. I shall return to it in my chapter on Beer-Hofmann.

All the characteristics of the identity crisis and its transcendence by mysticism of cosmogonic narcissism are recapitulated in a letter which Hugo sent in June 1895 to his friend Karg von Bebenburg. In the little garrison town where he was doing his military service, Hofmannsthal had an intense feeling of loneliness: 'A feeling of unspeakable and suffocating solitude, as if all that belonged not to life, real life, but to a strange place which I do not understand, which frightens me, and in which I have lost myself, God only knows how.'[83] This crushing loneliness made the young Hofmannsthal indifferent to the 'social problem', despite the abject poverty of the Slovak villages he saw: 'I do not know the "population". There is no population, I think, but only lots of different people, at least that is so here.'[84] It made the quarrel between nations suddenly seem quite futile. Moreover, the whole world seemed to have become incomprehensible: all abstract notions had lost their meaning. The same thing happens to Chandos at the beginning of his ordeal.

This distrust of hollow slogans is accompanied by a need to rediscover real life: 'Most people don't live in life, but in an appearance, a sort of algebraic formula, where there is nothing and everything is mere *signification*. I should like to feel intensely the being of all things, and be immersed in being – real, deep, meaning.'[85] Hofmannsthal dreamed of attaining to this unveiled being, as does Chandos in his mystical moments, by immersing himself in the presence of the humblest things, turning the most commonplace sensation into an epiphany, as when, 'one hot day, we go into the coolness of an entrance hall, over the still-damp tiles'.[86] Such revelations of the being of the world were worth more than any book, even the greatest, even the Bible. Then came the time

> when we become enamoured of ourselves and look so intently at our own reflection that we fall into the water, as they say Narcissus did; then we are on the right track, like children dreaming that they are sliding down their father's coat-sleeve into an enchanted world, between the glass mountain and the frog-king's pool. 'Self-love', I hear: in love with life, or perhaps God too – whatever you like.[87]

Few passages from the 1900s show so clearly the feeling that mysticism and narcissism could be a solution to the subject's identity crisis.

III

Narcissus and ornamentation: Klimt and Makart

One of the principal characteristics of 1900s style can be related to the theme of narcissism, and that is ornamentalism. As Jost Herman remarked, Jugendstil was not a revolt: it emerged from fin-de-siècle narcissism. Its world view savours of the same aestheticism as the decadence, symbolism and neo-Romanticism which attempted to react against the 'ugliness' and lack of formal rigour of the naturalist era. In both cases, little elites – and elites they believed themselves to be – took refuge in a world of pleasing appearances where there was no need to face the ever more pressing problems of technical, economic and social reality.[88] Speaking of the poet Richard Dehmel, Hermand observes that the decorative element and the monist vision are indissolubly linked, and he sums up certain traits common to Stefan George, Alfred Mombert and other poets: 'Finally they wished to immerse themselves in the vegetable element, as the culmination of an inverted metamorphosis. One of the essential symbols of this monist torpor is the figure of Narcissus, who, by contemplating his own face, lost sight of everything else and was turned into a flower by Aphrodite.'[89]

Before minor masters and imitators reduced it to mannerism, Jugendstil ornamentation was laden with profound meaning: it expressed man's original link with the world. It extended the lineaments of the human image to plunge it more deeply into a network of natural lines; it clasped and encircled the world around so as to regulate it according to the man who dwelt in it. This is *Leben*, the life which courses through the ornament and gives it dynamism. Ernst Bloch, in his essay 'The Mind of Utopia', in the chapter called 'Production of Ornament', contrasts the Egyptian and Gothic styles as paradigms: the first of a mineral and geometrical art showing the total domination of inorganic nature over life; the second of an art of organic effervescence, expressing a 'seizure of life' and a kind of 'second philosophy of nature'.[90] The ornamentalism of the 1900s undeniably belongs to the second category, Bloch's 'Gothic'.

Klimt's painting is one of the best examples of how this 'cosmogonic ornamentation' was put into practice. His famous portrait of Adela Bloch-Bauer is an ornamental orgy; the eye can scarcely distinguish the lines of the dress from those of the hangings; gold and silver are spread in as much profusion as on a Byzantine icon; the woman's face becomes almost secondary, merging with the decor. In his landscapes, devoid of any human image, natural forms become ornamental, and the treatment of colour is similar to that in Monet's 'Waterlilies', so much so that one has to look carefully at the profusion of motifs in order to distinguish the outlines of sky, earth and vegetation.

For Klimt, femininity corresponds to a state of fusion symbolized by ornamentation. Commenting on the paintings exhibited at the Vienna *Kunstschau* of 1908, the art critic Ludwig Hevesi emphasized

Klimt's way of painting hair: this proteiform element, the ornamental principle *par excellence*. An original material, infinitely malleable, which can be spun, curled, waved or plaited. Burning clouds which can take on any form, flash of lightning or serpent's tongue, climbing plant, inextricable entanglements, streaming veil and net spread wide. Here, we see [Klimt] draw on nature for this magical matter, the tress, the mane, the curl, as the raw material of an inventive imagination. In these simple sketches, we find in shorthand the natural germs of all his artistic imagination, dictated by a most lively life.[91]

For Ludwig Hevesi, here summing up the deepest conviction of Jugendstil, ornamentalism had nothing to do with artifice. Ornamentation, as mastered by the genius, was born 'under the dictates of life'. It made the life-force visible. There was nothing arbitrary about it: Hevesi speaks repeatedly of the numerous preparatory sketches from nature which made it possible to distil ornamentation from the abundance of real forms.

At the other end of the great chain of life, Klimt's universe was ruled by death: the old woman in the 'Three Ages of Life', the sometimes bloodless fragility of girls' bodies, the heavy, already wilting foliage of his landscapes. Klimt's work, as in the frescoes designed for the University of Vienna, is full of a feeling of *Vergänglichkeit*. Hevesi wrote in the article already cited:

> Look at his new picture 'The Kingdom of Death'. How many hours he spent this summer in Professor Zuckerkandl's dissecting rooms, drawing feverishly to extract from all that deathliness such a fixation, such a livid play of colour and line! Stylized corpses hover in their white shrouds, borne away by mysterious currents, and dark-blue serpents, thin and elastic, with golden heads like kings among worms, uncoil around them.[92]

'Ornamental narcissism' is stalked by nightmare. For, as Greek mythology reminds us, the narcissus is also the flower of the chthonic (subterranean, infernal) deities: seductive and fascinating, it can lead into death. Plutarch explained why: it has narcotic properties. Some even said that *narkissos* was derived from *narkè*.[93] In ornamentation, life and death are merged. Sometimes it fastens the living into a deathly frame; sometimes it drowns them in a current of life which is too much for them. Ornamentation is a perfect illustration of the distinction between life narcissism and death narcissism.

Hevesi made an interesting parallel between Hans Makart, the great decorator of the Ringstrasse, and the new art of the Secession. Under Hevesi's pen, Makart becomes a narcissistic demiurge dwelling in the omnipotence of his subjectivity:

> One essential quality of today's moderns is that they can once again see nature in an ornamental way. Nowadays they say 'ornamental'; before, one said 'decorative'.... Hans Makart had the courage – no, it was not courage – the stubbornness – no, it was not stubbornness either, simply an unconscious assumption which dwelt in him – to consider the whole world from a single viewpoint. His own. That is, to see the whole world as something decorative, where only appearances counted, and what was beneath them was of no consequence. He was without doubt the great original in a world bereft of originality.... The dream of the optic nerve: that, in sum, is the work of Makart.[94]

Here, the artist of Jugendstil, disciple of Makart, rejoins the pensive Narcissus described by Gide and the narcissistic artist analysed by Andreas-Salomé.

Jugendstil ornamentalism, whose Viennese representative was Klimt, was borne up by an artistic ideology which articulated an orphic and cosmogonic ambition – to make life speak through an ornamentation which espoused the half-hidden rhythms of nature; and by an eminently subjective perspectivism legitimized by genius: the language of ornamentalism founded a style which obeyed the creator's sovereign 'point of view'. According to this interpretation, ornamentalism is the distinctive mark of a 'Nietzschean' world view. Andreas-Salomé, speaking of the artist's mystic participation in the cosmic whole, went on to say that 'In the background is the idea that the universe is only a fiction created by man.'[95] It was that splendid illusion that she defined, in her theory of artistic narcissism, as 'a temporary return to the original fusion' and as a turning back to the self, 'not as it consciously relates to itself, but as it relates to the common background, the essential infancy of all individuals'.[96]

Part II
Crises of Masculine Identity

5
Schreber, Weininger, Hofmannsthal

I

Sexual differences and bisexuality

The three great affirmations of the deeper self against the vicissitudes of the psychological ego – 'oceanic feelings' of mysticism, the universal apperception of the genius and cosmogonic narcissism – have one thing in common. All three are modes of what D. W. Winnicott, in his study of 'the capacity to be alone', calls 'the orgasm of the ego', a pleasure similar to the ecstasy which marks 'the acme intervening in a satisfying relation with the ego'.[1] The adult can experience this state in aesthetic satisfaction or in friendship. The happy play of the child corresponds to that experience: it can then be compared to the interplay of bisexual love.

'That men and woman have a "predisposition to bisexuality" is not a new idea, either inside or outside the psychoanalytic field.'[2] If we try to compare and contrast pure masculine and feminine elements *vis-à-vis* the object relation, we can conclude that 'masculine' has the twofold meaning of 'actively relating to, or being related passively to' – what we can refer to as 'instinct drive' – while the purely feminine element 'is related to the breast or to the mother in a very different way: the baby becomes the breast (or the mother), and the object is then the subject', but without any kind of instinct drive. This relation of the purely feminine element to the breast illustrates the idea of 'subjective object', that is, an 'object which has not yet been repudiated as a non-ego phenomenon'.[3] Out of this experience of the subjective object will come that of the objective subject, a condition of the feeling of reality which forms the consciousness of an identity. So 'no feeling of self can be constructed which does not rest on the feeling of being. This feeling of being comes before the being-one-with because it has not yet had anything other than identity...This first experience inaugurates all the identification experiences which are to follow.'[4]

Thus we can complete the traditional conception, adopted by Freud, according to which masculine = active, feminine = passive, by stressing that feminine = being. It is this rootedness in being that man envies in woman because he thinks – perhaps wrongly – that the feminine element is self-evident. And Winnicott's conclusion is that 'when the girl element in the baby (boy or girl) or the patient discovers the breast, it is the self which has been found. . . . After being – doing and being done to. But first – being.'[5]

The malaise of scientific and technical civilization is revealed by the feeling of a loss of being and the attempt to restore the original community of self and world, the microcosm in harmony with the whole. Our short visit to Winnicott helps us to understand why, quite naturally, the individual identity crisis translates into a crisis of the masculine element and a nostalgia for the 'lost' feminine element – lost as paradise is lost.

Nostalgia for the feminine

It was this kind of reaction to the modern condition that Freud was criticizing at the beginning of his essay *Civilization and its Discontents*. How to explain the feeling of a relation between the subject and the world about him? By an obscure perception of the reign of the id beyond the ego? But the external frontiers of the ego are only banished – and then intermittently – by the state of being in love and in certain mental illnesses.[6] It might also be a distant memory of the first age of life, when the baby makes no distinction between its ego and exterior objects: of the desire for 'restoration of limitless narcissism'. However, Freud did not think that this 'oceanic' feeling was the essential dimension of religious feeling: 'It is very difficult for me to work with these almost intangible qualities,' he added.[7] Having rejected the viewpoint of Romain Rolland (who figures in this debate only as the representative of a sensibility which originated in fin-de-siècle mysticism), Freud found room for the classic concept of religious need as dependency and a demand for *paternal* protection. Thus Freud once again contrasted the law of the father with a fusional, *maternal* model.[8] The cure would aim to consolidate the ego and to tame affects by mastering them through the *logos* of words: an entirely opposite idea to that of deconstructing the frontiers of the ego and so restoring its contact with the non-ego. In modern civilization, with psycho-analysis playing a worthy part within it, Freud disputed the cultural value of 'primitive' feasts celebrating dionysian states. This may well be the reason why he always distanced himself from Nietzscheanism and from the representative writers of literary modernity.

The year 1903 saw the publication of two books destined for exceptional fame, both devoted to the masculine identity crisis: Daniel Paul Schreber's 'Memoirs of a Neuropath' and Otto Weininger's *Sex and Character*. The first is an autobiographical account of what Freud was to consider a typical case of paranoia. Schreber's masculine identity collapsed, he became a woman and was soon convinced of the prophetic value of his experience: his emasculation foreshadowed a renewal of humanity. Weininger, for his part, revealed the inextricable confusion of masculine and feminine in contemporary humanity. This bisexualization of culture disgusted him intensely when he realized that it was in fact the feminine element which was gaining ground and the masculine element which was in headlong decline. Weininger therefore vowed to struggle unremittingly against everything feminine he found in culture and in himself. He killed himself six months after the book was published, at the age of twenty-three, in October 1903. The careers of these two individuals are a spectacular illustration of what I mean here by the 'crisis of masculine identity'.

II

The feminization of Dr Schreber

In 1884–5, Daniel Paul Schreber went to Flechsig, a Leipzig psychiatrist, for a first course of treatment for 'hypochondria'. In 1893, he was fifty years old and his recent appointment to the important post of President of the Chamber of the Appeal Court at Dresden marked a solid professional success. 'The professional duties which devolved on me were enormous . . . so that after a few weeks I was already suffering from intellectual overstrain.'[9] Schreber dreamed that his nervous malady would recur, and 'one morning, while I was still in bed . . . I felt a sensation which had a very singular effect on me when I thought about it a little later, when I was fully awake. It was the idea that it must be very agreeable to be a woman undergoing the act of coition.'[10] A few days later, he went to Leipzig to attend the psychiatric clinic of Professor Flechsig.

This was the beginning of his astonishing experiences. Firstly he discovered the language of nerves:

> Beyond ordinary human language, there is also a sort of language of the nerves, which people in a normal state of health are normally unaware of . . . These words are spoken in silence (as in mental prayer, to which the faithful are exhorted from the pulpit), that is to say that a man incites his nerves to produce the vibrations which correspond to the desired words.[11]

At first, Schreber thought that his nerves were being manipulated by Professor Flechsig, who had usurped the action of God – God alone being normally capable of setting in motion, against the individual's will, the divine rays which released the language of the nerves.

But Schreber was soon resigned to 'the tendency, inherent in the universal order, towards the unmanning [*Entmannung*] of the human being who comes into lasting contact with these rays'.[12] For the plan which governed the universe had allowed for the possibility of renewing the human race after some catastrophe which would destroy humanity. The one surviving individual, the 'wandering Jew', would have to be emasculated and turned into a woman so as to bring children into the world. Schreber knew he was destined to be that last man after the final collapse of the cultural and moral decadence which was sapping the West. One of his visions showed him the particularly grave crisis afflicting the German people, especially Protestantism, which might well be the first casualty of the end of the world unless some warlike hero appeared to defend it. Schreber was equally worried by the rise of Catholicism, Judaism and the Slavs.[13]

At the same time, he learned that the world was afflicted with leprosy and plague. He talks of 'lepra orientalis', 'lepra indica', 'lepra hebraica', 'lepra aegyptica', and of blue plague, brown plague, white plague and black plague. During this time, Schreber's feminization proceeded apace, but the remains of his old self remained active: 'The "Jesuits", meaning no doubt the souls of former Jesuits, tried several times to put another 'nerve director' into my head which would modify the consciousness of my identity; the inside wall of my skull was covered in a new "cervical membrane" to blot out my memory of my real self. But with no lasting success.'[14]

In June 1894, Schreber was transferred to the clinic of Doctor Pierson and experienced 'the most amazing derangement of miracles'. At the end of the month he was moved again, this time to Sonnenstein's clinic. At this point Schreber took stock of his sexual metamorphosis: his emasculation had been turned aside from its real aim and used to humiliate him. The rays even went so far as to call him in mockery 'Miss Schreber'. Then he fought against the process of feminization. But the month of November 1895 was a turning point in his life:

> At that time, the signs of feminization on my body had become so plain that I could no longer delude myself about the immanent goal to which all this was leading. In the nights just preceding, if I had not thought it necessary to oppose it with all my will, obeying an impulse of masculine pride, my male sexual parts would really have retracted, so close was the miracle to its accomplishment.

The voluptuous feelings in Schreber's soul became so strong that he felt in his arms, his hands, then his legs, breasts, buttocks and all his other parts, the sensation of a female body:

> Thereafter I no longer doubted that the order of the world was imperiously demanding my unmanning, whether I liked it or not, and that in consequence I could no longer reasonably do other than to reconcile myself to the idea or my metamorphosis into a woman. The consequence of my unmanning could evidently be none other than a fertilization for the creation of a new humanity . . . From then on I marched under the colours of womanhood.[15]

Several chapters follow in which Schreber gives a minute description of the sound sensations he received, the singular language which was spoken to him, then his cosmogonic and theological concepts, and finally the close relationship which had developed between the world order, God and himself. Fearing lest some doubt be cast on his descriptions, he invited his critics to come and verify his metamorphosis for themselves. The last pages of Schreber's memoirs are a self-justification. He has, he explains, lost none of the scrupulous morality which distinguished him before his illness. The 'voluptuous feelings in his soul' are granted him for the salvation of the human race, not for his selfish pleasure. He is like the crusaders who wrote upon their banners

'God wills it.' What will become of him? God would be in considerable difficulties if Schreber were to die. In any case, until his death – an unlikely contingency – he feels he is destined for great things. He has no doubt that the tribunals will set him free and that humanity will revere his martyrdom as they did that of Jesus Christ.

In 1900, the Dresden tribunal had declared Schreber not responsible for his actions, and had had him shut up. It was between October 1900 and June 1901 that Schreber wrote most of his 'Memoirs', which were initially intended to convince the magistrates of his sanity. In 1902, he had his way and the detention was rescinded. Schreber left the asylum and went back to his family. The publication of his 'Memoirs' caused little interest, and his family got the unsold copies removed from sale. In November 1907, he was shut up again in a psychiatric clinic in Leipzig. He died in April 1911. In that same year, Freud published his important essay on Schreber,[16] and Jung also made some study of him.[17] Since then the Schreber case has been considered as one of the great classics in the annals of psychoanalysis and psychiatry. Jacques Lacan made constant reference to it, from his 1932 thesis 'On Paranoiac Psychosis and its Relationship to Personality' to his seminar on the psychoses in 1955–6. Among the sprinkling of interpretive essays independent of psychoanalysis we may mention that of Elias Canetti in 'Mass and Power'.[18]

Schreber's psychosis is a disturbing parody of the literary presentations of depersonalization and mystic or narcissistic reconstruction of the deeper self which we have seen figuring in Hofmannsthal, Rilke and Andreas-Salomé. When he spoke of a 'language of the nerves' that he had been hearing since the onset of his illness, Schreber was using a jargon much in vogue among his contemporaries: he was very well informed about the current state of psychological and psychiatric research, and his memoirs give evidence of a close reading of (for example) Kraepelin. Thus there is nothing startling about the apparent family likeness between Schreber's visions and Hermann Bahr's pronouncements on the nervous states of modern artists . . . As for Schreber's sombre prognostications about the decadence of the human race and the coming end of the world, they recall the literary discourse of 'decadence' which, like Schreber's imaginings, characteristically transformed personal crises into a generalized *Kulturkritik*.

The depersonalization syndrome, the dislocation of the 'self', inclines one to rank Schreber with the martyrs to the *unrettbares Ich*. On the other hand, his case gives us a better insight into one essential dimension of the deconstruction of the 'self', for example in Hofmannsthal's characters. The identity of the lost 'narrow self' is most often an identity connected with the masculine element, while the 'other states' to which the self aspires (mysticism, genius, narcissistic fullness) reactivate the feminine element. To describe this superficial and fragile identity, which his psychosis had swept away, Schreber used the suggestive expression 'flüchtig hingemachte Männer', cobbled-together men. These were the nurses, guardians and doctors who inhabited Schreber's new psychiatric universe and whom he heartily despised. But the deconstruction of the 'masculine' identity of the self could not but meet with virulent resistance from the unconscious, which in Schreber became so strong at one point that it was decided to leave him temporarily 'on the male side'. Freud has something to say on this episode of 'maaculine protest' in the sense given it by Alfred Adler.[19]

Hofmannsthal's 'Tale of the 672nd Night'

In this context we may reread Hofmannsthal's 'Tale of the 672nd Night' (1895) as the story of a sexual identity crisis in a masculine subject who, to his growing terror, finds himself invaded by femininity. In the most generally accepted interpretation, by Richard Alewyn,[20] this tale is a new parable on the theme of the restoration of the aesthete – egoist and prisoner in his artificial paradise – back to real life: the 'merchant's son' is seen as brother to Claudio in *Der Tor und der Tod*, torn from his dreams by the commanding force of life, which punishes him by appearing to him in the form of death. A variant of this interpretive schema takes the tale as a story of the 'crisis of maturity' in the artist or poet, who has to die to his aesthetic 'pre-existence' (Hofmannsthal's expression), losing his childish genius of mystical intimacy with the world, if he is to pass on to adult existence and acquire a stable identity.[21] But such readings do not adequately explain why the 'voyage of initiation' undertaken by the merchant's son takes the form of a fearful nightmare, a true 'descent into hell', as Marcel Brion puts it.[22]

The hero of the tale is a perfect example of narcissistic personality: 'Not long after reaching the age of twenty-five, the young son of a merchant, very handsome, with neither father nor mother, found living in the world and in society distasteful.'[23] He prefers his solitary existence to the company of his friends, and cannot bear the presence of a woman. He passes his time caring for his body and his pretty hands, and his image in the mirror is a source of great pride to him. His interior decor rivals that of des Esseintes; carpets, vases, lamps, carven wood and ornaments echo the forms of the world; 'In these interlacing ornaments he recognized an enchanted image of the inter-lacing marvels of the world.'[24] He finds real life in books and poetry, and his aestheticism culminates in his vision of a 'beautiful death': 'He would say "Your steps are taking you to the place where you must die," and would see himself, beautiful as a king lost out hunting, walking under strange trees towards an extraordinary and unknown destiny.'[25]

He has four servants. One is an old woman, once his nurse, who stands in for his lost mother; and there is a girl of about eighteen, who brings trays of fruit and pastries to his table every day. She is the incarnation of the feminine attractions which the merchant's son always tries to avoid: this female body seems to him 'the language of a wonderful, sealed world'.[26] And then there is the only man in his entourage, a servant he met at a reception given by the Persian ambassador, who seems to have a strong homoerotic attraction for the merchant's son: 'He showed a rare attachment to his master, anticipating his desires and intuitively guessing at his inclinations and repugnances, so that the latter felt an ever-growing inclination towards him.'[27]

The first grave disturbance in the existence of the merchant's son is caused by a young girl to whom, fulfilling a promise to his old governess, he gives shelter in his house. This girl, aged scarcely fifteen, seems to him sulky and incomprehensible. Why does she throw herself through the window in a moment of anger and hurt herself? When he comes to her bedside, he finds the childlike face disturbing:

> Suddenly she opened her eyes, gave him a freezing and hostile look, and then, compressing her lips with anger and overcoming her pain, she turned her face to the wall, so that she was lying on her wounded side. At that very moment, her livid face took on a greenish hue, she lost consciousness, and fell as if dead back into her former position.[28]

The real meaning of this childish 'anger' is not revealed until the beginning of part 2 of the tale. After receiving a threatening letter, the merchant's son also feels violent anger and realizes for the first time 'what had always made him angry as a child, his father's anxious love for his acquisitions, for the riches heaped under the vaults of his shop, the beautiful unfeeling children, which were the objects of all his seeking and his care.'[29] It was the same kind of anger which made the girl jump through the window: the jealousy of a child who feels abandoned by the father (or father substitute) in favour of his other 'unfeeling children', collector's items of the sort which now fill the house of the merchant's son as they once did his father's shop. The merchant's son had felt the same anger against his father; the girl is the double of his infant self. The violence she inflicted on herself, and which he could not understand, corresponds to the violence he is inflicting on himself by identifying with the image of his father and repressing his own desire to return to childhood, which would also be a return to the maternal, feminine sphere.[30]

At the beginning of part 2 of the tale, we realize that the aesthete's collections of pretty bric-à-brac and works of art owe their emotional value to an identification with the father. But for a long time, the merchant's son doubts this symbol of his father's way of life: 'He felt the vanity of things as much as their beauty; the thought of death never left him for long.'[31] The identification with the father takes the form of megalomaniac dreams of a 'great king': the merchant's son imagines himself dying like a king lost on the hunting trail, and delights in reading the glorious history of the wars of 'a very great king of long ago'.[32] Soon, this 'great king' is explicitly said to be a father image: when he understands his childish anger against the father who showed more affection to his riches than to his children, the hero realizes that 'the great king of long ago would have died if the realms he had conquered had been taken from him.'[33]

However much the merchant's son identifies himself with the father figure of the 'great king', his sense of self remains extremely fragile. The presence of his servants disturbs his solitude: they 'fawned on him like dogs, and although he seldom spoke to them, he still felt that they were constantly striving to serve him well. So he began to think about them from time to time.'[34] His uneasiness turns into a positive phobia in the course of the following summer, in the country house where he has settled with his servants; he believes they are spying on him, and can think of nothing else: 'He felt they were living more strongly, more intensely than he. For his own person he sometimes felt a faint tenderness or a certain astonishment, but they caused him a mysterious anguish.'[35]

More than once (in his annotations to *Sex and Character* and in a letter to Stefan Gruss),[36] Hofmannsthal compared this interior fragility of the merchant's son with a quotation from Keats, writing in 1818: 'When I am in a room with people if I ever am free from speculating on creations of my brain, then not myself goes home to myself, but the identity of everyone in the room begins to press upon me, so that I am in a very little time anihilated [*sic*].'[37] To Keats, and through him to Hofmannsthal, this fragility of the ego is characteristic of poetic genius, open to the world and to other people, pure sensibility.

The mention of Otto Weininger allows us to clarify what really afflicts the merchant's son. A few pages after his analysis of genius and his quotation from Keats (in *Sex and Character*), Weininger asserts that 'the absolute woman . . . is not conscious of her own identity.'[38] This makes femininity and genius strangely alike. Further on, in fact, Weininger goes so far as to acknowledge motherhood as an inferior kind of genius.[39] The creative genius, because of the fragility of his sense of self, is in fact profoundly feminized. In the first part of Hofmannsthal's tale the merchant's son is torn between his identification with father images (in his fantasies of the 'great king' and his love of beautiful things) and dislocation, that is, the feminization of his ego in presence of his servants. That is why they inspire him with a mixture of fascination and repulsion, while he feels a sort of homosexual attachment to his Persian servant.[40]

What Narcissus found in his mirror was a woman's face:

> Once he saw the girl in an inclined mirror; she was going through an adjacent room on a slightly higher level; in the mirror, however, she was coming at him from the deepest depths . . . What she seemed to be carrying with so much difficulty and solemnity was . . . the beauty of her own head with its heavy ornament of dark, living gold, wound between two great shells on either side of her smooth forehead, like a queen going to war.[41]

The warrior woman whom Narcissus sees in his mirror is perceived as a threat, an aggression. Thereafter there will be a 'masculine protest' against the attraction of the female. Unable to bear the physical presence of his fair serving maid, the merchant's son leaves the house and tries to calm himself by looking patiently for 'a flower whose form and scent, or a spice whose fleeting odour, were such that they would, for an instant, give him tranquil possession of that delightful charm which came from his serving girl, disturbed him and took away his peace.'[42] The flower and the aromatic plant are the fetishes with which he tries to mask the feminine body he finds so deeply disturbing.[43]

The story turns on one event: the merchant's son receives a curious letter. 'The letter bore no signature. It obscurely accused his servant of having committed, in the home of his former master, the Persian ambassador, an abominable crime. The unknown writer seemed to be nursing a violent hatred against the servant, and threatened him repeatedly.'[44] The narrator says no more about the crime the servant is accused of, about the threats, or about the writer of the letter. Is it a message to the merchant's son from his own subconscious? Was the servant's crime to arouse homosexual desire in his master? Is the letter a threat of feminization, an accusation of homosexuality? However that may be, it throws the merchant's son into a state of extreme panic.

Writers on the 'Tale' are fond of speculating on the meaning of this threatening letter.[45] The most valuable comments are by Eugene Weber, who recalls that the young Hofmannsthal wrote the story in the year of Oscar Wilde's trial.[46] In 1895 Wilde, returning from a journey in the company of his friend, Lord Alfred Douglas, found an insulting letter at his club from his friend's father. Wilde rashly took the father to court, but the outcome was disastrous for him: he was sentenced to two years in prison for immorality. The trial took place in the spring, and the newspapers, in Vienna as elsewhere, followed it closely. The first lines of the 'Tale' were written in April 1895. That is doubtless the real meaning of the letter which Hofmannsthal wrote to his father on 9 August: 'In this story I did not "mean" any more than is "meant" by any piece of newspaper gossip.'[47] Seen in this light, the message addressed to the merchant's son might well be of a similar kind to the letter received by Wilde.

The merchant's son leaves home in an attempt to get the matter cleared up. The tale then changes pace. While the first part describes the indolent existence and contemplative state of mind of the hero, a rapid succession of events ensues, ending in catastrophe. Things happen in obedience to a causality which is as imperious as it is mysterious. What inspiration guides the hero's steps into the most sinister quarters of the town, the street of prostitutes and among the slums? His curious wanderings through the sun-baked town remind us of Aschenbach, hero of *Death in Venice*, wandering through the old, plague-stricken streets of Venice, overmastered by homosexual desire.

Arthur Schnitzler, who was among the first to read Hofmannsthal's 'Tale', wrote to him in November 1895: 'The story ... bathes in a bluish dreamlight, with mysterious, half-hidden transitions, the singular mixture of precision in certain details and faintness in particular things which is so characteristic of dreams. And as soon as I see the adventures of the merchant's son as a dream, I find them most moving.'[48] Dorrit Cohn, taking Schnitzler literally, has suggested that this second part of the tale *is* a dream, all of whose elements are borrowed from the reality described in the first.[49]

This approach would explain why this second part topples over into fantasy. According to the analyses of Tzvetan Todorov, fantasy is in fact born of the reader's own hesitation and uncertainty: events which cannot be explained by the laws of the world we know may savour of madness, dream, or the supernatural.[50] As for the wanderings of the merchant's son, the fantasy is a perfect illustration of the analysis suggested by Freud in his 1919 essay on 'The Uncanny'. In it he says that one form of 'the uncanny' is connected with the theme of repetition connected with the subject's compulsion to repeat painful and upsetting experiences which he was unable to cope with the first time.[51] And indeed, the merchant's son in the 'Tale' goes in search of the feminine element which he could never encounter without anxiety in the first part of the story.

The genre of the short story after the fashion of the *Thousand and One Nights* was well suited to a narrative governed by the laws of dreams and the unconscious. In his 1906 essay on the *Thousand and One Nights*, Hofmannsthal wrote:

> In the youth of our hearts, in the solitude of our souls, we used to find ourselves in the midst of a great, mysterious city, menacing and alluring – Baghdad, perhaps, or Basra. Seduction and menace were strangely intermingled; our hearts felt a disquieting strangeness and nostalgia; we feared inner solitude, we were afraid of losing ourselves, and yet the courage of desire drew us on and sent us further along our labyrinthine path.[52]

The *Thousand and One Nights* let the reader through the *Porta Orientis* which for Hofmannsthal is in Vienna, the city of Freudian psychoanalysis: 'The Porta Orientis which leads to that mysterious inner Orient, the realm of the unconscious.'[53]

In his quest for the maternal, feminine element, the merchant's son goes into a jeweller's booth where a beryl, set in an ancient brooch, has caught his eye. He wants to buy the trinket for his old serving woman: 'Doubtless he had some day seen on her a similar trinket from the time of her youth.'[54] In the first sketch of the 'Tale', the brooch was intended for the young serving girl.[55] It is in the jeweller's booth that Narcissus again sees his female double in a mirror:

> His mind empty, he let his eye wander again over the old man's shoulder and light on a small hand-mirror of tarnished silver. Then, issuing from the depths of some interior mirror, the image of the girl came to meet him, flanked by the two dark heads of the bronze goddesses; he felt for an instant that her charm depended to a great extent on the humility and childlike grace with which her shoulders and neck bore up her head, the head of a young queen.[56]

This meeting with the feminine element of his own bisexual nature, which the first time he felt as a threat, an aggression, has now taken on the enchantment of childhood.

Leaving the jeweller's shop, the merchant's son decides to go through the backyard, and vanishes into a mysterious region which symbolizes erotic initiation – where pleasure and death, denoted by the 'infernal' flowers, are strangely close to each other: 'The merchant's son walked quickly along by the wall to the nearest greenhouse, went in, and found there a profusion of narcissi and anemones of rare and admirable species.'[57] The use of the greenhouse as a symbol of sexual deprivation has been shown by Roger Bauer to be common in fin-de-siècle literature, and we find it again here.[58] In Wilde's *Portrait of Dorian Gray* (1891), Dorian Gray sees through the panes of a greenhouse the threatening face of the brother of his former victim, Sibyl Vane. The merchant's son has a similar encounter:

> He was going slowly past the panes of the second greenhouse when suddenly he shivered with fear. For a human face pressed against the glass was looking at him ... The child, who was staring at him without moving a muscle, was frighteningly similar to the young girl of fifteen who lived in his house.[59]

As earlier in the tale, the girl is an incarnation of female innocence bruised by the inhibition which keeps the merchant's son a prisoner of his masculine identity. At the very moment of entering the female paradise, he becomes once again the tormentor of this child, the image of his own repressed femininity. He flees, full of anxiety and crushed by a feeling of guilt. He tries to go back, to rediscover the sheltered world of the aesthete and the 'great king':

> He ardently longed for a bed. With childish nostalgia, he thought of his huge, beautiful bed and dreamed of the beds that the great king of long ago had made for himself and his companions when they wedded the daughters of vanquished kings.[60]

This last vision of triumphant masculinity is in fact deceptive: in his panic flight from the female world, the merchant's son is flung back into the most bestial, elementary mannishness:

> By this time he had come to the low buildings which housed the soldiers. He did not realize it. Behind a barred window sat several soldiers with yellowish faces and sad eyes, who called some words to him ... But he did not understand what they wanted of him.[61]

What the soldiers called was no doubt what roughnecks say when they scent effeminacy. The masculine brutes gathering in the yard which the merchant's son now enters are like pitiable convicts, busy taking care of horses which are described as ugly, powerful and frightening, like the flesh-eating horses of the barbarian horde encamped before the old emperor's palace in Kafka's story *Ein altes Blatt* ('An Old Sheet of Paper'). One of these horses 'was trying to sink its huge teeth into the shoulder of the man who was kneeling before it, wiping its hoof'.[62]

We are irresistibly reminded of the fear of horses felt by Little Hans, the child of five whose phobia Freud was studying in 1909. Horses had a peculiar interest for Little Hans at the stage he had just reached, of discovering the anatomical differences between male and female. Fear of being bitten by a horse represented his castration anxiety, linked with a phobia for the female. It was in the same text that Freud, in a note, began his study of Weininger's case.[63]

Faced with the menacing horses in the barrack yard, the merchant's son feels with horror that his masculine ego is being effaced:

> At that moment, the horse turned towards him, and stared at him, shiftily laying
> its ears back and rolling its eyes horribly.... Before this hideous head, for a
> fleeting instant the merchant's son saw a long-forgotten human face ... And he
> knew it was the scowling face of a poor, ugly man whom he had seen, just once,
> in his father's shop. And that man had been scowling with terror, because
> people were threatening him, because he had a big piece of gold and would not
> say where he had got it from.[64]

Castration anxiety is inseparable from the image of the father: the hero is
recalling a scene in which, no doubt, his father had caught a thief red-handed
and had him thrown out of his shop. The humiliation of the culprit is equalled
only by the shattering omnipotence of the father.

The merchant's son stumbles and sends the beryl brooch rolling under the
horse's hoof. Buying the brooch had been the beginning of a quest for the
mother, for the female, soon to be broken off by the 'maaculine protest' of his
unconscious. He abandons the symbol of his desire for femininity as a
defeated enemy throws down his arms at the victor's feet, hoping perhaps for
mercy. But there is no mercy: 'He bent down; the horse kicked him savagely
in the groin, and he fell flat on his back.'[65] He has not escaped castration. He
dies pitifully, moaning 'like a little child, not with pain, but in distress, with
chattering teeth'.[66]

For the merchant's son, the destruction of his narrow narcissistic ego is not
an initiation rite which might lead to the return of his repressed femininity
and the enjoyment of total bisexuality. For this we must await the transgression of Lord Chandos, who opens himself to the feminine (via stages of
mystical fusion) to find salvation for the *unrettbares Ich*. When he tells how

> I could no more explain, in sensible words, what was this harmony which went
> through both of us – the whole world and myself – its floating suspense, nor
> how it became perceptible to me, than I could give an exact indication of the
> internal movements of my entrails or the stases of my blood,[67]

Chandos indeed seems to be living in a state very comparable to the voluptu-
ousness of the soul, the *Seelenwohllust* promised to Schreber once he had
reconciled himself to his new 'feminine' identity.

Schreber and Kulturkritik

Schreber's memoirs devote a good deal of space to maunderings over German
Protestantism and the Jews. Chapter 7, in which the crisis of the German
people, the rise of Catholicism, Judaism and the Slavs, and the outbreak of
epidemics of plague and leprosy are closely connected in a single context,
assumes a peculiar importance in this regard. Weininger, whose *Sex and
Character* could be called a formidable 'maaculine protest' against the threat of
feminization of the ego and of culture generally, confirms the close connection
between the masculine identity crisis, the fear of the feminine and certain
obsessions: the decline of German Protestantism, heavily invested with mas-

culinity, as opposed to Catholicism, which is 'feminine'; the connection between the Jewish (or Slav) element and generalized feminization; and the
theme of the fatal epidemic, which synthesizes all the other motifs. Klaus
Theweleit, through his research on the memoirs, personal writings, sentimental vagaries and sexual adventures of selected pioneers of the Third Reich
(Ernst Jünger, Ernst von Salomon, Lettow-Vorbeck, Rossbach and others),
has shown that the martial bearing of those manly heroes hid a feeble ego
which felt threatened by the 'bolshevik tide' or the 'Judeo-capitalist filth'
which they repeatedly confused with images of perverse femininity.[68]

Schreber's aim could be defined by adapting Winnicott's words: 'when the
feminine element in the patient discovers the breast, it is the self which has
been found.' By changing into a woman (signifying the liberation in him of the
repressed feminine element of his bisexual constitution), Schreber was seeking
an identification with the mother, allowing the rebirth of a true masculine
identity preferable to that of the *flüchtig hingemachte Männer* of which he
himself had been a specimen until his 'illness'. Schreber, in his madness,
turned this yearning into a megalomaniac vision, to give life to the Adam and
Eve of a renascent humanity, to compete with God by recreating the world.
Indeed, Schreber was worried by the idea of his own death: however would
God be able to manage without him?

This is the culmination of Schreber's psychotic narcissism. But comparable
fantasies can be found in turn-of-the century literature imbued with post-
Nietzschean philosophy. Rilke, for example, writing in 1898:

> The artist will not remain indefinitely on man's side. When the artist – more
> agile, more profound – knows wealth and procreative force, when he is experi-
> encing what today he can only dream of, man will gradually fade and die. The
> artist is eternity showing through the everyday.[69]

In the theme of the fusion of the artistic ego with the world which recurs
frequently in the writings of the young Rilke we can probably identify a desire
to restore the primary identification of early childhood associated with the
feminine element.

At the end of a study based for the most part on the Schreber case, Robert
J. Stoller concludes that the feeling of maleness and its progression into
masculinity are rather less firmly rooted in men than the feeling of femaleness
and femininity are in women. If this is true it is because men have, from the
beginning of life, a very intimate, fused relationship with the mother:

> Even in the most fortunate small boy, the feeling of belonging to the male sex
> disguises a more primitive oneness with the identity of the mother. In a small
> girl, this same oneness merely reinforces the feeling of femaleness . . . At bottom
> the attraction represented by a new oneness with the mother's femaleness
> terrifies and captivates men, it is a siren song. The Schreber case makes this
> plain.[70]

It was, I think, this attraction–repulsion that inspired a large part of the
literature, art and *Kulturkritik* of the turn of the century. It relates closely to a

crisis of modernization, interpreted and experienced as a too-exclusive affirmation of values connected with the masculine element. When Freud, in
Civilization and Its Discontents, undertook to define what he understood by
Kultur, he suggested a simple formula which would define as civilizing
(*kulturell*) 'all activities and resources which are useful to men for making the
earth serviceable to them, for protecting them against the violence of the
forces of nature, and so on'.[71] Thus his list of civilized values is headed by
scientific and technical rationality. A little later he emphasizes the other
fundamental aspect of civilization: it is a rule of law, to which all ('except those
who are not capable of entering a community') have contributed by the
sacrifice of their instincts, and which (with the same reservation) delivers
nobody up to brute force.[72]

Thus morality, codified as law, is immediately assimilated to a mastery
of one's own nature. Freud's definitions are classic, and do not aim for
originality. They have the merit of showing clearly that Freud's idea of
civilized values relates to the masculine element (mastery over the object). It
was just this point of view that was contested by aesthetic, *kulturkritisch*
modernism.

III

Weininger, Artaud and Kafka

Weininger's *Sex and Character* subsumes and carries to extremes the Western
tradition of misogyny, and his writings can be interpreted as symptomatic of
a repressive, authoritarian civilization grounded on the principle of male
domination – a reading central to my previous monograph on Weininger.[73]
But in fact *Sex and Character* has as much to say about men as about women,
about the anxieties of masculinity as about the 'inferiority' of the feminine.
Weininger's antifeminist diatribes betray a crisis of masculinity that was
strikingly evidenced by his suicide. *Sex and Character* is a cry for help and an
admission of weakness. Weininger only hates women (or femininity) because
he is afraid of them – or because he has a repressed longing to return to them.
He trumpets the laws of patriarchy just when he most fears to see the
imposition of something new and triumphantly matriarchal. He celebrates
the pomp and circumstance of masculinity to sharpen his denunciation of the
decadence of modern men. Finally, he latches on to the ideal of the genius,
which might have been able to free him from the impasse of *Sex and Character*
by restoring him to harmony with life, but which turns out to be against
nature.

August Strindberg regarded Weininger as a brother genius. In a letter of
1903 to Artur (*sic*) Gerber, a close friend of Weininger, we read: 'The
cynicism of life had become for him unbearable.'[74] Weininger refused to
compromise on his idealistic morality; it could be said that

> His ideal of love takes the form of a marriage of the heart, in which the bodily
> element is accepted, at most, as a passion of the soul. But this ideal was

constantly being undermined by a 'quasi-realism'. This tension makes the bourgeois very sensitive to bawdiness and pornography. He has a cynical smile on his lips.[75]

Weininger fulminated against the hypocrisy of Kantian morality: Kant himself had had great trouble in integrating conjugal sexuality into his ethic, tolerating it as a survival of animal nature into the age of practical reason. Weininger carried through to the end – which means into absurdity – the 'angelic' tendencies of Kantian ethics. His mystic quest was a quest for purity.

To this extent, Weininger was like Antonin Artaud, the 'lunatic' who used to spit on any woman he met in the corridors of the madhouse in Rodez, and then ostentatiously cross himself. Both their works (particularly if we think of Weininger's *Über die letzten Dinge*, 'On the Last Things') show the same fascination with astrology, alchemy and the occult; the same search for oneness, which tends to return to an original androgyny, a state which, as Artaud wrote in *Héliogabale*, 'brings together man and woman, the hostile poles, the ONE and the TWO, and marks the end of contradictions'.[76] Weininger's genius was 'the man-father, neither man nor woman'[77] of Artaud's dreams.

The experience of wholeness enjoyed by Weininger's genius-microcosm can be reduced to an experience of a void, a death in life, what Artaud called 'the appetite for not-being': 'The Solitary has avenged the Evil coming from the darkness of Women, by the force which he has newly reinvented. The force which he has allowed to detach itself has restored to him a converse force. / And it was a death-force. / All our Destiny is a Destiny of Death. One cycle of the world is complete.'[78] The rejection of woman, in Artaud as in Weininger, was a refusal to accept that there was in him 'something horrible which arises but which comes not from me, but from the darkness I have in me . . . and soon that's all there will be: the obscene mask of the one that grimaces between the sperm and the pooh.'[79] He would spiritualize the flesh, restore the masculine, deny his relationship to father and mother, scratch the body until it was clean, pure, devoid of sex and sexual organs: 'This means that the fruit of this death will be a *Higher Initiation* and that everything relating to sexuality will be burned away in this higher Initiation, its fire changed into Initiation. So as to restore everywhere the absolute Supremacy of Man.'[80]

As much as Artaud, Weininger's metaphysical misogyny recalls Franz Kafka: this time the connection has biographical support, for we know that Kafka was impressed by his reading of *Sex and Character*.[81] His horror of sexuality is expressed in his journal for 1913: 'Copulation considered as the punishment for the happiness of living together. To live in the greatest possible asceticism, more ascetically than any bachelor, is for me the only way of enduring marriage. But for her?'[82] A letter to Milena in 1920 even makes a Weininger-like connection between sexuality and Jewishness:

My body, often quiescent for years, was again shaken unendurably by this desire for a certain sordid little act, something rather repugnant, embarrassing, dirty: even in the best part of what was given me then, there was a little of that, a bad smell, a whiff of sulphur, a touch of hell. This impulse was something like the wandering Jew, carried along absurdly, journeying absurdly through an absurdly dirty world.[83]

There is a 'monkish'[84] tendency in the notes, dated 20 August 1916, which tabulate the comparative merits of the married man and the bachelor: the latter remains 'pure', he conserves his strength and concentrates on his work.[85] In Kafka's stories and novels, it is always women who incarnate the temptations and threats of sexuality which bring about the downfall of men.[86]

Sex and Character develops a metaphysics of masculinity in which the male principle is identified, to the point of absurdity, with the figures of intellect, creativity, liberty and will, cutting itself off more and more sharply from the body, instinct, life, nature. Following the masculine imperative brings one to a kind of death which seems to be not a void, but an absolute. Just like Schreber's 'Memoirs of a Neuropath', Weininger's treatise communicates the (no doubt typically masculine!) notion that it is infinitely easier to be a woman than a man. According to Weininger, a woman, to fulfil her destiny, simply has to abandon herself to the calls of nature, of the flesh, of instincts; to passivity, forgetfulness, the slumber of the mind, the will of the world, procreation. Whereas the destiny of man can be fulfilled only with a mighty and agonizing effort to realize the one command: 'Become a genius!'

Homosexuality and antisexuality: the impossible male

Everything in *Sex and Character* begins with bisexuality. The first part of the book shows the extraordinary initial confusion of the masculine and the feminine in every individual. The least little cell, the smallest globule in a human being, breaks down into the formula $xM + yF$. Weininger expounds this idea of the fundamental hermaphrodite with such vigour that many of his contemporaries credited him with its 'discovery' – which later caused a violent dispute between Weininger (posthumously!), Swoboda, Fliess and Freud. As late as 1924, Freud himself still felt obliged to point out: 'In lay circles the hypothesis of human bisexuality is regarded as being due to O. Weininger, the philosopher, who died at an early age, and who made the idea the subject of a rather unbalanced book . . . [there is] little justification for the claim.'[87]

Jean-Bertrand Pontalis has shown the importance of bisexuality to the dissidents and outsiders of psychoanalysis: Fliess, Adler, Jung, Groddeck, Ferenczi.[88] These differences over bisexuality often accompany serious disagreements on the subject of femininity. *Woman are the stronger sex, the first sex.* That is the message that emerges from behind the overt male chauvinism of *Sex and Character*. Weininger's notion of the evolution of the male is indeed a *via difficilior*, while women (or at least women who do not attempt to 'free themselves from their own femininity', as Weininger puts it) merely have to continue in their passive non-being. Bisexuality has different meanings for men and women. Masculine or feminine sexual identity is not just the result of an accentuation of one of the two sexes combined in the original bisexuality. Male or female ontogenesis and psychogenesis do not follow straightforwardly similar and parallel paths. Femaleness is the result of a passive process, maleness of an active process.[89]

Weininger's extraordinary demands on men must surely seem, to most of them, unacceptable. He had no illusions on that point:

> It would not be surprising if to many it should seem from the foregoing arguments that 'men' have come out of them too well.... The accusation would be unjustified. It does not enter the author's mind to idealise men ... it is a question of the better possibilities lying in every man.... There are, as has already often been demonstrated, men who have become women or who have remained women.[90]

Here Weininger meets Freud, who observed that by reason of the bisexual nature of individuals 'the majority of men are far behind the masculine ideal.'[91] If we take Weininger's theories to extremes we might end up saying that all human beings start by being (psychologically) women, and that the majority of them never leave behind this happy, but morally inferior, original state. The advent of masculinity requires 'masculine protest' (Adler's expression), and is never completely achieved. Manliness always remains to be conquered, on penalty of regression into the femininity which is always eager to reoccupy lost ground.

The desire for feminization which is expressed in Schreber's memoirs, the fear of female sexuality which inspires Weininger's theories and the identity crisis of the male hero in Hofmannsthal's 'Tale' are all expressed in themes or behaviour of a homosexual kind. Does this mean that we should attribute homosexuality to Weininger,[92] or to Hofmannsthal? Several recent critical studies have taken this step, and have seriously analysed the homosexuality which can be read between the lines of Hofmannsthal[93] or Kafka.[94] But some may find this diagnosis too reductive. I shall not attempt to pronounce on any particular case, but I shall examine the deconstruction of the masculine which seems to be closely connected with the very idea of modernity.

Already in Baudelaire we find this hatred of 'normal' sexuality, which 'is very like a torture or a surgical operation',[95] together with a violent misogyny bound up with longing for the lost *mundus muliebris* of childhood. As Gert Mattenklott has shown for the painter Aubrey Beardsley and for Stefan George,[96] homosexuality is only one of the names which could be given to the revolt against the 'natural' facts of sexuality, and to the feminization of art and literature, which stamp the modernity of the 1900s.

Gustav Mahler and Sigmund Freud: the meeting at Leiden

On 26 August 1910, Sigmund Freud met Gustav Mahler at Leiden and began on an analysis of the composer's *Mutterbindung*, his bond with his mother.[97] Freud later told Theodor Reik (letter of 4 January 1935) that he had spent a whole afternoon in Leiden analysing Mahler, and, as he had learned later, with impressive results. Mahler, Freud recounted, had thought the visit absolutely necessary, because his wife was just then rebelling against his absence of libido towards her. 'We made a very interesting survey of his life and discovered his amorous propensities, including his Mary complex (involvement with the mother); I took occasion to admire the man's clear-sightedness, amounting to genius,' Freud concluded.[98]

Jens Malte Fischer[99] hypothesizes that Freud adapted certain elements in his short analysis of Mahler for his 1912 essay on 'The Universal Tendency to Debasement in the Sphere of Love', which suggests that the love of certain persons remains divided between the two orientations that are conventionally called 'higher' and 'baser' love.

> Where they love they do not desire and where they desire they cannot love. They seek objects which they do not need to love, in order to keep their sensuality away from the objects they love; and, in accordance with the laws of 'complexive sensitiveness' and of the return of the repressed, the strange failure shown in psychical impotence makes its appearance whenever an object which has been chosen with the aim of avoiding incest recalls the prohibited object through some feature, often an inconspicuous one.[100]

According to this theory, Mahler's love life had deviated from its 'natural' object, his wife Alma, and turned towards the higher spheres of artistic creation and the ideal. In the train on the way home from Leiden, Mahler wrote a poem to Alma whose last verse contains a declaration of 'platonic' love, substituting for the wife an image of the immaculate Madonna, while the lover attains to a seraphic and immaterial felicity:

> *I love you!* it was the meaning of my life!
> How happily shall I sleep, far from the world, from dreams,
> *O Love me!* Prize of my assault!
> Saved, I am dead to the world – I am in harbour.[101]

This poem echoes the tone of a *Lied* Mahler composed in August 1901 to a poem by Rückert, 'Ich bin der Welt abhanden gekommen . . .' ('I have turned away from the world . . .'). It is interesting in this connection[102] to note the modification Mahler made to Rückert's poem, which ended: 'Ich leb' in mir und meinem Himmel! / in meinem Lieben, in meinem Lied' ('I live in myself and in my heaven! / in my love and in my song'). Mahler wrote 'Ich leb' allein in meinem Himmel . . .' ('I live only in my heaven . . .', or 'I live alone in my heaven . . .').

Mahler's Eighth Symphony, composed in the summer of 1906 and dedicated to Alma, ends in a 'Hymn: The Birth of Eros'. By combining two apparently very different texts – the 'Veni, Creator Spiritus' of Hrabanus Maurus, a ninth-century hymn celebrating the coming of the Holy Spirit at Pentecost, and the final scene of *Faust* – Mahler proclaims the oneness of Christian *caritas* and Goethe's creative Eros: 'Das Ewig-Weibliche / Zieht uns hinan' ('The Eternal Feminine bears us up'). Adorno was not impressed by the 'Eighth' and accused Mahler of sliding into 'decorative grandiosity'.[103]

For our present purpose, the most interesting aspect is the 'Parsifalian' atmosphere. This song to the glory of Eros (the title of the third movement) is in fact one of the most unfleshly of all the composer's works. The Nietzschean leanings of the young Mahler (who in 1895 had contemplated giving his Third Symphony the subtitle *Die fröhliche Wissenschaft*) gave way to the most ethereal mysticism when he undertook to celebrate love and women.

Alma Mahler-Werfel was left with a conjugal relationship which, she wrote in 'My Life', was an 'imposed asceticism' due to the composer's obsessive anxiety lest he waste valuable working time – his life was organized entirely around his artistic output. 'My strange marriage with that abstraction, Gustav Mahler, had kept me, for the first ten years of my conscious life, inwardly a virgin. I loved the mind of Mahler; his body remained for me a shadow.'[104] She adds a little later: 'He was celibate and was afraid of women. His fear of "abasing himself" was unbounded and he fled from life ... which is to say, from women.'[105]

Lawrence, Weininger, Bataille

It is known that the author of *Women in Love* and *Lady Chatterley's Lover* had read the works of Otto Weininger.[106] It is also known that Lawrence – albeit indirectly through Frieda Weekley (née von Richthofen) – had met with certain elements of German *Lebensphilosophie*, in particular Schwabing and his circle.[107] Lawrence's novels and essays develop a coherent metaphysics of sexuality and sexual difference[108] which combines certain prominent aspects of the 'modern crisis' of sexual identity. He can be closely compared with Weininger: both started from similar insights, opened themselves to a vision of evil and struggled to regain innocence and bring grace down upon earth.

Lawrence describes, as cruelly as Weininger, the destructive confrontation of man and woman and, to use his own words, 'the disintegrative effect of modern sex activity'. He goes on: 'So that at last I begin to see the point of my critics' abuse of my exalting of sex. They only know one form of sex: the nervous, personal, disintegrative sort, the "white" sex. ... the current sort of sex is just what I *don't* mean.'[109] Some passages from Lawrence equal Weininger's in misogyny. Hermione, in *Women in Love*, is an incarnation of repellent modern womanhood:

> In the life of thought, of the spirit, she was one of the elect. And she wanted to be universal. But there was a devastating cynicism at the bottom of her. She did not believe in her own universals – they were sham. She did not believe in the inner life – it was a trick, not a reality. She did not believe in the spiritual world – it was an affectation. In the last resort, she believed in Mammon, the flesh, and the devil – these at least were not a sham.[110]

The men Lawrence presents as harbingers of a new and virile race all show signs of antifeminism. Birkin, in *Women in Love*, goes in fear of 'dangerous female destructiveness'. He throws stones at the moon's reflection in the lake, hurling imprecations at Cybele, 'the accursed Syria Dea', the personification of aggressive female desire. He is suspicious of heterosexual love and tends to prefer 'Walt Whitman' camaraderie between men (symbolized by the boxing match between Birkin and Gerald). The scourge of modern life is the bisexualization of culture and the confusion of sexual characteristics. 'It's because th' men *aren't* men, that th' women have to be,' says the gamekeeper in *Lady Chatterley*.[111] And Birkin calls for the differences to be restored:

> There is now to come the new day, where we are beings each of us, fulfilled in difference. The man is pure man, the woman pure woman, they are perfect, polarised. But there is no longer any of the horrible merging, mingling, self-abnegation of love. There is only the pure duality of polarisation, each one free from any contamination of the other.[112]

Those of Lawrence's male characters who manage to win the war of the sexes and advance to cosmogonic eroticism must pass through a near-fatal ordeal. Birkin struggles to free himself from his destructive relationship with Hermione when he meets Ursula. The gamekeeper has had some unpleasant experiences, and at first spurns Lady Chatterley's advances. 'The Man Who Died', the title of a Lawrence story, sums up his idea that life is an initiation involving an encounter with death before one can resume living on a higher plane.

For Lawrence, as for Weininger, the sin which dogs all human life is the loss of original oneness and the severing of subject and object, male and female. Is there a way to regain the reconciled world as it was before the sins which the Bible calls by the one word *knew*? Weininger's 'wisdom' means living as a genius ('the universe and the ego have become one in him');[113] Lawrence's means acknowledging that 'there is nothing in me that is alone or absolute ... so that my individualism is really an illusion.'[114] It is the superficial (and, Weininger would say, typically feminine) affirmation of the individual and his petty, selfish wants that causes the dissevering of the subject and the world, and also the war between the sexes.

The ultimate experience, close to death, which Lawrence's heroes undergo is strongly reminiscent of Bataille's notion of inward experience:

> We find it hard to endure the situation which binds us to the chance individuality, the perishable individual that we are. At the same time as we have an anguished desire that that perishable individual should last, we are obsessed by a primary continuity which links us with being ... This longing governs the three forms of eroticism in all men.[115]

Georges Bataille distinguishes between the eroticism of bodies, the eroticism of hearts, and religious eroticism.

Weininger, in his nostalgia for primary continuity, sought the way of religious eroticism. Bataille goes on: 'Our heart faints at the idea that the discontinuous individuality in us will suddenly be snuffed out: however unimportant beings may be, we cannot without doing violence to ourselves imagine a threat to the being within.' In summer 1903 Weininger went through a shattering mystical ordeal which he confesses in *Über die Letzten Dinge* ('On the Last Things') and in the fragments of the *Taschenbuch*.[116] Here we find harsh bursts of symbols and a radical re-evaluation of the self which *Sex and Character* had naively placed at the centre of the universe: 'There is no self, there is no soul. The intelligible self is but vanity.'[117] The violent capsize which might have helped him out of the impasse of *Sex and Character* finally led him to suicide. A philosopher's end? More likely a truncated initiation.

To Lawrence, eroticism, before being a union between a man and a woman, is a union with the whole, with the vital flux, the divine. In his remarks on genius, Weininger seems to approach a similar conclusion. But his whole error, and his misfortune, consisted in a failure to distinguish between sexuality, which he rejected, and eroticism, a higher form of life acceptance, the affirmation of an individuality freed from the illusions of individuation. This necessary, but painful severance from an existence dominated by the I and governed by cerebral functions (which threatens to lead ultimately to suicide) in order to regain harmony with the immanent meaning of life seems to be crucial to male destiny. Without it the dialogue of the male and the female threatens to become the struggle of Thanatos and Eros.

IV

The fourth sex and the horror of women

In his *Das Sexualleben unserer Zeit* ('The Sexual Life of our Time', 1906), the Berlin sexologist Iwan Bloch included a chapter entitled 'Renunciation of Women' devoted to a phenomenon which he made a point of distinguishing from homosexuality. This new strand in contemporary sexual life had, he thought, been prefigured by Schopenhauer and oriented itself on Strindberg and Weininger. 'The enemies of woman today constitute a sort of "fourth sex" to which it is fashionable to belong.'[118] Bloch saw this misogyny, which was operative in the work of several contemporary scholars,[119] as the affirmation of a new 'masculine culture' and of 'the emancipation of men'. That paradoxical slogan was the title of a book by Norbert Grabowsky, published in 1897.[120] Bloch interpreted the appearance of a 'fourth sex' as revealing the upheavals which were marking 'the formation of a new kind of love relationship, more noble and more promising'.[121]

Arthur Schnitzler, in his journal for 1892, mentions a remark of the young Hofmannsthal concerning his 'horror of women' and 'sometimes [his] theoretical anxiety at never having felt any desire for women. I felt that at ten or eleven years old, sensual excitements, etc.' He added, addressing Schnitzler, 'What's more, your books make me afraid of women.'[122] Hofmannsthal's novel *Andreas*, begun in 1907, taken up and reworked several times up to 1927 and finally left unfinished,[123] can be interpreted as a sentimental education which details the anxieties and failures of a young man subjected to a crisis of sexual identity when faced with the disturbing faces of femininity. The concept of the novel, as it appears in the unfinished parts and fragmentary sketches assembled in the critical edition, is reminiscent of a *Bildungsroman*.[124] It is indeed with the intention of completing his education that Andreas von Ferschengelder's parents send him to Venice, with enough pocket money to pay for the journey and have an agreeable time. But Venice, in Hofmannsthal as in Thomas Mann's *Death in Venice*, is a place of perdition, a labyrinth where the youthful Andreas loses himself to such an extent that the 'novel of education' becomes the story of the collapse of a fragile personality, constantly under threat of psychopathological dissociation.[125]

This character is similar in many ways to the merchant's son in the 'Tale of the 672nd Night'; there are several notes in which Hofmannsthal makes that very comparison.[126] In the 1912 fragment called 'The Lady with the Lapdog', Hofmannsthal explains: 'The reason for making him undertake this journey: a slow and difficult convalescence after a spiritual crisis, traces of anhedonia, loss of a sense of values, confusion in his ideas.'[127] We recognize some of the principal symptoms of Chandos's spiritual ordeal. Andreas is divided into 'two different halves',[128] and this makes his character unstable. This schizoid tendency stems from the divergence between sensuality and 'ideal',[129] which strive for the mastery in Andreas, who is dominated at one moment by violent desires, at another by hatred of the flesh and the most ethereal aspirations. Hofmannsthal sums up the destiny of his hero: 'At first, becomes ready for love; then learns that mind and body are one. [Andreas] has always suffered from this dualism; first one, then the other seem to him empty of all value. At present he is learning to sense the one hiding behind the other, the one always bearing the other.'[130]

Was Andreas to achieve this planned inner healing, the reconciliation of two opposing tendencies, the harmonious consolidation of character? We can imagine a happy ending in which Andreas, having overcome his inhibitions and solved his inner conflict, returns to Austria, and this time successfully wins and keeps the love of Romana, whom he first met in Carinthia but lost through his mistakes and his clumsiness.[131] But we can also suggest that the novel is unfinished because Andreas's destiny remains fundamentally undecided. Hofmannsthal did outline some possible final reconciliations. But the fragments which give some idea of how the novel would have continued mostly convey discouragement and pessimism: 'Result of the stay in Venice: he feels, with terror, that he cannot return to his straitened existence in Vienna, that he has broken away from that life. But his new state causes him more anxiety than satisfaction.'[132]

The cleft subjectivity of Andreas is expressed in the story through the omnipresent theme of double personality. Gotthilf, the manservant whom Andreas rashly engages while staying at Villach, turns out to be a satanic double. His vulgar and titillating account of the erotic adventures of Count Lodron, his former master, deeply disturbs Andreas and provokes him to a waking dream of sexual violence.[133] Soon after, Gotthilf enacts the sadistic scenes of Andreas's nightmare when he rapes Romana and spreads terror through the household.[134]

Andreas is haunted by a painful memory of how, at twelve, he yielded to a cruel impulse and broke his little dog's back.[135] One of Gotthilf's evil deeds was to poison the hotel-keeper's dog.[136] He is indeed Andreas's diabolical double, the personification of his sadistic leanings, his aggressive and destructive sexuality, more inclined to rape than to love. The idealistic Andreas, in love with Romana, feels only repulsion and anxiety about sex. He looks on perplexedly as Romana sports with her goats,[137] and when, at nightfall, he creeps into Romana's room, his bold incursion ends in a rout. The double face of Andreas, now a pure and inhibited virgin, now a rogue capable of the basest tyranny, corresponds to a double image of woman, sometimes a love object beyond the reach of sexuality, sometimes a wanton, easily seduced and treated with sadistic scorn.

In Venice, Andreas becomes acquainted with Maria-Mariquita: 'the lady (Maria) and the tart (Mariquita) are . . . aspects of one and the same person, who are constantly dodging round each other.'[138] Maria inspires in men only a 'religious feeling, never love (Novalis)'; she feels only disgust for 'the act itself'.[139] Mariquita, on the other hand, is all sensuality, allurement, eroticism: she is an incarnation of 'the many faces of the demon'.[140] The character Maria-Mariquita had been suggested to Hofmannsthal by his reading of *The Dissociation of Personality* by the American psychiatrist Morton Prince.[141] The duality of mind and body, which caused the dissociation in Andreas's character at Villach, is this time transfered to a female character who combines in her person two types, the seductress and the madonna.[142]

The character of Sacramozo, the man from Malta, remains enigmatic due to the novel's unfinished state. An admirer of Maria, he becomes a teacher to Andreas. Under his authority, Andreas embarks on an initiation from which he should emerge regenerated.[143] And yet Sacramozo is deeply divided in himself. He is, says Hofmannsthal, experiencing 'the complete collapse of a man of forty';[144] he is suffering from 'impotence'.[145] He shares his young disciple's horror of sexuality: 'The man from Malta confessed that he had never touched a woman. Andreas admitted the same to him. The Maltese congratulated him on it.'[146] Another character in the novel portrays Sacramozo as a ridiculous and unsuccessful lover.

In the developing relationship between Andreas and Sacramozo there is certainly an important element of homosexual attraction. In the first scene of the novel, as soon as he arrives in Venice, Andreas reveals his unconscious homosexual leanings: meeting a masked gambler in the early hours, and seeing that the man is wearing nothing but a shirt under his cloak (he has gambled away all his other clothes), Andreas 'also involuntarily undid his travelling cloak'.[147] Several of Hofmannsthal's notes suggest that the relationship of teacher and pupil is tinged with homosexuality: the Maltese is successively compared to Stefan George, Winckelmann and Baron Charlus.[148]

The outcome sketched out in Hofmannsthal's notes is tragic: 'Sacramozo recognizes the right moment for a union of Andreas with Maria: it is that moment which he chooses to kill himself.'[149] 'The true act is suicide (Novalis),' Hofmannsthal wrote,[150] suggesting that this voluntary death is a mystic conversion, a dissolution of the ego in the universal.[151] It is this sacrifice –

doubtless an exorcism of homosexuality is also intended – which is intended to allow Andreas's regeneration and his ideal union with Maria, consummated beyond the sordid commerce of desire and the flesh; because the death of the Maltese is also the redemption of Maria, suddenly freed from her sensual other self. If such was to be the conclusion of the novel – but in the fragmentary state of the text we can only conjecture[152] – Andreas's crisis of sexual identity could only be resolved by marriage with the 'madonna' and the disappearance of the seductress, Mariquita – in short, by a complete neutralization of sexuality under a pretence of normalization.

Reading *Andreas*, one is tempted to say that sexual relations with women have become for men the most delicate, the most dangerous, the most uncertain of all undertakings – if not an impossible task. A letter from Hofmannsthal to Rudolf Pannwitz of 18 September 1917 suggests that despite appearances, the novel has some historical relevance:

> Although it is a purely personal story, the novel takes place in the year of the death of Maria Theresa. In that year, the hero is twenty-three; in the epilogue, in 1908–9 (Austrian uprising), he is an eminent official; his son is to be a diplomat, his grandson a deputy in the Paulskirche in 1848, so that all of it looks forward to the present.[153]

From this viewpoint the last generation of Andreas von Ferschengelder's descendants would be that of the young poets of Viennese modernism. Andreas's personal destiny, and all around him the confusion of relationships between the sexes, are distantly related to the historical changes which symbolically began with the death of Maria Theresa. Hofmannsthal's unfinished novel assumes the aspect of a reflection on modernity, particularly the overthrow of sexual codes and the still-unresolved redistribution of masculine and feminine roles.

6
The Feminine at Work in (Post)Modernity

I

Bisexuality and periodicity: the historical unconscious

In the first part of *Sex and Character*, Weininger paradoxically shows that the difference between the sexes, the opposition of masculine and feminine, does not answer to any empirical fact. Who, he asks, has not experienced one of those often lively discussions about 'men and women' or 'the liberation of women'? In such conversations and discussions, 'men' and 'women' are opposed with depressing monotony, 'like red and white balls'. And of course there can be no agreement, as always happens when the same word is used to denote different things, when the language does not match the concept:

> the improbability may henceforward be taken for granted of finding in nature a sharp cleavage between all that is masculine on the one side and all that is feminine on the other; or that a living being is so simple in this respect that it can be put wholly on one side or the other of the line. Matters are not so clear.[1]

The comparison with red and white balls is probably an echo of the linguistic scepticism of Ernst Mach, who in 'The Analysis of Sensations' gave this example of the inadequacy of words: 'The earth and a billiard ball are both spheres, so long as we agree to ignore everything which distances them from the spherical form, and so long as any greater precision is considered superfluous.'[2] 'Man' and 'woman', 'masculine' and 'feminine' are cultural constructs, chance ideas which help us to situate ourselves, but often lead us astray. The subject is perpetually out of phase with his sexed body.

These considerations did not deter Weininger from asserting, in the second part of *Sex and Character*, that if we wish to attain full knowledge of the opposition between the sexes we must accept that men and women are conceivable only as types: 'In plants and animals, the presence of hermaphroditism is an undisputed fact ... In the case of two human beings, however, it seems to be psychologically true that an individual, at least at one and the same moment, is always either man or woman.'[3] Weininger went on to discuss 'ideal types' (which he calls 'M' and 'W'). He speaks of masculine and feminine, not of men and women; though that does not save him from a massed counter-attack of ineffably trivial remarks on 'the inferiority of women'. And it is no real surprise to find, in chapter 8 of *Sex and Character*, some harsh and abrupt judgements on Jews. 'The Jew', like 'man' and 'woman', is a notion which nobody can actually define satisfactorily, but which everybody agrees on, especially when they are out to abuse it . . .

According to Weininger, the unconscious is historical. His theory of bisexuality is integrated with a theory of periodicity. Not only does the individual go through male and female stages (one of the ideas which Fliess accused Weininger and Swoboda of 'plagiarizing'), but above all – and this shows Weininger's originality – humanity goes through periods of greater or lesser gonochorism (complete separation of the sexes in individuals). 'There are times of lesser gonochorism when more masculine women and feminine men are born.'[4] Referring to Jacob Burckhardt, Weininger dubbed the Renaissance a period of lesser gonochorism. In his celebrated *The Civilization of the Renaissance in Italy*, whose influence on Nietzsche and the fin de siècle as a whole is well known, Burkhardt had noted that to understand Renaissance society it was essential to be aware that women were considered equal to men. If Renaissance Italians seldom spoke of the emancipation of women it was because it had naturally come about. Well-born women, like men, had to try to develop a distinct personality, complete in every respect:

> The highest praise which could then be given to Italian women was that they had the mind and courage of men. We have only to observe the thoroughly manly bearing of most of the women in the heroic poems, especially those of Boiardo and Ariosto, to convince ourselves that we have before us the ideal of the time. The title 'virago', which is an equivocal compliment in the present day, then implied nothing but praise.[5]

Thus there were periods when civilization was bisexual: Weininger identified them as the tenth, fifteenth and sixteenth centuries, then again the nineteenth and twentieth, periods which had seen the birth of more androgynous types, intermediate sexual forms. But one feels that Weininger is nonetheless putting his own dawning century on a lower cultural level than the Renaissance as seen by Burckhardt: whereas at that time women had had the principal masculine virtues, in his own time it was men who were acquiring female characteristics. He talks of 'the "secessionist" taste, which idealised tall, lanky women with flat chests and narrow hips. The enormous recent increase in a kind of dandified homo-sexuality may be due to the increasing effeminacy of the age, and the peculiarities of the Pre-Raphaelite movement may have a similar explanation.'[6]

The myth of the androgyne bears contradictory fantasies within itself. Sometimes it expresses a dream of omnipotence, total possession of the phallus – the archaic Zeus, bearded and breasted. At other times it exhibits the obliteration of the desiring subject and the negation of sex: the slender

Alexandrian adolescent, neither man nor woman. Bisexualization may lessen the difference between the sexes, enliven communication between them, increase the chances of concord, unity, real interchange – so long as the economic balance is not disturbed by excessive bisexualization, in which case Eros becomes increasingly vulnerable to destructive instincts, instinctive disruption becomes easier, and soon 'what seemed as if it would extend or create communication in fact severs it, and the happy introjection of opposite sexuality turns into a narcissistic fantasy of androgyny which is essentially toxic: which is the end of desirable and efficacious difference.'[7]

To Weininger, the bisexualization which he saw in 1900s culture meant aesthetic and moral decadence. He raged against this contemporary tendency, but he was not thinking of a restoration of traditional male dominance, having a horror of all sexuality. He dreamed of an unsexed hero whom he saw prefigured in Wagner's Parsifal. He expressed the fantasy of the 'neuter gender',[8] which emerges as no more than a death fantasy. This is the relevance of Weininger to our present purposes. He delineates with exceptional clarity one of the fundamental figures of modernity, which he experienced as a rise of the female and the deconstruction of the male.

The autumn of the patriarchs: Bachofen, Wagner and Nietzsche

The *Gründerzeit* (founding epoch), the time of Bismarck which prepared the fin de siècle, the apogee of economic expansion, European imperialism and scientific and technical progress, defined itself spontaneously in terms of heroic virility. Heinrich von Treitschke in his 'History of Prussia in the Nineteenth Century' gave this description of the young state on the threshold of its European career:

> It arose in its martial force, its youthful countenance still immature but strongly contoured, with bold and vigorous gaze, but without beauty, without grace or accomplished nobility of form . . . Legs apart like the colossus of Rhodes, it stood on the German lands, its feet planted on the threatened marches of the Rhine and the Niemen (Memel).[9]

The will to power was everywhere running free: in the cult of the genius and the great man whose supreme incarnation was Bismarck; in the antique monumentality of architecture and painting; in the confidence of progress and the fostering of warlike virtues, patriotism and *Kulturkampf*. Treitschke, as portrayed by the philosopher Dilthey, exemplifies the intellectual face of the *Gründerzeit*: 'It seemed that the time of blood and iron which was brewing in his youth and culminated in the German wars in his manhood years could have found no more impressive representative. Heroism dwelt in his very heart. Tall in stature, broad-shouldered, with powerful limbs . . .'[10]

Similar allegories or monumental figures seem characteristic of the spirit of the German *Reich*. It would be impossible to apply them unaltered to the Austro-Hungarian monarchy. One constant of the Habsburg myth is an emphasis on the feminine elements of 'Austrianness'. In his 1823 play 'The Fortunes and Fall of King Ottokar', Franz Grillparzer describes Austria as 'lying, a pink-cheeked youth, between the child Italy and the man Germany'.[11] Hofmannsthal expresses this aspect of the Habsburg myth most forcibly in his essay on the Empress Maria Theresa, whom he makes the foundress of Austrian identity: 'For us the "way things are", which began with her and is still going on, is pre-eminently important . . . If our existence has a particular brilliance, which the Germans feel when they come from their world into ours, it is because of her, in a more secret way than the historian's pen can convey.'[12]

Several times Hofmannsthal contrasts the 'virility' of neighbouring countries with the femininity of Austria. Thus in his 1905 essay 'Wir Österreicher und Deutschland' ('We Austrians and Germany'), he ends by alluding to two Viennese by adoption, Prince Eugene of Savoy and Beethoven, who typify 'what Austria has received from Europe and unhesitatingly made her own: from the West, the type of the clear mind, strength to act, unimpaired virility; from the North, the profundity of the German soul. Both surpass whatever she could find deep within herself, rich as those depths may be.'[13] Or in the little summary table of the German and Austrian national characters which he drew up in 1917 under the title 'Preusse und Österreicher' ('Prussians and Austrians'): '[Prussians:] virile in appearance. [Austrians:] minor (*unmündig*) in appearance.'[14]

The male colossus of the German *Gründerzeit* had feet of clay. Behind its display of virile strength, beneath its activist and bellicose eloquence, scepticism and renunciation were fermenting. They can be detected in Weininger's three great predecessors: Johann Jakob Bachofen, Richard Wagner and Freidrich Nietzsche.

The contradictions and longings of a culture dominated by masculine values emerge vividly from Bachofen's historical and anthropological opus 'Matriarchy: A Study of Religious and Juridical Gynocracy in the Ancient World' (first edition 1861).[15] This vast survey of the ancient Mediterranean civilizations traces the difficult birth of patriarchy, which Bachofen sees as the supreme achievement of Christian moral values. The destruction of Carthage and her matriarchal cults was the saving of humanity. Augustus and the Roman jurists completed the work begun by Scipio and Cato. In short, the phylogenesis of Western civilization as seen by Bachofen tallies with the schema of psychosexual ontogenesis suggested by Weininger: humanity, emerging from a prehistoric bisexuality, initially dominated by female characteristics, attains through masculine protest to its age of manhood, dominated by male characteristics.

Bachofen's contribution to the theory of modernity can scarcely be over-estimated. His view of ancient history traces the progress of humanity towards the Apollonian civilization of patriarchy. But Bachofen's cyclic vision leads to an uncertain future. The sceptre of Apollo could fall any day into the hands of Dionysos, the feminine god. Bachofen wrote, in a passage noted by Ernst Bloch, that the progress of sensuality everywhere corresponds to the dissolution of political organizations and to decadence in public life. In place of rich diversity, the law of democracy, the indistinguishable masses, and a kind of liberty and equality which makes distinctions according to the nature of organized civil society and relates to the corporeal and material side of human nature.[16]

For 'Bachofen the patrician', as Bloch called him, the return to the democratic values of matriarchy was a sign of decadence.

The opinions of this Christian patriarch are, in the last analysis, ambivalent. As Bloch observed, 'scarcely has matriarchy been exalted as "poetry in history" than the glory of Apollo begins to shine; Roman law is distinguished by "the superior purity of its paternal principle"; Christianity is seen as an absolute, the religion of the father ... Bachofen's heart is for matriarchy, his head for partriarchy.'[17] The final achievement of law comes when masculine reason recognizes *jus naturale* as the original foundation of the law, as an immanent material order. Now this natural law is profoundly related to matriarchal law. Bachofen himself concluded, in a lecture given in Basle in 1841, 'Set aside the divinization of human reason and the worship of idols created by man himself. If we wish to find peace, let us do as the ancient oracle commanded Aeneas: *Antiquam exquirite matrem.*'[18]

The neo-Romanticism of Ludwig Klages looks to the authority of Bachofen. Klages turns the male–female opposition into an antagonism of the mind (the modern evil) and the soul. For two generations of intellectuals, that of Nietzsche followed by that of Klages and Bloch, Bachofen's lesson was that as the nineteenth century drew to a close, modernity would be characterized by the return of the feminine into culture. A vision found also in the allegory of modernity suggested in 1888 by the critic Eugen Wolff: 'It is a woman full of wisdom, but pure, austerely loved as the spirit of the times, her robe blowing in the wind, her hair streaming around her, fearlessly marching onward.'[19] Bachofen (and Weininger was to pursue the theme) thought that femininity was sapping the foundations of moral order and faith in progress and in science, undermining the very values on which the *Gründerzeit* had rested.

Matriarchy is of the heart, patriarchy of the head. This formula could well be applied to Richard Wagner. Siegfried has bathed in authoritarian ideology for so long, as a paragon of aggressive virility, that it is hard to realize the obvious: the *Ring* tetralogy is a feminist story[20] which remorselessly points up the bankruptcy of maleness, whether coarse and unpolished (Siegfried) or entangled in its own devices (Wotan). The trouble all starts with the theft of the Rhinemaiden's gold and the betrayal of the love-principle for masculine values – possession, power, strength and glory. Erda, the wise divinity of the deeps, is consulted in the third act of *Siegfried* and concludes from this twilight of men that 'The acts of men darken my heart.'[21] Siegfried is an irresponsible oaf, odious at first but finally sympathetic. First we see his rough treatment of his foster-father, the unfortunate Mimir, although Mimir knows well enough what Siegfried lacks: 'Fool that I am, I have forgotten the most important thing: he should have learned to love me; that did not happen! How can I teach him fear?'[22]

Siegfried learns fear when he meets Brünhilde. But his first gesture of love, overlaid with brutality, is a sadistic impulse: he uses his sword to rend the Valkyrie's cloak. He was expected to redeem the corrupt kingdom of Wotan (like Parsifal in the realm of Amfortas). But Siegfried is pure male, and therefore limited, insufficient. He admits as much, naively, to Gunther: 'My sole inheritance was my own body, and I am using it up as I live.'[23]

Less than a year before he died, Wagner began an essay called 'Über das Männliche und Weibliche in Kultur und Kunst' ('On the Masculine and Feminine in Civilization and Art'). He wrote only a few lines, among them this: 'A civilization could only attain perfection if it did away with the separation between male and female.'[24] Wagner's works are overshadowed by the utopia of the androgyne. When he began the composition of *Parsifal*, he tried to give a musical rendering of the eucharist and said 'I should have to render the immaterial, a blending of voices, neither man nor woman, but neuter, in the highest sense of the word.'[25] Wagner was torn between the themes of androgyny, as a promise of happiness and reconciliation, and neuter gender, as a promise of redemption and purity – but also of death.

Nietzsche, Wagner's disciple and enemy, saw this clearly enough. In 'The Case of Wagner' he mocks at the 'Cagliostro of modernity' who draws on 'a nervous machinery' to bewitch his audiences: 'Wagner's *success* – his success with nerves, and therefore with women.'[26] 'Female Wagnerites' were the most redoubtable disciples of the 'master of Bayreuth',[27] and Nietzsche concluded with the following definition of Wagnerism: 'A Christianity adjusted for female Wagnerites, perhaps *by* female Wagnerites – for, in his latter days, Wagner was thoroughly *femini generis*.'[28]

Nietzsche poured scorn on the decadence of his times, of which the confusion and atrophying of sexual characteristics were, he thought, a symptom. Women were turning into viragos; men were going soft and evincing moral cowardice. The feminization of men and the virilization of women were making humanity culturally sterile, incapable of producing superior personalities. More than one passage in Nietzsche calls for a new opposition of sexual attitudes, a fertile polarity which would renew the libidinal tension between 'true' men and 'real' women. This segregation of the distaff side was to be one of the most deceptive expectations of Nietzscheanism.

We must understand that Nietzsche was only making the distinction in view of a closer union. Fragment 339 of the *Joyful Wisdom* puts us on the right track: 'But perhaps this is the greatest charm of life: it puts a gold-embroidered veil of lovely potentialities over itself, promising, resisting, modest, mocking, sympathetic, seductive. Yes, life is a woman!'[29] Dionysos, with whom Nietzsche eventually identified, drew his strength from his endurance and love of life. Dionysos, as Bachofen emphasized, is also the god of women, a sensual god, the master – and not a harsh master – of luxuriant nature and the liquid element.[30] One the one hand, Nietzsche was taking over a quasi-allegorical figure, Truth seen as a woman, or as the waving of a veil of modesty and female seduction. But on the other – as Jacques Derrida writes –

the philosopher, the credulous and dogmatic philosopher who believed in truth as much as he did in women,

> understood nothing either about truth, or about women. For if woman is truth, she knows that there is no truth, that there is no place for truth and that we do not have truth.... And in truth, the feminist females against whom Nietzsche fires so many sarcastic shafts are in fact men. Feminism is the operation by which woman tries to resemble man, the dogmatic philosopher, demanding truth, science, objectivity, that is, the illusion of manhood and the castration effect which goes with it.[31]

II

Viennese modernism: the battle of the sexes

Gründerzeit culture affected an aggressive masculinity: but for the three greatest fin-de-siècle interpreters of the modern condition, Bachofen, Wagner and Nietzsche, the feminine at work threatened male supremacy. To some contemporaries, the period around 1900 seemed to be a time of collapse of traditionally 'virile' assurances and values, which were yielding to 'unreliable sub-unities' and a redistribution of sexual roles in which the female apparently had the edge. Vienna is a good field for the study of this battle of the sexes: we can retrace the front lines, the offensives and counter-offensives of the masculine and the feminine among the circles of Young Vienna and the Secession, the 'antimodern moderns' (Kraus, Loos), the early expressionists and the 'modern ascetics' (Schönberg, Wittgenstein).

In 1891 the literary historian Rudolf Lothar published a study of contemporary trends. He said that materialism had proved a disappointment and that new religious attitudes had come to fill the void: return to the mysteries, to the truths hidden under the veil of symbolism. This trend, which he described as idealist, often accompanied a reaction against naturalism. He continues:

> Nervous sensibility is characteristic of the last years of our century. I am inclined to call this trend 'feminism', for everything goes to show that women's will to power, their desire to compete with men, has meant that the female hypersensitivity of gaze, of pleasure, of thought and of feeling, has been communicated to men and is taking them over.

Speaking of Paul Bourget, Lothar says: 'In a man of nervous temperament like Bourget, the wave of femininity which has passed over him is bringing him back to women and is constantly urging him to analyse women and women's hearts.'[32]

The Bohemian poet Peter Altenberg was acutely conscious of the affinities between shifting modern subjectivity and the 'feminine soul'. In his text called 'Autobiography' he wrote:

> I was nothing, I am nothing, I shall be nothing. But my life is passed in freedom, and I kindly allow noble and rich people to share in the events of this free, inner life by putting them on paper in the most condensed form possible.

I am poor, but I am myself! Myself in all! The man without concessions! . . . My life has been devoted, with unsurpassed enthusiasm, to that masterpiece of God which is 'the body of a woman'!³³

Altenberg is a mannerist version of the individualist 'genius' who affects and fosters the disintegration of the self, the 'chronic nervous weakness' confirmed by his family doctor as a dispensation (. . . from all obligations), the 'psychic dyspepsia', as a protest against convention and an art of poetry. His *unrettbares Ich* has a taste for brevity and extreme condensation of form, which he calls 'the telegraphy of the soul'.³⁴ The 'decadence' of the old human race bears the promise of a new humanity in harmony with life; and this utopian better life is inseparable from femininity: 'Never have I thought that anything in life had worth except women's beauty, the sweet and childlike grace of ladies. And I think that anyone who set a value on anything else in this world would be shamefully mistaken, and life would pass him by.'³⁵

This is how Hermann Bahr tells of his meeting with 'Loris', the young Hofmannsthal:

I am sitting in the café, reading, chatting . . . A young man comes up to me. He smiles, holding out his hand, a soft, caressing hand, the tender hand of a woman very much in love, which is insidiously pleasing to the touch like old, faded silk, and he says serenely, 'It is I, Loris . . .' Very young, just twenty, and utterly Viennese. A cherub, with the profile of a Dante, but a little gentler and softer, with more delicate and mobile features, as Watteau or Fragonard might have painted them . . . Merry, trusting brown eyes, like a young girl's, where a touch of reverie, of questioning hope, mingles with a naive coquetry which draws covert or sidelong glances.³⁶

The feminization of writing

In 'The Revolution of Poetic Language', Julia Kristeva, speaking of Mallarmé, launched the idea of a modernist 'feminization of writing'. By that she meant – to put it briefly – the hedonism of writers who turn away from meaning and abandon themselves to the enjoyment of trifles which sound pleasant but are empty, to harmonious nonsense.³⁷ We read in Mallarmé's *Symphonie littéraire* (1864):

Modern muse of Impotence, you who for so long have closed to me the familiar treasury of Rhythm, and condemn me (sweet torment) to do nothing but reread . . . I dedicate to you, as a mockery or (can I tell?) a token of love, these few lines from my life, written in the clement hours in which you did not inspire me with hatred for creation and the barren love of nothingness. Here you will find the delights of a purely passive soul which is still only woman, and which tomorrow may be mere beast.³⁸

In writing, the subject returns to the pre-Oedipal stage of maternal dependence. It enjoys the 'pleasure of nonsense' which Freud describes in his essay on the *Witz* (jokes) through a study of two cases in which this enjoyment was still, or once again, visible: 'the behaviour of a child in learning, and that of an adult in a toxically altered state of mind.'

> During the period in which a child is learning how to handle the vocabulary of his mother-tongue, it gives him obvious pleasure to 'experiment with it in play', to use Groos's words. And he puts words together without regard to the condition that they should make sense, in order to obtain from them the pleasurable effect of rhythm or rhyme.[39]

Théophile Gautier said of Baudelaire: 'For the poet, words, in themselves and independent of the meaning they express, have a beauty and value of their own, like precious stones which have yet to be cut and set in bracelets, necklaces or rings.'[40] Pursuing Freud's analysis, it could be said that 'modern' fin-de-siècle poetry is racked by a duality as defined by Baudelaire:

> The duality of art is the inevitable consequence of the duality of man. Consider, if you wish, the part which lasts eternally as the soul of art, the variable element as its body. This is why Stendhal – whose mind is daring, impudent, even repugnant, but its impertinence is a useful stimulus to meditation – came closer to the truth than many others when he said that *the Beautiful is only the promise of happiness*. No doubt this definition misses the target: it subjects the beautiful too much to the endlessly varying ideal of happiness; it is too ready to strip the beautiful of its aristocratic character.[41]

This duality could be expressed in terms of 'masculine protest' (the search for an aristocratic beauty), an opposition which, as Baudelaire himself says, disguises that of soul and body.

This opposition helps us understand how in Baudelaire worship of the *mundus muliebris* and hatred of women could exist side by side. Poetic inspiration makes the artist into a woman:[42] possessed by images of the world and by words, he offers and opens himself in an 'ineffable orgy . . . that sacred prostitution of the soul which gives itself entire, poetry and charity, to the revealed unforeseen, the passing unknown.'[43] Baudelaire's misogyny expresses an attempt to throw off this feminine side of the identity of the creative subject, to curb the aimless wanderings of the ego. Michel Butor puts it thus: 'Virility will be all the more striking as it is more willed – conquered, or more precisely, reconquered. It must be put to the test, constantly put to the test, arising in the midst of a femininity which threatens to swallow it.'[44] This masculine protest relates to the 'classical' rigour of Baudelaire's metrics.

On the one side, abandonment to the pleasure of words – the return to childhood, primary narcissism of language, fusion, femininity; on the other, work, rigour, discipline, the classical ideal: these were the two poles between which the young Hofmannsthal took up his pen. The feminization of writing was a permanent threat within poetic modernism; it would imply that the poet 'let the words write him', that discourse would function in place of the ego, unmastered, beyond the reach of censure, like an irrepressible pleasure,[45] the immanent genius of language replacing the genius of the artist. This temptation did exist in the poetry of Young Vienna. Its clearest manifestation is the poetry of Felix Dörmann.

In 1981, when he published *Neurotica*, his first book of poetry, Dörmann was twenty-one. In 1892 it was followed by *Sensationen*. Both were great successes, reprinted several times, but they also caused an outcry: copies of *Neurotica* were seized and suppressed by the Viennese courts on the grounds of immorality. Dörmann's poems, which no one nowadays would think comparable to Hofmannsthal's, are nonetheless frequently cited as a characteristic example of fin-de-siècle decadence. They exhibit its every excess: Wagnerian pauses, imitation of Baudelaire and Huysmans, mannerism, preciosity, worship of willowy Pre-Raphaelite women, *femmes fatales* and *belles dames sans merci*. His most famous poem is called 'Was ich liebe' ('What I Love'):

> I love the slender heavy narcissus
> with blood-red mouth;
> I love tormenting thoughts,
> pierced and wounded hearts;
> I love pale, blanched faces,
> tired-faced women,
> on whom speaks, in flaming tokens,
> the devouring furnace of the senses . . .
> I love what no one has chosen
> what no one could love:
> the intimacy of my own being,
> and all things strange and sick.[46]

The best writers of Young Vienna (Hofmannsthal, Schnitzler) had considerable reserves about Dörmann, whom all of them – even Hermann Bahr – looked upon as a lesser light with no real originality.[47] But they abruptly closed ranks when Karl Kraus let fly at him in an article published in February 1893 in the Berlin *Magazin für Literatur*.[48] Dörmann remained one of Kraus's favourite targets, and has pride of place in 'Die demolirte Literatur', a pamphlet from late 1896 which is directed against the whole Young Vienna movement.[49] Kraus's raillery in the earlier article culminates in the sentence, 'Manche seiner Poesien sind formell mannhaft, die meisten inhaltlich dörmannhaft' ('Some of his poems are manly in form, but most of them are dormanly in content').[50] This distinction between form and content is an early manifestation of Kraus's 'antifeminist' aesthetic, to which we shall return. He was in fact resuming the Baudelairean distinction between the body and the soul of art. To him, Dörmann represented a purely 'physical' poetry (purely woman), carried away by its own words and bereft of soul (masculine genius) – that is, of experience, real personal *Erlebnis*.

This lack of maleness in writing, of willed and calculated *poein*, was noted by Hofmannsthal when he read Amiel's *Journal* – with admiration and sympathy, but also some disapproval. He noted that Amiel, so prolix in his journal but incapable of executing the 'great work' he dreamed of, was like a sort of 'Raphael without hands . . . This excessive richness is really poverty; this universal will is no more than impotence despairing of its self-limitation . . .

A moving fluid, unable to find any form.'[51] Such was Hofmannsthal's judgement on Amiel's writings. He was, however, well aware of the modernity of this intimate journal, with its minute descriptions of the 'self-sickness' of an individualist who could stand as the prototype of the nervous sufferer from depersonalization, the Mach-style *unrettbares Ich* whom Bahr saw as the modern genius *par excellence*. It is interesting to note that Amiel's self-critical awareness of being a 'Raphael without hands', a 'shapeless fluid', finds spontaneous expression in fantasies of feminized writing:

> I can no longer vigorously embrace a grand whole: my power to combine, to continue, in a word to produce, has evaporated. I disseminate, scatter, volatilize what little activity and power I have left.... My passion for self-psychologizing without self-renewal has turned me into a contemplative consciousness, in fact it has emasculated me.[52]

And again: 'My dominating, if not my sole, interest has been my inner life, my awareness of the emotions and affections in the theatre of my soul. Feeling my life has been my usual way of living. Therefore I have lived in a feminine rather than masculine way.'[53] However, Amiel never attained to the pleasure of the soul which so ravished Dr Schreber: 'When I am writing it is like an interminable childbed, a labour which stubbornly works against itself, keeping only the pain of childbirth without granting itself the final delivery.'[54]

It is possible to reread the famous *Lord Chandos Letter* in the light of this fantasy of a feminized modernist literature. Chandos's happy state prior to his 'crisis' or 'ordeal', one of narcissistic fusion with Mother Nature, is expressed in the following image:

> It made no difference whether I was at my hunting lodge, gulping warm, frothy milk that some strapping farmhand had coaxed down into his wooden pail from the udder of a lovely, soft-eyed cow, or ensconced in the window seat of my study, drinking in sweet, frothy nourishment for the soul from one of my folios.[55]

This 'milk-feeding' scene 'functions as a scene of self-sufficiency and oral auto-erotism which encloses Chandos and begins the ordeal as a kind of anorexia.'[56] How can the 'paternal' inheritance of written culture be translated into the nourishment of the mother tongue – reading into feeding? A little later, during his 'ordeal', Chandos feels the words of his abstract, paternal language dissolve like putrid mushrooms in his mouth. The new language he glimpses at the end of the *Letter* prefigures a new kind of poetic writing, feminine and narcissistic. But that language would no longer serve for social intercourse and conversation: it consists of 'hieroglyphs', probably impossible to translate into ordinary words and syntax. The contrast, which persists until the end of the book, between the handsome rhetoric of Hofmannsthal as author and the 'feminized' language to which Chandos himself aspires betrays the failure of the writer faced with the transgressions of modernity. Hofmannsthal takes the deconstruction of language to a point of no return. On the edge of the abyss, seized with terror – the same terror which drove the merchant's son to 'feminize' himself – he retreats to the *terra firma* of classical expression.

The fantasy of the feminized writer[57] and artist recurs in a good many representatives of 1900s modernism. Thomas Mann wrote in *Tonio Kröger* (1903), 'All in all, is an artist a man? Ask the "woman"! I think that we artists all share a little in the fate of those "doctored" papal singers.'[58] Lou Andreas-Salomé noted in her 1899 essay on 'The Humanity of Women': 'It is not by chance that feminine traits are so often found in artists, or that they are so often accused of being effeminate.'[59]

Klimt and the matriarchal aesthetic

Bachofen's prophecy that the sceptre of Apollo might fall into the hands of Dionysos, and that the sensual chaos and primitive barbarism of matriarchy might resume their ascendancy, sweeping away the cultural gains of masculine, patriarchal civilization, seems to come true in the painting of Gustav Klimt. In 1894, the Austrian Minister for Education commissioned Klimt to design some frescoes for the ceilings of the new university. In 1900 he exhibited a preliminary sketch, 'Philosophy'. It scandalized most of the Viennese academics. In 1901, 'Medicine' caused even more violent reactions. In 1905, Klimt decided to resign officially from the ministerial commission and repaid the fees.

The minister had defined the proposed theme as 'The victory of light over darkness'.[60] Klimt's frescoes suggest something completely different. They savagely contradict positivism and confidence in progress. Philosophy no longer gives enlightenment to humanity, nor does medicine cure it of its ills; nothing remains, to give meaning to the world, but art and aesthetic contemplation. In 'Philosophy', an entranced priestess, crowned with vine leaves, leads the dreamy and lascivious dancing of female nudes who float with the currents of life. The fresco of 'Medicine' again shows humanity as being passively carried towards death. The terrible goddess Hygieia, a distant relative of the Cretan images in Minoan palaces, brandishes the caduceus like a bolt of lightning. Standing apart from the procession of humanity, a pregnant woman, her loins unashamedly exposed, counterpoints the skeletons of a *danse macabre*.

Though they did not say so openly, most of the university professors felt that Klimt's frescoes, far from glorifying the sciences in the service of progress in accordance with the ideas of liberal *Bildung*, expressed a pessimistic vision, sceptical and resigned. Humanity, unable to master nature through the wisdom of philosophers and the efforts of medicine, appeared to fall prey to all-powerful cosmic forces incarnate in matriarchal femininity.

A few years later, in 1908, in his private salon in the *Kunstschau*, Klimt exhibited sixteen paintings around the three great themes of humanity, woman and landscape. To illustrate humanity he presented 'The Kiss' (a couple embracing; only the woman is seen face on); 'The Three Ages of Life' (a woman as child, adult and in old age); a 'Danae', symbol of fertility; two

'Water-Snake' motifs (mermaids, nixes, naiads, nereids); a portrait of 'Two Sisters'; and four portraits of Viennese ladies, notably Adela Bloch-Bauer and Margaret Stonborough-Wittgenstein. Finally, six motifs from nature: undergrowth, gardens, fruit trees, flowers. Klimt's work as a whole was one vast homage to femininity, sometimes comforting and decorative, at other times menacing and destructive.

Along with the secessionist movement there developed a movement in the decorative arts. The output of the Wiener Werkstätte shows, with varying degrees of sobriety, how far Jugendstil ornamentalism had spread into every aspect of everyday life. Feminine allure was everywhere.[61] 'You want an ink-pot? Here it is: naiads bathing between two reefs, one containing the ink, the other sand. You want an ash-tray? Here it is: a serpentine dancer offers herself to your eyes, and you can stub out your cigar on the end of her nose.'[62] On the one hand the Secession haloed art and woman in aesthetical awe; on the other, the decorative arts celebrated the alliance between the creator and the prostitute – Baudelaire's second type of modernity. The factories were doing their best to woo the 'art lover'.

Antimodernist and antifeminist: Kraus, Loos and Weininger

The two pioneers of 'antimodern modernism' were Adolf Loos and Karl Kraus. The former progressively withdrew from the Secession and the ideology of the *Gesamtkunstwerk*, the 'total work of art'. His pamphlet 'Ornament and Crime' (1909) looked back over ten years of polemic. The latter had once frequented 'Young Vienna', especially the group around Arthur Schnitzler. His satire 'Die demolirte Literatur' ('Demolished Literature', 1896) led to an irretrievable break with that intellectual and artistic milieu. In his review *Die Fackel* ('The Torch'), founded in 1899, Kraus expounded his criticisms of Viennese aestheticism and paved the way for the second wave of modernism:

'These enthusiasts for "atmosphere" who are sprouting all over the place, like mushrooms after rain, go about ordering bizarre combinations of coloured sorbets or "mixes" in cafés ... "Secret nervousness" was their slogan, and they started scrutinizing their states of mind, trying to get away from anything that was clear and distinct.'[63] Kraus revolted against the worship of nuance, vagueness and convolution, and affirmed his hatred of slackness, confusion and languidity. In his collection of aphorisms, *Nachts* ('By Night'), he wrote first 'We are living at a time of transition, from high to low,' and then 'Businessmen are the panders of merchandise, popularizers the panders of knowledge, and intermediary forms the panders of pleasure.'[64] By 'intermediary forms' we are to understand homosexuality. Decadence, mercantilism, pretended knowledge, moral laxity – it all came to the same thing.

Like Schönberg in music, Kraus mistrusted 'transition'.[65] He called for frontiers to be redrawn. The first demarcation he demanded was between art and everyday life. One of his most famous aphorisms is:

Adolf Loos and myself – he literally, I in words – have done nothing other than show the difference between an urn and a chamber-pot, and that it is only this difference which allows culture to exist. As for the others, they can be divided into those who use an urn as a chamber-pot and those who use a chamber-pot as an urn.[66]

Loos had also been pleading since the end of the 1890s for a sound distinction to be made between art, craft and architecture. His long sojourn in the United States had convinced him that striving after the beautiful should not impinge on the double imperative of practical comfort and natural materials. Rather than endure the discomfort of a secessionist tripod he preferred a good old Biedermeier chair from Thonet's. He rebelled against the secessionist *Diktat* to craftsmen, architects and planners. *Could* life be made into a total work of art? In that case, he suggested, you had better get tram conductors to sing Wagner instead of blowing a whistle.[67] The worship of art seemed to him to be particularly pernicious in Vienna, because he thought it was throwing a veil over the profound lack of a culture capable of structuring a whole way of life, as in England or America.

In both Kraus and Loos, the opposition to ornamentation and mixing of genres (art and practical utility, literature and the press, the ornamental and the functional, etc.) assumed an antifeminist guise. Loos's article on 'Feminine Fashions' (1902) is revealing. He starts by declaring that everything noble in woman relates to a single aspiration, to take her place beside a great and strong man; he then states that this goal can only be achieved if the woman wins the love of the man:

> But a naked woman has no charm for a man . . . That is why she is compelled to arouse the man's sensuality by her clothes, to kindle an unhealthy sensuality in him, which comes only from the spirit of the age . . . Women's clothing is distinguished externally by ornament and colour. Women are backward in terms of vestimentary evolution. In the past, men also wore richly ornamented clothes. The magnificent evolution of our civilization this century has had the fortunate effect of outdistancing ornamentation. The lower the cultural level, the stronger the element of ornamentation.[68]

When *Sex and Character* appeared in 1903, Karl Kraus was twenty-nine. Weininger killed himself at the age of twenty-three. Between the suicide 'genius' and the editor of *Die Fackel* a posthumous alliance was born, to which Karl Kraus remained forever faithful. Weininger's antifeminism seemed to him part of his struggle against the lies and falsity of Viennese culture. But Kraus made one paradoxical correction to the conclusions of *Sex and Character*: 'It is as an admirer of womankind that I subscribe to his misogynistic arguments.'[69] Kraus approved of every aspect of Weininger's description of the female character: the feminine principle was irretrievably and uncompromisingly opposed to the masculine.

But where Weininger sees a mortal antagonism, Karl Kraus hails a creative polarity. Kraus adores the 'natural' woman, so repellently portrayed in *Sex and Character* – a repulsion which for Kraus becomes a predilection. But he loathes, despises and pours endless scorn on the 'modern woman': the emancipated woman, of course, but also the respectable middle-class lady sporting her qualifications from the 'ladies' academy' of good society. (One of Kraus's aphorisms runs: 'Sleep with him? Of course – but *no intimacy*!')[70] He wanted sensual, uncultured, amorous, insolent women like Wedekind's Lulu, whom he greatly admired. They would make it possible to reconcile genius and sex, mind and body, artist and woman – in a word, art and life: radical separation as a precondition for profound union. Full manhood – the genius – and pure womanhood – sex – would be restored, the society of effeminate men and mannish women would be destroyed, and real society built on its ruins.

Klimt followed the aesthetic trail blazed by Nietzsche. Kraus went back to the old Nietzsche of positive barbarism, the 'Eastern view of women', the return to a healthy polarization of the sexes. 'What makes women stupid is what in them does not conform to femininity,' we read in *Human, All Too Human*.[71] Kraus opposed modern 'nervousness', which was creating intermediary sexual forms, and demanded a return to a civilization dominated by masculine genius, fertilized by feminine life. Nietzsche had written:

> Classical Greek civilization was a civilization of men. Women had no other duty than to give birth to beautiful, powerful bodies, where the spirit of the father lived again with as little interruption as possible, and thereby to put up a resistance to the growing nervous overexcitement of a highly developed civilization. That is what kept Greek civilization youthful for so comparatively long: for in Greek mothers the genius of Greece was constantly returning to nature.[72]

Continence or chaos were the alternatives offered by Weininger at the end of *Sex and Character*. Either a war between the sexes, in which women would do their best to shatter the ethical and cultural aspirations of men by dragging them back again and again into the sin of promiscuity; or the heroism of the genius, of whom Parsifal, repelling Kundry's advances, was the model. Ernst Gombrich has ironically observed that Loos's attacks on the Secession had the puritanical tones of a Cicero defending the virtues of Attic eloquence, sober and disciplined, against the baroque innovations of fashionable orators. Cicero alluded to women's natural beauty, which had no need of jewellery and paint.[73]

The ascetic modernist: Schönberg and Wittgenstein

The other family of modernist Viennese creative artists worshipped an ascetic ideal. In what Schönberg called 'the emancipation of dissonance', in the demarcation of silence which, Wittgenstein says in the *Tractatus*, protects ethics and aesthetics against the prevarications of propositionality, we find this elitist curbing of the senses. While it is possible to speak of a musical Jugendstil, detectable in Schönberg's first phase, the successive stages of his reform of composition are an affirmation of the logical and the rational against the sensual and the mystical.[74] Similarly, Loos, faced with the chinoiserie of the Secession, hit back with japonisme, 'less is more', a purging of modernism.

Schönberg despised the 'cowardice' of Richard Strauss, because he had recoiled from the new vistas opened up by *Salome* (1905) and *Elektra* (1908). Their integral chromaticism implied an extreme feminization of the musical atmosphere (both Strauss's heroines sing in the register of high hysteria): over the harsh dissonances he had brought forth, Strauss had spread some perfect harmonies and so kept up an appearance of tonality which Schönberg considered 'hypocritical', demanding an 'emancipation of dissonance' which meant that he was ready to sacrifice harmony.[75] Similarly Weininger, who denounced the illusions of love, which 'strives to cover guilt, instead of conquering it ... the "something" folds the "nothing" in its arms and thinks thus to free the universe of negation and drown all objections.'[76] And similarly Karl Kraus, who mocked at the hollow rhetoric of a purely decorative morality which hid the 'criminal' treatment of prostitutes by bourgeois men.[77]

In 1938, Theodor Adorno also made use of formulae borrowed from sexual morality when he contrasted the 'decline of listening' in popular music with the exigencies of the avant-garde. He observed that a pretence of asceticism had too long served the reactionary repression of a certain degree of aesthetic severity, and that asceticism had now become the distinguishing mark of advanced art:

> Not, indeed, through an archaizing parsimony with means, an exaltation of impoverishment, but by the strict exclusion of all 'culinary' complaisance, suited to immediate consumption, as if the sensual in art could not contain an intellectual element which shows in the work as a whole and not in isolated motifs! Art gives negative evidence of this possibility of happiness which is now being corrupted and shackled by a positive and only partial anticipation of happiness. All 'easy', pleasant art has become illusory and false: what is presented as a kind of pleasure no longer arouses anything but nausea.[78]

Nietzsche expressed a similar opinion: 'Dissonance and harmony in music: ... pain and contradiction are the truth of being. Pleasure and harmony are its appearance.'[79] Asceticism had become characteristic of a certain kind of modernity. This is probably why Schönberg cited Weininger among his moral mentors in the preface to his *Treatise on Harmony*.

The linguistic asceticism advocated in Wittgenstein's *Tractatus* recalls Schönberg's musical reforms. The latter rejected prefabricated musical units, and forced himself to write note by note, using the smallest possible units: isolated intervals, short motifs. Similarly Wittgenstein, writing to Ludwig von Ficker: 'In my book I have given a solid status to what many people today make empty speeches about – by keeping silent about it.'[80] The life and thought of the young Wittgenstein showed a distinct ascetic tendency (he became progressively less austere as he advanced towards the *Philosophical Investigations*): his admiration for the ageing Tolstoy, his penitential sessions working in a monastery and as a village schoolteacher, his refusal of the family fortune, his obsession with sin. (Certain biographers have drawn attention to the homosexuality which caused him so much anguish.)[81]

The moderns could, like Gustav Klimt at times, sink into nightmarish dreams of a cosmogonic eros in travail with a new world, a world of dethroned masculinity. Or, like Karl Kraus, they could resist, hoping to overcome the crisis of civilization and artistic creation by the virility of genius. In music, Schönberg stood firm against the kinds of feminizing and sensual images which make for easy listening, but at the price of 'regression', which eventually led the composer into the impasses of tonality; he returned finally to the law of the father with *Moses and Aaron*. Postmodernism was to direct its fire at the supposed lack of warmth of such music, its aridity and difficulty. Can we not find such a reaction even in Alban Berg, as the feminine advances back into *Lulu* or the *Concerto in Memory of an Angel*?

III

The feminine in civilization, as seen by Freud

The 'feminine at work' amid the modern crisis of civilization was equally apparent in the sociopolitical sphere. In Freud's *Civilization and its Discontents*, woman appears when it becomes clear that Eros cannot live happily with *Kultur*.[82] Freud's thinking here is fundamentally similar to Bachofen's. In the beginning (says Freud), women laid the foundations of civilization by their defence of love and sensuality, but they soon became obstacles to the progress of culture as it advanced beyond the narrower interests of family and sex. After that it was men, with their greater capacity for sublimation, who handed on the torch of progress, until now 'the woman finds herself forced into the background by the claims of civilization and she adopts a hostile attitude towards it.'[83]

Women, says Freud, can be a safeguard against totalitarian threats to the individual: in the great artificial groupings, the church and the army, there is no place for women as sex objects. Love relationships between men and women must be excluded from those organizations. When direct sexual drives control individual behaviour they work against group formation. The Catholic church was well advised to demand celibacy of its priests: 'Love for women breaks through the group ties of race, of national divisions, and of the social class system, and it thus produces important effects as a factor in civilization,' Freud concluded.[84]

Women as obstacles to civilized progress or as safeguards of civilization: such, it seems, are the two leading parts Freud assigns to them in the play of *Kultur*. But they could also be seen as a symptom of the crisis of social organization.[85] In *Group Psychology and the Analysis of the Ego* (1921) Freud advances a theory of social relations. He resurrects his earlier notion that the murder of the father forged the links between members of primitive tribes: shared regret for this collective murder created a feeling of belonging, 'all men together'. This act of mourning restores the father at the centre of the group: the ego, originally its own narcissistic ideal, transfers its ego ideal on to the image of the father. Thus individual egos are identified with a collective ego ideal. Women had no direct part in the murder of the father; they do not join in this sort of masculine idealization which binds men to one another (which means that social bondings remain intrinsically homosexual, as can be seen in the two best-organized groups, the army and the church). Freud even suggests that the homosexual is particularly likely to identify with the group,[86] as he shows diagramatically (see the figure).[87]

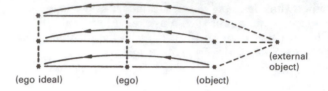

(ego ideal)   (ego)   (object)   (external object)

We could pursue Freud's reasoning a little further and ask whether an 'idealization crisis' affecting the 'external object' (father image, headman, *Führer*) might not cause the ego to fall back on its 'object', that is, woman (the mother). The death of a king, a revolution, a crisis of authority (which might start as an excess of authority) would all be likely to cause a dislocation of the group (bound together by identification with the ego ideal/father image) and a return of individuals towards the feminine. Two hypotheses could be advanced (free speculation based on Freud). In the first case the excessive authority of the father figure would trigger an attempt to replace him with a feminine object, a mother figure: this gives us Schreber and, as we shall see, also Otto Gross. The 'law of the mother' (matriarchy) would then substitute, in a more or less illusory way, for the 'law of the father'. In the second case, the loss of authority of the father figure would send the ego back to its (feminine) object and trigger a 'masculine protest', a desire to 'save the father', defend him (like Parsifal going to the aid of the aged Amfortas) against threats against him, which would most likely come from the female. This second case would be Otto Weininger's.

Adler, Groddeck, Simmel and Benjamin

Alfred Adler paid particular attention to the link between 'feelings of inferiority' and 'masculine protest'. The abusive supremacy of the masculine principle is a 'cancer' in our society, he wrote in 1910;[88] the individual will to power, be the individual man or woman, produces a desire to be a man. Adler calls this aspiration, common to both sexes, 'psychic hermaphroditism'.[89] Neurosis appears whenever this masculine protest is compromised by real life and 'feminine' characteristics – submissiveness, passivity, etc. – are reinforced within the subject.

Wilhelm Stekel, following Adler, made a detailed study of the various disturbances resulting from this inner masculine/feminine conflict: homosexuality, frigidity in women, impotence in men...[90] The will to power, to which Adler, directly inspired by Nietzsche, gave the widest possible interpretation, could have no more spontaneous expression, no other *modus dicendi*, than the 'jargon of sexuality' or 'sexual fiction'[91] through which the subject could recount – to himself and to others – his own story and that of the whole world around him, its violence, confrontations and sexual complexities.

Rereading the troubled history of European civilization since the turn of the century, as encoded in the voluminous outpourings of *Kulturkritik*, we notice the obsessive *leitmotif* of male–female confrontation. The deconstruction of traditionally masculine values and the challenging of authoritarian integrality inspired, on the one side, utopian prophecies of feminine redemption, and on the other, pessimistic and reactionary demands for the restoration of the old male–female polarity.

George Groddeck accorded the feminine a positively messianic significance. The last two chapters of his book 'A Woman's Problem' (published in 1903) are entitled 'The Woman' and 'The Child': 'The future is with women. The brain of man is gathering dust. Only women are barbaric enough to transform our worm-eaten culture. . . . Let her become self-aware. The future of humanity is in her womb. Man is disappearing, but woman is eternal.'[92] What Groddeck calls for is matriarchy indeed:

> Sacred depths are slumbering in woman. But who can awaken them? Since the world began woman has been taught to serve; when will she learn to reign? . . . Let women grow, freed from all male passions and male thoughts! Immeasurable streams of new ideas will gush forth, new religions will spring up, new gods, new worlds. . . . The civilization of the stronger sex, of women, is awakening.[93]

But the coming of a feminized civilization will have a deeper meaning: humanity's return to childhood, the lost paradise of bisexuality, the all-powerful ego in symbiosis with the external world, the play of creation. Here we meet again the great theme of sensibility which is integral to turn-of-the-century Nietzschean *Lebensphilosophie*. 'The world will die if it grows wise,' said Groddeck in 'A Woman's Problem'.[94] The child being (which to Groddeck is almost the same as the female being) is opposed to the male being and the adult being, as life according to nature is opposed to modern civilization. We shall see that some of Otto Gross's ideas were very similar to Groddeck's.

The last chapter of Georg Simmel's essay 'Philosophical Culture' (1911) is entitled 'Female Culture'. He asks what is the meaning and importance of contemporary feminism. The movement would, he says, be on the wrong track if it demanded *equality* with men in modern society. Instead it should aim to deepen the essential differences and develop the specific abilities of women, which have hitherto been stifled, repressed, devalued by male cultural supremacy. If women had the chance to pursue their own vocation fully, they would be the complement, the corrective and the renewal that would breathe new life into tottering Western civilization.

> If the new freedom demanded by women led to an objectivization of the female being similar to that of the male being which civilization has already produced,

and not to a repetition by women of masculine contents ... then indeed a new continent of civilization would have been discovered.[95]

But what does Simmel mean by 'female being'? In reality, nothing other than what was meant by the antifeminist Weininger. The female characteristics which *Sex and Character* holds up for execration reappear, more or less, in Simmel as a panacea for modern ills. Weininger's nightmare is Simmel's utopian dream. The two theorists share a common assumption: that nothing in civilization can be considered asexual, unconnected with sexual difference.

In the correspondence of Walter Benjamin we find this passage from 1913:

> For my part, to tell the truth, I here avoid all concrete allusions and prefer to speak of masculine and feminine: how utterly intermingled they are in a human being! ... Europe is made up of individuals, each of them with elements of masculine and feminine – not of men and women. Who knows how far the profound nature of women really extends? What do we know of women? As little as we do of youth. We still have no experience of any women's civilization.[96]

The young Benjamin's remarks reveal a line of thought similar to Simmel's, but more subtle, because it takes account of how bisexuality can at any time dislocate the sexed subject from its deeper identity.

Two decades after these youthful pronouncements, Benjamin's work on nineteenth-century Paris was to show how, as Christine Buci-Glucksmann puts it:

> Starting from the new imaginative outlook which stemmed from Baudelaire (the prostitute, the barren woman, the lesbian, the androgyne, as allegories of modernity), which had their origins in the nineteenth-century utopianism (Saint-Simonism, feminism à la Claire Demar, history of sects) and their posterity in Berg's *Lulu* and the pubescent flower-children of the Jugendstil, Benjamin reconstructed a whole system of genuinely modern imagined femininity.[97]

Baudelaire had a particular attraction for Benjamin because his socioenonomic analyses were as penetrating as his imagination. For example, the new status of women in big cities – where the difference between the sexes was becoming less and less perceptible in work and in everyday life, where the 'aura' of womanhood was dwindling into a publicity image for the masses or into prostitution – seemed inseparable from the lyrical experience of the 'feminized' poet who identified with his heroines in protest against modern life.

As Benjamin saw it, Baudelaire had formulated more clearly and consciously than any other critic of modernity the idea that modernization inevitably overturned sexual identity and that this had profound cultural consequences. And in Baudelaire, as in most men who paid attention to this process, the most virulent antifeminism, the 'masculine protest' against the feminization of culture, was combined with a tendency to identify with certain favoured female figures. Fascination with certain 'damned' heroines (the prostitute, the lesbian), and with all situations that subverted accepted sexual roles, expressed a revolt against bourgeois 'phallocracy' and aspiration towards sexual revolution.[98] In Benjamin's *Passagen-Werk* can be found

> the aim of deducing from a hermeneutics of sexual behaviour the evolution of a whole society; drawing from the exploration of a sphere of the most intimate lived experience a theory of the historical constitution of the subject. This design is similar to Foucault's in his *History of Sexuality*. For the latter, indeed, Benjamin's 'Baudelaire' served as an example.[99]

From the Great War to the rise of fascism: collapse and reaction of virility

The First World War had been, in the words of the sexologist Magnus Hirschfeld, 'the greatest sexual catastrophe which has ever befallen civilized man'.[100] Traditional institutions had collapsed (in 1919 Paul Federn was talking about a 'society without fathers'),[101] and nineteenth-century values had been tragically refuted by the butcheries of 1914–18. Those chaotic years had emancipated women, who were forced to work in factories, hospitals and public services while their husbands were away at the Front. The ordeal had also undermined masculinity. The traumatic neuroses of soldiers had even led them into collective hysteria, whole units in fits of tears or vomiting. Freud had much to say about the profound rejection of masculine roles imposed by the war.[102] When they returned home, demobilized soldiers felt that their world had been turned upside-down. Joseph Roth, in 'The Capuchins' Crypt', recounts the misfortunes of Lieutenant Trotta, who finds that his wife Elisabeth has turned independent, earning her own living and reluctant to accept patriarchal authority back into the conjugal sphere. Trotta tries to save the situation by fathering a child. But he loses all the same, because Elisabeth leaves home to live with a lesbian artist with *short hair* and a boyish look. In 1931 Robert Musil brought out a malicious little attack on psychoanalysis which he called 'A Threat to Oedipus'.[103] What, asked Musil, could 'nostalgia for the mother's breast' mean in a civilization where women had become radically masculinized and femininity had altogether ceased to be a refuge for men? Would Oedipus yield his place to Orestes, concluded Musil, murdering his mother to avenge the betrayal of his father?

Fascism, then, gave males a chance of revenge against a femininity which had lent its countenance to modernity. Futurism set the tone of this 'conservative revolution'. Marinetti's manifesto, in 1909, proclaimed, 'We want to glorify war – the only hygiene for the world – patriotism, the destructive acts of the anarchist, beautiful Ideas that kill and contempt for women.'[104] Giovanni Papini wrote in 1912:

> Look at the Italian literature of today and you might think that all the males were dead, and that only females were able to write. No talk of petticoats or anatomical differences: I am a Weiningerite! There are spiritual sexes as well as physical ones. When I say 'male', I mean strength, energy, sternness, pride;

when I say 'female', I mean softness, tenderness, easy pleasure, the minor key, facile tears, spiritual babble and swooning musicality.[105]

The token futurist woman was represented by Valentine de Saint-Point, the pseudonym of Anna-Jeanne-Valentine-Marianne Desglans de Cessiat-Vercell, a great-niece of Lamartine. In 1910 she brought out an essay entitled 'A Woman and Desire', with reference to Schopenhauer, Nietzsche and Wagner. Her 'Futurist Woman's Manifesto' (1912) proclaimed that it was absurd to divide humanity into men and women. It was really made up of masculinity and femininity:

Ages of fertility, when the greatest number of heroes and geniuses springs forth from the teeming soil, are ages rich in masculinity and virility.... Ages which denied the heroic instinct and, turning to the past, were lost in dreams of peace, were ages dominated by femininity. We are living at the end of one such era. What women, just as much as men, most need is virility.... In the feminized age we live in, only the opposite extreme can be salutary: our proposed model must be the brute.[106]

IV

(Post)modernity and transsexuality, from Schlegel to Musil

In recent studies of contemporary 'postmodernity', such themes as the feminization of culture, the male identity crisis and the return of a widespread androgynity have returned in strength. They are operative, for example, in Gilles Lipovestsky's book *L'ère du vide: Essais sur l'individualisme contemporaine*. In my discussion of narcissism I showed that the crisis of the 1970s and 1980s, as seen by Lipovetsky (whose ideas I take as representative of a certain type of contemporary sociological discourse), repeated certain themes already strongly evident in fin-de-siècle Vienna: 'Widening of the private sphere, erosion of social identity, ideological and political disaffection, accelerated destabilization of personality, individualist revolution ... The great axes of modernity have been attacked; technological and scientific optimism has collapsed ... now we are ruled by the void.'[107] The echo of Mach's *unrettbares Ich* and Broch's *Wert-Vakuum*, responses to the crisis of Viennese culture in 1900, is quite unmistakable.

Paradoxically, Lipovetsky, with an irony better suited to our own time than the fevered prophecies of a Weininger, reawakens some of the terrors which were already lurking in *Sex and Character*: it is the same impression of ethical chaos triggered by rampant sensuality:

In the face of contemporary erotic inflation and pornography, feminists, moralists and aesthetes unite in a sort of unanimous denunciation.... But what if that is not the really important thing, what if pornography itself is only one face of temptation? Is it not in fact a way of overthrowing the archaic order of Law and Taboo, sweeping away the coercive order of Censure and repression?[108]

This 'face of temptation' was to fin-de-siècle eyes, from Bachofen onwards, the face of woman; and the reign of Eros, matriarchy.

This eroticization of culture accompanies a collapse of traditional values:

> The opposition of sense and nonsense is no longer so piercingly clear: it ceases to be so radical when faced with the frivolity or futility of fashion, leisure and advertising. In an age of spectacle, clear antimonies – truth and false-hood, beauty and ugliness, reality and illusion – are obscured, antagonisms become uncertain, and we begin to realize, *pace* our metaphysicians and anti-metaphysicians, that it is now possible to live without any aim or meaning.[109]

Weininger suggested a detailed phenomenology of this mode of human living when he analysed his ideal of the feminine: alogical, amoral, insensible to the demands of Art, perfect nonsense, astonishing absurdity: such is woman, that is, the feminine element in humanity's bisexual make-up, in *Sex and Character*.

On the subject of disappearing frontiers between the masculine and the feminine, Lipovetsky emphasized that feminism is destabilizing fixed oppositions and undercutting stable frames of reference. One of the oldest anthropological divisions, and its associated conflicts, are disappearing. There is no longer war between the sexes, but the whole world of sex, with its coded oppositions, is coming to an end: 'The more feminists question the nature of the feminine, the more it fades and is lost in uncertainty; the more women cast off whole areas of their traditional status, the more maleness itself loses its identity.'[110] The relatively homogeneous classifications of sex are being replaced by ever more fleeting identities.

In a world in which 'the dialectic of the One and the Other [is giving way to] a resemblance of the sexes,'[111] individualism is seeking the way of an androgynous Ego, self-sufficient and complete. Better solitude than constraint and dissatisfaction! A new kind of relationship between the sexes is beginning:

> The model of resemblance, along with the return to the self, seems to have eliminated the problem of power. As God is no longer of importance in the West, it is becoming impossible to say what powers the one sex does have over the other, now that both have access to the economic, political, social, cultural, or whatever sphere it may be.[112]

There is, apparently, only one type of power remaining, that of one individual over another. Procreation is the sole power that women still keep to them-selves. But biotechnology and genetic manipulation are beginning to offer unexplored vistas for dreams (or nightmares) of transsexual procreation . . .

What earlier in the century was called the feminization of civilization, and we would rather call its bisexualization, figured in the expectations of early Romantic modernism as a liberating utopia. In Schlegel's *Lucinda* the opposition of the sexes is the major obstacle to a new humanity, an obstacle which must be overcome. 'The male condition, condemned to division and analysis, must unite with the female, on the side of nature and innocence. This reconciliation prefigures the restoration of our society in crisis.'[113] Nietzsche, in the course of his generalized critique of ideas of emancipation and romanticism, stressed the ambivalence of the 'modern' ideal of cultural bisexuality: seen as a levelling of sexual characteristics, it meant the extinction of all human creativity and, eventually, all life; seen as a pact between Dionysos and Ariadne – dynamic bisexuality – it held the promise of a superior will to power.

Wagner, intent on recreating in art the lost unity of the modern national community, often had recourse to sexual metaphors: poetry, a manly inspiration, and music went together like husband and wife; melody coupled with the People. The revolution called for by Wagner was to herald a new 'communism', meaning the community of *Volk* and Nature. The new total work of art (*Gesamtkunstwerk*), the crucible of artistic unity and political liturgy, would have a 'religious' function. The poet, the myth-maker, the man, would impregnate music, the woman. In his narcissistic fantasies of omnipotence, the musician-poet Wagner, bearer of both masculine and feminine principles, the complete genius, presents himself as the androgyne.[114] In the *Ring* tetralogy, the original union of the arts in the circle of the three Rhine-daughters is broken by Alberich 'the Jew'. Siegfried is the incarnation of the poet, the virile creator, and he couples with Brünhilde, who is music. But the masculine principle is dominant: the woman is doomed to sacrifice and death.

The catalyst was probably Ludwig Feuerbach and his treatise on 'The Essence of Christianity' (1841). Feuerbach is an example of the metaphysical quest for wholeness: his interpretation of Christ as 'half man, half woman' and his presentation of Judaism as the 'egoistic religion' impressed Wagner, who also took from him the notion of 'communism'. Whereas, in Wagner's early essays, the maleness of poetry dominates the androgynity of the *Gesamtkunstwerk*, after 1854, when he had read Schopenhauer, the musical, feminine element gradually acquired metaphysical superiority. But Wagner in his last years had a horror of decadence, and combined ideas of sexual and 'racial' regeneration with an ever more pronounced misogyny and antisemitism. Parsifal rejects union with the 'Jewess' Kundry. His is an angelical and asexual androgyny, prototype of a new humanity which has transcended sexual and racial divisions. Wagner's narcissistic fantasies in *Parsifal* are unbridled: the androgyne genius has vanquished time and become God.

In Wagner, the myth of the androgyne seems to produce nothing but illusion and regression. But we should no doubt distinguish more clearly between the androgyne and the hermaphrodite. Franz von Baader insisted on the importance of this distinction.[115] The hermaphrodite is the juxtaposition and sum of masculine and feminine powers, active bisexuality: the male becomes all-powerful by annexing all the virtues it once envied in the female – beauty, fertility, familiarity with nature. Thus we should speak of Wagner as hermaphrodite rather than androgynous, for in him the male was dominant and the union with the female meant possession and submission; the theme of the reconciliation of opposites points only to a truly totalitarian nostalgia, incapable of adjusting to the idea of difference. The androgyne, on the other hand, is not a coexistence of opposites but a transcending of them.

Creative anachronism or a lifeless neuter? The optimistic view is represented by Michel Maffesoli in *L'ombre de Dionysos: Contribution à une sociologie de l'orgie* ('The Shadow of Dionysos: Contribution to a Sociology of Orgies'): 'the morality of work becomes relative, more stress is laid on the body, polymorphism wanders, ideology is distanced, links of love are forged.' Should one see in this a flight into privacy or a mark of decadence? 'I do not think so,' replies Maffesoli. 'If the orgy is a denial of abstract History, it is also an affirmation of history as it is lived day by day.'[116] The opposite view is held by François Roustang, who pauses in his account of Casanova to say, 'One cause of madness is certainly the incapacity to discern sex, because it means inability to maintain the difference between the sexes. Because if the latter were to disappear, it would take with it one of the cultural yardsticks for distinguishing between individuals.'[117]

Is the 'coming god' Dionysos, who deconstructs individuation and drags men and women indiscriminately into his orgies, abolishing the difference of sex and freeing humanity from its divisions to set it on the road to new and creative distinctions?[118] Or will it be Isis/Osiris, the incestuous couple of Musil's poem of 1923?

> On leaves of stars the boy was sleeping
> (tranquil silver moon)
> and the sun's wheel-hub
> turning, watched him.
> The red wind blew from the desert
> and no sail came to shore.
>
> Then softly the sleeper's sister
> took away his phallus to eat,
> and gave him in exchange her gentle heart
> her red heart, and set it in him.
> Then in a dream the wound healed
> and she ate the cherished phallus ...[119]

In *The Man Without Qualities*, the meeting of Ulrich and his sister Agatha renews the myth of Isis and Osiris:

> What Ulrich said was: 'There's not only the myth of the human being divided into two. We might also take Pygmalion, or Hermaphroditus, or Isis and Osiris: with slight variations it's always the same thing. It goes back a very long way, this desire for a *doppelgänger* of the opposite sex, this craving for the love of a being that will be entirely the same as oneself and yet another.[120]

In the love of the 'Siamese twins' Ulrich intermittently attains to the mystical 'other state' which is the fulfilment of the individualist ethic, a feeling of solipsistic pleasure and omnipotence far more perfect than can be offered by the love of the Other.

Hermaphroditic love is the ultimate atrophy of the ego and of individualism, internalized alterity, the ego usurping the divine wholeness. Agatha is the missing link in Ulrich's ego-knowlege of satisfaction and fulfilment: 'The cleft in him becomes visible. He is filled with infinite anguish ... Agatha is his autism,' noted Musil in his journal.[121] And a little later, 'The love between brother and sister must be stoutly defended. Anders [Ulrich] feels it very deeply, as part of his rejection of the world. It is one of the few chances of union that are granted him.'[122]

But this 'other state' turns out to be as near to death as to life. 'When it comes down to it, all still-lifes show us the world on the sixth day of Creation, when God and the world were still close, without men coming between them!' observes Ulrich, not without uneasiness, for he senses 'a strange analogy' between the life he has led since his encounter with Agatha and the art of still-life, and it all suddenly seems to him comical: 'But is not the strange charm of the still-life comical in itself? A sort of airy necrophilia?'[123] The descriptions of the androgynous other state in *The Man Without Qualities* are bathed in the same moonlight as the 'Isis and Osiris' poem. The world seems to have come to a petrified stop: 'Spring and autumn, speech and silence, the magic of life and of death, were mingled . . . Their hearts seemed to have stopped, to have issued forth from their breasts to commune with the silent procession. 'Then my heart was taken from my breast,' a mystic once said. Agatha remembered those words.'[124]

The 'reign of the millennium' which Ulrich and Agatha enter at the end of Musil's novel is a disturbing allegory of the relation between the masculine and the feminine in the postmodern age. The early Romantics began breaking down the barrier between the sexes with a view to emancipating and liberating a new creative potential, the bisexualization of society and culture; they upset the libidinal equilibrium of love and the beauty of difference. The fantasy of androgyny came down on the side of death narcissism. The transsexual state did not necessarily change life by ending the war between the sexes; perhaps it only caused confusion and promiscuity leading to sexual indifferentiation. That is one possible approach to 'postmodernity' as a resolution of all contrasts into one grey generality. Jean Baudrillard says that the postmodern world has embarked on a process of growing indifferentiation: 'Economy becomes transeconomy, aesthetics transaesthetics, sex transsexual – all converging by a transverse and universal process in which no discourse can stand any longer as a metaphor for another.'[125]

The redistribution of masculine and feminine did not renew harmonious communication between the sexes, but turned individuals back to autism, illusory self-sufficiency – which was really a prison. In this denial of sexual difference, the greatest loss was suffered by the male: the castration of Osiris lets Isis assume the male into herself by eating the phallus of her brother. The removal of the phallus, the poem seems to suggest, lets them exchange bodies and offer their hearts in homage. But in the novel the hearts are carried away in the 'silent procession' of a funeral.[126]

7

Law of the Father, Law of the Mother, and Otto Gross

I

Great is Diana of the Ephesians

In a short essay of 1912, entitled 'Great is Diana of the Ephesians',[1] Freud communicates his notes on Sartiaux's archaeological study of *Dead Cities of Asia Minor*. He pays particular attention to the cult of Artemis at Ephesus. About eight centuries BC, Ionian immigrants took over the city and discovered the Asiatic cult of Oupis, whom they equated with their goddess Artemis. The temple of Artemis, several times destroyed and rebuilt, notably after the fire started by Erostratus, was one of the most popular pilgrim sites of antiquity: the Lourdes of Asia Minor, as Freud calls it.

In AD 54 the apostle Paul, a Jewish convert to Christianity, came to preach at Ephesus. The new faith was a grave threat to the cult of Artemis and to the whole tourist industry, Freud says. Angry craftsmen organized a protest march led by Demetrius, with the slogan 'Great is Diana of the Ephesians'. The church Paul founded at Ephesus did not long remain faithful to him, and turned instead to John, who came to Ephesus in the company of Mary, mother of Christ. Soon they constructed a basilica dedicated to her whom Freud calls 'the new mother-goddess of the Christians'.[2] The old pilgrimage began again, with no less success than in the time of Oupis or Artemis, and lasted until the advent of Islam.

The history of the pilgrimage of Ephesus had a more recent epilogue in the visions of a nun, Anna Katharina Emmerich (1774–1824); Clemens Brentano acted as her secretary from 1819 to 1824. Katharina Emmerich proved capable of describing the house of Mary at Ephesus, and her visions were confirmed by the archaeologists. After that, the house of the Virgin at Ephesus once again became a favourite place of pilgrimage. Thus St Paul's religion, the law of the father, had never managed to supplant the matriarchal cult of Oupis-Artemis-Mary.

St Paul had clashed with Demetrius – the man of Demeter – the defender of feminine values. Freud's essay can be interpreted as a parable of the resistance which psychoanalysis had to be prepared to meet. 'Freud guessed that at the very heart of the analytical movement, people like Demetrius would be legion.'[3] Otto Gross, Freud's troublesome disciple, was one of them. His career and his theories deserve our attention here, for they are the exact antithesis of the life and works of Otto Weininger. To the same degree as Weininger was antifeminist and ascetic, Gross was 'feminist' and a supporter of 'sexual immoralism'. But the two sets of works and the two characters have something in common – the fundamental insight that the crisis of modern civilization was essentially a crisis of masculine values which faced European humanity with an alternative: masculine or feminine. Weininger believed it was possible to cling to the law of the father. Gross directed all his wishes towards the coming of the law of the mother.

Otto Gross, 'sexual immoralist'

In his early works, Otto Gross (who was born in 1877) concentrated on a psychiatry based on neurophysiology; but already, under the influence of his father, the criminologist Hans Gross, professor at the University of Graz,[4] he was turning to the great problems of ethics and social life. His 1902 book on 'Secondary Cerebral Functions' had made his name known in psychological and psychoanalytical circles. Ernest Jones dates the first meeting between Sigmund Freud and Otto Gross to 1904.[5] Without turning his back on organic psychiatry (Wernicke remained his favourite authority), Gross had for several years been incorporating Freudian concepts into his work, making a very singular and unorthodox synthesis of classic psychiatry and psychoanalysis.

In 1907 he published a study entitled 'The Theme of Ideogeneity in Freud and its Meaning in Manic-Depressive Insanity According to Kraepelin',[6] in which he remained faithful to the outlook of psychophysiological monism. He sought an organic equivalent to each of the processes examined by Freud (symbolization, repression, etc.). The mortar between the bricks of Wernicke, Freud and Kraepelin was the vitalist doctrine of Hans Driesch.[7] He saw affects as reactions of the organism and the psyche adapting to new situations. Any unusual stimulus disturbs the individual's vital rhythms. This disturbance of equilibrium (traumatism) makes the nervous elements dissociate from their specific functions and return to a state comparable to that in the embryo, reopening all potentials for structural and functional development. The organism seeks the equilibrium best suited to it. Through inhibition mechanisms it rejects certain choices until it finds a way of reacting which suits it, and settles into a new equilibrium. This return to stability is an adaptation mechanism which is accompanied by feelings of pleasure. Otto Gross adds, 'The best expression for this biological principle is Nietzsche's "will to power".'[8]

He concludes that any affect, as a process of biological regulation, must be traversed to the bitter end, without impediment, if we wish it to develop far enough to form a new and durable programming. But here he encounters the problem of the individual adapting to the conditions of his own life, particularly social constraints. The demands of society are an impediment to individual mechanisms of regulation.[9] On one essential point, Otto Gross is opposed to the Freudian view: Gross seeks the principal source of psychic disturbance not in sexuality, but in the individual's more or less successful adaptation to society.

He added a footnote to this debate:

> The essential aspect of the causes suggested by the Freudian interpretation is psychic *conflict* in general and *not* the sexual aspect as such, as is so often wrongly believed. Latterly this widespread error has been brilliantly corrected by C. G. Jung. Sexual causation is quite independent of the fundamental aspects of Freud's theory of ideogeneity; it is no more than a deduction from empirical cases.

Even while ranking himself with the 'Jungian' psychoanalysis, Otto Gross paradoxically agrees with Freud. By trying Freud's method in his practical experiments, he explains, he firmly expected to find that the validity of Freud's theories on the sexual origins of 'inner conflicts' would be restricted to a very specific and severely limited class of patients. But, he went on, Freud's observations were vindicated in every case ... And he concludes: 'I am more than ever convinced that the privileged causative role of sexual conflicts is a result of environment, an expression of contemporary mores and their effect on the individual.'[10] For Gross, the treatment of neuroses required an understanding of the conflict in the interaction between the individual and society. The 'sexual problem' was really a social problem. It condensed all the hidden violence and the contradictions of civilization. Individual crises were a reflection of a collective crisis. Did this mean that individuals could only be cured by a change in social behaviour? Gross was convinced that it was so, and this was soon to bring him into open conflict with society.

On 25 September 1907, Jung wrote to Freud:

> Dr Gross tells me that he puts a quick stop to the transference by turning people into sexual immoralists. He says the transference to the analyst and its persistent fixation are mere monogamy symbols and as such symptomatic of repression. The truly healthy state for the neurotic is sexual immorality. Hence he associates you with Nietzsche. It seems to me, however, that sexual repression is a very important and indispensable civilizing factor, even if pathogenic for many inferior people. Still, there must always be a few flies in the world's ointment. What else is civilization but the fruit of adversity? I feel Gross is going along too far with the vogue for the sexual short-circuit, which is neither intelligent, nor in good taste, but merely convenient, and therefore anything but a civilizing factor.[11]

This mistrust of Otto Gross's ideas and character did not deter Freud from admitting him to the Psychoanalytical Congress in Salzburg at the end of April 1908. But in February 1909 Jung again expressed his disapproval, this time in a letter to Ernest Jones: 'I believe that in publicly announcing certain things one would saw off the branch on which civilization rests; one undermines the impulse to sublimation ... The extreme attitude represented by Gross is decidedly wrong and dangerous to the whole movement.'[12]

In 1906, Gross settled in Munich. He soon became well known in the intellectual, artistic and political circles of Schwabing, where he was the accredited representative of psychoanalysis. His concepts of 'erotic immoralism' were, not unnaturally, enthusiastically endorsed by his bohemian cronies. Erich Mühsam, for example, recalled Gross as 'the most notable of Freud's disciples'.[13] The Schwabing circle had a favourite holiday resort, the village of Ascona in the Tessine Alps, the meeting place of all who belonged to what in modern Germany is called the 'alternative' subculture.[14] Gross was a frequent visitor.

In Munich he began on an affair with Else Jaffé-von Richthofen, a friend of his wife Frieda Schloffer, who was pregnant at the time. In 1907 Else, already mother of two children, had a baby boy, born at almost the same time as Otto's legitimate son; both sons of the same father, they received the same name, Peter. And at more or less the same time Gross was involved with Frieda Weekley-von Richthofen. (Martin Green has published the evidence for these liaisons with the consent of the von Richthofen sisters.)[15] This polygamy put into practice the 'sexual immoralism' from which Gross the psychiatrist expected true inner liberation. Other rumours were circulating as well: in 1906 his name was mentioned in connection with the mysterious suicide of the anarchist Lotte Chattemer at Ascona. Gross was suspected of having given her the drugs which caused her death, and encouraged her to kill herself.

From the beginning of his adventures, Gross served as both foil and example to many contemporaries who had only a vague idea of psychoanalysis. For some he was a striking confirmation of the immorality which the prejudiced discovered in Freudian ideas. For others he offered a fertile interpretation of the 'message' of psychoanalysis which could connect with other *Weltanschauungen*, fashionable world-views such as Nietzscheanism, vitalism, and various ideas on social reform and revolutionary action.

Among those whose suspicions of psychoanalysis were confirmed by Otto Gross's excesses was Max Weber, the sociologist.[16] There had been much talk about Gross in Heidelberg circles via the von Richthofen sisters. Else Jaffé had encouraged him to submit an article for Weber's journal of sociology. The reaction was a violent one, as Marianne Weber tells in her biographical record. At Easter 1907, she had given a lecture to the Congress of Social Protestants of Strasburg on 'Problems of the Principle of Sexual Ethics'.[17] This lecture was, according to Marianne, full of most elevated ideas which had been inspired by the sight of a young and brilliant disciple of Sigmund Freud 'interpreting the theories of the master in his own way and drawing radical conclusions, preaching a sexual communism beside which the so-called "new ethics" seemed a very mild affair'.

Max Weber, Marianne explaines, was dismayed by the appalling effects this 'Dr X' had had on certain people. He immersed himself in Freudian theory and acknowledged its importance, but without accepting the interpretation given it by certain apostles of psychoanalysis, whose excesses were threatening the highest values of life. Therefore Weber rejected Gross's article on the grounds that the theories of S. Freud have greatly changed in the last few years, and in my judgement (though I am no expert) they have not yet reached their final form... There is no doubt that Freud's ideas on a whole range of phenomena in the history of civilization, particularly religion and social behaviour, may turn out to be extremely important – even if, in the eyes of cultural historians, they are far from possessing the universality which, in their understandable enthusiasm and in the thrill of discovery, Freud and his followers attribute to them.[18]

Weber went on to say that the applicability of psychoanalysis to the humane sciences would have to be more closely examined, with further case studies, to ensure that Freud's disciples did not lapse into amateurism or pseudo-scientific speculation. He concluded, referring to Otto Gross, that he should bear in mind the boundaries which separated scientific study from an exceedingly suspect kind of militancy. Later, in his studies of the sociology of religion, Weber was to try and accommodate his theories to the 'shock' of that encounter.[19]

Otto Gross spent the spring of 1908 as a patient at the Burghölzli clinic under the directorship of Carl Gustav Jung. He was being treated for drug abuse. Since his youth he had been taking opium, cocaine and morphine. He had been treated at the Burghölzli before, in 1902. While the detoxifying treatment was in progress, Jung also undertook to psychoanalyse Gross. The 'cure' took a peculiar turn: Jung worked on it furiously, spending several hours a day with Gross, in learned conversation about the problems of psychoanalysis. Finally, the analysis proved abortive, to the infinite consternation of Jung: Gross, who had been admitted to the Burghölzli on 11 May, escaped on 11 June by climbing over the wall. Jung, whose psychoanalytical talents were seriously questioned after this affair, never forgave Gross and pronounced on his patient one of the direst possible psychiatric verdicts – *dementia praecox*.[20]

The 'escape' from the Burghölzli was a turning point in Gross's career. He shifted definitively to the side of revolt and marginalization. The diagnosis of *dementia praecox* remained a millstone round his neck and he was looked on as a sick man, or even a madman, a menace to public order. But he never ceased to regard himself as a psychoanalyst and to defend his own idea of psychoanalysis against his detractors. The bizarre case of Elisabeth Lang, in autumn 1908, gave him a chance to publicize his very personal conception of the role of psychoanalysis and psychoanalysts.

On 10 October 1908 Maximilian Harden's Berlin journal *Die Zukunft* published a sort of open letter by Gross, entitled 'Parental Violence'. It tells[21] how he treated Elisabeth Lang, a young lady who had quarrelled with her family, and how he strove in vain to explain the situation to her parents. They entrusted their daughter to another doctor and forbade her to see Gross, but he continued to see her secretly to continue the analysis. Finally the parents had their daughter confined in a psychiatric clinic in Tübingen. His protest against the parents' 'abuse' of their authority over their daughter gave Gross a chance to outline his concept of psychoanalysis.

The task of psychoanalysis, he explains, is to resolve repressed psychic

conflicts deriving essentially from the antagonism between personal development and outside pressures which is characteristic of childhood. What Gross
calls 'the suggestions of upbringing' (using the word in the same sense as in
'hypnotic suggestion') causes inner conflict between 'the private and the alien'
(*das Eigene und das Fremde*). The expression recalls Max Stirner's *Der Einzige
und sein Eigentum* ('The One and his Property', 1845), which is known to have
influenced the anarchist movement. Successful psychoanalysis, says Gross,
cancels out the effects of upbringing, restores mechanisms of individual self-
regulation and consolidates individual values. He stresses that, from this point
of view, the notion of 'health' is relative and can vary from one individual to
another.

At that time Gross was believed to be intimate with anarchist groups in
Munich and Ascona. Emanuel Hurwitz has published Swiss and German
police reports in which Gross is suspected of anarchist militancy and anti-
militarism, and also of drug trafficking and drug-taking. Since 1907 he had
been acquainted with the Munich painter and anarchist Sophie Benz. In the
summer of 1910 he was living with her in Ascona. Her psychotic state became
worse and worse; she killed herself in March 1911. Here again, as after the
suicide of Lotte Chattemer, Gross's complicity was suspected.

He found himself back in a psychiatric clinic, being treated for depression
and drug addiction. In late March 1911 he was transfered to the Steinhof
clinic near Vienna. (Its new buildings had been opened in 1907; they are
dominated by the impressive church built by Otto Wagner, one of the best
examples of Viennese Jugendstil.) All Gross's medical tratment was paid for
by his father, who exhorted the clinic's directors to give his son the best of
comfort during his stay. At the end of June 1911, Gross left again for Zurich.
He intended to join his friend Erich Mühsam to found an 'anarchist academy'
at Ascona . . . In August he was being hunted by the police of Zurich canton.
His father had the search called off. In October 1911 he was back in Vienna;
next spring, in Florence; in 1913, he settled in Berlin.

'Degenerates are the salt of the earth'

During this troubled period Otto Gross brought out an important book,
'Psychopathological Inferiorities': a 122-page volume which was published in
Vienna in 1909 by Braumüller, who had also published *Sex and Character*. Its
style bears witness to Gross's unique way of thinking: all the stages of
his medical experience, almost without exception, are recapitulated and syn-
thesized into a rather precarious harmony. The psychiatrists Wernicke and
Anton are still favourite sources of reference; nonetheless, the discoveries of
Freudian analysis are hailed, from the first page, as fundamental.

Elsewhere Gross turns readily to Nietzsche. His vision of psychosomatic
parallelism inspired this synthesis: every event in psychic life has its equivalent
biological process. The governing idea is still to maintain equilibrium: the
individual in the course of normal development adapts himself and resolves
the conflicts between ego and non-ego by reconstituting his equilibrium

afresh at every stage. In the course of psychopathological development, physiological and psychological weaknesses may rob the individual of this ability to overcome such ordeals. The conflicts cause pathological states: Gross details the principal types, which leads him to a reassessment of the nomenclature of psychopathological afflictions.

The erudite and technical detail in many chapters may make them almost unreadable today, for they assume a certain familiarity with now-forgotten psychiatric theories; but the last chapter, where Gross's tone becomes more personal and he formulates all the value judgements on which his research has been based, is all the more fascinating and raises questions which are still relevant today. He targets the viewpoint of his own father, Hans Gross, who in 1905 had published an article called 'Degeneration and Deportation',[22] and he summarizes its arguments in the book. Gross the elder had expressed his uneasiness at the contradiction he perceived between nature, selecting those living creatures best suited to survival and eliminating the unsuitable (this is a 'social Darwinist' speaking), and nurture, which does its best to 'save' those individuals and give them the chance to reproduce, thereby creating a risk of racial degeneration.

Gross the younger calls Nietzsche as a witness against this position and holds that nurture does not merely counter the process of natural selection, but can even redefine and amend the criteria for that selection, preventing the blind excision of every deviation from the norm. For it is precisely the deviation from the norm which makes genius – the opposite of degeneration – possible: genius represents the capacity of the human type to evolve towards unprecedented, superior forms. And yet the boundary between genius and degeneracy seems so uncertain ... Gross uses this disturbing resemblance as an argument, proclaiming that 'the degenerate are the salt of the earth!' On one point he does yield to the Darwinists: he acknowledges the hypothetical *variability* of the human race. But he rejects all hasty judgements of the cultural value of apparently 'degenerate' types. They have a way of adapting to archaic social conditions which are incompatible with modern life. Their apparent inability to cope with the latter should not blind us to the fact that they may represent the future of civilization. They are, says Gross in his concluding sentence, the 'raw material' of future evolution.

Here, Gross takes his stance in the great debate on decadence which had absorbed intellectuals since Nietzsche and the literary 'decadents'.[23] Is the genius a superior degenerate? Is degeneration the breeding ground of higher civilizations, even the mark of modernity? This discussion, so early in the century, affected most of the works of *Kulturkritik* (for example, Max Nordau's essay 'Entartung' – 'Degeneration'), as well as works of psychiatry from Morel and Lombroso onwards, and literary fictions (almost all Mann's novels deal with the subject). Otto Gross, in his book written in 1909, voices his agreement with Nietzsche in *Human, All Too Human*: 'Ennoblement through degeneration ... It is on the more unrestricted, more uncertain and morally weaker individuals that depends the *intellectual progress* of such communities ... Deviating natures are of the utmost importance wherever there is to be progress.'[24]

It is plain to see that Gross's essay on 'psychopathological inferiorities' answers to a need of self-justification and goes sheer against the conservative ideology represented by his father, Hans Gross. The son's whole life appears to have been dominated by his revolt against parental authority, but also by a constant dependence on paternal assistance. At the worst moments of his existence, Gross got from his parents the money which enabled him to survive, the protection or good word which saved him from police – or psychiatric – ill-treatment. Nonetheless, the last three years of Hans Gross's life, from 1913 to 1915, were to see incessant and violent warfare between him and his son.

Hans Gross had become the greatest authority on penal and criminal law in the Habsburg monarchy. Before taking up an academic career he had been thirty years an examining magistrate, and his published work drew on this first-hand experience. His 'Practical Handbook of Criminal Investigation' (1883) presented criminology above all as a multidisciplinary science, and gave evidence of an encyclopaedic curiosity and erudition worthy of Sherlock Holmes for anything which might contribute to 'scientific policing'.[25] Since 1905 he had been Professor of Criminology at the University of Graz. In his institution he had set up a 'museum of crime' for the edification of magistrates and police officers. In 1899 he had founded, and subsequently edited, the journal *Archiv für Kriminal-Anthropologie und Kriminalistik*.

Freud cites Hans Gross's *Criminal Investigation* (1898) in his *Psychopathology of Everyday Life*.[26] In his article 'Diagnostic Establishment of the Facts and Psychoanalysis', first published in Gross's *Archiv* in 1906, Freud pointed out the importance of psychoanalysis in criminal investigations and proceeded to the famous comparison between the practitioner and the examining magistrate; he spoke with respect of Hans Gross's school.[27] The latter was keenly interested in the sciences of psychology and psychoanalysis as adjuncts to criminal investigation. At Graz, he worked closely with his colleague Richard von Krafft-Ebing, whose *Psychopathia sexualis* had a 'penal' chapter.

In most cases when he felt called on to make a value judgement, Hans Gross showed an unyielding severity, for example when writing of gypsies:

> All those who know them agree that they are a compound of vanity, vulgarity, coquetry, seriousness and indifference. They have not a trace of manly intelligence, but this makes them all the more cunning and deceitful. Their most striking traits are servility, insolence, unreliability, total shamelessness and infinite laziness. If we consider their character as a whole, we can easily understand the actions of gypsies. Their cowardice, above all, seems to me an essential element.[28]

As one might expect, Gross was actively against prostitution, homosexuality, sexual 'perversions' and pornography, even when the latter masqueraded as literature: novels which spread moral infection must be suppressed. The danger, as he saw it, came from degeneracy, which increased the number of deviants from the norm. Effeminate men and viragos, but also tramps, revolutionaries, anarchists and even thieves were all, in his eyes, degenerates. In 1905, in the conclusion of the study which Otto Gross was to attack in

1909, Hans Gross suggested that these degenerates should be deported to the colonies, perhaps to South-West Africa or the Pacific Islands.

II

The revolution of matriarchy

In 1913, Otto Gross settled in Berlin. He joined the adherents of Franz Pfemfert, editor of the journal *Aktion*, one of the most important in the Expressionist movement. It was in this journal that he published his manifesto, 'How to Survive the Crisis of Civilization', in April 1913. Its three pages were presented as a reply to the anarcho-syndicalist Gustav Landauer, who had made an attack on psychoanalysis. The clarity of its political message makes this article into a turning point in Gross's thought. 'The psychology of the unconscious', he declared roundly, 'is the psychology of revolution. None of the revolutions of history succeeded in establishing the freedom of the individual. They hung fire and ended in a pressing desire to belong and to conform to what was generally accepted as normality.'[29] Today, Gross continued, it was finally becoming clear that the root of all authority was the family, and that collusion between sexuality and authority, as in the patriarchally governed family which was still the norm, enslaved the individual.

Periods of cultural crisis, said Gross, were connected with challenges to marriage and family ties: this led to talk of decadence, but the original sin of reducing women to slavery in the name of procreation was forgotten. He concluded: 'Today's revolutionary, who thanks to the psychology of the unconscious can see relations between the sexes in the light of a free and happy future, struggles against rape in its most elemental form, against the father and against patriarchy. The coming revolution is a revolution of matriarchy. And its form and methods are unimportant.'[30] Gross's manifesto seems foresighted: it foreshadows the aims of the Freudian Left in the 1920s,[31] the aims of Erich Fromm, Wilhelm Reich and Otto Fenichel, and later, Herbert Marcuse. The reference to the antagonism between matriarchy and patriarchy also places Gross among the revolutionary descendants of Johann Jakob Bachofen, following August Bebel (*Women and Socialism*, 1879) and Friedrich Engels (*The Origins of the Family, Private Property and the State*, 1884), both of whom acknowledged Bachofen's influence. Later Ernst Bloch, Max Horkheimer, Fromm and Reich were to pay their own homage to Bachofen,[32] but they made no mention of Gross.

A few weeks later, in May 1913, Gross took up the defence of psychoanalysis, again in *Aktion*, against the author Ludwig Rubiner, who had written that creative minds needed 'a new mythology, not psychology', and that psychoanalysis could only *cure* weak characters (such as impressionist artists and women . . .), not 'inspire the strong-minded'. Gross, answering Rubiner, recalled a remark Freud had addressed to him at the Psychoanalytic Congress in Salzburg: 'We are doctors and we wish to remain doctors.' Gross rejected that concept and continued, 'We now know that the contribution [of psychoanalysis] has been infinitely more important.' Up to then the artist had been alone in penetrating the secrets of the unconscious; from now on he would have to take account of psychoanalysis. Gross ended with these words: 'Ludwig Rubiner betrays a fatal error of appreciation when he contrasts woman with the free spirit. I think that the first real revolution will be that through which woman, freedom and spirit will become one.'[33]

At the end of 1913, further short but important articles by Gross appeared in *Die Aktion*. In 'The Effects of Society on the Individual'[34] he again placed himself under the authority of Nietzsche, presenting Freud as the latter's direct heir. He repeats that the conflict between the self and society gives rise to conflicts within the self. Sexuality is the preferred ground for this trespassing by society on the terrain of the individual, and women are its first victims. The 'Remarks for a New Ethics' are still more provoking. On the grounds of the original bisexuality of individuals, Gross advises not only complete tolerance of homosexuals, but even the nurturing of homosexual tendencies in as many people as possible. Declaring that marriage is rape and enslavement of women, he calls for 'the destruction of monogamy and its even deadlier form, polygamy'[35] as a preliminary to founding new relations between the sexes and freeing individuals from their subjective solitude.

On 9 November 1913 Gross was arrested at the Berlin home of his friend Franz Jung by the Prussian police and expelled from that country back to Austria. Hans Gross, who up to then could boast of having used his influence in high places to protect his son against the police forces of Europe, had finally 'lost patience' and asked the Berlin police to intervene. On the Prussian frontier Otto Gross was handed over to the Austrian police and interned, on Hans Gross's instructions, in a private psychiatric home in Tulln. Hans Gross obtained an expert psychiatric opinion, signed by two doctors, which declared Otto Gross mad and not responsible, and advised that he should be confined. On 9 January 1914 the Graz tribunal confirmed this opinion and designated Hans Gross as his guardian.

In December 1913 a press campaign in support of Otto Gross and against Hans Gross had started. Franz Pfemfert's *Die Aktion* in Berlin and the journal *Revolution* in Munich had brought out special issues in tribute and support.[36] They included articles by Ludwig Rubiner, Blaise Cendrars, Erich Mühsam, Johannes R. Becher, Jakob van Hoddis, René Schickele, Else Lasker-Schüler and other leading lights of the Expressionist movement. Soon the big newspapers were reporting this sensational affair. Even the *Mercure de France* and *L'intransigeant* were talking about it.[37] The governors of the Tulln institution began to fear that Gross's friends would organize his escape, and on 25 January 1914 the 'patient' was transferred to the Troppau home in Silesia. Gross nonetheless managed to send an open letter to Maximilian Harden, editor of the Berlin journal *Die Zukunft* which had published his article on 'Parental Violence' in 1908. This time it was his own case that Gross described to *Zukunft*'s readers. He began with a touching description of the troubles of his wife, Frieda Gross, and his son Peter, whom Hans Gross had taken it upon himself to separate from each other. Then he went over the principal offences which had led to his arrest and confinement.

He admitted that in 1906 he had supplied Lotte Chattemer with the poison she had used to commit suicide at Ascona. He also mentioned the suicide of Sophie Benz, which he called a case of psychosis, and declared that his only error was not to have had Benz interned in time in a psychiatric home – for which, he said, he should be praised rather than blamed. And since he was also accused of being a threat to public order, he declared:

> I am not satisfied with the existing social order...If it is considered that normality means conforming to the existing order, then my dissatisfaction could be interpreted as a sign of mental disturbance. But if by 'normal' one understands the fostering of all the innate potentialities of man, and if one knows intuitively and from experience that the existing social order makes this supreme accomplishment of the individual and of humanity impossible, then it is the man who is satisfied with the existing order who will be considered inferior.[38]

Gross remained a prisoner in the home at Troppau until 8 July 1914. He then went to Bad Ischl, where Wilhelm Stekel undertook to treat him. The latter, in his tribute to Gross published in 1920, was to challenge Jung's diagnosis and conclude that Gross was suffering from a grave neurosis complicated by drug addiction; he had never met with such a waste of so outstanding a talent.[39]

Family history: the Grosses and the Schrebers

We may remember here that Daniel Paul Schreber's 'Memoirs of a Neuropath' was written as an apologia intended to persuade his judges to end his confinement in a psychiatric home and restore his liberty. In an 'Appendix' to his memoirs, Schreber published some reflections on the subject, 'Under what conditions can a person judged insane be confined in a hospital establishment against his manifest wishes?'[40] Since coming to terms with the mysterious ordering of the world which had doomed him to become a woman in order to save mankind, Schreber had always thought that his 'martyrdom' should be admired as a saint's and that the judicial authorities would eventually have to acknowledge that he was right.

Otto Gross's visions of the 'revolution of matriarchy' are strongly reminiscent of Schreber. In his last work, 'Three Studies of Mental Conflict', Gross talks of the inner wealth of bisexuality in men and says that men should foster their latent homosexuality, rediscover and cultivate the buried feminine in themselves. We might say that Gross's theories are a 'ratiocinated' form of the message contained in the madness of Dr Schreber.

What Daniel Paul Schreber and Otto Gross have in common is surely the crushing presence of the father, both loved and feared, a model for identification and a target of revolt. Schreber's father, Daniel Gottlieb Moritz Schreber (1808–61), had the same authoritarian character as Otto's father, Hans Gross. Both fathers set an ideal of order and social progress alongside a predilection for the most harshly repressive methods. Schreber the elder, an orthopedist and pediatrician, and a specialist in corrective gymnastics, was the author of popular works such as 'Medical Gymnastics in Your Own Room' (*Ärztliche Zimmergymnastik*) and 'Callipaedia, or Beauty Education through Natural and Balanced Encouragement of Normal Bodily Attitudes' (*Kallipaedie oder Erziehung zur Schönheit durch naturgetreue und gleichmässige Förderung normaler Körperhaltung*). His whole method rested on a systematic use of constraint and punishment. The orthopedic accessories which he recommended to parents and teachers, and which are illustrated in the plates of his textbooks, resemble instruments of torture.

He gave minute descriptions of the corporal punishments which were to be administered to children every time they fell short of good behaviour. The prevention and repression of infant masturbation was an obsession of his, and his precepts were part of a ruthless struggle against the 'growing laxity of morals' and the 'degeneracy of the modern world'.[41] Most of the racier details in the psychotic visions of Schreber the younger spring from the vagaries of his father's discipline. And Freud – who showed the greatest respect for Schreber senior, as indeed he did for Hans Gross[42] – interprets the delirium of Schreber the younger as showing the workings of the father complex, the ambivalent relationship with the father which is one essential feature of the Oedipus complex.[43]

Otto Gross's career was also intepreted in terms of a *Vaterkomplex*. An only son (whereas Schreber the younger had had an elder brother, who had committed suicide), Gross had been brought up 'like a prince', on the evidence of Else Jaffé.[44] A spoiled child, considered 'exceptionally gifted' and educated far in advance of his years, he helped his father's research in his early years at university and was protected by him in his career (so soon to be broken off) at the University of Graz; his early love affairs were chaperoned by him; he could only live for, and against, his father. The death of Hans Gross on 9 December 1915 was a blow from which he was never to recover. In the description by Franz Jung:

> His father was dead. He had to follow another course of treatment for abuse of cocaine. There was no one now to confine and threaten him. He realized that he had lost his mainstay. He gave up his work, ceased to face up to the material necessities of existence, could no longer live independently. All inhibitions seemed to have fallen away from his behaviour, which took on a distinctly infantile character. He seemed doomed to an early death. For whole weeks, even months, he wandered through Vienna, without a penny, without shelter, living off chance meetings in cafés.[45]

Daniel Paul Schreber's father had died in November 1861, at the age of fifty-three (his son was then nineteen). It was at the age of fifty-three, in November 1895 (according to 'Memoirs of a Neuropath'), that Schreber junior, who had been in a psychiatric hospital for two years, found his womanhood coming fast upon him and 'resigned himself' to this fate. In both Schreber and Gross, the death of the father caused a destructuring of personality and a regression to a primitive, pre-Oedipal psychic state of identification with the mother.

Matriarchy, heaven or hell? Gross and Beer-Hofmann

At the beginning of the First World War, Otto Gross worked as a volunteer in various hospitals, firstly in Galicia and then in Vienna, Slavonia and in the Banat district of Romania. There, at Temesvár, he once again had to be hospitalized because of drug abuse, at the end of 1916. He remained under treatment at Temesvár for six months; in May 1917 he was transferred to the Steinhof clinic near Vienna, and left there soon after having been declared unfit for war service. He lived with his mother in Munich, then in Vienna. He travelled a great deal, staying in Prague, Budapest and Berlin. On 11 February 1920 Otto Gross was found, overcome with hunger and cold, on a Berlin pavement. He was treated for pneumonia and drug abuse at the sanatorium at Pankow. He died on 13 February 1920. He was buried, 'by mistake' according to Emanuel Hurwitz,[46] in the Jewish cemetery in Berlin.

These last years were especially dark, shadowed with war, wanderings, poverty, solitude and drugs – not to mention the judicial bother stemming from the care order of January 1914 – and yet he never ceased his regular output of work. In 1914 his study of 'The Symbolism of Destruction' appeared in the *Zentralblatt für Psychoanalyse und Psychotherapie*, whose editor was Wilhelm Stekel. Between 1915 and 1918 Gross, together with Franz Jung, was on the editorial committee of the Berlin journal *Die freie Strasse*, which stood midway between Expressionism and Dadaism. In 1917 and 1918 he was often to be seen in Prague, where he met Max Brod, Franz Kafka and Franz Werfel. In his last years, in Berlin, he contributed to the journals *Das Forum*, *Die Erde*, *Rätezeitung* and *Sowjet*. And in 1920, probably not long after his death, there appeared his little book 'Three Studies of Mental Conflict', the most polished and attractive version of the salient ideas in the last phase of his thought.

The article on the 'Symbolism of Destruction' was based on observations Gross had made at Troppau, in the asylum in which he had been confined in 1914; and on the novel 'Comrades!' by Franz Jung, in which a woman cries, 'I hate all women. I would rather be a man and a homosexual.' In every case he presents, Gross brings out the rejection of sexual relations, seen as a rape of the woman. This rejection is, he says, ethical in nature. It is a response to the organization of the sexual drive in terms of raping and being raped. Gross's theoretical comments draw heavily on Alfred Adler, Wilhelm Stekel and Sabina Spielrein. Central to his analysis is the inner conflict between sadism and masochism, which in his eyes is connected with the position of women in society and the family. Now this patriarchal order was established at the price of a victory of violence over matriarchy. This, Gross affirms, is shown by the latest research on anthropology:

> Matriarchy guarantees women economic, and therefore sexual and human, independence from a particular man, and gives women as mothers a direct responsibility to society: the future is in their hands. The mythologies of all peoples preserve the memory of a prehistoric state of free matriarchy in the idea of a golden age of justice and an original paradise.... The hope of a better future for humanity must lie in a return to the freedom of matriarchy.[47]

Gross develops the same ideas in his article 'The Communist Ideal in the Symbolism of Paradise', which appeared in the Viennese journal *Sowjet* in 1919. He compares the childhood of the individual, rich in spontaneous potential which is repressed or channelled by education, with the childhood of humanity, lost since the advent of civilization, which sacrificed the freedom of the mind to the affirmation of power – power over nature and over men. Material culture and authoritarian institutions developed to the detriment of the free development of personality. Humanity still has a nostalgic longing for the ancient golden age, the paradise of Genesis, characterized above all by free relationships between beings – beginning with that between man and woman. Marriage and the reduction of women to dependency provoked the Fall. The establishment of patriarchy was the original sin: it was not sexuality as such, but rather a perversion of the deeper meaning of sexuality, now caught in the fetters of good and evil. The biblical story of paradise lost shows that by turning away from matriarchy, mankind sinned against the divine will and caused a cultural catastrophe.

The communist revolution, then, must restore the matriarchal order. For matriarchy, says Gross, prevents the relationship between the sexes from lapsing into a moral or legal obligation, or into an economic and social constraint. It protects sexuality against the corruption brought into it by the spirit of domination. It makes sexual unions 'clean of all contract and all authority, clean of all marriage and all prostitution'.[48] At a blow, the basis of social authority would be destroyed and the economic problem solved: for in matriarchy, society as a whole is bound to provide for mother and child. The true liberation of women implies the suppression of the patriarchal family and the removal of maternal responsibility to the public sphere.

In the conclusion to his article, Gross remarks (in a note) that the originator of Genesis must have been thinking of the struggle between the authoritarian and theocratic monotheism of the Prophets and the worship of Astarte, which decided the fate of ancient Israel and its sphere of influence:

> The worship of Astarte at that time must have gathered to itself all that was left of women's freedom and dignity. The orgy, as an act of worship, still asserted the positive judgement of matriarchal society on sexuality, and the priestess was an incarnation of the ancient spirit of female supremacy. To destroy the worship of Astarte, the prophets imposed the religious monopoly of men on Jewish culture, so that the characteristic abasement of women became part of the vision of the Jewish, Christian and Muslim worlds. It is in this exclusive sense, as the first white terror unleashed against women's freedom, that Judaism was later allied to Hellenism.[49]

The violently anti-Jewish and anti-Christian tone of this passage, as well as the implicit reference to Bachofen, recall the new 'paganism' of Ludwig Klages or Alfred Schuler. They saw Judaism, throughout the history of civilization, as a victory of the *logos* and of patriarchy over the soul and the cosmogonic eros. Gross had met Klages at Schwabing and heard of the ideas discussed in the *Kosmische Runde* by the friends and disciples of Stefan George.[50]

One of the most remarkable literary representations of the matriarchal cult of Astarte – the *dea syria* – is in Beer-Hofmann's tale *Der Tod Georgs* ('George's Death'), published in 1900. Paul, the hero, is the very type of the fin-de-siècle aesthete, egocentric and narcissistic.[51] 'His will to live engenders a new life': this remark, from Georg Lukács's essay on 'George's Death' in *Soul and Form*,[52] points out one of the main threads in the text. Paul, dissatisfied with his life, tormented by the boredom, melancholy, distraction, expectancy and irresolution of his existence, is unexpectedly visited by his friend George, whom he has not seen for a year. George is Paul's opposite: adventurous and ambitious in character, vigorous (the text alludes repeatedly to his athletic physique and suntanned face), successful in everything, with a brilliant medical career in front of him. He is real life, in contrast to Paul, and that evening, after an afternoon spent in George's company, Paul realizes the danger he is in: of being a failure, of being left behind by the flood-tide which is leading George on to fortune.

That same night, while Paul pursues his gloomy thoughts, George suddenly dies in the next room. He, the force of nature so envied in the first chapter, is in the third no more than a corpse which Paul must accompany on the train to the town where it is to be buried. After the destruction of that impossible ideal, other responses to life begin to stir in Paul. In the last chapter, he will know the revelation which will consolidate this feeling of life restored, stronger and more sure of itself: the voice of his Jewish blood and an individualistic conversion to a sort of 'aesthetic Zionism'. Thus 'George's Death' is really the story of a return to life, the rebirth of Paul.

At the beginning, Paul is kin to all those 'unsavable egos', an *unrettbares Ich* similar to Lord Chandos at the beginning of his 'ordeal', or the merchant's son in the 'Tale of the 672nd Night'. The decisive step on his journey back to life is taken in the second chapter. This chapter, the strangest and most fascinating one in the book, describes certain dreams Paul has on the night of George's death. The two most important ones involve a return to the feminine element in the two forms most typical of the 1900s: the willowy, pre-Raphaelite woman and the menacing *femme fatale*, the Astarte. In his first dream, Paul is engaged to a young woman he met in a field of daffodils, who dies of a consumption as mysterious and ineluctable as that of Maeterlinck's Melisande or Barrès's Bérénice.

At the start of his second dream, Paul sees a temple in Hierapolis in Syria, on a rocky height, surrounded by a double wall of Cyclopean masonry. In the Holy of Holies reigns a goddess whose description recalls the Judiths and Salomes of Gustave Moreau, or the 'Astarte Syriaca' of Dante Gabriel Rossetti:[53]

Surrounded by gilded statues of gods, the great goddess was seated in a chariot drawn by lions, covered with precious stones, a crown shaped like a fortress on her head. By night, when the flashing of the water-blue and fire-coloured gems grew dim, an unknown jewel in her crown lit up the temple. The goddess's open eyes looked into the eyes of whoever approached and followed him around the room wherever he went.[54]

In the temple, richly ornamented with gold (thanks to the offerings brought by the girls and boys who prostitute themselves for the goddess in the sacred groves near the river), the pilgrims crowd in to celebrate the erotic 'feast of spring' (*Ver sacrum* was the name of the journal of the Viennese Secession). The priests, eternally young, are eunuchs devoted to fleshly enjoyments. On the meadow before the temple gates there is a monumental phallus of red sandstone. On this meadow pyres are built, on which offerings are laid. After nightfall the crowds throng to the sacred meadow, cries are heard and perfumes are scattered. The orgy begins. In the waves of rejoicing, a few perish, crushed by the trampling crowds or pushed over the precipice by the surging human tide. The orgy creates a crowd dynamic which drowns out individuality: 'The crowd knew and felt more strongly than individuals. The deep and ardent meditations of the daytime had bound it together into one; that which no individual could sense dwelt in the perceptions of all . . . they wanted to feel, feel themselves live at last.'[55]

The orgy is a variant on Nietzsche's Dionysian principle in *The Birth of Tragedy*: it abolishes the *principium individuationis*. The woman whom the dreamer, now part of the crowd,[56] has made love to dies in his arms, slain by the very violence of her pleasure: 'While loins quivering with desire turned to him and greedily drank the burning torrent of new life, he did not see that under his kisses the parted lips were growing slowly cold and that the eyes, drowning but not in pleasure, were gazing fixedly at the sky.'[57] As in the first dream, in which the frail woman dies to give life to Paul, the body which has given pleasure to the dreamer is swallowed up in death – the ultimate 'transgression' (in Bataille's sense) of this sacred orgy.

For the archaeological detail of this dream, written with a luxuriance reminiscent of Flaubert's *Salammbô*,[58] Beer-Hofmann used chiefly the *De Dea Syriaca* of Lucian and Burckhardt's *Age of Constantine the Great*.[59] He was also following Bachofen's theories on matriarchy, representing life within the sanctuary as a paradise in which human beings lived in harmony with nature, without seeking to master her by technology. But in his tale, the goddess Astarte assumes the guise of a 'phallic mother' (in a literal sense, since the phallus of red sandstone is erected in the sacred meadow before the temple), more frightening than beneficent, and the orgy turns into a sinister press of bodies in which death cuts them down without troubling to count its victims.

Otto Gross's idea of matriarchal utopia remained imprecise and ill-thought-out. His description of the worship of Astarte seems too naively idyllic. Beer-Hofmann's story on the same theme goes further. He clearly shows the ambivalence of matriarchy as a response to the crisis of masculine identity. The plans for the feminization of culture, defended lucidly enough by Gross and crazily by Dr Schreber, betray a longing to return to the mother's breast, fascination with the idea of a euphoric fusion with the feminine element, pleasure mingling with male transsexual erotic passivity. But Beer-Hofmann's tale and Schreber's phobias clearly show that these promises of ecstasy and inner liberation cannot overcome the disquiet caused by the phallic mother, the terror of the loss of identity she might inflict.

'When he is deprived of the breast, the child has a foreboding of what the loss of his penis might mean . . . and his behaviour in adulthood rests on this twofold foundation in the remote past: the euphoria of fusion associated with intolerable anxieties, both experienced in a total dependence on the woman.'[60] Gross saw only one face of matriarchy – the smiling face. He refused to see the other face of the Great Mother, the devourer, phallic, the castrator. He ought to have realized that the 'law of the mother', so often hailed as part of the utopian sexual revolutions of the new century, was no less harsh than the law of the father which he saw as the source of all evil.

III

Franz Werfel and Max Brod against Otto Gross

Otto Gross's influence on the literature of the twentieth century was no less – perhaps greater – than his influence on the history of psychoanalysis. At every stage in his life he moved in circles frequented by representative modernist and avant-garde writers; on all of them he made a profound impression. The two authors he knew best, Leonhard Frank (1882–1961) and Franz Jung (1888–1963), give him pride of place in their novels and memoirs. D. H. Lawrence mentions him in *Twilight in Italy*.[61] During his Munich years he also knew Johannes R. Becher, Karl Otten, Walter Hasenclever and Oscar Maria Graf, and these encounters left their mark on their poems and novels. In Prague in 1917, the arrival of Otto Gross caused a well-attested sensation in the circle of Franz Werfel, Max Brod and Franz Kafka. Finally, in Berlin in 1919, Gross's theories influenced the Dadaist group, as is shown in particular by the evidence of Raoul Hausmann. This literary influence of Gross's has been the subject of a special study.[62] I shall pay particular attention to his encounter with Werfel, Brod and Kafka, since the image these writers give of him helps us to a better understanding both of the ceaseless anguish he was enduring at the time he was developing his theories on matriarchy, and of the reasons for his failure.

Franz Werfel's view of Otto Gross was ambivalent, though disapproval takes precedence over fascination. In his novel 'Barbara, or Piety' (1929),[63] part of which concerns the intellectual and social disarray resulting from the First World War, there is a character called Gebhart who lives in an environment of women and drugs, and who says that

> All forms of existence and of the state, all political institutions, rest on authoritarianism and date from the fatal moment when natural matriarchy was destroyed by power-crazed patriarchy. This fatal error has been perpetuated and increased incessantly up to our own time. Its latest violent consequence was the world war, that bloody homage to the religion of power.[64]

Gebhart sees Moses, the prophets, Plato and Christ as belonging to the genealogy of that power, which is no more than an instinct for rape and is marked by respect for the father, monotheism and monogamy. Gebhart prefers Babylonian religion, the worship of Astarte; he calls for a 'sexual revolution' alongside, and as part of, the communist and anarchist one. He is accused of murder after giving poison to a depressive, suicidal young woman. He lives in a dirty, neglected apartment, but rules over a harem of women whose erotic life is governed by him, on the basis of orgies in the house of a young war widow who has fallen under his influence.

Gebhart's favourite pastime is to hold forth on the subject of eroticism. He has particular praise for homosexuality:

> In his eyes it had a great part to play in the spiritual life of humanity. It was homosexuality which raised our instincts above the merely animal. It alone allowed the two sexes to know and appreciate each other. The man who did not feel in himself, by an instinct of homophilia, any reason to be loved as a man, remained uncouth and violent. It was the homosexual side of his character which permitted him to understand, and dearly respect, the love of women.[65]

These fair words do not, however, prevent Werfel's Gebhart from culpably neglecting his own child, to whom he has not even given a name . . .

Max Brod's view of Otto Gross, as expressed in his novel *Das grosse Wagnis* ('The Great Challenge', 1918), is even more negative. After a devastating war, a few deserters and refugees found a utopian colony, Liberia, ruled over by a certain Dr Askonas. This character, married but surrounded by mistresses, preaches the inner liberation of individuals:

> I distrust any act which a man inflicts on himself to his own disadvantage. Overcoming oneself would be all very well, if the victory were not at the same time a self-defeat. The decay of love, a castrated and confined humanity, a world declining into abstractions . . . those are the fruits of self-defeat! . . . To this we sacrifice our love and happiness![66]

Dr Askonas arouses the suspicions of the novel's hero: 'Who is this Dr Askonas? A redeemer who sacrifices himself to his own dream? Or a traitor, a criminal disguising his baser instincts under a messianic cloak?'[67] The story ends badly. We soon realize that Liberia is a prison camp governed by a terrifying authority. The inhabitants of Liberia revolt against Askonas, and the camp is eventually obliterated by the war going on around it. Realizing the failure of his utopia, Askonas cries, 'One should never think of saving humanity until one has accomplished the task of making one's self pure!'[68]

Kafka between Gross and Weininger

In a letter to Milena, written at Merano on 25 June 1920 (published in 1983), Franz Kafka tells of his encounter with Gross in 1917. Milena must just have told Kafka of Gross's death in February 1920. Kafka wrote back:

> I scarcely knew Otto Gross, but I felt that something important was reaching out to me under a cloak of ridicule. The lost air of his friends and family (his wife,

his brother-in-law, and even the baby, mysteriously silent among the travelling cases – which were to stop him falling out of bed when left alone – drinking black coffee, eating fruit or anything that was offered) rather reminded me of the disciples' lost look at the foot of the Cross. On that day I had just got back from Budapest, where I had been with my fiancée, and I was travelling, completely exhausted, towards Prague, where I was to suffer a haemorrhage. Gross, his wife and his brother-in-law had taken the same night train. . . . Gross was telling me something through almost the entire night (with a few short pauses, during which he was probably injecting himself); at least, that is what I thought, because to tell the truth I did not understand a word of it. He explained his ideas to me on the basis of a Bible passage which I did not know, but out of cowardice and fatigue I did not tell him this. He went on and on examining this passage, bringing in new elements, seeking my approval. I nodded mechanically as his face swam before my eyes. In any case, even with a clear head I doubt if I would have understood what he was telling me, my thoughts are cold and slow . . . At Prague I only caught one further glimpse of him.[69]

Gross had suggested that Kafka should join with him and some other friends in founding a journal to be called *Blätter zur Bekämpfung des Machtwillens* ('Journal for Combatting the Will to Power'), and it seems that Kafka was rather taken with the project. For example, he wrote to Max Brod in November 1917: 'If a journal did once tempt me for quite a time, it was that of Dr Gross, because it seemed to me – that evening, at least – to be born of the flame of a certain personal sympathy. A sign of a common aspiration and of personal sympathies – that is probably all that a journal can be.'[70]

Apart from these anecdotes, what can we discern of a possible influence of Otto Gross on Kafka? The unusual violence of the conflict between Gross the father and Gross the son, the weird mixture of revolt and dependence in Otto's relations with his father could not but seem familiar to the author of *Letter to his Father*.[71] (Hans Gross was professor of penal law and criminology at the University of Prague at the time when Kafka was a student in the same faculty;[72] we may well imagine that when he met the son, he had not yet forgotten the father.) We should probably not be content with Kafka's disillusioned judgement on his conversations with Gross in his letter to Milena of June 1920. Elsewhere he notes, for example, that 'Gross was probably not wrong, in so far as I understand him.'[73]

By examining the representation of sexuality and relationships between men and women in *The Castle* in the light of a reading of Otto Weininger alongside Otto Gross, Hartmut Binder has given a particularly intriguing view of that work.[74] Not that we need agree with him when he speaks, without clearly defining what he means by the word, of an 'influence' of Weininger and Gross on Kafka. But in Kafka's last great novel we may indeed find ideas which had been central to Weininger and Gross. This rapprochement of 'Parsifalian' antifeminism and feminist matriarchy is not as paradoxical as it appears. Fear of women and adulation of the feminine have the same root; the crisis of masculine identity.

Arriving in the village, K. is hailed as a liberator by the women who are subject to the (patriarchal?) law of the castle. 'How lucky for us that you came!' says Olga, and Pepi describes him as 'a hero, a liberator of girls', while Frieda, from the first, gives herself to him and finds the courage to defy Klamm, the powerful chief secretary of the castle who regulates the erotic life of the village. And K. himself seems to accept this role of lover and liberator: 'You ought to leave Klamm and be my mistress,' he tells Frieda in chapter 3. But at the last, 'captivated by all the women and girls of the village, but unable to form any full and free union, K. bungles the castle as Ulysses would have bungled his return if his "sentimental education", one of the aims of his ten years of trial, had been as lamentable a failure.'[75]

These women, subject to the law of the castle to the point of humiliation, nevertheless show an instinctive intelligence and connivance with the Gentlemen of official rule who give them an ascendancy over the men of the village, which is ruled by a sort of matriarchy. But

> this superiority, before which all men must bow, gains the women neither happiness nor freedom; they exercise it collectively, by the force of their sex rather than through their personal worth, so that at bottom they seek only to be delivered from it. Hence the comically reciprocal hope of salvation: K. wants to be saved by the women, but they look to him as a liberator.[76]

The disappointed women whom K. has loved and left fall back under the power of the castle, and turn out to be as much its accomplices as its victims. The love of Frieda, Olga, Amalia and Pepi does not carry K. on any further, but on the contrary seems to hold him back and turn him away from his goal.

However, the solitary man seems just as much condemned to failure, unable to give a direction to his life. Law of the father or law of the mother? Both seem lost and reduced to caricatures: Klamm, the unworthy bureaucrat, on the one side; Gisa, the sadistic schoolmistres who tyrannizes over Schwarzer, on the other. Though seemingly reduced to the status of inferiors, the women in *The Trial* and *The Castle* turn out to be closely connected with the sources of power: they know all the ins and outs of the Tribunal and find their way into the highest spheres of the Castle. The village is certainly under the governance of patriarchy, but the Gentlemen who exercise the power seem deep down to be subject to a matriarchy which is all the more sovereign for the way it remains mysterious.[77] As if the two Ottos, Weininger and Gross, were at long last standing back to back.

8

Electra, Antigone and Ariadne

I

Mycenae, Knossos, Vienna

The historicism of the Ringstrasse and the Viennese modernism of the 1900s have one thing in common: their constant reference to Antiquity and archaeology. Marthe Robert's observation on the education of Sigmund Freud applies to most of the Viennese intellectuals of his generation and the one which followed:

> Latin and Greek took up a third of the classes in the lower forms, but from the fourth form onwards half the time was devoted to them, while German had only a subordinate position . . . Although it assumes unusual proportions in Freud, the cult of Antiquity was by no means an exceptional phenomenon in his time: it was very widespread among the Germans, as among the assimilated Jews who found in it one of the few pieces of neutral ground on which to meet their hosts.[1]

All the Viennese modernists were soaked in Latin, Greek and ancient history. In his tribute 'An einen alten Lehrer' ('To an Old Teacher'), Karl Kraus declares: 'Latin and German: you taught me them. / If I owe German to you, it is because I studied Latin. / What German became to me, when I / Learned to read your beloved Ovid!'[2]

The personality of Theodor Gomperz (1832–1912), author of the illustrious textbook *Griechische Denker* (1896–1906), dominated Viennese university life; his son Heinrich Gomperz (1873–1942), author of *Grundlegung der neusokratischen Philosophie* ('Foundations of Neo-Socratic Philosophy', 1897), had a direct influence on Hugo von Hofmannsthal and the writers of 'Young Vienna'.[3] In 1897, Rudolf Lothar described them as 'neo-Socratics', disciples of Heinrich Gomperz, devotees of irony and of a philosophy which interpreted the world and life as a game.[4] Hofmannsthal gave solemn expression to the profound affinity between Viennese modernity and classical antiquity: 'If we consider Wieland's concept of Antiquity alongside that of Nietzsche or Jacob Burckhardt, we realize that we, more even than other nations, are approaching Antiquity as a magic mirror in which we expect to glimpse our own faces in a strange and purified guise.'[5]

Now Viennese modernism is marked by a change of paradigm. While the return to Antiquity by the liberal generation of the 1850s and 1860s looked to classical Greece and Rome, as well as to the Renaissance, as symbolizing a view of the world based on reason, with trust in Progress and grounded in the harmonious enlightenment of the human race, the Young Vienna generation turned rather to the primitive and archaic periods with which it felt more in sympathy. Here I shall concentrate on one particular aspect of this change of approach: the fascination with the Creto-Mycenaean civilization as a source of legends, mythologies and forms.

Freud, Schliemann, Evans

From the 1870s onwards the pre-Hellenic civilizations, which until then had for the most part remained mysterious, known essentially through the Homeric writings, began to yield their secrets. Heinrich Schliemann was excavating in 1868 in Ithaca, from 1870 onwards at Troy (Hissarlik), and at Mycenae in 1874. It was in 1876 that he discovered the famous Mycenaean tombs and their treasures. Schliemann intended to pursue his investigations in Crete, at Knossos, but he died in 1890. The great Cretan discoveries are due to Sir Arthur Evans, mostly between 1900 and 1905. But it was Schliemann's digs which represented for his contemporaries the most exciting of archaeological adventures.[6] We may recall Wilibald Schmidt, the teacher of classical literature in Fontane's novel *Frau Jenny Treibel*, following Schliemann's campaigns with as much passion as if they were the victories of a Napoleon.

Like Fontane's Wilibald Schmidt, Sigmund Freud was closely interested in the progress of archaeology in Troy, Mycenae and Crete. In May 1899 he wrote to Fliess: 'I have bought myself Schliemann's *Ilios* and enjoyed the account of his childhood. The man found happiness in finding Priam's treasure, because happiness comes only from fulfilment of a childhood wish.'[7] In December of the same year he announced in the following terms his success in analysing a patient: 'Buried deep beneath all his fantasies we found a scene from his primal period ... It is as if Schliemann had dug up another Troy which had hitherto been believed to be mythical.'[8] And in August 1901, he wrote again to Fliess.

> Have you read that the English excavated an old palace in Crete (Knossos) which they declare to be the real labyrinth of Minos? Zeus seems originally to have been a bull. Our old god, too, is said to have been worshipped as a bull prior to the sublimation imposed by the Persians. This is cause for all sorts of thoughts too premature to write down.[9]

In his 1931 essay on female sexuality, Freud was to give the key to his fascination with Creto-Mycenaean archaeology:

We have, after all, long given up any expectation of a neat parallelism between male and female sexual development. Our insight into this early, pre-Oedipus phase in girls comes to us as a surprise, like the discovery, in another field, of the Minoan-Mycenaean civilization behind the civilization of Greece. Everything in the sphere of this first attachment to the mother seemed to me so difficult to grasp in analysis – so grey with age and shadowy and almost impossible to revivify – that it was as if it had succumbed to an especially inexorable repression.[10]

The discovery of the 'becoming-woman' phase preceding the Oedipus complex put Freud in the same situation *vis-à-vis* his researches as the archaeologists of the Greek world faced with the enigma of Linear B (finally to be deciphered by Michael Ventris in 1953); how could psychoanalysts have continued for so long to ignore the importance and lastingness of the little girl's attachment to her mother?[11]

A footnote in Freud's last major work, *Moses and Monotheism*, returns to the theme of Cretan matriarchy:

Evans assumes that the final destruction of the palace of Minos at Knossos too was the consequence of an earthquake. In Crete at that period (as probably in the Aegean world in general) the great mother-goddess was worshipped. The realization that she was not able to protect her house against the assaults of a stronger power may have contributed to her having to give place to a male deity, and, if so, the volcano god had the first claim to take her place. After all, Zeus always remains the 'earth-shaker'. There is little doubt that it was during these obscure ages that the mother-goddesses were replaced by male gods (who may originally perhaps have been sons). The destiny of Pallas Athene, who was no doubt the local form of the mother-goddess, is particularly impressive. She was reduced to being a daughter by the religious revolution, she was robbed of her own mother and, by having virginity imposed on her, was permanently excluded from motherhood.[12]

Theseus versus the Minotaur – from Nietzsche to Klimt

The justification for this metaphor identifying the Creto-Mycenaean element with a 'matriarchal' phase, apparently to the exclusion of male power, is to be found in Bachofen, who devoted a whole chapter of his book on matriarchy to the Cretan world. The interpretation can be traced back as far as Nietzsche: a fragment from 1869–70 proposes the antithesis 'Platonic State – Cretan State, as the State of music'.[13] The philosopher who, in his last moments of semi-lucidity, signed some of his letters simply 'Dionysos', had chosen for his mystic companion Ariadne, one of the daughters of Minos, king of Crete. Abandoned on Naxos by the vanquisher of the Minotaur and then (according to the most optimistic version of the myth) rescued by Dionysos, she could be presumed to have become the wife of the god of music and intoxication, and the priestess of his temple.

These references to Bachofen, Freud and Nietzsche allow us to make more sense of the mythological scenes chosen by Gustav Klimt for the poster of the first exhibition of the 'Secession' in 1898.[14] Carl Schorske, in his comments on this poster, emphasizes Klimt's aggressively insistent exaltation of youth, and his desire for liberation.[15] Theseus killed the Minotaur to free the children of Athens: Schorske reminds us that a psychoanalytic interpretation allows us to identify the bull as a father image.[16] Thus he understands Klimt's graphics as a rallying call to the 'Oedipal rebellion', the rising of the young against the old. We might add that the slaying of the bull 'totem' by Theseus would, if interpreted along the lines of Freud's *Totem and Taboo*, constitute a civilizing act. This scene of the conflict with the Minotaur expresses much more than the old conflict of the ancients and the moderns: it illustrates – in direct line with Nietzsche's *Thoughts Out of Season* – the conviction that the false culture of the fathers (that of the *Gründerzeit* and its Viennese variant, the Ringstrasse) was merely an avatar of barbarism, while the renewal of the Secession was bringing humanity back to true civilization.

But this upper part of Klimt's poster, the combat of Theseus and the Minotaur, cannot be isolated from the whole; it must be considered in relation to the vertical element which shows a warlike, helmeted Athene, armed with a lance and a shield bearing an archaic head of Medusa. Let us bear in mind that Athene was heir to a Mycenaean divinity who protected the dwelling of the kings: the famous lion gate at Mycenae is in the shape of a monumental Cretan altar on which rest the hind paws of two lionesses, for Athene was also the lady of the wild beasts.[17] She can be identified with the Potnia of Knossos, mistress of the labyrinth, a chthonic deity associated with trees (the olive, symbol of fertility), serpents (connected with her other title, Hygieia, goddess of health) and birds (the owl); this Athene-Potnia was warlike, and either her breastplate or her shield bore the aegis, the skin of the Gorgon she had killed and flayed during the battle against the Giants. Aeschylus speaks of her as a bold leader of battles: she smote the giants Pallas and Enceladus and invented the war-dance (*komos*). She was the protectress of heroes: Diomedes, Achilles, Ulysses, Telemachus, Herakles, Perseus – and, of course, Theseus.

It was only after a rather long evolution that Athene became, in the classical age, the goddess of reason and harmony. Originally she was very close to Medusa. The Gorgon's head which Athene, in the earliest sources, uses to frighten her enemies may originally have been her own. Only later, when her outward appearance and her character underwent the Hellenic metamorphosis which turned her into an Olympian deity, did her terrifying Gorgon aspect become dissociated from her and was opposed to her as an antagonistic principle doomed to defeat.[18]

The presence of Pallas Athene on Klimt's poster is thus doubly justified: she is on her own ground, mistress of the labyrinth, and she is protecting the hero. But her deadly gaze and the hideous Gorgon face which she bears on her aegis connect her with the terrible and all-powerful Cretan mother goddess. On the one side, then, we have Theseus' fight with the Minotaur: the Oedipal scene, presenting the law of the father and the affirmation of the manly values of renewal; on the other side, the figure – more dominant than protective – of the archaic Athene, attending on the triumph of the youthful hero so as to place him under the law of the mother.

Under the eye of the war goddess, Theseus no longer appears as a triumphant liberator, but as a vulnerable, threatened man, of the race described in the second of Nietzsche's *Thoughts Out of Season*:

> the men and the times that serve life in this way, by judging and annihilating the past, are always dangerous to themselves and others . . . It is an attempt to gain a past *a posteriori* from which we might spring, as against that from which we do spring; always a dangerous attempt, as it is difficult to find a limit to the denial of the past, and the second natures are generally weaker than the first.[19]

Klimt's metaphor for modernity is thus paradoxical: it is the threatened son who kills the father who is stronger than he.[20] The gaze of Pallas Athene seems to illustrate Walter Benjamin's words: 'The face of modernity itself smites us with an immemorial gaze. As the gaze of Medusa was to the Greeks.'[21]

'To decapitate = to castrate', wrote Freud in his essay on 'Medusa's Head': 'The terror of Medusa is thus a terror of castration that is linked to the sight of something. Numerous analyses have made us familiar with the occasion for this: it occurs when a boy, who has hitherto been unwilling to believe the threat of castration, catches sight of the female genitals.'[22] One need only glance through the handsome gallery of heads of the Medusa in the catalogue of the exhibition *Zauber der Medusa*[23] to realize the incomparable originality of Gustav Klimt amidst the 'mannerism' of the 1900s. He chooses the archaic visage of the Gorgon, who, associated with Pallas Athene, the fair and terrible, incarnates more than the deadly attraction of the female, more than a 'bizarre androgyne [who] has kept all the attractions of a manly soul in a charming woman's body' (Baudelaire describing the 'armed Pallas sprung from the head of Zeus'):[24] incarnates, in fact, the matriarchal principle of the law of the mother in its challenge to the law of the father, the idea of a feminization of culture in modernity and the deconstruction of masculine values.

This 'Creto-Mycenaean Athene' reappears, full face, with the archaic Gorgon's head on her breastplate, in the 1898 picture entitled 'Pallas Athene';[25] and again, as the serpent goddess Hygieia, in the 'Medicine' fresco intended for the University of Vienna, which, as Werner Hofmann has noted, celebrates the triumph of 'Dionysian' art rather than that of health.[26] In November 1898 the art critic Ludwig Hevesi wrote of 'Pallas Athene':

> The breastplate, the scaly aegis of Athena, aroused the liveliest indignation. A thousand malevolent eyes saw at once that the face of Medusa which serves as the fibula or the aegis, that scaly covering of myth, was the same as had already drawn the sarcasms of all Vienna on to the Secession poster of the previous spring. This 'facies', as it had often been called, with its protruding tongue, was indeed a faithful imitation of the most ancient Medusa heads, rendered with very genuine archaism; but the good citizens of our nineteen urban districts took it for a puerile product of the delirious imaginings of the Secessionists, intended merely to cause a sensation. . . . Every scale of the aegis has different shades of colour. The tones of blue and violet harmonize in the subtlest way, they suggest

the steely blue (*kuanos*) of the breastplate of a Homeric hero. And in the midst there is the gleam of gold, true gold with no alloy of copper, the yellow Mycenaean gold of the Atrides.[27]

A comparison of this Klimt work with the statue of Pallas Athene made by Karl Kundmann to crown the fountain designed by Theophil Hansen for the approach to the new Vienna Parliament[28] shows the profound difference between the interest which the Secession and Young Vienna took in ancient Greece and the neo-classical rhetoric of the creators of the Ringstrasse. Kundmann's statue (which was not erected in its present position until 1902, nearly twenty years after the Reichsrat building was finished) follows the Hellenistic stylistic tradition. It symbolizes the wisdom which is to guard and guide the *polis*. A symbol turned to mockery by the paralysis of the parliamentary system in Cisleithania: faced with open conflict between nations and the obstructiveness of political factions, the Emperor Franz Josef was resigned to periodically suspending the activities of the Reichsrat!

II

Hofmannsthal's Elektra

When he embarked on *Elektra*, Hugo von Hofmannsthal was determined to break with the tradition of humanizing antiquity which went back to Goethe: 'I had in mind a style which would be at the other end of the spectrum from *Iphigenia*, and of which it could never be said [what Goethe had said] that "this Hellenizing piece seemed to me, on a second reading, infernally human." '[29] Hofmannsthal stood against Winckelmann and Goethe and with Nietzsche, Erwin Rohde, Jacob Burckhardt on the one side, and Josef Breuer and Sigmund Freud on the other.[30] In his stage directions, Hofmannsthal tells producers to avoid any kind of archaeological accuracy, 'these pseudo-antique banalities which are more likely to bore than to impress an audience'.[31] The Mycenaean setting he saw rather as 'oriental'. The palace of the Atrides had to give the audience 'that impression which makes the great houses of the Orient so strange and mysterious'.[32] He wanted windows 'given, by the painter's skill, that air of dissimulation and watchfulness proper to the Orient',[33] and costumes which 'should conjure up the atmosphere of oriental tales'.[34]

This merging of the 'Mycenaean' into the 'oriental' brings into view, close beneath the Greek surface, a concept inherited from the 'oriental renaissance'[35] of the early Romantics and the Basle circle. According to this interpretation, classical Hellenism had been essentially an ordering of 'oriental chaos': 'Their "culture" was for a long time a chaos of foreign forms and ideas – Semitic, Babylonian, Lydian and Egyptian – their religion a battle of all the gods of the East . . . The Greeks gradually learned to organize the chaos,'[36] wrote Nietzsche (influenced by Rohde and Bachofen) at the end of the second of his *Thoughts Out Of Season*.

Nietzsche's predilection for Dionysian Greece, which he found more suggestive than classical Athens, had always been perceptible in Hofmannsthal.[37] Thus he wrote in his 1892 essay on Swinburne:

> not just Hellenism when it achieved the controlled clarity and grace of the dance . . . but the old, Orphic Greece, shadowed by passion. The passions ran to and fro like Maenads, barefoot, their hair blowing in the wind; life bore the mask of Medusa, with enigmatic, disturbing eyes; as in the mourning for Adonis, the worship of Cybele, the intensest quiverings of life mingled with those of death; and the god Dionysos walked, laughing and deadly, through a frightening world teeming with life.[38]

This decorative and mannerist version of Nietzscheanism reached its more accomplished expression in Hofmannsthal in his libretto for *Ariadne auf Naxos*.

In *Elektra*, Hofmannsthal immerses us in a more sombre and tragic atmosphere. His leaning towards orientalism brings him back to Hölderlin,[39] from whom he took the epigraph for his other great adaptation of Greek tragedy, 'Oedipus and the Sphinx'.[40] On 28 September 1803, Hölderlin wrote to his publisher, Friedrich Wilmans: 'I hope to give my public . . . a more vivid idea than usual of Greek art by stressing the oriental character which it always denied.'[41] Hölderlin's view is explained by his letter to Böhlendorff of 4 December 1801:

> I believe that the clarity of the exposition was originally as natural to us as the fire of heaven to the Greeks. For this very reason, it must be easier to surpass them through flights of passion . . . than in their Homeric presence of mind and their gift for exposition. This seems a paradox. But I repeat . . . as civilization advances, the purely national element will always be the lesser advantage. That is why the Greeks are less masters of the sacredness of emotion, because it was native to them, while from Homer onwards they excelled in exposition, for that extraordinary man had enough soul to steal, for the good of his Apollonian kingdom, the Junonian sobriety of the West, and also to appropriate the foreign element. With us the converse is true.[42]

In translating Sophocles, Hölderlin[43] – like Hofmannsthal a century later – did his best to bring out the principle which remained hidden in the original. The translation must rekindle the 'fire of heaven' that had been snuffed out by 'Junonian sobriety'. That is why both Hölderlin, in his translation of *Antigone*, and Hofmannsthal in *Elektra* lay particular stress on motifs of fury, madness, savagery and intoxication. Hofmannsthal in so doing draws on the psychiatric and psychoanalytical literature and turns Elektra into a great 'hysteric'.

Thus the road leading away from convention follows the reverse direction to the Greek development. In Hölderlin and Hofmannsthal, modernism has come to terms with the archaic. Now, what Hölderlin called 'the patriotic inversion of all modes of representation',[44] by which he probably meant a cultural revolution of ethics, aesthetics and politics, finds spontaneous allegorical expression in a female figure. Antigone is 'antitheos', meaning that she acts like one who, 'in the purposes of God himself, seems to be acting against God, and, while obeying no law, acknowledges the spirit of the Most High'.[45] Nor does the spirit of modernity obey any law; and it seems unwilling to accept any other allegory than that of active femininity. The moderns, from Hölderlin to Hofmannsthal, were imitating a Greece which had perhaps never existed and which was thus strictly inimitable. The modernists' imitation was in fact pure originality. It followed the model of self-formation, a kind of creativity traditionally attributed to genius,[46] and which from then on always wore a woman's face.

From Hölderlin's Antigone to Elektra, or from the modern to the postmodern

There is, however, one fundamental difference between Hölderlin's *Antigonä* and Hofmannsthal's *Elektra*. In Hölderlin, the woman bearing the 'fire from heaven' clashes with a powerful male figure: Creon, the representative of the ancient and now unendurable law. Antigone, crushed by him, becomes a martyr to a democratic ideal of insurrection. But Hofmannsthal, when he penetrates through to the deepest levels and rediscovers, beneath Sophocles, the previous, 'oriental' stage of Hellenic culture, brings us back to the archaic matriarchy described by Bachofen. As Maximilian Harden observed after the play's premiere in Berlin in 1903, the male roles are altogether secondary, and all the author's attention is concentrated on the female characters. Hofmannsthal agreed: 'As regards my *Elektra* he [Harden] said the only relevant thing I have ever read on the subject: that is, that it would be a better play and a purer work of art if Orestes had been kept out of it altogether.'[47]

The force opposed to Elektra is not the male world of law, but the terrifying *Magna mater*, Clytemnestra. The invisible ghost of Agamemnon, murdered by this sanguinary mother, obsesses conscience and memory. But it is the mother who rules. And that rule knows no law, but follows the course of a blind and chaotic violence. As Bachofen said (when he was giving voice to his reason and not his heart, as Ernst Bloch would have put it), archaic matriarchy is no more than anarchy and barbarism.

Quite recently Christa Wolf, in *Kassandra* (1983) and in her essay *Voraussetzungen einer Erzählung: Kassandra. Frankfurter Poetik-Vorlesungen* ('Proem to a Story: Cassandra. Frankfurt Lectures on Poetry'), has given an example of a feminist interpretation of Creto-Mycenaean mythology along the lines of Bachofen. But Wolf seems far removed from 1900s modernism: she feels herself closer to the 'modernity' of 1800 (her *Kein Ort, nirgends* – 'No Place, Nowhere' – of 1977 leaves no room for doubt on this point), and drew on it to interpret the contemporary situation in the former German Democratic Republic. It will come as no surprise, therefore, that Wolf's insights follow the line of Hölderlin's *Antigonä* rather than Hofmannsthal's *Elektra*.

Unlike Carl Jung, who postulated an 'Electra complex' to mark the existence of parallel attitudes to parents in both sexes,[48] Freud refused to accept the idea of a female equivalent to the Oedipus complex: 'We have an impression here that what we have said about the Oedipus complex applies with complete strictness to the male child only and that we are right in rejecting the term "Electra complex" which seeks to emphasize the analogy between the attitude of the two sexes.'[49]

While the Oedipus conflict was part of becoming a man and was, to Freud, the very foundation of all human civilization, the relationship between mother and daughter belonged to an archaic universe previous to all culture, which had to be swept away before humanity could know any moral law. Freud acknowledged no 'law of the mother'. The play of *Elektra* probes the fearful mystery of the ambivalent and violent relationship between daughter and mother; but if it is true (as Hofmannsthal himself was to affirm in 1916, perhaps trying to pour a little water on the 'fire from heaven' which his 1903 *Elektra* had kindled)[50] that Elektra 'through her hatred, is working for the return of harmony in the world',[51] her reference to a lost law puts her on the father's side: 'She is the father (he is not, save for her); she is the mother (more than the mother herself is): she is the whole house.'[52]

The abdication of men, feminism, and Rosa Mayreder

The first modernism, that of Hölderlin, set a woman, Antigone, against a corrupt, but still all-powerful male world. The Viennese (post)modernism of 1900, as represented by Hofmannsthal, finds no masculine role which is still worthy or capable of standing against Electra. The authoritarian world of Creon still had a certain coherence. In the world of Aegisthus, in the ruined palace of Agamemnon, Electra alone – for the feeble Orestes is of small help to her – must rebuild 'the whole house': masculine values have been swept away, but the utopia of matriarchy has been irreversibly discredited by the barbarity of Clytemnestra. The law of the father is abolished, and men seem incapable of resuming responsibility for the world order for which they were once chiefly answerable.

In her 1905 essay *Zur Kritik der Weiblichkeit* ('Critique of Femininity'), the Viennese feminist Rosa Mayreder traced the consequences of the profound crisis of masculine identity within modernism. She went so far as to suggest that contemporary feminism could no longer be explained or justified simply as a movement for the emancipation of women struggling against male abuses of power, but was the result of changes in men themselves.[53] Our culture, she wrote, has become feminized. The more men have access to culture and refinement, the more their way of life resembles that of women. Modern warfare leaves no place for the traditional 'warrior virtues': as a disciplined and technical butchery, it savours of supreme passivity. (Here Mayreder is thinking of modern war as described in Zola's *La Débâcle*.)[54] The ostentatious virility which was still exhibited in certain all-male gatherings, such as the student clubs in the university, now seemed merely odious and ridiculous. 'Offices, counters, ticket-booths, workshops, are so many coffins for virility. For virility, the life of great cities is one vast tomb.'[55]

Our Western civilization, Mayreder repeats, is suffering because archaic myths of virility linger on in it. While other cultures place the priest or scholar at the top of their scale of values, modern European man resents his intellectualization as a decline or nervous illness.[56] In a word, Mayreder concludes, men and women in the modern world are separated only by trifling details.[57] But men are weakened by one serious handicap: they remain prisoners of the traditional dualism of body and mind, incapable of harmonizing their intellectual drives with their sexual role – which makes them see women as a threat, or an object to be conquered.[58]

Mayreder's studies lead to a rather paradoxical view of the feminist movement: it is not just a movement of conquest, for men have abandoned all their citadels; nor essentially one of revolt, for the modern world is suffering more from the vacuum left by the collapse of male values than from their authority. 'Since men have turned into women,' cried Mayreder, 'women have no choice but to occupy the ground they have abandoned.'[59] On the other hand, women had no interest in further weakening men, now that they had become so unsure of themselves; on the contrary, they should help them to regain an equilibrium which would allow relations between the sexes to become creative once more. Modern woman faced the immense task of renewing the dialogue between men and women, and crossing the gulf created by a now exhausted patriarchal tradition.[60] The masculine identity crisis was not a consequence of feminism putting men on the defensive,[61] but the opposite: feminism was born because women had to reconstruct a whole civilization on the ruins deserted by men.

This brought Mayreder into conflict with Lou Andreas-Salomé (the two women had met in Vienna in the winter of 1896–7).[62] According to the latter, woman can be seen as a self-sufficient, self-enclosed, sovereign being, who looks down on man 'like an old, blue-blooded aristocracy firmly settled in its lands and its family seat'.[63] Mayreder said that this was 'the extreme of frigid and egoistic feminism borne up by the insatiable lust for domination'.[64] But, paradoxically, Andreas-Salomé's theories on the rooted femininity of life and nature, more vegetative than inclined to abstraction, lead back to men's misogynistic view of women. In support of Mayreder here we may quote this passage from Andreas-Salomé's journal kept during her year at the school of Freud, and inspired by a discussion of Otto Weininger's ideas: '[Men] would be the weaker sex as seen from the position of woman, who is narcissistic and cultureless, woman who perhaps never attains the final insights of the mind but instead finds her being in the intuitive knowledge of life and mind. Woman – the fortunate animal.'[65]

Deep down, Mayreder adds, this type of narcissistic woman is well suited to modern man, torn between the body and the mind, for she, too, is torn in her way. She suffers from a contradiction between her kind of eroticism, dominated by submission and passivity, and her need to affirm her superiority.[66] She submits in order to dominate. Mayreder accused Andreas-Salomé of practising what Joan Rivière, in 1929, was to call 'the masquerade of womanhood': feminine qualities worn as a mask to hide a profound masculinity capable of intimidating any lover.[67] This was a common complaint of Andreas-Salomé's detractors, including even her severe biographer, Rudolph Binion.[68] Andreas-Salomé's masochist tendencies are shown, for example, in the novella

'Debauchery', published as a sequel to *Fenitschka* in 1898. The heroine, an artist who lives as an 'emancipated' woman, dreams of being trampled on, as in an engraving by Max Klinger, 'Time Destroying Glory', in which a young man in armour is slaying a young woman lying at his feet.[69]

To escape this war footing between the sexes, which tinges male eroticism with sadism and female eroticism with masochism, Mayreder called for a 'genius of eroticism' which would lead each sex to a better intuitive understanding of the other.[70] This notion of erotic genius brings us back to the utopia of the androgyne. At the beginning of her essay 'Critique of Femininity', Mayreder had attempted to do justice to Weininger. She did not attack him with the outrage and repulsion which at the time was the ordinary reaction of intellectual feminists to *Sex and Character*.[71] On the contrary, she stressed that the first part of the book, which revealed the bisexuality of every individual reduced to the equation xM + yF, had opened up promising avenues which were unfortunately not explored in the second part of *Sex and Character*. She pleaded for a readiness for cultural transformation of a Nietzschean kind, the coming of a new human race of 'intermediary forms' which would cast off the 'tyranny of norms' and leave behind the archaic opposition of male and female.[72]

It will be no surprise to us to find that Lou Andreas-Salomé more or less annexes the mythic figure of the androgyne to the female. She sees it as incarnate only in the mother ('The firmest union of masculinity and femininity is comprised by motherliness, where woman conceives and bears and also generates, protects and governs the offspring'),[73] in the poetic genius (Rilke),[74] and in the philosophical genius (Nietzsche)[75] – this last being, according to Andreas-Salomé's profound conviction, a feminized masculine type. But for Mayreder, the androgyne of modernity was neither predominantly male nor predominantly female, but a genuine *synthesis*,[76] and so uniquely able to renew communication between the sexes.

III

Nietzsche, Ariadne and Lou Andreas-Salomé

'*Vita femina*' is the title of Fragment 339 of the *Joyful Wisdom*, which Nietzsche ended with these words: 'Yes, *life is a woman!*'[77] In *Nietzsche Against Wagner* he repeated, 'musica is a woman'.[78] The identification of the Dionysian element as *feminine* is one of the constants of Nietzsche's theories and imaginings.[79] Lou Andreas-Salomé seemed predestined to have an irresistible attraction for him, since she came to him already wearing the mask of the 'genius of life', the supreme manifestation of womanhood in his eyes. 'Perhaps you too feel that as both "thinker" and "poet" I must have had a certain foreboding of L.?'[80] was Nietzsche's reply, on 25 July 1882 to Peter Gast, who had written, 'She [Lou] will draw many things forth from you.' Lou had haunted Nietzsche's imagination since long before he met her . . .

The European intellectuals who were so easily conquered by Lou Andreas-

Salomé were affected by her as if by a 'collective hallucination'.[81] Its importance can be measured if we remember that the themes of decadence and male identity crisis were expressed, for Nietzsche and his contemporaries, as a diagnosis: inability to cope with life. This is the *taedium vitae* described by Paul Bourget in his 'Essays on Contemporary Psychology': 'How is it that this "delicate monster" [Baudelaire's "ennui"] has never yawned so loudly as in the literature of our century, in which so many conditions of life have come to perfection, unless it is because that very perfection, which had so complicated our souls, has made us incapable of happiness?'[82]

Woman, 'the fortunate animal' as Andreas-Salomé called her, appeared before the philosopher bearing her poem 'Lebensgebet' ('Prayer of Life'), which she had written in Zurich shortly after leaving Russia, and in which Nietzsche thought he saw 'A commentary upon the *Joyful Wisdom* ... a sort of *basso continuo*':[83]

> I love thee, enigmatic life –
> Whether thou makest me exult or weep,
> Bring me happiness or pain,
> I love thee in all thy cruelty.[84]

One chapter in Guy de Pourtalès's essay 'Nietzsche in Italy' was called 'Mademoiselle Lou at Naxos'.[85] We should beware of identifying Ariadne too hastily with Lou: it would be as arbitrary as the more commonly accepted idea that Cosima Wagner was the key to the character of Ariadne.[86] 'Who knows, but I, who Ariadne is!' cries Nietzsche in *Ecce Homo*.[87] It may be suggested that Ariadne was, in Nietzsche's personal mythology, what Lou had been in his actual life: an incarnation of the greatest potential of human life under the law of Dionysos.

'Abandoned by the hero, I dream of the Superman', says Ariadne in a fragment from summer 1883.[88] Deserted on Naxos by Theseus, Ariadne finds in her new sufferings the resources for the ultimate transcendence which will lead to her fulfilment by Dionysos. She is freed from that love, that impulse of pity which once impelled her to help Theseus escape from the labyrinth. She is no longer a maiden in love, but a solitary. Her sufferings are equal to those of the philosopher in *Zarathustra*: 'such things have never been written, never been felt, never been *suffered*: only a God, only Dionysos suffers in this way. The reply to such a dithyramb on the sun's solitude in light would be Ariadne.'[89]

Dionysos, or the ordeal of the labyrinth

Left abandoned on Naxos, Ariadne knows an anguish equal to that of the Enchanter, the 'Penitent in spirit' encountered by Zarathustra, 'the poet and magician who at last turneth his spirit against himself, the transformed one who freezeth to death by his bad science and conscience'.[90] Karl Reinhardt, in his 1935 study on the lament of Ariadne, pointed out that in this chapter of

Thus Spake Zarathustra, the 'Penitent in spirit', one of the faces of nihilism, makes the same lamentation as Ariadne in the *Dithyrambs of Dionysos*.[91] The words are indeed the same,[92] but the conclusion is very different in the two texts. In *Zarathustra*, the 'Penitent in spirit' is given a beating and dismissed as a jester and forger by Zarathustra. In the dithyramb, Ariadne sees Dionysos arise before her, saying, 'Ariadne, be wise':

> Little ears thou hast, my ears:
> Put in them these wise words!
> Must one not first hate himself, who would love himself?
> I am thy labyrinth.[93]

These little ears are not listening for a Master, and certainly they do not want to hear precepts of Christian morality, such as enter into the big ears of an ass. Little ears receive only what they want to hear – what they must hear.[94] It is now Dionysos who is the labyrinth of Ariadne. The solitary girl of Naxos is lost in the labyrinth of grief, as the 'Penitent in spirit' was lost in the labyrinth of the mind. But from this adventure Ariadne emerges victorious, regenerated by the experience of active nihilism and guided towards the Dionysian life; whereas the Penitent remained locked in his own passive nihilism, full of resentment and the desire for death.[95]

Philosophy and the Dionysian life are a 'labyrinth' experience. The strong man (*Der Starke*) 'plunges into a labyrinth, he multiplies a thousandfold the dangers which life itself already brings with it; not the least of which is that no one can see how and where he loses his way, becomes isolated, and is torn to pieces by some minotaur of conscience.'[96]

From this mortally dangerous expedition, only human beings as strong as Ariadne can escape unharmed (but even they may succumb, as in the other version of the myth retained by Racine: 'Ariadne, my sister, wounded with what love / Didst thou die on the shore where thou wast left'):

> 'Under certain circumstances I love mankind' (and [Dionysos] referred thereby to Ariadne, who was present). 'In my opinion man is an agreeable, brave, inventive animal, that has not his equal upon earth, he makes his way through all labyrinths. I like man, and often think how I can still further advance him, and make him stronger, more evil, and more profound . . . also more beautiful.[97]

The womanhood of Ariadne seems better armed than the hero for the ordeal of the labyrinth – that is, of life. But she cannot find her way until she has broken the bonds of love which held her to Theseus. It seems that solitude – with all the sacrifices it entails – is a necessary prelude to the meeting with Dionysos. Maybe even human love between a man and a woman is finally one of those 'Christian' virtues which must be swept away by the Dionysian transmutation of values. As Gilles Deleuze has written, 'so long as Ariadne loves Theseus, and is loved by him, her womanhood remains imprisoned, bound by the thread. But when the Dionysios-Bull approaches, she learns the true affirmation, the true lightness.'[98] Man – the human male – must, it seems, be kept away from the 'superhuman' couple.

Hofmannsthal, in his treatment of the Ariadne-on-Naxos motif, took as much care to distance himself from Ringstrasse aesthetics as Klimt did with his archaic portrayals of Athene. One of the most famous paintings by Hans Makart, now in the Belvedere gallery in Vienna, is called 'The Triumph of Ariadne' (1873–4). In this painting, Ariadne, splendidly naked, towers over a group of intoxicated fauns and nymphs, the incarnation of the myth of Viennese hedonism, like the heroine of a mythological light opera in the style of Offenbach or Johann Strauss. Hofmannsthal, on the other hand, sees in Ariadne the incarnation of ethereal womanhood, halfway between the *femme fatale* and the frail woman of 1900s aesthetics. His Bacchus is no rampant Silenus, but a handsome, shy adolescent – out of which Richard Strauss, who was closer at heart to Offenbach than to the spirit of Viennese modernism, was to make a *Heldentenor* verging on the ridiculous.

Did Nietzsche think he had found his Ariadne in Lou Andreas-Salomé? His meeting with Lou in 1882[99] can be seen as an *Urszene*, a 'primal scene' of the meeting between the *femme fatale* and her male victim, which happened again and again all through our period. If the woman is *fatale* it is because the alliance of beauty with cruelty belongs to the very nature of *vita femina*, the Dionysian life. And if man is finally the victim, it is because his masculinity deserves no better than to be destroyed and 'transcended'.

Nietzsche-Dionysos wanted to make Ariadne into his disciple. This is his account of the episode:

> Chatting on in this way, I gave myself up wholly to my teaching, for I was happy to have someone who would go on listening to me. But at that very moment, Ariadne lost patience – the episode happened during my first sojourn on Naxos – and said, 'But Sir! You speak German like a pig!' 'Take back that "pig", my goddess! You underestimate the difficulty of saying elevated things in German!' 'Elevated!' cried Ariadne, horrified, 'but it was pure positivism! Elephantine philosophy! A conceptual mishmash, the leavings of a hundred philosophies! Whatever did you mean by it?' And so saying, she fidgeted with her famous thread, which had once guided Theseus through the labyrinth. Thus it was revealed that Ariadne was two thousand years behind in her philosophical development.[100]

The master was scolded by his pupil: the sort of 'Dionysian' thinking towards which Nietzsche was striving could not be taught, lest it petrify into a new dogmatism. Ariadne, two thousand years 'behind', was two thousand years ahead on the journey which took the mind away from the dusty philosophical literature which had piled up since Plato, back to the true thinking at the dawn of Greek philosophy.

This disciple may have had little ears, but her hearing was keen. She unmasked Nietzsche-Dionysos as a parody of the real Dionysos. By behaving like a triumphant seducer (resuming the role of Theseus!), Nietzsche-Dionysos had disappointed her. For the transmutation of values and the attainment of superhumanity were a perpetual quest, never achieved, forever renewed. The task was not to escape the labyrinth, like Theseus, but to become oneself 'labyrinthine'. It was such a man that Ariadne was awaiting: 'A labyrinthine man never seeks truth, but always his Ariadne – whatever he may tell us!'[101]

Ariadne represented something quite different from the classical Egeria, the helping womanhood which offers the saving thread to the male hero and then bows down before him. She was really the beginning of the *femmes fatales* of the 1900s:

> 'Ariadne,' said Dionysos, 'Thou art a labyrinth: Theseus lost himself in thee; there is no longer any thread; what now does it profit him that the Minotaur devoured him not? For what now devours him is worse than the Minotaur.' 'Thou flatterest me,' Ariadne replied, 'but my patience is at an end; with me all heroes must come to their doom; that is the last word of my love for Theseus: I send him to his doom.'[102]

In the famous photograph taken in Jules Bonnet's studio in Lucerne in 1882, in which we see Lou Andreas-Salomé in a carriage drawn by the docile pair, Paul Rée and Friedrich Nietzsche, it is Lou who has the whiphand. She tells in her autobiography how Nietzsche set up this photograph in the smallest detail. In May 1913 she was to note in her journal, written while in the school of Freud, that Nietzsche was a 'sadomasochist unto himself'.[103]

In this sense, Karl Kraus was to be thoroughly 'Nietzschean'. According to one of his aphorisms: 'A man with an artist's imagination can be masochistic with a real woman and sadistic with an unreal one. The latter will be ill-treated so as to strip her of her anti-natural culture, until the female reappears. But when the former is already present, one can only fall on one's knees.'[104] Though not forgetting his whip when he goes among 'modern' women, the man holds out his rods to be beaten when he meets with archaic, untouched femininity, which is so much superior to a now fully decadent maleness.

From the viewpoint of the Nietzschean transformism of Peter Altenberg, who was hailed by Egon Friedell with an *Ecce poeta*[105] which echoes the *Ecce homo*, the future of an improved humanity required the extinction of masculinity. In 1896 he wrote to Ricarda Huch: 'I am indeed an enemy of "man". I believe that the "Saviour in him" will never awake and will always be kept asleep . . . by his solid bourgeois sense of the business of life.'[106] A good many representatives of Viennese modernism bear this stamp of 'antivirilism'. As an aphorism in *Die Fackel* declared, 'I am not *for* women, but *against* men.'[107]

Part III
Masculine – Feminine – Jew

9

A Triangle of the Times

I

The woman and the Jew: Weininger, Schopenhauer, Baudelaire and Groddeck

The challenge to cultural values and images traditionally assigned to the masculine and the feminine, and its connection with individual symptoms of a crisis of sexual identity, has been revealed as one of the great themes of modernity at the turn of the century, particularly in Viennese circles. We have seen how men (or fictional male characters) were seeking a redefinition of their sexual identity: sometimes by a 'masculine protest' against the femininity they discovered in themselves, or against the feminization of modern culture; sometimes by a 'cult of the feminine', linked with criticism and 'decon-struction' of masculine values.

There is a second theme which seems to be closely, perhaps indissolubly, linked with the first: the crisis of Jewish identity at the end of a century of emancipation, at a time when the assimilation which had seemed almost complete was being brutally contested by antisemitism. Between forgetfulness of Judaism, which could go so far as to repress all Jewishness, and a return to Judaism, which could take a religious, political or merely cultural form, individuals traced their own very different paths, which I shall attempt to follow in the next few chapters.

To all appearances it was in Otto Weininger that the close connection between these two themes, the crisis of sexual identity and the crisis of Jewish identity, was most forcibly shown. All Weininger's work is a search for oneness: the oneness of the individual and the *Volk*, the oneness of the perceiving subject and the world-as-object, the oneness of body and soul, the oneness of life with a higher level of being. And the intrusion of evil is represented by Weininger in terms of severance. Contemporary individualism was atomizing society into floating subjectivities; science and technology were cutting human beings off from the macrocosm to which they belonged;

sexuality was turning the flesh into a 'foreign body'. Weininger rejected life lived by the rules of decadence and could only accept an existence which was all transcendence, conversion and rebirth. The forces of evil included anything which was an obstacle to this. In *Sex and Character* they wear the mask of the Eternal Feminine and of the Jew.

In his last fragments and aphorisms Weininger could still write lucidly that 'hatred of women is never anything more than man's imperfectly controlled hatred of his own sexuality.'[1] Similarly, the antisemitism of Weininger – a Jew – crystallized everything he hated about himself, since his Jewishness cast doubt on the Wagnerian, *völkisch* authenticity to which he aspired. From the masochistic violence which he projected on to the objects of his 'scientific' knowledge (his 'bio-characterization' of the woman and the Jew), he drew an intense guilt feeling, which he eased by inveighing against 'Jewish' science – which would have to include his own science – with its tendency to analyse and decompose reality instead of trying to understand and respect it.

The partial identity of the antisemitic and antifeminist elements constitutes the originality of Weininger's writings. But it is not unique in the genre. It is found also in Schopenhauer, or in D. H. Lawrence, with a similar significance.[2] In Schopenhauer, the evil declares itself alongside the desire to live; but there is a possible other reality, beyond this will-to-the-world, one older than original sin: we are at the hinge of two worlds. Human knowledge can place itself at the disposal of the will to live, but it can also open the way of redemption which requires the abolition of that desire – via aesthetic contemplation or the experience of pain, which leads finally to pity for the absurd sufferings of life.

However, it is not easy to reach this 'knowledge of the third kind', and that is the fault of woman: she 'fundamentally is only there to ensure the survival of the race, which is where her usefulness ends'.[3] Woman ensures the continuance of the will to live, obeying an obscure necessity which endlessly restores the life-force. Similarly, according to Schopenhauer, 'Judaism has the fundamental characteristics of realism and optimism which are closely bound together and are, in fact, the necessary conditions of theism.'[4] Realism naively confuses phenomena with things-in-themselves, and so cuts itself off from the intuition of the highest level of Being (Weininger was also to say that the Jew could never attain to the genius of contemplation). Schopenhauer found optimism as distasteful as he did procreation (for Weininger, the Jew and the woman were the two enthusiasts for the hollow idea of progress). Finally, theism postulated a creator to whom mankind must show a servile gratitude: Schopenhauer could not but despise such womanish piety.

In Baudelaire we find an almost identical schema. Woman seems to exist in order to remind man constantly about the identity of life and desire. The poet's 'misogyny' expresses his rejection of the natural conditions of existence, seen as a perpetual fall, as against the spontaneous materialism of woman, who 'does not know how to distinguish soul and body. She is as simplistic as the animals.'[5] The God of the church, author of that Creation ruled by the evil perpetuated by the desire for love, himself appears effeminate: he is the 'most prostituted of beings',[6] says Baudelaire, speaking of 'the femininity of the church as a reason for its omnipotence'.[7] The ideology (also entirely feminine) of progress makes him feel only disgust: 'By progress I understand the progressive diminution of the soul and the progressive domination of matter.'[8] And in *Mon coeur mis à nu* we find this strange sequence of thought: 'From the infamy of printing, a great obstacle to the development of the Beautiful. / A fine conspiracy to organize for the extermination of the Jewish Race. / The Jews, *Librarians* and witnesses of *Redemption*.'[9] Claude Pichois insists in a note: 'There is no implication of antisemitism.'[10] Maybe not; but from Schopenhauer to Baudelaire and Weininger, misogyny and antisemitism develop according to an analogous 'logic'.

All that Schopenhauer, Baudelaire and Weininger most hated, especially in themselves, they projected on to the Jew. The woman and the Jew were two faces of the same temptation, the temptation to 'resign oneself to exile, take root in a shameful soil, connive at downfallen nature, make do with a belittled destiny'.[11] Be it noted that in this perspective the connections which structure the triangle of Masculine, Feminine and Jew are as much the result of chance as of necessity. Thus Georg Groddeck, in his essay 'The Double Sex of the Human Being' (1931), writes of the Jews: 'There is no people on earth which is so manifestly male.' The orientation of the triangle, in which the Masculine can be at the top (Weininger) or at the bottom (Groddeck) – though the Jew is *invariably* at the bottom – depends on the personal equation. Weininger is obsessed with the fantasy of an excess of femininity; Groddeck (not unlike Otto Gross) by an obsessive *lack* of femininity.

What matters is that the Jew is always identified with obstacles – ultimately, obstacles to a vision which tends to deny and look beyond the inadequacies of the human condition. Groddeck interpreted in these terms the symbolism of Jewish circumcision:

> The prepuce is cut away to eliminate all female semblance from the sign of maleness: for the prepuce is female, it is the vagina in which the male glans is buried ... But it is not so for the Jews: if they cut away the prepuce, they thus eliminate the bisexuality of the man, and take from the male its female character. Thus, for the sake of the bisexual divinity, they renounce their innate divine semblance: by circumcision, the Jew becomes mere man. Consider the special character of the Jew: there is no people on earth which is so manifestly male.

By 'male', Groddeck understands nothing heroic, or even positive. He goes on:

> If we take man for what he is, a needy, unfree being, bound a thousand times by the everyday, who is only occasionally capable of anything higher, and then only for a brief exalted instant; a being whose strength resides not in exaltation, but in subjection to the legal – then we must conclude that the Jews have, so far as is possible, repressed the feminine.[12]

Otto Weininger had said the exact opposite: the evil for him was not repression of the feminine, but an excess of it.[13] None the less, Groddeck and Weininger share a rejection of the 'human, all too human' and a demand for the 'superhuman'. According to Roger Lewinter, who has well expounded Groddeck's view while criticizing his implicit anti-Judaism, circumcision does indeed repress all sign of femininity in a man: for the human being it means renouncing a bisexual interplay which would be sacrilegious, a fantasy of rivalry with God. The distance which separates and defines creature and creator must not be crossed: 'Judaism is in fact a kind of humanism: an opting for being-in-this-world from which the potentially superhuman – the bisexual – is excluded.'[14]

Antifeminism, antisemitism and castration complex

It was with reference to Otto Weininger that Sigmund Freud, in a note to his essay on 'Little Hans: Analysis of a Phobia in a Five-Year-Old Child' (1909), connected antifeminism with antisemitism and associated them both with castration. Freud had just summed up the difficult problem which lay behind Little Hans's phobia:

> The piece of enlightenment which Hans had been given a short time before to the effect that women really do not possess a widdler was bound to have had a shattering effect upon his self-confidence and to have aroused his castration complex. For this reason he resisted the information, and for this reason it had no therapeutic results. Could it be that living beings really did exist which did not possess widdlers? If so, it would no longer be so incredible that they could take his own widdler away, and, as it were, make him into a woman![15]

This text has a peculiar importance for the history of psychoanalysis: the analysis of Little Hans was decisive in Freud's discovery of the castration complex.[16]

It is therefore not unimportant that this discovery was immediately followed (in a note) by the formulation of a theory of the common origins of antifeminism and antisemitism:

> The castration complex is the deepest unconscious root of anti-semitism; for even in the nursery little boys hear that a Jew has something cut off his penis – a piece of his penis, they think – and this gives them a right to despise Jews. And there is no stronger unconscious root for the sense of superiority over women. Weininger (the young philosopher who, highly gifted but sexually deranged, committed suicide after producing his remarkable book, *Geschlecht und Charakter*), in a chapter that attracted much attention, treated Jews and women with equal hostility and overwhelmed them with the same insults. Being a neurotic, Weininger was completely under the sway of his infantile complexes; and from that standpoint what is common to Jews and women is their relation to the castration complex.[17]

A year later, in the essay 'A Childhood Memory of Leonardo da Vinci', Freud again connected the castration complex, antifeminism and antisemitism: 'Under the influence of this threat of castration he now sees the notion he has gained of the female genitals in a new light; henceforth he will tremble for his masculinity, but at the same time he will despise the unhappy creatures on whom the cruel punishment has, as he supposes, already fallen.'[18] At this point, Freud adds in a note that he considered it incontestable that this was one root of the antisemitism (*Judenhass*) which was so nakedly and irrationally shown among Western peoples: 'circumcision is unconsciously equated with castration. If we venture to carry our conjectures back to the primaeval days of the human race we can surmise that originally circumcision must have been a milder substitute [*Milderungsersatz*], designed to take the place of castration.'[19]

In his later works Freud was to broaden and deepen his theory of anti-semitism. But the castration complex remained an essential element: 'among the customs by which the Jews made themselves separate, that of circumcision has made a disagreeable, uncanny [*unheimlich*] impression, which is to be explained, no doubt, by its recalling the dreaded castration and along with it a portion of the primaeval past which is gladly forgotten,'[20] repeats Freud in *Moses and Monotheism*. Evidently this Freudian approach to antisemitism caused a certain amount of embarrassment even in psychoanalytical circles. Otto Fenichel, for example, in his 'Elements of a Theory of Antisemitism' (1946), introduces his account of Freud's theory with these words, which seem intended as an 'excuse' for the master's incongruities:

> of course, I have no intention of defending a thesis according to which anti-semitism is no more than the fact that the uncircumcised despise the circumcised as non-male and fear lest the circumcised avenge themselves by circumcising them in their turn. Things are a little more complicated than that, and circumcision is only one of the many customs which were felt to be uncanny [*unheimlich*].[21]

Be it noted that the thesis which Fenichel says is simplistic can only be imputed to Freud if we limit ourselves to the footnotes to 'Little Hans' and 'Leonardo da Vinci'. At the most developed stage of his thinking on this subject, in *Moses*, the castration complex is *not* the sole unconscious root of antisemitism, but only one of the deepest among other causes.

Another essential work for the psychoanalytical theory of antisemitism is that of Rudolph M. Loewenstein, begun in France in 1941 and published in French in 1952. Despite its title, 'Psychoanalysis of Antisemitism', the book devotes comparatively little space to the psychoanalytical approach as such. Political, economic and religious aspects in fact take up many more pages. Loewenstein discusses Freud's theory of the castration complex and shows that, in certain individuals, the neurosis has been constructed upon passive tendencies repressed in childhood. These passive neurotics often overcompensate by trying to identify with heroes, or with strong and virile men, and imitate them: 'They fear that the psychoanalyst may try to weaken them, unman them or change them into women. Curiously, at such moments the Jewist psychoanalyst may be seen either as a Mephisthophelean being or as an effeminate, castrated man. The fact that the Jews are circumcised – in a way, mutilated – inspires a certain awe.'[22] Thus these neurotics show the unconscious terror – which psychoanalysts see as being well-nigh universal among boys – of being emasculated, mutilated, castrated, as a punishment for their forbidden desires. We can see that Loewenstein has slightly modified the thrust of Freud's theory: he reduces the importance of the castration complex as a root of antisemitism to the hatred and fear of psychoanalysis – and the psychoanalyst – which overwhelm the patient, who tends to identify the discipline as a 'Jewish science' and the doctor as an '*unheimlich* Jew'.

In the *Acta* of the Fourth Congress of the Deutsche Gesellschaft für Psychotherapie und Tiefenpsychologie (held in Wiesbaden, 5 May 1962), which centred on the study of antisemitism, the notion of castration complex does not figure very prominently. Alexander Mitscherlich defined antisemitism as a 'disease of prejudice' which was endemic and could reawaken at any moment.[23] Such an approach makes us wonder what specific contribution psychoanalysis can make to the struggle against antisemitism. The question is all the more justified in that, as Martin Wangh states in the same *Acta*, antisemites do not seek to be cured: on the contrary, they see their passion and 'conviction' as an eminently 'healthy' sign and a pillar of their personal sanity. Wangh even observes that if the psychoanalyst dwells on the problem of antisemitism during a treatment, the patient will tend to put his doctor down as a 'Jew', and never come back.[24]

During the Wiesbaden congress several contributors attempted to 'correct' Freud on the theme of castration. Thus Béla Grunberger declared that the Jew was assimilated to a castrated being not because he was circumcised, but because he was outside society.[25] And Martin Wangh substituted a sociological argument for Freud's theory, seeing the common ground between women and Jews as being their inferior social status.[26]

I do not intend to discuss here the validity of the connection which Freud, citing Weininger as an example, made between the castration complex and antisemitism; rather I would point out that psychoanalysis, by establishing a link between the masculine, the feminine and the Jew, was reformulating in its own terms one of the central themes of turn-of-the-century *Kulturkritik*. Freud does not simply parallel the Jew and the feminine. Some fundamental differences stand out: while Freud sees the female as having a characteristically feeble superego, the Jew dwells under the law of an imperious superego which, as is explained in *Moses*, nourishes the feeling of endless guilt which is native to the Jewish psyche. While Freud's discussion of women (like Weininger's) allows for a fair variety of configurations (the hysteric, the narcissistic woman, etc.), his examinations of the Jew present a single psychological type, fixed and unchanging from Moses onwards.

But at the same time, this fixed approach is a common element, within the Freudian corpus, of his work on both women and Jews. A woman of thirty, says Freud in his 1930 lecture on 'Femininity', 'often frightens us by her psychical rigidity and unchangeability. Her ego has taken up final positions and seems incapable of changing them for others.'[27] Similarly, 'the Jewish people is almost the only one which still exists in name and also in substance. It has met misfortunes and ill-treatment with an unexampled capacity for resistance; it has developed special character-traits and incidentally has earned the hearty dislike of almost every other people.'[28] Thus there would be an 'eternal Jew' as well as an 'eternal feminine'.

Freud's theory of the castration complex as a root of antisemitism lends itself quite readily to a feminist interpretation. Thus Margarete Mitscherlich, in her collection of essays 'Peaceable Women: A Psychoanalytical Study of Aggressiveness by Sex', calls one chapter 'Antisemitism: A Male Malady?' Recalling that symbolic castration in Freud is the common denominator in problems of self-image, Mitscherlich states that the unconscious psychic motives of antisemitism really appertain only to men. If women succumb to antisemitism it is not so much because of their castration worries, psychic conflicts and projections, but through identification with masculine prejudice.[29]

One of the most recent variations on the triangle of 'masculine/feminine/ Jew' has come from Jean-François Lyotard in his 1988 essay 'Heidegger and the "Jews"'.[30] The author discusses what he calls 'the silence kept to the end by the philosopher of Todtnauberg over the extermination of the Jews', and concludes that 'we can find in Freud an articulation of this immemorial paradox.'[31] Reminding us that Freud sees sexual difference as arousing the same terror in a boy as the head of Medusa, Lyotard suggests that 'something similar to sexual difference plays in Western (European) thought this role of an immanent terror, not identified as such, unrepresentable, with an unconscious affect.'[32]

This 'role', then, is assigned to the Jews, 'the people of the other', '"a people" other than peoples'.[33] From this point of view 'Western antisemitism is not its xenophobia, it is one of the ways its culture ... can combat the original terror and actively forget it.'[34] To talk of Jews after Auschwitz faces modern sensibilities with the unspeakable, the indescribable (which Lyotard attempts to tackle in terms of the 'sublime' of Kantian aesthetics). Thus the shifting and secret relationship between sexual difference and Jewish identity, so heavily emphasized by the Viennese modernists, has found an unexpected relevance in the writings of one of our postmodernist theorists.

From bisexuality to ambivalence – Jew and non-Jew

In psychoanalysis the strongest link between the female and the Jew is the gaze of the antisemite, whose phobia, like that of the antifeminist, derives from the castration complex. If we bear in mind the hypothesis of psychic bisexuality, male antifeminism would mean merely the hatred of men for the feminine element within themselves. Could we go so far as to conceive a psychic duality, Jew and non-Jew, which would be common to all individuals in the same way as bisexuality? Otto Weininger seems to have come very close to this hypothesis. At the beginning of *Sex and Character* he states that he will not be talking about men and women, but about masculine and feminine 'substances', 'ideas' of manliness and womanliness. Similarly, in part 2, chapter 13, of his book, Judaism becomes 'an idea in the Platonic sense', and Weininger claims that 'there are Aryans who are more Jewish than Jews.'[35]

Weininger thus arrives at a new explanation of antisemitism: those who hate Jewishness most are those most deeply involved in it. Only philosemites are perfectly free from Jewishness; and they, says Weininger, do not know of what they speak. Richard Wagner must have had a lot of the Jew in himself to have attained to such a noble antisemitic rage (just as, in Weininger's explanation, he drew on the feminine parts of his temperament for the inspiration to create Kundry): 'Thus,' concludes Weininger, 'the fact is explained that the bitterest antisemites are to be found among the Jews themselves.'[36] In 1888 even Nietzsche himself had unhesitatingly taken up the rumours current in Germany about the mysterious Jewish ancestry of Richard Wagner . . .[37]

Around 1900 the adjective 'Jewish' was applied in the most arbitrary way. Carl Dallago, for example, described Hermann Bahr as a 'cosmopolitan Jew'.[38] And Bahr himself defined the Viennese as 'Judaified', which was not intended as a compliment. The 'real' Jew, Bahr explained (without making clear what he meant by 'real'), has no power over the city of Vienna. And that is a pity, Bahr adds, because the Viennese could do with his sense of effort, enterprise, the seriousness of life (which makes us think that Bahr has in mind the poor, industrious *Ostjuden* who remained faithful to orthodoxy):

> Everything that is productive, great and strong about the Jews, Vienna dislikes. But the Jew who desires to be a Jew no longer, the traitor who abandons his race, the comedian who mimics another race – they are akin to Vienna. The artificial side of uprooted existences which, emptied of all their past, puff themselves up with greedy draughts of present and future, windbags swelling day by day, capable of *being* nothing but *seeming* anything – has always attracted the Viennese. The Viennese finds himself in them: in this sense we could say that he is completely Judaified. He already was, even before the first Jew ever came here.[39]

For Bahr, just as there was a typically Viennese self-hatred (*Wiener Selbsthass*), comparable with the *jüdaischer Selbsthass*, there was a resemblance between the 'degeneration' of the assimilated Jew and the decadence of the modern Viennese.

There are in Freud some traces of a theory close to Weininger's, which would put the Jew/non-Jew dualism at the very heart of the Jewish psyche and thus make antisemitism the hatred of the individual for the Jewishness in himself. Freud in fact introduces that duality into Moses himself by suggesting that he was an Egyptian. He seems to be following Weininger and interpreting antisemitism as an inner struggle of the Jews when he writes to Arnold Zweig on 18 August 1933: 'People will do anything to defend themselves against castration, and perhaps this is another clever way to hide a certain resistance to one's own Jewishness. Our great master Moses was, after all, a raving antisemite and made no secret of it. Perhaps he really was Egyptian.'[40]

Here it is tempting to pursue Weininger's intuition, which reduced all antisemitism to a subjective interior antagonism between Jewishness and non-Jewishness, just as all antifeminism came down to a protest of the male against his own femininity. Hitler himself decreed that German citizens should go back to the third generation to make sure that there was not, concealed in their ancestry, some Jewish ancestor who might pollute the race, and this obsession with racial purity seemed inseparable from the fear of women, who were capable of any treachery towards German blood: 'Women', Hitler declared, 'brought sin into the world, and the ease with which they yield to the lustful artifices of subhuman near-animality is the principal cause of the pollution of Nordic blood.'[41] One of the fantasies making up the antisemite's phobia may well be the fear of discovering that he or she is Jewish . . . Just as the misogynist trembles at the thought of being revealed as a woman.

II

The dialectic of reason and the misunderstandings of emancipation

Another theoretical approach which helps us to understand the link which modernity has established between the female and the Jew is prefigured in the *Dialektik der Aufklärung* (*Dialectic of Enlightenment*) by Theodor W. Adorno and Max Horkheimer. In this book, written between 1942 and 1944 and published in 1947, the emphasis is on the fundamental conflict between man and nature, inside and outside the individual. Contemporary capitalism and the authoritarian state, brutal manifestations of one man's domination over other men, appear as 'the revenge of nature for the cruelty and exploitation that Western man had visited upon it for generations'.[42]

These reflections develop ideas which had already been examined by Horkheimer in 'The Beginnings of the Bourgeois Philosophy of History',[43] where the concept of science and technology in the age of the Renaissance was related to political domination: corresponding to the concept of nature as a domain to be conquered and mastered was a concept of man as an object of domination. Several contributors to the *Zeitschrift für Sozialforschung* had gone into the same theme in the 1930s. In 1937 Leo Löwenthal, for example, studied the 'pre-fascist' sensibilities of the novelist Knut Hamsun and emphasized that, in liberalism, nature seemed to be above all a reality that mankind must master so as to increase his material wealth. Latterly, Löwenthal added, it was becoming an ideal which must console men for the disappointments inflicted on them by a collective existence. The individual, transfigured by the superior function attributed to him by liberal philosophy, aspires to submit as a passive element to the all-powerful totality of life. But, Löwenthal remarked, 'The ideal of a life in conformity with nature is characterized by Hamsun's biological idea of erotic relations. In this ideology sentimentality and brutality are constantly being directly juxtaposed in a combination that truly belongs to the authoritarian type of the present.'[44] In 1934 Erich Fromm published 'The Sociopsychological Significance of the Theory of Matriarchy' in the same journal; he repeated that in a patriarchal society the domination of nature and the subjection of women were two sides of the same coin.[45]

The *Dialektik der Aufklärung* takes up this theme in the part entitled 'Juliet, or *Aufklärung* and Morality':

The domination of nature is reproduced within humanity.... As in the case of original inhabitants enslaved inside the earliest states, as with the natives in the colonies, inferior to their conquerors in organization and arms, as with the Jews among the Aryans, the inability of women to defend themselves gives them a sort of legal entitlement to the oppression they endure. Sade anticipates the thoughts of Strindberg.[46]

The originality of Adorno and Horkheimer's research consists in the close link they make between the destinies of women and Jews as 'victims' of the *Aufklärung*:

the signs of impotence, hasty and ill-coordinated movements, the agony of the creature, its panic, arouse the appetite of the murderer. The declaration of hatred towards woman as an intellectually and physically inferior creature, marked on the brow with the seal of servitude, is also a declaration of hatred towards the Jew. It is written on the face of women and Jews that they have been kept far away from power for thousands of years. They live, although they could have been eliminated: their suffering and their weakness, their greatest affinity with nature under the oppression they endure: that is their element.[47]

A little further on in their book, in the chapter on 'Elements of Anti-semitism: the Limits of *Aufklärung*', Adorno and Horkheimer return to the parallel between the Jew and the woman. Jews, they explain, represent, at the very heart of a modern society cut off from nature, the memory of an archaic way of life; for liberalism has granted them property without power. Such was the import of the Declaration of the Rights of Man: it promised happiness even to those who did not have power. The conclusions which Adorno and Horkheimer draw from this may seem paradoxical. Because the deceived masses foresaw that this universal promise would remain a lie as long as social classes continued to endure, they erupted. They repressed their desire for this kind of 'happiness without power' and denied, all the more furiously, the mere possibility of such happiness. Against everything which suggested to them that the idea could indeed be realized, they were doomed to repeat the repression of their own aspirations:

He who provokes such a repetition, even if he is himself in misery, Ahasver the Wandering Jew or Mignon – the foreign element recalling the promised land, the beauty evoking the sex rejected as an accursed and repugnant animal, representing promiscuity – all that attracts the destructive hatred of civilized individuals who have never been able to reach the end of the painful civilizing process.[48]

According to this vision, the Jew, like the woman, is a standing provocation for those who live with the 'discontents of civilization' as described by Freud. The idea that female sensuality is a menace to throne and altar is not new. We should, however, appreciate the originality of this interpretation of the Jew as incarnating the utopia of happiness without power. Elsewhere in the same chapter, Adorno and Horkheimer generalize their insight: the Jew represents the utopias of riches without labour, fatherland without frontiers and religion without myth. This inverts and makes positive the image of the usurious and parasitic Jew, who benefited from an 'unjustified enrichment' at others' expense – the cosmopolitan and 'faithless' Jew who lurks in the antisemitic imagination . . .

Jews, then, like women, are a form of 'human being according to nature' whose existence is a kind of challenge to the instrumental rationality of the modernity derived from the Enlightenment. This presence, which non-Jewish society feels as a provocation, then arouses reactions of censure and repression which nourish antisemitism. A paradoxical conclusion, since the *Dialektik der Aufklärung* elsewhere adopts the less original view that the Jews were so identified with the scientific mind, the ethics and politics of the Enlightenment, that they were virtually indistinguishable from the latter and were 'responsible' for them in the eyes of various anti-liberal movements from the end of the nineteenth century.

If certain aspects of the 'Elements of Antisemitism' are debatable, on one point at least the approach of Adorno and Horkheimer remains exemplary, and has guided a good deal of research into the history of antisemitism: the nineteenth century's failure to emancipate the Jews on the lines of the *Aufklärung*, and the inability of liberalism to supply a lasting answer to the 'Jewish question', were inevitable from the outset due to deficiencies in the doctrine of the Enlightenment. That was indeed the link between the fate of women and of Jews, between antifeminism and antisemitism: the woman and the Jew were the two main 'beneficiaries' of the Enlightenment notion of emancipation, but in both cases this idea was too hedged with qualifications to be successfully implemented.

In her biography of Rahel Varnhagen, Hannah Arendt paralleled these two great movements of emancipation to show the 'traps and illusions' in both,[49] not only through the reactions of her contemporaries to Rahel Varnhagen-Levin's 'career', but also through the identity crisis which she endured: 'Her identity was doubly negative: shame for her Jewish birth was rooted in shame for her sex. To be a woman was to be on the margin of society – ill-born.'[50] It was in a similar spirit to that of Arendt and Horkheimer–Adorno that Hans Mayer wrote his *Aussenseiter* ('Outsiders'), which begins with a chapter on 'Outsiders and *Aufklärung*' and unambiguously states that 'This book starts from the premise that the bourgeois *Aufklärung* was a failure.'[51]

Mayer broadens the comparison by adding to Jews and women a third group of 'outsiders' involved in the failure of the Enlightenment: homosexuals. These comparisons have been resisted: it has been pointed out that women are half of humanity and cannot conceivably be eliminated, while Jews have usually been treated as a minority. Others have said that Jews are born, while homosexuals are made, and have suggested that there are many other kinds of 'existential outsiders' within the European tradition.[52] Sander L. Gilman has compared modern psychopathological descriptions of women, Jews and blacks: there is no shortage of similarities.[53] None the less, few themes have been so central to reflections on the modern crisis of civilization, since the turn of the century, as the crises of masculine, feminine and Jewish identity.

The historian Reinhard Rürup has assembled a good deal of evidence to support the insight common to Horkheimer, Adorno, Arendt and Mayer, establishing a causal link between the implementation of the 'enlightened' idea of emancipation and the birth of modern antisemitism. Why was German culture, which was one of the first to give a clear and determined form to the idea of emancipating the Jews – before the French Revolution – also one of the nations most fertile in antisemitic theories and policies between the end of the nineteenth century and 1945?

This question applies equally to Austria. We must remember that on the eve of the French Revolution, Vienna set Europe an example of liberal legislation for the emancipation of Jews. The 'edict of tolerance for Viennese Jews' (*Toleranzpatent für die Wiener Juden*) signed by Josef II on 2 January 1782, a year after the publication of the treatise 'On the Civil Improvement of the Jews' (*Über die bürgerliche Verbesserung der Juden*) by the Prussian Christian Wilhelm von Dohm, was one of the first reforms of the period concerned with the 'Jewish question' (*Judenfrage*). This edict does, however, have an understandable mercantilist bias. Jewish finance and commerce had to be put to the best possible use for the prosperity of the monarchy. Josef II's policy of tolerance (and edicts for tolerance similar to the Viennese one were promulgated in several other provinces of the monarchy) was also intended to compete with the king of Prussia, so as not to seem less 'enlightened', and in order to safeguard the loyalty of the Jews in the frontier provinces.[54]

Nonetheless Vienna, at the end of the eighteenth century and through the first three-quarters of the nineteenth, did indeed seem to be favourable ground for Jewish assimilation. And yet it was in Vienna that, from the early 1880s onwards, the first antisemitic mass movements were formed which were eventually to guide the destinies of the German world in the twentieth century. The value of Rürup's studies is that they point out the 'original defects' in the concept of Jewish emancipation bequeathed by the *Aufklärung*, which go a long way towards explaining the failure of that generous intention. The first problem was that the emancipation was essentially conceived as an *assimilation* of the Jews to German culture: 'The Jew is, after all, more a man than a Jew,' wrote Dohm.[55] But in practice this concept was reduced to the grim demand for the Jew to be 'un-Jewed'.[56]

Even the relationship between Kant and Moses Mendelssohn, though it was based on mutual admiration and sympathy, was not without some ambiguity. A note in the 'Conflict of Faculties' expresses some doubts as to Mendelssohn's good intentions. Kant has been suggesting a 'purging' of the Jewish religion and has come to the following conclusion: 'The euthanasia of Judaism is pure moral religion, renouncing all the ancient dogmas.'[57] He observes in a footnote:

Moses Mendelssohn rejected this notion [of a general conversion of the Jews] in a way which does honour to his *intelligence* (by an *argumentatio ad hominem*). 'So long as God, from Mount Sinai, does not abrogate our law as solemnly as he gave it to us between the stars and the lightning,' he said, 'and that day will never come, we are bound to that Law'; by which he doubtless meant, 'Christians, first take away the Judaism from your *own* faith; after which we will also renounce ours.' It is true that, by this stern demand, he is destroying all hope of even the slightest alleviation of the burdens which oppress his fellow Jews (although probably he only thought a very small proportion of them to be essential to his faith): let them decide if that does honour to his *good intentions*.[58]

Kant thinks that if religions, purged by reason, are to converge on a universal moral ideal, this will involve the 'euthanasia of Judaism': by keeping to their faith and refusing to be completely 'un-Jewed', the Jews lay themselves under the suspicion of not playing fair in the game of *Aufklärung*.[59]

The debate which had divided intellectuals since the end of the eighteenth century bore on the way in which emancipation should be implemented: should rights and liberties be granted the Jews all at once, considering that these rights and liberties could be neither subdivided nor restricted; or were the Jews still not ready to enjoy the status of free citizens with equal rights? The French Revolution decided on immediate and complete emancipation by the law of 13 November 1791. In the German states and Austria, it was the idea of progressive integration, controlled by the authorities, which prevailed. This proved to be a fatal step.

As early as 1809, Wilhelm von Humboldt, in a report to the Prussian Ministry of the Interior, stressed the disadvantages of a policy of progressive emancipation. An immediate and complete emancipation seemed to him the only reasonable solution. For, he insisted, the state had neither the means nor, especially, the will to undertake the 'education' of the Jews for citizenship. Moreover, he said, 'progressive abolition implies a justification for the discrimination that it claims to be abolishing, in every area in which segregation persists. The newly granted freedoms will in fact redouble awareness of the continuing restrictions, and thus abolition will work against itself.' Thus, Humboldt continued, only an open attitude from the state would allow the prejudices in society to be effectively combatted; and without it the people would always consider 'good' Jewish fellow-citizens to be the exception.[60]

This far-sighted warning was not heeded. The great majority of German governments, and that of Austria, opted in the nineteenth century for a gradual emancipation, considering for one thing that the Jews were not ready for immediate integration, and for another that society was still not willing to open to them. The Austrian bureaucracy of the *Vormärz* took care to accumulate interminable reports and inquiries in which the pros and cons of Jewish emancipation were weighed up with delicate precision. But the cons generally weighed heavier and no firm decisions ensued. During this time there was a flood of pamphlets and studies hostile to emancipation, which remained the order of the day but was never really executed.[61] It was not until more than half a century later that the emancipation of the Jews seemed on the brink of achievement (in Austria this event can be dated to the liberal constitution of December 1867; in Germany, to the law of 16 April 1871 which extended to the whole *Reich* the law abolishing the last elements of discrimination, adopted by the Norddeutscher Bund in 1869).[62] But when emancipation seemed finally to have been achieved, the age of antisemitism had already begun.

Two things had aggravated the inherent defects of this progressive emancipation. Firstly, the multiplicity of German states meant that the status of the Jews varied wildly from one region to another. The prejudices opposed by civil law in one state were enshrined in the law in the next. Antisemites could denounce the excesses of liberalism in one place by pointing out the archaisms which survived in another. Secondly, in Austria in particular the rights and liberties seemed to have been 'granted' to the Jews by the good pleasure of the authorities: even when its status had been largely liberalized, the Jewish sect remained dependent on the tutelage – sometimes protective, sometimes arbitrary – of the administration. In 1900, in Vienna, the antisemitic burgomaster Karl Lueger gave cynical expression to this bygone paternalism when he pronounced his celebrated formula, '*I* will decide who is Jewish' ('Wer ein Jud' ist, bestimme ich'), while at the opposite end of the scale the Emperor Franz Josef posed as a protector of the Jews, as the chief *Staatsvolk* of the monarchy at a time when all ills were due to nationalism ... In the Austro-Hungarian monarchy, the memory of the most brutal repression was still very much alive at the very time when the authorities were making a great display of mildness. Less than forty years before Josef II's 'edicts of tolerance', in 1744, the Empress Maria Theresa had threatened to expel all Jews from Prague ...

German and Austrian liberals, then, had demanded – often successfully – that the Jews should renounce their religious identity in a sort of euthanasia, while denying them the complete and immediate emancipation which would have helped them to integrate. Thereby they had exposed the assimilation programme to a double danger: German and Austrian Jews had sacrificed a large part of their identity to enter into German culture, and yet they were doomed to remain *Gastvolk*, a 'guest people' dependent on the goodwill of their hosts. Freedom and equal rights remained a delusion, for at the same time the archaic notion of the ghetto was maintained by the restrictions and inequalities of the laws still in force.

It is clear that throughout the nineteenth century there was a similar dialectical relationship between Enlightenment ideas on the emancipation of women and antifeminist reactions. The *Aufklärung* made great plans for the education of girls so as *progressively* to remove inequalities. But the emancipated woman, a standing contrast to most others, seemed like an aberration of modern civilization, a flying in the face of nature. The weakness· of the thinking behind the emancipation of women was that it was couched in terms of equality between the sexes, that is, the assimilation of feminine roles to masculine ones; and so it was constantly being challenged on the basis of theories of the essential difference, or even total polarization, of the male and the female.

The 'enlightened' approach to emancipation was all the more vulnerable to criticism and mockery in that it still followed a self-styled 'universal' reasoning which in reality was exclusively masculine. The founding fathers of the *Aufklärung* had had little to say on the subject. Kant's *Pragmatic Anthropology* repeats most of the clichés of traditional misogyny. The nineteenth-century emancipation of women, precarious and often challenged as it was, went side by side with the rise of antifeminism.

Femininity, Jewishness and modernity

If 'the dialectic of *Aufklärung*' explains the difficulties in the way of the two great modern drives for emancipation, that of women and that of Jews, the psychological and psychoanalytic approach shows us another essential aspect of this development, which was again common to the destiny of women and of Jews in the modernist period. Just as antifeminism was symptomatic of a profound crisis of individual masculine identity in revolt against the female within itself, and this individual crisis turns out to be linked to a general crisis of culture, similarly antisemitism was symptomatic of a crisis of individual and social identities under the effects of modernization.

It might be said that antisemitism was the protest of society against a liberalism with which it had first appeared to identify, but had then denied. The antisemitic intellectual was often an ex-liberal who was projecting his anti-liberal self-hatred on to the Jew. The prototype of the ex-liberal antisemite is Richard Wagner, who wrote in his essay 'Das Judentum in der Musik' ('Jewishness in Music'):

> When we fought for the emancipation of the Jews, we were really fighting far more for an abstract principle than for a real case; just as our liberalism was only a rather short-sighted attitude of mind, since we were struggling for the freedom of the people without knowing the people, without even wanting any real contact with them – in the same way our zeal for equal rights for the Jews was fed by a general ideal rather than by a real sympathy; however much we spoke and wrote about the emancipation of the Jews, any real close contact with them inspired in us an involuntary repugnance.[63]

When putting 'Viennese modernism' into its historical and social context we saw that the economic and demographic growth of the Habsburg capital greatly disturbed two fundamental elements in the traditional Viennese microcosm. Economic liberalism threatened the prosperity of the small tradesman or craftsman, and the stock-market crash of 1873 bankrupted many a small or modest business; the popularity of the Christian socialist movement, soon to supplant the Liberal Party, rested on its hostility to 'big capital', and as it was anti-capital, so it was anti-liberal. The growth in population was perceived by the Catholic Austrian majority as a threat to its identity, and in particular, to its social and cultural supremacy. Ethnic and linguistic minorities were becoming more and more prominent, especially the Jews from the East and the Czechs. In 1900 about 7 per cent of the population of Vienna were Czech speakers; in the tenth urban district, where many of the Czech community lived, the proportion reached 20 per cent.[64] The 'anti-Slavism' of Austrian Germans developed in parallel with antisemitism.

The social tensions within the capital were a minor echo of the national conflicts which were tearing the monarchy apart (in 1893, Karl Lueger had flung into an election speech that 'We have become islets of Judeo-Magyars,'[65] a strange combination of anti-Hungarian nationalism and anti-semitism). At that time, 80 per cent of Viennese were professing Roman Catholics – an overwhelming majority, or so it seems at first sight. And yet the 20 per cent of non-Catholics were seen by clerics as a provocation: they spoke of an end to Christianity and inveighed against the atheism of modern times . . .[66]

All the anxieties of social milieux threatened by economic modernization, and all the old fears of traditionalists with their talk of decadence, found a common outlet in antisemitism. A speech by Lueger during a parliamentary debate on the 'Law defining the civil status of Jewish confessional communities'[67] is particularly revealing of the amalgam of preoccupations which converged on antisemitism:

> In Vienna the Jews are as numerous as the sands of the sea; wherever you go, Jews, nothing but Jews; if you go into the Stadtpark, nothing but Jews; if you go to a concert, nothing but Jews; if you go to a ball, nothing but Jews; if you go to the university, nothing but Jews. So we will not cry 'hep, hep, hep!' [the rallying cry of German antisemites[68]]; but we will revolt against the fact that all Christians are oppressed and that in place of the old Austrian Christian empire a new realm of Palestine is being founded. Therein lies the cause of antisemitism. It is not a hatred for individuals, or against some poor little Jew. No, honourable Members, we feel hatred only against the big capital which is crushing us and which is in the hands of the Jews.[69]

The fantasy of a 'feminized' culture which so terrified Weininger – and lured Groddeck and Otto Gross – finds a parallel in the fantasy of a 'Jew-ridden' culture and society which became a commonplace of anti-liberal *Kulturkritik* from the last third of the nineteenth century. In Weininger himself (and in his principal admirer, Karl Kraus), as in the ideological precursors of Nazi *Weltanschauung* (Houston Stewart Chamberlain, Adolf Josef Lanz von Liebenfels, Alfred Rosenberg), and in the sayings of most of the chief representatives of the fascist movement, the two themes appear to be closely connected.[70] In Rosenberg's 'Myth of the Twentieth Century', the racial chaos which has allowed the Jews to infiltrate the Germanic *Volk* in all kinds of ways, and the sexual chaos which has plunged male and female roles into anarchy, are side by side. 'Little men trotting furtively along in patent-leather shoes and mauve stockings, covered in bracelets and dainty rings, with blue shadow on their eyes and rouge under their noses' – that is Rosenberg's picture of the bastard offspring of modern Germany. The emancipation of the Jews (who are poisoning the Germanic race) and the emancipation of women (who are sapping the virility of men) are the two main causes of decadence.[71]

Schnitzler on Jews, women and antisemites

Central to the dramatic and narrative works of Arthur Schnitzler is this same parallel – created by the vicissitudes of emancipation, its promises, contradictions and disappointments – between the Jews and the women of modern times. Through his 'Viennese imagery'[72] Schnitzler presents us with the principal incarnations of bourgeois womanhood at the turn of the century: integrated woman (girl of good family or virtuous mother); old maid; libertine;

prostitute; woman of the world and *femme fatale*; seductive child-woman (*das süsse Mädel*); hysteric; and 'liberated' woman.[73]

Successfully emancipated women are rare in Schnitzler: we might point to Marcolina in the story 'Casanova's Return', who combines charm and wit with a freewheeling sexual life and a high level of artistic and scientific sophistication, and who inflicts a crushing defeat on the seducer, Casanova. But the fact that Schnitzler sets this story in eighteenth-century Italy probably suggests that such an ideal of female emancipation would be impossible in the Vienna of 1900 . . . Most of Schnitzler's women who have distanced themselves from the stereotypes dictated by social convention seem doomed to a lonely and embittered existence, threatened by depression and suicide.

The world of the assimilated Jews, beset with antisemitism, is the other favoured ground for Schnitzler's observations and reflections. It is in the play *Professor Bernhardi* (1912) that he goes furthest in denouncing antisemitism: he invents a sort of Dreyfus affair transplanted into the world of Viennese medicine. Schnitzler does more than analyse Jewish reactions to antisemitism: he also dissects the mental machinery which makes a non-Jew speak and act like an antisemite. The long short story 'Lieutenant Gustl' is particularly revealing, for 'just as the innermost secrets of the individual are laid bare, Schnitzler finds a void instead of a self. The inner monologue has merged with the sayings of others, of a social category.'[74]

Lieutenant Gustl is subjected to a series of humiliations. He is bored by a concert and becomes aware of his cultural and social inferiority. Then, in the foyer of the concert hall, he is roundly rebuked by a 'civvy', a baker by trade – a nasty blow to the narcissism of a uniformed soldier imbued with the code of honour proper to his caste. How can he avenge this 'insult' from an adversary whose condition is too lowly for satisfaction to be demanded? Must the 'dishonoured' soldier kill himself? This tragi-comic inward struggle makes Gustl reflect on all his disappointments as a social pariah: his father, a petty official in inglorious retirement; a sister who cannot be married off for lack of a dowry; his own failure in his studies, his reason for joining the army.

Gustl's inner monologue passes through fleeting visions of sadistic triumph over a weeping woman;[75] misogynistic scorn of another woman who has been too 'easy';[76] and, as counterpoint, happy memories of a male – probably homosexual – friendship as experienced in a barrack-room.[77] For the time being he has to make the best of a liaison with a milliner who is being kept by another man, richer than he:

> In any case, he must be a Jew! He must be, since he's in banking and has a black moustache . . . And they say he's a lieutenant in the reserve! Well, he'd better look out if he comes on exercises with my regiment. All the same, to think that they still let these Jews become officers – so much for antisemitism![78]

Gustl's feeling of social failure brings on a crisis of masculine identity which drifts spontaneously towards antisemitism.

Schnitzler's finest and most subtle analysis of the identity crisis in assimilated Viennese Jews is condensed into the novel *Der Weg ins Freie* (1908);

the title, 'The Road to Freedom', stresses the idea of a failed liberation, an abortive emancipation. The novel encapsulates the most typical reactions of Jews to modern antisemitism.[79] Doctor Stauber, a Social Democrat member of parliament who has been publicly insulted by antisemites, chooses exile and leaves Vienna to continue his medical researches abroad. Salomon Ehrenberg, a wealthy industrialist, rallies to the Zionist cause, deliberately cultivates a Yiddish accent and talks of going to Palestine (though in fact he never leaves Vienna), while his wife and daughter Else keep a cultivated salon on the Ringstrasse, and his son Oskar tags along with his friends, members of the non-Jewish Viennese *jeunesse dorée*, and dreams of having his Jewishness forgotten.

Theresa Golowski becomes a militant Social Democrat and sacrifices her woman's happiness to the demands of politics. Leo Golowski is also a Social Democrat, but above all a Zionist. The old musician, Eissler, has composed waltz tunes which are supposed to be quintessentially Viennese. The writer Heinrich Bermann (whom most critics see as a portrait of the author) suffers terribly from the atmosphere of antisemitism, so much so that he occasionally lapses into *jüdischer Selbsthass* (Jewish self-hatred); but he feels no attraction to Zionism and accepts that Vienna and Austria are the only *Heimat* to which he can be bound.

None of the Jews described here by Schnitzler with such compassion and understanding has a satisfactory answer to the 'Jewish question'. The novel has no 'message' unless it be the awareness of the contradictions and insufficiencies of all these reactions by assimilated Jews to antisemitism. Schnitzler has no solution to suggest; the final impression is pessimistic. The cause of *Aufklärung*, the only one Schnitzler ever believed in sincerely,[80] seems lost.

One aspect of the novel may be emphasized for our purposes: the paralleling of the Jewish crisis of identity with the failure of the love between Georg von Wergenthin and Anna Rosner. The failure of von Wergenthin, an aristocrat, represents various aspects of 'decadence': the decline of Austria (he is the son of a high-ranking diplomat, and his powerlessness to carry on the family inheritance symbolizes the renegation of the monarchy's elite); the crisis in artistic creation (he is a composer with a high ideal of 'pure art', but never gets beyond a few musical trifles and suffers from lack of inspiration); and the crisis of masculinity, for he is incapable of answering the challenge of life as represented by Anna's love and the child she bears.

At the beginning of the novel, von Wergenthin appears akin to the decadent and individualistic aesthetes who people the literary world of Young Vienna. His liaison with Anna Rosner follows the same laws as Anatol's love affair with the *süsses Mädel* of the suburbs. Von Wergenthin is obliged to leave the centre of Vienna, the first district, where he lives, when he visits the Rosner family in their modest suburban dwelling. But Georg is no disillusioned cynic like Anatol; as an impassioned Wagnerian he sees himself and Anna as a second Tristan and Isolde. On the afternoon when their son dies, Georg occupies himself by playing over the score of the opera. But that death, after which Georg finally breaks with Anna, is a punishment for the 'error of

Narcissus'. He has never seen anyone but himself; he has never really become aware that Anna has a life of her own. Even the child seemed to him a reflection of himself: 'Contrary to what Georg had expected, his face was not wrinkled and ugly like an old dwarf's. It really was a human face, a child's face, calm and beautiful, and Georg knew that its features were a faithful reflection of his own.'[81] The death of this child reveals Georg's refusal of life.

Many years before the publication of 'The Road to Freedom', Lou Andreas-Salomé had written to Schnitzler:

> It is striking how pathetic the men in your works seem in comparison with the women – so unimpressive that one is tempted to ask if you are not to some extent calumniating your own sex. The man, good or bad, regularly appears less interesting. And all those women are in a way superior to him, even if only because of the innocence of their insignificance . . . Man and woman, placed thus side by side, go together like disease and health.[82]

Thus 'The Road to Freedom' develops two parallel themes: the Jewish crisis of identity and the male crisis of identity. Schnitzler's first readers noticed this feature of the book, which some thought was a weakness. In June 1908 the critic Georg Brandes wrote to Schnitzler: 'Have you not written two books in one? The liaison of the young baron with his mistress is one thing; the new situation of the Jewish people of Vienna, faced with antisemitism, is another, which, it seems to me, is not necessarily connected with the former.'[83] Schnitzler's answer justified the construction of his novel in terms of an overwhelming inner necessity: 'As I worked on it I did feel that it was going to turn out that way; but I could not – and would not – do otherwise.'[84]

It was a necessity of the same order, dictated by a certain historic situation and its reflection in literature – *Kulturkritik* pyschology and philosophy – which convinced me that the 'triangle' of masculine, feminine and Jew was part of the underlying structure of Viennese modernism.

Part IV
Crises of Jewish Identity

10
The Assimilated Jews of Vienna

If we ask questions about our Jewish identity it means we have already lost
it. But it also means that we are still clinging to it; for otherwise we should
not ask such questions. Between that 'already' and that 'still' there
stretches a kind of tightrope along which the Jewishness of Western Jews
is now dangerously venturing.

Emmanuel Levinas

I

Assimilation, conversion, liberalism

After the culmination of the Enlightenment, marked by the 'Edict of tolerance
of Viennese Jews' of 2 January 1782, the status of Jews regressed from year to
year until 1848.[1] However, there was still 'tolerance' for the initiatives and
responsibilities of Jews who served the monarchy. Ennobled Jewish families
like the Eskeles and the Arnsteins were pre-eminent in social, artistic and
political circles. The *Haskala* (the Enlightenment within Judaism) had dominated the years of the *Vormärz*. A few Hebrew journals and other writings
were published in Vienna. But among the Jewish social elite the idea of
assimilation was beginning to prevail, and was already clashing with the
orthodoxy of the *Ostjuden*, though their numbers were still few. The Jews
of the Enlightenment had brought into their synagogues the *Wiener Ritus*,
intended to offer Viennese Catholics the reassuring sight of a modernized
Judaism – and also to keep the allegiance of the 'modern' Jews, who were
becoming less and less inclined to hold to the ancient rites.

This policy was to bear fruit: in Vienna, Jewish assimilation was rarely seen
in religious terms. Conversion to Catholicism was understandable in cases of
urgent need, perhaps for professional reasons (actors and actresses, among
others, had to bow to this social demand if their career was to progress); or it
could happen in the case of a mixed marriage. Between 1868 and 1903 some
9,000 Viennese Jews were converted. This was a far larger number than in
other cities of the monarchy, and larger than that for Berlin.[2] But the total of
conversions never surpassed 10 per cent of the total number of Jews. Moreover, only half the converts became Catholics. A quarter chose Protestantism
(a particularly likely choice among intellectuals, who thus declared their
willingness to quit the Jewish community without yielding to opportunism).
Another quarter remained 'without confession' (*konfessionslos*). As was to be

expected, it was among the bourgeois and petty bourgeois that conversions were most numerous; they remained very rare among the *Ostjuden*.[3]

To the culturally assimilated Jews, a Jew who converted to Catholicism (*Taufjude*, the title of a pamphlet by Fritz Wittels),[4] cut a somewhat inglorious figure. In 1913, Karl Kraus (who converted to Catholicism on 8 April 1911) inveighed against 'renegades' as much as against antisemites: their 'egoism', he wrote, had nothing in common with the 'secret altruism' of the true convert, 'who works for the future and smooths the path of future generations'.[5] Kraus took the work 'secret' literally: though his journal *Die Fackel* sometimes reads like a private diary, he says nothing in it about his conversion, breaking his vow to be candid with his readers.

For the Jews, as for the monarchy as a whole, 1848 had been a historic turning point. In Vienna the Jewish intellectuals, in particular the medical students (the only faculty open to Jews before 1848), had played a leading role in the revolutionary events. Adolf Fischhof (1816–93) was the leading light, and remained until his death the grand old man of Austrian liberalism; but he was also something of an incubus, since he was a Jew and remained an ardent reformer even when the liberal club was merely out cynically to defend the interests of the upper middle class.[6] The few months of revolutionary agitation following March 1848 had revealed the antisemitism of some workers and petty bourgeois, who disliked the demands for equal rights, were frightened by competition from Jewish artisans and tradesmen, and accused the Jewish bank of collaborating with Metternich. Nonetheless, the Reichstag had had the time to vote for the abolition of the Judensteuer (poll tax on Jews). The 1849 constitution had recognized the right to existence of the Jewish community, but Franz Josef had abrogated this constitution in 1851, and discrimination seemed very likely to return.

With the early military difficulties of the monarchy in 1859 (the Italian war and Solferino), which forced the authorities to make political concessions, liberalism gained ground in Austria. However, the abolition of the corporate order in 1859 turned out to be a poisoned chalice for the Jews: fear and resentment of Jewish competition, which could now develop free from hampering regulations, was to turn into a popular mass movement. The second blow to the monarchy in 1867 (the war with Prussia and Sadowa) made a fresh constitutional reshuffle unavoidable; in May 1868 it was followed by an interconfessional law which proclaimed religious freedom and attenuated the effects of the 1855 Concordat with the Vatican (which was to be revised in 1871).

It could be said that the golden age of Austrian liberalism lasted for scarcely twenty years, from 1859 to the end of the 1870s. After the crash of 1873 liberalism became unpopular. In 1879 the Liberals suffered a severe electoral defeat, and the new Taaffe government was a gathering of all the forces traditionally most distrustful of Jews: clerical, aristocratic, Slav, Polish and conservative Czech. The extension of the franchise in 1882 brought down the last liberal bastions in Austria. Liberalism survived only in Vienna, thanks to the emperor, who helped by delaying for four years, until 1897, the appointment of the Christian Socialist burgomaster Karl Lueger, one of the first prominent antisemitic agitators of the twentieth century. By 1900 liberalism had completely lost its foothold in Austrian politics.[7]

The 'modern' Jews of Vienna had trusted to liberalism and rested all their hopes on it. Adolf Jellinek (1821–93), Chief Rabbi of Vienna from 1865 and the symbol of a generation brought up on enlightened rationalism, declared in 1870 that 'Judaism consecrates and sanctifies the ideals of modern society, bringing healing and trust, peace and reconciliation, to suffering, erring humanity.'[8] Jellinek interpreted the law of the Jews as a promise of union between Jews and non-Jews. He worked towards a time when Judaism would, as he put it, be free 'from petty and insubstantial external oddities and archaic customs' and be revealed as 'a religion of the mind and heart; of holiness, justice, liberty and charity'.[9] He preferred to be called priest rather than rabbi. His successor, Moritz Güdemann (1835–1918), defended principles which were steeped in liberal thinking: as a disciple of Graetz, Bernays and the *Wissenschaft des Judentums* he was opposed to the Zionism of Theodor Herzl, which to him seemed a treacherous form of assimilation; he rejected all forms of Jewish nationalism (which he saw as curbs on Judaism) and emphasized the educational aspects of the Jewish tradition.[10]

The social organization which was officially recognized as representing Viennese Jews, the Israelitische Kultusgemeinde, was by all accounts closer to the assimilated Jews of the aspiring middle class than to the *Ostjuden*, and it, too, remained faithful to the liberal ideal – which meant hostile to all forms of nationalism, including Zionism.[11] Many accused it of taking an insufficiently hard line against antisemitism, and several groups seceded from it so as to defend Jewish interests in Vienna and Austria more vigorously. An example was Josef Samuel Bloch, rabbi of a working-class district of Vienna called Floridsdorf, who was elected to the Reichsrat in 1883 (representing a Galician constituency); he was editor of the *Österreichische Wochenschrift* and in 1886 founded the Österreichisch-Israelitische Union.[12] Another was the business-man Sigmund Mayer, one of the leading lights of this Austrian-Israelite Union, who commented in his memoirs: 'I had completely forgotten that I was a Jew. But at present the antisemites are forcing me to make that unpleasant discovery.'[13] The Israelitische Kultusgemeinde was implacably hostile to the initiatives of Bloch, which they saw as dangerously provocative; they thought it wiser to come to terms with Lueger, whose antisemitism was frankly open to negotiation. But the Taussig affair was to expose the contradictions of this liberal policy. Theodor von Taussig, director of the important Boden-Creditanstalt bank and member of the governing committee of the Kultusgemeinde, had advanced substantial credit to the Tsarist government at a time when it was tolerating or even encouraging antisemitic pogroms in Russia. In 1906 Taussig, faced with an indignant campaign by Jewish nationalists and Zionists, was forced to resign from all his responsibilities within the Viennese Jewish community.[14]

German nationalism, Jewish nationalism

The Austrian tradition of liberalism went hand in hand with a policy of centralism and Germanization. It exploited the effective alliance between assimilated Jews, seen as the ideal *Staatsvolk*, and Austrian Germans. But the liberal club was careful to do nothing which might confirm its reputation for being 'accommodating' to Jews, and its opposition to antisemitism often seemed timid.[15] The standing contradiction between 'pluralist' rhetoric and the actual policy of favouring the ruling minority over provincial 'nationalities' had contributed a good deal to the electoral downfall of liberalism. The majority of the Jews of the Austrian part of the empire took for granted the cultural and political pre-eminence of the Austrian Germans. In 1877 Jellinek said, rather incautiously, that 'Jews have a particular affinity with the German nation: they look for an Austria founded on a strong centralized government.'[16] It is easy to see why Franz Josef made every effort to contain the antisemitism within his domains.

Paragraph 19 of the Basic Law (*Staatsgrundgesetz*) of 21 December 1867 declared that 'All peoples [*Volksstämme*] of the state have equal rights and every people has an inalienable right to maintain and defend its nationality and language.' But this proved no help to the Jews of Austria-Hungary, for they were not recognized as a 'nation'. The laws never spoke of Jews, but only of the 'Israelite confession', and Yiddish did not have the status of a national language. At the end of the nineteenth century, it was allowed that the Jews did constitute a *Volk*: a highly reputable encyclopaedia entitled *The Peoples of Austria-Hungary* devoted a whole volume to them.[17] But the debate on the right and capacity of the monarchy's Jews to define themselves as a nation on an equal footing with other peoples had been at the centre of numerous controversies since the 1880s.[18]

It is scarcely necessary to say that the Jewish liberal reaction to this question was a negative one. By contrast, in 1882 some Jewish students of the University of Vienna had founded a nationalist Jewish association, the Kadimah,[19] which imitated the other nationalist student groups in every respect. For example, it resumed the custom of the 'duel of honour' with sabres, thus registering a protest against the antisemitic students who were trying to deprive Jews of the right to demand satisfaction (*Satisfaktionsfähigkeit*). The militancy of this association – it actively solicited support from leading personalities – obliged a substantial number of Jewish intellectuals and academics to take a stance on the 'Jewish question'. The long letter written in 1894 by Freud's friend Josef Breuer, in answer to an appeal from Kadimah, gives a clear idea of the attitude – a cautious one *vis-à-vis* this 'Jewish nationalist' movement – of an assimilated Jew who defined himself as *natione germanus, gente judaicus*.[20] The Zionist ideal as restated by Theodor Herzl was to change the premises of the debate.

Jews in Viennese culture

Long after the electoral collapse of liberalism, the Viennese Jewish establishment continued to defend its principles. It had a tool fit for the purpose: the quality press. This included *Die Presse*, founded by August Zang and known later as *Neue Freie Presse* under the editorship of Max Friedländer and his successor, Moritz Benedikt; Moritz Szeps's *Neues Wiener Tageblatt*, founded in 1867, a favourite with Crown Prince Rudolf; the *Wiener Allgemeine Zeitung*, founded in 1880 (its first editor was Theodor Herztka, a former head of the economics section of the *Neue Freie Presse*). Most congenial to the Jewish bourgeoisie was the *Neue Freie Presse*. The poet Stefan Zweig tells how he was interviewed as a young man by Theodor Herzl, head of the literature section, who was

> the oracle of my fathers and the asylum of heads crowned by an unction sevenfold ... In Vienna, there was really only one daily paper of the first rank, the *Neue Freie Presse*, which with its dignity, its cultural priorities and its political prestige occupied much the same place in the Austro-Hungarian monarchy as *The Times* in the English-speaking world, or *Le Temps* in France.[21]

Benedikt's most obdurate intellectual adversary was Karl Kraus, who had turned his back on the *Neue Freie Presse* to found his own journal, *Die Fackel* ('The Torch'). The inflated rhetoric of Benedikt and his editors was an invitation to satire, for it ill disguised the inability of liberal ideology to face up to contemporary problems. This would-be humanist and universalist style actually concealed attitudes favourable to the ruling classes and the German minority. Finally, throughout the 1914–18 war Benedikt and his newspaper had been in the first ranks of the war party, faithful to the alliance with the German *Reich*.

The other refuge for Jews who remained nostalgically faithful to liberalism, even after its fall from power, was in *Bildung* and its privileged auxiliary, art, seen as a secular substitute for religion as a source of human values. For this liberal generation, the Ringstrasse was an open-air museum of artistic heritage for the edification of all peoples. The Jewish bourgeoisie had confidence in art (or at least in art which was officially approved by academics) as a guarantee of the success of assimilation. 'Wherever we went,' wrote Stefan Zweig in his memoirs, 'we heard adults around us discussing the Opera or the Burgtheater. We had no need to fear opposition from our parents: theatre and literature were reckoned as innocent passions, unlike card-playing or chasing women.'[22]

With the lucidity which shines so painfully through his blindness, Weininger correctly observes that Jews seemed to have a particular gift for journalism (a talent which he attributed to 'The extreme adaptability of the Jews ... the "mobility" of their minds, their lack of deeply rooted and original ideas, in fact the mode in which, like women, because they are nothing in themselves, they can become everything').[23] He is right again when he says that culturally speaking, 'Judaism, at the present day, has reached its highest point since the time of Herod.'[24] This insight makes his chapter on the Jews more disturbing than any run-of-the-mill antisemitic libel. As Gershom Scholem remarked with reference to Kurt Tucholsky,[25] the gaze of *Selbsthass*, when turned on modern Jewry, is far more hurtful than that of conventional antisemitism.

Recently several sociologists have attempted to probe the importance of Jewish intellectuals and artists in the cultural life of Vienna, an importance out of all proportion to their number. It emerges that Jewish families had taken the whole educational system by storm, as the 'noblest' means of social betterment and assimilation, in the last third of the nineteenth century. In all the high schools (*Gymnasien*) of Vienna taken together, 30 per cent of the pupils around 1900 were Jews. In the districts with the highest Jewish populations (the first, second and ninth) the proportion was spectacularly higher: 40 per cent, 75 per cent and 60 per cent respectively. The case of 'Leopoldstadt' (the second district) is typical: in 1900 Jews constituted some 34 per cent of the population, but 75 per cent of the high school pupils were from Jewish families. The figures were no less impressive in the girls' schools.[26]

In the University of Vienna around 1900, almost a quarter of the law students and over half the medical students were Jewish.[27] If we add to this the fact that in professional life,[28] almost three-quarters of Viennese Jews were in liberal professions or salaried professions in the tertiary sector (commerce, services, etc.), we have to conclude that in 1900 the Viennese Jews were not only the richest potential source of cultural output – taking into account their high educational level – but also an indispensable part of its public: readers of newpapers and books, theatre-goers, music-lovers . . .

II

Jewish youth: pan-Germanist, Wagnerian, Nietzschean

The Jewish bourgeoisie, both high and low, sent their children to high school and university to acquire the *Bildung* which, according to liberal belief, would firmly integrate them into modern society. It is easy to understand how the political – and moral – downfall of Austrian liberalism made the generation which reached university age about 1875 question the old, optimistic definition of *Bildung*. The history of the 'Pernerstorfer circle' and the association Leseverein der deutschen Studenten Wiens[29] is a good illustration of the conflict which, at about that time, was setting sons against fathers:[30] sons who were now looking for a social, cultural and political renewal of the liberal ideology of the Viennese *Gründerzeit*.

In the beginning, the Pernerstorfer circle, founded in 1867, numbered a few students from the Vienna Schottengymnasium: Engelbert Pernerstorfer (one of the few non-Jews in the group), Victor Adler, Heinrich Friedjung. These young men were dissatisfied with the liberal ideology, which they thought too individualistic, too indifferent to social problems, too cosmopolitan and too flatly rationalistic. They sympathized with the socialist movement, stood with German nationalism against Habsburg policies, and defended 'new values': nature, country, art, the new mythology and the *Volk* were the guiding notions of their movement, which declared for Nietzsche and for Wagner. At the University of Vienna, the Pernerstorfer circle became the intellectual core of the Leseverein der deutschen Studenten, founded in 1871, which rapidly acquired considerable influence. Among the students who frequented the private discussions and public debates of the circle was Siegfried Lipiner (who was to become famous through his correspondence with Nietzsche, and later with Wagner, and was to meet both of those geniuses), Richard von Kralik,[31] the future founder of Gralbund ('League of the Grail'),[32] and also the musicians Gustav Mahler and Hugo Wolf.

The Leseverein der deutschen Studenten Wiens was essentially and enthusiastically pan-Germanic, Nietzschean and Wagnerian. For this reason it was regarded with distrust by the university authorities. In 1876 the philosopher Franz Brentano came to give a lecture to the Pernerstorfer circle. He had been made professor at the University of Vienna in 1874.[33] He represented a rationalist and scientific view of philosophy opposed to the new Nietzscheanism. In his lecture, on the question 'What kind are the philosophers most likely to leave their mark?',[34] he attempted to bring his audience back to reason and dethrone the thinker of the hour, Nietzsche. These wise words were not sufficient to calm the livelier spirits of the Leseverein, and the association was finally dissolved in December 1878 for 'subversive machinations' and threats to public order. Many former members of the association were to reappear beside Georg von Schönerer at the founding of the Deutsche Volkspartei and the drafting of the 'Linz programme' (1882) of that anti-liberal, pan-Germanist and populist party.

At that time, Schönerer was not yet an overt antisemite. The outbreak of political antisemitism in Vienna dates from the early 1880s. It was to confound the individual strategies of assimilated Jews. The history of the Pernerstorfer circle and the Leseverein der deutscher Studenten Wiens shows that the new generation of Viennese Jews, the one which reached the age of twenty in or around 1880, was spontaneously attracted to German nationalism and idolized Nietzsche and Wagner. From the beginning of the 1880s, the antisemitism which was irreversibly warping that pan-Germanist ideology of cultural renewal and the *Volk* forced the Jews to redefine, willy-nilly, their Jewish identity. Some turned to the revolutionary social-democratic movement, others to Jewish nationalism and then to Zionism; yet others refused to admit the failure of assimilation as an ideal and were to practise a sort of 'extreme assimilationism', sometimes approaching what has been called *jüdischer Selbsthass* (Jewish self-hatred); others again were to try and face up to the new world order by falling back on individualism and the subjective quest for a new personal equilibrium.

Roots of Austrian antisemitism

There were several ingredients to 'traditional' Austrian antisemitism: anti-Jewishness could be aristocratic,[35] but it was chiefly clerical. Antisemitic Catholic writings were legion: from the pamphlets 'The Talmudic Jew' (1871) by Canon August Rohling and 'A Ritual Murder Proven' (1893) by the priest Josef Deckert, to the *Wiener Kirchenzeitung*, a newspaper founded in 1848 by Sebastian Brunner, which became steadily more anti-Jewish from the 1860s onwards.[36] They rekindled the antisemitism smouldering beneath certain popular religious customs, and nourished the 'churchy neuroses' alluded to by Friedrich Heer in his provokingly titled book 'God's First Love: Two Thousand Years of Judaism and Christianity. The Genesis of the Austrian Catholic Adolf Hitler'.[37] Those active in the fight for social Catholicism against 'untamed' capitalism (fostered by Baron Karl von Vogelsang and his newspaper *Vaterland*) readily stooped to antisemitic arguments.

The hostility of some national groups against the Jews who supported the dominant 'nations' (Austro-German in the Austrian zone, Hungarian in the other half of the monarchy) had long been an ingredient of Austro-Hungarian antisemitism. But from the end of the nineteenth century it acquired a series of new elements which explain the emergence of 'modern' antisemitic political movements: the pan-Germanist faction of Georg von Schönerer, whose political career ended in failure, but who propagated unusually violent antisemitic ideas through Austria; and especially the Christian Socialist Party led by Karl Lueger, one of the first politicians to have deliberately exploited antisemitic demagoguery as a tool in his bid for power.[38]

The growth in the number of Viennese Jews doubtless helped to stir up xenophobia and, in the poorer districts, fear of Jewish competition. In 1857 there were 6,217 Jews officially registered in Vienna, 2.16 per cent of the total population. After Jews were granted freedom of movement and settlement throughout the monarchy, immigration into Vienna increased rapidly. In 1880 there were 72,588 Viennese Jews (10.06 per cent); 118,495 in 1890; 146,926 in 1900; 175,318 in 1910. It would be wrong, however, to postulate a direct causal link between Jewish immigration and antisemitism. It would probably be fairer to say that antisemitism made the Viennese aware of the growth in the Jewish population. For antisemitic observers – and sometimes the Jews themselves – were undeniably inclined to exaggeration. For example, some descriptions give us the impression that there was a positive horde of Galician Jews in the capital; in reality, careful study of the geographical origins of Viennese Jews proves that Galicians never made up more than a quarter of them.[39]

Some facts have been verified by research: for example, the relative concentration of Jews in certain districts or even certain blocks (20 per cent in the first urban district, 34 per cent in the second, the 'Leopoldstadt', 21 per cent in the ninth), which could give the impression of a new 'ghetto'.[40] On the other hand, any talk of the Jews being dominant in the press, banking and the liberal professions, or of their being unusually wealthy, is usually exaggerated or misconceived. Statistics – which are hard to establish with precision from contemporary documents, for some Jews became converted and certain Jewish interests, especially after 1890, hid behind pseudonyms to escape the malice of the antisemites – confirm that there was a large number of Jews in professional circles.[41] But this fact is not easy to interpret. Was there a 'Jewish lobby'? The truth is that many observers and historians progressed, and still progress, too hastily from a self-evident fact (for instance, that the percentage of Jews in journalism *was* vastly higher than that in the population as a whole) to a shaky pronouncement on the 'preponderance of Jews' in the press.

We can no longer be satisfied with the methods used, for instance, by Hans Tietze, who wrote in 1933 of certain fields of activity (piling in as examples the trade in grain and in antiques, clothes manufacture, the press and operetta), 'These sectors are largely in Jewish hands. There is no need to quote any facts or names in support of this observation.'[42] Excessive reliance on preconceived ideas may lead to mere repetition of the prejudiced affirmations of antisemites. One of the earliest pundits of German antisemitism, Wilhelm Marr (who is credited with inventing the word *Antisemitismus*),[43] accused the press of being the tool of what he called, in the title of his book published in 1879, 'The Victory of Judaism over Germanness', while the third issue of his *Antisemitische Hefte* (1880) was entitled, 'Readers of German Newspapers, Open your Eyes!'[44] Did Karl Kraus, in his tireless struggle against the evils wrought by Jewish thought and Jewish money in the Viennese press, bring yet more grist to the antisemitic mill on one of their favourite themes? We can scarcely refrain from asking ourselves the question.

As early as 1900 the theme of 'Jews, Jews everywhere' had become commonplace in descriptions of Vienna. It became a virtual obsession, maintained by some more enthusiastically than others. A French observer, Ulysse Robert, commented unfavourably in his *Voyage à Vienne*, published in 1899:

> If Jews do not have the influence here that they have in France, they are none the less masters of trade and finance. One need only look around the Stock Exchange. They are a force to be reckoned with, because they are also numerous. Some estimate them at 75,000, others at 100,000. One of my Viennese friends said, referring to the Jews, 'They breed like rabbits.' It was a good description. However, since the antisemitic movement has begun to grow in the last few years, the Jews have had the sense to understand that the best thing for them to do is lie low. Otherwise they would be broken without mercy.[45]

Jakob Wassermann, who too readily betrays a *jüdischer Selbsthass*,[46] makes very similar observations:

> Soon I realized that the whole of public life was dominated by the Jews. The banks, the press, the theatre, literature, high society, everything was in their hands ... I was amazed to see the number of Jewish doctors, lawyers, clubmen, snobs, dandies, proletarians, comedians, journalists and writers ... German Jews had brought me to expect more of a bourgeois overlay, more discretion. In Vienna I could never be free from a certain shame. I was ashamed of their manners, ashamed of their behaviour.[47]

The long-assimilated Viennese Jews were themselves embarrassed by the newcomers. In his journal for 1882, Theodor Herzl noted that one of the treacheries of Dühring, the German antisemite, had been to deliberately confuse Jews in general with *Ostjuden*. He concluded that antisemitism would disappear in the course of 'progress', which would eliminate the handicaps of this backward minority.[48] In a paper later published by his son Heinrich, Theodor Gomperz pointed out the lack of solidarity among the various Jewish Viennese milieux in the 1870s: on the one side there was a tightly knit coterie of families who had settled before 1848; at the other extreme were the more recent immigrants from the eastern provinces.[49]

The shame these 'poor relations' caused the assimilated Jews is examined by Arthur Schnitzler in *Der Weg ins Freie* (1908), in which one of the characters, Heinrich Bermann, declares:

> I cannot deny that I am peculiarly sensitive to the faults of the Jews. That is probably because of the upbringing I and all of us – including the Jews – have had, which systematically inculcated that critical and vigilant attitude in us. Since our youth we have been encouraged to find specifically Jewish qualities especially ridiculous or repulsive, which is not true of the peculiarities of other individuals. I will not hide the fact that when a Jew acts in a ridiculous or uncouth way in my presence, I feel horribly embarrassed and wish I could sink through the floor.[50]

Weininger felt this shame too. There is no other explanation for the passages in *Sex and Character* which accuse the Jew of being 'the opposite of a gentleman', and declare that he prefers to hide in the bosom of his fellow-Jews, bend to the family's laws and accept an arranged marriage for the sake of money.[51] Evidently Weininger is here thinking of the *Ostjuden*, whom Joseph Roth was to describe with compassion and understanding in his *Juden auf Wanderschaft* ('Wandering Jews').[52]

New trends in antisemitism

The other new element in fin-de-siècle Vienna was the arrival *en masse* of German-inspired antisemitism, influenced both by Wagnerianism and by racist anthropobiology in the service of a reactionary *Kulturkritik*. Houston Stewart Chamberlain (1855–1927) lived in Vienna from 1889 to 1890.[53] His *Weltanschauung* fed on both positivist science (he had studied biology under the eminent Jewish Viennese scientist Julius von Wiesner) and Wagnerian ideology. To all that he added the German Idealist philosophy of Fichte and Kant. He wrote a book on the latter in 1908, presenting the Königsberg philosopher as a hero of the Prussian race, in opposition to Hermann Cohen who, at the same period, saw Kant as demonstrating the convergence of German mind and Jewish tradition.[54] Chamberlain was in fact Weininger's model. The chapter on the Jews in *Sex and Character* draws heavily on 'The Foundations of the Nineteenth Century' which Chamberlain had just (1909) brought out in Vienna and which is dedicated to Julius von Wiesner. This dedication, a strange one for what was to become a textbook of German antisemitism, in itself tells us a good deal about the pitfalls of the 'German–Jewish dialogue'.

The first place in Vienna to be contaminated by pan-Germanist ideology was the university. It was there that the agitator Georg von Schönerer recruited most of his henchmen. The German student corporations began to exclude Jews from their ranks in the late 1870s;[55] 'Teutonia' and 'Libertas' introduced antisemitic clauses into their statutes as early as 1877–8. The definition of 'Jew' which lay behind these exclusions foreshadows the Nuremberg laws: any descendant of Jewish parents is a Jew, a declared confession making no difference. The word 'Aryan' was increasingly used to mean a non-Jewish German, and no allowance was made for converted Jews.

Antisemitism was part of the 'correct' attitude in university circles. In 1875 the famous professor Theodor Billroth wrote in a pamphlet 'On the Teaching and Apprenticeship of Medical Disciplines': 'We sometimes completely forget that the Jews are a quite distinct nation, and that a Jew can no more become a German than can a Persian or a Frenchman.'[56] A while later, in 1891, Billroth revised his views and joined the association against antisemitism (Verein zur Abwehr des Antisemitismus): following a sadly familiar process, an intellectual who had provided antisemitism with arguments, and more importantly respectability, eventually turned away in disgust from 'vulgarly' antisemitic manifestations.

Hermann Bahr, who had begun as a rabid antisemite at a time when he was known for his pan-Germanist harangues and his ardent Wagnerianism (he was one of the leaders of the demonstration in Vienna to mark the death of Wagner in 1883), published in 1894 a collection of interviews with about forty writers, scientists and politicians, German, French, English and Austrian, antisemitic and philosemitic, on the nature and ultimate causes of antisemitism. This book[57] is by a Bahr who has repented of his youthful sins. He is, as he explains in a foreword, attempting to make antisemitism more understandable the better to oppose it. The pros and cons of the phenomenon, and almost all the possible approaches to it, are set out; psychological, socioeconomic and religious interpretations are offered pell-mell. The book is packed so tightly that Bahr's contemporaries cannot have found it particularly enlightening. But it does confirm one important observation: by the last decade of the nineteenth century, the synthesis of all the components of 'modern' antisemitism had been completed.[58]

Bahr noted in a foreword that 'Antisemitism is sufficient unto itself. It is not a means to an end. The only purpose of antisemitism is antisemitism. One is antisemitic for the sake of it. It can be intoxicating.'[59] He compared this sort of antisemitism to a drug or mystique. He thought it was one of the many symptoms of a return to religious sectarianism (others being occultism and spiritualism) which he had examined in his earliest writings on decadence and the fin de siècle.[60]

This 'antisemitic religion' was showing itself in Vienna around 1900 amid a proliferation of sects and chapels which was as grotesque as it was disquieting. One was the offspring of Adolf Josef Lanz von Liebenfels (1874–1954), sometime Cistercian novice at the abbey of Heiligenkreuz, editor of the journal *Ostara*, who revived the swastika and proposed to re-establish the order of Templars so as to muster the Aryans in their struggle against the Jews and other 'inferior races'.[61] Another was the sect of Guido List (1848–1919), founder of the journal *Ostdeutsche Rundschau*: he was the inspiration behind the 'German Union' (Bund der Germanen), founded in 1886 by followers of Schönerer, and the propagandist of 'Aryosophy', a belief founded partly on the racism of Gobineau and partly on the theosophy of Madame Blavatsky.[62] We could also mention the devotees of Arthur Trebitsch, a Viennese Jew, born like Weininger in 1880, who pushed the *jüdischer Selbsthass* to such lengths that he imagined he was being persecuted by an 'Israelite Alliance' and beseeched doctors to come and measure his skull to confirm that he really had all the anatomical characteristics of an Aryan.[63]

These various antisemitic sects, each with its own petty prophet, would deserve no serious attention were it not that their 'antisemitic mystique' had a profound effect on Adolf Hitler while he was studying in Vienna, from 1907 to 1913; he says himself, in *Mein Kampf*, that they were the 'granite foundation' of his racist *Weltanschauung*.[64] Other intellectual phenomena seen in turn-of-the-century Vienna show that the racist maunderings of a Lanz or List could have a direct influence on cultural policy. The case of the 'Aryan theatre' of Adam Müller-Guttenbrunn is revealing. He was a theatre critic and *Kulturkritiker*, with ideas similar to List's. At the time when he was in charge of the Raimundtheater he had affected liberalism and been a friend of Bahr's; in 1898 he became director of the 'Kaiserjubiläums-Stadttheater' (now the Volksoper). With the support of the city council under Lueger and the antisemitic newspapers *Deutsches Volksblatt* and *Kikeriki*, he aspired to regenerate Viennese culture by eliminating from his repertory all Jewish authors and actors, giving preference to plays illustrative of 'Aryan' culture – Germanic and virile – and encouraging new plays with a 'message' useful to the pan-Germanist and antisemitic cause. But his tactical ineptitude and his inability to keep the trust of his earlier admirers, and above all the disfavour of audiences, forced his resignation in 1903.[65]

Jewish reactions to antisemitism

In retrospect the antisemitism of the turn of the century seems almost benign. Stefan Zweig, looking back amid the heat of the Second World War on 'yesterday's world', saw little to complain of in those good old days. Verbal violence in the university had been followed up by a few fisticuffs and some nasty treatment of Jews. But in politics, anti-Jewish diatribes had seemed little different from the routine swapping of insults between nations – Germans and Czechs, for example. In the economic sphere, Jewish interests had been safeguarded and had been strong in some key sectors, in spite of all those who demanded a return to discrimination. In public life it had been known that there were invisible quotas hampering the advancement of Jews, especially in the army and the higher administration. But even the antisemitic Lueger, once installed as mayor, had not dreamed of implementing his programme in full. Many Jews had friendly feelings towards Lueger; Rabbi Josef Samuel Bloch said of him that 'of all our enemies, Lueger gave me the least anxiety.'[66]

The older generation of Jewish intellectuals did not take anti-Jewish trouble-makers very seriously. Daniel Spitzer (1835–93), famous for his 'Promenades in Vienna' which appeared regularly in the *Neue Freie Presse* from 1865 to 1871 (Herzl succeeded him as literary editor), wrote in an editorial of 1886 that all this anti-Jewish agitation was distracting attention from the real problems: public health, education, road-building. It was the voice of a rearguard liberal . . .

The wounds of antisemitism were none the less deep. As Arthur Schnitzler wrote,

> It was no longer possible for a Jew, especially a Jew in the public eye, to forget that he was Jewish, for others did not forget it – either the Christians or, still less, other Jews. One either had to be appear as insensitive, intrusive or arrogant, or as susceptible, timid and afflicted with persecution mania. And even if one kept enough detachment and poise to avoid both those attitudes, it was as impossible to remain completely indifferent as it is for a man whose skin has been anaesthetized, but who has to look on with open and wide-awake eyes as he is scratched, even cut, with a dirty scalpel until the blood runs.[67]

In what follows I am going to trace the crises of identity of some prominent Viennese Jews: Sigmund Freud, Theodor Herzl, Karl Kraus and Richard Beer-Hofmann. We shall see that certain specific features of Viennese modernity can be understood only if we bear in mind the profoundly disturbing effects of the outbreak of antisemitism from the 1870s onwards.

This applies, for example, to 'art for art's sake' and the Viennese aestheticism on which Carl E. Schorske's researches have thrown such a new light: 'Aestheticism, which elsewhere in Europe took the form of a protest against bourgeois civilization, became in Austria an expression of that civilization.'[68] Devotion to art and literature as a school for the man of goodwill was of the fathers' generation. The sons had the same passion, but they radicalized it: Stefan Zweig speaks of a 'monomania, a fanatical cult of the arts, a tendency to overvalue aesthetics to the point of absurdity'.[69]

Viennese aestheticism was not, of course, the prerogative of Jewish intellectuals. But it can be seen to assume a unique existential significance for them once it is interpreted as a reaction to the loss of political structures and of possible sociocultural identification, as throwing the individual back on certain refuges: beauty, introspection, dreams. It is then easy to see why these Jewish writers were in such a good position to go further than others in pursuing (and at the same time criticizing) the flight from the world and the denial of reality which is 'art for art's sake'. What we call Viennese modernity meant first living through a crisis of subjectivity, and then reacting against it. Some authors explicitly linked the crisis with Jewishness: Weininger saw 'decadence' as the natural vocation of the Jewish character, which acted as the secret agent of decay. For Beer-Hofmann, on the other hand, realization of his Jewish identity served as an escape from nihilism. Both these attitudes – Weininger's *jüdischer Selbsthass*[70] and Beer-Hofmann's 'cultural Zionism' – expressed a revolt against the intellectual climate of Vienna.

The artificial paradise of 'art for art' was not the only aesthetic expression of the Jewish crisis of identity. Leon Botstein,[71] taking up a hint from Theodor Adorno, shows how the pessimism of Mahler, who did not believe in assimilation, led him to break with the serene and 'reasonable' aesthetic of Mendelssohn and introduce a sort of musical *Sprachkritik*, questioning the classical criteria of beauty and preferring motifs of anguish, despair and death. The ruthless exposure of contradictions was also to be a concern of Schönberg, who on this point could be called a successor to Mahler. It will be understood that according to this approach, which could also be applied to Kraus and Wittgenstein, *Sprachkritik* indirectly expressed a loss of transparency and of confidence in the virtues of 'liberal' assimilation.

III

Individual strategies: Zweig, Hertzka, Popper-Lynkeus

Jewish reactions to Viennese antisemitism were neither unitary nor mutually acceptable.[72] They did not increase solidarity among Jews but, on the contrary, an even greater dispersion of individual and collective strategies, and of breakaway groups of every conceivable persuasion.[73] The particular cases to be examined in the following pages do not exhaust the infinite number of ways in which Viennese Jewish intellectuals took up the challenge of antisemitism.

We should, for example, pay attention to Stefan Zweig, who offers us an example of what Claudio Magris calls 'a vague and imprecise cosmopolitanism, an inspiration to universality often drowning in rhetoric and dilettantism'.[74] In 1913 Karl Kraus held up for ridicule this ironical portrait of Stefan Zweig by Leo Feld:

> This slim, elegant young man, with a fine-drawn, nervous face which might be that of a poet or of a bank clerk; this dynamic and enterprising temperament which never departs from the careful politeness of the well-brought-up son of bourgeois parents, overflowing with ideas artistic, political, scientific and industrial, who is to be found today in Canada, tomorrow in Mariazell, today working on a poetic fresco of the past, a few days later examining plans for the Panama Canal; this poet, musician and philosopher, who supplies a great publisher with brilliant projects, who writes editorials and poems, who translates from the French and adapts scripts for the cinema; always in love, and at home among crowds of friends in Paris, Prague, Brussels, Rome, Komotau, Madrid or New York.[75]

Presumably this cosmopolitanism offset the impossibility of belonging to the Austrian nation, doubly impossible owing to the decay of all national cohesion in Austria-Hungary and to antisemitism. Hannah Arendt remarks that this cosmopolitanism was like one of those international passports which gives you free entry to every country in the world, except your own.[76]

This no doubt explains Zweig's astonishing admiration for Émile Verhaeren, and later for Romain Rolland, whom he regarded all his life, with exaggerated deference, as a spiritual mentor.[77] Sometimes Zweig was misled by his own almost unreasoning cosmopolitanism. After hailing Verhaeren as a 'pan-European', he was shattered to discover in 1914 that his Belgian idol was an anti-German patriot, capable – it had to be admitted – of violently antisemitic pronouncements.[78] Zweig's mistaken belief that the pacifist movement could rest all its hopes on enlightened friendships between great writers was allied to his own inconsistency: he himself fell prey to nationalism during the early months of the war, as is shown by his private diaries and his astonishing and disquieting open letter 'To my Friends Abroad' which appeared in the *Berliner Tageblatt* on 19 September 1914.[79] The Jewish identity crisis as manifested in Zweig found a solution in internationalism; the solution was illusory.

This unconscious compensation strategy is not unrelated to the supra-national ideology espoused by the Habsburg monarchy in reaction to the irresisitible rise of nationalist movements. In Bahr's journal we find this reflection: 'Perhaps the new Austrians have it in them to invent an apolitical man, cut off not only from all nationality, but even from all States, a sort of new Jew.'[80] This sentence is echoed in Nathan Birnbaum's definition of the Jews (1915) as 'the Austrian people': 'As the only cultured people which has long been completely international, they seem positively predestined to approve of Austria, and to love her.'[81] This paradoxical identification of the old 'wandering Jew' with the myth of a supranational Austria was also to emerge in the thought of Joseph Roth.

It could also be shown how the longing for a liberalism now forever lost drew some Jewish intellectuals into a sort of utopianism which took up the old creed of rationalism and progress and projected it into ideas for splendidly unattainable 'cities of the future'. Thus Theodor Hertzka, the former econ-omics editor of the *Neue Freie Presse*, and the first – and ill-starred – general editor of the new liberal paper of 1880, the *Wiener Allgemeine Zeitung*: in his utopian novel *Freiland* (1889) he detailed plans for a new colony in Africa which would realize the 'best of all worlds' according to the liberal creed. A romantic expedition to Africa inspired by this novel was a resounding failure. The 'Freiland-Bewegung' founded by Hertzka was taken up in Germany by the pharmacist Franz Oppenheimer, and attracted a few hundred adherents before coming to a lamentable end shortly before the First World War.[82] And Theodor Herzl himself chose, like Hertzka, to expound his ideas in the form of a utopian novel, *Altneuland* ('Old-and-New Land', 1902), whose title was an echo of *Freiland*.[83] As for the Zionist utopia, it was destined to become a reality . . .

Josef Popper-Lynkeus defined himself as a realist: hence the title of his collection of short stories, 'Fantasies of a Realist' (1899). But his economic, social and political theories none the less breathed a utopian spirit. This engineer, an expert on steam engines, who was also skilled in aeronautics and electrical science, remained faithful to the tradition of the liberal *Aufklärung*, witness his enthusiastic study of Voltaire published in 1905. The guiding principle of all his theories is the absolute respect for life and the rights of the individual. For example, he wrote a book of reflections on war and military service to make the point that the state had no right to dispose of the life or liberty of its citizens, and to suggest a system of voluntary recruitment.

Popper-Lynkeus saw no need to develop a personal philosophy: he referred his readers and supporters to the anti-metaphysical positivism of Mach. His own social reform movement was from the first closely linked with the Austrian 'monism' over which Mach presided.[84] Popper-Lynkeus called himself a socialist, but his utopia was nevertheless a capitalistic one, though it placed its greatest hopes on state intervention as guarantor of social justice and economic commonsense. His system of 'compulsory food service' (*Allgemeine Nährpflicht*) is an amalgam of social security and military enonomics, mixing ideas drawn from physiocracy and *Lebensreformbewegung* (a return to the 'natural' balance between resources and requirements), from Malthus (Popper-Lynkeus advocated euthanasia and abortion as precautions against overpopulation), and from 'enlightened' *dirigisme*. In the early 1920s he enjoyed an immense reputation in Austria and Germany, and his inspiration lay behind the whole movement of *Allgemeine Nährpflicht*.

This scholarly and utopian engineer is the very incarnation of what has been called the 'second *Aufklärung*' which blossomed in Vienna around 1900,[85] rivalling the new party *Weltanschauungs* and the assorted nationalist, antisemitic and *völkisch* 'Kulturkritiker'. For Popper-Lynkeus himself, devotion to this 'second *Aufklärung*' was inseparable from his identity as an assimilated Jew, son of a small tradesman from the Kolin ghetto in Bohemia, born in 1838 and settling in Vienna in 1861, full of the hopeful liberal spirit of 1848.

Until 1881 Josef Popper always claimed to be 'without confession', but then he read, and was deeply disturbed by, an antisemitic treatise by Eugen Dühring. His own tract, 'Bismarck and Antisemitism' (1886),[86] was written in answer to Dühring. In it he recommends the founding of a Jewish state as the solution to antisemitism, while mercilessly excoriating the faults of the 'Jewish race' in a way any antisemite might have been proud of. To the end of his life he remained faithful to the Zionist movement. But on the outbreak of the First World War his chauvinistic and militaristic attitudes (on the part of a pacifist in favour of abolishing compulsory military service!) laid bare the contradictions of a Jewish identity profoundly assimilated to German culture.

Jews and socialism

To complete our survey of assimilated Viennese Jewish intellectuals in their reactions to antisemitism, which provides the framework for the more detailed case studies to follow, we must not omit to mention one of the paths most often trodden by intellectuals in revolt against the political and social bankruptcy of liberalism: that of revolutionary socialism. Victor Adler's progress along it was entirely typical.[87] Born in Prague in 1852, he attended the Schottengymnasium and was a founder member of the famous Pernerstorfer circle; a pan-Germanist and Wagnerian, co-author with Schönerer and Friedjung of the 'Linz manifesto' (1882) of the National German Party, founding father of the Austrian socialist movement, Adler had originally been impelled by a twofold passion: anti-liberalism (merging with anti-capitalism) and assimilation to a *Kultur* regenerated by Nietzsche and Wagner.

Victor Adler's contradictory responses to all questions relating to the 'Jewish problem' and antisemitism can be explained by his intellectual roots. He converted to Protestantism in 1878, believing that complete assimilation of the Jews was the best possible end, and socialism the best means to that end; but he did not hesitate to borrow for his own purposes the popular cliché of the 'capitalist Jew', the enemy of the people, and made allusion to an 'objective alliance' between Lueger and Rothschild.

The Austrian Social Democratic Party suffered from a fundamental contradiction. The considerable number of assimilated Jews in its upper echelons gave antisemites the excuse to refer to it as a 'Jewish conspiracy'.[88] And yet those same party leaders felt bound to avoid any pronouncement or action which might make them look like 'lackeys of the Jews' – *Judenknechte*, a favourite word with antisemites – observing a kind of neutrality on the 'Jewish problem' and hoping that antisemitism would disappear of its own accord after the triumph of socialism.[89] Austrian Social Democrats were careful not to take up too rigid a stance in notorious cases, from the Dreyfus affair to the Hilsner scandal; and they did not attempt to hide their hostility to Zionism and every form of Jewish nationalism, which they described as 'petty bourgeois' and reactionary.

The matter of Galicia clearly revealed the contradictions of social democracy. A Galician Social Democratic Party had been founded in 1897.[90] It was led by militants from the assimilated Jewish bourgeoisie. One of them, Max Zetterbaum, explained in an article entitled 'Class Conflicts Among the Jews'[91] that the enemies of the Jews were, on the one hand, the corrupt and cynical Jewish bourgeoisie, and on the other, the obscurantist forces of orthodoxy, Hassidism and Jewish national renewal. Defending Jews *as* Jews, the party leaders were never tired of saying, would only exacerbate antisemitism.

At the 1897 Congress of the Social Democratic Party, Victor Adler was attacked on this question by a Galician militant, Jakob Brod. The substance of his challenge was: should we not be defending the proletarian Jews of Galicia instead of merely denouncing Jews as capitalists?[92] In 1902, in the seminal work by the socialist Otto Bauer, 'Social Democracy and the Problem of Nationality',[93] we can still read that the Jews were a 'nation without a history', a 'sickly culture' whose development was going in the opposite direction from the other rising nationalities of the Habsburg monarchy, and that they would soon disappear from the East, as they had already disappeared from the West...

The 'Jew without qualities'

My description of the position of Jewish intellectuals in turn-of-the-century Vienna does not claim to be a complete catalogue, any more than do the chapters which follow. Such an inventory would undoubtedly have become enormous because of the great variety of Jewish reactions to antisemitism. My aim has been rather to show how the collapse of the liberal order, which had promised individuals a rational and foreseeable integration into society, obliged each and every one to face up to the new cultural and social disorder as best he could. Some shrank from this, even into the despair of *jüdischer Selbsthass*. To keep a balance of mind, every individual had to develop, both consciously and unconsciously, a personal, psychological and intellectual strategy for building a new identity.

The last certainties about Jewish identity were indeed to be found in antisemitism. The assimilated Jew seemed doomed to become an 'imaginary Jew'.[94] Jewishness became a perpetual process of quest, questioning and invention. What a century earlier had seem to be defined by the most un-bending of laws became uncertain and indeterminate. What had been one of the elementary characteristics of the individual – like his or her sex – now became part of their most intimate being. Every combination, however para-doxical, and every progression, however tortuous, was now possible.

The ever more insubstantial identity of the assimilated Jew makes him a prototype of the postmodern self: unstable, solitary, free if it so chooses from coercive ideologies, autonomous and yet constantly harassed by the gaze of the other, constantly tempted to abdicate the uncomfortable privilege of being a 'man without qualities' and identify itself, perhaps over-hastily, with any certainty which may be offered.

11

Sigmund Freud and Theodor Herzl: In the 'New Ghetto'

I

Freud between two cultures

Sigmund Freud (born in 1856) and Theodor Herzl (born in 1860) belonged to the same generation of Viennese intellectuals. Their fathers had looked to the progress of civilization and the Enlightenment to assure the success of assimilation as it had been defined, in the German world, by Moses Mendelssohn: to keep the Jewish faith ('enlightened', like Christianity, by reason), while unreservedly accepting German culture. Both fathers had confidence in liberalism. They refused to let antisemitic disturbances worry them unduly. After reading 'The Jewish State', which was published in 1896, Jacob Herzl wrote to his son that the Zionist ideal would soon be seen to be unnecessary, since antisemitism would have disappeared from Austria.[1] Freud tells this anecdote in *The Interpretation of Dreams*:

My parents had been in the habit, when I was a boy of eleven or twelve, of taking me with them to the Prater. One evening, while we were sitting in a restaurant there, our attention had been attracted by a man who was moving from one table to another and, for a small consideration, improvising a verse upon any topic presented to him. I was despatched to bring the poet to our table and he showed his gratitude to the messenger. Before enquiring what the chosen topic was to be, he had dedicated a few lines to myself; and he had been inspired to declare that I should probably grow up to be a Cabinet Minister. I still remembered quite well what an impression this ... prophecy had made upon me. Those were the days of the 'Bürger' [Middle-Class] Ministry. Shortly before, my father had brought home portraits of these middle-class, professional men – Herbst, Giskra, Unger, Berger and the rest, and we had illuminated the house in their honour. There had even been some Jews among them. So henceforth every industrious Jewish schoolboy carried a Cabinet Minister's portfolio in his satchel. The events of that period no doubt had some bearing on the fact that up to a time shortly before I entered the University it had been my intention to study Law.[2]

Eduard Herbst, Minister for Justice; Karl Giskra, Interior Minister; Josef Unger and Johann Nepomuk Berger, ministers of state: all were in various cabinets in the era of the Liberals from 1867 to 1879. Just after the defeat at Sadowa (1867), the Habsburg monarchy had at last seemed disposed to make certain political concessions. The promises broken in 1848 were, it seemed, about to be fulfilled. Young Sigmund's family, like most other families among the assimilated Jews, was optimistic for the future.

Marthe Robert has described Freud's education, which placed him 'between two cultures', but in fact closer to German *Kultur* than to Jewish tradition. On 20 February 1930 Freud wrote to A. A. Roback:

> You will doubtless be interested to learn that my father actually came from a Hassidic background. When I was born he was forty-one, and his links with his native country had been broken for almost twenty years. My education was so little Jewish that I am even unable to read your dedication, which I can see is written in Hebrew letters. In later years I have often had occasion to regret my lack of knowledge in this respect.[3]

Marthe Robert, commenting on this passage, suggests that Freud's father, cut off from tradition by the sudden move to the city from a small rural community, had enough living Jewishness still alive in himself not to feel dangerously uprooted, whereas he bequeathed to his children only some fragments of folklore and a few humiliating memories: they were left with a dead past, an uncertain future, and a present which had to be entirely re-made.[4] One humiliating incident is that of the cap in the mud, recounted in *The Interpretation of Dreams*:

> On one such occasion, he told me a story to show me how much better things were now than they had been in his days. 'When I was a young man,' he said, 'I went for a walk one Saturday in the streets of your birthplace; I was well dressed, and had a new fur cap on my head. A Christian came up to me, and with a single blow knocked off my cap into the mud and shouted: "Jew! Get off the pavement!"' 'And what did you do?' I asked. 'I went into the roadway and picked up my cap,' was his quiet reply.[5]

Although Jacob Freud did not give his son any religious education,[6] the Freud family remained faithful to certain Jewish customs.[7] In a letter written on 17 March 1873 to his friend Emil Fluss, young Sigmund tells how he had acted with his sisters in a play for the feast of Purim, a day of rejoicing to commemorate the deliverance of the Jews from their persecutor Haman.[8] He goes on to emphasize that the feast of Purim fell that year on 13 March, the Ides of March when Brutus murdered Caesar.[9] We might remark on Freud's slight mistake with the Roman calendar; but it is more interesting to see how freely he interprets a Jewish custom, comparing it with Roman history to bring it round to the theme he was himself most passionate about: the Jews' revolt against tyranny and their liberation. Throughout his life the same creative freedom can be seen at work in Freud's interpretations of the Bible and of Jewish tradition.

It is nonetheless true that Freud had no deep knowledge of Judaism, though he had certainly studied Hebrew and the scriptures at school (his Hebrew teacher, Samuel Hammerschlag, became one of his best friends). Although he often showed a remarkable familiarity with the Bible (but such familiarity was not confined to German *Jews*: it is characteristic of true *German* culture, from Goethe to Thomas Mann), he sometimes betrays a surprising ignorance, as in a letter to Martha (21 September 1907) in which he describes a visit to the Roman catacombs, says that he noticed many drawings of the seven-branched candlestick, and adds 'I think it is called a menora[h]', hesitating over both the word and its spelling.[10]

Freud's patchy acquaintance with Jewish culture may explain certain pre-conceptions about Jewish religion which are to be found in his writings. As Léon Poliakov has observed in connection with *Moses and Monotheism*, his interpretation of the ancestral religion, which he knew only imperfectly, is warped by the Christian culture in which he lived, which was accustomed to contrast the legalism and rigour of the Old Testament with the maternal tenderness of the New.[11] Two major preconceptions recur constantly: that Judaism was the 'religion of the father', while Christianity had 'matriarchal' tendencies; and that Judaism was essentially rationalist in contrast to the 'mystical' tendencies of Christianity.

These judgements, to which we shall return, are certainly debatable. In any case we may observe that they bear some resemblance to antisemitic clichés: 'For the Christian imagination,' Poliakov writes, 'the deicide Jews exemplified the type of cruel, infanticidal fathers.'[12] Similarly, the idea that 'the Jewish mind was incapable of mystical thought' crops up in many modern antisemitic writings, in which the 'Aryan' – especially the Germanic – mind is suggested to be essentially 'mystical'. The beliefs and prejudices of Christians with regard to Jews probably influenced Freud more than he cared to admit. For example, Sander L. Gilman has found remarks in letters to Fliess (20 July and 15 October 1897) which seem to show that at one time Freud, like Fliess, believed in the existence of 'male menstruation' and observed it in his own self-analysis. Gilman points out that since the Middle Ages, 'male menstru-ation' had been regarded as a 'Jewish disease'.[13] Freud, under the influence of Fliess, seems to have taken seriously – at least for a few months – one of the most racist hypotheses in the medical repertoire.

It is probable that Freud's real 'religion' was not Judaism but classical antiquity. He knew Homer, Sophocles, Virgil and ancient history better than the scriptures and the history of Judah. It is worth remembering that in his final school examinations he had to translate forty-three lines of Sophocles' *Oedipus Rex*. And his uncle by marriage, Jacob Bernays, was one of the greatest Greek scholars of his day. 'What did Freud see on the Acropolis?' asks Guy Rosolato; and he answers: 'He saw the Temple was no more... Staring at the emptiness through the gathering of ruined columns led him to another temple which was no more... For he was bound to notice the affinities between the Parthenon and the Temple of Jerusalem.'[14]

From Jacob to Theodor Herzl

In his 'A Disturbance of Memory on the Acropolis', a letter written in January 1936 to Romain Rolland, Freud described how far he still had to go before he could be assimilated to *Kultur*: 'Our father had been in business, he had had no secondary education, and Athens could not have meant much to him. Thus what interfered with our enjoyment of the journey to Athens was a feeling of *filial piety*.'[15] This 'superiority of the sons', a mixture of pride and guilt, was probably not felt so keenly by Theodor Herzl, since Jacob Herzl's family in Budapest had already attained to an elevated social and cultural position. When Theodor was born, in 1860, his family was well off, 'enlightened' in religion, liberal in politics and German in culture. Its Jewishness went no further than what the assimilated Jew and Greek scholar Theodor Gomperz would have called 'un pieux souvenir de famille'.[16]

The Herzls remained practising Jews, going regularly to the synagogue in Pest and keeping the chief religious festivals at home. But they only respected the food laws when their grandfather, Simon Loeb Herzl, from Semlin in Slavonia, came to visit. Herzl, like most young Jews of his social class, celebrated his Bar-Mitzvah, though his family called it simply 'confirmation'. The Herzls, like the Freuds, spoke in terms of Jewishness (*Jüdischkeit*), but not of Judaism (*Judentum*).[17]

In 1873 Jacob Herzl was ruined by the Vienna stock-market crash. In the next few years he managed to regain his prosperity. Theodor's literary vocation became apparent early, exemplifying the genealogical schema so well described by Stefan Zweig:

> In the Jewish world, the desire for wealth usually runs out after two, at most three, generations of the same family; and the most powerful dynasties find their sons little inclined to take over the banks, factories and prosperous businesses of their fathers. It is no coincidence that Lord Rothschild is an ornithologist, Warburg an art historian, Cassirer a philosopher, Sassoon a poet; they have all obeyed the same unconscious call to free themselves from the thing that has put Judaism in such narrow confines, the cold desire to make money; perhaps it also expresses their secret desire to escape into the realms of the mind from what is specifically Jewish – to become part of universal humanity.[18]

Herzl's first steps in literature show a whole-hearted allegiance to German culture.[19] In 1874 he founded a school literary society ambitiously named *Wir* ('We'). After leaving the Realschule he went to the Protestant high school in Pest (the Evangelisches Gymnasium), the most 'German' of the educational establishments in the Hungarian capital, and where there was a majority of Jewish boys of good family. In February 1878, after the death of Theodor's sister Pauline, the whole Herzl family moved from Budapest to Vienna. In the autumn of that year Theodor entered the law faculty of the University of Vienna.

Freud, antisemitism, and Nietzscheanism

In his 1925 autobiography, Freud wrote:

> When, in 1873, I first joined the University, I experienced some appreciable disappointment. Above all, I found I was expected to feel myself inferior and an alien because I was a Jew. I refused absolutely to do the first of those things. I have never been able to see why I should feel ashamed of my descent, or, as people were beginning to say, of my race. I put up, without much regret, with my non-acceptance into the community; for it seemed to me that in spite of this exclusion an active fellow-worker could not fail to find some nook or cranny in the framework of humanity. These first impressions at the University, however, had one consequence which was afterwards to prove important; for at an early age I was made familiar with the fate of being in the Opposition and of being put under the ban of the 'compact majority'. The foundations were thus laid for a certain degree of independence of judgement.[20]

His disappointment was all the more acute in that he, like most Jewish students, felt an instinctive sympathy for the German nationalist movement. This appears clearly from his political dream about the 'Count of Thun':

> A crowd of people, a meeting of students. – A count – (Thun or Taaffe) was speaking. He was challenged to say something about the Germans, and declared with a contemptuous gesture that their favourite flower was colt's foot, and put some sort of dilapidated leaf – or rather the crumpled skeleton of a leaf – into his buttonhole. I fired up – so I fired up, though I was surprised at my taking such an attitude.[21]

A few pages later, Freud emphasizes: 'In the dream, I was *surprised* at my German-nationalist attitude.'[22]

It has been established that Freud was a member of the Leseverein der deutschen Studenten Wiens from his entry into the university in 1873 until the association was dissolved in 1878.[23] Among Freud's fellow members was Victor Adler, the future leader of the Austrian Social Democrats, who appears in the 'dream of Count Thun'. From the late 1870s onwards, the antisemites were trying with increasing success to 'infiltrate' the Leseverein. This was the climate of the University of Vienna during Freud's years of study there. It is easy to understand the 'keen disappointment' he felt at the antisemitic drift of the German nationalistic movement to which he had instinctively rallied.

One wonders if Freud was at the Leseverein meeting of January 1874 at which Franz Brentano gave his lecture in defence of scientific rationalism, which was in part an attack on Nietzsche. It is known that Freud attended Brentano's official lectures with great enthusiasm, as is shown by his letters to Eduard Silberstein.[24] Brentano's influence on Freud was to prove lasting: indeed it was he who taught that psychology could not afford to ignore 'internal perception,' made possible through memory, and that it was doomed to failure if it took account only of physiology.[25] But Brentano's influence on Freud probably went even deeper than this. It was to help turn him away from the 'Nietzschean' *Weltanschauung* and towards an insistence on the *wissenschaftliche Weltauffassung.*[26]

Bearing in mind the prevailing atmosphere of the Leseverein der deutschen Studenten Wiens, it may be presumed that Freud very soon came to hear of Nietzsche: he knew Siegfried Lipiner very well, for example.[27] Freud's reservations about Nietzsche, which he never abandoned, go back to this period; they owe something to Brentano's influence,[28] but also undoubtedly to the misunderstandings which clouded the relationship between 'Nietzscheanism' (which was in fact a popular, not to say inaccurate, version of what Nietsche actually said) and Judaism.

Most young Jewish admirers of Nietzsche went through a violent crisis in their Jewish identity, beginning with Lipiner himself. For them, Nietzscheanism belonged with Wagnerism. In December 1883 and the first three months of 1884, Josef Paneth, a friend of Freud's, paid a visit to Nietzsche,[29] and the two men spoke at length about Judaism. Paneth sent a most reassuring message to his family: Nietzsche was certainly not in the least antisemitic.[30] But Franz Overbeck said in his memoirs, after emphasizing Nietzsche's spontaneous liking for Paneth, that 'Nietzsche was a resolute enemy of antisemitism . . . All the same, when he speaks frankly his judgement on the Jews sounds much harsher than anything said by the antisemites. His antipathy to Christianity is essentially grounded in antisemitism.'[31]

This evidence reopens the argument about the complex relations between Nietzsche and the Jews. Here I shall confine myself to suggesting that the feeling of profound 'incompatibility' between affirmation of Jewish identity and acceptance of Nietzscheanism may have influenced Freud's attitude to the philosopher. On his own admission, he felt great interest in him, but he also pretended not to know him;[32] – not to *want* to know would probably be a better way of putting it.

The shock of antisemitism sent the young student Sigmund Freud into a phase of profound political discouragement: 'In politics I have fallen so low that I can no longer even say that I have an opinion,' he wrote on 7 March 1875 to his friend Silberstein, who had been discussing his social democratic friends; and in the same letter Freud added, 'I should like to know if your social democrats are as revolutionary in philosophical and religious matters; I think that their attitude on that point is the best indication of whether their character is really profoundly radical.'[33] This evidence clearly confirms Schorske's suggestion that Freud, disappointed by political action, was to use other means – science and 'radical' thinking – of settling his account with a society which sought to deny Jews any place.[34]

Herzl, a Wagnerian among the antisemites

In the autumn of 1878, when he began to study law, Theodor Herzl was at first in sympathy with German nationalism. In 1881 he joined the student corporation Albia, whose tone was predominantly pan-Germanist and Wagnerian. Herzl decided to resign from Albia in 1833, after the famous festival organized on 5 March 1883 by the student corporations as a tribute to Wagner, who had died in Venice on 13 February. Albia, represented by Hermann Bahr, had had the last word, and Bahr had given a speech demanding the restoration to the German *Reich* of the German territories of the Habsburg monarchy, a speech which led to his lifelong expulsion from the University of Vienna.[35]

In the winter semester of 1878–9, the student corporation Libertas had added to its statutes an article making it impossible for Jews, even if converted, to be considered as German, or in consequence, to be admitted to the corporation. Herzl, who had requested an 'honourable discharge' (*honorige Entlassung*) was, in the student jargon of the time, quite simply 'turfed out' (*geschasst*). His private diary witnesses to the trauma of this exclusion: 'Ah! People do not know how much misery and pain and despair this "young man full of hope" carries hidden under his waistcoat. Doubt and despair!' he wrote on 13 April 1883.[36]

II

Freud: social confinement and Jewishness

For Freud, as for Herzl, the shock of the antisemitism he met at the university was of decisive significance. It revealed the fragility of the social and political gains of liberalism, the persistence of the hatreds of which Freud's father had been a victim in the 'cap-in-the-mud' episode. In the twenty years from 1880 to 1900, before the publication of *The Interpretation of Dreams* and the foundation of psychoanalysis, Sigmund Freud was forced to redefine his identity as an assimilated Jew in view of the by now obvious bankruptcy of the liberal assimilationist ideology.

One temptation seemed to have been put aside forever, that of conversion. Freud knew that such an easy – perhaps even cowardly – solution was of little use now that pan-Germanist antisemites were beginning to scrawl their racist slogan on the walls of Vienna: 'Was der Jude glaubt, ist einerlei. / In der Rasse liegt der Schweinerei' ('Who cares what the Jew believes? As a race they are swine').[37] Later he was to advise Max Graf, the father of his future patient 'Little Hans', against having his son baptised. Max Graf recalls:

> When my son was born, I wondered if I should not save him from antisemitic hatred ... and bring him up in the Christian faith. Freud advised me against it: 'If you do not let your son grow up as a Jew,' answered Freud, 'you will deprive him of those sources of energy which nothing else can replace. He will have to fight as a Jew and you must foster in him all the energy he will need for that fight. Don't deprive him of that advantage.'[38]

If Ernest Jones is to be believed, it seems that Freud only once throught of converting to Protestantism, for convenience's sake, to get married 'without having the complicated Jewish ceremonies he hated so much'.[39] Elsewhere, however, Jones says that Freud never really seriously considered the idea.[40]

At that time Freud was also learning to answer the delicate question of his national affiliations. It was a somewhat thorny question for a Viennese Jew, since the Austro-Hungarian national identity, mauled by the nationalist movements, was gradually losing all substance, but the Jews were not recognized as one of the nations of the monarchy in the 1867 constitution, and German nationality, which ought to have attracted a Jew imbued with Germanic *Kultur*, was denied the Jews by the antisemites.

Freud's sojourn in Paris in 1886 was marked by one revealing incident. General Boulanger had just been appointed Minister for War. At a reception to which Freud was invited, the neurologist Gilles de la Tourette described for him the fearful revenge which the French were shortly to exact from the Germans. Freud told him that he did not feel involved, being neither German nor Austrian, but Jewish.[41] In a letter to his wife, telling of this incident, Freud comments further: 'I always find such conversations very painful, for I feel they arouse the Germanness in me that I long ago decided to repress.'[42] George Sylvester Viereck reports a remark by Freud, made in the course of an interview in 1926, which sums up the whole problem: 'My language is German. My culture, my attainments are German. I felt myself German intellectually until I noticed the growth of anti-Semitic prejudice in Germany and in German Austria. Since that time, I consider myself no longer a German. I prefer to call myself a Jew.'[43] The price Freud paid for this 'decision' – to be nothing other than Jewish – during the difficult years between his university career and the foundation of psychoanalysis was what Marthe Robert has called a certain 'social confinement':[44]

> Freud could have made friends with one of those liberal Christians – few, but courageous – who were the open enemies of the antisemitic agitators ... and, after all, he was not actually forced to take a wife from a family well known for its orthodoxy, proud of its 'sages' and its past. But to all appearances he liked being among his own people.[45]

His best friends of those years were Samuel Hammerschlag, Josef Breuer and Wilhelm Fliess.

In 1897 he joined the Viennese branch of the Jewish association B'nai B'rith. Thirty years later, in 1926, he was to write to the association to thank them for celebrating his seventieth birthday, and he then recalled his state of mind in 1897:

> I felt as though I were despised and universally shunned. In my loneliness I was seized with a longing to find a circle of picked men of high character who would receive me in a friendly spirit in spite of my temerity. Your Association was pointed out to me as the place where such men were to be found.
>
> That you were Jews could only be agreeable to me; for I was myself a Jew, and it had always seemed to me not only unworthy but positively senseless to deny the fact.[46]

Dennis B. Klein has shown how, especially in the years between 1897 and 1902, Freud took an active part in the business of the association, giving many lectures and leading some discussions; his earliest disciples were recruited from its ranks.[47]

Freud against religion

Nonetheless Freud's affection for Jewish life and culture was allied to an undeviating hostility towards all religion, including Judaism. In 1882 Freud met an old Jewish stationer in Hamburg who had remained faithful to the teachings of Isaac Bernays, the former spiritual leader of the Jewish community in Hamburg and the grandfather of Freud's fiancée, Martha. He wrote to her describing the incident on 23 July 1882. Marthe Robert comments:

> Because of the illusion that it was helping to preserve, the Haskala was no more defensible than any other modern attempt to rejuvenate the prehistory of thought (Freud was to say elsewhere that he still preferred the old catechism to such attempts at modernization); but in so far as it taught how to do justice 'to the increased demands of logic', it prepared for the advent of 'our god Logos', the only divinity to which the inventor of psychoanalysis could and would make sacrifice in exchange for a real hope of progress.[48]

In the school of Brücke and Meynert, Freud had become a man devoted to laboratories and to research, a convinced positivist for whom science was the only religion. It is there, perhaps, that we should seek the 'nationality' of the man who would be 'neither German, nor Austrian': Freud the Jew assimilated himself to the transnational community of rationality. As a Jew he was an outsider in any nation; as a research scientist he was a citizen of the world of science. His social and political 'confinement' was in fact compensated by his intellectual membership of the universal *Logos*. This gives to Freud's 'assimilation' the deeper meaning which the assimilation of Jewish intellectuals in the German world had had since the time of Moses Mendelssohn, and which has been clearly described by Hannah Arendt in her essay on '*Aufklärung* and the Jewish question':[49] assimilation to the ethics and epistemology of the Enlightenment.

Peter Gay has laid great stress on the anti-religious – one might even say 'Voltairean' – aspect of Freud's intellectual outlook, concluding that if he did identify with Judaism it was in an 'aggressively secularized' way.[50] This 'aggressiveness' was aimed particularly at whatever in religion savoured of the irrational, miraculous or dogmatic. Freud as psychoanalyst was to make every attempt to 'demystify' religious belief, from his studies of hysteria (in which, following Charcot, he saw an explanation for certain miracles and mystical experiences) to his last book on Moses, with its stress on 'Moses the man'.

This distancing from religion became a positive allergy when Freud met with rituals and festivals. Jones tells how in 1884 he went to the synagogue for the marriage of his friend Paneth to Sophie Schwab: 'He gazed at the scene with a fascinated horror and then wrote a letter of sixteen pages describing all the odious detail in a spirit of malign mockery.'[51] In all Freud's writings, religion, or its appurtenances of church, ritual and clergy, are savagely criticized. In *Moses and Monotheism* he contrasts the clergy of the early Jews with 'Moses' men':

> It had become the main function of the priests to develop and supervise the ritual, and besides this to preserve the holy writ and revise it in accordance with their aims. But was not all sacrifice and all ceremonial at bottom only magic and sorcery, such as had been unconditionally rejected by the old Mosaic teaching? Thereupon there arose from among the midst of the people . . . the Prophets.[52]

While Freud respected the 'enlightened' religion of Moses (who seems to be the spiritual ancestor of the Haskala of Isaac Bernays), he had an overwhelming hatred for all rituals and dogmas.

This fundamental cast of mind in Freud throws a great deal of doubt on studies into sources which claim to find in the Jewish mystic tradition[53] or in the Talmud some of the 'inspiration' of psychoanalysis.[54] A letter written by Freud in 1910 in answer to a Jewish student, A. Druyanov, is revealing: 'My attention has frequently been called to the observations in the Talmud about the problems of dreams. But I must say that the approximation to the understanding of the dream among the Ancient Greeks is far more striking.'[55] The best way to establish a link between Freud's Jewish identity and the genesis of psychoanalysis is probably not to attempt the chancy and unreliable search for analogies between Jewish doctrine and some aspect or another of psychoanalytic theory. The approach I prefer is to try and show how Freud's 'Jewishness', taken not to refer to a strictly religious definition of Jewish identity, influenced the decisive choices in his life, and his intellectual options.

Herzl: from assimilation to Zionism

Jacob Freud left the Galician Schtettel in about 1844 and moved to Freiberg, in Moravia, then to Leipzig, then in 1859 to Vienna, to the Leopoldstadt quarter (there were many Jews there, some of them recent immigrants who were very badly off – but we should not confuse the Leopoldstadt of the *Gründerzeit*, which was still a middle-class district, with the proletarian quarter it was to become in the twentieth century).

In 1878, the Herzl family also came to the Leopoldstadt. Theodor's father, after the ruin of 1873, started a new career as a stockbroker on the Viennese market. But young Theodor's roots in Jewish tradition were even more fragile than Sigmund Freud's: his awareness of his own Jewishness was less spontaneous and less precise, his assimilation to German culture and nationality more exclusive. Thus Herzl's formative years, from the time he entered the university in 1878 to his Zionist 'conversion' in 1895, were full of temptations and changes of direction which did not afflict Freud during the same period.

During those years Herzl was torn between two identities which represented strategic decisons on his road to success. His law studies seemed to have fitted him for a career as a lawyer or politician; he was always to keep a certain 'legalistic' outlook, even in his Zionist writings. It might be said that a good deal of his later thinking was aimed at establishing *legal* grounds for the Jews to aspire to a 'national homeland', basing the legitimacy of the coming Jewish state on the notion of states of emergency and legitimate self-defence, and describing minutely the great, liberalistic legal principles which were to govern the new state.[56] This essentially political and juridical approach to the Jewish problems was to seem unsatisfactory to *Kulturzionisten* such as Ahad Haam (Asher Ginsberg) and Martin Buber, who preferred to look to Jewish cultural and religious tradition for the justification of the Jewish state. But it was the very knowledge and awareness of that tradition which was most lacking in Herzl.

Herzl's other ambition was literature. He aimed to conquer the two chief bastions of success in Vienna: to be a newspaper 'chronicler' (that is, write the fiction serial), ideally for the *Neue Freie Presse*, and to have his plays put on in Viennese theatres, if possible the Burgtheater. In the 1880s he turned himself into a dandy whose elegance and distinction quite eclipsed those of Schnitzler. He joined the young 'moderns'. Success seemed just round the corner: his 'chronicles' in various Viennese newspapers became increasingly popular;[57] in October 1891 the *Neue Freie Presse* sent him to Paris as official correspondent; when he returned, in the autumn of 1895, he became chief literary editor of the *Neue Freie Presse*. This position gave him a good deal of intellectual and political influence, which he used to promote the Zionist cause; his success in the theatre was less remarkable, but some of his plays were indeed put on at the Burgtheater ('The Fugitive', 1889; 'The Lady in Black', 1890; 'I Love You', 1900).

Until 1895 Herzl seemed far removed from Zionism. He remained convinced that the Jews must become totally assimilated to the German people. When in 1883 he read the newly published antisemitic treatise of Eugen Dühring on 'The Jewish Question as a Racial Problem', he agreed with Dühring's description of the defects of contemporary Judaism, and only disagreed with Dühring's view in so far as he (Herzl) insisted that these deformations had historical causes.[58] While he was in Paris, the Dreyfus affair and the fanaticism of Edouard Drumont made him aware of the seriousness of antisemitism and the urgency of the 'Jewish question'.

But his first reactions show a profound confusion. At one moment he was proclaiming that half-a-dozen duels with the leading antisemites – Prince Lichtenstein, Lueger, Schönerer – would be enough to end matters. If he were killed, his will would be found to contain a grandiose denunciation of this scourge of modern life. If he killed his adversary, he would be hailed as a hero. At another moment he was dreaming of persuading the Pope to convert the Austrian Jews to Catholicism *en masse*, at a ceremony in the Stefanskirche in Vienna.[59] If we read Herzl's diaries we can see that the threat of *Selbsthass* was never completely overcome. As late as 5 July 1895 he was writing: 'For the rest, if I wished to be anything, it would be a Prussian nobleman of an old stock.'[60]

A few days earlier, on 2 June 1895, he had paid his first visit to Baron Hirsch in the Rue de l'Elysée in the attempt to win him over to the idea – still vague in Herzl's own mind – of a Jewish state. Afterwards he wrote to the Baron, who had taken him for an unrealistic dreamer: 'Believe me, the policies of a nation are impelled by imponderable and imperceptible factors ... Remember whence came the German Reich: from dreams, songs, visions, black, red and gold ribbons – and in a short time. Bismarck shook the tree that the dreamers had planted.'[61]

At that moment, as he was beginning to visualize the Exodus of European Jews towards a promised land – wherever it might be – Herzl identified himself with Bismarck. A few days later, on 22 June, he wrote to the former Reich Chancellor asking for an interview. Later, he had a chance to urge on the Emperor the advantages of Zionism for the pan-Germanist cause: a Jewish state would be a spearhead of German interests and European culture in the Near East; moreover, it would relieve Germany of a good many of those Social Democrats of which the *Reich* was so anxious to be rid. Herzl's Zionism begins to look like the result of a crisis of identity in an assimilated Jew who was always to remain faithful to his preferred culture, which was German. From this viewpoint his Zionism would be the Jewish, 'neo-liberal' version of pan-Germanism.

We might even go so far as to suggest that Theodor Herzl had in mind a Judaism rejuvenated by Zionism on the Wagnerian model of a 'modern mythology' which would allow the restoration of a lost community. He did not see Judaism primarily as a religion. Moreover, we know that his Zionist plans were to meet with opposition from most Jewish clergy, both the orthodox and those rabbis who favoured an enlightened, modern rite. The former thought that political Zionism had mistaken the purely spiritual meaning of Zion; the latter that Herzl's projects would imperil all the gains of assimilation. For Herzl, Judaism was a national identity, with its own history and mythology, just like the other nationalities of the monarchy – the Magyars, for example.

In 1898, for the solemn inauguration of the Second Zionist Congress in Basle, Herzl selected some music from *Tannhäuser*. Heinrich Rosenberger, his secretary, asked jokingly: 'Would an assembly of antisemites have applauded the work of a Jewish composer as vigorously?'[62] Herzl's passion for Wagner's opera is expressed in his diary entry for 5 June 1893:

> This evening, at the opera, I had another chance to see what is in fact a mass phenomenon. There were people concentrating for hour after hour, without moving, in conditions of the greatest discomfort, and for what? For something which can be neither weighed nor measured: sounds, music, visual impressions. At all the ceremonies which will mark our arrival in our own country, I want to arrange for magnificent music to be played.[63]

Here we recognize the 'imponderables' that Herzl had mentioned in his letter of justification to Baron Hirsch. The Judaism which served to justify Zionism can be seen here as a 'nationalist' choice similar to the choices made by peoples of Austria-Hungary who refused to assimilate to an ever more evanescent Habsburg national identity.

The notion of a pan-Germanist Wagnerian Zionist seems somewhat contradictory. But it is probably not much more so than the ideas of Lajos

Kossuth, the historic leader of Hungarian nationalism, who swore exclusively by the Magyar blood – although he had little of it in his veins, being a descendant of a ruined family of the Slovak petty nobility. (This, incidentally, confirms that the *Blut und Boden* movement, despite its name, had nothing to do with either blood or soil and would be better called a *cosa mentale* . . .) Like a good number of the assimilated Jews of his time,[64] Herzl found Wagnerism supremely comforting because it promised the restoration of a national community which had been lost to the secularized liturgies of the *Gesamtkunstwerk*. Here we return to Herzl's early, literary vocation. We shall see shortly that he dreamed of putting on a play, with special effects, to be called *Moses*. We may be tolerably sure that he would have sought inspiration for this work from the master of Bayreuth.

III

Freud and Herzl: the meeting in the dream of 'My son, the Myops'

Freud was never to meet Herzl, who died on 3 July 1904. But thanks to Leo Goldhammer, we know that on 28 September 1902 Freud sent Herzl a copy of *The Interpretation of Dreams*, asking him if he could arrange for a review of it to appear in the *Neue Freie Presse*. He wrote a dedication 'With the respect that I – like many others – have borne for years for the poet and defender of our people's rights.'[65] We could see this as an attempt by Freud to reawaken public interest in the *Traumdeutung*, which up till then had been moderate. The chief literary editor of the *Neue Freie Presse* was, it seems, not specially impressed by the compliment, for no review of the book ever appeared in the paper.

In one of his lectures at the University of Vienna, in 1905 or 1907, Freud apparently described a dream of his in which Herzl had appeared, as Goldhammer tells us: in this dream, Herzl was a majestic figure with a black beard and sad eyes, and spoke urgently to Freud, who was deeply disturbed and asked himself how he could save the Jewish people.[66] But the only indirect mention of Herzl in Freud's published works is connected with the dream of 'My son, the Myops', which is examined in two parts in the *Traumdeutung*:

Another time I had a dream that a man on the staff of the University said to me: 'My son, the Myops.'[67] . . . Here is the missing main dream, which introduces an absurd and unintelligible verbal form which requires an explanation.

On account of certain events which had occurred in Rome, it had become necessary to remove the children to safety, and this was done. The scene was then in front of a gateway, double doors in the ancient style (the 'Porta Romana' at Siena, as I was aware during the dream itself). I was sitting on the edge of a fountain and was greatly depressed and almost in tears. A female figure – an attendant or nun – brought two boys out and handed them over to their father, who was not myself. The elder of the two was clearly my eldest son; I did not see the other one's face. The woman who brought out the boy asked him to kiss her good-bye. She was noticeable for having a red nose. The boy refused to kiss her, but, holding out his hand in farewell, said 'AUF GESERES' to her, and then 'AUF UNGESERES' to the two of us (or to one of us). I had a notion that this last phrase denoted a preference.[68]

In the commentary which follows, Freud explains:

This dream was constructed on a tangle of thoughts provoked by a play which I had seen, called *Das neue Ghetto* ['The New Ghetto']. The Jewish problem, concern about the future of one's children, to whom one cannot give a country of their own, concern about educating them in such a way that they can move freely across frontiers – all of this was easily recognizable among the relevant dream-thoughts.[69]

The ambiguities of the 'New Ghetto'

Das neue Ghetto was a play that Herzl had written in Paris, just as the Dreyfus affair was coming to light, in autumn 1894; it was published in 1897 in the Zionist journal *Die Welt*, founded by Herzl in June 1897, and was finally performed at the Vienna Carltheater in January 1898.[70] The première was on 5 January. According to Didier Anzieu, the dream of 'My son the Myops' dates from 'the week from 29 December to 4 January 1898, or the days immediately preceding or following'.[71] Freud would thus have dreamed this dream at the very time of the Viennese première of the 'New Ghetto' – a rare leisure activity for Freud, whose biographers tell us that he seldom went to the theatre. A letter to Wilhelm Fliess (4 January 1898) indicates that Freud dreamed about the play (whose subject must have been well known to the Viennese; the author's name alone was enough to arouse thoughts of the whole Jewish problem) *before* having seen it: 'On Wednesday, we shall go with your entire family (Bondy, Rie) to a Jewish play [*Judenstück*] by Herzl in the Carl Theater – a first night, which has already played a role in my dreams.'[72]

Between 1894 and 1898 – between Herzl's writing the play and its performance in Vienna – political Zionism had officially come to birth. *Das neue Ghetto* is a genuinely transitional work. It is an eloquent, but not particularly original, study of the 'Jewish question': the only 'reason' for antisemitism seems to be the financial power of the Jews; everything else seems to savour of an inexorable and inexplicable fate which exposes the Jews to the hatred of their non-Jewish fellow citizens. When Herzl was writing the play, which is accepted as one of his more successful dramatic works, his view of the world was still one of deeply pessimistic resignation.

In October 1894, in a review of Alexandre Dumas the Younger's play *La femme de Claude*, Herzl rejected the idea of Zionism and poured scorn on the character of Daniel the Jew, who dreams of seeing his people return to the land of their ancestors: 'If perchance the Jews returned "home", they would see straight away that they had long lost their community of being. Centuries ago they took root in new homelands (*Heimaten*) and were nationalized (*nationalisiert*): they are different from one another, keeping some things in common only because of the pressures which everywhere surround them.'[73] Herzl's reservations are revealed by the successive changes he made to the last scene of *Das neue Ghetto*. In the first draft the last words of the dying hero are, 'Jews, my brothers, you will only be allowed to live again if you have learned to die.'[74] Schnitzler, who was one of the first to read the manuscript, wrote to Herzl on 17 November 1894: 'There was a time when Jews were burned at the stake in thousands. They knew how to die. And they haven't been let live – because of that. Thus your play goes astray at the very end of the journey it has made with such vigour.'[75]

In the first published version (in *Die Welt*), Herzl corrected and had printed: 'Jews, my brothers, you will only be allowed to live again if you . . .' – the disputed phrase was replaced by an ellipsis. It was this somewhat enigmatic version which was adopted for the 1898 performances and is found in the *Gesammelte zionistische Werke*.[76] Thus it is clear that *Das neue Ghetto* contains no Zionist message. In 1898, it was only Herzl's fame as the leader of the political Zionist movement which could have influenced interpretation of the play.

Das neue Ghetto is set in Vienna. In Act I, Jakob Samuel, a young lawyer, is celebrating his marriage with Hermine, the daughter of Rheinberg, a Jewish speculator and parvenu who speaks strongly accented German. This is the world of the assimilated Jews who have lost their historical 'roots'. There is even a converted Jew, Bichler, who is gently reproved by the rabbi at the feast. During the ceremony in the synagogue, the young ladies do nothing but look at and compare one another's fashionable dresses. At the end of Act I, Jakob and the rabbi, Friedhammer, have an argument: the rabbi observes that the disappearance of the ghetto has exposed the Jews of today to the dangers of a Christian society which is hostile to them. He thinks that there may even be a good side to antisemitism, for it encourages Jews to fall back on themselves and rediscover their own religion and traditions. Jakob, on the contrary, wants to get out of this 'new ghetto'. The conversation ends thus:

> *Jakob*: We must get out of the ghetto!
> *The rabbi*: I tell you that we cannot! . . . Woe to him who leaves the ghetto![77]

This passage is interesting because it shows how starkly Herzl's ideas had diverged from Jewish religion, even before he became a Zionist. As David Ben Gurion was to say, Zionism is a revolt against Jewish tradition.

In Act II, Jakob is visited by his old friend Franz, a Viennese Catholic, who has come to tell Jakob that he must break with him, and that he is going to join an antisemitic group – out of conviction, but also to further his career. Jakob feels he has been flung back into the ghetto which he wanted to escape. A little later, a worker comes to see him who is a militant Social Democrat (Jakob has often defended members of this party without asking a fee). The worker has come to complain about conditions in a mine at Dubnitz, and asks for Jakob's support for a planned strike. The mine happens to belong to Baron von Schramm, an antisemite and personal enemy of Jakob. Moreover, the Jews on the stock-market are speculating on the Dubnitz coal mines because von Schramm is in debt, and Jakob has got wind of these financial manoeuvres.

Jakob disinterestedly supports the strike. When work stops in the Dubnitz mine the result is a flood, and part of a tunnel collapses, killing several miners, including the one who had asked for Jakob's support in Act II. Jakob's involvement has unintentionally played into the hands of the Jewish speculators: the Dubnitz shares collapse. Baron von Schramm is ruined and all his mines are for sale cheap to Jakob's Jewish 'friends'. Von Schramm blames Jakob for this, and challenges him to a duel. Jakob dies of his wound. The rabbi had warned him: in Act III he asked Jakob, 'Why do you feel called on to meddle in the miners' affairs?'[78] and then told him the story of Moses ben Abraham in the sixteenth century – how he heard cries before the gates of the ghetto of Sbira, went out to offer help, and was himself killed by the antisemites.

The lesson of the 'New Ghetto' is really somewhat confused and resigned. Perhaps Rabbi Friedheimer is actually right when he advises the Jews not to leave the ghetto. Pushing the idea to its limits, is Zionism itself to be a future ghetto, freely chosen – unlike the ghettos which were forced on Jews after the Diaspora? Jakob's humanitarian and political solidarity with the striking miners turns out, against his expectations, to play into the hands of the Jewish stock-market speculators. Whatever he does, Jakob seems doomed to a 'commitment to the Jews' which he rejects and which is grist to the antisemitic mill. Herzl brings out no convincing broader view in this play, although we should bear in mind that no one in January 1898 could have been unaware of the progress of the Zionist cause.

In truth the play came out of the personal crisis which Herzl was going through in 1894. The character of Jakob is strongly autobiographical: his marital difficulties recall Herzl's own (his endless globe-trotting was also an attempt to escape home life); Jackob's indignant reaction to his well-off family's careless, 'nouveau riche' attitude is very like the author's own. Herzl pushed his satire on the assimilated Jews of the Viennese financial world so far that Schnitzler, alluding to something Jakob says to his friend ('Now you can see why the Jews are dogs!'), remarked:

There your intention is clear – so clear that it shocks me! Similarly, the 'Jew with no sense of honour' whom you mention is by no means to my liking. Give your Jakob a little more inner freedom: the general idea is not enough, and it will make the character all the more sympathetic, don't you think? And I say again: one feels the lack of a self-assured Jew in your play, it seems to me. It is not true at all that all Jews go about like that, sometimes with a defeated air, sometimes inwardly corrupt. There are others – and those are the very ones the antisemites hate most. Your play is courageous; I should like it to be provoking as well.[79]

With his usual lucidity the anti-Zionist Karl Kraus, in articles of 15 and 16 January 1898, pointed out this major weakness in Herzl's play:

Nonetheless, the author of the 'New Ghetto' has unexpectedly alienated the sympathy of antisemites. In the setting of the financial world seen from a

Christian Socialist viewpoint, he has committed the error of not denying the possibility of heroic instincts, and has created the character of the noble Doctor Samuel [Jakob], who could not but shock that very element in the audience which would have been inclined to defend the author against Jewish attacks.[80]

Kraus's suggestion that Herzl had satirized the assimilated Jews from the viewpoint of Lueger's antisemitic party was a cruel one, but there is no denying he was right.

Hermann Bahr's review of *Das neue Ghetto* appeared in *Die Zeit*. Bahr, sometime 'comrade' of Herzl in the Albia student corporation, the impassioned antisemite of the famous Wagnerian festival of 5 March 1883, had repented only very recently, if we are to believe the confident assertion of his biographer: '[From 1890] he took every opportunity to combat antisemitism.'[81] He began by retracing Herzl's own career, describing the earliest plays with their would-be 'French spirit', their elegant lightness and 'champagne sparkle' (*das Moussierende*), which had nevertheless seemed too affected and artificial. Since then, went on Bahr, after his sojourn in Paris, Herzl had become more serious. Bahr then explained his own interpretation of Zionism as a realization that assimilation was illusory:

The best Germans among them seem foreign to Germans by birth: shadow-Germans, as it were, without German blood. They are German in mind: they have German ideas and German concepts. But they lack German instincts. And as they have lost their Jewish instincts, how can they live? That is why they wander, half-human beings, cut off from their best source of strength, creatures reduced to mere mind, strange and uncanny [*unheimlich*] to others, unendurable to themselves.

Bahr concluded that Zionists believed that a Jew could never become a true German or a true Frenchman, and that a Jew who tried to do so would lose the best of himself and gain nothing: 'I believe that a man can have nothing nobler in himself than the assured energy of the instincts of his race. It is to them that he must remain faithful, it is them he must cherish, each to his own. Jews, remain Jews! Do not surrender, be proud.'[82] Bahr then gave his strong approval to Herzl's 'heroic conception' of Zionism.

We may note in passing the nationalistic drift of what Bahr was saying: he saw nascent Zionism as a 'romance of national energy'. 'A Jew can never become a true German or a true Frenchman': this was the – alarming – lesson Bahr drew from 'The New Ghetto'. It showed slack thinking on the part of this 'pope among critics'. But it also showed the dangerous ambiguity of the message of Herzl's play.

Freud's dream of 'My son, the Myops' has been variously interpreted.[83] Here I shall concentrate on the elements in it which help us recreate the answer Freud unconsciously gave to the question raised by Herzl's play: where can Jews go when their country of assimilation casts them out, when they can neither return to the ghetto which they thought they had escaped nor leave it without risking their lives? Herzl was, of course, dramatizing the problem. In

1898 Jews could still live well enough in Austria, in spite of a few unpleasant-nesses. But the question had been asked. Herzl asked it and Freud's uncon-scious answered it. We might even say that this coded response of 1898 foretells in every detail the one which he finally made forty years later, in June 1938.

As Marthe Robert has pointed out, the dream came to Freud during a period of inner crisis, sustained and to a certain degree aggravated by con-temporary events: the repercussions of the Dreyfus affair in France and the slow rise of Austrian antisemitism.[84] At about the same time, on 9 February 1898, Freud wrote to Fliess: 'Zola keeps us very much in suspense. A fine fellow, someone with whom one could communicate. The lousy behavior of the French reminds me of what you said on the bridge of Breslau about the decay of France, remarks which at first I found quite disagreeable.'[85] The 'certain events which had occurred in Rome' must surely have had some connection with antisemitism. The Rome he was talking about was the capital of the Catholic church, the institution under whose cloak Freud had sought a lasting protection. In February 1938 he could still write to Marie Bonaparte: 'We have no other choice but to hold out here. Will it still be possible to find safety in the shelter of the Catholic Church? *Quien sabe?*'[86]

Long before that, in the dream of 1898, Rome is already clearly the enemy, and Freud does not dream of going there so as to share in her culture: he is there, but she casts him out and forces him to share the tragic fate of the Jewish people.[87] In his commentary, Freud compares the Yiddish words 'Auf Geseres/Auf Ungeseres' with the pairing *Gesäuert/Ungesäuert* (leavened/unleavened): 'In their flight out of Egypt the Children of Israel had not time to allow their dough to rise, and, in memory of this, they eat unleavened bread to this day at Easter.'[88] The flight from Rome – that is, from Catholic Vienna – is assimilated to the flight out of Egypt where Joseph had given shelter to his aged father and brothers. In the dream, Freud knows that he is not only Joseph, Pharaoh's protégé, but also Joseph, youngest son of the patriarch.

But what of the Promised Land? In a footnote to his commentary, Freud adds: 'The situation in the dream of my removing my children to safety from the city of Rome was distorted by being related back to an analogous event that occurred in my own childhood: I was envying some relatives who, many years earlier, had had an opportunity of removing their children to another country.'[89] Didier Anzieu's explanation is that Jacob, his young wife and the two children of his second marriage (Sigmund and Anna) went 'one way', to Vienna. This was the unfortunate direction (*Geseres*). The two children of the first marriage (Emanuel, with his wife and children, and Philip) went another way, to Manchester: the fortunate direction (*Ungeseres*). 'The desire under-lying the final "preference" of the dream is as follows: if I had gone with the other side of the family to England, if I had been Emmanuel's son, I should have escaped antisemitism.'[90]

The Myops dream shows a profound feeling of solidarity with the people in exile, and in this almost Biblical scene Freud seems more than ever part of his nation. But Marthe Robert remarks that 'as always, appearances are half-deceptive, for if he fully accepts the fate of the Jews, he nonetheless complains of it.'[91] Is there a sort of 'geographical slippage' by which Freud substitutes England for Palestine, Albion for Zion? In *The Interpretation of Dreams*, Freud introduces one paragraph of his commentary on 'My son, the Myops' by quoting Psalm 137, which begins: 'By the rivers of Babylon we sat down and wept.' Freud actually wrote, 'An den Wassern Babels sassen wir und weinten.' Alexander Grinstein notes that Freud was quoting from Swinburne's poem 'Super flumina Babylonis', published in 1869: 'By the waters of Babylon we sat down and wept.'[92] The German 'an den Wassern' seems closer to 'by the waters' than to the Bible, which has 'rivers'. Freud was dreaming of an English Zion.

While drawing on biblical imagery, Freud also remained faithful to his identity as a Jew of the Diaspora, and preferred not to make the complete break which would have led him to Zionism. In 1938, when the Viennese Society for Psychoanalysis decided to transfer its headquarters to whatever city Freud might settle in, he commented as follows: 'After the destruction of the Temple in Jerusalem by Titus, Rabbi Jochanan ben Sakkai asked for permission to open a school at Jabneh for the study of the Torah. We are going to do the same. We are, after all, used to persecution by our history, tradition and some of us by personal experience.'[93] This anecdote is yet another example of the superimposing on Hebraic tradition of the choice of England as a refuge. Freud, on his way to London, had the feeling that he was perpetuating, *in his own way*, a Jewish tradition.

In this context it may be noted that it was on 29 September 1897[94] that Freud joined the Jewish association B'nai B'rith – at about the same time, that is, as the personal crisis which was expressed in the Myops dream. B'nai B'rith ('Sons of the Alliance') had been founded in 1843 in New York. The mission it espoused was educational and humanitarian, and it saw itself as secular, cosmopolitan and faithful to the liberal tradition of assimilation. For example, at the end of the nineteenth century it was doing its best to help Jewish immigrants to the United States by subsidizing lessons in 'Americanization'.[95]

If we accept that the question in the Myops dream is the choice of a new country for an emigré Viennese Jew and his family – a choice between Vienna and Zion – then we should attach a good deal of weight to Freud's concluding remark: 'After the child had turned to *one side* to say farewell words, he turned to the *other side* to say the contrary, as though to restore the balance.'[96] The idea was basically to leave Rome without returning to Jerusalem, not to be 'myopic', to see both sides. For the other dimension of the dream is connected with the argument over bisexuality and the importance of bilateral symmetry which had set Freud against Fliess:

At this time my friend had been telling me his views on the biological significance of *bilateral symmetry* and had begun a sentence with the words 'If we had an eye in the middle of our foreheads like a Cyclops...' Hence the appearance in the dream of '*Myops*' (and, behind it, 'Cyclops') and the reference to *bilaterality*. My concern about one-sidedness had more than one meaning: it could refer not only to physical one-sidedness but also to one-sidedness of intellectual development.[97]

I might be tempted to add that it may also be the fear of a one-sided development of Jewish destiny, rejection of Zionism as much as assimilation.

Jacquy Chemouni, in her commentary on the Myops dream, makes much of the fact that Freud does not mention Herzl's name when alluding to 'The New Ghetto'. Freud speaks only of 'ein im Theater gesehenes Schauspiel *Das neue Ghetto*'.[98] This 'forgetfulness' probably does betray some conflict. Freud deliberately avoids Herzl's name, and this means he avoids having to pronounce on the Zionist question. He even avoids the name of Zion which is at the centre of Psalm 137, which goes on 'By the rivers of Babylon we sat down and wept, yea, we wept, when we remembered Zion,' while verse 5 contains the famous line, 'If I forget thee, O Jerusalem . . .'[99]

Freud's Promised Land: Zion or Albion?

The Myops dream, as I read it, expresses the fear and presentiment of inevitable exile. But the 'Promised Land' it offers is that of English civilization. This interpretation gives full meaning to the 'hatred of Vienna' so often observed in Freud's writings. It was in the years immediately before and after *The Interpretation of Dreams* that Freud made repeated complaints against Vienna (letters to Fliess, 22 September and 7 December 1898, 11 March and 16 April 1900).[100] Freud's love for England, however, always remained constant. He never ceased to envy his half-brother, who had been able to emigrate there, and Jones tells us that England always remained his favourite country.[101] He first visited it at the age of nineteen. Jones adds that this visit confirmed Freud's old admiration for Oliver Cromwell, whose name he bestowed on his second son.[102] In *The Psychopathology of Everyday Life*,[103] Freud confessed that he would rather have been Emanuel's son, for life would then have been much easier.[104]

More than once, in his letters to his fiancée, Martha, he mentions the idea of going to live in England (occasionally he also suggested the United States or Australia). Particularly striking in this connection is a letter of 16 August 1882:

> I am aching for independence, so as to follow my own wishes. The thought of England surges up before me, with its sober industriousness, its generous devotion to the public weal, the stubbornness and sensitive feeling for justice of its inhabitants, the running fire of general interest that can strike sparks in the newspapers – all the ineffaceable impressions of my journey of seven years ago, one that had a decisive influence on my whole life, have been awakened in their full vividness . . . Must we stay here, Martha? If possible let us seek a home where human worth is more respected. A grave in the Centralfriedhof is the most distressing idea I can imagine.[105]

These ideas are already apparent in the long letter that Freud wrote to his friend Silberstein on 9 September 1875, on his return from England: 'I would prefer to live there rather than here, in spite of the fog and the rain, the drunkenness and the conservative outlook,' he wrote, adding that he had sworn to remain faithful to the spirit of those Englishmen he admired, 'Tyndall, Huxley, Lyell, Darwin, Thomson, Lockyer, etc.'[106]

Freud in Rome: Michelangelo's 'Moses'

After the publication of *The Interpretation of Dreams* and the birth of psycho-analysis, in the first decade of the twentieth century, Freud's Jewish identity seems to have stabilized. Following on a period of retreat and dreams of escape, the time now seemed ripe for the 'conquest of Rome': the Rome which, in the Myops dream, he had been bound to flee, seemed to lie open to the founder of psychoanalysis. Between 1895 and 1898, Freud visited Italy five times, but never went as far as Rome.[107] He seemed to be inhibited about it. In *The Interpretation of Dreams* he analyses four dreams which centre on Rome. At one point he compares the ever-frustrated wish to enter Rome to the story of 'An impecunious Jew [who] had stowed himself away without a ticket in the fast train to Karlsbad. He was caught, and each time tickets were inspected he was treated more and more severely.'[108] Clearly one of the elements in these 'Roman dreams' is the forbidden desire for assimilation.

Another element in them is the revolt against antisemitism:

Hannibal . . . had been the favourite hero of my later school days. Like so many boys of that age, I had sympathized in the Punic Wars not with the Romans but with the Carthaginians. And when in the higher classes I began to understand for the first time what it meant to belong to an alien race, and anti-semitic feelings among the other boys warned me that I must take up a definite position, the figure of the semitic general rose still higher in my esteem. To my youthful mind Hannibal and Rome symbolized the conflict between the tenacity of Jewry and the organization of the Catholic church.[109]

By renouncing any possible vengeance on the Romans[110] – by abandoning the legal studies which, according to the prophetic public poet of the Prater, might have led the young Jew to a seat in the Cabinet – Freud was giving up the attempt to conquer Rome by force. But, he asks himself in *The Interpretation of Dreams*, quoting Jean Paul, 'Which of the two, it may be debated, walked up and down his study with the greater impatience after he had formed his plan of going to Rome: Winckelmann, the Vice-Principal, or Hannibal, the Commander-in-Chief?'[111] In 1901 it was the author of the *Traumdeutung*, the man of science: Winckelmann was to enter at last into Rome.

On 19 September 1901 Freud wrote to Fliess:

It was an overwhelming experience for me, and, as you know, the fulfilment of a long-cherished wish . . . It was slightly disappointing, as all such fulfilments are when one has waited for them too long, but it was a high-spot in my life all the same. But, while I contemplated ancient Rome undisturbed . . . I found I could not freely enjoy the second Rome; I was disturbed by its meaning, and, being incapable of putting out of my mind my own misery and all the other misery which I know to exist, I found almost intolerable the lie of the salvation of mankind which rears its head so proudly to heaven. I found the third, Italian Rome hopeful and likeable.[112]

The 'second Rome', the capital of Catholicism, could not charm Freud as could the ancient city.

To dispel the uneasiness caused by the pomp of Catholicism and the lies of assimilation, Freud went in the course of this first stay in Rome to see the statue of Moses carved by Michelangelo for the tomb of Pope Julius II. In that work, the artist – no Jew – had pressed the founder of Jewish tradition into the service of the Catholic faith. Was this not sacrilege to a Jew? How could there be an effigy of one who had forbidden the worship of idols? Freud thought that Michelangelo had taken desacralization yet further: his Moses was not the Moses of the Bible, but something quite different, the result of the artist's own feeling and his readiness to take liberties with scripture and alter the character of that godlike man.[113] Freud came to the surprising conclusion that Michelangelo's Moses is superior to the Moses of history or tradition:[114] he has mastered his passions, shattered his own anger (and not the Tablets of the Law), and shown true force of character.

At the beginning of his study of Michelangelo's 'Moses' (first published anonymously in *Imago*), Freud reviewed the numerous critical works devoted to the statue. This tedious enumeration does not include the poem 'Michelangelo und seine Statuen' by Conrad Ferdinand Meyer (published in 1882), although it succinctly suggests the same interpretation as Freud's. 'You grasp your beard, Moses, with a powerful hand, / But rise not from your seat,' wrote Meyer, and ended his comparison of various sculptures with this address by Michelangelo to his statues:

> You represent, my children, the gesture of pain,
> But without pain!
> It is thus that the spirit set free
> Broods on the vanquished sufferings of life.[115]

The stoic ideal of self-control in suffering can be perfectly expressed only through art: this seems to be Meyer's idea.[116] It is very close to Freud's vision. And knowing that Meyer was one of Freud's favourite authors,[117] one is tempted to believe that the poem had not escaped his attention, and might have influenced his study of Michelangelo's 'Moses'.

By 'assimilating' Moses to Renaissance aesthetics, the genius of Michelangelo had administered a sort of 'correction' to Jewish tradition which raised it to the height of a humanist universal and freed it from all the limitations imposed by the authority of scripture. We may well think that Freud, writing this, was identifying with Michelangelo as much as with Moses (it is usually the second aspect which is emphasized).[118] Was not his own kind of genius seeking to assimilate Jewish identity to a universal ethical and scientific ideal? Would not his later study of *Moses and Monotheism* seek to create a distance from the Bible with as much freedom as Michelangelo's work, and to raise

Moses to an intellectual and moral level 'higher' than that of the Moses of tradition?

Joseph, son of Jacob

Moses was to remain the biblical figure with whom Freud most readily identified. But at the outset of his career in psychoanalysis, he was just as fond of comparing himself to Joseph.[119] Moses was the masterful father, Joseph the obedient son – like Freud, a son of Jacob. Carried off as a slave to Egypt, he was successfully assimilated, and his skill in the reading of dreams made him the minister of Pharaoh. As Freud himself observed in a footnote to *The Interpretation of Dreams*, 'It will be noticed that the name Josef plays a great part in my dreams . . . My own ego finds it very easy to hide itself behind people of that name, since Joseph was the name of a man famous in the Bible as an interpreter of dreams.'[120]

One of the characters named Joseph in *The Interpretation of Dreams* is the Austrian emperor who initiated the Enlightenment and gave the Viennese Jews their earliest freedoms. Freud mentions the equestrian statue of that emperor, which is to be seen near the Hofburg in Vienna, in the 'Non vixit' dream,[121] where he also alludes to Josef Paneth, the friend and colleague who died young. Joseph, who had the key to dreams, was also an enlightened minister. He was finally to be the favourite son of Jacob and would give his whole family a triumphal welcome into Egypt.

William McGrath has pointed out that Ludwig Philippson, the editor and annotator of the Bible bequeathed by Jacob Freud to his son, saw Joseph as an avatar of Moses:[122] the dazzling success of his assimilation into Egypt had enabled him to put the Jewish family in a place of safety. His cunning and compromise were necessary so that Moses, the strong-minded rebel, could act to emancipate the Jewish nation. Joseph the wise, the interpreter of dreams, had in the end accomplished a decisive political achievement. Through him, the revolutionary ambition of the young Freud, frustrated during his university years, and the scientific ambition of the founder of psychoanalysis came into a perfect synthesis.

Freud, entering into Rome, might well have thought that he was following in Joseph's footsteps: he had achieved the necessary assimilation while keeping his Jewish identity; he had brought out his *Interpretation of Dreams* and could claim his rightful place in the scientific world. The way now lay open to Moses, the object of one of his earliest Roman excursions when he went to see the tomb of Julius II in the basilica of San-Pietro-in-Vincoli.

12

Each a Modern Moses

Freud's Jewish identity after 1914

The First World War momentarily stirred nationalist feelings in Freud which had been 'repressed' since his youth.[1] But on 9 November 1915 he wrote to Ferenczi: 'As for the downfall of Old Austria I can only feel deep satisfaction. Unfortunately I don't consider myself a German-Austrian or Pan-German.' This did not mean that he felt any more sympathy for the new, victorious nations: 'I should like to feel a great deal of sympathy for the Hungarians, but I can't bring myself to. I can't get over the ferocity and the lack of sense in that quite uncultivated people.'[2]

The crises which shook the European democracies in the 1920s and 1930s, the powerful surge of mass antisemitism in Germany and Austria, were to force Freud to confront once again the problem of his Jewish identity. The situation was very different from what it had been in the 1880s and 1890s: Freud was the director of an international scientific movement whose fame was ever increasing. And the 'Jewish question', too, had changed a good deal. Political Zionism had had some success: the 'Balfour Declaration' dates from 2 November 1917; the Hebrew University of Jerusalem was founded in 1918, and Jewish emigration to Palestine was gathering momentum.

During the time of his dispute with 'the Christian C. G. Jung', Freud had more than once written as if psychoanalysis had something to do with a specifically Jewish turn of mind. There is a series of pronouncements along those lines in his correspondence with Karl Abraham through 1908, including this from 3 May:

> Please be tolerant and do not forget that it is really easier for you than it is for Jung to follow my ideas, for in the first place you are completely independent, and then you are closer to my intellectual constitution because of racial kinship, while he as a Christian and a pastor's son finds his way to me only against great inner resistances. His association with us is the more valuable for that. I nearly

said that it was only by his appearance on the scene that psycho-analysis escaped the danger of becoming a Jewish national affair.[3]

This remark demonstrates Freud's tendency to consider Jung as the type of the 'non-Jewish intellectual', and himself, by contrast, as the typical Jew. This inclination grew stronger after his break with Jung. It could be said that from then onwards, the more Freud distanced himself from Judaism and all other religions, the more he was to suggest that his attitude as such was entirely Jewish.[4]

Abraham replied to Freud's letter on 11 May 1908:

> I freely admit that I find it easier to go along with you rather than with Jung. I, too, have always felt this intellectual kinship. After all, our Talmudic way of thinking cannot disappear just like that. Some days ago a small paragraph in *Jokes* strangely attracted me. When I looked at it more closely, I found that, in the technique of apposition and in its whole structure, it was completely Talmudic.[5]

It is not certain that Freud fully approved of Abraham's remarks: witness his reply in 1910 to Drujanov, the student who had questioned him about the Talmud. When Freud, at this stage, conceded that psychoanalysis was a 'Jewish science', he was not referring to any particular point in his theories, but to a state of mind. We find the following in a letter he wrote to Abraham on 26 December 1908:

> The opportunity of demonstrating our skill comes eventually, even if it should fail in this particular case . . . I expect a huge defensive din to arise from the case history of a boy of five which is to be the first article in the *Jahrbuch*: I have the proofs here for correction. German ideals threatened again! Our Aryan comrades are really completely indispensable to us, otherwise psycho-analysis would succumb to anti-Semitism.[6]

During the inter-war years it seems that Freud ceased to emphasize the 'Jewishness' of psychoanalysis and laid more stress on its universality: one of his patients, Smiley Blanton, reported him as saying that psychoanalysis, as a science, was neither Jewish, nor Catholic, nor pagan.[7] In 1926 he spelled this out in two important letters. To Enrico Morselli, who had just brought out a book entitled *La psicoanalisi*, he wrote regretting that Morselli had shown such reluctance to accept psychoanalysis, but saying that he had enjoyed his essay on the Zionist question. He added:

> I do not know if you are right to see psychoanalysis as a direct product of the Jewish mind, but if such were the case I should not feel in the least ashamed of it. Although I have for a long time been distanced from the religion of my ancestors, I have never lost the feeling of belonging to my people, and I am pleased to think that *you* call yourself the pupil of one of my fellow-Jews, the great Lombroso.[8]

Sympathetic to Zionism, belonging with the Jews, Freud remained sceptical about any interpretation which made psychoanalysis into a product of the 'Jewish mind': that is the attitude which may be deduced from this letter.

Being a Jew: conviction and mystery

In a letter to Jones in March of that same year, Freud defined his Jewishness as 'a private matter' which he put on the same footing as his belief in telepathy and his taste for tobacco, and considered to be 'inessential [*wesendsfremd*]' to psychoanalysis.[9] A couple of months later, in May 1926, he was writing his letter of thanks to the B'nai B'rith:

> What bound me to Jewry was (I am ashamed to admit) neither faith nor national pride, for I have always been an unbeliever and was brought up without any religion though not without a respect for what are called the 'ethical' standards of human civilization. Whenever I felt an inclination to national enthusiasm I strove to suppress it as being harmful and wrong, alarmed by the warning example of the peoples among whom we Jews live.

He added that there were a good many other elements which made the attraction of Jews and Jewishness irresistible:

> many obscure emotional forces, which were the more powerful the less they could be expressed in words, as well as a clear consciousness of inner identity, the safe privacy of a common mental construction. And beyond this there was a perception that it was to my Jewish nature alone that I owed two characteristics that had become indispensable to me in the difficult course of my life. Because I was a Jew I found myself free from many prejudices which restricted others in the use of my intellect; and as a Jew I was prepared to join the Opposition and to do without agreement with the 'compact majority'.[10]

Here there is a clear conviction of Jewish identity, but the exact nature of that identity remains mysterious. Freud's admission is paradoxical. At the end of the passage quoted above, 'Jewishness' is merely a favourable condition for the discovery of psychoanalysis – favourable, but neither sufficient nor, probably, necessary. But Freud also speaks of a 'psychic construct'; he clearly rejects the 'biological' definition of Jewishness, as he does again, implicitly, in a letter to Arnold Zweig of 8 May 1932: 'it is impossible to say what heritage from this land [Palestine] we have taken over into our blood and nerves (as is mistakenly said).'[11] While awaiting further enlightenment, Freud was content to accept a degree of secrecy and mystification.

This attitude emerges, for example, when he speaks of creative genius (at the end of his essay on Leonardo),[12] or of women,[13] As late as 1936, in a letter to Barbara Low remembering his colleague, the English psychoanalyst Eder, who had just died, Freud wrote: 'We were both Jewish and both knew that we had in common, deep down, this miraculous thing which is still beyond all analysis and which makes the Jew.'[14] But it was seldom that Freud scented a 'mystery' without attempting to solve it. After many delays – as happened with femininity – he resolved in *Moses and Monotheism* to meet the question of Jewish identity head on. (As for 'the enigma of woman', he had penetrated it in his 1931 essay on 'Female Sexuality' and his 1932 lecture on 'Femininity'.)

Freud's preface to the Hebrew translation of *Totem and Taboo* (December 1930) makes a fairly clear announcement of his desire to solve the 'mystery' of Jewish identity by means of psychoanalysis. No reader of this translation, says Freud, will find it easy to put himself in the position of the author, who does not understand the sacred tongue, is totally divorced from the religion of his fathers – as from every other religion – and who has none the less never denied belonging to his people:

> If the question were put to him: 'Since you have abandoned all these common characteristics of your countrymen, what is there left to you that is Jewish?' he would reply, 'A very great deal, and probably its very essence.' He could not now express that essence clearly in words; but some day, no doubt, it will become accessible to the scientific mind.

The final paragraph of this preface states that *Totem and Taboo* is about the origins of religion and morality, but does not adopt any Jewish viewpoint or make any exception in favour of Judaism: 'the author hopes, however, that he will be at one with his readers in the conviction that unprejudiced science cannot remain a stranger to the spirit of the new Jewry.'[15] This is more of a threat than a promise: if the 'new Jewry' does not find psychoanalysis to its taste, this will not stop Freud from attempting to solve the question of Jewish identity independent of any national – particularly Zionist – or religious considerations.

Freud and Zionism

In the 1920s and 1930s, Freud's attitude to Zionism became clearer. On 10 December 1917 he wrote to Karl Abraham: 'The only thing that gives me any pleasure is the capture of Jerusalem and the British experiment with the chosen people.'[16] Freud was always to cherish a deep admiration for Lord Balfour – who, for his part, thought that Bergson, Einstein and Freud were the three Jewish thinkers who had most profoundly influenced the modern world. Freud sent him a copy of his 'Autobiography' via Ernest Jones.[17] In 1934 Freud told a patient, Joseph Wortis, that he was not a Zionist – at least, not in the same way as Einstein. But he did acknowledge 'the great attraction' of a centre of Jewishness in the world to be a rallying point for Jewish ideals. If this place had been in Uganda, the project would not have had the same value, Freud conceded: the sentimental importance of Palestine was immense. He added: 'For a time I feared that Zionism might give an opportunity to revive the ancient religion, but people who have been there assure me that young Jews, in general, are not religious, which is a good thing ... But all this has nothing to do with psychoanalysis.'[18] Thus, while not contesting the legitimacy of Jewish aspirations to a homeland, Freud declared his preference for a secular Jewish state. Nonetheless Zionism did not really win his full support. In a letter to Friedrich Thieberger of 25 April 1926 he wrote, 'I am not altogether sympathetic towards Zionism, but I cannot judge its chances of success, or the dangers which it may have to face.'[19]

As for public commitment, Jacquy Chemouni's study of Freud's dealings with Jewish and Zionist associations shows that he was widely solicited by them. If it was a cultural or humanitarian organization he would not reject the offer. He refused only to be seen as 'an ideal Jew, a guide for Israel', as he put it.[20] Commenting on the flood of congratulatory messages which had reached him on his seventieth birthday, he wrote to Marie Bonaparte on 10 May 1926: 'Jewish associations from Vienna and elsewhere, the University of Jerusalem (of which I am a trustee), in fact the Jews in general, have fêted me as a national hero, although as far as the Jewish cause goes my sole merit is never to have denied my Jewishness.'[21] On his seventy-fifth birthday, compliments were again to be showered on him by official Jewish and Zionist representatives in the hope that his glory would reflect on their cause. The Grand Rabbi of Vienna, David Feuchtwang, for example, addressed his congratulations to 'the great Jewish scientist', adding that 'Perhaps the last roots and germs of your intellectual construction are to be sought in the Jewish terrestrial realm – perhaps. The author of *The Future of an Illusion* is closer to me than he thinks.'[22]

If Freud had agreed to become one of the trustees of the Hebrew University of Jerusalem, it was in pursuance of his hope that the Jewish state in Palestine would be based on a cultural ideal rather than on religion and national feeling.[23] In the correspondence between Arnold Zweig and Freud there is much talk of Zionism. Freud regretted that his friend found it so important to feel he belonged to a nation. He found it hard to understand Zweig's personal anguish, torn between his love–hate relationship with Germany and his enthusiastic Zionism. On 8 May 1892 he warned Zweig against the mirages of Palestine: 'Palestine has never produced anything but religions, sacred frenzies, presumptuous attempts to overcome the outer world of appearance by means of the inner world of wishful thinking.'[24] And on 18 August 1932 he wrote expressing his astonishment that Zweig should be yielding to 'the illusion that one has to be a German. Should we not leave this God-forsaken nation to themselves?'[25] That is probably what had always puzzled Freud about Herzl: Zionism seemed to him a compensation for national feelings frustrated by antisemitism. Freud himself had never been so deeply infected by the 'disease of Germanness', so he did not feel the need for a Zionist antidote.

II

Moses the Egyptian: Freud, Schiller, Goethe, Heine and Popper-Lynkeus

Moses and Monotheism was the work of Freud in exile. The first preface to part 2, 'written before March 1938 in Vienna', alludes to the protection of the church: 'We are living here in a Catholic country under the protection of that Church, uncertain how long that protection will hold out.'[26] Freud goes on to explain that the work is not to be published during its author's lifetime: 'So long as it lasts, we naturally hesitate to do anything that would be bound to arouse the Church's hostility.' [27]

As in the Myops dream, Freud had had to flee from Rome. Once in London there was no further need to delay publication:

> In the few weeks of my stay here I have received countless greetings ... And in addition there arrived, with a frequency surprising to a foreigner, communications of another sort, which were concerned with the state of my soul, which pointed out to me the way of Christ and sought to enlighten me on the future of Israel.[28]

Thus the messages of welcome – some more welcome than others – tended to put Freud back face to face with the dilemma of assimilation versus Zionism, whereas all his pronouncements and writings to date had shown that he claimed the right to choose a 'third way'. In this context his book on Moses begins to look like a final and indirect piece of self-justification. In it Freud paradoxically affirms that his fidelity to Jewish tradition has involved him in a historical and psychological reinterpretation of scripture which may seem heretical. In this last great work he explains, for the last time, that his choice of Diaspora in the spirit of *Aufklärung* is a return to the sources – a return no less legitimate than that of Zionism.

Freud's theory that Moses was an Egyptian is certainly the weak point of the book. But it is also what he found most important in it: the more he insists that his 'Egyptian Moses' is not the real source of his troubles, the more the reader is inclined to think that it is – the sore point to which the author returns again and again.[29]

In fact, whether he knew it or not, Freud's insistence on Moses's Egyptian origins was an echo of an old Enlightenment polemic.[30] In the summer of 1789, as part of a series of lectures at the University of Jena entitled 'An Introduction to World History', Schiller gave a course on 'The Sending of Moses'. He said that Moses had been the first to achieve the modern synthesis between religion and the state. The religion of Moses had created a unity which the law by itself could not establish; it expressed the truth in a language the people could understand; it worked for the emancipation of the people and the triumph of reason (*Vernunft*) in history. Thus Moses was the remote ancestor of the contemporary *Aufklärung* (Enlightenment).[31]

Schiller had in mind a work by Carl L. Reinhold, a Freemason and follower of Kant, a professor at the University of Jena. In *Die Hebräischen Mysterien oder die älteste religiöse Freimaurerey* ('The Hebrew Mysteries or the Oldest Religious Freemasonry', published in Leipzig, 1788, under the pseudonym Br. Decius), we read that 'among the Hebrews who came out of Egypt, everything was Egyptian, from the gold and silver vessels that they carried off in secret to the wisdom of their guide and lawgiver.' Reinhold in his turn was pursuing the arguments of Manetho, an Egyptian priest of the Hellenistic era (third century BC).[32] Schiller, following Reinhold, explained how Moses had discovered in the Egyptian cult at Hieropolis the earliest manifestation of the Supreme Being. His stroke of genius had been to pass off this 'Egyptian invention' as the God of the Hebrew nation. It was a kind of 'ruse of history' for the benefit of reason.

It is not certain that Freud knew this text of Schiller's, but there is every reason to believe that he did, given his familiarity with the German classics. In any case the comparison is interesting, and throws some light on Freud's probable intentions in declaring that Moses was of Egyptian origin. By constructing this 'historical romance',[33] Freud was turning Moses into a sort of proto-Freemason, a pioneer of Enlightenment rationalism, a sort of 'enlightened despot' who used the cloak of religion to deliver to a still uncultivated people, the primitive Hebrews, an audaciously progressive and modern message. All in all, Moses's achievement had been the opposite of 'religious' (in the pejorative sense a 'Voltairean' like Freud would give to that word): it had furthered a 'secular concept of life and a progression beyond magical thinking, a rejection of mysticism', as Freud wrote in a letter of 14 December 1937.[34]

This vision, reminiscent of Schiller's and influenced by Reinhold, connects with a tradition within the French Enlightenment (Voltaire's *La philosophie de l'histoire* of 1765, Nicolas Antoine Boulanger's *Recherches sur l'origine du despotisme oriental* of 1761, etc.) which tended to see the founders of Judeo-Christian religion as manipulators who were not above using cunning and lies to rouse people from their spiritual torpor and impose their new way of worship.

Though Freud does not mention Schiller's essay, he does devote a good deal of attention to Goethe, whose authority he cites in support of the second hypothesis Freud proposes with no other proof than his own conviction: that Moses was murdered in the wilderness. Goethe wrote his 'Israel in der Wüste' ('Israel in the Wilderness') in 1797;[35] its gestation can be followed through his letters to Schiller.[36] Goethe applied to the Book of Exodus a method of historical criticism inspired by his universalist theism.

Freud certainly owes a good deal to Goethe's description of Moses as irascible, cunning and occasionally violent. But he does not follow Goethe's suggestions as to Moses's 'faults': his cruelty and lack of breeding (Goethe makes Moses a shepherd's son, but to Freud he is of noble birth and right-hand man to the pharaoh Akhenaton); his bad leadership and poor strategy. 'Unfortunately,' Goethe wrote, 'Moses had even less ability as a general than as a sovereign... He was not equal to his great task.'[37] His Moses finds it harder and harder to make people obey him; rebellions come thick and fast; he destroys Aaron when he revolts against him, but is finally killed in another uprising. This is Goethe's explanation of how Moses came to be murdered in the wilderness.

Freud owes more to Goethe than the mere hypothesis. He also took from him the idea of a radically *humanized* Moses. At the end of his work, Goethe anticipates the criticisms of those who may accuse him of denigrating one of the greatest figures in the Bible:

It is not any particular ability or skill which really makes the man of action, but his personality, on which everything depends in such circumstances. Character is founded on personality, not on ability. . . . And we readily admit that the personality of Moses, after his first crime of blood, and through all his acts of cruelty until his death, gives a highly significant and fitting image of a man impelled by his nature towards the greatest ends.[38]

It was probably from Goethe that Freud got his idea of stressing 'Moses the man'. Perhaps the faults described by Goethe are settled by Freud on the *other* Moses in his historical romance, the Madianite Moses whom he contrasts with Moses the Egyptian. The Madianite Moses is the prophet of Yahweh, who 'was probably in no respect a prominent being. A coarse, narrow-minded, local god, violent and bloodthirsty.'[39]

Thus Freud's 'rationalized' and 'humanized' Moses harks back to the great masters of the *Aufklärung*. He is a link with the biblical interpretations of historical critics in the Age of the Enlightenment, who made Moses into a prototype of the *Aufklärer*. There is a witness to this interpretation in a letter Hölderlin wrote to his brother on 1 January 1799: 'Kant is the Moses of our nation: he led it out of its slumber in Egypt into the lonely wilderness of his speculations, so that it brought back from the sacred mountain the vigour of the Law.'[40]

Heinrich Heine's own intellectual journey brought him to a similar vision. Freud, in a footnote to *Moses*, alluded to Heine's intuition: 'Who suggested to the Jewish poet Heine in the nineteenth century AD that he should complain of his religion as "the plague dragged along from the Nile Valley, the unhealthy beliefs of Ancient Egypt"?'[41] Freud is quoting from the poem 'The New Israelite Hospital of Hamburg' (1843). Heine was then going through his violently anti-religious and anti-Jewish phase. Freud used Heine's bitter jest as one more argument in favour of his theory of Moses's Egyptian origins.

In fact no such idea had been in Heine's mind. In his 1843 poem he had enumerated the three plagues which afflicted the Jews: poverty, disease and Judaism. He said that 'The worst of the three is the last. / The hereditary, thousand-year disease, / The plague dragged along from the Nile Valley, . . .'[42] In an essay on 'The Musical Season of 1844', in which he mentions that Meyerbeer was Jewish, Heine develops the notion by making Spontini say: 'Accursed Pharaoh! You are responsible for my misery. If you had not let the Children of Israel leave the land of Egypt, or if you had let them all drown in the Nile, I should not have been crowded out of Vienna by Meyerbeer and Mendelssohn.'[43] Heine subsequently revised his judgement of Moses and, in his later writings, showed him as a great educator of the human race, while still contrasting Egyptian obscurantism with the enlightened Mosaic law.[44] Freud was mistaken in thinking that Heine had divined that Moses was an Egyptian. But he was invoking the authority of a poet who, like him, had included Moses among the precursors of the *Aufklärung*.[45]

Josef Popper-Lynkeus, who worked entirely within the Enlightenment tradition, wrote a short story entitled 'The Son of the King of Egypt' (in his collection 'Fantasies of a Realist'), in which he advanced a hypothesis which Freud must have found attractive. Popper, too, suggested an Egyptian Moses, or, more precisely, a Moses born of a pharaoh and a Jewess. Jean Starobinski writes: 'Freud had not formulated the idea that Moses might be a Jewish-Egyptian half-breed; what source could have suggested it to him? But was it not an attractive variation on the family romance? Popper brought forth from a "mixed union" the very man who was to decree the laws to safeguard Jewish identity.'[46] Starobinski adds that this would make Moses's struggle against his father, the pharaoh, into a variant of the Oedipal conflict; but that Popper's inspiration was predominantly 'pan-national' and universalistic. By making Moses into the son of an Egyptian, Popper-Lynkeus was disputing all notions of Jewish 'particularism' and reducing the genealogy of the 'chosen people' to fully human proportions and contingencies. This latter aspect also assumes great importance in Freud's book on Moses.

Around Lagarde and Chamberlain

When Israël Doryon embarked on his study of 'Freud and Hebrew Monotheism: *Moses and Monotheism*', he asked Freud if Popper-Lynkeus had in fact influenced him. Doryon published Freud's three replies, confirming that Popper-Lynkeus might very well have influenced him, although it was a long time since he had read 'Fantasies of a Realist', and the idea of Moses as a 'half-Egyptian' was less bold than that of 'Moses the full Egyptian'. In the first of his letters, written from London on 7 October 1938, Freud added this interesting detail: 'When it [my book on Moses] was already in print, to my surprise I discovered this thesis [that Moses was Egyptian] in the writings of the all-too-famous Houston Stewart Chamberlain'.[47] Chamberlain had indeed written in 'The Foundations of the Nineteenth Century' that Moses was sprung not from Judah but from the Tribes of Israel; and he added parenthetically, 'if he was not purely and simply an entirely non-Semitic Egyptian'.[48]

Chamberlain's specious distinction between Israel and Judah was a mere device intended to strip the Jews of all their prestigious contributions to culture by attributing them to another people, less unworthy of the respect of an antisemite. All Chamberlain's published writings illustrate the reversal of Enlightenment tradition into an early twentieth-century counter-Enlightenment: his 1905 book on *Immanuel Kant* makes that philosopher into an heir and hero of the Germanic *Weltanschauung*, while his *Goethe* (1912) insists that the whole of the Weimar master's works were animated by a rejection of Judaism.[49] One of Chamberlain's other books was devoted, more logically, to *Richard Wagner*.

In support of his suggested 'Egyptian Moses', Chamberlain quotes a sentence from Ernest Renan declaring that 'Moses must be considered almost as an Egyptian', and Maspero's comment on an Egyptian tradition making Moses into a priest called Osarsyph who had fled from Heliopolis. This unexpected convergence between Freud and Chamberlain proves that Freud's book on Moses was in truth taking him on to dangerous ground and risking the gravest misunderstanding . . . That is, alert readers of *Moses and Monotheism*, published in 1939, could scarcely avoid the comparison with Chamberlain. This was all the more likely in that another leading antisemitic Germanist thinker, the orientalist Paul Lagarde (1827–91), whose *Deutsche Schriften* (1878, 1881) were extensively quarried by Chamberlain and his followers,[50] had already advanced the same thesis in 1880 in a learned article entitled 'Erklärung hebräischer Wörter' ('Explanation of Hebrew Words').[51] Lagarde accepted Manetho's interpretation of the Flight out of Egypt – Manetho having been the first to identify Moses with the Egyptian Osarsyph.

It is clear, then, that from the end of the nineteenth century the idea of Moses as an Egyptian had become commonplace among antisemites, having been launched a century earlier, in an anti-dogmatic spirit, by certain historical critics of the Bible. It cannot be denied that Freud's determination to cast doubt on the Jewishness of Moses betrays a certain animosity towards traditional Judaism. We may recall his letter to Arnold Zweig of 18 August 1933 (it is not to be found in the official edition, but a significant extract is given by Max Schur): 'Our great master Moses was, after all, strongly antisemitic and made no secret of it. Perhaps he was really Egyptian.'[52]

Certain commentators on this delicate question have, like Paul Roazen, unhesitatingly spoken of a 'hatred of his own Jewishness'[53] which makes of Freud a representative of *jüdischer Selbsthass* (Jewish self-hatred) – a theme to which we shall return in connection with Karl Kraus. Otto Weininger, with whom Freud had had a brief but memorable encounter,[54] had been a spectacular example of that pathological state which Theodor Lessing (another of Freud's *bêtes noires*) had attempted – without much success – to explain theoretically in his study *Der jüdische Selbsthass*, published in 1930. In this book Lessing makes Freud, along with Adler, a follower of Paul Rée (a Jew with antisemitic inclinations) and of Nietzsche, opining that in any case all that needed saying had already been said by Herbart and Theodor Lipps. Elsewhere, in his essay *Europa und Asien*, he indulged in a thoroughgoing critique of psychoanalysis.

Ernest Jones tells us of the encounter between Lessing and Freud. In July 1931, Freud told Eitington that in his leisure moments he had composed a 'hate list' of seven or eight names, of which he mentioned only one, Theodor Lessing, who had recently dedicated to him a book which Freud described as 'repulsive'. The dedication of 'Jewish Self-Hatred' in fact read 'In devotion from an opponent'. In 1936 Kurt Hiller wrote a biographical essay on Lessing. Freud replied to his letter: 'To me he was to the depths of my being antipathetic', and then gave his own thoughts on Jewish self-hatred: 'It may come about through someone hating his father intensely and nevertheless identifying himself with him; that results in the self-hatred and the splitting of personality.' He added, 'Don't you think that the self-hatred as shown by Th. L. is an exquisitely Jewish phenomenon? I really think it is.'[55] Strange remarks, which seem to justify Lessing while at the same time vehemently rejecting him.

Freud's theory of antisemitism and the psychopathology of Judaism

Some of the most interesting passages in *Moses and Monotheism* are devoted to outlining a theory of antisemitism. Freud says that the main reasons for antisemitism lie with the Jews themselves. This may surprise those who believe, with Sartre, that 'antisemitism is not a Jewish problem, it is *our* problem.' Setting aside certain reasons for antisemitism which he himself believes to be secondary (that Jews are strangers in their host countries, are in the minority and cultivate 'small differences'), Freud returns to his oldest idea on antisemitism: that it is due to the fear of castration engendered by the rite of circumcision.[56]

Freud then details some other fundamental causes of antisemitism, introducing some fresh ideas:

1 The antisemite makes the following accusation:

> They will not accept it as true that they murdered God, whereas we admit it and have been cleansed of that guilt. It is easy therefore to see how much truth lies behind this reproach. A special enquiry would be called for to discover why it has been impossible for the Jews to join in this forward step which was implied, in spite of all its distortions, by the admission of having murdered God. In a certain sense they have in that way taken a tragic load of guilt upon themselves; they have been made to pay heavy penance for it.[57]

On the previous page Freud had said that at the core of the Jewish self-image there was undeniably a feeling of guilt born of repressed hostility to God. Thus this self-image had 'the characteristic – uncompleted and incapable of completion – of obsessional neurotic reaction-formations.'[58]

2 The Jews' feeling of being a 'chosen people' exposed them to resentment from other nations: 'I venture to assert that jealousy of the people which proclaimed itself the first-born, favourite child of God the Father, has not yet been surmounted among other peoples even today.'[59]

3 'And finally, the latest motif in this series, we must not forget that all those peoples who excel today in their hatred of Jews became Christians only in late historic times, often driven to it by a bloody coercion. It might be said that they are all "mis-baptised". . . . Their hatred of Jews is at bottom a hatred of Christians.'[60]

It will be noted that only the last of the 'reasons for antisemitism' quoted above is external to the Jews themselves. All the others are more or less concerned with Jewish 'responsibility'. At the end of *Civilization and its Discontents*, Freud suggests that it might be possible to construct a 'pathology of cultural communities'.[61] In that sense the *Moses* is a pathology of Judaism as a religion. The aim is perhaps to loosen the tyranny of the Mosaic superego in order to free the Jews from their 'obsessional neurosis', which has engendered a grandiose self-image, but is also responsible for the most painful 'discontent of civilization' as far as the Jews themselves have been concerned – and for the hostility of neighbouring cultural communities. By saying that the choosing of the Jewish people was not done by God himself, but by a non-Jew, Moses, the inventor of the letter of the Jewish law, Freud seems to have been attempting to relativize the very idea of Election. It is made to seem a consequence of *human* history, and therefore contingent, rather than a manifestation of the divine will.

It is worth attempting to place this aspect of Freud's *Moses* in the context of psychiatric and psychological pronouncements from the nineteenth century and the 1900s concerning the 'degeneracy of the Jews'.[62] 'On Idiocy and Mental Derangement among German Jews' was the title of an article by M. Boudin, published in 1863 in the *Bulletin de la Société d'Anthropologie de Paris*.[63] The author argued that endogamy was the explanation for the prevalence of derangement among the Jews. Jean-Martin Charcot took up the same theme in 1889, in his *Leçons du mardi à la Salpêtrière*: 'Nervous diseases of all sorts are incomparably more frequent among Jews.'[64] Richard Krafft-Ebing echoed the same prejudice in his manual of psychiatry of 1879.[65] This medical description of 'Jewish neurosis' was passed on to the psychoanalysts by Isidor Sadger, who at a meeting of the Viennese Society for Psychoanalysis on 30 January 1907 attributed the said predisposition to 'the tendency to rumination which has characterized them for thousands of years (study of the Talmud etc.)'. Similarly, at the meeting of 11 November 1908 Paul Federn said that 'neuroses are more prevalent among Jews.'[66]

Several other Zionists echoed this scientific 'rumour'. Thus in 1902 Martin Engländer published in Vienna an essay on 'Morbid Symptoms Particularly Prevalent in the Jewish Race',[67] and suggested that Jewish neurasthenia might be a relic of persecution excited by the nervous strain of modern living. Cesare Lombroso made some concessions to this approach in his study 'Antisemitism and Modern Science' (1894),[68] and Max Nordau, one of the first in the German world to make *Entartung* into a slogan for the age, called on the Jews to regenerate themselves mentally and physically so that they could be bold and muscular like Germanic athletes.[69] The chorus was swelled by one psychiatrist who was in contact with the psychoanalysts. In 1918 Rafael Becker, a Jew who worked at the Burghölzli clinic, delivered to a Zionist group in Zurich a paper on 'Jewish Nervousness: Its Forms, Aetiology and Treatment'.[70] Becker saw assimilation as the main root of the evil; Jews, if 'uprooted', suffered from an inferiority complex leading to self-hatred.

We might say, with Jean-François Lyotard, that in *Moses* 'Freud is attacking not only Christianity, reclassified (as in *Totem and Taboo*) as a totemism, but also primitive Judaism', presented not just as an obsessional neurosis – that, for Freud, went for all religions – but as a genuine *psychosis*.[71] By refusing to admit to the original parricide, Jews were shutting themselves into a denial of reality. Freud paints a gloomy picture of Judaism, showing how the narcissistic feeling of having been 'chosen' accompanies a profound self-accusatory melancholy: to excuse God they accuse themselves, or proclaim that they deserve no better, etc. Certain passages even directly recall Nordau's voice deploring the degeneracy of the Jews in comparison with the Greek or German heroes: 'The pre-eminence given to intellectual labours throughout some two thousand years in the life of the Jewish people has, of course, had its effect ... Harmony in the cultivation of intellectual and physical activity, such as was achieved by the Greek people, was denied to the Jews.' Freud concludes, however, that 'In this dichotomy their decision was at least in favour of the worthier alternative.'[72]

In his 'Pathology of Judaism', Freud lays special emphasis on the necessity of defusing the 'chosen people' fantasy which is exposing the Jews to the jealousy of non-Jews, and in particular of Germans, who have been subject to a strangely similar fantasy since the birth of pan-Germanism. This, if we follow René Major's remarks on this subject,[73] would explain why contact between Jews and Germans sparked off a particularly inexorable antisemitic hatred.[74]

These new insights deriving from Freud's book undoubtedly have a certain anti-Judaistic flavour – even if, as we have seen elsewhere, Freud does declare Judaism superior to other religions. This anti-Judaism is part of Freud's antipathy towards religion in general. However ill-considered it might have appeared in 1939, it should not be taken for 'Jewish self-hatred'. For, as the evidence already adduced makes clear, Freud always spoke of his own Jewishness without the slightest pejorative overtone. But he probably thought that the 'spirit of the new Judaism' to which he alludes in his preface to the Hebrew translation of *Totem and Taboo* ought to shake free of Jewish tradition and put itself in harmony with a scientific civilization – which to Freud meant a civilization cured of its religious illusions.

As Jacques Lacan emphasized in his seminar on 'The Ethics of Psychoanalysis', 'everything depends on the distinction between Moses the Egyptian and Moses the Madianite . . . Moses is the Great Man, the legislator, and also the politician, the rationalist . . . Beside him is Moses the Madianite, the son-in-law of Jethro, whom Freud also calls the man of Sinai, of Horeb . . . inspired, obscurantist.'[75] Freud considered that Judaism could only be 'saved' if it bore the face given to it by Moses the Egyptian as a precursor of the scientific mind, a religion leading inexorably towards the transcending of all religion.

Freud probably hoped that the disappearance of the religious 'illusions' of Judaism would put a stop to antisemitism. He returned to the problem one last time in a short study published in 1938, 'A Comment on Antisemitism'.[76] In it he quotes at length from a non-Jewish author's defence against antisemitism, and mentions in conclusion a book by Heinrich Coudenhove-Kalergi, *Das Wesen des Antisemitismus* ('The Essence of Antisemitism'), first published in 1900. Freud mentions that the book has been reprinted (in 1929), with a preface (he describes it as 'admirable') by the author's son Richard. This 'last word' on antisemitism seems to suggest that no one had made a better job than Coudenhove-Kalergi of refuting it, and pleading for dialogue between Christian and Jew.

We may look more closely at one aspect of the book which throws some light on Freud's own point of view: Coudenhove-Kalergi thought that the essence of antisemitism was primarily *religious*. Other aspects of the phenomenon – even contemporary racism, which seemed so remote from any religious outlook – are seen as more or less indirect consequences of anti-Judaism. It is probable that Freud shared that conviction: that the root of the evil was primarily religious. The struggle against antisemitism naturally and inevitably took the form of a fight against *all* religions, on behalf of the scientific outlook.

III

Freud's Moses: a defiant fable

The originality of Freud's ideas on Moses rests on two hypotheses – that the 'great man' was Egyptian and that he was murdered by the Jews – which have rather differing epistemological status within the book itself. The second hypothesis, of the murder of Moses, follows on from what we might call a structural analysis of the biblical text, and from a theoretical necessity emerging from the conclusions of *Totem and Taboo*, which are summarized in the third part of *Moses and Monotheism*.[77] Freud claims to find 'proof' of this murder in the works of Goethe and the historian Ernst Sellin. It must be admitted that Freud picks and chooses the theories which suit him in Sellin's work, simplifying and distorting his arguments and refusing to acknowledge that in other works Sellin had reconsidered his hypothesis that Moses was murdered.[78] In fact Freud relies just as much, or more, on specifically 'psychic' evidence[79] revealed by psychoanalysis and accessible in no other way.

Moses as an Egyptian is an even more delicate question. While the importance of the murder hypothesis for the solidity of Freud's theoretical evidence is obvious, it seems at first sight to be little more than unjustified obstinacy which impels him to pursue the question 'Was Moses an Egyptian?' in such detail through the first and second parts of the book. He did once write to Arnold Zweig, in a moment of depression, that it 'is not the essential point, though it is the starting point,'[80] and he finally admitted that 'here someone might ask what we gain by tracing Jewish to Egyptian monotheism. It merely pushes the problem a little further back: it tells us nothing more of the genesis of the monotheist idea. The answer is that the question is not one of gain but of investigation.'[81] It is a distinctly unsatisfactory reply, and we might retort that while what is finally gained from his 'demonstration' is, at least to a casual glance, obscure, what Freud has *lost* by it seems, on the contrary, obvious.

By his determined defence of the 'Egyptian' theory Freud compromised the scientific credibility of the whole book in the eyes of even the best-disposed theologians and historians.[82] The opinion of Martin Buber on the subject is typical: 'That a scholar as eminent in his own field as Dr Freud should be capable of publishing so unscientific a book, rashly based on groundless hypotheses, is both astonishing and regrettable.'[83] We may even wonder if Michel de Certeau is not being over-optimistic when, discussing the non-scientific nature of Freud's 'history' in *Moses and Monotheism*, he speaks of a rejection of 'official history'. De Certeau quotes from a letter from Freud to Arnold Zweig on the subject of Elias Auerbach's historical study of 'The Wilderness and the Promised Land'; in the letter Freud states that 'In short, his Moses is not my Moses; he did not break with tradition to reveal a repressed prehistory.' But Freud goes on to say, 'My opinion about the weakness of my historical construction was confirmed and it was this which rightly made me desist from publishing the work.'[84]

In the correspondence between Freud and Arnold Zweig, about the time the *Moses* was being written, there is much discussion of the methods and techniques for writing historical novels. In 1934, Zweig told Freud, in Vienna, that he was thinking of writing a historical novel about Nietzsche, and he asked his friend's advice.[85] For various reasons, Freud tried to deter Zweig from this attempt, giving various reasons why he thought such a work could never succeed. He explained, in particular:

> It seems to me that we touch here on the problem of poetic licence versus historical truth. I know that my feelings on this point are thoroughly conservative. Where there is an unbridgeable gap in history and biography, the writer can step in and try to guess how it all happened. In an uninhabited country he may be allowed to establish the creatures of his imagination. Even when the historical facts are known but sufficiently remote and removed from common knowledge, he can disregard them.[86]

These lines written to Zweig seem to contain the artistic credo which Freud himself followed when composing the *Moses*. A little later, in another letter to Zweig, he announced that he intended to call his book 'Moses the Man, An Historical Novel' (30 September 1934). This confers great importance on a preliminary sketch for the foreword to *Moses and Monotheism* discovered by Yosef Hayim Yerushalmi, which proves that Freud did indeed give this subtitle ('An Historical Novel') to his 1934 manuscript. The sketch reads, 'Thus, one undertakes to treat each possibility in the text as a clue, and to fill the gap between one fragment and another according to the law, so to speak, of least resistance, that is – to give preference to the assumption that has the greatest possibility.'[87] This is very revealing of Freud's method. He added that he wished to execute a *Charakterstudie*, that is (as Yerushalmi puts it) 'to deduce the character of the Jews from that of Moses'.

Thus Freud's occasional defiance of the scientific method in *Moses* could be interpreted as the use of poetic licence by a historical novelist, a *Dichter* whose creative labours savour as much of *Phantasieren* as of *Wissenschaft*. This is the suggestion of Ilse Gubrich-Simitis,[88] who sees Freud's last great work as a 'daydream' (*Tagtraum*: note that Freud, at least until he wrote *Der Dichter und das Phantasieren* ('Creative Writers and Day-Dreaming'), in 1908,[89] used *Tagtraum* and *Phantasieren* as virtual synonyms to refer to artistic or literary creation). This 'daydream', Gubrich-Simitis avers, expressed Freud's reaction to the traumas of Nazi antisemitism and exile. It allowed him to relax his intellectual and emotional self-censorship and to accomplish his desire to make a grandiose redefinition of his own personal identity, based on a 'heretical fidelity' to Judaism and on the saga of his own family. It also allowed him to fill in certain gaps in the theoretical edifice of psychoanalysis: for example, it develops the 'traumatic' aetiology of neuroses and the explanations of antisemitism and of Jewish identity. Freud is saying that daydreams, like ordinary dreams, feed on impressions left by events which occurred in childhood: thus, Gubrich-Simitis concludes, writing *Moses* must have helped Freud to overcome the anguish caused by Nazi persecution, which had reactivated his infantile neuroses,[90] and to fulfil his rejection of all kinds of dependence – on mother, family, religion or whatever – and his pressing desire for self-sufficiency.

To describe *Moses and Monotheism* as a 'historical novel' or a 'daydream', as Freud and his interpreters have done, could, however, be misleading if we went on to conclude that the work is merely the product of a personal whim, a response to a purely individual crisis. In truth – and herein resides the greatness of the work – Freud's own preoccupations meet up with a funda-mental tendency of the assimilated, believing German Jew in modern society. This emerges clearly from an essay by Shulamit Volkov entitled 'The Invention of a Tradition'.[91] Volkov defines Jewish identity in a modern context as a 'cultural system' (using the term in the same way as the historian Thomas Nipperdey used it to refer to the German Protestants and Catholics in the nineteenth and twentieth centuries, implying that modern Germany was a 'bicultural society'). Volkov stresses that assimilation, as the Enlightenment conceived it, aimed at much more than a modernization of Jewish religion: it also sought a sweeping reform of every aspect of Jewish life. Similarly, Zionism, while opposed to the aims of assimilation, itself aimed to regenerate the Jewish 'cultural system' in all its aspects. Now these various efforts to modernize and regenerate Jewish identity were, in fact, *inventing* a tradition which diverged perceptibly from orthodoxy and drew on a whole arsenal of modern historicism and scientific approaches in order to invent a Jewish history (the task of the *Wissenschaft des Judentums*), a Jewish ethic, a Jewish aesthetic, able to mount a challenge to Germanic *Kultur*. Inventing a Jewish ethic suited to the modern context meant incorporating 'liberalism' and the 'scientific mind' into Jewish 'tradition'.

Seen in the light of Volkov's essay, Freud's historical novel – Freud's daydream – seems to be obeying a supra-individual law, for it follows very closely the original direction taken by the attempt to assimilate Jews into the German world. This assimilation would lead not to a loss of identity, but to the invention of a new Jewish tradition capable of sustaining a reborn confidence in Jewish identity.

A close examination of the sources – historical, theological and literary – used by Freud for his *Moses* reveals that, for most of his arguments, he was able more or less to rely on the works he had assembled. Only the 'Egyptian' hypothesis was unshared by any of these authors. His criteria for sifting through others' ideas, retaining some, rejecting others, were dictated by his preconceived idea. Sometimes he even quotes an author's words out of context, even to the point of giving them an entirely different meaning.[92] The historian E. Meyer, for example, is often quoted, although Meyer denied that there was any trace of Egyptian influence on Jewish religion.

In *Moses and Monotheism*, especially when he undertakes to prove the 'great man's' Egyptian origins, Freud was in fact manipulating his sources. None the less, he cherished a rather naive hope that some archaeological windfall would come to justify him in the teeth of all and sundry. Hence the passionate interest in the excavations at Tell el-Amarna which emerges from his letters to Arnold Zweig.[93] (As early as 1904 the discovery of the 'code of Hammurabi' at Souza had inspired a lecture given by Freud to the B'nai B'rith; Dennis Klein sees in this the first germ of inspiration for Freud's reinterpretation of Moses.)[94] This doubt over the status of 'psychic evidence' revealed by psychoanalysis has a certain similarity with Freud's nostalgic fondness for reductionist experiments on the model of the exact sciences, which sometimes appears in his work as a counterpoint to its metaphysical enthusiasms.

As if to forestall the inevitable objections, Freud filled the *Moses* with cries of *mea culpa*, the scholar caught *in flagrante delicto* of theoretical imprudence:

> I am very well aware that in dealing so autocratically and arbitrarily with Biblical tradition – bringing it up to confirm my view when it suits me and unhesitatingly rejecting it when it contradicts me – I am exposing myself to serious methodological criticism and weakening the convincing force of my arguments.[95]

> I have already laid stress on the factor of doubt in my introductory remarks; I have, as it were, placed that factor outside the brackets and I may be allowed to save myself the trouble of repeating it in connection with each item *inside* them.[96]

> To my critical sense this book, which takes its start from the man Moses, appears like a dancer balancing on the tip of one toe.[97]

It would be easy to find many more such exhibitions of (false) modesty, calculated to disarm the over-positivist reader.

Was it only a joke?

Were all these attempts at proof really only a joke? In the tenth of his *Introductory Lectures on Psychoanalysis* (1916), 'The Symbolism of Dreams', Freud had already alluded to Otto Rank's 'myth of the birth of the hero', a study to which he returns in the *Moses*. In 1916 he had written:

> If one rescues someone from the water in a dream, one is making oneself into his mother, or simply into *a* mother. In myths a person who rescues a baby from the water is admitting that she is the baby's true mother. There is a well-known comic anecdote according to which an intelligent Jewish boy was asked who the mother of Moses was. He replied without hesitation: 'The Princess.' 'No,' he was told, 'she only took him out of the water.' 'That's what *she* says,' he replied, and so proved that he had found the correct interpretation of the myth.[98]

This is, in condensed form, the earliest version of Freud's theory that Moses was Egyptian. To introduce this somewhat sacrilegious variant on Jewish history, Freud took shelter behind the harmless face of a Jewish story. As suggested in *Jokes and their Relation to the Unconscious*, this spared him the need to repress the unpleasant affect (to a Jewish audience), while overcoming the automatic defence mechanisms of the unconscious.[99] As in Jewish humour, there is a masochistic element[100] in *Moses*, which challenged one of the fundamental convictions of the Jews in the very hour that the whole world was turning against them. And as in the young Jewish boy in Freud's anecdote, so in *Moses* there is a good deal of provocation and enjoyment of the game of historical hypothesis.

Why all this research and labour, undertaken with great effort and in the most unfavourable circumstances? The only possible answer is that *Moses and Monotheism* touches on the author's most intimate concerns. This historical construct is a sort of 'waking dream' which pursued the founder of psycho-analysis towards the end of his life, just as *The Interpretation of Dreams* had marked the founding of the discipline. And there are certain fundamental themes common to both books: in particular, family descent and Jewish identity. Even more than a 'historical novel', *Moses* is a family romance in which Freud, for the last time, reconstructs his personal identity.

By challenging Moses's Jewish birth Freud was challenging his own descent. In *The Interpretation of Dreams* he had tried to free himself from the image of a Jewish father who had confined his existence within the intolerable limits of inferior birth.[101] He had affirmed that it was possible to find his own way, which would be neither that of assimilation nor that of Zionism. Forty years later 'Freud had a last impulse of revolt against the inexorable fate which closely confines every man within his origins, his race, and his name.' He had already said many times that he did not consider himself an Austrian or a German. Now he was even suggesting that he was not a Jew in the usual meaning of the word. 'He wished only to be nobody's son from nowhere, the son of his own works.'[102]

In the genealogical fantasies of the *Traumdeutung*, Freud's father had merged into the figure of Garibaldi, or that of Hamilcar Barca, father of Hannibal. Paul Roazen has pointed out how readily Freud indulged in fantasies of self-creation, descanting away from his natural family. Freud returned a good many times to this fantasy of the fatherless child. In his book on Leonardo he even mentions an Egyptian legend that vultures were born of the wind: Leonardo was a vulture-child, because he had been brought up far away from his natural father. 'Freud unconsciously considered himself his own father,' Roazen concludes.[103]

In *Moses*, Moses's master, the pharaoh Akhenaton, converts to monotheism and changes his name: 'he erased it [the now detestable name of the God Amon] . . . from every inscription – even when it occurred in the name of his father, Amenophis III'.[104] Similarly, Moses the Egyptian breaks with his family, and, as Eugène Enriquez puts it, poses as the parthogenetic engenderer of his own chosen people. 'Moses chooses his people, the people kill him, but by doing so set him up as the father: thus the sons choose their own father. The father has chosen them. In their turn they choose to be the sons of such a father.'[105]

This also, incidentally, reminds us of why Freud presents Judaism as a religion further advanced in rationality and more faithful than others to the law of the father: the son can choose the father only if intellect has asserted its superiority over the senses. For the senses, only motherhood is recognizable or has any importance.[106] This no doubt explains one curious 'omission' from the *Moses*. In 1912 Karl Abraham had written an article for *Imago* on

'Amenhotep IV (Ekhnaton)'.[107] This article also suggested that Amenhotep had been a precursor of Moses. But Abraham had laid great emphasis on the decisive role of the pharaoh's mother, Queen Tiy, and seen Amenhotep's work as a reform of the paternal heritage under the influence of his mother. We are almost tempted to conclude, with Estelle Roith,[108] that this aspect of Abraham's article, which was scarcely compatible with Freud's *idée fixe* (monotheism as the law of the father), explains the conscious or unconscious 'censuring' of Abraham's article in *Moses and Monotheism*.

Sigmund Freud and Thomas Mann as 'biblical' novelists

One little detail in the *Moses* may surprise readers: tucked away in a footnote[109] is a reference to the 'romance of Shakespeare's origins'. Marthe Robert has given a humorous description of the quite passionate interest which Freud took in learned discussions about Shakespeare's origins; Freud himself preferred to think of him as a gentleman of high birth.[110] But it is rather surprising to find this as a digression in a book about Moses. Let us bear in mind that if Freud 'chose the Jewish people as his own', this fantasy had nothing to do with any sort of abasement. Freud assures us that in Egypt Moses was an aristocrat of very high rank. And later he draws attention to the very respectable ancestry of which German Jews could boast: 'In many places dominated by anti-semitism today the Jews were among the oldest portions of the population or had even been there before the present inhabitants. This applies, for instance, to the city of Cologne, to which the Jews came with the Romans, before it was occupied by the Germans.'[111]

This digression on Shakespeare brings us back to the 'English hypothesis' already advanced in connection with the Myops dream: while he was working on *Moses and Monotheism*, Freud perhaps tended unconsciously to conflate Egypt, land of Moses and his 'enlightened' monotheism, and England. In a letter to Ernst Freud of 12 May 1938, a few days before his departure for England, he wrote: 'I sometimes compare myself to old Jacob, who was also taken by his children to Egypt in his old age, as Thomas Mann is to tell us in his next novel. Let us hope that no flight out of Egypt will ensue, as it did then. It is time that Ahasuerus found a place of rest.'[112] This reminds us of Freud's frequent contacts with Thomas Mann at the time he was working on the *Moses*.

Much attention has been paid to the influence of psychoanalysis on the tetralogy *Joseph and his Brothers* and the novel *Das Gesetz* ('The Law'), which Mann wrote in 1943 and whose subject is indeed Moses. But the influence of Mann on Freud seems to have been somewhat neglected. The first novel of the tetralogy, *The Stories of Joseph*, appeared in 1933, and the second, *Young Joseph*, in 1934. Freud could also have become acquainted with *Joseph in Egypt* (1936) before publishing his own work on *Moses* – of which the first two parts, including 'If Moses was Egyptian', appeared in 1937 in *Imago*. In January 1937 Freud had been visited by Mann in Vienna.[113]

The similarities between the novelist's picture of Egypt and the Egypt of

Freud's Moses are striking. The authors set their historical novels in exactly the same period, the reigns of Amenhotep III and Amenhotep IV, at the end of the fourteenth century BC. For Mann this is the time of Joseph; for Freud, that of Moses. It makes little difference, in fact, since both take what liberties they like with history, while both claiming that their conjectures are supported by the most unassailable evidence!

The discovery of the clay tablets of Tell el-Amarna, in 1888, had given Egyptologists a substantial body of evidence about the reigns of Amenhotep III and IV. Most of the tablets are letters, in cuneiform script, from officials in the provinces of Syria and Canaan, and from Asiatic vassals of Pharaoh. One of the most powerful of Amenhotep IV's governors was Johamu, a sort of viceroy of Palestine, who lived in a palace in the Nile delta. In 1903 the archaeologist Hugo Winckler had suggested that this Johamu could be identified with the biblical Joseph, and had connected him with Amenhotep IV Ekhnaton. Freud and Mann had both used A. Erman's *Dia ägyptische Religion*, Freud referring to the Berlin edition of 1905 and Mann to the Tübingen edition of 1923, revised by H. Ranke.[114] Erman, like Winckler, had made a connection between Johamu and Joseph. Freud, unlike Mann, paid it no attention.

Freud, reading the earlier volumes of *Joseph and his Brothers*, and later in his conversations with Thomas Mann, must have been impressed by the novelist's strong contrasting of the biblical and Egyptian worlds. Old Jacob is still living in a mythical universe, without chronology or individuality, in which the self yields to the accomplishment of the divine will. Joseph, on the other hand, assimilates totally to the Egyptian world which has received him, and which Mann in the third novel, and even more strongly in the fourth, equates with English and American civilization.

The last volume in the series, Mann explained in a lecture given in 1942, 'was born under an American sky, more particularly under the sunny sky of California, so similar to that of Egypt'.[115] Hans Mayer has commented that Thomas Mann's Joseph, when he rises to be Pharaoh's minister, behaves like an American capitalist businessman, in the Protestant spirit as defined by Max Weber.[116] Be it noted that Weber, for his part, considered Judaism as one of humanity's first decisive steps along the road to ethics and rationalism, leading ultimately, in his view, to Protestantism itself.[117] Which, all in all, is not so very different from Freud's concept.

Comparisons are not explanations, and I shall proceed no further with this parallel between the Freud's 'Egyptian novel of Moses' and Thomas Mann's 'Egyptian novel of Joseph'. I shall retain only the tendency, common to both authors – both going through a troubled period of flight and exile – to conflate biblical Egypt with the modern English-speaking world. If it is true that Freud identified with Moses, as has been convincingly shown many times (from Marthe Robert to Marianne Krüll),[118] then we may talk of 'Sigmund Freud the Egyptian' – which in our hypothesis would be 'Freud the Englishmen', making *Moses and Monotheism* into an attempt to reconcile the irreconcilable, Freud the Jew and Freud the Englishman, substituting for Zionism a call from the Diaspora to the land of freedom.

Moses the Egyptian and Freud the Englishman

Leaving for London, Freud would thus have felt that his youthful dream had come true: he was to live in England, the land of his old hero Cromwell, the home of the modern scientific mind – and leave Austria and Vienna, the *Heimat* where life had been so difficult, and finally impossible. One of Freud's last remarks was in defence of one of his 'personal myths': on 16 November 1938, when he was living in Maresfield Gardens, he wrote in answer to the editor of *Time and Tide*, who had asked him to take part in an investigation into antisemitism. Freud ended his letter, 'I feel deeply affected by the passage in your letter acknowledging "a certain growth of anti-semitism even in this country". Ought this present persecution not rather give rise to a wave of sympathy in this country?'[119] For Sigmund Freud, Jew, Viennese and anglophile, it was impossible to imagine the land of Disraeli as anything other than a Jewish Promised Land.

Thus Freud had repeated the journey he had made as a nineteen-year-old, when he had visited his half-brother Emanuel at his home in Manchester – the brother twenty years older than he, who might have been his father and could have given him an easier life. The fantasy of Moses the Egyptian expresses the desire for another birth, by which Jewishness would have been not a fate but a choice, the choice already made by Moses himself, a choice conforming to reason and the progress of humanity. Just as Freud wanted the freedom to choose for himself the country in which he was to live, without obeying the imperatives of Zionism.

Theodor Herzl, the Viennese Moses

In 1898 Theodor Herzl, outlining the plan for an opera to be called *Moses*, described his hero in the following terms:

> A great man, out of the ordinary, full of vital force and humour, inwardly tormented but firmly sustained by his will, not too preoccupied by the purpose of the journey . . . The aged Moses constantly sees the return of Korah, the golden calf, and the same caravans of slaves. Exhausted by all this, he must still carry them along with ever-renewed enthusiasm. It is the tragedy of a leader [*Führer*] who is not a misleader [*Verführer* – 'seducer'].[120]

In his book 'The Jewish State' (1896), Herzl had explained that

> The 'Society of Jews' is the Jews' new Moses. But the undertaking of the great governor [*Gestor*] of the Jews of old is to our own what a superb oratorio of earlier days is to a modern opera. We play the same tune with many, many more violins, flutes, harps, cellos and double-basses, electric spotlights, scenery, choruses, splendid sets, and a cast of the highest quality.[121]

On 18 August 1895, Herzl proudly noted in his journal that Gudemann had said to him, 'You remind me of Moses.'[122] Shortly before his death, Herzl is supposed to have told a friend about a childhood dream of his: when he was twelve he had dreamed that the Messiah appeared before him, took him in his arms and carried him off to heaven. Upon the shining clouds they saw Moses, whose face bore the features Michelangelo had given him. The Messiah said to Moses: 'This is the child on whom I called in my prayers,' and Moses said to the young Theodor, 'Go, tell the Jews that I shall come soon and accomplish miracles and marvels for my people and for the whole world.' This anecdote was told by Reuben Brainin, who used to add that he wondered if Herzl had really dreamed this dream in his childhood or whether he was indulging his adult imagination.[123]

Casting Herzl as Moses had become commonplace among his contemporaries. The painter E. M. Lilien, a Zionist and follower of Beardsley, used to portray him as a combination of Wotan and Moses bearing the Tablets of the Law.[124] Rabbi Chajes, critical of the influence of modern nationalism on Herzl's Zionism, used to say he was like a Moses who had grown up at Pharaoh's court.[125] And the German poet Börries von Münchhausen sang an antisemitic song of rejoicing which antiphrastically praised the Zionists for emptying Germany of her Jews: 'O Moses of our days! God give you the victory!'[126]

However much he identified with the ancient Moses, Herzl intended to act as a modern statesman and businessman. In the Myops dream Freud had recalled how, in their flight out of Egypt, the Jews had had no time to leave their dough to rise, and that in memory of this they still ate unleavened bread at Passover. Herzl did not intend to be so hasty: 'Moses forgot to take the cooking-pots of Egypt. We shall take thought for that,' he confided to his journal in July 1895.[127] This is why he insisted in 'The Jewish State' that the core of the 'Society of Jews' should consist of 'the worthy English Jews to whom I confided my plans in London'.[128] The modern Moses was to be backed by City of London capital and the practical English mind.

Freud had never met Herzl except in dreams. In 1913, nine years after the death of the founder of the Zionist movement, Freud was visited by his son, Hans Herzl, come in search of advice. Hans was uncertain whether to follow in his father's footsteps and attend the Eleventh Zionist Congress. Freud, according to Hans Herzl's biographer, encouraged him to shake off his father's influence, and added,

> Your father is one of those men who have turned dreams into reality. People of that type, the Garibaldis and Herzls, are very rare, and dangerous. I shall say only that they are at the other extreme from my own scientific work. My job is to strip dreams of their mystery, make them clear and ordinary. They do the opposite: they command in the world, but remain on the other side of the psychic mirror. My work is psychoanalysis; theirs is psychosynthesis.[129]

These words – perhaps largely apocryphal – would incline us to see Herzl and Freud as lifelong opposites. However, what they have in common is no less striking. Both Freud and Herzl saw England as the only country in Europe deserving of Jewish trust. One, it is true, was bound for

Zion, while the other was finally to take the road to London, but they both cherished the same ideal: the building of a liberal, cosmopolitan world, a world without antisemitism, in which the Jews could freely follow their own paths without being deprived of the fruits of Progress – scientific, technical and cultural progress for Herzl, 'spiritual progress' ('Fortschritt in der Geistigkeit') for Freud. The dream the two Viennese intellectuals had in common was doubtless the restoration of the liberal order which had been irrevocably lost in Austria at the end of the 1870s, and the rediscovery of the lost paradise of their youth, those 'better days' that their fathers had once told them were yet to be.[130]

13

Karl Kraus, or the Undiscoverable Jewish Identity

I

A crown for Zion

On the first page of the first issue of his journal *Die Fackel* ('The Torch'), in April 1899, Karl Kraus expressed his intentions succinctly under the headline 'Was wir umbringen', meaning both 'What we are publishing' and 'What we are killing'. At the end of the same issue there were several pages of publicity for his two founding manifestos, the intellectual groundwork of *Die Fackel*: 'Demolished Literature' (1897)[1] and 'A Crown for Zion' ('Eine Krone für Zion', 1898). These were pamphlets in which Kraus had completed the break with two groups to which he could easily have belonged: literary 'Young Vienna' and the Zionists. Kraus's ego instinctively knew what it was 'against'; only later was *Die Fackel* to declare its own values and find its own way.

The first of these pamphlets, 'Demolished Literature', can still be read with pleasure today, for its ferocity rings true and it is lucid in its denunciation of the more ridiculous elements of cultivated fin-de-siècle decadence. The other, 'A Crown for Zion', seems on the contrary indefensible. A brief summary: Zionism usurped the purposes of the antisemites, driving the Jews out of Vienna into a 'new ghetto' by arousing antisemitic passions which would otherwise soon have been forgotten. Zionism, the invention of well-off, well-assimilated Jews, is encouraging the poor Jews of Central Europe to have expectations which will inevitably be disappointed. Intellectuals – aesthetic, 'modern' and cut off from Jewish tradition – are suddenly beginning to talk of the Bible and the prophets. Zionism has come along just as the benefits of assimilation and social democracy are beginning to look as if they could solve the Jewish problem of discrimination and poverty. At the Basle congress, people went on about Palestine without even knowing where it was, and the irreducible heterogeneity of the Diaspora showed up in the babble of languages spoken by the delegates. Will Theodor Herzl, the future king of Zion, be doomed to reign over a multinational empire subject to linguistic regimentation similar to that of Franz Josef? Will everyone have to learn Hebrew? Will they have to create a national culture out of nowhere?

Against these absurd and dangerous visions of utopia – as he considered them – Kraus restated the virtues of assimilation. To put an end to anti-semitism, in his view, it would be enough to eliminate the remains of Jewish separateness which were being perniciously encouraged by rabbis, especially in the eastern provinces. Instead of sending them on a wild-goose chase to Palestine, the Jews' situation in Europe should be improved. Kraus denied that he was speaking opportunistically: he was not protecting the gains of the well-off Jewish bourgeoisie but pleading for the poor Jews of Galicia, who could be helped only by social democracy and not by Zionist 'lies'.

One does not have to be anti-Zionist[2] to see merit in several of Kraus's criticisms. Herzl had undoubtedly been infected with *Realpolitik*, negotiating with the Prussian Kaiser and the Russian Tsar, cunningly manipulating the aspirations of the Jewish masses of Eastern Europe, colluding with the colonial ambitions of the great powers, suggesting to Wilhelm II the grandiose plan for the Baghdad railway, dreaming of a vigorous settlement of Palestine once Uganda had proved out of reach. But the blindness shown in 'A Crown for Zion' is frightening: the idea that Zionism breeds antisemitism; the trumpeting of unbridled assimilation; the call to eliminate the Jewish religious culture of Eastern Europe; the absence of any real feeling of solidarity between the Jew, Karl Kraus, son of the assimilated bourgeoisie, and 'the others' – and above all, the unawareness of the real dangers of contemporary antisemitism.

Frightening, too, is the cruel vigour of the presentation: despite his pretentions to an unequalled mastery of language and style, Kraus recklessly adopts his enemies' manner of speaking. Scarcely in the best of taste are remarks like 'Wir haben es ... mit der Schule der Ahasveristen zu tun', meaning 'We are dealing with the school of the Ahasverists' – a pun on 'Ahasver', the name of the Wandering Jew, and 'verists', naturalist ('snivelling') writers.[3] No better is 'Es liegt neuerdings ein Verdienst darin, keine geradlinige Nase zu besitzen, und man kann sie nicht hoch genug tragen': 'It has lately become creditable not to have a straight nose, and one cannot hold it high enough' (meaning 'be arrogant enough').[4]

The uses of antisemitism

Every issue of *Die Fackel* was to pursue these ideas of Kraus's: why attack the antisemites when it was Jewish and liberal corruption in finance and the press that was causing all the trouble? Kraus had no belief in 'Jewish solidarity': Jewish liberals and antisemites were in collusion.[5] In October of 1899, the year when *Die Fackel* was launched, and when Kraus was identifying himself more and more closely with the opponents of Dreyfus in the famous Dreyfus affair, he officially abandoned the Jewish community. Sigurd Paul Scheichl[6] believes that from that moment onwards the problem of assimilation became less prominent in *Die Fackel*. I think the opposite is true. That problem lurked behind all Kraus's writings to the end of his life; it even got worse. His reactions to the Dreyfus affair are particularly revealing.[7]

Attempts have been made to justify Kraus's attitude throughout the Dreyfus affair by relating it to *Die Fackel*'s battle against the perversions of modern journalism. Thus Helmut Arntzen, in his essay 'Karl Kraus and the Press', says that Kraus was not talking about the Dreyfus affair itself, but about the way it was being reported. Exactly what was being said was less important to him than showing *how* the press had seized on the Dreyfus trial, how it was describing it.[8] Arntzen sees it as a virtue of Kraus's that he denounced the 'Dreyfus kitsch' of the *Neue Freie Presse* and highlighted the hidden motives of such 'sentimentality'.

These arguments have some weight. But they skate over the fact that it was possible to criticize the compromises and bad taste of the liberals in the *Neue Freie Presse* without reneging on support for Dreyfus. Arthur Schnitzler's attitude is proof of this. On 9 September 1899, Schnitzler wrote from Ischl to his friend Gustav Schwarzkopf. Amidst various pieces of news we find the following reflection: 'Mercier and the other swine are positively driving me to fury – in spite of the *Neue Freie*.' Like Kraus, Schnitzler, a convinced Drey-fusard with a visceral loathing for Mercier (the French Minister for War), felt the need to hold aloof from the *Neue Freie Presse*, because its unvarying and melodramatic support for Dreyfus made it hard to keep track of what was really happening at the trial. But, while Schnitzler shared Kraus's irritation over journalistic exploitation of sympathy for Dreyfus, he also (in the same letter) passed a severe judgement on his fellow Viennese:

> His attitude towards the antisemites is the most repulsive thing I have ever seen. If it had been inspired by clear-sightedness and a concern for fairness – but all in all it is nothing but servility, a bit like something I witnessed one day on the trams, when a pathetic little Jewish commercial traveller got out of Lueger's way with a 'Please go first, Herr Doktor,' and seemed really surprised when Lueger didn't actually kick his backside. In a word, little Kraus's attitude towards the antisemites is . . . typically Jewish.[9]

We must, of course, temper this judgement by pointing out that Viennese intellectuals did not attach the same importance to the Dreyfus affair as did their opposite numbers in Paris: it was far off, a complicated matter, some-thing for the French themselves to sort out while others followed it through the press reports. However, Viennese intellectuals did react to it according to their own political bent.[10] Those with the strongest liberal inclinations were instinctively in sympathy with Dreyfus: the doyenne of Austrian letters, Marie von Ebner-Eschenbach (1830–1916), and her colleague and contemporary, Peter Rosegger (1843–1918),[11] together with Bertha von Suttner (1843–1914), the leading light of the pacifist movement,[12] were all firm Drey-fusards. So were those of the 'moderns' who were most politically aware: Sigmund Freud, Arthur Schnitzler, and also Rudolf Steiner, the founder of anthroposophy.

The young aesthetes of the Viennese avant-garde seem to have been more or less indifferent: there is not a trace of the Dreyfus affair in the writings and letters of Hugo von Hofmannsthal, which shows his 'apolitical' bent – and also his tendency to repress anything which threatened to raise the 'Jewish question'. (We shall refer again to this tendency when we examine how Hofmannsthal reacted to the conversion of his friend Richard Beer-Hofmann to Zionism.) In contrast, among opponents of antisemitism – especially in Rabbi Josef Samuel Bloch's journal *Österreichische Wochenschrift: Centralorgan für die gesammten Interessen des Judenthums*[13] – and among Zionists like Herzl and Nordau, interest in the Dreyfus affair was naturally very considerable.

This reminder of the situation in Vienna makes Karl Kraus's own position more comprehensible: his sarcastic comments ran directly counter to the liberals and Zionists, but he was also shaking his 'Young Vienna' friends out of their apolitical torpor – in pursuit of which he seemed not unwilling to find himself hobnobbing with antisemitic Austrian journalists.

Karl Kraus the 'intellectual', and the language of pamphlets

The assimilationist creed summarized in 'A Crown for Zion' was not much different from the one propagated, in its own fashion, by the *Neue Freie Presse*. That organ spoke for an assimilated Jewry which was willing to come to terms with an ever more antisemitic society. Kraus was loud in his criticisms of such compromise. But what had he to set against the stratagems of the liberal Jewish bourgeoisie? Only the utopia of an 'authentic' assimilation whose rationalism seemed tragically unrealistic as the new century sank slowly into racist antisemitism. Kraus was projecting on to his own time ideas inherited from the *Vormärz*, the Restoration which lasted from the Congress of Vienna until 1848: up to the end of the liberal period they had kept a certain plausibility, but they were distinctly out of date by the time Kraus was founding *Die Fackel*.

It is striking how far this *Vormärz* outlook impregnates the whole of Kraus's output and ideology: his nostalgia for a strongly hierarchical, aristocratic society, his adoration of Nestroy and his liking for Kürnberger all bear witness to the phenomenon. So, deep down, does his idea of what the press ought to be. Here again, the Dreyfus affair served to reveal a new style of cultural and political life characterized by the increasing importance of the press. It showed the power of the big newspapers in spreading the virus of a social disease such as antisemitism and in manipulating public opinion. But on the other hand, Émile Zola's intervention had also shown that mass-circulation newspapers could be the most effective way for an intellectual to influence events. The ambivalence of the leading newspapers, both means of manipulation and weapons for the truth, stood clearly revealed.

Kraus was unwilling to perceive that ambivalence. He could accept only the former aspect: the threatening face of the big newspapers, stupefying and enslaving minds. This diabolical image forced Kraus into an incessant, hopeless struggle, a blanket condemnation, an unyielding refusal. He dreamed of restoring the press to the state of innocence it had been in before 1848, under the vigilant censorship of Metternich, with a limited circulation: a press without opinions or political purposes, going from day to day in pursuit of stylistic elegance and giving plenty of room – perhaps too much – to literary, theatrical and artistic criticism (to which Kraus would have added linguistic criticism, keeping watch over the correctness of the German language used by his contemporaries!).

But times had changed. Everywhere Karl Kraus saw lies and scandal. 'The Torch' burned through the corruption, harking back deliberately to Rochefort's *La lanterne*. Rejecting the pugnacious style proper to a committed intellectual of Zola's stamp, Kraus opted for the 'language of pamphlets' as analysed by Marc Angenot; in fact he exemplifies all its characteristics:

> The paradoxical idea the pamphleteer has of his task, the dim view of the world which to him is axiomatic, the established conjunction of verbal 'persuasion and violence', the interconnection of truth, liberty and solitude, the idea that a pamphlet must always speak against Authority and Power while imitating their features in a terroristic way – all these characteristics tend to block or distort the critical faculty.[14]

A pamphleteer gives an idea of himself as a solitary conscience, courageous, often rash. His self-appointed status as a chivalrous defender of the truth does something to mitigate his uncomfortable lack of social legitimacy. His strategy is based on a break with his original milieu, but it is most often against that milieu, rather than against his natural enemies, that he does battle.

Thus Kraus based his literary personality on the break with Young Vienna, and his career as a journalist on his challenge to the liberal press. His natural enemy, antisemitism, was not his favourite target. ' "Commonplaces" become his opinions, the opinions which the polemicist has noisily sworn to defend to the death.' Similarly *Die Fackel*, though without any clear pronouncement on the subject, 'defended' the idea that Dreyfus might be guilty, as was commonly and unthinkingly believed. 'Such an operation reactivates the myth of the independence of the Mind, which by *fiat* of the individual will can free itself from material constraints and those of popular opinion.'

Kraus extended that individualism into the worship of 'genius' which he imposed on his readers. As pamphleteer he equated opposing ideologies with 'scandal'. His adversaries were not merely 'wrong', they were liars and imposters, their errors tantamount to moral perversion. This sort of pessimism gives pamphleteers a 'dim view of the world': 'From Henri Rochefort to Maurice Clavel, pamphleteers have often been ideologists identified as "left-wing", but their "independent outlook" often puts their contemporaries in serious doubt about the "progressive" character of their attitudes.'[15] Could it be said that Kraus, who thought that the 'last days of humanity' were being reported in the columns of the *Neue Freie Presse*, was a left-winger? Surely not! A right-winger then? Yes – and no.

From one *obiter dictum* to the next, the pamphleteer showed little fear of self-contradiction. He unmasked the hypocrisy of society and the law courts, gave himself anticlerical airs, but took up the argument against Dreyfus;

though often anti-monarchic and anti-militaristic, he occasionally had dreams of an authoritarian regime which would ensure that the right side triumphed. 'This ideological to-ing and fro-ing is sustained by a strong "feeling" of inner coherence. The pamphlet, a symptom of the contradictory position of the intellectual in modern society and an illusory transcendence of that position, seems to be the *simulation* of a radical state of mind, a travesty of analysis into confusion and resentment.'[16] These observations of Marc Angenot are based on a collection of evidence which does not include *Die Fackel*. On many points, however, they can be applied to the 'intellectual power' exercised by Karl Kraus. They may explain why such an admirer of *Die Fackel* as Elias Canetti could both pay tribute to it as a 'school of resistance' and disapprove of the pamphlet style which turned its readers into an 'aggressive and hate-filled mob'.[17]

II

Jewish 'self-hatred'

Karl Kraus's anti-Jewish opinions, which often put him in the same camp as the antisemites, did not go unnoticed by his contemporaries. Theodor Lessing, in his essay *Der jüdische Selbsthass*, defined Kraus as 'the most shining example of Jewish self-hatred'.[18]

Kraus replied to Lessing in an issue of *Die Fackel* entitled 'Why "The Torch" Has Not Appeared' (July 1934). Speaking of himself in the third person, Kraus wrote,

> He could easily continue to retreat a little further from every accusation, referring to the notice on the cover of *Die Fackel* [for years the cover had read, 'The editor does not desire any form of communication from readers'], which applies even when no issue appears, and which is in fact a sign of vitality, a resolve of self-preservation against all forms of intellectual aggression – as opposed to the widespread opinion in psychological circles that his aversion to intellectual interchange is a desperate act of 'Jewish self-wounding'. It is anything but that, and I, who as editor of *Die Fackel* have followed the inner journeyings of the author for many long years – both the conscious processes and those of the unconscious, which can be ferreted out by the curious – I can assure you that his cricitism of Jewry has not the slightest element of that 'Jewish self-hatred' which has in fact been aroused recently by a certain cultural historian, and which has always served as a compensatory fable for gossip-mongers and literary rejects.[19]

Lessing's essay is a moving book, written as an autobiographical confession – for the author himself acknowledges having suffered at one time from *jüdischer Selbsthass*. He could be criticized for suggesting that 'self-hatred' is a distinctive element in the 'Jewish character'. However, Lessing's insight seems to be correct if it is refined, first by limiting the chronological framework within which it applies,[20] and secondly by giving a little more sociological precision to Lessing's largely anecdotal descriptions. This twofold refine-

ment has been carried out in several recent studies, in particular by Hans
Dieter Hellige in his edition of the correspondence of Walther Rathenau and
Maximilian Harden.[21]

The parallel between Kraus and Harden makes it possible to correct an
error of outlook by Arnold Zweig, who in a 1927 essay entitled 'Caliban'
suggested that *jüdischer Selbsthass* was a Viennese speciality. In the Habsburg
capital, he says, non-Jewish culture and ways of living do indeed still have
immense prestige. But what German ideal could the Jews of Berlin identify
with? The Brandenburg Junker, the Prussian officer, the industrialist and the
functionary were not exactly inspiring![22]

Against the idea that *jüdischer Selbsthass* was a phenomenon unique to the
Austrian ancien regime could be set the declarations of Albert Memmi, whose
Tunisian roots were fairly remote from Vienna: 'I was not far removed from a
frightful feeling that must be called by its proper name, self-hatred...
This self-destructive fury, so to call it, is much commoner than is generally
believed... Self-rejection can affect and corrode everything in a human being:
body, language, traditions, religion, culture...'[23] Memmi, it is true, was
not seeking to convey that Jews were the only victims of this psychological
torment: 'The Jew has his judeophobia as the negro has his negrophobia, and
women their antifeminism, all the logical outcome of self-rejection.'[24]

Karl Kraus's first two major pamphlets attacked, at one and the same time,
art for art's sake, the aestheticism and self-absorption of the youths of Young
Vienna (in 'Demolished Literature'); and the Zionists (in 'A Crown for Zion').
At that time Kraus had a (distant) sympathy with the Social Democrats, but
soon, under the influence of *jüdischer Selbsthass*, he swung over to aristocratic
conservatism. That put him in the midst of the quadrilateral of typical reactions
by an assimilated Jew faced with antisemitism: aestheticism (which he rejected),
Zionism (also rejected), socialism (for which he had some sympathy) and
antisemitic neo-conservatism, with which he finally allied himself.

Zionism, seen as a 'dissimulation' strategy in reaction to the failure of
assimilation, also sometimes forged unexpected links with neo-conservative
ideology. We have already alluded to Max Nordau, who denounced the
'degeneracy' of the moderns in terms strongly reminiscent of those used by
reactionaries and racists, and recommended that the Jewish race, enfeebled by
centuries in the ghetto, should be licked into shape by physical education and
fresh air. As for Vladimir Jabotinsky, he was to borrow some of the worst
deviations of German nationalism and, in the 1920s, openly adopt the fascist
model.[25] It was via such suspect infiltrations that certain elements in Zionism
and in the *jüdischer Selbsthass* – both extreme reactions to the failure of liberal
assimilation – maintained a distant dialectical relationship.

Karl Kraus and the antisemites: Chamberlain, Weininger, Lanz-Liebenfels

Kraus's *jüdischer Selbsthass*, whose psychological and social roots we have just
been examining, was elevated into a doctrine by two authors, Houston Stewart

Chamberlain and, above all, Otto Weininger. But the ambivalent relationship between Kraus and the racist Lanz von Liebenfels shows how this 'metaphysical' antisemitism was constantly threatening to lapse into the crudest 'biologism'.

Between 1901 and 1902 Kraus published two articles and two letters by Chamberlain. The oddest of these is doubtless the article entitled 'Catholic Universities',[26] which Kraus thought so important that he devoted an entire issue of *Die Fackel* to it. It would take too long to recap all the tortuous arguments of Chamberlain, who claimed that the modern world was threatened by two principles, Rome and Jerusalem, and concluded that Catholicism and Protestantism would do well to make an alliance. What is important for our purposes is the passage in which Chamberlain describes the threat from 'Jerusalem'. It was diffuse; it could wear court dress or carry a red flag. It could worm its way into any milieu. It was always a will to possession and to power. It created nothing, but ruined and destroyed what it conquered: art and tradition. Its most fearsome weapon was the press.[27]

However reluctantly, we must concede that Chamberlain's antisemitic harangue echoed a good many of Kraus's own beliefs, as summarized by Sigurd Paul Scheichl: 'Kraus's attitude to Judaism developed in perfect harmony with his *Kulturkritik* in so far as the Jews seem to be part of all the contemporary phenomena which he judged unfavourably: liberalism, liberal corruption of the press and the economy, forgetfulness of nature in bourgeois morality.'[28]

Edward Timms has explained the reasons for this disturbing convergence of Kraus and Chamberlain. When Kraus sent Chamberlain the proofs of his article for correction, he pointed out that the text was a little too short to take up all thirty-two pages of an issue of *Die Fackel*. He suggested that Chamberlain should add a few extra remarks to the criticism of 'Jerusalem' and stress the corrupting role of the press. Kraus even enclosed with his letter his own 'rough outline' of the subject. Chamberlain readily agreed to the suggestion. Thus Kraus was in part the hidden co-author of this antisemitic pamphlet.[29] The forces of evil called 'Jerusalem' were to reappear in May 1916, under the name 'Israel', in Kraus's poem 'Prayer to the Sun of Gideon'.[30]

If Chamberlain seems to have been very important to Karl Kraus, the influence on Kraus of *Sex and Character* was equally profound, both in building up his mythology of the feminine and in his concept of genius, culture, modernism, psychoanalysis – and also Jewry.[31] On some essential points, Weininger's antisemitism draws on Chamberlain's 'The Foundations', from which he borrowed the vision of a radical conversion which would redeem Jewry in the same way as Jesus Christ in his act of 'foundation'. The *Kulturkritik* outlined in *Sex and Character* suggests that once the Jew entered into culture he began to twist it away from its proper direction. Just as Wagner was furious to see good old German music, the pure soul of the *Volk*, fall into hands too skilful to be wholly honest, so Weininger claimed that science, the noble Faustian striving towards what Goethe had seen as a scientific cosmology, had been reduced by Jewish scientists to a pitiable exercise in disintegrative manipulation. They had turned gold into base metal.

This passage in *Sex and Character*[32] clearly shows that Weininger saw the Jew as an agent of the modernization which was bringing about the 'disenchantment of the world' (to use Max Weber's expression) and working towards a narrowly instrumental scientific and technical rationalism. Weininger here is a perfect model of 'reactionary modernism', falling back on neo-Romantic tradition to escape the withering of rationalism when confined to 'positivist' uses. Hatred of Jews is an expression of discontent with contemporary civilization, a rejection of modernity. (This explains the apparently ludicrous comparison which Weininger, following Wagner, makes between the Jew and the Englishman.)[33] The superman of the Weininger sort (a variant on the 'Aryan myth' as detailed by Léon Poliakov)[34] is a microcosmic genius, a new Novalis destined to restore a wisdom based on sympathy between the individual soul and the 'soul of the world'.

Weininger's fulminations against the Jews convey a criticism of the illusions and frustrations of the *Aufklärung*. He has even been compared to Theodor Adorno with his critique of the Enlightenment.[35] The *jüdischer Selbsthass* of Karl Kraus also has that dimension: an anguished revolt against the contradictions of modern rationalism, of a civilization which claimed to be following Progress while preparing- for war and the 'last days of humanity'. The real villain of this apocalypse would always, in the end, be the liberal Jew, in his various capacities: politician, journalist, speculator; traitor-scientist and destroyer of Nature; traitor-psychologist and destroyer of Genius;[36] traitor-artist and destroyer of Culture.

Liberal *Bildung*, Weininger declared, could no longer serve the modern Jew as a secularized religion. It is not surprising that he should have directed his most vigorous and bitter attacks against Schiller, the great German author who, as Gershom Scholem has pointed out, was almost worshipped by the assimilated Jews of the liberal era.[37] 'Can't they see the total flatness of his plays, their metaphysical nullity?' wrote Weininger. 'He is one of the originators of the hypocritical enthusiasm of the worshippers of Progress who are so numerous amongst today's Jews.'[38] It was this very article on Schiller, which was included in Weininger's posthumous book 'Last Things', that was reprinted by Kraus on the first page of *Die Fackel* for 11 November 1909.[39]

It has often been said – for example, by Sigurd Paul Scheichl – that neither Chamberlain nor Weininger was racist in the strictest sense of the word, since they did not have a narrowly biological concept of Jewishness. This is partly correct, for these two antisemitic authors do respect the possibility of true 'conversion'. But only partly true. Chamberlain has a racist dimension derived from Gobineau and Darwin, and the whole of the first part of *Sex and Character*, it should be remembered, is based on biological (pseudo)science.

The same could be said of Kraus. His *kulturkritisch* judeophobia was constantly threatening to drift into racism. As Kraus's *jüdischer Selbsthass* and reactionary sympathies reached their apogee, just before the First World War and into its early stages, *Die Fackel* began to exhibit some very disquieting features. Indignation against Moriz Benedikt assumed the force of a 'Revelation of the corrosive tendencies of his race'.[40] In an article entitled 'Die Historischen und die Vordringenden. Ein Wort an den Adel' ('The Old

Nobility and the Parvenus: A Word to the Aristocracy'),[41] Kraus warned the aristocracy against the mingling of blood which could come about through their excessively trusting relationship with the Jews. For, he explained,

> How can a race whose ambition is insulted if it is accused of desiring only worldly goods not also desire the spiritual goods which, in our radically changed existence, are (are they not) the cheapest ornaments for other people? If a day comes – and it has come – when values become wholly mercantile, it must still be possible to take them off the market so as to rob the eternal marketeers of their pleasure: let the aristocracy show its mettle by withdrawing from them, let it turn its back on society as a ghetto of new-made nobilities.[42]

In May 1917 Kraus thundered alarmingly against the 'Jewish scoundrels, these poets of a nation not their own'[43] – a curious way to denounce the bellicosity of a handful of state-sponsored rhymsters! We may draw attention to the antisemitic tendencies[44] of certain scenes in his play 'Last Days of Mankind': for example, the tableau in the 'Epilogue' entitled 'Master of the hyenas'. There are many indications that Kraus's 'judeophobia', both in the years before the Great War (his conversion to Catholicism dates from 1911) and in the early 1920s, was getting dangerously close to racist antisemitism.

All the elements in this apogee of Kraus's *jüdischer Selbsthass* appear clearly in 'Er ist doch ä Jud' ('Ain't he a Yid?'), of 1913.[45] In it, Kraus replied to a reader who had asked him if he thought he had never himself had any 'Jewish peculiarities', and what he thought of the opinions of racist antisemites such as Lanz von Liebenfels, who maintained that one could never 'get away from one's race'. Kraus insisted at the outset that he did not feel qualified to pronounce on racial questions. But he added that in all races there might be exceptional individuals who could rise to a 'superior state'. As far as he personally was concerned he declared: 'Not only do I believe, but I feel it as a staggering revelation, that not one of the qualities which we nowadays recognize as Jewish is found in me.' And at the same time he is insisting that the language of *Die Fackel* is infinitely superior to that used by the antisemites!

For the rest, he added, the faults of the Jews have become universal, beginning with materialistic greed. Kraus admits that the 'renegade' Jews who converted out of self-interest deserved the contempt and the attacks of anti-semites. But he considered himself far above such opportunism, asking:

> Do you really believe that I would 'deny' Jewry, whence I came, so as to move among counts, officers and bishops, for example? Certainly I do not seek to deny that for me, whose political convictions – if I have any – go back to before the French Revolution, counts, officers and bishops are more likely in principle to improve the human race than speculators, psychologists and journalists.

After this confession of reactionary faith – which, as we have said, is a typical corollary of the *jüdischer Selbsthass* – Kraus gave voice to a Weiningerian idea: 'The alpha and omega of my political opinions is to blame the ruin of the world and especially of the state – the state, which in truth is the catalyst of chaos and effeminate decadence – on the unmanly attitude of mind which casts doubt on all the faiths in the world.'[46] As in Weininger, antisemitism and antifeminism are inextricable.

After proclaiming his antipathy to Schnitzler and his admiration for Else Lasker-Schüler and Peter Altenberg, Karl Kraus concluded that 'Race is a thing I cannot make sense of.' And because the reader whose question had prompted the whole essay had referred to Lanz von Liebenfels, Kraus cited the latter as an example of how far the racists themselves were contradictory in their judgements. Lanz von Liebenfels, in an issue of *Der Brenner* devoted to Kraus,[47] had described the latter as 'the saviour of Aryo-Germanity', and in his own journal, *Ostara*, he called him 'a Jew of the blond, Mongol type', the type which had produced many a genius, including Spinoza. Kraus poured scorn on Lanz von Liebenfels's absurdities, but nevertheless quoted his opinions with a certain gratification, saying that he was not an agitator but a 'researcher' (*Forscher*).

The respect widely paid to Lanz von Liebenfels, who was twice invited to contribute to *Der Brenner*,[48] is incomprehensible to us today. The journal *Ostara* was a monument to racist fanaticism and primary antisemitism. It recommended itself to its readers on the cover in the following terms: 'The reading matter of the blond people is – in an age which tenderly nurtures effeminates and inferior races and is mercilessly eliminating the heroic blond race – the rallying point of all idealists raised in the quest of beauty, truth, reasons for living, and God.'[49] The interest and consideration shown by Karl Kraus, and also by Ludwig von Ficker, to Lanz von Liebenfels prove how far antisemitism, in the first years of the twentieth century, had become a linguistic game acceptable to certain intellectuals.

In 1934, in the famous issue on 'Why "The Torch" Has Not Appeared', Kraus asked the disturbing question:

> Pen-pushers are strangely mistaken when they ask if the silence of *Die Fackel* might mean that it approves of its ideas being touted by national socialism, or if this success has been enough to stifle its expressions of horror at the ill-treatment meted out to an innocent group of Jews. Can the author help it if his defence of humanity, his allying himself with nature and the spirit against the destructive forces of a deviant intelligence and a misunderstood technology, have been usurped, as if his work not only served it, but was devoted to it exclusively through an aryogermanism whose preoccupations remain alien to him?[50]

The question was indeed fundamental, and could have been put to a good many other European intellectuals in sympathy with reactionary neo-conservatism; but it was also an admission of failure, coming from a writer who had claimed to be fighting against the moral corruption of his times.

Kraus in the 1930s: regrets and contradictions

The most astonishing thing about the Karl Kraus of the 1920s and 1930s was not the inevitable and urgent adjustments which the rise of fascism and

Nazism forced him to make to his antisemitic beliefs. On the contrary: the most astonishing thing is his obstinate refusal to renounce his pre-war dogma that the Jews and 'the Jewish spirit' in civilization would be the scourge of the twentieth century, and his continuing rejection of Jewish 'solidarity'. When in 1930 Arnold Zweig asked him to sign an international petition against the repression of Russian Jews who taught or studied Hebrew, Kraus refused, explaining that the defence of German in Germany seemed to him more pressing than the defence of Hebrew in Soviet Russia. He concluded by pointing out a grammatical error in the text of the petition, which quite damned it in his eyes![51]

In 'Why "The Torch" Has Not Appeared', Kraus complained that the need to be different had been described as proof of some shameful association. He saw this as an unpleasant tendency of the psychoanalytical mind:

> On the contrary, he feels compelled to say that in spite of everything, amidst the free play of intellectual irony, in the worship of profaned and polluted life, he gratefully acknowledges the elementary force of incorruptible Jewishness, which he loves above all things, as something which remains immune to race and class and cash-box, mobs and gutters, and to all the hatred between traffickers and troglodytes.[52]

And yet, a few lines earlier, he had pronounced the cruellest and most absurd opinion imaginable:

> As for his criticism of the inferior Jewish types who, in literature as in psychology, commit cruel acts of vengeance against the spirit and nature, it seems to him that these misdeeds – with all the consequences for the soul and the language that Aryan naivety has long since absorbed as part of the same attack – are not less serious, within the history of ideas, than the violence which more readily excites compassion for human suffering.[53]

He really seems to think that the supposed 'crimes' of Jews against culture are on a par with Nazi crimes against Jews!

III

Salome: *Jewishness and 'sexual perversions'*

Karl Kraus's *jüdischer Selbsthass* dominated even his sexual life. I have already referred to the masochistic character of his eroticism: his fantasies of woman-kind took the form of the faithless, destructive *femme fatale*, of the demons described by Otto Weininger or of Franz Wedekind's Lulu.[54] In Karl Kraus's relationship with Sidonie Nádherný von Borutin this masochism combined with a typical element of *jüdischer Selbsthass*: a fascination with the aristocracy, which Kraus dreamed of joining. He was to be disappointed, for Sidonie was always to reject the idea of marrying a Jew as being incompatible with her aristocratic pretentions – as her friend, Rainer Maria Rilke, rather nastily pointed out to her when he realized she was in love with Kraus. In her childhood commonplace book, to the question 'What do you hate most?', Sidonie had answered 'The Jews.'[55]

The contradictions of his Jewish identity so tormented Kraus that they biased his judgement in one of his greatest *causes célèbres*, his unceasing struggle against the hypocrisy of bourgeois manners, against the assimilation of certain types of sexual behaviour (adultery, prostitution, homosexuality) to crimes subject to the penal code, and against the trespassing of public order into private life. *Die Fackel* was never tired of pillorying 'Judeo-Christian morality', and Kraus constantly emphasized its Jewish dimension. Like Weininger in *Sex and Character*, he accused the Jewish bourgeoisie of reducing marriage to a monetary transaction got up by a set of go-betweens. This criticism of Jewishness was connected with prostitution. It should not be forgotten that the problem of the 'white slave trade' organized by Jewish panders in Galicia and Bucovina, and the large proportion of Jewesses among the prostitutes of Vienna, was a cause of concern to contemporaries. Bertha Pappenheim was to make the struggle against prostitution one of the objectives of her Jüdischer Frauenverein. In 1892, fourteen antisemitic Christian Socialist members of the Reichsrat had proposed a motion demanding energetic measures against the prostitution supposedly being organized by the Jews.[56] In such a climate we can see why Kraus's interest in the problem of prostitution was not unconnected with his animosity against Jewry.

His reactions to the performance in Vienna of Oscar Wilde's *Salome* at the end of 1903 are particularly revealing. The Deutsches Volkstheater of Vienna had revived a production from the Berlin Neues Theater, with Adele Hartwig as Salome. Autumn 1903 had seen the suicide of Otto Weininger, which much preoccupied Kraus: Weininger had instantly become one of the 'doomed geniuses' celebrated in *Die Fackel*. The issue for 23 December 1903, which opened with a review of the Volkstheater's *Salome*, also contained a letter from Weininger's father.[57]

Oscar Wilde was, after Shakespeare, the English writer whom Karl Kraus most passionately and unswervingly admired.[58] But in that year of 1903, mention of Wilde in *Die Fackel* could not be dissociated from discussion of homosexuality. In the issue of 2 December Kraus had referred to a study of 'Sexual Life in England' and the reviews of it in the German press, emphasizing that the Germans had good reason to envy the British for their superiority in 'the culture of sexual perversion' which had nurtured the genius of Oscar Wilde.[59]

Kraus began his discussion of the Viennese performance of *Salome* in his usual way, by criticizing the article on it which had appeared in the *Neue Freie Presse*. On this occasion his target was Freidrich Schütz. That critic had introduced his review in the *NFP* with some moralizing considerations on the misfortunes of Wilde, that brilliant representative of English culture who had been damned by sexual perversions. Kraus expressed in the strongest terms his rage against this right-thinking imbecile. Schütz's only concern, he declared, was to proclaim loud and clear that he was not 'one of *them*'. As for

Kraus himself, he said that in passionately pleading the homosexual cause, he took a malicious pleasure in hinting that he might indeed be one of *them* ...

Kraus then changed the subject and tackled Wilde's presumed antisemitism. Schütz had opined that Wilde showed the Jews in a very unflattering light: Herod as an incestuous father, Herodias an unnatural mother, Salome a hysterical girl, and the Jews in general as sexual perverts, or just grotesque. Schütz thought that the Volkstheater production had pushed this even further by making the Jews speak with the Galician accent of the *Ostjuden*, the *mauscheln*. Kraus thought that Schütz's article breathed the very spirit of the *Neue Freie Presse*: on the one side, mealy-mouthed puritan preaching about homosexuality, on the other, the seizing of any slight pretext to defend the Jews. Kraus's sarcastic reaction shows that if he, for his part, was quite willing to risk being seen as a friend of homosexuals, he energetically refused to be taken for one of *those* Jews ...

In fact, Schütz's article had clear-sightedly revealed something which was to dog *Salome* through Germany and Austria, as was soon to be confirmed by Richard Strauss's operatic adaptation. As Sander L. Gilman has shown,[60] successful performances of *Salome* in the German world always meant the accentuation of certain Jewish stereotypes, often bordering on outright anti-semitism. Gilman points out that the sexual 'perversions' rampant in Herod's court (homosexual tendencies, incest, hysteria) echoed the catalogue of anomalies which late nineteenth-century psychiatrists considered to be more frequent among Jews (especially the *Ostjuden*) than among other ethnic groups.

By his ardent defence of Wilde's *Salome* and his vicious attack on 'the right-thinking Jew of the *Neue Freie Presse*', Kraus was killing two birds with one stone. First, he was allying himself with the artistic avant-garde and confirming his commitment to the cause of sexual freedom. Secondly, he was once again unmasking the 'Jews of the *NFP*' and brandishing, as a manifesto for modernism, a play which German adaptation had tinged with antisemitism.

Kraus versus Heine: the hidden language of the German Jew

The fundamental element in the aesthetic and in the ethics (for him they were the same thing) of Karl Kraus was his cult of language. 'Tell me how you speak and write and I'll tell you who you are' might have been the adage behind all the combats he engaged in *Die Fackel*. And one of the founding manifestos of his *ars poetica* and his ethical and political endeavours was the piece written in August 1911 (at the height of Kraus's 'reactionary' period) and entitled 'Heine and his Consequences'. This essay, one of the most unjust he ever wrote, can only really be understood if it is seen as yet another symptom of *jüdischer Selbsthass*. By choosing as target *the* German Jewish poet most commonly attacked by the antisemites, Kraus was giving a token of his entire 'assimilation' and differentiating himself – he, who might well have passed as one of the German writers most deeply indebted to Heine's satirical cast of mind and verbal virtuosity – from a model with whom he could not endure to be compared. This, no doubt, explains the singular attitude of Kraus towards Heine: the fear of being associated with Heine the Jew.

From the beginning of the century Kraus always spoke of Heine in the context of antisemitism and of his own struggle against the 'corruptions' of Jewry.[61] The essay 'Heine and his Consequences' appropriates a goodly number of commonplaces from the antisemitic polemic against the poet. First, cosmopolitanism and Frenchiness: 'Without Heine there would be no literary journalism. It is a French disease which he has brought back to us.'[62] Then his lack of a deep feeling for nature:

> But the reader who considers a poem as a revelation from a poet deep in the contemplation of nature, and not from nature deep in the contemplation of the poet, will confine himself to appreciating him as a technician skilled in the expression of joy and pain, and a gifted stage-manager of readymade ambiances.

This lack of a real feeling for nature was attributable to Heine's 'uprooted-ness'; Kraus preferred Detlev von Liliencron, who 'had only a provincial vision [*Landanschauung*, a play on *Weltanschauung*, world view]. But it seems to me that he was more cosmic in his Schleswig-Holstein than was Heine in the entire universe.' And lastly comes the overtly antisemitic complaint: 'In faith as in unbelief, Heine can never rid himself of his mercantile outlook.' None the less Kraus seeks to put himself above vulgar antisemitism: 'Alas! That mean-minded hatred for Heine which attacks the Jew does not touch the poet, and bleats to the sound of a sentimental melody even without the aid of the musician.'[63]

In October 1915 Karl Kraus returned to Heine in two articles published successively in *Die Fackel*: 'The Enemies, Goethe and Heine' and 'The Friends, Heine and Rothschild'. Kraus was reacting to an article by Hirth, editor of Heine's letters, which had appeared in the *Österreichische Rundschau* under the title 'Heine and Rothschild'. Karl Kraus's main aim was to attack the literary mania of Germanists who buried their great authors under an avalanche of 'Complete Works', determinedly publishing even very unim-portant writings. But he took the opportunity for an incidental comparison between the 'true' poet Goethe and the hapless poetaster Heine, and to dilate on the 'famillionaire' tone of the correspondence between Heine and Rothschild.[64]

Kraus's real grudge against Heine was that he 'talked Jewish', used the 'jargon' which was one of *Die Fackel*'s pet targets. Even in the pre-war *Die Fackel* the use of jargon cloaked a symbolic function. Its untiring mockery of Jewish German – no longer Yiddish, but not yet German – really implied that the relationship between Jewish intelligence and the spirit had been vitiated through the former's troubled relationship with language.[65] In November 1912, a few months after his essay on Heine, Kraus brought out in *Die Fackel* the little play called *Harakiri und Feuilleton*, which consists of an imaginary dialogue set in the editorial office of the *Neue Freie Presse*. In his introduction he emphasizes that the characters are talking in dialect. The play was not, he said, trying to make out that the real denizens of the liberal press actually spoke that dialect, at least not in so exaggerated a form. 'But I admit that I would have been unable to give any other kind of speech to characters who by race or education are a hundred leagues away from such a dialect. For it is their very soul which speaks that dialect.'[66] Kraus took up the same theme in 'Er ist doch ä Jud':

> I do not know what the specifically Jewish things are nowadays . . . But if there was only one, the sing-song intonation they use when discussing and going about their business, I would say that the others could be discerned in it too, for it is the intonation which makes such a nice accompaniment to the clink of coin. It is the language of the world and its desires, and it is quite justifiable to see it as characteristically Jewish.[67]

Studies of modern German antisemitism have arguably failed to lay sufficient emphasis on *linguistic racism*. Sander L. Gilman, in his study on 'Antisemitism and the Hidden Language of the Jews', has gathered an imposing body of evidence on this singular aspect of racism, which goes far beyond mere criticism of accent, intonation or vocabulary.[68] Jewish idiom had characteristics which were all the more striking in that they were disguised. The Yiddish of the *Ostjuden*, and the bastard German spoken by Jewish immigrants from the eastern provinces,[69] were not the most worrying phenomenon in the ears of antisemites. They were more anxious to hunt down the 'Jewish jargon' which masqueraded as the purest and most irreproachable German.

In their ears the Jew, even when he spoke German perfectly – better than the Germans – still spoke Jewish. This subversion was deadly dangerous to the German of Luther and Goethe: in the mouth of the 'German Jew' it lost its profundity, its expressive force, its 'immanent metaphysic'. Gilman has shown the grip which this obsession took on Wilhelm Marr, Eugen Dühring, Heinrich von Treitschke and even Theodor Billroth, who in his 1876 pamphlet on 'The Teaching and Study of the Medical Sciences' declared that the most perfectly assimilated Jew still talked Jewish, even if he dazzled his hearers by the apparent elegance of his German.[70]

Many assimilated German-speaking Jews reacted to this aspect of contemporary antisemitism with an absolute obsession with linguistic purity and correctness. Eduard Engel's book *Sprich deutsch! Ein Buch zur Entwelschung!*[71] (roughly 'Speak German! How Not to Be an Alien!') was the work of a Jew who had become an arbiter of linguistic purity against the infiltrations of French and Jewish, or *mauscheln*, jargon. Such purism could lead to *jüdischer Selbsthass*. A German Jewish writer lived in dread of being caught out in *mauscheln*. In his *Beiträge zu einer Kritik der Sprache* ('Contributions to a Critique of Language'), Fritz Mauthner savagely attacked Jewishness, which he accused of having introduced the superstition of words and the fetishism of language, and also the Jews, who would always be an alien tribe in Germany so long as they went on 'jargonizing' in the language of 'Mauschel' (the Hebrew-Yiddish version of Moses, meaning the poor Jew).[72] In *Sex and Character*, Otto Weininger declares that Jews – like women – don't know what 'speaking' is: they chatter a lot, but they don't *say* anything.[73]

One of the most surprising of Theodor Herzl's writings, from 1897, is called *Mauschel*. In it he fulminates against the assimilated Jews who were behaving as anti-Zionists, who, he wrote, made him feel utterly sick: 'Mauschel is a caricature of humanity, something unspeakably horrid and repugnant.' This Mauschel was the curse of the Jewish race, for the antisemites equated him with the genuine Jews. But the Zionists would get the better of him: 'the second arrow of Zionism shall pierce the breast of Mauschel!' Herzl concluded,[74] at the end of a tirade which echoes the most grating clichés of antisemitism.

Fear of 'Mauschel', the double who seemed to slumber within every assimilated Jew, could lurk even in the unconscious. When Josef Breuer described the symptoms of the hysteria suffered by Anna O., he emphasized her loss of the German language. Sometimes she spoke in a foreign language, such as English, but she also occasionally used what Breuer calls a 'disjointed jargon', probably a mixture of German and Yiddish.[75] (Later, Bertha Pappenheim, alias Anna O., translated several Yiddish books for German readers.) In *The Interpretation of Dreams*, and even in *Jokes and Their Relation to the Unconscious*, Freud avoids quoting Yiddish sentences and even words, preferring to translate all the Jewish stories into good German. The 'Myops' dream is one of the few cases where he 'writes Yiddish'. The jargon of his unconscious, *Auf Geseres, auf Ungeseres*, betrays his linguistic conscience. The 'correct usage' of German was one of the first things to go when the identity of a German Jew was under threat.

The 'Wagnerianism' of Karl Kraus and the mystique of language

When he raged against Heine, it was 'Mauschel' who was Karl Kraus's real target. But this kind of polemic was almost certain to become an echo of Richard Wagner's tirade against Mendelssohn. In his essay 'Judaism in Music', Wagner deplored 'The effect the Jew has on us through his *language*; and that is the starting point of my reflections on Jewish influence in music. The Jew speaks the language of the nation in which he has dwelt from generation to generation, but he speaks it always as a foreigner.'[76] This, according to Wagner, is why Jews are incapable of creating poetry: 'In that language, in that art, the Jew can only imitate, but never really write, or create works of art.'

The Jew is even more alienated from true *song*, and consequently from music, than from the poetic word. Even an assimilated and cultivated Jew cannot attain to true poetry or music, for they, says Wagner, are rooted in the instincts of the *Volk* to which the Jew is ever a stranger. He can only assume the outward characteristics of a nation's art, so that 'Jewish music often makes the same impression on us as – for example – a poem of Goethe would if it were offered to us in Jewish jargon.'

The most typical example of this, for Wagner, is Mendelssohn, in comparison with the great masters of German music, Bach, Mozart or Beethoven. By the end of the essay Mendelssohn's bogus creativity has burgeoned into a malady affecting all of contemporary art: 'Impotence is lodged in the very soul of our art.' Outside the musical domain Wagner claims contemporary poetry as an example. He uses Heine as the symbol of this age 'in which our poetry has become lies'. This over-gifted Jew has cast over German poetry the mantle of his Jesuitic hypocrisy, his analytic spirit and his mockery. 'He was the conscience of Jewry, just as Jewry is the bad conscience of our modern civilization.'

But Wagner, like all antisemites, made an exception for one Jew who consoled him for all the Mendelssohns and Heines: this was the writer Ludwig Börne. The Jew, says Wagner, must cease to be a Jew. Börne has managed it. But it is precisely his example which shows us that such redemption cannot be sought by the complacent and the facile: its price is 'distress, anguish, suffering and pain in abundance'. And Wagner exhorts the Jews: 'Take part wholeheartedly in this work of redemption which grants rebirth through self-destruction, for it is thus that we shall be able to merge into one unity! But you must know that you have only one way of deliverance from the curse which is upon you: the deliverance of Asahuerus – annihilation.'[77]

Wagner's essay was to be echoed tirelessly in the nineteenth and twentieth centuries by all antisemites. Thus in 1909 the music critic Rudolf Louis, in 'German Music of Our Time', spoke of Gustav Mahler's 'expressly and fundamentally Jewish character'. If his music had a frankly Jewish accent, it might seem 'foreign' and even 'exotic'; but alas! it could only use Jewish-German jargon – *mauscheln*.[78]

Wagnerian Jews (Otto Weininger, for example) had only to follow the trail blazed by Wagner's Börne. Assimilation, which liberalism and the *Aufklärung* had seen as a rational choice, was to be restaged as a mystic conversion. We might say – however paradoxically in connection with an admirer of Offenbach! – that Karl Kraus was, in his way, a 'Wagnerian Jew'. But Kraus sought in language the mystery which was to bind the Jewish writer in communion with German culture.

This insight throws fresh light on Kraus's linguistic eroticism, which takes masochism as the way to the most exquisite pleasures. 'Nothing can forbid me writing what forbids me writing.'[79] How to overcome this poetic 'impotence' which antisemites saw in Jews and which *jüdischer Selbsthass* internalized as a permanent query? 'The more closely you look at a word, the more distantly it looks at you' is one of Kraus's aphorisms.[80] This is not, as Walter Benjamin said, 'a Platonic love of language', but the same 'anguish of mortal love' which Kraus knew in his relationship with Sidonie Nádherný – as Nike Wagner has observed.[81] A proximity which is really distance, an intimacy which reserves the right to strangeness, arousing ambiguous feelings, that doubt which Kraus so often mentions in connection with his work on language.

If we interpret Kraus's 'mysticism' of language as an attempt to exorcize *jüdischer Selbsthass* through writing, the thousands of pages of *Die Fackel* begin to look like a sort of Great Wall of China raised against the invading hordes of the antisemites, but above all against inner doubt – both of which disputed Kraus's right to belong to *German* language and literature. In his battle with

Heine he was fighting his own double, the (Jewish) German writer who surely resembled him most. Kraus, like Heine, was constantly heckled by antisemites who accused him of 'writing Jewish' in *Die Fackel*.

Karl Kraus's letter of 21 April 1933 to the producers of Radio Cologne shows his perfect awareness of the vanity of his attempt to assimilate to German culture: asked to publish his translation of Shakespeare's sonnets, he replied, 'We must draw your attention to the fact that this adaptation of the sonnets of Shakespeare by Karl Kraus has in fact been published in German, but without the necessary proviso that it is in fact a translation from the Hebrew; and if you prefer a translation directly into German, you certainly ought to make do with that of Stefan Georg.'[82]

Kafka on Kraus

Franz Kafka's opinion proves that Karl Kraus's case, far from being anomalous, was quite representative of the tormented Jewish identity of some of the century's major writers in the German language. After reading 'Literature, or This Will Really Surprise You', a 'magical operetta' by Kraus, published in 1921, which contained merciless parodies of (in particular) Franz Werfel, Kafka wrote to Max Brod:

> It seemed to me to strike extraordinarily true, right to the heart ... No one can talk jargon like Kraus, though in this Jewish-German world no one can really do anything other than talk jargon, in the widest sense – the only sense it should ever have – as an appropriation, which may be noisy, silent or tormented, of someone else's possession which one has not acquired, but which has been seized with a (rather) hasty hand, and which remains someone else's possession, even when there is not the slightest linguistic error to be found.

Why, asks Kafka, are Jews so irresistibly attracted by this language which 'has never been less varied than it is now; perhaps it has even lost some diversity'? Is the 'decadence' of German to be blamed on the strong Jewish presence in its literature? This rush to assimilate to the German language speaks to the 'relationship young Jews have with their Jewishness, the terrible inner state of these generations: this is what Kraus in particular recognized so clearly.'

And Kafka goes on, in this same letter to Brod, to give an impressive description of the situation which may lead to *jüdischer Selbsthass*:

> This father complex on which more than one is spiritually fed has nothing to do with the innocent father, but with the father's Jewishness. For the most part, those who began to write in German wanted to get away from Jewishness, generally with the vague approval of their fathers (it is the vagueness which is so disgusting); they wanted to, but their hind feet were still stuck to their father's Jewishness, and their front feet could not find any new ground. The resulting despair was their inspiration.[83]

14

The 'Cultural Zionism' of Richard Beer-Hofmann

I

Assimilation without illusion

If the Jewish identity of Karl Kraus seems tormented and paradoxical, that of Richard Beer-Hofmann (1866–1945) is the exact opposite: perfectly assured. Like all the assimilated Jews of his generation, he came up against the prevailing antisemitism at the university, in the army, and in everyday life. But he, unlike Herzl or Kraus, was not induced by his experiences to question his Jewish roots. In fact, one discovers with surprise that descriptions of Viennese antisemitism are by no means prominent in the autobiographical fragments under the title *Paula*, written between 1941 and 1945 in New York and dedicated to the memory of his wife, Paula Lissy, who died in Zurich in October 1939. The Beer-Hofmann family had fled from Nazi Austria on 20 August 1939. In 1936, Richard had made a journey to Palestine at the invitation of Zionist organizations.

He bore the name of his father, Beer, and of his cousin, Hofmann. His ancestors, who according to family tradition had come from Cologne and Trier, were by the beginning of the seventeenth century living in southern Moravia, where by the end of the eighteenth century they were firmly settled as clothmakers. Richard's father had come to study law at the University of Vienna. Another branch of the Beer family had been living in Vienna for even longer: Hieronymus Beer, a doctor of the University of Padua, had become a professor of forensic medicine and psychiatry there in 1848.[1]

Richard's mother had died at his birth in 1866. His father Hermann Beer, a young lawyer, entrusted him to the family of Aloïs Hofmann in Brünn (Brno), where he spent his childhood and youth. In 1880, at fifty, Aloïs sold the Hofmann factory in Brünn and bought three apartment blocks near the Ringstrasse, where they settled. The income from the apartments allowed the Beer-Hofmann family to live as well-off Viennese bourgeois. Hermann Beer, meanwhile, had in 1869 set up as an advocate in the Habsburgerstrasse, where he was to practise until 1896.[2] The entire family kept to the Jewish faith,[3] but Richard's memoirs give no indication that he received any more detailed religious education than was customary in assimilated Jewish bourgeois families.

In 1880 he entered the Akademisches Gymnasium, a prestigious high school in the first quarter of the city where Arthur Schnitzler had been a pupil from 1871 to 1879, and where Hugo von Hofmannsthal was to be found from 1884 to 1892. At that time more than 45 per cent of the pupils were from Jewish families.[4] In his memoirs Schnitzler describes the atmosphere in the school, especially the uproar and indifference which marked the two compulsory hours of Jewish religious education.[5] In 1883 Beer-Hofmann entered the university, becoming a doctor of law in 1890. His father hoped to take him on as an associate, but the son repeated the conflict we have seen so many times in these pages, and which was analysed by Stefan Zweig: he refused to accept a 'bourgeois' career and devoted himself to literature.

A theme common to the biographies of Freud, Herzl, Kraus, Kafka and others is the dissatisfaction of 'sons' with the strategy of assimilation – naively optimistic or (as described in the 'Letter to his Father') too vague and indecisive – pursued by 'fathers'. Biographical evidence shows that in Beer-Hofmann's case the opposite was true: the father warned the son not to be too trusting. In 1890, the year Richard took his doctorate, he did a period of military service in the barracks at Brünn; his adoptive father wrote advising him not to struggle against his fatigue, but rather to report sick. He added, 'If *you* think the fatherland is so precious, well, *I* do not. – A fatherland which delivers us up defenceless to a raging mob, and which even seems to delight in our sufferings, and only treats us as equals with respect to our obligations, but keeps all the rights for itself.'

And nine years later, when Hilsner, a Jew, was tried for 'ritual murder' at Polna, Aloïs Hofmann wrote to Richard: 'The prosecutor, slightly embarrassed, made out that he was guilty of a ritual murder and a certain Dr Baxa (who was representing the victims) repeated this idea without any embarrassment whatever. The antisemitic papers *D.V.* [*Deutsches Volksblatt*], *D. Ztg* [*Deutsche Zeitung*] and *Vaterland* [*Vaterland. Zeitung für die österreichische Monarchie*] are jubilant because it seems that we have now proved that Jews are athirst for Christian blood.'[6]

Perhaps Aloïs Hofmann's disillusioned lucidity spared the young Richard the shock and ordeal of *jüdischer Selbsthass* which so many of his fellows suffered when their trust in assimilation, inherited from fathers of the liberal generation, was brutally shattered.

Prince of Young Vienna

Richard Beer-Hofmann's literary career was governed by his close friendship with Hugo von Hofmannsthal. They first met in the autumn of 1890; Hofmannsthal's last letter to Beer-Hofmann is dated Rodaun, 15 July 1929, the day of his death. In 1919 Hofmannsthal wrote a fervent avowal of friendship to Beer-Hofmann:

When I look back, I see three people whose kindness to me I can never forget: my father; another infinitely good man and great character now gone from among us [Eberhard von Bodenhausen]; and yourself. I am very fond of you, Richard . . . I like everything about you, Richard, everything: your look, your voice, your face – which I can no longer see in the flesh, but in a quite different and much more complicated way – your hands, your gravity, your jokes, your approval – ah, how much! but also your disagreement . . .[7]

When they first met Hofmannsthal was still a pupil at the Akademisches Gymnasium and Beer-Hofmann had just taken his doctorate. He became his friend's mentor.

Beer-Hofmann belonged to the elite of 'Young Vienna', devotees of dandyism and the higher thought. Everyone remembered him for his impressive assurance and Olympian superiority. Rudolf Borchardt later wrote a poem to him comparing him to a king in triumph. Erich von Kahler was to recall his superior attitude, before which everything seemed to yield, the easy life his wealth allowed him to lead, and his princely bearing.[8] Felix Salten described him:

He dressed with the most exquisite nobility, refined elegance and the subtlest taste, which always had something provoking about it. Every day he displayed in his buttonhole a flower carefully selected to suit the atmosphere. He had (and still has) such an irresistible eloquence, such a luminous and penetrating mind, that at the time I dubbed him 'the patron of intelligence'. At first he did not even seem to want to write: one had the impression that he felt above all that.[9]

This narcissistic halo could make Beer-Hofmann seem a little too distant, even from his closest friends, as is shown by the curious letter Hofmannsthal addressed to him on 30 June 1893:

Am I worth no more than an old crushed sardine tin full of wood shavings and rusty nails? Am I an old checked handkerchief, bloodstained and greasy, to be thrown away? I hope those two objects come to your mind when you are about to sink your nose into a perfumed hyacinth, or are nibbling at Neopolitan almonds wrapped in a poem by Barbey d'Aurévilly and steeped in eternal light.[10]

In June 1892, Hofmannsthal had thanked Beer-Hofmannsthal for lending him Barbey d'Aurévilly's 'On Dandyism and George Brummel'.[11]

Richard Beer-Hofmann was to preserve this aristocratic style throughout his sojourn in Vienna. In the autumn of 1906 he moved with his family to the wonderful villa built for him by the architect Josef Hoffmann (whose most notable work is the famous Palais Stoclet in Brussels), Hasenauerstrasse 59 in the 'Cottage' district of the residential suburb of Döbling.[12] Beer-Hofmann had the star of David inscribed on the facade. This house, one of the most remarkable artist's residences of the turn of the century, was confiscated by the Nazis in 1939, and was unfortunately demolished in the late 1960s.

Beer-Hofmann's literary output was small, but his works were always hailed by his contemporaries as great events: two novellas in the decadent style in 1893 ('Camelias' and 'A Child'); a few poems (in particular, the 'Lullaby for Myriam' of 1897, dedicated to his daughter born in September of that year); the story 'George's Death' (1900), which literary historians see as his most important work; an Elizabethan drama, inspired by a play by Philip Massinger and Nathaniel Field, 'The Count of Charolais' (1904); and some essays, such as the 'Discourse on Mozart' of 1906. Later came the dramatic cycle 'The History of King David' and a few stagings at the Burgtheater in the 1920s and 1930s.

Truth to tell, Beer-Hofmann's creativity seems to have gone through some periods of eclipse which worried his friends and admirers. In his conversations with Werner Vordtriede he said frankly that his literary vocation had never been very deep, but added that 'in that circle [of Hofmannsthal, Schnitzler and Bahr] everyone was convinced that I would be a writer and a good one. I enjoyed unlimited credit, not only before I had published anything, but even before I had written anything at all.'[13] Hofmannsthal's letters to him contain some positive exhortations: 'Dear Richard, do force yourself really to work, I beg you,' he wrote in 1894; and six years later: 'I am very worried to think that once again you have given up work.'[14] Like Hofmannsthal's other friend, Leopold von Andrian, whose poetic output remained exceptionally slender, Beer-Hofmann seems to have been smitten by the malady of Lord Chandos, who avowed himself unable to take up his pen.

The two novellas from 1893 express the quintessence of Viennese 'decadence' and dandyism, as does Schnitzler's *Anatol*. In 'Camelias', Freddy, a thirty-eight-year-old bachelor, leaves a ball in the early dawn, returns home, and contemplates breaking with his mistress so as to marry Thea, a girl of seventeen, with whom he has just fallen in love; but the thought of a bourgeois marriage frightens him and he abandons the project, instead sending his usual bouquet of camelias to Franzy, his mistress, the type of the *süsses Mädel* of the suburbs so often represented by Schnitzler. Freddy is a dandy haunted by the fear of growing old; his bedside book is Mantegazza's 'The Hygiene of Love', with its talk of venereal diseases and sexual impotence...

In 'A Child', Paul is looking for an excuse to get rid of his mistress, a soubrette called Julie. When she tells him of the death of their child, who had been put out to nurse in the country, he thinks the moment has come. But he cannot stop himself from thinking about the dead child he never knew. To cast off this tormenting thought he goes to the village where the child died and finds peace in meditating on the ineluctable course of destiny. Paul lives in an apartment of the Ringstrasse district, decorated in the 'Makart' style characteristic of the *Gründerzeit*. He likes looking down on the boulevards from his balcony, and in the novella Beer-Hofmann gives some descriptions which, according to a contemporary critic, 'rank among the best things ever written in Vienna and about Vienna'.[15] The consoling thoughts which calm Paul after the child's death are inspired by a monist world view akin to *Lebensphilosophie*, in which existence and death are part of the great cycle of life.

This novella ('A Child') contains in embryo all the themes of Beer-Hofmann's later work: criticism of the 'decadent' lifestyle, brutally shattered by the intrusion of death (as in 'George's Death'); the 'voice of the blood' which awakens after the child's death and which was to lead Beer-Hofmann to affirm his Jewish identity; and the presence of an aesthetical metaphysics of post-Nietzschean inspiration which gives his works a sort of profundity, but also the over-density which, when allied to an extremely elaborate style, makes 'George's Death' difficult to read. Even in connection with 'A Child' Hofmannsthal remarked to his friend that 'in the last two chapters, reflection and philosophical meditation take centre-stage . . . and these chapters really seem superfluous.'[16] Lou Andreas-Salomé wrote to Beer-Hofmann in the same spirit, comparing his novellas to Schnitzler's, and concluded, 'You are more of an artist and philosopher, while he is more of a writer.'[17]

Beer-Hofmann and Herzl

In Richard Beer-Hofmann's early writings there are no traces of any thoughts about Jewish identity. But of all the intellectuals of Young Vienna he took the most interest in the Zionist movement gathering around Theodor Herzl. When 'The Jewish State' appeared in 1896 he wrote to the author: 'More even than all that was *in* your book, I found what was behind it sympathetic. At last, someone who does not carry his Jewishness with resignation, like a burden or misfortune, but shows pride at being the legitimate heir to an ancestral culture.'[18] This message of support in fact reveals the disagreements between Herzl and Beer-Hofmann. The latter avoids mentioning Zionist politics: the evidence available shows clearly that he was against political Zionism[19] and that his affirmation of Jewish identity was a matter of being aware of Jewish *culture*, defending and illustrating it.

This was indeed Herzl's weakness: he was guided by no infallible instinct for the continuity of any Jewish tradition, but rather by the will to overcome his own identity crisis through the political means available in 1900: nationalism and *Realpolitik*. In his reply to Beer-Hofmann, Herzl in fact betrays a certain anxiety: 'Is it true that you support the ideas expressed in my little book? I should be proud to have aroused enthusiasm in people like you.'[20] The relationship remained distant, and the two men never became friends, for all Herzl's hopes.

In 1897, Beer-Hofmann wrote his 'Lullaby for Myriam', a meditation on life and death, rather melancholy in tone, dedicated to his newborn child. The last verse clearly sounds the note of Jewish identity as experienced by the author:

> Myriam, do you sleep? Myriam, my child,
> We are but the banks, and beneath us flows
> The blood of people past and gone, flowing towards those still to come,
> Blood of our fathers, full of anxiety and pride.
> And we, all of us are there. Who feels lonely?
> You are their life – their life is yours –
> Myriam, my life, my child – sleep![21]

The theme of the blood linking the ephemeral individual to the eternal race of the Jewish people; pride in response to anxiety; individualism and rootedness in a historic community; Jewishness as a mode of Life (in the fullest sense of that word in the aesthetics of *Leben*): all themes which recur in 'George's Death', published in 1900 after Beer-Hofmann had worked on it for several years, while also composing (from 1898) the first sketches for his dramatic cycle 'King David'.

II

The affirmation of Jewishness in 'George's Death'

We have already mentioned 'George's Death' in connection with narcissism as a response to the individualist's crisis of identity, then again in connection with the orgiastic dream of the cult of Astarte in the second chapter of the story. Now we shall dwell in particular on the conclusion to the work, which describes Paul's inner conversion. On the threshold of the third chapter, Paul, the dreamer, returns to conscious life. The awakening is a sore trial for him: will the surge of life he has rediscovered in the dream world ebb away into reality? Since the first scene in the story, the strange night when George lay dying while Paul lay awake, then went to sleep in the next room, existence has seemed gloomy and difficult. The last pages of the book show how the aspirations of the dream and the demands of reality may finally be reconciled.

Paul takes a walk one autumn evening in the park at Schönbrunn. He meets two women, a young girl accompanied by her mother. This girl reminds him of the one he glimpsed during the walk described in chapter 1, during the evening when George had just gone to sleep and was soon to die in Paul's apartment. In chapter 2, Paul had dreamed about that woman, that he was married to her and was already watching her on her death-bed.

Now, in the park at Schönbrunn, he remembers the dream and the reminder triggers the unpredictable and mysterious mechanism of what Proust calls 'involuntary memory': 'The memory of a dream which he had had several months earlier, during the August night when George had died, had been reawakened by his meeting with those two women, and they vanished from his existence as if their mission had now been accomplished.'[22] At the end of a dizzying and unexpected succession of memories snatched from the void, a succession of free associations, what comes back clearly to Paul's mind is – his Jewish identity.

His 'dream memory' reveals to him the dissociation which afflicts him, the gulf between the world of dreams and the unconscious, and the world of reality:

> He had been flung into a foreign, incomprehensible world, where he lived his waking life; that of which he was not conscious acted on him, and that which he did was lost in the unknown. Whereas the world in which he dreamed had been born of him: the boundaries of its skies and continents had been drawn by him. There he knew everything and everything related to him.[23]

Paul wonders about the links uniting dreams and reality. Would it be better never to wake up again, like George – to die so that the dream could endure and vanquish reality?

In life, life seems to be lost. Outside the dream world, Paul's narcissism seems to be stripped of all its cosmogonic depth and relapses into mere egocentricity:

> Paul went up to the edge of the pool; mirrored in the still water he saw his own face, clear but darker and sadder than in real life, looking back at him . . . In all things he had sought only himself and in all things he had found only himself . . . He had been proud and turned away from other people . . . without ever thinking that life – an imperious master – might come up behind him, seize him, and order him threateningly to 'Play with me!'[24]

Suddenly Paul is ashamed of the bogus life he has been leading, and the memories trooping through his mind seem to belong to somebody else.[25]

And yet Paul feels that only in himself can he find salvation: 'All happiness and good luck were contained within the narrow frame of his solitary life; nothing else could help him.'[26] The intuitive notion of a 'third world' where dream and reality can be reconciled brings him the longed-for relief. This superior form of existence seems to him distant and inaccessible – and also close by, as present within him as is his own blood. In it he feels caught up in a 'great and solemn whirling' to the rhythm of 'eternal laws'. There, 'united to the whole, necessary and indispensable to the whole, each of his acts was a ministration, and his sufferings meant a kind of dignity, and death was perhaps a mission.'[27] Like the protagonist of 'A Child', who regains his serenity when he understands that the death of his child is a necessary part of life, Paul in 'George's Death' succeeds in reconciling his own narrow self with the mystery of the world. The worship of life goes alongside the worship of death, which appears to be the redemption of individual existence.

Paul, listening to the voice of his own blood, reaches a sort of consciousness of a third kind which resolves the contradictions between dream and reality. A few pages later, Beer-Hofmann clarifies the outlines of Paul's vision. The intuition of the great cycle of the world turns into an intuition of the Jewish genealogy of which he is himself a part:

> Wandering ancestors, the dust of all those marching armies with their hair and beards, their clothes in rags, burdened with every humiliation, hated by all, rejected even by the lowliest – but never denying themselves . . . and behind them all, a people, not begging for mercy but winning, through a lofty struggle, the blessing of their god; crossing the seas, conquering the deserts, and always as filled with the awareness of their just god as their veins were with blood . . . And he also was of their blood.[28]

The most obvious meaning of 'George's Death' links it with the group of writings by Hofmannsthal and Schnitzler. These works, while carrying the 'decadent' style to its highest perfection, criticize a way of life where egoism leads to cynicism, and aestheticism distracts art from its regenerating vocation:

from 'The Death of Titian' to 'The Tale of the 672nd Night', from *Anatol* to *La Ronde*. This was to be the central theme of Georg Lukács's essay on Beer-Hofmann, 'The Moment and Form', in his 1911 book *Soul and Form*. Lukács had been personally acquainted with Beer-Hofmann, and he sees 'George's Death' in much the same way as does Hermann Broch in his essay on 'Hofmannsthal and his Times': as both the quintessence of, and a judgement on, Viennese aestheticism and impressionism.[29] It is interesting to note that Lukács pays no particular attention to the protagonist's eventual 'conversion' – probably because of the embarrassment felt by contemporaries at this unusual way of approaching the problem of Jewish identity.

The 'conversion' which ends 'George's Death' echoes the process traced by Maurice Barrès in his novelistic trilogy 'Self-Worship' (*Le Culte du Moi*), which progresses naturally from the deepening of the individual ego to the discovery of a collective ego: 'The individual is guided by the same law as his race . . . A whole race culminates in me,' declares Barrès in 'A Free Man' (1889). This is paralleled by the shift in the register of Paul's narcissism in Beer-Hofmann's tale.

As in 'Young Vienna' literature, so in the French writings of the 1890s we find a movement of reaction against decadence which takes the form of a rejection of individualism.[30] In 1895, Gustave Le Bon was teaching, in *La psychologie des foules* ('Crowd Psychology'), that if a civilization is to be born then there must be a cohesion of ideals, language and 'historic race', whereas primitive barbarism reduces society to a collection of individuals. What characterized contemporary decadence, for Le Bon, was the fact that

> the race is progressively losing what constituted its cohesion, its unity, its strength. The individual may be growing in personality and intelligence, but at the same time the collective individualism of the race is being replaced by an excessive development of individual egoism, together with an enfeeblement of character and a lessening of the capacity for action.[31]

Calls for the 'sacrifice of the self' were becoming more insistent. As early as 1891 the philosopher Gabriel Séailles was writing that 'Anyone who tries to rise above life in a lordly manner may fall lower than the beasts, into the poverty of an individual ego which can endure only the illusion of existence.'[32] Gide's André Walter calls on people to get outside themselves: 'do not shut yourself up in your own life, your own body: make your soul host to others.'[33] Maurice Barrès called on this same generous impulse: the *culte du moi*, self-worship, implied a duty to transcend that self and link it with the landscape, the race, the dead. This transcendence led to some attitudes characterisic of the early years of the new century: anti-intellectualism, worship of energy – especially 'national energy' – and religious conversion.

Paul's enlightenment, in Beer-Hofmann's story, is not so much a religious conversion (Jewishness is seen rather as a historical and cultural tradition) as the discovery of a 'national energy' hidden deep within the modern individual. This energy draws into him the powerful current of life, more durable and less illusory than the erotic orgies of the Syriac worship of Astarte which had figured in Paul's dream in chapter 2.

Culte du moi *and criticism of the decadent 'Jewish mind'*

In 1891 Hugo von Hofmannsthal gave the Viennese reading of *Culte du moi* by Maurice Barrès. His point of departure – as with Beer-Hofmann's Paul – is a recognition that 'we are suffocating our own selves. One can be quite happy in such a life, but in reality one is hideously miserable. One is a shadow, animated by alien blood, an alien slave under the gaze of the masters, who are barbarians.' The soul aspires to a salvation which would mean 'living one's individuality to the full and taking possession of one's self'.[34] In Barrès's trilogy of novels the hero, Philippe, meets Bérénice, an encounter which Hofmannsthal interprets as a first approach to the 'wholeness of life': 'A sister of the naiads and dryads, of Melusine and the Lorelei: such is Bérénice, the queen of the garden, emanation of the soul of that land. She is the incarnation of the whole unconscious, all the melancholy and tenderness which is in the air.' Hofmannsthal compares the harmony amidst which Bérénice dwells in her garden with the contented vegetating of Virginie (heroine of Bernardin de Saint-Pierre's famous novel *Paul et Virginie*) in her tropical jungle. He interprets Philippe's attraction to Bérénice as a nostalgia for the lost paradise and 'a Goethe-inspired religion of harmony with nature', but also as an 'Indo-Christian worship of suffering'. He concludes that 'Philippe has a presentiment of fusion in the knowledge of the Whole.'[35]

Paul's first dream in chapter 2, of which the erotic Astarte-worship is a part, tells of his engagement and marriage to a 'frail woman' who is soon carried off by death. This girl, who first appears in 'George's Death' in a meadow full of daffodils, is to be Bérénice to Paul's Philippe. Through her he glimpses the mystery of life, where death and life mingle and merge, and she reminds him of his childhood: as she lies dying, he reads the *Thousand and One Nights* and marvels at the sweeter life led by its characters,[36] a wonder which recalls his enjoyment of reading as a child.[37] In Paul's dream, the wife dies just as Bérénice dies in Barrès's novel. Barrès wrote:

> Her face and hands, pale as the sheets between which she lay, still had that faint air of secrecy which we had always seen in her.... 'Bérénice will perish,' I thought, 'but I will keep the best of her. I have taken over her feeling for life, her submission to instinct, her insight into nature; I am the first stage in her immortality.'[38]

What Hofmannsthal called the 'Indo-Christian worship of suffering' becomes in Beer-Hofmann a Judeo-Christian worship. The author's hints pass unnoticed at a first reading, for until the last few pages there is no indication that Paul is a Jew. But certain details in the young wife's death agony recall the meeting of Judas with Christ. (Let us note in passing a biographical detail: Paula Lissy, Beer-Hofmann's wife, was a Christian who converted to Judaism after several years of marriage.)[39] 'On the pale blue of the coverlet fell the crossed black shadow of the casement,' Paul notices as he enters the dying woman's bedroom.[40] A little later, the body of the young woman is washed in vinegar and water; then Paul, who feels responsible for her death, kneels beside her and kisses her hands – the kiss of Judas.[41]

Even more clearly than in Barrès, the death of the 'frail woman' in Beer-Hofmann is a religious sacrifice: she, the innocent, dies for Paul, whose sin was to remain deaf to the call of life. At this stage Paul's only Jewish traits are the negative ones with which modern *Kulturkritik* saddled the Jew: analytical, sceptical intellectualism opposed to naive faith and instinct.

> Sometimes with a single smile, or with cunning words which seemed mere jest, he damaged what had seemed [to the girl] untouchable. He was taking away her faith in a good god who watched over her destiny and leaving her only a gnawing desire for that lost belief; where she had been walking on solid ground, her mind free from all presentiment, he had made her hear the dark turbulence at the bottom of the abyss, and had taught her to ask questions and to see her own existence with doubting eyes. Trustingly she had offered to him what her poor childlike mind considered to be her most noble and immutable possessions; and when he had held them up to the light, in his cold and searching fingers, all their brilliance had fled, and what she had thought would shed eternal radiance was no more than a string of tawdry beads.[42]

A little later, the heavy silence in the dying girl's bedroom is shattered by the cries of children playing in the garden, who come to press their curious faces against the window. Paul reacts furiously to this noise and intrusion. He shakes his fists at the children so violently that he breaks a windowpane and cuts his hand. For a moment, the faces stuck against the window had seemed to him 'disfigured and shapeless, like the features of unborn children'.[43] Here again, Paul comes over as life-denying, turning his young wife into a 'woman without a shadow' (in the sense in which Hofmannsthal uses the phrase).

As I have already emphasized, it is only on a second reading that we can give this dream of Paul's an ethical and religious dimension. But the minuteness with which Beer-Hofmann worked on his text inclines me to think that the resemblance is not coincidental. This makes Paul's 'conversion' at the end of the story seem to be more than a sudden enlightenment stemming from his Jewish blood. It also means a passage from what Kierkegaard would have called demonic individualism, opposed to the meaning of life and in conformity with the caricature of the modern 'Jewish mind', into a kind of life lived under the joint auspices of *Leben* and true Jewishness. Seen from this perspective, the critical debate which has repeatedly erupted, from Schnitzler onwards, over the coherence of the story and the seemingly abrupt transition from the main part of the text to the final revelation of Jewish destiny may seem superfluous.[44]

Thus it would be too limiting to read 'George's Death' as a critique of aestheticism and narrow individualism;[45] the 'deadly disease' which afflicts Paul at the beginning of the story, against which he struggles in his dreams and from which, in his final illumination, he is delivered, also assumes the hidden dimension of a pathological study of the assimilated, secularized Jewish mind whose salvation must involve a return to the cultural roots of Jewishness. Beer-Hofmann's originality lies in the way he has combined, and virtually merged, two themes: that of the transcending of the deadly selfishness of aestheticism and the return to true life, and that of the return of the 'Jewish mind' to 'the spirit of Jewishness'. The parallel helps us to understand the meaning which Beer-Hofmann attributes to the affirmation of Jewish identity: it means the transcending of individuation and the restoration of the great whole. It is a mode of the dionysian exaltation described by Nietzsche in *The Birth of Tragedy*, and as such it is an 'aesthetic phenomenon'.

In such a context the dream about the erotic worship of the *Dea Syria* begins to look like a temptation similar to that described by Flaubert in *The Temptation of Saint Anthony*, combining the extremism of the Nicolaitans ('to rid ourselves of the lusts of the flesh, we indulge it to the point of exhaustion') with the 'sacrilegious delirium of murder and lust' of the Carpocratians. Flaubert's Queen of Sheba, like Beer-Hofmann's Astarte, is depicted with a lushness recalling a painting by Moreau, while the man who accompanies his Ennoïa-Helen declares, 'I have come to destroy the law of Moses, to overturn rules and purify impurities; I am he who teaches the vanity of works.'[46] The Astarte dream also recalls the dream of Gustav von Aschenbach in chapter 6 of *Death in Venice*, a dionysian orgy for which Thomas Mann drew directly on sources published by Erwin Rohde, the friend of Nietzsche, in his *Psyche*.[47]

A jotting among Beer-Hofmann's notes for 'The Young David' proves that in his imagination the sacred prostitution at Hieropolis was associated with biblical passages about the courtesans of Canaan (for example, Genesis 34 and 38):

> Ashtaroth at Bashan, centre of the cult of the ancient Asiatic nature-divinity Astarte, worshipped in Canaan under the name Astar, Astoret (which gives the Aramaic Aphtoret and the Greek Aphrodite). A famous centre of the cult was Hieropolis in Syria. Lucian, *De dea Syriaca*. She is the mother of the gods, goddess of procreation and fertility.[48]

Thus Paul's dream is a worshipping of the Golden Calf, a defiance of the law of Moses. This point in the story has two contradictory inspirations: the dionysian principle described by Bachofen, Jacob Burckhardt and Nietzsche, and biblical Judaism. Whereas in the closing pages, as Paul turns back to the Jewish tradition, the two inspirations converge and finally merge: affirmation of life and fidelity to Jewishness.

The dead, ornamentation and life

I have emphasized that Paul's conversion in 'George's Death' answers to the same need for self-transcendence, the same reaction against decadence and individualism, as does Barrès's *Le culte du moi*. There is another point of contact between the two authors: in both, the individual's realization of collective identity involves an encounter with the dead. This macabre element in Barrès's imagination, which frequents cemeteries and funerary monuments in search of the *frisson* of national energy, reduces the individual to a link in the long chain connecting the living with the dead.

Martin Buber, in his 1963 preface to Beer-Hofmann's collected works, stressed the omnipresence in them of death:[49] the dead child in the novella 'A

Child'; the pessimistic view of death, still unknown to the newborn child, in 'Lullaby for Myriam'; and the rule of *Thanatos* in 'George's Death'. George dies in the prime of life, while Paul, before his final conversion, is one of the 'living dead', his whole life petrified by aestheticism;[50] Paul dreams of a dying woman and an erotic orgy whose supreme outrage is the violent death of the woman he has lain with, and regains consciousness of his own Jewishness when he hears the voice of blood speak to him of the dead corpses that pave the way of the Chosen People.

The death theme is illustrated in 'George's Death' by a medical allegory reminiscent of that devised by Gustav Klimt. In the train which is taking him to the town where George is to be buried (the story adds that the coffin is travelling in the same train), Paul reflects on what George's career as a professor of medicine might have been like.[51] Far from imagining a triumph over death and suffering, Paul sees George among sick and dying people who call to him in desperation while he meditates stoically on the fragility of all that is human, becoming the very incarnation of the 'therapeutic nihilism' which William Johnston has claimed as one of the essential characteristics of the 'Austrian mind'.[52] George, as a doctor, follows almost word for word the suggestions given by Nietzsche in a fragment in *The Twilight of Idols* entitled 'A Moral for Doctors': 'they should no longer prepare prescriptions, but should every day administer a fresh dose of *disgust* for their patients.'[53] In the same way Klimt, in his fresco which was supposed to celebrate medicine and embellish the ceilings of the University of Vienna, created a *danse macabre* led by death, in which human knowledge seemed a small thing indeed.

In Beer-Hofmann the aesthete tormented by the thought of death is soothed by acceptance of a 'monist' vision of the universe which allows him to perceive the profound oneness of death and life in the great cycle of becoming. The realization of his Jewish heritage completes this soothing vision by assuring the individual that he has a presence in the world and a place between lives that are past and lives that are to come.

'George's Death' is a perfect illustration of the theory of Jugendstil ornamentalism which I advanced in my earlier chapter on 'Narcissus'. It confirms the close relationship between the 'second' – orphic and cosmogonic – direction of narcissism and the dense ornamentation of this typical work of 1900s style. We have seen that Paul, who at first is the very type of the fin-de-siècle Narcissus, suffers from a sort of perceptive disorder: 'What his subjectivity perceived instantly lost its autonomy; what his senses grasped, his imagination transformed into an ornamentation totally subordinate to his subjectivity.'[54] His gaze makes all ornamentation deadly.

In the oft-cited passage in which Paul first meets the 'frail woman' whom he marries and who is soon to die, the woman against her background of flowering meads seems already lifeless:

She seemed almost fleshless; there remained only her white silhouette, its differing lines standing out against the flowers and tangled stems of the tapestry sewn with narcissi. From the woodshore where, under the thick foliage where the sun could never penetrate, the hard snow of winter lingered under the brown and rotting leaves, blew a little cold wind, and she hunched her shoulders and shivered.[55]

This description has some typically Jugendstil elements: the woman with her white dress and parasol, against a background of snow and white narcissi; the floral decor, like a wallpaper motif (Beer-Hofmann actually says 'narzissenübersäte Tapete'); the thick tangle of wavy lines which submerge the outline of the human character in a greater whole; the absence of depth and perspective, reducing the image to two dimensions as in a landscape by Klimt;[56] the idyll of the *locus amoenus*, threateningly precarious (the fragility of the woman's silhouette and the icy wind which blows so menacingly from out of the wood).

In this story, ornamentation has a twofold significance: it is symptomatic of the solipsism of the aesthete who turns all beings and all things into ornaments subject to the decrees of his sovereign preferences, but it is also a sign. It reveals the mightly coherence of all things, man and nature, the human body and the things around it. Ornamentation is the link which keeps the human microcosm in the bosom of the macrocosm. Paul's meeting with the 'frail woman' takes on this double significance: her death, for which he feels mysteriously responsible, is a punishment for his inability to enter into union with life, but it is also (to paraphrase Barrès's description of Bérénice's death) 'the first stage in a return to life'. The Astarte dream, which shows us the opposite pole of femininity in the mind of the 1900s – the *femme fatale* – allows him to go on to a second stage.[57]

In the two dreams, the orgy of ornament is a sign that life is reviving and flowing through the whole, smudging the outlines of individuation and immersing the subject in a wider world. It is not by chance that Beer-Hofmann's hero experiences this broadening of self through a dream. For dreams, as Freud often remarked, are a narcissistic phenomenon answering to an absolute egocentricity.[58] However, in Beer-Hofmann's story these dreams have a surprisingly *objective* effect (so much so that the reader sometimes has difficulty in telling what belongs to the waking world and what to dreams). This is because the narcissism at work in Paul's slumbers essentially fol-lows the 'other direction' studied by Lou Andreas-Salomé, that of primary narcissism which contains the great anthropocosmic and monistic unities which are lost to the age of individuation.

Narcissism and the 'group illusion'

The dream about the erotic orgies in the temple of the *Dea Syria* also reveals the other inclination of Paul's narcissism, which leads the subject to seek fusion with the crowd, following a mechanism studied by Freud in his 1921 essay *Group Psychology and the Analysis of the Ego*.[59] This mechanism, as explained by Janine Chasseguet-Smirgel, springs from the fundamental dif-ference between the ideal of the ego, heir to the primary narcissism, and the superego, heir to the Oedipus complex. The former is an attempt to regain a lost omnipotence, the latter (in the Freudian view) issues from the castration complex. The former inclines to restore the illusion, the latter to promote reality. The superego cuts the child off from the mother, the ideal of the ego impels it to merge with her.[60] Now, group phenomena tend towards the elimination of the superego. The individual in a group can relax the repression of unconscious tendencies which are the basis of all morality and obey a new authority (that of the group) which allows the accomplishment of desires which are normally repressed.

Didier Anzieu, in a study of 'group illusion', draws an analogy between 'groups' in this sense and dreams[61] which is particularly enlightening when applied to Beer-Hofmann's story, since it is actually in a dream that Paul, the narcissist, merges with a group and so takes part in an erotic orgy. Anzieu sees, in the group as in the dream, a threefold regression: the group tends to regress towards primary narcissism; the ego and superego no longer exercise control; the id takes over the psyche via the ideal ego which 'attempts to fuse with the all-powerful mother and introjectively restore the first, lost love object. The group becomes, for each of its members, a substitute for that lost object.'

This shows us the real inner meaning of the 'matriarchy' which governs Hieropolis in Paul's dream. The group illusion defends the subject against castration anxiety, removes the father figure and the superego, proclaims the advent of the all-powerful mother, and satisfies the desire for primary fusion. The abandoning of the superego explains the readiness of the subject, once merged with the group, to take part in atrocities like the killing of the individuals who are trampled and assaulted during the sacred orgy.

Narcissism and Jewishness

Not once but twice the vigour of life which the dream seemed to have restored is shattered by death. The erotic orgy ends horribly, and Paul's dream concludes with the death of the 'frail woman'. To give Paul's narcissism a final appearance of 'life', Beer-Hofmann ends with his conversion. The 'life of the third kind' on which Paul enters will be lived according to the laws and prophecies of the Bible. This time, narcissism broadens and deepens into a religious dimension. Thus any interpretation of *Der Tod Georgs* which sees a chasm between Paul's narcissistic existence at the beginning and his final discovery of a Jewish identity does not seem to be acceptable. It cannot really be called even a transcending of narcissism.[62] Paul's awareness of his Jewish identity emerges as a *prolongation* of his initial narcissism.

For it is to himself, to the call of his own blood, the feeling of belonging which awakens in him, that Paul owes this, as it were, 'immanent grace'. And it would not be too far-fetched to say that the ornamental register is maintained in this conversion which introduces the final twist in the story. In her memoirs, Olga Schnitzler recalls a conversation between Theodor Herzl and Richard Beer-Hofmann:

Herzl was dreaming of a Palestine on entirely European lines, which he described in these terms to his friend Beer-Hofmann: 'We shall have a university and an opera house, and you shall go to the play in evening dress with a white gardenia in your buttonhole.' But Beer-Hofmann, whose idea of his ancestral home was better thought out, protested laughingly, 'Heavens, no! When we get there I want to go about in a white silk burnous, covered with gold chains and wearing a turban with a diamond brooch.'[63]

This 'Zionist pose' was entirely consistent with fin-de-siècle dandyism.[64] That, in particular, was what provoked Karl Kraus's rather too cruel mockeries in 'A Crown for Zion': 'They have recovered astonishingly fast from the age-long sufferings of the Jews, which now helps them to assume a thousand extraordinary attitudes.'[65]

'Reserved blood': Thomas Mann

A comparison between *Der Tod Georgs* and Thomas Mann's novella *Wälsungenblut* ('Reserved Blood') brings out the originality of Beer-Hofmann's linkage between the themes of narcissism and Jewish identity. In Thomas Mann's story, written in 1905, the twins Siegmund and Sieglinde Aarenhold are Jewish. The first version of the text makes this explicit: after the incest scene, Sieglinde, alluding to her 'official' fiancé, cries, 'Now don't you think we've made a proper fool of that goy?'[66] Later Mann cut out this sentence, with its Yiddish word, to end the scandal provoked by the first version, in which some readers had detected an antisemitic satire on the author's Jewish in-laws and their circle.

Whatever the autobiographical relevance, Mann was describing in this story a case of 'Jewish sexual perversion' typical of the prejudices, frequent in Christian thinking (and which became a *topos* of literature, anthropology and psychology), relating to the endogamy and incestuous marriages which were supposed to be causing the 'degeneracy' of the Jewish race and the perversion of 'Jewish sexuality'. The Jewishness of Siegmund and Sieglinde is one of the acutest symptoms of Decadence.

There are details in the story which show that Siegmund Aarenhold's narcissism feeds on his awareness of belonging to a 'different race'. He feels that his Jewish identity is a sign of election. A true dandy, he spends hours in front of his mirror so as to choose the perfect tie for his suit and wonder at his own singularity: 'None of that seemed to him pointless, for he thought that if a nonchalant manner, soft boots and open collars were suitable for fair-haired aristocrats, he owed it to himself to be more exacting, impeccably dressed from head to foot.'[67] Beckerath, Sieglinde's fiancé, is a specimen of the ill-dressed, fair-haired aristocrat:

'Beckerath,' said Sieglinde, 'wears all his ties, even the coloured ones, with little knots according to last year's fashion.'

'Beckerath,' Siegmund replied, 'is the most vulgar creature whom ever my eyes beheld. . . . Moreover, I would ask you not to refer to that Teuton again this evening.'[68]

During a performance of Wagner's *Die Walküre*, Sieglinde and Siegmund Aarenhold identify with their two namesakes, descendants of Wotan, sublime carriers of divine blood who are offset by the brutish Hunding.[69] When he returns to his rooms, Siegmund Aarenhold looks again in the mirror:

> Eye to eye with himself, he gazed at his own face. He examined every feature, minutely, curiously. . . . He stayed so for a long time, studying the marks of his origin in every feature: the slightly hooked nose, the full, soft lips, the prominent cheekbones, the thick, curly dark hair, forcibly parted and falling over the temples; finally, his eyes under their beetling brows.[70]

Thomas Mann's ironic presentation of the twins as a caricature of Wagnerian decadence evidently does small honour to Siegmund's 'Jewish narcissism'. He remains narrowly egocentric, as unfruitful as the artistic teaching which he undergoes from one of the foremost artists of his time, although his drawings reveal his lack of talent. For Beer-Hofmann's Paul the discovery of Jewish identity accompanies a 'cosmogonic' intensification of his narcissism. His feeling of historic solidarity with his people's destiny turns the choosing of a people into a solemn obligation.

III

The cultural Zionism of Beer-Hofmann and the reservations of Hofmannsthal and Schnitzler

Beer-Hofmann's 'inner conversion', which he experienced in much the same way as his character Paul, seems to have established his narcissism immovably. Erich von Kahler, remembering his friend in Vienna, speaks of his 'singular solitude, his subjective self-distancing from the world, contrasting with his existential rooting in the world and in the community of his ancestors',[71] which remained unaffected even by Nazi persecution and exile. Reading what Beer-Hofmann said on his first and last visit to Palestine, in 1936, we could almost describe it as subjective Zionism, a Promised Land of the mind:

> I have been at home in the Promised Land for thirty years. For one cannot write on biblical themes without living in a community of soul with Palestine. I have lived in the land of Palestine, and this existence has always been for me a reality [*Realität*], but a reality above the real world [*Wirklichkeit*].[72]

In Beer-Hofmann's later works, this inner Zionism, such a sturdy prop to individual narcissism, is expressed though the theme of *election* which is at the centre of the dramatic cycle 'History of King David', especially the prologue, 'Jacob's Dream', on which he had been working since 1898 and which was performed in autumn 1918 in Berlin and in April 1919 in Vienna.[73] This work, which is not unlike a mystery play, is the author's challenge to the contemporary world, riven with war and antisemitism. Jacob sets up a direct and unmediated relationship with God, who appears to him in a dream. He returns to reality strengthened and convinced of the permanence of his election. This biblical piece can be compared with Stefan Zweig's *Jeremiah*, published in 1917 and performed in Zurich.[74] Faced with the same European catastrophe, Zweig adopts an emotional tone which tends to sink into tearful grandiloquence, whereas Beer-Hofmann seems reluctant to yield to the emotions of the moment and maintains an air of religious solemnity.

It was, however, this play which at first displeased Hofmannsthal and drew from him the only letter which was slightly aggressive in all his forty-year correspondence with Beer-Hofmann. It is dated Easter Sunday, 20 April 1919:

> Your play made a strange impression on me. As I think back on it, the feature which is most alien to me, the tendency to chauvinism and national pride – which, to speak with the assurance and infatuation of a personal viewpoint, I cannot but see as the root of all evil – becomes clearer to me and perturbs me almost as much as would an alien or evil feature in a fair and beloved face.[75]

Hofmannsthal adds that he felt the same uneasiness when he discovered Beer-Hofmann's play 'The Count of Charolais': the killing of the count's wife seemed to him a piece of 'incomprehensible inhumanity'. 'The Count of Charolais' features a character called 'the red-haired Jew', a creditor of the count, who demands his due and cries vengeance for the persecution of the Jews.[76] It was probably this passage, as much as the 'inhumanity' of the count (which is explicitly condemned in the play), that Hofmannsthal found so disturbing.

In Hofmannsthal's next letter he tried to go back on these assertions and blame them on a fever which had kept him in bed. On 7 May 1919 Beer-Hofmann replied in a letter whose length (over a dozen pages) shows how much Hofmannsthal's attacks had hurt him. He tried to defend himself against the accusation of chauvinism and national pride by emphasizing that Jacob's election did not imply exclusion of all others, but that 'everyone must feel of equal importance to God's plans,' and there was no desire for power and domination in Jacob's mind. Then he wrote:

> When a man who has been through unspeakable sufferings hears himself say, 'What you have endured is not without meaning – and your sufferings will not last forever,' do you see that as national pride or chauvinism? Do you not rather remember the passage from Saint Matthew's Gospel: 'Jesus saith unto them, Did ye never read in the scriptures, The stone which the builders rejected, the same is become the head of the corner' [Matthew 21:42]? The subtitle of 'Jacob's Dream' could have been 'The Elect' or 'The Pious Man' (Heimann once suggested to me, in passing, 'The Artist').[77]

In his following letters Hofmannsthal tried to win Beer-Hofmann's pardon for his outburst of Easter 1919 by heaping praise on his writings.

This interchange is interesting above all for what it tells us about Hofmannsthal. For that author never tackled the question of his own Jewish identity, except in a very oblique fashion, and his dialogue with Beer-Hofmann goes to show how far he repressed it. To be quite accurate, we should point out that Hofmannsthal's ancestry was only a quarter Jewish,[78] but his contemporaries took little account of such restrictions: the anthology 'Jews in the German Cultural Sphere', finished in 1934, gave Hofmannsthal pride of place. Even earlier, in 1912, Moritz Goldstein had included Hofmannsthal in the 'Germano-Jewish Parnassus'.[79]

In his essay on 'Hofmannsthal and His Times', Hermann Broch gives a subtle analysis of the 'inner antisemitism' of the assimilated Jew, in which he detects

> a phenomenon of 'two-level narcissism'. Even after a successful assimilation spanning several generations, they remained attached (though only in the darkest areas of the unconscious) to their initial 'splendid isolation'. The world of the assimilated, which had long since acquired the familiarity of a native land, is thus mentally kept at a distance which makes it into a foreign country. The assimilated Jew thus feels himself elect to a superior degree. He is chosen among the chosen people.[80]

Beer-Hofmann's Jacob could have been called 'The Elect' or 'The Artist': it was just this kind of election, which made him into the prince of poets, which so exactly suited Hofmannsthal. But the election of the Jew must, as Broch points out, remain 'in the darkest areas of the unconscious' so as to reinforce the narcissism of this psychological type. Hofmannsthal's aggressiveness towards his friend Beer-Hofmann stems precisely from the way the latter revealed what ought to have remained hidden. Hofmannsthal related the problem to nationalistic struggles, and took refuge in the universalist ideology being propagated officially by the Habsburg powers and adopted by a fair number of Cisleithan assimilated Jews: a universalism which in fact masked an objective alliance between assimilated Jews and Austro-Germans.

Hofmannsthal's political development, which was to lead him into calling for a 'conservative revolution' by 1927,[81] savours of the paradox which Gershom Scholem detected in Rudolf Borchardt: 'This extraordinarily gifted man, sure that he had annihilated all that was Jewish in himself, became the most eloquent spokesman of German traditionalism and cultural conservatism.'[82]

Nevertheless, in spite of these manifest divergences, the voyages of self-discovery made by Hofmannsthal and Beer-Hofmann were undeniably similar. Both these erstwhile representatives of Young Vienna passed from dream to reality, from the world of ornamentation to that of contemporary society, by recourse to cultural tradition: for Beer-Hofmann it was an individualist variant of Zionism, for Hofmannsthal a return to the European theatrical tradition of the seventeenth century and to Catholic ideology. For Leopold von Andrian, it was a reformulation of the myth of Eternal Austria, its hierarchy modelled on the divine order.

Contemporaries were not deceived. In his diary for 1919, Hermann Bahr, sometime propagandist for Young Vienna, already almost forgotten, noted that 'Jacob's Dream' savoured of the old baroque theatre whose sole vocation, he

said, was to 'show forth God, thank God, celebrate God'.[83] This opinion
has the merit of pointing out that, beyond their differing conceptions of
Jewish identity, Beer-Hofmann and Hofmannsthal were both deeply rooted in
Austrian tradition. For Beer-Hofmann's originality surely lies in the fact that
he used his talents to defend and illustrate not only a Jewish identity, but also
a Viennese cultural identity.

It could even be said that in a way, Beer-Hofmann's 'cultural Zionism' fits
in with the logic of a multinational empire. In Musil's *The Man Without
Qualities* Count Leinsdorf, an eminent representative of the official ideology,
passes on the following reflections to Ulrich:

> The whole Jewish question would disappear in a twinkling if the Jews would
> only make up their minds to speak Hebrew, go back to their old Hebrew names
> and wear Oriental garb . . . Frankly, a Galician Jew who has just come and made
> a fortune in Vienna doesn't look quite the thing, on the Esplanade at Ischl, got
> up in Tyrolean costume, with a chamois-tuft in his hat. But just put him in a
> long flowing robe, as costly as you like as long as it covers the legs, and you'll see
> how admirably his face and the great sweep of his temperamental gestures go
> with such a style of dress! All the things that people make jokes about now
> would be in their proper place – including the expensive rings they like to wear.
> I am opposed to assimilation of the kind the English nobility practise. It's a
> tedious and uncertain process. But give the Jews back their true character, and
> you'll see what a gem they turn out to be, positively an aristocracy of a rare and
> different kind among the peoples gratefully thronging round His Majesty's
> throne – or if you'd rather picture the thing in everyday terms, quite clearly,
> pacing along our Ringstrasse, which is unique in the world because there in the
> midst of the highest degree of West-European elegance one may also see a
> Mohammedan in his red fez, a Slovak in his sheepskin, or a bare-legged
> Tyrolean.[84]

In context it is clear that this Count Leinsdorf is steeped in the resolute
antisemitism proper to his aristocratic calling. But the words the author here
puts in his mouth renew the subtle debate over the dialectic relationship
which connects Zionism – even in its 'cultural' guise – with antisemitism.

Another friend of Richard Beer-Hofmann's, Arthur Schnitzler, had from
the first expressed some reservations over the final conversion in 'George's
Death'. On 2 March 1900, having explained his doubts about the coherence
of the story, which seemed to him like a necklace of precious stones without
a connecting thread, he wrote: 'Somewhere in the fourth chapter lurks a
corroding trickery: you cannot be unaware of it. You suddenly change register,
and it sounds magnificent – but that does not prove anything.'[85] There follow
some criticisms of the frequent shifts from reality to dream in the story
(which, says Schnitzler, means one has to read the whole thing two or three
times before it becomes clear), and of the style, which he found too oratorical
and dramatic in places.

For reasons very different from Hofmannsthal's, Schnitzler also failed to
appreciate the 'subjective Zionism' of Beer-Hofmann. Doubtless he thought it

an attitude too irrational and too close to religious thinking to attract a free-thinker like himself. He was also suspicious of definitive solutions. His own novel 'The Road to Freedom' (*Der Weg ins Freie*), which gives the most complete panorama of Viennese Jewry, in fact suggests that none of the reactions to antisemitism and the crisis of assimilation (socialism, Zionism, exaggerated assimilationism, individualism, etc.) was entirely satisfactory. To one with so lucid – and in a way despairing – an awareness of contemporary problems, so critically undecided, Beer-Hofmann's conversion must perforce have seemed unconvincing.

The 'Young Jewish' movement: Martin Buber and Richard Beer-Hofmann

Closest to Beer-Hofmann, all in all, was the 'Jungjüdische Bewegung', the Young Jewish movement – containing in its title the favourite word of the times, *jung* as in 'Jugendstil' and 'Young Vienna'. One of its most illustrious members was Martin Buber (who was to write the preface to Beer-Hofmann's complete works in 1963). Born in Vienna in 1878, brought up in Lemberg, Buber had entered the University of Vienna in 1896; his thesis was supervised by Friedrich Jodl and Laurenz Müllner. (Otto Weininger had submitted his doctoral thesis, which was reworked as *Sex and Character*, to the same two professors.) During his time at university he had adopted the style of the aesthetes of Young Vienna, attended with them the lectures of Ernst Mach, and had published articles on Altenberg, Schnitzler and Hofmannsthal. Thus Buber and Beer-Hofmann began their careers in much the same way. And their 'Zionist conversions' show some points of similarity.

The ideas of Buber, and other representatives of the Jungjüdische Bewegung, on the unique creativeness of the Jewish mind give us a better understanding of Paul's enlightenment in 'George's Death'. In his essay on 'Creators, the People and the Movement' (*Die Schaffenden, das Volk und die Bewegung*, 1902), Buber wrote:

> The movement of a people is their acceding to fertility. By belonging to a people, an individual is constantly being enriched and strengthened; and also by the 'movement' of his people, when there really is movement, i.e. when the individual can share in the blossoming of thousands of germinating souls, related to his own, and in the general activating of the fruitfulness of his blood and of his race.[86]

This ideology of renewal and youth is directly inspired by Nietzsche.

Buber was following in the footsteps of the neo-Hebraic writer Micha Josef Berdyczewski, whose often rudimentary Nietzscheanism nourished his favourite theme of Jewish nationalism.[87] A whole artistic, literary and philosophical movement among young Jewish intellectuals was to embellish what Buber called the 'Jewish renaissance'. It was in order to promote this, he wrote to Herzl in August 1911, that he had accepted the editorship of the newly founded Zionist journal *Die Welt*.[88] The other pillars of this 'Young Jewish' revival in the German world were the journal *Ost und West* and the Jüdischer Verlag publishing house (founded by the painter and illustrator Ephraïm Moses Lilien, the poet Berthold Feiwel, Martin Buber and some other intellectuals), which published the *Jüdischer Almanach*. It could be said that in these circles the essence of Jugendstil ideology and aesthetics was applied to the defence and embellishment of a modern Jewish culture. One of the principal sources of inspiration for the whole movement was Nathan Birnbaum, author of essays on 'The National Renaissance of the Jewish People in its Homeland as a Way of Solving the Jewish Question' (1893) and 'Jewish Modernism' (1896), and an enthusiastic advocate of the writer Ahad Haam.[89]

This variant on Zionism, which took as its priority the cultural affirmation of Jewishness (as against the *Realpolitik* practised by Theodor Herzl), made no secret of its debt to Nietzsche. Certain 'Zionist cultural' declarations even echo the ideology of blood and race. In his introduction to the *Jüdischer Almanach* Feiwel wrote:

> Thus Jewish themes and the Jewish viewpoint, in all their forms, are to be found here: sometimes deeply rooted in the people and its tradition, as usually happens with the works of Jews from the East; sometimes consciously brought forth from European culture to rally modern national Jewry, as in the works of the Zionists of Western Europe. To this we must add the works of writers and artists from Western Europe who, unconsciously or without following an overtly nationalist impulse, give their work a specifically Jewish tone by reason of the racial component within themselves.[90]

One of the great literary successes of the Jüngjudischer Bewegung was the publication in 1900 of a (distinctly equivocal) work called *Judas*, by Börries von Münchhausen, with illustrations by E. M. Lilien.[91] Karl Wolfskehl, a disciple of Stefan George, and Stefan Zweig were among the most celebrated contributors to the *Jüdischer Almanach*. Beer-Hofmann's 'Lullaby for Myriam' was very frequently reproduced in the journals of this movement.[92] The conclusion of 'George's Death' belongs in this same context, the 'Jewish cultural renaissance'.

From Nietzsche to Jewish mysticism

Martin Buber's doctoral dissertation, presented in 1904 in Vienna, was entitled 'Contributions to the History of the Problem of Individuation';[93] it is a study of Nicolas de Cues and Jacob Böhme, influenced by Schopenhauer and especially by Nietzsche, and it shows that Buber shared in the preoccupations of the whole intellectual generation examined in the first four chapters of the present book. Their ideas followed two fundamental tendencies: the *principium individuationis* had to be transcended and a creative individualism affirmed. In 1900 Buber devoted an entire article to Nietzsche,[94] saying that the latter had imagined a type of heroic human who is his own creator, but also transcends himself. Instead of sterile altruism, Buber continues, Nietzsche had proclaimed the egoism of self-development. According to Buber, the superman opposes to the God who began the world a god of becoming, a god partly created by superhumanity, and who represents the final end of the evolution foreseen by Nietzsche.

After his discovery of German and Jewish mysticism, this 'god of becoming' fused in Buber's mind with the 'realized god' of the mystic communion, and later still, with the god with whom mankind is in dialogue. As he himself explains:

> Since 1900 I have been under the influence of German mysticism, from Magister Eckhart to Angelus Silesius, for whom the foundation of being, the nameless and impersonal Divine, first comes to 'birth' in the human soul – then by the later developments of the Kabbalah, which teach that man can acquire the power to unite the God above the world with his own immanent 'Chekhina'; thus was born in me the thought of a realization of God by man; man seemed to me like the being through whose existence the absolute, immutable in its truth, can acquire the character of a reality.[95]

This vision of theogonic individualism gives us a better understanding of the process which moves Paul, at the end of Beer-Hofmann's 'George's Death', from death narcissism to life narcissism, from constricted individuation to creative individuality, from egocentric dream to mystic religiosity. It is not really a conversion to the Jewish religion. Gershom Scholem has rightly emphasized this distinction, which is both the strength and the weakness of Buber's thought: the opposition between religion and religiosity, official Judaism and underground Judaism, which explains why (as Scholem puts it) the young Buber had a profound aversion to the Law and the Halakah in all its aspects. Not only (still according to Scholem) did Buber deny it any place in authentic Judaism, he also – as a Romantic – considered it as a power hostile to life.[96]

Let us note that this approach to Judaism via the mystical is the exact opposite of Freud's: Freud, for his part, saw Judaism as the most anti-mystical of religions. He would add that it was the religion which most explicitly proclaimed the law of the father. But Buber's contemporaries were alive to the *feminine* tone which emerged from his conception of religiosity. Gustav Laudauer saw him as 'an awakener and defender of a specifically feminine thought, without which there will be neither renewal nor rejuvenation of our culture in its terminal decline'.[97] Earlier, Lou Andreas-Salomé, another 'godless mystic' of the 1900s, had suggested in an audaciously syncretic essay entitled 'Jesus the Jew'[98] that Christ owed to Judaism his religion of the here and now, his message of love which, she said, meant fusing God and creation in a loving unity. A rapprochement which shows clearly that Judaism itself, if interpreted in a more or less liberal fashion, was not immune to the 'feminization of culture' so characteristic of the turn of the century. And the great rabbi of Vienna, Adolf Jellinek, emphasized in his book 'Studies and Sketches:

The Jewish Race: An Ethnographical Study' (1869) the profoundly 'feminine' characteristics of Jewishness: vivacity, quick thinking, chameleon adaptability, but also vindictiveness, a capacity for violent hatred, vanity and superficiality, and a lack of originality in scientific research.[99] Thus it is clear that the comparison between femininity and Jewishness was common currency, and not only amongst the antisemites.

Beer-Hofmann's hero, like Buber, discovers the god of the Jews within his subjective ego. This god is synonymous with 'life', 'blood', the *Volk*. Subjectivity emerges, 'dionysian', from the confines of individuation to become the creator of God. This is the meaning behind Beer-Hofmann's remark that his play 'Jacob's Dream' might well have been subtitled 'The Artist'. The Jacob who enters into a dialogue with God (Beer-Hofmann's stage directions envisage the voice of God booming down from the flies of the Burgtheater) is an Artist who creates God.

Buber's cultural Zionism – and the same formula could be applied to Beer-Hofmann – comes down to this:

> Create! The Zionist who feels all the sanctity of that word, and lives by it, is a man of the highest stature in my eyes. To create new works out of the depths of an ancestral singularity, the unique and incomparable force of blood, so long in chains and reduced to unproductiveness, that is the ideal we must lay before the Jewish people. To create the monuments to its own essence! To let its destiny burst forth in a new vision of life![100]

To attain to such creativity, the individual had first to penetrate into himself, get back to his own 'essence', seek and find his own self.

In this perspective dogma has small importance, provided the individual can find the god who is speaking to him. In Buber's anthology 'Ecstatic Confessions', which was published in 1909 but which he had begun to assemble in 1903, he gives pride of place to the German mystics and the Hassidim. But it also includes assorted European mystics, Chinese Taoism, Egyptian, Byzantine and Indian mysticism, Arabian and Persian Sufiism,[101] across the centuries from the sixth to the nineteenth. This mystic sensibility was quite indifferent to theological rigour; it could even suit itself to an atheist. Thus Fritz Mauthner, that great sceptic, noted after an encounter with Buber: 'Personality of exceptional worth. Polish Jew. Friend of Landauer. Atheistic Zionist.'[102] The Jewish mysticism of Buber and Beer-Hofmann is one variant on the Nietzschean heritage of the early twentieth century. Paul, in 'George's Death', could take his place among the characters in *The Man Without Qualities*. (Musil quotes copiously from Buber's 'Ecstatic Confessions' in the descriptions of mystical states – some parodic, some serious – which abound in the novel.)[103] For his self-identification as a Jew is a response to the modern crisis of identity which everyone in Musil's novel wrestles with as best he can. Ulrich, the man whose identity is a perpetual project, would probably have felt sympathy for that cultural Zionist. But he would certainly have condemned Paul's way of restoring identity as an illusion.

The 'call of blood' which Paul thinks he can perceive in himself: is it a dream, a hallucination? The final sentences of the story seem to introduce a doubt over the nature of the hero's Zionist revelation:

> How thick the fog was, how far away the town! But in spite of all his weariness, Paul felt serene and sure of himself. As if a powerful hand had been laid on his to reassure and guide him; as if he felt the beating of that powerful pulse. But what he felt was only the beating of his own blood.[104]

After the long dreams of chapter 2, which on a first reading were hard to distinguish from reality, comes a reality which seems to belong to the imagination. Is this Jewish identity, discovered instantaneously in a sort of solitary enlightenment, really a waking dream, a 'self-made fiction'? Beer-Hofmann adds nothing to the narrative which could resolve the reader's doubts. Tomorrow, perhaps, Paul will no longer hear that 'voice of blood' so clearly. His sense of a Jewish identity remains, irremediably, fragile.

Conclusion:
The (Post)Modern Indeterminacy of
Identity

What are we playing at? Wittgenstein

What was most notable about the Viennese modernists was that before they made the crisis of identity into a theme for their works of theory, literature or art, they lived it, experienced it as a loss of identity of themselves as subject, followed by a reconstruction which was often precarious. To most of them the 'modern condition' seemed the result of the fading and loss of traditions, the triumph of forces of disorganization and disintegration, putting every individual into a state of uncertainty and disorientation which was hard to overcome.

Ludwig Wittgenstein was one of those who best expressed, retrospectively, this 'Austrian mind', when he wrote, for example:

> Earlier physicists are said to have found suddenly that they had too little mathematical understanding to cope with physics; and in almost the same way young people today can be said to be in a situation where ordinary common sense no longer suffices to meet the strange demands life makes. Everything has become so intricate that mastering it would require an exceptional intellect. Because skill at playing the game is no longer enough; the question that keeps coming up is: can this game be played at all now and what would be the right game to play?[1]

Jacques Bouveresse, commenting on Wittgenstein's allusions to the modern condition, points out that 'in no case can a "play on language" be the outcome solely of a concerted creation or transformation: it must have a "natural" basis, represent some sort of spontaneity.'[2] This anti-conventional view, which made Wittgenstein hostile to (for example) various attempts to create a universal language such as Esperanto, cast doubt on the notion that a man could, freely and by the sole exercise of his reason, create a way of life for himself which fell outside a given, accepted, supra-individual mould. Any game of language, to be confirmed as viable, must make reference to the 'fair' game whose rules cannot be decided arbitrarily.

In his projected preface to the *Philosophical Remarks*, Wittgenstein, after declaring his 'antipathy' towards the dominating tendency of European and American civilization (*Zivilisation*), compares culture (*Kultur*) to a huge organism within which each man has his place, so that every individual activity reinforces the cohesion of the whole. He goes on: 'In an age without culture, on the other hand, forces become fragmented and the power of an individual man is used up in overcoming opposing forces and frictional resistances; it does not show in the distances he travels but perhaps only in the heat he generates in overcoming friction.' The death of a culture does not mean the disappearance of human values, he adds, and concludes: 'yet the fact remains that I have no sympathy for the current European civilization and do not understand its goals, if it has any.'[3]

A passage from Gustav Janouch's conversations with Franz Kafka echoes these ideas of Wittgenstein's:

> The people of the Bible are individuals assembled by a law. Now, the masses of today resist any kind of assembly. They tend to scatter because no law governs them internally. That is the engine of their unceasing movement. But where are they going to? And where have they come from? Nobody knows. The more they move, the less they get anywhere. They spend their energies in vain. They think they are advancing, but they are only running on the spot and falling into the void.[4]

Is not Kafka's idea of a vanished and unknowable law, in a world which is nevertheless governed by implacable and absurd legality, comparable to Wittgenstein's ideas on the modern condition as a game which one has to play without a hope of discovering the rules?

Wittgenstein is a cultural pessimist: the dislocation of the sociocultural order obliges individuals to make their own way in solitude, with enormous expenditure of energy and in danger of exhausting themselves in useless struggles even before they can throw off the shackles of a disorganized civilization. This pessimism is wholly characteristic of the 'Austrian mind' common to the Viennese of the 'second generation', which reached literary and theoretical maturity around the First World War or in the 1920s and 1930s: Hermann Broch, Robert Musil, Wittgenstein and others. Their *Kulturkritik* picks up and develops themes which had been prefigured, or even clearly formulated, around 1900 – by Hofmannsthal, for example.

Wittgenstein, like all assimilated Jewish intellectuals, found his Jewish identity a problem,[5] and the influence of Weininger and Kraus is perceptible in his somewhat deprecating remarks about it: 'When you can't unravel a tangle, the most sensible thing is for you to recognize this and the most honourable thing, to admit it. [Antisemitism.] What you ought to do to remedy the evil is *not* clear. What you must *not* do is clear in particular cases.'[6] If we add that at some periods of his life Wittgenstein was combatting his homosexual tendencies[7] by taking refuge in a kind of ascetism of a Weiningerian (or Tolstoyan) sort, we can see that his crisis of Jewish identity was coupled with a crisis of sexual identity.

The importance of these two factors to Wittgenstein's philosophy is some-times thought by his interpreters to be negligible, or even denied altogether.[8] However, my study of some of the other figures in this book goes to show that the consequences of this double crisis of identity may have been much more serious than is commonly acknowledged, not only for Wittgenstein's intellectual personality, but also for the fundamentals of his thought. Some of his preoccupations are surely inseparable from the crisis of identity: his interest in Weininger[9] and in psychoanalysis,[10] his mystical tendencies, but also his reflections on genius, on the self, and on ethics.

Most 'Viennese modern antimodernists', representatives of modernity, have been reluctant to see the crisis of culture in nakedly political terms. They have analysed it rather in terms of (usually individualistic) aesthetics, ethics, psychology or logic. Wittgenstein, who (like Joseph Roth) looked back nostalgically on a well-ordered world where everyone had his place, found modernity uncultured because it had lost its power to integrate, and left individuals in a state of confusion. The only ones who can keep their balance and personal creativity are those whom Nietzsche calls the strong men, that is the most moderate, who need neither convictions nor religion, who are able not only to endure, but to accept, a fair amount of chance and absurdity, and are capable of thinking in a broadly disillusioned and negative way without feeling either diminished or discouraged.[11] Of this 'strength', this wisdom, Freud was perhaps an example.

Chaos and the void: Hermann Broch

Broch's trilogy of novels, 'Sleepwalkers' (1930–2), shows individuals lost in the void left by the collapse of tradition. The only choice left to them is between a commitment which may be naive, derisory or dangerous, amidst a plethora of new religious or political communions, and the radical and immoral cynicism of the *arriviste* Hugenau – or the solitary and pessimistic individualism of the intellectual observing the modern world. In his later essay on 'Hofmannsthal and his Times', Broch was to make the cultural 'void' into a canvas on which to paint the individual destinies of the Viennese fin de siècle.

Broch, like Wittgenstein, analyses contemporary decadence in terms of a collapsing edifice of collective values without which there can be no culture worthy of the name. Modernity is an anarchy of individualist values which coexist but are unaware of one another, or even mutually exclusive. The theoretical epilogue of 'Sleepwalkers' shows that after the 'disintegration of values' (*Wertzerfall*), nothing is left but individual spheres of value creation. This dispersal atomizes and pulverizes culture until it is reduced to a 'void' in which individual value subsystems float without coherence. Here Broch is returning to the sources of criticism of 'decadence'. Paul Bourget, in his 'Essays on Contemporary Psychology', had compared society to an organism which 'resolves itself into a federation of cells. The individual is the social cell. . . . If the energy of the cells becomes independent . . . the anarchy which

ensues constitutes the decadence of the whole.' Bourget immediately trans-
posed this analysis into the creative domain so as to define the 'style of
decadence', 'in which the unity of the book dissolves to leave room for
the independence of the page, the page dissolves to leave room for the
independence of the sentence, and the sentence to leave room for the independence of the word.'[12] Nietzsche had borrowed this idea of Bourget's and
applied it to Wagner.[13] Broch draws the fullest consequences from this
critique of modernity, showing that the dispersal of culture into a multitude of
tiny individual entities dooms to failure any kind of rational moral or political
action which a reformer (head of state, 'great man' or committed intellectual)
might undertake. Even the idea of a *Kulturkritik* developed by a great thinker
on the part of some ancient or modern order seems desperate, ridiculous or
dangerous amidst the chaos of the world.[14] At the same time, each of the
solipsistic atoms which cluster together to form society shows itself to be
unstable and manipulable, responsive to the call of the irrational as soon as
some political or religious *Führer* appears who is able to destabilize the
libidinal equilibrium of the individual and initiate collective movements of
identification: such might be the conclusion of 'Sleepwalkers'.

Broch's essay on Hofmannsthal gives us 'the life plan of a creator who has
vigorously perceived the vacuum of values which surrounds him and sets his
own personality up against it'.[15] The building blocks of that personality,
according to Broch, were Jewish assimilation, the narcissistic self-absorption
of the child prodigy, then of the aesthetic 'genius', and finally the affirmation
of salvation by the ritual of art, which Broch finds unsatisfying: 'Is this not
most uncomfortably close to Wagner? This supreme sublimation of theatrical
style, in the sublimation of language into music, does it not foreshadow
the total work of art [*Gesamtkunstwerk*]?'[16] What saves Hofmannsthal from
becoming like the false prophet of Bayreuth is what Broch calls his 'anguish':

[In] his *Lord Chandos Letter*, full of anguish, obsessed by chaos ... we can
foresee the dangers which were beginning to stir in the dissolution of norms
created by the void ... He was trying to hold on to what existed – still existed –
and that is why, in his art as in his life, he had to cling to tradition ... He was
not unaware that in the last analysis he was assimilating to the void.[17]

The joyful apocalypse: from pessimism to utopia

We have studied the 'modern' crisis of culture, which manifests itself in the
destabilization of individual roles and identities, through two aspects which
turn out to be particularly representative: the questioning of masculine identity by the deregulation of old sexual codes of behaviour and feeling; and the
avatars of Jewish identity, dissolved into assimilation, then brutally reawakened
by the provocations of antisemitism, and finally reconstructed through
each individual's subjectivity via a process of 'working through' (Freud's
Durcharbeitung) which may be more or less difficult, often dramatic, and
sometimes unsuccessful. These two paradigms for the loss of culturally prede-
termined identities, for the uncertain and endlessly indecisive redefinition of

difference and for the subject's assumption of responsibility for the disorder of the world all point us towards a more precise definition of Viennese modernity in the spirit of Hermann Bahr's aphorism of 1889: 'modernity is everything that follows on the bankruptcy of individualism: everything which is no longer there, but is in course of becoming.'[18]

This approach serves to confirm my hypothesis that Viennese modernity from 1900 onwards prefigured some of the great themes of 1970s and 1980s *Kulturkritik*, and to explain the singular fashion for things Viennese which swept Europe and North America during those years. In France it was set in motion by the 1975 special number on 'Vienne, début d'un siècle' ('Vienna, opening of a century') of the journal *Critique*; and the movement reached its apogee with the exhibition 'Vienne, 1880–1938' at the Pompidou Centre in Paris in 1986. With hindsight we might say that French interest in the Germanic world shifted momentarily away from the Weimar era, whose fascination had been felt in the 1950s and 1960s, towards this era in Vienna.

This shift coincided with a feeling of disaffection on the part of the thinking public against revolutionary commitment and critical theories of society. After having celebrated *homo politicus*, people were taking more interest in the *homo psychologicus* put forward by Carl Schorske, pioneer of Viennese studies, as the hero of a modernity conceived as what Heinz Kohut, in another context, called a 'reshaping of self'. Historical change does not only oblige the individual to forge himself a new identity: it also compels whole social groups to rethink or replace vanishing belief systems. Liberal culture, as Schorske reminds us, believed in rational man who would become, thanks to physical science, master of nature, and thanks to moral science, master of himself. In the modernism of 1900, the man of reason, as a universal ideal, gave ground to a more unstable and changeable individual, in search of new ways of life, and always afraid of seeing his individualism engulfed in new kinds of community.[19]

Some years ago Henri Meschonnic poked fun at the 'operation "Joyful Apocalypse"' set up by the organizers of the 'Vienne 1880–1938' exhibition at the Pompidou Centre: 'This cradle of modernity has become a coffin. I suggest that if you look closely you will find it is your own.'[20] As the twentieth century draws to an end, said Meschonnic, it chooses to see modernist Vienna as a period dominated by decadence and by a premonition of the 'last days of humanity', coming to believe that, to borrow a phrase from E. M. Cioran, 'in history, only the periods of decline are really interesting.'[21] In fact, it all pointed to a morbid attraction towards decrepitude and decline.

However, the pessimism of Broch or Wittgenstein, faced with the vacuum of modern culture and the difficulties of the individual, forced to seek a footing without any collective norm to hold on to, must not blind us to the fact that the general deconstruction of identities, felt with dizzying and anxious intensity in modernist Vienna, also carried within it the utopias which could regenerate the human race. Habermas reminds us that Adorno used to cite the famous 'nervous debility' of Peter Altenberg as an example of individuation pushed to extremes, the last refuge of a private life removed from the grasp of every power, every totalitarian allegiance, an anticipation of a freer humanity.[22]

Similarly, there are more ways of looking at the prodigious cultural and linguistic heterogeneity of the Habsburg monarchy than to allude to its inevitable dissolution in an age of triumphant 'national identities'. One could, for example, point out the democratic potential of the multicultural and multilingual pluralism which made such true 'Europeans' of certain intellectuals of the old Austria-Hungary.[23] It is true that this potential was not perceived by contemporaries, who considered the polyethnic plurality of the monarchy much more as a weakness – especially in comparison to the German *Reich* – than as the crucible of a new, transnational cultural code.

In an essay on 'Individuality' which figures in the collection *Pròdròmòs* (1906), Altenberg proclaimed that 'In so far as an individuality has some *raison d'être*, if only the appearance of one, it must not constitute anything other than a prototype, an anticipation within some organic evolution of humanness in general, following the natural course of the potential evolution of all humanity.'[24] Later, Egon Friedell was to present his essay on Altenberg as a 'natural history' of the changing human species.[25] The exercise by which individual existence is stripped barer and barer, ever more anticonformist and marginal, creates a *tabula rasa* on which to rebuild a better kind of life, freed from all the conventions of culture. There dwelt in Altenberg, behind the lackadaisical, nonchalant poetic bohemian, a sort of ironic prophet.

Thomas Mann, who appreciated Altenberg's work, said that his pose was a parody of Nietzsche's *Ecce homo*.[26] And indeed Altenberg used to parade as a sort of Zarathustra of the Café Central ... The new type of humanity which he claimed to represent, or at least prefigure, was evidently nothing like the 'strong' Nietzschean superman. Rather he exhibited an indeterminate and fluctuating self, a floating space, unfixed, undirected, open to any scenario, any seduction, permanently in formation, typifying indeed the new individualism of the era of the void.

Lou Andreas-Salomé, who had become acquainted with Altenberg while staying in Vienna in autumn 1905, wrote, 'When one was in his company, one thought neither of a woman nor of a man, but of a creature of a third kind.'[27] In the same tone, Egon Friedell declared, in a piece written for Peter Altenberg's fiftieth birthday, 'He has the imagination and feelings of a woman, but exercises them with the superior intelligence of a man. He has, to use a metaphor, a brain whose matter is feminine, but its structure is masculine.'[28] As for his Jewishness, Altenberg[29] defined it in *Pròdròmòs* by readapting, in jest, the theme of the 'dissolving Jewish mind': 'There are two sorts of men: those who in their way bring grist to the mill of the Creator as he works on the purification of humanity, and those of the 'après moi le déluge' type – Christians and Jews, more or less.'[30]

Like Broch, who analysed the crisis of modern culture in terms of a 'degradation of values' – that is, the fragmenting of collective norms into little atomized value systems cut off from one another; like Wittgenstein, who observed that a culture worthy of the name must show each individual his own place, whereas the modern condition delivered each to his own fate – so

Robert Musil, speaking through Ulrich, declares that at the end of a century of scientific and technical progress, 'all the order we have gained in detail, we have lost again overall, so that we have ever more orders (in the plural) and ever less order (in the singular).'[31] Hermann Broch, in his tribute to Musil, described *The Man Without Qualities* as a romantic conception related to that of 'Sleepwalkers', defining Musil's theme as 'The exhaustion and quasi-mystical process of dissolution of a culture, the collapse of a complex edifice of values.'[32]

Shifting identity

Robert Musil, in his search for a better way of life, a new ethics, is constantly insisting on the need to remain in a state of subjective availability, to leave one's character (that is, the sum of one's 'qualities') unfinished, so as to allow for possible new combinations. A life appears as 'a collection of moral attitudes which have been sketched out, but left aside and not lived, which at one time or another appeared to us as possibilities; beside which a man can be thought to have reached his adult ethic without really knowing why. Beside visions of the world which might have contained more happiness.'[33] What Musil calls 'moral fruitfulness' (*moralische Fruchtbarkeit*) means an ability to change, to obey a sort of mystical intuition which shows the ordering of the world in a new light, unhampered by any fixed identity. The law of true morality is in perpetual metamorphosis; it is not a fixed code, but a series of creative recombinations. Freed from the roles and identifications which society seeks to impose on him, the man without qualities stands revealed as the man of the possible, of experiment, who does not fear to see his identity in constant process of reshaping. He prefers this indeterminate liberty to all the certainties which enslave the other characters around him.

Musil took literally Nietzsche's demands for 'that excess which gives the free spirit the dangerous prerogative of being entitled to live by *experiments*' (preface to *Human, All Too Human*),[34] and the proclamation that 'We ... want to look as carefully into our experiences, as in the case of a scientific experiment, hour by hour, day by day! We ourselves want to be our own experiments, and our own subject of experiment' (*The Joyful Wisdom*).[35] Accordingly, Musil presents in *The Man Without Qualities* a 'utopia of experimentation' which means that 'a change in one of the elements is observed together with the effects that it would cause in that compound phenomenon we call life.'[36] Modern individuals are bound to become 'autopoietic systems',[37] constantly recreating themselves, and to proceed inexorably to the selective reorganization of the disorder in the world and in their own lives. 'What, then, alone, can our teaching be?' asked Nietzsche in *The Twilight of Idols*. And he answered his own question: 'That no one gives man his qualities, neither God, society, his parents, his ancestors, nor himself.'[38] One would think that nothing was more firmly and irrevocably fixed than sexual identity, which prompted Freud himself to say, 'Anatomy is destiny, to paraphrase a saying of Napoleon's.'[39] Nothing looked more constricted and immutable than Jewish identity: Freud remarking that of all the Mediterranean peoples the Jewish people were almost alone in remaining unchanged, like a fossil out of biblical times, across the ages. How many of the ethical and aesthetic values of our cultural tradition – and how many acts of oppression, how many crimes against humanity – have been grounded in these differences, these blindingly obvious distinctions!

But Viennese modernity discovered, signed and sealed the ruin of those former certainties. The androgynism of the modern psyche and the henceforth inextricable interpenetration of Jew and non-Jew created the most vertiginous state of confusion. Should we speak of decadence and extinction of culture, or of a creative and liberating redistribution? The middle years of the twentieth century saw an impassioned restoration of those lost identities: fascists and Nazis reconstructed 'feminine nature' only to enslave it, 'the Jew' in order to exterminate him. After this relapse into barbarism, culture still continued to live under the aegis of those restored certainties; it revived the goals of emancipation from the age of the Enlightenment, and repeated some elements of nineteenth-century 'struggle'.

As the twentieth century draws to a close it seems that we have tired of our attempts to replay the eighteenth and the nineteenth centuries: we are back in a situation similar to that of the Viennese modernists. Once again sexual identities are becoming confused, and the 'Jew' defined only by the imagination. The example of Vienna shows that this indeterminacy can be extremely fruitful, allowing for recombinations of unbelievable variety and richness – so long as no new reaction comes to cut short our postmodern game of self-invention.

Notes

Abbreviations

Lou Andreas-Salomé
NaD 'Narzissmus als Doppelrichtung', *Imago: Zeitschrift für Anwendung der Psychoanalyse auf die Geisteswissenschaften* 7.4 (1921), pp. 361–86.

Richard Beer-Hofmann
GW *Gesammelte Werke*, with preface by Martin Buber (Frankfurt, 1963).
TG *Der Tod Georgs*, ed. Hartmut Scheible (Stuttgart, 1980).

Hermann Broch
SzL *Schriften zur Literatur 1, Kommentierte Werkausgabe*, ed. Paul Michael Lützeler, vol. 9.1 (Frankfurt, 1975).

Sigmund Freud
GW *Gesammelte Werke in achtzehn Bänden* (vols 1–17, London, 1940–52; vol. 18, Frankfurt, 1969).
SE *The Standard Edition of the Psychological Works of Sigmund Freud*, ed. and trans. James Strachey et al. (London, 1953–74).

Hugo von Hofmannsthal
GW *Gesammelte Werke in zehn Bänden*, ed. Gerd Schoeller and Rudolf Hirsch (Frankfurt, 1979–80).
D2 *Dramen II, 1892–1905*.
D5 *Dramen V, Operndichtungen*.
EGB *Erzählungen, Erfundene Gespräche und Briefe; Reisen*.
GD1 *Gedichte, Dramen I, 1891–98*.
LCL *The Lord Chandos Letter* (1902), trans. Russell Stockman (Marlboro, Vermont, 1986).
RuA *Reden und Aufsätze* (vol. 1: 1891–1913; vol. 2: 1914–24; vol. 3: 1925–1929, *Aufzeichnungen*).

Ernest Jones
LWSF *The Life and Works of Sigmund Freud* (3 vols, London, 1953–7).

Robert Musil
GW2 *Gesammelte Werke II, Prosa und Stücke, Kleine Prosa, Aphorismen, Autobiographisches, Essays und Reden, Kritik*, ed. Adolf Frisé (Reinbeck/Hamburg, 1978).
MoE *Der Mann ohne Eigenschaften*, ed. Adolf Frisé (Reinbeck/Hamburg, 1978).

MWQ The Man Without Qualities, trans. Eithne Wilkins and Ernst Kaiser (3 vols, London, 1953).

Friedrich Nietzsche
KSA Sämtliche Werke, Kritische Studienausgabe in 15 Banden, ed. Giorgio Colli and Mazzino Montinari (Berlin/New York, 1980).
CW Complete Works, ed. Oscar Levy (Edinburgh/London, various years).

Rainer Maria Rilke
SW Sämtliche Werke, ed. the Rilke-Archiv, Ruth Sieber-Rilke, Ernst Zinn (6 vols, Frankfurt, 1955–66).

Daniel Paul Schreber
DeN Denkwürdigkwiten eines Nervenkranken, ed. Peter Heiligenthal and Reinhard Volk (2nd edn, Frankfurt, 1985).

Otto Weininger
GuCh Geschlecht und Charakter (reprint, Munich, 1980).
SC Sex and Character, authorized translation (London, 1906).

Chapter 1   Reflections on Viennese Modernity

1 Rudolf Haller, *Studien zur österreichischen Philosophie* (Amsterdam, 1979); cf. Alberto Coffa, 'Le positivisme logique, la tradition sémantique et l'a priori', in *Le cercle de Vienne. Doctrines et controverses*, ed. Jan Sebestik and Antonia Soulez (Paris, 1986), pp. 81–102; Joëlle Proust, 'Alberto Coffa et la tradition sémantique', *Archives de Philosophie*, no. 50 (1987), pp. 353–8; Rudolf Haller, 'Remarques sur la tradition sémantique', *Archives de Philosophie*, no. 50 (1987), pp. 359–69; J. C. Nyiri (ed.), *Von Bolzano zu Wittgenstein. Zur Tradition der österreichischen Philosophie* (Vienna, 1986).

2 Roger Bauer, *Der Idealismus und seine Gegner in Österreich*, Beiheft zum *Euphorion*, no. 3 (Heidelberg, 1966), pp. 61ff. Werner Sauer's *Österreichische Philosophie zwischen Aufklärung und Restauration. Beiträge zur Geschichte des Fruhkantianismus in der Donaumonarchie* (Amsterdam, 1982) suggests that Bauer's arguments should be modified in view of the fact that there was a pre-existing Austrian tradition of 'Kant reception'.

3 Bauer, *Idealismus*, p. 37.

4 Cf. Franz Brentano, *Über Ernst Machs 'Erkenntnis und Irrtum'*, ed. Roderick M. Chisholm and Johann C. Marek (Amsterdam, 1988). On Mach see *Ernst Mach, Werk und Wirkung*, ed. Rudolf Haller and Friedrich Stadler (Vienna, 1988).

5 Hermann Bahr, *Rede über Klimt* (Vienna, 1901), p. 12. Cf. Donald G. Daviau, 'Hermann Bahr and the Secessionist Art Movement in Vienna', in *The Turn of the Century: German Literature and Art, 1890–1915*, ed. Gerald Chapple and Hans H. Schulte (Bonn, 1981), pp. 433–62. On the aesthetic debates on the Viennese modernists, cf. Bernhard Kleinschmidt, *Die 'gemeinsame Sendung'. Kunstpublizistik der Weiner Jahrhundertwende*, Münchener Studien zur literarischen Kultur in Deutschland 8 (Frankfurt/Berne, 1989).

6 Hermann Bahr, *Selbstbildnis* (Berlin, 1923), p. 127.

7 Gotthart Wunberg, 'Deutscher Naturalismus und österreichische Moderne, Thesen zur Wiener Literatur um 1900', in *Verabschiedung der (Post)-Moderne?*, ed. Jacques le Rider and Gérard Raulet (Tübingen, 1987). Cf. Jens Rieckmann, *Aufbruch in die Moderne. Die Anfänge des Junge Wien* (Königstein, 1985). For the

earlier period (1875–90) see Karlheinz Rossbacher, *Literatur und Liberalismus. Zur Kultur der Ringstrassenzeit in Wien* (Vienna, 1992).

8   Carl E. Schorske, *Fin-de-Siècle Vienna: Politics and Culture* (London, 1979), p. 186.

9   *Leo Baeck Institute Year Book*, vol. 2 (London, 1957).

10   Schorske, *Fin-de-Siècle Vienna*, p. 201.

11   Hugo von Hofmannsthal, *RuA*, vol. 3, p. 383.

12   Georges Rodenbach, *Bruges la morte* (1909).

13   Robert Musil, *Der Anschluss an Deutschland* (March 1919), in *GW2*, pp. 1039, 1041.

14   Cited in Werner Hofmann, *Gustav Klimt und die Wiener Jahrhundertswende* (Salzburg, 1970), p. 11.

15   Hermann Bahr, *Wien* (Stuttgart, 1906), p. 9.

16   Cf. Paul-Laurent Assoun, 'Freud et le lien viennois', *Austriaca: Cahiers Universitaires d'Information sur l'Autriche*, no. 21 (1985), pp. 11–19.

17   Sigmund Freud, *The Complete Letters of Sigmund Freud to Wilhelm Fliess, 1887–1904*, ed. and trans. Jeffrey Moussaieff Masson (Cambridge, Mass., 1985), p. 57.

18   Ernest Jones, *LWSF*, vol. 1, p. 323.

19   Hugo von Hofmannsthal/Richard Beer-Hofmann, *Briefwechsel* (Frankfurt, 1972), p. 59.

20   Hugo von Hofmannsthal, *Briefe, 1900–9* (Vienna, 1937), p. 356.

21   Peter Berner, Emil Brix and Wolfgang Mantl (eds), *Wien um 1990. Aufbruch in die Moderne* (Vienna, 1986), p. 14. The volume *Die Wiener Moderne, Ergebnisse eines Forschungsgespräches der Arbeitsgemeinschaft Wien um 1900 zum Thema Aktualität und Moderne*, ed. Emil Brix and Patrick Werkner (Vienna/Munich, 1990) pursues the analyses initiated in *Aufbruch in die Moderne*; see in particular the essay by Moritz Csaky, 'Die Moderne'.

22   Albert O. Hirschman, *Deux siècles de rhétorique réactionnaire* (Fayard, 1991) takes no account of this central European variant. See also Herbert Matis, *Österreichs Wirtschaft 1848–1913. Konjunkturelle Dynamik und gesellschaftlicher Wandel im Zeitalter Franz Josephs I* (Berlin, 1971); Ernst Bruckmuller, 'Die verzögerte Modernisierung. Mögliche Ursachen und Folgen des "österreichischen Weges" im Wandel des Agrarbereiches', in *Wirtschafts- und sozialhistorische Beiträge. Festschrift für Alfred Hoffmann*, ed. Herbert Knittler (Vienna, 1979), pp. 289–307.

23   Cf. Jacques Le Rider, 'Allemagne, Autriche et Europe centrale', *Le Débat* 67 (Nov.–Dec., 1991), pp. 105–26.

24   Cf. David F. Good, *The Economic Rise of the Habsburg Empire 1750–1914* (Berkeley/Los Angeles, 1984).

25   Cf. John Komlos, *Die Habsburgermonarchie als Zollunion. Die Wirtschaftsentwicklung Österreich-Ungarns im 19. Jahrhundert* (Vienna, 1986).

26   Cf. Kurt W. Rothschild, 'Wurzeln und Triebkräfte der Entwicklung der österreichischen Wirtschaftsstruktur', in *Österreichs Wirtschaftsstruktur, gestern, heute, morgen*, ed. Wilhelm Weber (Berlin, 1961).

27   Cf. Franz Baltzarek, Alfred Hoffmann, Hannes Stekl, *Wirtschaft und Gesellschaft der Wiener Stadterweiterung* (Wiesbaden, 1975), vol. 5 in the series *Die Wiener Ringstrasse. Bild einer Epoche*, ed. Renate Wagner-Rieger; Carl E. Schorske, 'The Ringstrasse', ch. 8 of Schorske, *Fin-de-Siècle Vienna*.

28   Renate Banik-Schweitzer and Gerhard Meissl, *Industriestadt Wien. Die Durchsetzung der industriellen Marktproduktion in der Habsburgerresidenz* (Vienna, 1983).

29   Ibid., p. 147.

30   Hans Bobek and Elisabeth Lichtenberger, *Wien. Bauliche Gestalt und Entwicklung seit der Mitte des 19. Jahrhunderts* (Vienna, 1966).

31 Peter Feldbauer, *Stadtwachstum und Wohnungsnot* (Vienna, 1977), p. 39.

32 Reinhard E. Petermann, *Wien im Zeitalter Kaiser Franz Josephs I* (3rd edn, Vienna, 1913), p. 160. On immigration and cultural, ethnic and linguistic minorities in Vienna see Michael John and Albert Lichtblau, *Schmelztiegel Wien – einst und jetzt. Zur Geschichte und Gegenwart von Zuwanderung und Minderheiten* (Vienna/Cologne, 1990).

33 Josef Ehmer, 'Wiener Arbeitswelten um 1900', in *Glücklich ist, wer vergisst...? Das andere Wien um 1900*, ed. Hubert C. Ehalt, Gernot Heiss and Hannes Stekl (Vienna, 1986), p. 197.

34 Alfons Petzold, *Das rauhe Leben* (Graz, 1979); Max Winter, *Das schwarze Wienerherz. Sozialreportagen aus dem frühen 20. Jahrhundert* (Vienna, 1982); cf. Emil Klager, *Durch die Quartiere der Not und des Verbrechens* (Vienna, 1908); Stefan Riesenfellner (ed.), *Arbeitswelt um 1900. Texte zur Alltagsgeschichte von Max Winter* (Vienna, 1988).

35 Johan Böhm, *Erinnerungen aus meinem Leben* (Vienna, 1953).

36 Hedwig Lemberger, *Die Wiener Wäscheindustrie* (Vienna, 1907); *Die Arbeits- und Lebensverhältnisse der Wiener Lohnarbeiterinnen, Ergebnis und stenographisches Protokoll der Enquete über Frauenarbeit* (Vienna, 1897).

37 Cf. *Vom Tagwerk der Jahrhundertwende. Bilder der Arbeit, 1870–1930* (Vienna, 1985). See the photographs by Hermann Drawe in *Vienne, 1880–1938. L'apocalypse joyeuse*, ed. Jean Clair, catalogue, Pompidou Centre (Paris, 1986), pp. 390ff.

38 Donald J. Olsen, *The City as a Work of Art: London, Paris, Vienna* (New Haven, 1986) makes a systematic comparison of the three capitals.

39 Cf. Maren Seliger and Karl Ucakar, *Wien, politische Geschichte. 1740–1934* (Vienna and Munich, 1985).

40 Robert Musil, *MWQ*, vol. 1, p. 4; *MoE*, p. 10.

41 Cf. Renate Banik-Schweitzer, 'Berlin–Wien–Budapest. Zur sozialräumlichen Entwicklung der drei Hauptstädte in der zweiten Halfte des 19. Jahrhunderts', in *Die Städte Mittel Europas im 19. Jahrhundert*, ed. Wilhelm Rausch (Linz, 1983), pp. 139–54; Peter Hanak, 'Verbürgerlichung und Urbanisierung. Ein Vergleich der Stadtentwicklung Wiens und Budapests', in *Gesellschaft, Politik und Verwaltung in der Habsburgermonarchie, 1830–1918*, ed. Ferenc Glatz and Ralph Melville, Veröffentlichungen des Instituts für europaische Geschichte Mainz 15 (Wiesbaden/Stuttgart, 1987), pp. 203–35.

42 Jean-Paul Bled, *François-Joseph* (Paris, 1987), p. 458; cf. Bled, *Les fondements du conservatisme autrichien, 1859–79* (Paris, 1988).

43 Cf. John Boyer, 'The Position of Vienna in a General History of Austria', in *Wien um 1900*, ed. Berner et al., pp. 205–20; on the Czechs in Vienna see Monika Glettler, *Die Wiener Tschechen um 1900. Strukturanalyse einer Minderheit in der Grosstadt* (Munich/Vienna, 1972); Glettler, *Böhmisches Wien* (Vienna, 1985).

44 Claudio Magris, *Der habsburgische Mythos in der österreichischen Literatur* (German trans., Salzburg, 1963).

45 *Die Habsburgermonarchie, 1948–18*, vol. 2: *Verwaltung und Rechtswesen* (Vienna, 1975), pp. ixff.

46 Wolfgang Mantl even speaks of 'strikingly modern bureaucratic and technocratic structures', in *Wien um 1990*, ed. Berner et al., p. 252.

47 Robert A. Kann, 'Die habsburgermonarchie und das Problem des übernationalen Staates', in *Wien um 1900*, ed. Berner et al.

48 Hermann Broch, *SzL*, p. 158.

49 Carl E. Schorske, 'Politics and the Psyche: Schnitzler and Hofmannsthal', ch. 1 of Schorske, *Fin-de-Siècle Vienna*.

50   Cf. Werner Hofmann, 'Die Emanzipation der Dissonanzen', in *Verabschiedung*, ed. Le Rider and Raulet, p. 130.

51   Rudolf Borchardt, 'Rede über Hofmannsthal', in *Reden*, ed. Marie Luise Borchardt, R. A. Schröder and S. Rizzi (Stuttgart, n.d.), pp. 50–60, reprinted in *Die literarische Moderne, Dokumente zum Selbstverständnis der Literatur um die Jahrhundertwende*, ed. Gotthart Wunberg (Frankfurt, 1971), pp. 142ff.

52   Friedrich Nietzsche, *Ecce Homo*, see *CW*, vol. 17, p. 115; *KSA*, vol. 6, p. 350.

53   Hofmannsthal, *RuA*, vol. 1, p. 60.

54   Werner Hofmann, *Gustav Klimt und die Wiener Jahrhundertwende* (Salzburg, 1970), p. 22.

55   'Er ist doch ä Jud', *Die Fackel*, no. 386 (Oct. 1913).

56   Quoted in Charles Rosen, *Schönberg* (London, 1976), Preface.

57   Theodor W. Adorno, 'Funktionalismus heute', lecture given to the assembly of the Deutscher Werkbund, Berlin, 23 Oct. 1963, in *Ohne Leitbild, Parva Aesthetica* (Frankfurt, 1967), p. 104. Similarly, in his *Ästhetische Theorie* (Frankfurt, 1970) Adorno parallels Loos with contemporary technocrats (p. 96). On the biographical relations between Adorno and the Viennese milieu see Heinz Steinert, *Adorno in Wien. Über die (Un-)Möglichkeit von Kunst, Kultur und Befreiung* (Vienna, 1989).

58   Cf. Wagner, *Moderne Architektur* (first edition, Vienna, 1895; the fourth and subsequent editions bore the title *Die Baukunst unserer Zeit*).

59   Peter Haiko and Renata Kassal-Mikula, *Otto Wagner und das Franz Josef-Stadtmuseum. Das Scheitern der Moderne in Wien*, exhibition catalogue of the Historisches Museum der Stadt Wien (Vienna, 1988).

60   Heinz Geretsegger and Max Peintner, *Otto Wagner, 1841–1918. Unbegrenzte Grosstadt. Beginn der modernen Architektur* (Salzburg, 1964).

61   Hermann Bahr, *Briefwechsel mit seinem Vater*, ed. Adalbert Schmidt (Vienna, 1971), p. 154, letter of 14 March 1887.

62   Charles Baudelaire, *Oeuvres complètes*, ed. Claude Pichois (Paris, 1976), vol. 2, p. 696.

63   Ibid., p. 695.

64   René Huyghe, *L'esthétique de l'individualisme à travers Delacroix et Baudelaire*, Zaharoff lecture for 1955 (Oxford, 1955), p. 15.

65   Louis Dumont, *Essais sur l'individualisme* (Paris, 1983); Gilles Lipovetsky, *L'ère du vide. Essais sur l'individualisme contemporain* (Paris, 1983).

66   Jean Baudrillard, 'Modernité', in *Encylopaedia Universalis*, vol. 12 (Paris, 1985).

67   Jacques Le Goff, 'Antique (Ancien)/Moderne', in Le Goff, *Histoire et mémoire* (Paris, 1988), pp. 59–103.

68   Alain Touraine, *La société postindustrielle* (Paris, 1969); Daniel Bell, *The Coming of Post-Industrial Society* (New York, 1973).

69   Ihab Hassan, *The Dismemberment of Orpheus: Towards a Postmodern Literature* (New York, 1971); Charles Jencks, *The Rise of Post-Modern Architecture* (London, 1975).

70   'Jean-François Lyotard. Réécrire la modernité', *Cahiers de Philosophie*, no. 5 (Lille, 1988); issue no. 6 (1988), 'Postmoderne. Les termes d'un usage', examines the question in detail.

71   Jürgen Habermas, *The Philosophical Discourse of Modernity*, trans. F. Lawrence (Cambridge, 1989), ch. 4, pp. 83–105.

72   Ernst Behler, 'Friedrich Schlegels theorie des Verstehens: Hermeneutik oder Dekonstruktion?', in *Die Aktualität der Frühromantik*, ed. Ernst Behler and Jochen Horisch (Paderborn, 1987), pp. 141–60.

73   Jean-François Lyotard, *La condition postmoderne* (Paris, 1979), p. 63. See also

Jacques Le Rider, 'La postmodernité', *Commentaire* 54 (Summer 1991), pp. 283–91.

74 Ibid., p. 68.
75 Paris, 1983. Guy Scarpetta, in *L'impureté* (Paris, 1985) emphasizes that the reference to Vienna was intended to help French intellectuals free themselves from post-war ideologies. Cf. William M. Johnston, 'Modernisme et post-modernisme dans la pensée de l'Autriche fin de siècle', in *Le génie de l'Autriche-Hongrie*, ed. Miklós Molnar and André Reszler (Paris, 1989), pp. 173–89. In *Vienne à Paris. Portrait d'une exposition* (Paris, 1989), Nathalie Heinrich and Michael Pollak give a sociological analysis of the impact of the Pompidou Centre exhibition.
76 To adopt an idea of Alain Renaut (*L'ère de l'individu*, Paris, 1980), it was during the reign of the individual that the subject as conceived by the *Aufklärung* finally died. In fin-de-siècle Vienna the neutralization of the political subject reinforced the triumph of individual values, and caused a real desocialization of the in-dividual. It seemed to bear out the prophecies of Tocqueville and Benjamin Constant concerning 'the liberty of the moderns': 'From now on, almost all the joys of the Moderns will be within their private existence' (Constant, *De la liberté chez les Modernes*, ed. Marcel Gauchet, 2nd edn, Paris, 1989, p. 44).
77 Georg Simmel, *Philosophische Kultur* (1923, reprinted Berlin, 1983), p. 152.

Chapter 2   Individualism, Solitude and Identity Crisis

1   Jürgen Habermas, 'Der Eintritt in die Postmoderne', *Merkur* 37.7 (Oct. 1983).
2   Arthur Schopenhauer, *Die Welt als Wille und Vorstellung*, in *Sämtliche Werke*, ed. Wolfgang von Löhneysen (Darmstadt, 1974), vol. 1, p. 495.
3   Thomas Mann, *Buddenbrooks*, trans. H. T. Lowe-Porter (London, 1924), part 10, ch. 5.
4   Friedrich Nietzsche, *CW*, vol. 3, pp. 45, 49, 50; *KSA*, vol. 1, pp. 44ff.
5   Nietzsche, *KSA*, vol. 11, p. 642.
6   Ibid., vol. 2, p. 349.
7   Ibid., vol. 3, pp. 123–4.
8   Nietzsche, *CW*, vol. 10, p. 64; *KSA*, vol. 3, p. 396.
9   Nietzsche, *KSA*, vol. 12, pp. 502–3.
10 Georg Simmel, *Grundfragen der Soziologie (Individuum und Gesellschaft)*, vol. 4: *Individuum und Gesellschaft in Lebenanschauungen des 18. und 19. Jahrhunderts (Beispiel der philosophischen Soziologie)* (Berlin/Leipzig, 1917), p. 83; cf. Patrick Watier, 'Individualisme et sociabilité', in *Georg Simmel, la sociologie et l'expérience du monde moderne*, ed. P. Watier (Paris, 1986), p. 237; David Frisby, *Fragments of Modernity: Theories of Modernity in the Works of Simmel, Kracauer and Benjamin* (Cambridge, 1985) (on the notion of individualism see pp. 44ff.); François Léger, *La pensée de Georg Simmel* (Paris, 1989), pp. 202ff.
11 Simmel, *Grundfragen der Soziologie*.
12 Georg Simmel, 'Exkurs über die Soziologie der Sinne', in Simmel, *Soziologie. Untersuchungen über die Formen der Vergesellschaftung* (Leipzig, 1908), p. 658.
13 Philippe Ariès and Georges Duby (eds), *Histoire de la vie privée*, vol. 4: *De la Révolution à la Grande Guerre*, ed. Michelle Perrot (Paris, 1987), p. 416.
14 Julien Freund, in *Georg Simmel*, ed. Watier, p. 247.
15 Wilhelm Dilthey, 'Die Selbstbiographie', in section 3 of *Der Aufbau der ges-chichtlichen Welt in den Geisteswissenschaften*, vol. 7 of *Gesammelte Schriften*

(Leipzig/Berlin, 1927), pp. 199–200; cf. Hans-Joachim Lieber, 'Geschichte und Gesellschaft im Denken Diltheys', in *Kulturkritik und Lebensphilosophie, Studien zur deutschen Philosophie der Jahrhundertwende* (Darmstadt, 1974).

16 Raymond Aron, *La philosophie critique de l'histoire* (Paris, 1969), p. 74.
17 Nietzsche, *CW*, vol. 4, p. 223; *KSA*, vol. 4, p. 231.
18 Ibid., pp. 212–13; p. 221.
19 Ibid., vol. 17, pp. 25–6; vol. 6, pp. 275–6.
20 Cf. Eberhard Lammert, 'Nietzsches Apotheose der Einsamkeit', in *Nietzsche-Studien* 16 (1987), pp. 47–69; Herbert Roeschl, *Nietzsche, poète de la solitude* (Paris, 1960).
21 Quoted in Geneviève Bianquis, *Nietzsche devant ses contemporains* (Monaco, 1959), p. 221.
22 Cf. Werner Hamacher, 'Disaggregation of the Will: Nietzsche on the Individual and Individuality', in *Reconstructing Individualism*, ed. Thomas C. Heller, Morton Sosna and David Wellbery (Stanford, 1986), pp. 128ff.
23 Nietzsche, *KSA*, vol. 13, pp. 84–5. (Nietzsche cites Baudelaire in the original French.)
24 Cf. Karl Pestalozzi, 'Nietzsches Baudelaire-Rezeption', *Nietzsche-Studien* 7 (1976), pp. 158–88; Mazzino Montinari, 'Aufgaben der Nietzsche-Forschung heute: Nietzsches Auseinandersetzung mit der französischen Literatur des 19. Jahrhunderts', *Nietzsche-Studien* 18 (1989).
25 Georges Blin, *Baudelaire* (Paris, 1939), pp. 17ff.; John E. Jackson, 'D'une solitude à l'autre' (on Rousseau, Baudelaire and Rimbaud), in *Passions du sujet. Essais sur les rapports entre psychanalyse et écriture* (Paris, 1990), pp. 171ff.
26 Jean-Paul Sartre, *Baudelaire* (1st edn 1947; Paris, 1963), p. 21.
27 Rainer Maria Rilke, *Das Florenzer Tagebuch* (Frankfurt, 1982), p. 29.
28 Rudolf Kassner, *Narciss. Oder Mythos und Einbildungskraft* (1928), in *Sämtliche Werke*, ed. Ernst Zinn and Klaus E. Bohnenkamp, vol. 4 (Pfullingen, 1978).
29 Rainer Maria Rilke, *SW*, vol. 6, p. 861.
30 Richard Beer-Hofmann, *GW*, p. 144.
31 Hugo von Hofmannsthal, *RuA*, vol. 1, p. 144.
32 Robert Musil, *MWQ*, vol. 1, p. 7; *MoE*, p. 12. See Renate Mohrmann, *Der vereinsamte Mensch. Studien zum Wandel des Einsamkeitsmotivs im Roman von Raabe bis Musil* (Bonn, 1974); Gert Mattenklott, 'Der subjective Faktor in Musils Törless', in *Robert Musil*, ed. Renate von Heydebrand (Darmstadt, 1982), pp. 250–80.
33 Musil, *MWQ*, vol. 2, pp. 453–4; *MoE*, p. 664.
34 Hugo von Hofmannsthal, *GD1*, p. 23; Beer-Hofmann, *GW*, p. 654.
35 Cited in Manfred Diersch, 'Vereinsamung und Selbstentfremdung als Lebenserfahrung Wiener Dichter um 1900', in *Deutsche Literatur der Jahrhundertwende*, ed. Viktor Zmegac (Königstein, 1981), p. 85.
36 Ibid., p. 86.
37 Ibid., p. 88.
38 The Austrian Academy of Sciences has published the volumes for 1879–92 (Vienna, 1987), 1909–12 (1981), 1913–16 (1983) and 1917–19 (1985).
39 Fritz Mauthner, 'Nietzsche', in Mauthner, *Sprache und Leben. Ausgewählte Texte aus dem philosophischen Werk*, ed. Gershon Weiler (Salzburg/Vienna, 1986), section 11, pp. 52–4; Elisabeth Bredeck, 'Fritz Mauthners Nachlese zu Nietzsches Sprachkritik', *Nietzsche-Studien* 13 (1984), pp. 587–99.
40 Fritz Mauthner, *Beiträge zu einer Kritik der Sprache* (Frankfurt/Berlin/Vienna, 1982), vol. 1, pp. 39–40.

41 Robert Musil, *Tagebücher*, ed. Adolf Frisé (Reinbeck/Hamburg, 1976), book 21, 1920–6, pp. 615–23.
42 Ludwig Klages, *Vom kosmogonischen Eros* (Munich, 1922), pp. 69, 72.
43 Lou Andreas-Salomé, *Gedanken über das Liebesproblem, Neue Deutsche Rundschau*, XII (1900), in *Die Erotik. Vier Aufsätze*, ed. Ernst Pfeiffer (Munich, 1979), p. 69.
44 Andreas-Salomé, *Die Erotik*, pp. 102ff.
45 Rainer Maria Rilke, *Letters to a Young Poet*, trans. M. D. Herter Norton (New York, 1934), p. 54.
46 Rainer Maria Rilke, Eighth Duino Elegy, in *SW*, vol. 1, pp. 714–15.
47 Otto Weininger, *SC*, p. 162; *GuCh*, p. 142.
48 Ferdinand Ebner, *Das Wort und die geistigen Realitäten* (Frankfurt, 1980), pp. 154ff.; cf. Daniel Eckert, 'Der gespiegelte Spiegel. Sexualität und Subjekt-theorie bei Otto Weininger', in *Gegen den Traum vom Geist*, International F. Ebner Symposium 1981, ed. Walter Methlagl, Peter Kampits et al. (Salzburg, 1985), pp. 182–90; and papers by Michael Benedikt, Daniel Eckert and Peter Kampits in *Otto Weininger, Werk und Wirkung*, ed. J. Le Rider and N. Leser (Vienna, 1984).
49 Hugo von Hofmannsthal, 'Das Tagebuch eines Willenskranken' (1891), in *RuA*, vol. 1, p. 117.
50 Cf. Gotthart Wunberg, *Der frühe Hofmannsthal, Schizophrenie als dichterische Struktur* (Stuttgart/Berlin, 1965). Similarly, Wolfram Mauser places notions of 'disturbed identity' and 'crisis of adolescence' at the heart of his book *Hugo von Hofmannsthal. Konfliktbewaltigung und Werkstruktur. Eine psychosoziale Interpretation* (Munich, 1977).
51 Hermann Bahr, 'Die Krisis des Naturalismus', in *Das junge Wien. Österreichische Literatur- und Kunstkritik, 1887–1902*, ed. Gotthart Wunberg (Tübingen, 1976), vol. 1, pp. 145–9 (and cf. Bahr's allusions to Bourget from 1889, ibid. *passim*); Hugo von Hofmannsthal, 'Zur Physiologie der modernen Liebe', in *RuA*, vol. 1, pp. 93–8.
52 Paul Bourget, *Essais de psychologie contemporaine*, vol. 1 (1883; definitive enlarged edn Paris, 1901), p. 13.
53 Cited in Rainer Hank, *Mortifikation und Beschwörung. Zur Veranderung ästhetischer Wahrnehmung in der Moderne am Beispiel des Frühwerkes Richard Beer-Hofmanns* (Frankfurt/Berne/New York, 1984), p. 38.
54 Ibid., p. 39.
55 Hugo von Hofmannsthal and Leopold von Andrian, *Briefwechsel*, ed. Walter H. Perl (Frankfurt, 1968), p. 86.
56 Hugo von Hofmannsthal, 'Aufzeichnungen aus dem Nachlass' (1889), in *RuA*, vol. 3, p. 313.
57 Peter Altenberg, *Wie ich es sehe* (1896; 4th edn Berlin, 1904), p. 226.
58 For the relationship between Nietzsche and Bourget, see the studies cited in note 24 above.
59 Nietzsche, *KSA*, vol. 2, p. 204.
60 Hermann Bahr, 'Die Überwindung des Naturalismus' (1891), in *Das junge Wien*, ed. Wunberg, vol. 1, p. 158;
61 Sigmund Freud, *SE*, vol. 9, pp. 181–204; *GW*, vol. 7, p. 148.
62 Cf. Peter Gay, *The Bourgeois Experience. Victoria to Freud*, vol. 2: *The Tender Passion* (New York/Oxford, 1986), p. 351; cf. David Frisby, 'Neurasthenia', in *Fragments of Modernity in the Work of Simmel, Kracauer and Benjamin* (Cambridge, 1985), pp. 72–7.
63 Carl E. Schorske, *Fin-de-Siècle Vienna* (London, 1979), p. 22.

64 Paul Ricoeur, 'Individu et identité personnelle', in _Sur l'individu_, collected essays (Paris, 1987), p. 55; cf. Odo Marquardt and Karl Heinz Stierle (eds), _Identität, Poetik und Hermeneutik_, vol. 8 (Munich, 1979); Alex Mucchielli, _L'identité_ (Paris, 1986); Annette M. Stross, _Ich-Identität zwischen Fiktion und Konstruktion_, Historische Anthropologie 17 (Berlin, 1991).

65 Manfred Frank, _Die Unhintergehbarkeit von Individualität_ (Frankfurt, 1986). In the same book Frank discusses Viennese postmodernism; cf. his ' "L'absence de qualités" à la lumière de l'épistémologie, de l'esthétique et de la mythologie', _Vienne, 1880–1938, Revue d'Esthétique_, NS no. 9 (Toulouse, 1985), pp. 105–17; Manfred Frank and Anselm Haverkamp, _Individualität, Poetik und Hermeneutik_, vol. 13 (Munich, 1988).

66 Paul Ricoeur, _Temps et récit_, vol. 1 (Paris, 1983). Earlier, Emile Benvéniste had written in _Problèmes de linguistique générale_ (Paris, 1966) that 'it is through language that the individual subject constitutes himself as such' (vol. 1, p. 260).

67 Wilhelm Schapp, _In Geschichten verstrickt. Zum Sein von Mensch und Ding_ (1953; 3rd edn Frankfurt, 1985), p. 190.

68 Cf. Michel Neyraut, Jean-Bertrand Pontalis, Philippe Lejeune et al., _L'autobiographie. VIe Rencontres Psychanalytiques d'Aix-en-Provence_ (Paris, 1988); John E. Jackson, 'Mythes du sujet: a propos de l'autobiographie et de la cure analytique', ch. 2 of _Passions du sujet_, pp. 59ff.

69 Cf. Claus Vogelsang, 'Das Tagebuch', in _Prosakunst ohne Erzählen. Die Gattungen der nicht-fiktionalen Kunstprosa_, ed. Klaus Weissenberger (Tübingen, 1985), pp. 185–202. On the vogue for private diaries around 1900 see also 'The Private Experience', ch. 6.4 of Peter Gay, _The Education of the Senses_, vol. 1 of _The Bourgeois Experience_ (New York/Oxford, 1984–6).

70 Gunther Stern [G. Anders], 'Pathologie de la liberté. Essais sur la non-identification', in _Recherches Philosophiques_ (1936), pp. 22–54.

71 Cf. the study of _The Man Without Qualities_ by Anne Longuet-Marx in Marie-Louise Roth, _Robert Musil_ (Paris, 1987); Hartmut Boehme, _Anomie und Entfremdung. Literatursoziologische Untersuchungen zu den Essays Robert Musils und seinem Roman Der Mensch ohne Eigenschaften_ (Kronberg, 1974).

72 Ludwig Wittgenstein, _Vermischte Bemerkungen_, ed. Georg Henrik von Wright (Frankfurt, 1977), p. 21.

73 The expression is from Paul-Laurent Assoun's 1985 introduction to the French translation of Musil's _Beitrag zur Beurteilung der Lehren Machs_ ('Towards an Evaluation of the Doctrines of Mach').

74 André Green, 'Atome de parenté et relations oedipiennes', in _L'identité_, ed. Claude Lévi-Strauss (1977; Paris, 1987), p. 82.

75 Alain de Mijolla, _Les visiteurs du moi. Fantasmes d'identification_ (Paris, 1981).

76 Jean Florence, 'Les identifications', in Monique David-Menard, Jean Florence, Julia Kristeva et al., _Les identifications. Confrontation de la clinique et de la théorie de Freud à Lacan_ (Paris, 1987), p. 152; cf. issue 38 of the review _Topique_ (Paris, 1986), entitled 'Constructions de l'identité'.

77 Florence, 'Les identifications', pp. 115–16.

78 Ibid., pp. 165–6.

79 Ibid., p. 185.

80 Sigmund Freud, _SE_, vol. 19, p. 28 n2; _GW_, vol. 13, p. 256 n2.

81 Henrik Ibsen, _Peer Gynt_, trans. Michael Meyer (London, 1963), p. 154.

82 Cf. J. Le Rider, 'Avant-propos' to Otto Weininger, _Des fins ultimes_ (Lausanne, 1981, p. 15), the French translation of _Über die letzten Dinge_.

83 _Über die letzten Dinge_ (reprint, Munich, 1980), pp. 18–19.

84 Nicole Berry, _Le sentiment d'identité_ (Paris, 1987).

85 The influence of Nietzsche on the early Hofmannsthal has been studied by H. Jürgen Meyer-Wendt, *Der frühe Hofmannsthal und die Gedankenwelt Nietzsches* (Heidelberg, 1973), and by Hans Steffens, 'Hofmannsthal und Nietzsche', in *Nietzsche und die deutsche Literatur*, vol. 2, *Forschungsergebnisse*, ed. Bruno Hillebrand (Tübingen, 1978), pp. 4–11.
86 Nietzsche, *CW*, vol. 16, p. 36; *KSA*, vol. 6, p. 91.
87 Nietzsche, *CW*, vol. 16, p. 110; *KSA*, vol. 6, pp. 151–2.
88 Gottfried Benn, 'Nietzsche nach fünfzig Jahren' (1950), in *Essays, Reden, Vorträge*, vol. 1 of *Gesammelte Werke in vier Bänden*, ed. Dieter Wellershof (Wiesbaden, 1959), p. 492.
89 Cf. Alexander Nehamas, *Nietzsche: A Life as Literature* (Cambridge, Mass., 1985), pp. 150ff. Jacques Derrida observes that 'Autobiography is stamped with something not unconnected with the "eternal return" in Nietzsche': *L'oreille de l'autre. Autobiographie, transferts, traductions*, writings and discussions ed. Claude Lévesque and Christie V. McDonald (Montreal, 1982).
90 Nietzsche, *CW*, vol. 4; *KSA*, vol. 6, p. 255.
91 Nietzsche, *CW*, vol. 10, p. 270; *KSA*, vol. 3, p. 570.
92 Nietzsche, *CW*, vol. 4, p. 183; *KSA*, vol. 4, p. 193.

Chapter 3   The Mystic and the Genius

1 Georges Gusdorf, *L'homme romantique* (Paris, 1984), p. 26.
2 Ibid., p. 28.
3 Immanuel Kant, *Werke*, ed. Wilhelm Weischedel, vol. 2 (Darmstadt, 1956), p. 344.
4 Cf. Horst Hillermann, 'Zur Begriffsgeschichte von "Monismus"', *Archiv für Begriffsgeschichte*, no. 20 (1976), pp. 14–35.
5 Otto Weininger, *SC*, p. 164; *GuCh*, pp. 214–15.
6 Weininger, *SC*, p. 154; *GuCh*, pp. 198–9.
7 Ernst Mach, *Die Analyse der Empfindungen* (the first edition in 1886 was called *Beiträge zur Analyse der Empfindungen*), 6th edn (Jena, 1911), p. 24, note 1.
8 Cf. Manfred Diersch, *Empiriokritizismus und Impressionismus. Über Beziehungen zwischen Philosophie, Ästhetik und Literatur um 1900 in Wien* (2nd edn, Berlin, 1977); Judith Ryan, 'Die andere Psychologie. Ernst Mach und die Folgen', in *Österreichische Gegenwart. Die moderne Literatur und ihr Verhältnis zur Tradition*, ed. Wolfgang Paulsen (Berne/Munich, 1980), pp. 11–24; Adalbert Schmidt, 'Die geistigen Grundlagen des Wiener Impressionismus', in *Jahrbuch des wiener Goethevereins* (1974), pp. 90–108.
9 William M. Johnston has discussed this question in *The Austrian Mind: An Intellectual and Social History* (Berkeley, 1972), pp. 181ff.
10 Hermann Broch, *SzL*, p. 153.
11 Robert Musil, *Beitrag zur Beurteilung der Lehren Machs* (Reinbeck/Hamburg, 1980), p. 44.
12 Ernst Mach, *Die Mechanik, in ihrer Entwicklung historisch-kritisch dargestellt*, 4th edn (1901), p. 519.
13 Mach, *Die Analyse der Empfindungen*, p. 299.
14 Cited in Paul-Laurent Assoun, 'Freud et le lien viennois', *Austriaca*, no. 21 (1985), p. 23.
15 David Hume, *Treatise of Human Nature* (1739–40; Harmondsworth, 1969), book I, part 4, section 6, p. 300.
16 Hermann Bahr, 'Das unrettbare Ich', in *Dialog vom Tragischen* (Berin, 1904),

p. 93; also in Bahr, *Zur Überwindung des Naturalismus*, ed. Gotthart Wunberg (Stuttgart, 1968), p. 189.

17 Cf. Gotthart Wunberg, 'Mach und Hofmannsthal', in *Der frühe Hofmannsthal. Schizophrenie als dichterische Struktur* (Stuttgart/Berlin, 1965), pp. 30–3.

18 Hugo von Hofmannsthal, *EGB*, p. 461; *LCL*, p. 11.

19 Hofmannsthal, *EGB*, p. 465; *LCL*, p. 19.

20 Hofmannsthal, *EGB*, pp. 466–7; *LCL*, p. 22.

21 Wunberg, *Der frühe Hofmannsthal*, pp. 106ff.

22 Hugo von Hofmannsthal, *RuA*, vol. 3, pp. 390–1.

23 Hofmannsthal, *EGB*, p. 467; *LCL*, p. 23.

24 Cited in Wunberg, 'Mach und Hofmannsthal', p. 116.

25 Rudolf Kassner, *Sämtliche Werke*, ed. Ernest Zinn, vol. 1 (Pfullingen, 1969), p. 31.

26 Rudolf Kassner, *Das physiognomische Weltbild* (Munich, 1930), p. 249.

27 Document by Hofmannsthal published in *Merkur* 9 (1955), pp. 965ff.; cf. Gerhart Baumann, *Rudolf Kassner – Hugo von Hofmannsthal. Kreuzwege des Geistes* (Stuttgart, 1964).

28 Cf. Wolfdietrich Rasch, 'Aspekte der deutschen Literatur um 1900', in *Zur deutschen Literatur seit der Jahrhundertwende. Gesammelte Aufsätze* (Stuttgart, 1967), pp. 1–48.

29 Rainer Maria Rilke, *SW*, vol. 5, p. 233.

30 Hofmannsthal, *EGB*, pp. 469–70; *LCL*, pp. 28–9.

31 Georg Simmel, *Hauptprobleme der Philosophie* (Leipzig, 1910), p. 15.

32 Hermann Bahr, *Prophet der Moderne. Tagebücher 1888–1904*, ed. Reinhard Farkas (Vienna, 1987), p. 48.

33 Published in Berlin in 1903.

34 Fritz Mauthner, *Gottlose Mystik* (Dresden, n.d.), p. 129.

35 Cf. Fritz Mauthner, *Sprache und Leben*, ed. Gershon Weiler (Salzburg, 1986), pp. 47ff.

36 Ibid., p. 189 (extract from *Die drei Bilder der Welt*, Erlangen, 1925).

37 Mauthner, *Sprache und Leben*, p. 195.

38 Ibid., pp. 208–9.

39 *Meister Eckeharts Schriften und Predigten*, ed. Gustav Landauer (Berlin, 1903). On Magister Eckhart's fortunes at the turn of the century cf. Jochen Schmidt, *Ohne Eigenschaften. Eine Erläuterung zu Musils Grundbegriff* (Tübingen, 1975), pp. 53–63.

40 *Die Eitelkeit und Unsicherheit der Wissenschaften*, ed. Fritz Mauthner (Munich, 1913).

41 Cf. Fritz Mauthner, *Der letzte Tod des Gautana Buddha* (Munich/Leipzig, 1913).

42 Mauthner, *Sprache und Leben*, p. 253 (extract from *Der Atheismus und seine Geschichte im Abendlande*, 4 vols, Stuttgart/Berlin, 1920–3).

43 Mauthner, *Sprache und Leben*, p. 255 (extract from *Die drei Bilder der Welt*).

44 Ludwig Wittgenstein, *Tractatus Logico-Philosophicus*, trans. D. F. Pears and B. F. McGuinness (London, 1961), p. 37; cf. Allan Janik and Stephen Toulmin, *Wittgenstein, Vienne et la modernité* (Paris, 1978), chs 5 and 6.

45 Wittgenstein, *Tractatus*, pp. 149–51; cf. Jacques Bouveresse, 'Mysticisme et logique', in *Wittgenstein: la rime et la raison. Science, éthique et esthétique* (Paris, 1973), pp. 21ff.

46 Cited in Kurt Wuchterl and Adolf Hübner, *Ludwig Wittgenstein in Selbstzeugnissen und Bilddokumenten* (Reinbeck/Hamburg, 1979), p. 53.

47 Cf. Jacques Le Rider, 'Musil et Maeterlinck', in *Bruxelles–Vienne, 1890–1938*, ed. Fabrice van de Kerckhove (Brussels, 1987), pp. 38–47.

48 Bahr, 'Die Decadence' (1891), in *Studien zur Kritik der Moderne* (Frankfurt, 1894).

49 Paul Bourget, *Essais de psychologie contemporaine* (1883; definitive expanded edn Paris, 1901), p. 7.
50 Letter from Hermann Broch to Daniel Brody, 27 July 1930, in Hermann Broch, *Briefe 1 (1913–1938)*, in *Kommentierte Werkausgabe*, ed. Paul Michael Lützeler, vol. 13.1 (Frankfurt, 1981), p. 97.
51 Assoun, 'Freud et le lien viennois', pp. 182–3.
52 Cf. Schmidt, *Ohne Eigenschaften*.
53 Robert Musil, *MoE*, p. 753.
54 Quoted in J. Le Rider, *Le cas Otto Weininger. Racines de l'antiféminisme et de l'antisémitisme* (Paris, 1982), p. 94.
55 Weininger, *GuCh*, pp. 101–2.
56 Ibid., *GuCh*, pp. 220–1.
57 Otto Weininger, *Taschenbuch*, ed. Artur (sic) Gerber (Leipzig/Vienna, 1919), reprinted in the Munich edn of *GuCh* (1980), pp. 601ff.
58 Cf. Jean-Louis Vieillard-Baron, 'Microcosme et macrocosme chez Novalis', *Les Études Philosophiques* (April/June 1983), pp. 195–208.
59 Bahr, *Prophet der Moderne* , p. 69.
60 Weininger, *SC*, p. 182; *GuCh*, pp. 233–4.
61 Weininger, *SC*, p. 183; *GuCh*, p. 236.
62 Friedrich Schlegel, Fragment 16 of the *Athenaeum*; 'Athenäums-Fragmente', no. 16, in *Charakteristiken und Kritiken I, 1796–1801*, ed. Hans Eichner, vol. 2 of *Kritische Friedrich Schlegel Ausgabe*, ed. Ernst Behler (Munich/Paderborn, 1967), p. 148.
63 Georg Simmel, *Lebensanschauung. Vier metaphysische Kapitel* (2nd edn, Munich/Leipzig, 1922), pp. 193, 226; cf. Simmel, *Das individuelle Gesetz. Philosophische Exkurse*, ed. Michael Landmann (new edn, Frankfurt, 1987).
64 Marie-Louise Roth, 'Robert Musil zum Problem der Ethik', in *Gedanken und Dichtung. Essays zu Robert Musil* (Sarrebruck, 1987), pp. 75–97.
65 Musil, *GW2*, p. 1017.
66 Quoted in Roth, 'Robert Musil zum Problem der Ethik', p. 88.
67 Quoted in ibid., p. 76.
68 Musil, *GW2*, pp. 1076ff.
69 Friedbert Aspetsberger, 'Anderer Zustand, Für – In – Musil und einige Zeitgenossen', in *Robert Musil. Untersuchungen*, ed. Uwe Baur and Elisabeth Castex (Königstein, 1980), pp. 46–66.
70 Hofmannsthal, *RuA*, vol. 3, pp. 40–1.
71 Jochen Schmidt, *Geschichte des Genie-Gedankens*, vol. 2: *Von der Romantik bis zum Ende des Dritten Reichs* (Darmstadt, 1985), pp. 129–68.
72 Johann Willibald Nagl, Jacob Zeidler and Eduard Castle (eds), *Deutsche-öster-reichische Literaturgeschichte*, vol. 4: *Von 1890 bis 1918* (Vienna, 1937), p. 1806.
73 Schmidt, 'Von der Romantik', p. 188.
74 Cf. the first part of the thesis by Hildegard Châtellier, 'Conservatisme et fascisme. Esthétique et idéologie dans l'oeuvre théorique de la droite littéraire en Allemagne de 1890 à 1933' (doctoral dissertation, University of Paris IV-Sorbonne, 1986).

Chapter 4   Narcissus

1 Christopher Lasch, *The Culture of Narcissism* (New York, 1979).
2 Gilles Lipovetsky, *L'ère du vide. Essais sur l'individualisme contemporain* (Paris, 1983).

3   Cf. Richard Sennett, *The Fall of Public Man* (New York, 1976); and the contributory volume *Pathologies of the Modern Self: Postmodern Studies on Narcissism, Schizophrenia and Depression*, ed. David Michael Levin (New York/London, 1987).

4   Charles Baudelaire, *Le peintre de la vie moderne*, in *Oeuvres complètes*, ed. Claude Pichois, vol. 2 (Paris, 1976), p. 719.

5   Charles Baudelaire, *Les paradis artificiels*, in *Oeuvres complètes*, vol. 1 (Paris, 1975), p. 440.

6   Lou Andreas-Salomé, NaD.

7   In French as Lou Andreas-Salomé, *Carnets intimes des dernières années, 1934–36*, trans. Jacques Le Rider (Paris, 1983).

8   Lou Andreas-Salomé, *Friedrich Nietzsche in seinen Werken* (1894), ed. Ernst and Thomas Pfeiffer (Frankfurt, 1983), pp. 263–4.

9   Ibid.

10   Lou Andreas-Salomé, *Lebensrückblick. Grundriss einiger Lebenserinnerungen*, ed. Ernst Pfeiffer (5th edn, Frankfurt, 1974), p. 9.

11   Lou Andreas-Salomé, *Mein Dank an Freud. Offener Brief an Professor Freud zu seinem 75. Geburtstag* (Vienna, 1931), pp. 9–20.

12   Cf. Andreas-Salomé, *Carnets*, p. 40.

13   Andreas-Salomé, *Mein Dank an Freud*, p. 17.

14   Ibid., p. 24.

15   Walter Gebhard, *Der Zusammenhang der Dinge. Weltgleichnis und Naturverklärung im Totalitätsbewusstsein des 19. Jahrhunderts* (Tübingen, 1984).

16   Hugo von Hofmannsthal, 'Aufzeichungen aus dem Nachlass, 1894', *RuA*, vol. 3, p. 376.

17   Paul-Laurent Assoun, *Introduction à l'épistémologie freudienne* (Paris, 1981), pp. 39–50.

18   Sigmund Freud, *GW*, vol. 13, p. 57.

19   *Sigmund Freud and Lou Andreas-Salomé: Letters*, ed. Ernst Pfeiffer, trans. William and Elaine Robson-Scott (London, 1972), p. 32 (letter of 30 July 1915).

20   Goethe (actually Georg Christoph Tobler), 'Die Natur', in *Werke, Hamburger Ausgabe*, ed. Erich Trunz (7th edn, Munich, 1975), vol. 13, p. 45.

21   Sigmund Freud, *SE*, vol. 21, pp. 64–5; *GW*, vol. 14, p. 422.

22   David James Fisher, 'Sigmund Freud and Romain Rolland: The Terrestrial Animal and His Great Oceanic Friend', *American Imago* 33.1 (1976), pp. 1–59.

23   Paul-Laurent Assoun, 'Freud et la mystique', in *L'entendement freudien. Logos et Anankè* (Paris, 1984), pp. 101–35.

24   Marie Moscovici, 'Une femme et la psychanalyse', introduction to Lou Andreas-Salomé, *L'amour du narcissisme. Textes psychanalytiques*, trans. into French by Isabelle Hildenbrand (Paris, 1980), pp. 21–2.

25   *Sigmund Freud and Lou Andreas-Salomé: Letters*, ed. Pfeiffer, pp. 60–1.

26   Andreas-Salomé, NaD, p. 362.

27   NaD, p. 363.

28   NaD, p. 369.

29   *The Freud Journal of Lou Andreas-Salomé*, trans. S. A. Leavey (London, 1965), pp. 56–7.

30   Rose-Maria Gropp, '*Das Weib* existiert nicht', in *Lou Andreas-Salomé*, ed. Rilke-Gesellschaft (Karlsruhe, 1986), pp. 46–54.

31   Andreas-Salomé, NaD, p. 366.

32   Ibid., pp. 366–7.

33   Ibid., p. 367.

34   Ibid. Andreas-Salomé's article in *Imago* was in fact the first (partial) publication

of Rilke's poem. She quotes only the second poem called 'Narziss' ('Dies also: geht von mir aus...') – in Rainer Maria Rilke, *SW*, vol. 2, pp. 56–7; but she omits the fourth verse ('Was sich dort bildet...'), the second line of verse 5, the last line of verse 6, and the whole of the seventh and final verse ('Hob es sich so in ihrem Traum herbei...'). These omissions by Lou Andreas-Salomé suppress all mentions in Rilke's poem of the women Narcissus had seduced.

35 Rainer Maria Rilke, 'Narcissus'.

36 Cf. Rainer Maria Rilke, Second Duino Elegy, in *SW*, vol. 1, p. 689.

37 Marcel Kunz, *Narziss. Untersuchungen zum Werk R. M. Rilkes* (Bonn, 1970); Hanspeter Zürcher, *Stilles Wasser. Narziss und Ophelia in der Dichtung und Malerei um 1900* (Bonn, 1975).

38 Cf. Rainer Maria Rilke, 'Dame vor dem Spiegel' (1907), in *SW*, vol. 1, p. 624.

39 Here I refer the reader to my article 'Le narcissisme orphique de Rainer Maria Rilke', *Europe*, no. 719 (March 1989), pp. 104–20. There I analyse the affinities between Rilke, Andreas-Salomé and Kleist's 'On the Puppet Theatre'. (On this point cf. Elisabeth Lenk, *Die unbewusste Gesellschaft*, Munich, 1983, pp. 72–7, an interpretation of Kleist's essay in the light of the narcissism theory; Rudiger Görner, 'Zur Kleist-Dichtung der späten Lou Andreas-Salomé', in *Lou Andreas-Salomé*, ed. the Rilke-Gesellschaft, pp. 80–91.)

40 Jean Laplanche and Jean-Bertrand Pontalis, *Vocabulaire de la psychanalyse* (Paris, 1967), p. 264.

41 Heinz Henseler, 'Die Theorie des Narzissmus', in the series Kindlers Psychologie des 20. Jahrhunderts, *Tiefenpsychologie*, vol. 1: *Sigmund Freud. Leben und Werk*, ed. Dieter Eicke (Basle, 1976), pp. 453–71; Heribert Wahl, *Narzissmus? Von Freuds Narzissmustheorie zur Selbstphilosophie* (Stuttgart, 1985).

42 André Haynal, preface to *Le narcissisme. L'amour de soi*, in the series Les Grandes Découvertes de la Psychanalyse (Paris, 1985), p. 15.

43 André Green, *Narcissisme de vie, narcissisme de mort* (Paris, 1984); cf. *Die neuen Narzissmustheorien: Zurück ins Paradies?*, ed. Psychanalytisches Seminar Zurich and Gabi Dörmann-Höh (Frankfurt, 1981).

44 Henseler, 'Theorie des Narzissmus'.

45 Sigmund Freud, *The Ego and the Id*, in *SE*, vol. 19, p. 45; *GW*, vol. 13, p. 275. Cf. 'Das grosse Reservoir der Libido', appendix 2 in Freud, *Studienausgabe*, ed. Alexander Mitscherlich, Angela Richards and James Strachey (Frankfurt, 1975), vol. 3: *Psychologie des Unbewussten*, pp. 327–30.

46 Sigmund Freud, *Outline of Psychoanalysis*, in *SE*, vol. 23, p. 150; *GW*, vol. 17, pp. 72–3.

47 Sigmund Freud, *Narcissism: An Introduction*, in *SE*, vol. 14, pp. 76–7; *GW*, vol. 10, p. 142.

48 Sigmund Freud, *Totem and Taboo*, in *SE*, vol. 13, p. 89; *GW*, vol. 9, pp. 110–11.

49 Ibid., p. 110.

50 Sigmund Freud, 'A Case of Paranoia', in *SE*, vol. 12; *GW*, vol. 8, p. 302 (Freud quotes a maxim of Rumi as adapted by Rückert).

51 Sigmund Freud, *Group Psychology and the Analysis of the Ego*, in *SE*, vol. 18, p. 124; *GW*, vol. 13, p. 38.

52 Mikkel Borch-Jakobsen, *Le sujet freudien* (Paris, 1982), pp. 77ff.

53 Freud, *Narcissism*, in *SE*, vol. 14, pp. 88–9; in *GW*, vol. 10, p. 155.

54 Ibid., in *SE*, p. 89; *GW*, p. 156.

55 Sarah Kofmann, *L'énigme de la femme. La femme dans les textes de Freud* (Paris, 1980), p. 67.

56 Jacqueline Cosnier, 'Lou Andreas-Salomé et la sexualité féminine', *Revue Française de Psychanalyse*, no. 37 (1973), pp. 65–78.

57   Cf. Angela Livingstone, 'Essays on Love and Woman', ch. 9 of *Lou Andreas-Salomé* (London, 1984).
58   Sigmund Freud, *Instincts and Their Vicissitudes*, in *SE*, vol. 14, pp. 118–19; *GW*, vol. 10, p. 226.
59   Monique Schneider, *Freud et le plaisir* (Paris, 1986), p. 56.
60   Freud, *Instincts*, in *SE*, vol. 14, p. 136; *GW*, vol. 10, p. 229.
61   Sigmund Freud, *Civilization and its Discontents*, in *SE*, vol. 21, p. 145; *GW*, vol. 14, p. 506.
62   Freud, *A Childhood Memory of Leonardo da Vinci*, in *GW*, vol. 8, p. 170.
63   Cf. Sigmund Freud, *GW*, vol. 8, p. 417.
64   Lou Andreas-Salomé, 'Der Mensch als Weib' (1899), in *Die Erotik*, ed. Ernst Pfeiffer (Munich, 1979), p. 22.
65   Andreas-Salomé, NaD, p. 386.
66   Rilke, *SW*, vol. 1, pp. 275–6.
67   Hermann Bahr, *Prophet der Moderne. Tagebücher 1888–1904*, ed. Reinhard Farkas (Vienna, 1987), p. 68.
68   In my article 'Le narcissisme orphique de R. M. Rilke' (see note 39 above), I emphasize the 'Narcissus satisfied' myth of the 1900s with reference to Rudolf Kassner and Robert Musil, with a survey of the Narcissus myth after Ovid (from Plotinus to Rousseau). German Idealism and Romanticism, which marked the triumph of the individualist principle, were sometimes dominated by the narcissistic fantasy of integrating the whole of reality into the self, as Hartmut Böhme and Gernot Böhme have shown in relation to Kant, Fichte and Schelling: *Das Andere der Vernunft. Zur Entwicklung von Rationalitätsstrukturen am Beispiel Kants* (2nd edn, Frankfurt, 1985), pp. 124ff., 160ff. In my article I also mention Goethe's *Werther*, Schlegel's *Lucinda* and Brentano's *Godwi*. For the 1900s I show the resurgence of 'Orphic narcissism' in Gide, Wilde and Valéry, and also later in Bachelard and Marcuse.
69   Leopold von Andrian, *Der Garten der Erkenntnis*, ed. Walter H. Perl (Frankfurt, 1970), p. 58. Cf. Gerhart Baumann, 'Leopold Andrian; "Das Fest der Jugend"', in *Vereinigungen, Versuche zu neuerer Dichtung* (Munich, 1972), pp. 1–35; Jens Rieckmann, 'Narziss und Dionysos: Leopold von Andrian "Der Garten der Erkenntnis"', *Modern Austrian Literature* 16.2 (1983), pp. 65–81; Ursula Renner, *Leopold von Andrians 'Garten der Erkenntnis'. Literarisches Paradigma einer Identitätskrise in Wien um 1900* (Berne, 1981). When he wrote this novella, Andrian was also embarking on a work, never finished, which he called 'Buch der Weltanschauung'. This metaphysical sketch retraces the creation of the world and suggests that the universe was born of self-love. Original matter, desiring to see its own beauty, created the universe to that end. The creation of the world would therefore be the result of a 'perversion'. Humans, too, Andrian wrote, came forth from this original matter; human narcissism, particularly that of the artist, corresponds with world narcissism, and culminates in knowledge of the cosmos. MS TuA (Tagebücher und Aufzeichnungen), 'Buch der Weltanschauung', Marbach no. 47, Deutsches Literaturarchiv/Schiller-Nationalmuseum.
70   Andrian, *Garten der Erkenntnis*, p. 4.
71   Ibid., p. 32.
72   Green, *Narcissisme de vie*, p. 198.
73   Andrian, *Garten der Erkenntnis*, p. 42.
74   Otto Rank, 'Der Doppelgänger', *Imago*, no. 3 (1914), pp. 97–164; reprinted in *Psychoanalytische Literaturinterpretationen*, ed. Jens Malte Fischer (Tübingen, 1980), pp. 104–88.

75 Hugo von Hofmannsthal, *GD1*, pp. 282–3.
76 Ibid., p. 291.
77 Ibid., p. 287.
78 Ibid., p. 288.
79 Jens Rieckmann, 'Narziss und Dionysos'.
80 Hugo von Hofmannsthal, *Der Tor und der Tod*, in *GD1*, p. 297.
81 Hugo von Hofmannsthal, *EGB*, p. 464.
82 Ibid., p. 463.
83 Hugo von Hofmannsthal/E. Karg von Bebenburg, *Briefwechsel*, ed. Mary E. Gilbert (Frankfurt, 1966), p. 80.
84 Ibid.
85 Ibid., p. 81.
86 Ibid., pp. 81–2.
87 Ibid., p. 83.
88 Jost Hermand, afterword to *Lyrik des Jugendstils*, ed. Jost Hermand (Stuttgart, 1964), p. 64.
89 Ibid., pp. 70, 72.
90 Cf. Ernst Bloch, *Geist der Utopie, bearbeitete Neuauflage der zweiten Fassung von 1923, Gesamtausgabe*, vol. 3 (Frankfurt, 1964), pp. 32–40; Gérard Raulet, *Natur und Ornament. Zur Erzeugung von Heimat* (Darmstadt-Neuwied, 1987), pp. 91–100. In an essay entitled 'Linienkunst', *Ver Sacrum*, no. 5 (Vienna, 1902), pp. 111–22, Franz Servaes showed the connection between the Nietzschean cult of *Leben* and secessionist ornamentalism. Cf. Jürg Mathes (ed.), *Theorie des literarischen Jugendstils* (Stuttgart, 1984), pp. 95ff.
91 Ludwig Hevesi, *Acht Jahre Sezession* (Vienna, 1906; reprint Klagenfurt, 1984), p. 449.
92 Ibid.
93 Pierre Hadot, 'Le mythe de Narcisse et son interprétation par Plotin', *Nouvelle Revue de Psychanalyse*, no. 13 (1976), p. 84.
94 Hevesi, *Acht Jahre Sezession*, pp. 266–7.
95 Andreas-Salomé, *Friedrich Nietzsche*, p. 264.
96 Andreas-Salomé, NaD, p. 381.

Chapter 5   Schreber, Weininger, Hofmannsthal

1 Masud R. Khan, 'L'orgasme du moi dans l'amour bisexuel', *Nouvelle Revue de Psychanalyse*, no. 7 (1973), pp. 315ff.
2 D. W. Winnicott, 'Clivage des elements masculins et féminins chez l'homme et chez la femme', *Nouvelle Revue de Psychanalyse*, no. 7 (1973), p. 301. In *Making Sex: Body and Gender from the Greeks to Freud* (Harvard University Press, 1990), Thomas Laqueur shows that two traditional models of discourse on sexuality coexist and are opposed in Western tradition, one based on a 'single sex' and one on 'two sexes'. He believes that since the eighteenth century the two sexes have been seen as radically distinct both anatomically and physiologically: *sex* is fundamental, whereas social *gender* is merely an expression of it. But in Freud we find some traces of the 'single sex' model. Freud, and still more the Freudians, describe the body as being unisexual. Whereas social, medical and political discourse are still pervaded by the notion that the two sexes are biologically distinct, Freud asks how woman develops away from her childhood bisexual inclinations. To Freud, 'man' and 'woman' denote not the 'natural' sex but the

'theatrical' gender which forces individuals into the roles society and culture demand of them.

3   Winnicott, 'Clivage', p. 308.
4   Ibid., p. 309.
5   Ibid., p. 314.
6   Sigmund Freud, *SE*, vol. 21, pp. 57–145; *GW*, vol. 14, pp. 423ff.
7   Freud, *GW*, vol. 14, p. 430.
8   Jacqueline Cosnier, 'Freud et la féminité', in *Destins de la féminité* (Paris, 1987), pp. 47–8.
9   Daniel Paul Schreber, *DeN*, p. 31.
10 Ibid., pp. 30–1.
11 Ibid., p. 37.
12 Ibid., p. 40.
13 Ibid., pp. 61–2.
14 Ibid., p. 69.
15 Ibid., pp. 123–4.
16 Sigmund Freud, *SE*, vol. 12, pp. 3–84; *GW*, vol. 8, pp. 239–320.
17 C. G. Jung, *Wandlungen und Symbole der Libido. Beiträge zur Entwicklungsgeschichte des Denkens*, 1911–12.
18 Elias Canetti, 'Der Fall Schreber', in *Masse und Macht* (Hamburg, 1960), pp. 500–33.
19 Sigmund Freud, *SE*, vol. 12, p. 42; *GW*, vol. 8, p. 277.
20 Richard Alewyn, *Über Hugo von Hofmannsthal* (4th edn, Göttingen, 1967), pp. 174ff. Waltraud Wietholter, *Hofmannsthal oder Die Geometrie des Subjekts: Psychostrukturelle und ikonographische Studien zum Prosawerk* (Tübingen, 1990), has suggested a new interpretation of the tale which emphasizes the motifs of alchemism and the occult; this allows a new interpretation of the beryl brooch.
21 Jens Rieckmann, 'Von der menschlichen Unzulänglichkeit: zu Hofmannsthals *Das Märchen der 672. Nacht*', *German Quarterly* 54 (1981), pp. 298–310.
22 Marcel Brion, 'Andreas de Hugo von Hofmannsthal', in *L'Allemagne romantique*, vol. 4, *Le voyage initiatique*, II (Paris, 1978), pp. 240–60; cf. M. Brion, 'Versuch einer Interpretation der Symbole im *Marchen der 672. Nacht*', in *Deutsche Erzählungen von Wieland bis Kafka*, ed. Jost Schillemeit (Frankfurt, 1966).
23 Hugo von Hofmannsthal, *EGB*, p. 45.
24 Ibid.
25 Ibid., p. 46.
26 Ibid., p. 48.
27 Ibid.
28 Ibid., p. 47.
29 Ibid., p. 52. This passage may be compared with an autobiographical note by Hofmannsthal, dated 1904 (*RuA*, vol. 3, pp. 457–8).
30 Cf. Dorrit Cohn, '"Als Traum erzählt": The Case for a Freudian Reading of Hofmannsthal's *Märchen der 672. Nacht*', *Deutsche Vierteljahresschrift für Literaturwissenschaft und Geistesgeschichte* 54.2 (1980), p. 291: 'The girl becomes a magnified reflection of his own repressed self'; cf. also Marlies Janz, *Marmorbilder. Weiblichkeit und Tod bei Clemens Brentano und Hugo von Hofmannsthal* (Konigstein, 1986), chapter on the *Märchen*, pp. 128–48.
31 Hofmannsthal, *EGB*, p. 46.
32 Ibid., p. 49.
33 Ibid., p. 53.
34 Ibid., p. 46.
35 Ibid., p. 49.

36 In 1906 or 1907 Hofmannsthal noted in a copy of Weininger's *Sex and Character* (1906 edition), in the margin alongside a Keats quotation in one of Weininger's notes – 'The merchant's son' (cf. Hugo von Hofmannsthal, *Sämtliche Werke, Kritische Ausgabe*, vol. 28. *Erzählungen I*, ed. Ellen Ritter (Frankfurt, 1975), notes, p. 210). The same quotation from Keats figures in a letter dated January 1907 to Stefan Gruss (Hofmannsthal, *Briefe 1900–9*, Vienna, 1937, p. 254).

37 Cf. David D. Perkins, *English Romantic Writers* (New York, 1967), p. 1220.

38 Otto Weininger, *SC*, p. 147; *GuCh*, p. 240.

39 Weininger, *SC*, p. 233; *GuCh*, p. 308.

40 In the first sketch of the 'Tale' Hofmannsthal described 'the servant' as 'aged forty-eight, face berry-brown like the dictator Sulla', *EGB*, p. 64.

41 Ibid., pp. 50–1.

42 Ibid., p. 51.

43 This is still clearer in the first sketch for the tale, ibid., pp. 64–5.

44 Ibid., p. 52.

45 Cf. Bernhard J. Dotzler, 'Beschreibung eines Briefes. Zum Handlungsauslösenden Moment in Hugo von Hofmannsthals "Märchen der 672. Nacht"', in *Hofmannsthal-Forschungen*, vol. 8 (Freiburg, 1985), pp. 49–54. His interpretation seems to me to be too general and imprecise.

46 Eugene Weber, 'Hofmannsthal und Oscar Wilde', in *Hofmannsthal-Forschungen*, vol. 1 (Basle, 1971), pp. 99–106; cf. Sander J. Gilman, 'The Pervert: Wilde in Germany', in *Disease and Representation: Images of Illness from Madness to AIDS* (Ithaca, NY, 1988), pp. 156–62. Gilman talks of 'Oscar Wilde's image as the homosexual writer *par excellence* in the German-speaking lands' around 1900.

47 Hofmannsthal to his father, 9 August 1895, in Hofmannsthal, *Briefe I. 1890– 1901* (Berlin, 1935), p. 167.

48 Arthur Schnitzler to Hofmannsthal, 26 November 1895, in Hugo von Hofmannsthal/Arthur Schnitzler, *Briefwechsel*, ed. Thérèse Nickl and Heinrich Schnitzler (Frankfurt, 1964), pp. 63–4.

49 Cohn, '"Als Traum erzählt"'.

50 Tzvetan Todorov, *The Fantastic: A Structural Approach to a Literary Genre*, trans. Richard Howard (Ithaca, NY, 1973), p. 25.

51 Freud, *SE*, vol. 17, pp. 234–52; *GW*, vol. 12, pp. 248ff.

52 Hofmannsthal, *RuA*, vol. 1, p. 362; cf. Wolfgang Köhler, *Hugo von Hofmannsthal und 'Tausandundeine Nacht'* (Berne/Frankfurt, 1972). Paul, the hero of Beer-Hofmann's *Der Tod Georgs*, is reading the *Thousand and One Nights* (Beer-Hofmann, *GW*, Frankfurt, 1963, pp. 531–2). Hermann Broch observes that the narrative style of the young Hofmannsthal is similar to that of the oriental tale (Brock, *SzL*, p. 321).

53 Hofmannsthal, *RuA*, vol. 2, p. 195.

54 Hofmannsthal, *EGB*, p. 54.

55 Ibid., p. 65.

56 Ibid., p. 54.

57 Ibid., p. 55.

58 Roger Bauer, *Das Treibhaus oder der Garten des Bösen. Ursprung und Wandlung eines Motivs der Dekadenzliteratur*, Akademie der Wissenschaften und der Literatur, Mainz (Wiesbaden, 1979): on Hofmannsthal see pp. 18ff.

59 Hofmannsthal, *EGB*, p. 56.

60 Ibid., p. 59.

61 Ibid., pp. 59–60; in the first sketch of the 'Tale', Hofmannsthal gave a rather different meaning to the soldier's cry: 'They asked him if he wanted to buy some tobacco, they bothered him' (p. 65).

62　Ibid., p. 60.
63　Freud, *SE*, vol. 10, p. 36 n1; *GW*, vol. 7, p. 271.
64　Hofmannsthal, *EGB*, p. 61.
65　Ibid.
66　Ibid., p. 62.
67　Ibid., pp. 469–70.
68　Klaus Theweleit, *Männerphantasien* (2 vols, Frankfurt, 1977–8).
69　Rainer Maria Rilke, *Florenzer Tagebuch* (1898; Frankfurt, 1982), p. 29. These visions were probably influenced by Nietzsche's *Birth of Tragedy*, where the genius in action is conflated with the 'Urkünstler der Welt' (Nietzscke, *KSA*, vol. 1, pp. 47–8).
70　Robert J. Stoller, 'Faits et hypothèses. Un examen du concept freudien de bisexualité', *Nouvelle Revue de Psychanalyse*, no. 7 (1973), p. 153.
71　Freud, *SE*, vol. 21, p. 90; *GW*, vol. 14, p. 449.
72　Freud, *SE*, vol. 21, pp. 94–5; *GW*, vol. 14, p. 455.
73　Jacques Le Rider, *La cas Otto Weininger. Racines de l'antiféminisme et de l'antisémitisme* (Paris, 1982); enlarged German translation *Der Fall Otto Weininger* (Vienna, 1985).
74　August Strindberg to Artur (*sic*) Gerber, 8 December 1908, in Otto Weininger, *Taschenbuch und Briefe an einen Freud*, ed. Artur Gerber (Vienna/Leipzig, 1919), p. 101; also in Weininger, *GuCh*, p. 651.
75　Peter Sloterdijk, *Kritik der zynischen Vernunft* (Frankfurt, 1983), p. 480.
76　Antonin Artaud, *Héliogabale ou l'anarchiste couronné*, in *Oeuvres complètes*, vol. 7 (Paris, 1967), pp. 105–6.
77　Antonin Artaud, *Les Tarahumaras*, in *Oeuvres complètes*, vol. 9 (2nd edn, Paris, 1979), p. 13.
78　Antonin Artaud, *Les nouvelles révélations de l'Être* (1937), in *Oeuvres complètes*, vol. 7, p. 171.
79　Artaud, *Les Tarahumaras*, pp. 24–5 (this part of the work, 'Le rite du Peylots chez les Tarahumaras', was written at Rodez in 1943).
80　Artaud, *Les nouvelles révélations de l'Être*, p. 159.
81　Heinz Politzer, *Franz Kafka: Parable and Paradox* (Ithaca, 1962); Hartmut Binder, *Kafka in neuer Sicht* (Stuttgart, 1976), pp. 374ff.
82　Franz Kafka, *Tagebücher 1910–1923*, in Kafka, *Gesammelte Werke*, ed. Max Claude David, vol. 7 (Frankfurt, 1976), p. 231.
83　Franz Kafka, letter of 9 August 1920, in *Briefe an Milena*, enlarged edn ed. J. Born and M. Müller (Frankfurt, 1983), pp. 197–8.
84　Gerald Stieg, 'Kafka und Weininger', in *Dialog der Epochen. Studien zur Literatur des 19. und 20. Jahrhunderts*, Festschrift for Walter Weiss, ed. Eduard Beutner, Josef Donnenberg, Adolf Haslinger et al. (Vienna, 1987), pp. 88–100.
85　Franz Kafka, *Hochzeitsvorbereitungen auf dem Lande*, in *Gesammelte Werke*, vol. 6, p. 173.
86　Rainer Stach, *Kafkas erotischer Mythos. Eine ästhetische Konstruktion des Weiblichen* (Frankfurt, 1987).
87　Sigmund Freud, *Three Essays*, in *SE*, vol. 7, p. 143 n1; *GW*, vol. 5, p. 43 n1.
88　In *Nouvelle Revue de Psychanalyse*, no. 7 (Paris, 1973), p. 20.
89　Cf. 'Le corps', part 1 in *Le fait féminin*, ed. Evelyne Sullerot (Paris, 1978), pp. 27–218.
90　Weininger, *SC*, pp. 301–2; *GuCh*, pp. 403–4.
91　Freud, *SE*, vol. 19, p. 258; *GW*, vol. 14, p. 30.
92　Andreas Puff-Trojan, 'Im Zeichen des Androgynen. Weininger, Serner und die

Folgen einer Bewegung', in *Das Lila Wien um 1900*, ed. Neda Bei, Wolfgang Forster, Hanna Hacker and Manfred Lang (Vienna, 1986), pp. 97–107.

93 Jens Rieckmann, 'Ästhetizismus und Homoerotik: Hugo von Hofmannsthals "Das Bergwerk zu Falun"', *Orbis Literarum*, no. 43 (1988), pp. 1–11.

94 Günter Mecke, *Franz Kafkas offenbares Geheimnis. Eine Psychopathographie* (Munich, 1982); Ramon G. Mendoza, *Outside Humanity: A Study of Kafka's Fiction* (Lanham, NY/London, 1986); Evelyn Torton Beck, 'Kafka's Triple Bind: Women, Jews and Sexuality', in *Kafka's Contextuality*, ed. Alan Udoff (Baltimore, 1986), pp. 342–88.

95 Charles Baudelaire, 'Fusées', in *Oeuvres complètes*, ed. Claude Pichois, vol. 1 (Paris, 1975), pp. 651–2.

96 Gert Mattenklott, *Bilderdienst. Ästhetische Opposition bei Beardsley und George* (2nd edn, Frankfurt, 1985), pp. 325–6.

97 Cf. Henry-Louis de La Grange, *Gustav Mahler, chronique d'une vie*, vol. 3: *Le génie foudroyé (1907–1911)* (Paris, 1984), pp. 770ff.; Ernest Jones, *LWSF*, vol. 2, pp. 88–9; Jens Malte Fischer, 'Ein Spaziergang. Sigmund Freud und Gustav Mahlers Leiden', *Merkur* 42.9–10 (Sept.–Oct. 1988), pp. 775–87.

98 Quoted in Fischer, 'Ein Spaziergang', pp. 783–4.

99 Ibid., p. 786.

100 Freud, *SE*, vol. 11, p. 183; *GW*, vol. 8, p. 82.

101 Quoted in Fischer, 'Ein Spaziergang', p. 787.

102 Hans H. Eggebrecht, *Die Musik Gustav Mahlers* (Munich, 1982), p. 274.

103 Cf. Theodor W. Adorno, *Mahler: eine musikalische Physiognomik* (Frankfurt, 1960).

104 Alma Mahler-Werfel, *Mein Leben* (Frankfurt, 1960), p. 37.

105 Ibid., p. 40.

106 Émile Delavenay, *D. H. Lawrence, l'homme et le genèse de son oeuvre* (Paris, 1969), and 'D. H. Lawrence, Otto Weininger and Rather Raw Philosophy', in *D. H. Lawrence: New Studies* (London, 1984).

107 Martin Green, *The Von Richthofen Sisters* (London, 1974).

108 Éliane Amado Lévy-Valensi suggests a systematic reconstruction in *Les niveaux de l'être et de la connaissance dans leur relation au problème du mal* (Paris, 1962).

109 D. H. Lawrence, *Apropos of Lady Chatterley*, in Phoenix edition of *Lady Chatterley's Lover* (London, 1960), p. 34.

110 D. H. Lawrence, *Women in Love* (Cambridge critical edn, 1987), p. 293.

111 Lawrence, *Lady Chatterley's Lover*, p. 274.

112 Lawrence, *Women in Love*, p. 201.

113 Weininger, *SC*, p. 170; *GuCh*, p. 221.

114 D. H. Lawrence, *Apocalypse* (Harmondsworth, 1974), p. 126.

115 Georges Bataille, *L'érotisme* (Paris, 1957), p. 22.

116 Weininger, *Taschenbuch und Briefe*.

117 Otto Weininger, *Über die letzten Dinge* (reprint Munich, 1980), p. 184.

118 Iwan Bloch, *Das Sexualleben unserer Zeit* (3rd edn, Berlin, 1907), p. 532.

119 Paul Julius Moebius, *Über den physiologischen Schwachsinn des Weibes* (4th edn, Halle, 1902); Heinrich Schurtz, *Altersklassen und Männerbünde* (Berlin, 1902); Benedikt Friedländer, *Renaissance des Eros Uranios* (Berlin, 1904); Edwin Bab, *Frauenbewegung und Freundesliebe* (Berlin, 1904).

120 Norbert Grabowsky, *Die Zukunftsreligion und Zukunftswissenschaft auf Grundlage der Emanzipation des Mannes vom Weibe* (Leipzig, 1897).

121 Bloch, *Sexualleben*, p. 538.

122 Arthur Schnitzler, Journal, 23 October 1892, in *Hofmannsthal-Forschungen III*.

Arthur Schnitzler: Hugo von Hofmannsthal, Charakteristik aus den Tagebüchern, ed. Norbert Altenhofer and Wolfram Mauser (Freiburg, 1975), p. 17.

123   Cf. Hofmannsthal, *Roman-Biographie (Andreas, etc.)*, vol. 30 of *Sämtliche Werke, Kritische Ausgabe*, ed. Manfred Pape (Frankfurt, 1982).

124   Fritz Martini, *Das Wagnis der Sprache, Interpretationen deutscher Prosa von Nietzsche bis Benn* (Stuttgart, 1954).

125   W. G. Sebald, 'Venezianisches Kryptogramm. Hofmannsthals *Andreas*', in *Die Beschreibung des Unglücks. Zur österreichischen Literatur von Stifte bis Handke* (Salzburg/Vienna, 1985), pp. 61–77. Waltraud Wietholter decodes 'Andreas' as a 'hermetico-alchemical cryptogram'.

126   Hofmannsthal, *EGB*, p. 305.

127   Ibid., p. 287.

128   Ibid., p. 265.

129   Ibid., p. 287.

130   Ibid., p. 291.

131   This is suggested e.g. by Richard Alewyn, *Über Hugo von Hofmannsthal*, p. 130.

132   Hofmannsthal, *EGB*, p. 308.

133   Ibid., p. 211.

134   Ibid., pp. 255ff.

135   Ibid., pp. 232–3; Ritchie Robertson, 'The Theme of Sacrifice in Hofmannsthal's "Das Gespräch über Gedichte" and "Andreas"', *Modern Austrian Literature* 23.1 (1990), pp. 19–33.

136   Hofmannsthal, *EGB*, p. 234.

137   Ibid., p. 217.

138   Ibid., p. 274.

139   Ibid.

140   Ibid., p. 277.

141   Morton Prince, *The Dissociation of Personality: A Biographical Study in Abnormal Psychology* (New York, 1906); on Hofmannsthal's reading of this book cf. Alewyn, *Über Hugo von Hofmannsthal*.

142   On the image of the Madonna in the nineteenth century cf. Stéphane Michaud, *Muse et madone. Visages de la femme de la Révolution Française aux apparitions de Lourdes* (Paris, 1985).

143   Hofmannsthal, *EGB*, p. 272.

144   Ibid., p. 300.

145   Ibid., p. 283.

146   Hofmannsthal, *Roman-Biographie*, p. 23.

147   Hofmannsthal, *EGB*, p. 199.

148   Hofmannsthal, *Roman-Biographie*, pp. 160, 179, 201.

149   Hofmannsthal, *EGB*, pp. 283–4.

150   Ibid., p. 284.

151   Ibid., p. 285.

152   Achim Aurnhammer, *Androgynie. Studien zu einem Motiv in der europäischen Literatur* (Cologne/Vienna, 1986), pays some attention to *Andreas* (pp. 246–58). He emphasizes the frequent incidents of transvestism in the story by which women are taken for men and vice versa, and suggests that Hofmannsthal was inspired by an 'androgynous ideal'.

153   Letter cited in Hofmannsthal, *Roman-Biographie*, p. 369.

Chapter 6   The Feminine at Work in (Post)Modernity

1   Otto Weininger, *SC*, pp. 2–3; *GuCh*, pp. 4–5.
2   Ernst Mach, *Die Analyse der Empfindungen* (5th edn, Jena, 1906), p. 5.
3   Weininger, *SC*, p. 79; *GuCh*, pp. 97–8.
4   Ibid., p, 90.
5   Jacob Burkhardt, *The Civilization of the Renaissance in Italy*, trans. S. G. C. Middlemore (3rd edn, London, 1950), p. 343.
6   Weininger, *SC*, p. 73; *GuCh*, p. 90.
7   Christian David, 'Les belles différences', *Nouvelle Revue de Psychanalyse*, no. 7 (1973), pp. 248–9.
8   Cf. André Green, 'Le genre neutre', *Nouvelle Revue de Psychanalyse*, no. 7 (1973), pp. 251ff.
9   Heinrich von Treitschke, *Deutsche Geschichte im 19. Jahrhundert* (3rd edn, 1892), vol. 1, p. 47.
10   Wilhelm Dilthey, 'Erinnerungen an deutsche Geschichtsschreiber', *Gesammelte Schriften*, vol. 11 (Stuttgart, 1960), p. 223. This Prussian 'masculinity' was a favourite theme with Julius Langbehn, e.g. in *Rembrandt als Erzieher* (Leipzig, 1890). Langbehn wrote: 'In the marriage between Prussia and Germany it is unquestionably Prussia who takes the husband's part' (p. 203). Nietzsche makes the same diagnosis on Bismarck's Germany in *The Twilight of Idols*: 'It is no superior culture that has ultimately become prevalent with this modern tendency, nor is it by any means delicate taste, or noble beauty of the instincts; but rather a number of virtues more manly than any that other European countries can show' (in *CW*, vol. 16, p. 50; *KSA*, vol. 6, p. 102).
11   Franz Grillparzer, *König Ottokars Glück und Ende*, in *Sämtliche Werke*, ed. Peter Frank and Karl Pörnbacher, vol. 1 (2nd edn, Munich, 1969), p. 1037.
12   Hugo von Hofmannsthal, 'Maria Theresia', in *RuA*, vol. 2, pp. 452–3.
13   Hugo von Hofmannsthal, 'Wir Österreicher und Deutschland', in *RuA*, vol. 2, pp. 395–6.
14   Hugo von Hofmannsthal, 'Preusser und Österreicher', in *RuA*, vol. 2, p. 460.
15   Johann Jakob Bachofen, *Das Mutterrecht. Eine Untersuchung über die Gynaikokratie der altern Welt nach ihrer religiösen und rechtlichen Natur*, ed. Hans-Jürgen Heinrichs (Frankfurt, 1975).
16   Cf. Ernst Bloch, 'Bachofen, Gaia-Themis und Naturrecht', ch. 15 of *Naturrecht und menschliche Würde*, in Bloch, *Gesamtausgabe*, vol. 6 (Frankfurt, 1961), pp. 126–7.
17   Ibid., p. 119.
18   Bloch, *Naturrecht und menschliche Würde*, p. 114.
19   Eugen Wolff, 'Die jüngste deutsche Literaturströmung und das Prinzip der Moderne', in *Die literarische Moderne. Dokumente zum Selbstverständnis der Literatur um die Jahrhundertwende*, ed. Gotthart Wunberg (Frankfurt, 1971), p. 40.
20   Cf. Dieter Schickling, *Abschied von Walhall. Richard Wagners erotische Gesellschaft* (Stuttgart, 1983).
21   Richard Wagner, *Siegfried*, ed. Wilhelm Zentner (Stuttgart, 1973), p. 74.
22   Ibid., p. 33.
23   Richard Wagner, *Gotterdämmerung*, ed. Wilhelm Zentner (Stuttgart, 1969), p. 24.
24   Richard Wagner, 'Über das Männliche und Weibliche in Kultur und Kunst', in *Mein Denken*, ed. Martin Gregor-Dellin (Munich, 1982), p. 410.

25   Richard Wagner, *Das braune Buch. Tagebuchaufzeichnungen 1861–1882*, ed. Joachim Bergfeld (Zurich/Freiburg, 1975), p. 245.

26   Friedrich Nietzsche, *CW*, vol. 8, pp. 13–14; *KSA*, vol. 6, p. 23.

27   Nietzsche, *CW*, vol. 8, p. 41; *KSA*, vol. 6, p. 44.

28   Nietzsche, *CW*, vol. 8, p. 50; *KSA*, vol. 6, p. 51.

29   Nietzsche, *CW*, vol. 10, p. 269; *KSA*, vol. 3, p. 569.

30   Luce Irigaray, *Amante marine. De Friedrich Nietzsche* (Paris, 1980).

31   Jacques Derrida, *Epérons. Les styles de Nietzsche* (Paris, 1978), pp. 40, 50. Cf. David Farrell Krell, *Postponements: Woman, Sensuality and Death in Nietzsche* (Bloomington, 1986); Sarah Kofman, 'Des femmes', in *Nietzsche et la scène philosophique* (Paris, 1979), pp. 285–94.

32   Rudolf Lothar, 'Kritik in Frankreich' (1891), in *Das junge Wien*, ed. Gotthart Wunberg (Tübingen, 1976), vol. 1, p. 211.

33   Peter Altenberg, 'Autobiography', in *Was der Tag mir zuträgt* (Berlin, 1901).

34   Egon Friedell emphasized that the brevity of Altenberg's texts was what made them 'modern': 'Peter Altenberg. Zu seinem 50. Geburtstag. Am 8 März 1909', in Friedell, *Abschaffung des Genies, Essays bis 1918*, ed. Heribert Illig (Vienna/Munich, 1982), p. 58.

35   Altenberg, 'Autobiographie'.

36   Hermann Bahr, 'Loris', in *Die Überwindung der Naturalismus*, ed. Gotthart Wunberg (Stuttgart, 1968), p. 161.

37   Julia Kristeva, *La révolution du langage poétique* (Paris, 1974). John E. Jackson, *Passions du sujet* (Paris, 1990), develops the idea that the process of literary creation is fundamentally 'bisexual': the feminine images of engendering (pregnancy, birth) are balanced by the masculine images of shaping and imprinting. Language, which is feminine in nature, is worked on by writing, which is masculine. This idea was suggested by Paul Federn in his comments on Freud's lecture on Leonardo, given to the Viennese Society for Psychoanalysis on 1 December 1909: 'The bisexual inclinations of genius have often been pointed out: a great artist must be a *father*, but also a *mother*.' See *Protokolle der Wiener Psychoanalytischen Vereinigung*, ed. Herman Nunberg and Ernst Federn, vol. 2: *1908–10* (Frankfurt, 1977), p. 318.

38   Stéphane Mallarmé, *Oeuvres complètes* (Paris, 1945), p. 261.

39   Sigmund Freud, *SE*, vol. 8, p. 125; *GW*, vol. 6, p. 140.

40   *Baudelaire par Théophile Gautier*, ed. Claude-Marie Senninger (Paris, 1986), p. 145.

41   Charles Baudelaire, 'Le peintre de la vie moderne', in *Oeuvres complètes*, ed. Claude Pichois (Paris, 1976), vol. 2, pp. 685ff.

42   Leo Bersani, *Baudelaire and Freud* (Berkeley/Los Angeles/London, 1977), pp. 11–15.

43   Charles Baudelaire, 'Le spleen de Paris', XII, 'Les foules', in *Oeuvres complètes*, vol. 1, p. 291.

44   Michel Butor, *Histoire extraordinaire. Essai sur un rêve de Baudelaire* (Paris, 1961), p. 85; cf. Pierre Emmanuel, *Baudelaire, la femme et Dieu* (2nd edn, Paris, 1982); Tamara Bassim, *La femme dans l'oeuvre de Baudelaire* (Neuchâtel, 1974).

45   Cf. the remarks by Michèle Montrelay on writing and femininity in *L'ombre et le nom. Sur la féminité* (Paris, 1977).

46   Felix Dörmann, 'Was ich liebe', from *Neurotica* (1891), in *Die Wiener Moderne. Literatur, Kunst und Musik zwischen 1890 und 1910*, ed. Gotthart Wunberg (Stuttgart, 1981), p. 57.

47   Cf. Jens Malte Fisher, 'Felix Dörmann: Sensationen', in *Fin de siècle. Kommentär*

zu einer Epoche (Munich, 1978), pp. 114–24; Jens Rieckmann, 'Lyrik aus der Dekadenz', in *Aufbruch in die Moderne, die Anfänge des jungen Wien* (Königstein, 1985), pp. 111–24.

48 Karl Kraus, 'Wiener Lyriker', in *Frühe Schriften, 1892–1900*, ed. Johannes J. Braakenburg, vol. 1 (Munich, 1979), pp. 89–91.

49 Karl Kraus, 'Die demolirte Literatur', in ibid., vol. 2, pp. 285–6.

50 Kraus, 'Wiener Lyriker', p. 91. Here Kraus was writing about Richard Specht, a rival of Dörmann's.

51 Hugo von Hofmannsthal, *RuA*, vol. 1, p. 114.

52 Henri-Frédéric Amiel, *Du journal intime*, ed. Roland Jaccard (Brussels, 1987), p. 71.

53 Ibid., p. 78.

54 Ibid., p. 98.

55 Friedrich Kittler points out the socioeconomic realities which fed this fantasy of feminized writing: *Aufschreibesysteme, 1800–1900* (Munich, 1985), pp. 356ff.

56 Hofmannsthal, *LCL*, p. 17.

57 Cf. Dominique Tassel, 'En lisant *Une Lettre*', *Poétique*, no. 66 (1987), p. 147.

58 Thomas Mann, *Tonio Kröger*, in *Sämtliche Erzählungen* (Frankfurt, 1963), p. 233.

59 Lou Andreas-Salomé, 'Der Mensch als Weib' (1899), in *Die Erotik. Vier Aufsätze*, ed. Ernst Pfeiffer (Munich, 1979), p. 22.

60 Werner Hofmann, *Gustav Klimt* (Salzburg, 1970), pp. 22–3; Carl E. Schorske, *Fin-de-Siècle Vienna* (London, 1979), pp. 226–7, 231–43.

61 On this see Claude Quiguer, *Femmes et machines de 1900. Lecture d'une obsession modern style* (Paris, 1979); and the contributed volume, *Ornament und Askese im Zeitgeist des Wien der Jahrhundertwende*, ed. Alfred Pfabigan (Vienna, 1985).

62 Adolf Loos, 'Keramika', in *Trotzdem. 1900–31* (1st edn 1931), ed. Adolf Opel (Vienna, 1982), p. 59.

63 Kraus, 'Die demolirte Literatur', p. 278.

64 Karl Kraus, 'Nachts. III Zeit', *Die Fackel*, nos 389–90 (mid-Dec. 1913), p. 37; *Aphorismen*, in *Schriften*, ed. Christian Wagenknecht (Frankfurt, 1986), p. 343.

65 Nike Wagner, *Geist und Geschlecht. Karl Kraus und die Erotik der Wiener Moderne* (Frankfurt, 1982), p. 54.

66 Kraus, *Aphorismen*, p. 341; 'Nachts'.

67 Burkhardt Rukschcio and Roland Schachel, *Adolf Loos* (Salzburg, 1982), p. 51.

68 Adolf Loos, 'Damenmode', in *Ins Leere gesprochen* (1st edn 1921), ed. Adolf Opel (Vienna, 1981), p. 130.

69 Karl Kraus, 'Kehraus', *Die Fackel*, no. 229 (2 July 1907), p. 14; *Aphorismen*, p. 51.

70 Karl Kraus, 'Abfälle', *Die Fackel*, no. 202 (30 April 1906), p. 2; *Aphorismen*, p. 19.

71 Nietzsche, *KSA*, vol. 2, p. 671.

72 Ibid., pp. 213–14.

73 Ernst Gombrich, *Ornament und Kunst. Schmucktrieb und Ordnungssinn in der Psychologie des dekorativen Schaffens* (Stuttgart, 1982), pp. 71–2; cf. Roger Bauer, in 'Décadence: histoire d'un mot et d'une idée', *Cahiers Roumains d'Histoire Littéraire*, no. 1 (Bucharest, 1978), pp. 55–70.

74 Reinhard Gerlach, *Musik und Jugendstil der Wiener Schule, 1900–1908* (Laaber, 1985).

75 Charles Rosen, *Schönberg* (London, 1976), pp. 31ff.

76 Weininger, *SC*, p. 302; *GuCh*, p. 402.

77 Cf. Karl Kraus, *Sittlichkeit und Kriminalität* (Vienna, 1908).

78   Theodor W. Adorno, *Dissonanzen* (Göttingen, 1956), p. 13.
79   Nietzsche, *KSA*, vol. 7, p. 202.
80   Ludwig Wittgenstein, *Briefe an Ludwig von Ficker*, ed. Georg Henrik von Wright and Walter Methlagl (Salzburg, 1969), p. 35.
81   William W. Bartley III, *Wittgenstein, A Life* (Philadelphia, 1973). (Specialists have expressed doubts about this book.)
82   Paul-Laurent Assoun, *Freud et la femme* (Paris, 1983), p. 192.
83   Sigmund Freud, *Civilization and its Discontents*, in *SE*, vol. 18, p. 141; *GW*, vol. 14, p. 463.
84   Sigmund Freud, *Group Psychology and the Analysis of the Ego*, in *SE*, vol. 18, p. 116; *GW*, vol. 13, pp. 158–9.
85   Paul-Laurent Assoun, 'La femme, "symptôme" de l'organisation sociale', in *Le sexe du pouvoir. Femmes, hommes, pouvoirs dans les organisations*, ed. Nicole Aubert, Eugène Enriquez and Vincent de Gaulejac (Paris, 1986), pp. 394–409.
86   Freud, *SE*, vol. 18, p. 141; *GW*, vol. 13, p. 159.
87   Ibid., p. 116; p. 128.
88   Alfred Adler, 'Trotz und Gehorsam', *Monatshefte für Pädagogik und Schulpolitik* 2.9 (1910), pp. 321–8; cf. Almuth Bruder-Bezzel, *Alfred Adler. Die Entstehungsgeschichte einer Theorie im historischen Milieu Wiens* (Göttingen, 1983), pp. 85ff.
89   Alfred Adler, 'Der psychische Hermaphroditismus im Leben und in der Neurose', *Fortschritte der Medizin* 28.16 (1910), pp. 486–93.
90   Cf. Wilhelm Stekel, works published in the series Störungen des Trieb- und Affektlebens (Berlin/Vienna): 1, *Nervöse Angstzustände und ihre Behandlung* (3rd edn, 1924); 2, *Onanie und Homosexualität. Die sexuelle Parapathie* (1st edn, 1917; 3rd edn, 1923); 3, *Die Geschlechtskälte der Frau* (2nd edn, 1921); 4, *Die Impotenz des Mannes. Die psychologischen Störungen der männlichen Sexualfunktion* (2nd edn, 1923); etc.
91   Alfred Adler, *Über den nervösen Charakter* (4th edn 1928; Frankfurt, 1972), p. 122. Adler took the term 'fiction' from Hans Vaihinger, *Die Philosophie des Als Ob* (1911).
92   In French in Georg Groddeck, *Un problème de femme*, trans. Roger Lewinter (Paris, 1979), p. 123. Cf. Jacquy Chemouni, 'Un monde humain issu de la femme', in *Georg Groddeck, psychanalyste de l'imaginaire* (Paris, 1984), pp. 287–303.
93   Groddeck, *Problème de femme*, pp. 124ff.
94   Ibid.
95   Georg Simmel, *Philosophische Kultur* (3rd edn 1923; Berlin, 1983), p. 238; *Schriften zur Philosophie und Soziologie der Geschlechter*, ed. Heinz-Jürgen Dahme and Klaus Christian Köhnke (Frankfurt, 1985); Jean-Louis Vieillard-Baron, 'L'image de la femme dans l'oeuvre de Georg Simmel', in *Georg Simmel, la sociologie et l'expérience du monde moderne*, ed. Patrick Watier (Paris, 1986), pp. 281–5; Lewis A. Coser, 'Georg Simmels vernachlässigter Beitrag zur Soziologie der Frau', in *Georg Simmel und die Moderne. Neue Interpretationen und Materialien*, ed. Heinz-Jürgen Dahme and Otthein Rammstedt (Frankfurt, 1984), pp. 80–90; Gabriella Bonacchi, 'La culture de la femme. Ambigüité et fonction critique d'une figure classique de l'ère moderne: Georg Simmel', in *Femmes et fascismes*, ed. Rita Thalmann (Paris, 1986), pp. 31–40; Cornelia Klinger, 'G. Simmels "Weibliche Kultur" wiedergelesen', *Studia Philosophica* 47 (1988), pp. 141–66, and *Georg Simmel*, Cahier du GRIF 40 (Paris, 1989).
96   Walter Benjamin to Herbert Belmore, 23 June 1913, in *Briefe*, ed. Gershom Scholem and Theodor W. Adorno (Frankfurt, 1966), vol. 1, pp. 65–6; cf. Christine Buci-Glucksmann, 'Féminité et modernité: Walter Benjamin et

l'utopie du féminin', in *Walter Benjamin et Paris*, ed. Heinz Wismann (Paris, 1982), pp. 403–20 (cf. Christine Buci-Glucksmann, 'Walter Benjamin et l'ange de l'histoire. Une archéologie de la modernité', in *L'écrit du temps*, no. 2 (Paris, 1982), pp. 45–85, and *Walter Benjamin und die Utopie des Weiblichen* (Hamburg, 1984)).

97 Buci-Glucksmann, 'Feminité et modernité', pp. 404–5.
98 Dolf Oehler, *Pariser Bilder I. Antibourgeoise Ästhetik bei Baudelaire, Daumier und Heine* (Frankfurt, 1979), pp. 241ff.
99 Michel Espagne and Michael Werner, 'Bauplan und bewegliche Struktur im Baudelaire. Zu einigen Kategorien von Benjamins Passagen-Modell', *Recherches Germaniques*, no. 17 (1987), p. 104.
100 Magnus Hirschfeld, *Sittengeschichte des Weltkrieges* (2 vols, Leipzig, 1930), p. 437; cf. Alfred Pfoser, 'Verstörte Männer und emanzipierte Frauen', in *Aufbruch und Untergang. Österreichische Kultur zwischen 1918 und 1938*, ed. Franz Kadrnoska (Vienna, 1981), pp. 205–6.
101 Paul Federn, *Die vaterlose Gesellschaft. Zur Psychologie der Revolution* (Vienna, 1919).
102 Cf. K. R. Eissler, *Freud und Wagner-Jauregg vor der Kommission zur Erhebung militärischer Pflichtverletzungen* (Vienna, 1979).
103 Robert Musil, 'Der bedrohte Oedipus', in *GW2*, pp. 528ff.
104 Giovanni Lista, *Futurisme. Manifestes, documents, proclamations* (Lausanne, 1973), p. 87.
105 Cf. Alberto Cavaglion and Michel David, 'Weininger und die italienische Kultur', in *Otto Weininger, Werk und Wirkung*, ed. Jacques Le Rider and Norbert Leser (Vienna, 1984), p. 42.
106 In Lista, *Futurisme*, pp. 329–30.
107 Gilles Lipovetsky, *L'ère du vide* (Paris, 1983), pp. 8–12.
108 Ibid., p. 33.
109 Ibid., pp. 43–4.
110 Ibid., p. 80.
111 Elisabeth Badinter, *L'Un est l'Autre. Des relations entre hommes et femmes* (Paris, 1986), p. 305.
112 Ibid., p. 340; also Elisabeth Badinter, *XY. De l'identité masculine* (1992), which concludes that 'the boundaries of masculine and feminine have become blurred. And from now on every man must ask himself what his true identity is. Men, mutilated, torn between contradictory images, forever required to repress an essential part of themseles, are a dying breed.... Prelude to a completely new kind of harmony between the sexes.' These insights of Badinter's are confirmed by Evelyne Sullerot, *Quels pères, quels fils?* (Paris, 1992): she writes that sexual liberation and women's liberation have meant that 'patriarchy has been buried without ceremony and without regret', and that in this war 'fathers are the biggest losers' (p. 254). Further confirmation is found in the contributory volume *Des hommes et du masculin*, ed. Bulletin d'Information des Études Féminines (Lyon, 1992), especially in Marc Chabot's essay, 'Genre masculin ou genre flou'.
113 Gerard Höhn, '*Lucinde* ou le nouveau (dé-)règlement', *Romantisme*, no. 20 (1978), p. 28.
114 Jean-Jacques Nattiez, *Wagner androgyne. Essai sur l'interprétation* (Paris, 1990).
115 See the numbers of *Cahiers de l'Hermétisme* entitled 'L'Androgyne' (1986) and 'L'Androgyne dans la litterature' (1990).
116 Michael Maffesoli, *L'ombre de Dionysos. Contribution à une sociologie de l'orgie* (Paris, 1982), p. 209.

117   François Roustaing, *Le bal masqué de Giacomo Casanova* (Paris, 1984), p. 67.
118   Manfred Frank, *Der kommende Gott. Vorlesungen über die Neue Mythologie* (Frankfurt, 1982), p. 20.
119   Robert Musil, 'Isis und Osiris' (April-May 1923), in *GW2*, p. 465; cf. Achim Auernhammer, 'L'androgyne dans *L'homme sans qualités*', *L'Arc*, pp. 35–40, and *Androgynie* (Cologne/Vienna, 1986), pp. 285–99; Jacques Perronnet, '"Isis et Osiris" ou le discours mythique', in *Cahier de L'Herne Robert Musil* (Paris, 1981) (*L'Herne*, no. 41), pp. 225–9.
120   Robert Musil, *MoE*, part 3, ch. 25, p. 905; *MWQ*, vol. 3, p. 282.
121   Robert Musil, *Tagebücher*, ed. Adolf Frisé (Reinbeck/Hamburg, 1976), vol. 1, p. 598.
122   Ibid., p. 601.
123   Musil, *MoE*, part 3, ch. 51, pp. 1230–1. (The projected translation of this concluding part of *MWQ* was never published.)
124   Musil, *MoE*, part 3, ch. 52, p. 1232.
125   Jean Baudrillard, *La transparence du mal. Essai sur les phenomènes extrêmes* (Paris, 1990), pp. 15–16.
126   Musil, *MoE*, p. 1235.

Chapter 7   Law of the Father, Law of the Mother, and Otto Gross

1   Sigmund Freud, 'Great is Diana of the Ephesians', in *SE*, vol. 12, pp. 342–4; *GW*, vol. 8, pp. 360–1.
2   Ibid., p. 343; p. 361.
3   Paul-Laurent Assoun, *L'entendement freudien. Logos et Ananké* (Paris, 1984), p. 134.
4   On the life and works of Otto Gross, see Emanuel Hurwitz, *Otto Gross, Paradies-Sucher zwischen Freud und Jung* (Zurich, 1979); cf. Jacques Le Rider, 'De la psychanalyse à la révolution. Le destin d'Otto Gross (1877–1920)', introduction to Otto Gross, *La révolution sur le divan*, trans. Jeanne Etore (Paris, 1988).
5   Ernest Jones, *LWSF*, vol. 2, p. 33. Part of what Jones says is inaccurate, in particular the last sentence: 'In the First World War he enlisted in a Hungarian regiment, but before it was over his life came to an end through murder and suicide.'
6   Otto Gross, *Das Freudsche Ideogenitätsmoment und seine Bedeutung im manisch-depressiven Irresein Kraepelins* (Leipzig, 1907).
7   Hans Driesch (1867–1941), biologist, famous for his work on the embryology of sea-urchins, author of philosophical works beginning with his book *Naturbegriffe und Naturteile* (1904). Gross refers in particular to *Vitalismus als Geschichte und Lehre* (1905).
8   Gross, *Freudsche Ideogenitätsmoment*, p. 14.
9   Ibid., pp. 14–15.
10   Ibid., pp. 7–8.
11   *The Freud–Jung Letters*, ed. W. McGuire, trans. R. Manheim and R. F. C. Hull (London, 1974), p. 90; Sigmund Freud and Carl Gastav Jung, *Briefwechsel* (Frankfurt, 1974), pp. 99–100.
12   Jones, *LWSF*, vol. 3, pp. 157–8.
13   Erich Mühsam, *Namen und Menschen. Unpolitische Erinnerungen* (1st edn Leipzig,

1931; Berlin, 1977), p. 117. Gross's influence on Mühsam was considerable: see Hurwitz, *Otto Gross*, p. 114.

14 Cf. *Monte Verità. Antropologia locale come contributo alla riscoperta di una topografia sacrale moderna*, ed. Harald Szeemann (Milan, 1978); Robert Landmann, *Ascona Monte Verità* (Frankfurt/Berlin, 1979).

15 Martin Green, *The Von Richthofen Sisters* (London, 1974).

16 Wolfgang Schwentker, 'Leidenschaft als Lebensform. Erotik und Moral bei Max Weber und im Kreis um O. Gross', in *Max Weber und seine Zeitgenossen*, ed. Wolfgang J. Mommsen and W. Schwentker (Göttingen, 1988), pp. 661–81.

17 Marianne Weber, *Max Weber, ein Lebensbild* (Tübingen, 1926), p. 376.

18 Ibid., pp. 376–7.

19 Max Weber, *Gesammelte Aufsätze zur Religionssoziologie* (Tübingen, 1963), vol. 1, p. 560.

20 See Hurwitz, *Otto Gross*; Le Rider, 'De la psychanalyse à la révolution'.

21 Otto Gross, 'Elterngewalt', *Die Zukunft* 65 (1908), pp. 79–80.

22 Hans Gross, 'Degeneration und Deportation', *Politische und Anthropologische Revue* (Autumn 1905); Otto Gross, *Über psychopathologische Minderwertigkeiten* (Vienna/Leipzig, 1909).

23 Roger Bauer, 'Décadence: histoire d'un mot et d'une idée', *Cahiers Roumains d'Histoire Littéraire*, no. 1 (1978), pp. 55–70; and Bauer, 'Décadence bei Nietzsche. Versuch einer Bestandsaufnahme', in *Literary Theory and Criticism*, Studies in Honour of René Wellek, ed. Joseph P. Strelka (Berne/New York, 1984), pp. 35–68.

24 Friedrich Nietzsche, *CW*, vol. 7, pp. 207–8; *KSA*, vol. 2, pp. 187–8.

25 Hans Gross, *Handbuch für Untersuchungsrichter, Polizeibeamte, Gendarmen, usw.* (Graz, 1893); *Criminal Investigation* (1898; London, 1962).

26 Sigmund Freud, *Psychopathology of Everyday Life*, in *SE*, vol. 6, p. 254n; *GW*, vol. 4, p. 164.

27 Sigmund Freud, 'Tatbestandsdiagnostik und Psychoanalyse' (1906), in *GW*, vol. 7, p. 7; the first edition was published in Gross's journal *Archiv für Kriminal-Anthropologie und Kriminalistik* 26 (1906).

28 Hans Gross, *Die Erforschung des Sachverhalts strafbarer Handlungen* (Munich, 1902), p. 54.

29 Otto Gross, 'Zur Überwindung der kulturellen Krise', *Die Aktion*, 2 April 1913, p. 386.

30 Ibid., p. 387.

31 Russell Jacoby, *The Repression of Psychanalysis: Otto Fenichel and the Political Freudians* (New York, 1983) – on Gross, pp. 40–5.

32 Hans Jürgen Heinrichs (ed.), *Materialien zu Bachofens 'Das Mutterrecht'* (Frankfurt, 1975).

33 Otto Gross, 'Ludwig Rubiners "Psychoanalysis"', *Die Aktion*, 14 May 1913, pp. 506–7.

34 Otto Gross, 'Die Einwirkung der Allgemeinheit auf das Individuum', *Die Aktion*, 22 Nov. 1913, pp. 1091–5.

35 Otto Gross, 'Anmerkungen zu einer neuen Ethik', *Die Aktion*, 6 Dec. 1913, p. 1142.

36 *Die Aktion*, 20 Dec. 1913; *Revolution*, 20 Dec. 1913.

37 Hurwitz, *Otto Gross*, p. 33.

38 Otto Gross, 'Der Fall Otto Gross', *Die Zukunft*, 28 Feb. 1914, p. 306.

39 Wilhelm Stekel, 'In Memoriam', *Psyche and Eros* 1 (July 1920).

40 Daniel Paul Schreber, *DeN*, pp. 251–61.

41   William G. Niederland, 'Schreber: Vater und Sohn', in Niederland, *Der Fall Schreber* (Frankfurt, 1978), pp. 75–88.
42   Freud, *SE*, vol. 12, p. 51; *GW*, vol. 8, pp. 286–7.
43   Ibid., p. 59; p. 291.
44   Hurwitz, *Otto Gross*, p. 49.
45   Franz Jung, 'Von geschlechtlicher Not zur sozialen Katastrophe' (1923), in *Otto Gross. Von geschlechtlicher Not zur sozialen Katastrophe*, ed. Kurt Kreiler (Frankfurt, 1980), p. 135.
46   Hurwitz, *Otto Gross*, p. 306.
47   Otto Gross, 'Über Destruktionssymbolik', *Zentralblatt für Psychoanalyse und Pychotherapie* (ed. Wilhelm Stekel) 4.11–12 (Aug.–Sept. 1914), p. 533.
48   Otto Gross, 'Die kommunistische Grundidee in der Paradiessymbolik', *Sowjet, kommunistische Monatsschrift*, no. 2 (Vienna, July 1919), p. 21.
49   Ibid., pp. 26–7.
50   Hurwitz, *Otto Gross*, pp. 112ff.
51   Hartmut Scheible has strongly emphasized the narcissism in his afterword to 'George's Death' and in the chapter 'Das Weltreich des Narziss' in his book *Literarischer Jugenstil in Wien* (Zurich, 1984), pp. 93–117.
52   Georg Lukács, *Soul and Form* (London, 1974), p. 111.
53   Dante Gabriel Rossetti, 'Astarte Syriaca (Venus Astarte)', painting of 1877 in Manchester City Art Gallery, no. 1891–5. Cf. Maria Teresa Benedetti, *Dante Gabriel Rossetti* (Florence, 1984), p. 325 and plate 24.
54   Richard Beer-Hofmann, *TG*, p. 33.
55   Ibid., p. 31.
56   Paul, the dreamer, is clearly identified at this point in the text: see Hartmut Scheible's afterword, in ibid., p. 142.
57   Beer-Hofmann, *TG*, p. 33.
58   Flaubert noted while working on *Salammbô* that at Carthage 'religion turns on two ideas, Baal and Astarte: the one terrible and bloodthirsty, the other voluptuous and orgiastic.' Quoted in Anne Green, *Flaubert and the Historical Novel: Salammbô Reassessed* (Cambridge, 1982), pp. 44, 50.
59   Rainer Hank, *Mortifikation und Beschwörung. Zur Veränderung ästhetischer Wahrnehmung in der Moderne am Beispiel des Frühwerkes Richard Beer-Hofmanns* (Frankfurt/Berne/New York, 1984), p. 122.
60   Béatrice Marbeau-Cleirens, *Le sexe de la mère et les divergences des theories psychanalytiques* (Paris, 1987), p. 38; cf. Wolfgang Lederer, *La peur des femmes, ou Gynophobia*, trans. Monique Manin (Paris, 1980).
61   D. H. Lawrence, *Twilight in Italy* (London, 1916); Green, *The Von Richthofen Sisters*, p. 60.
62   Jennifer E. Michaels, *Anarchy and Eros: Otto Gross' Impact on German Expressionist Writers*, Utah Studies in Literature and Linguistics 24 (New York/Berne/Frankfurt, 1983); a first approach to the subject was suggested by Arthur Mitzman, 'Anarchism, Expressionism and Psychoanalysis', *New German Critic*, no. 10 (1977), pp. 77–104.
63   Franz Werfel, *Barbara oder die Frömmigkeit* (Frankfurt, 1988).
64   Ibid., pp. 347–8.
65   Ibid., p. 352.
66   Max Brod, *Das grosse Wagnis* (Leipzig/Vienna, 1918), p. 155.
67   Ibid., p. 173.
68   Ibid., p. 252.
69   Franz Kafka, *Briefe an Milena*, new enlarged edn, ed. J. Born and M. Müller (Frankfurt, 1983), pp. 78–9.

70 Letter to Max Brod, November 1917, in Franz Kafka, *Briefe 1902–1924* (New York, 1958), p. 196.
71 Thomas Anz, 'Jemand musste Otto G. verleumdet haben... Kafka, Werfel, Otto Gross', *Merkur*, no. 2 (1984), pp. 184–91.
72 Walter Müller-Seidel, *Die Deportation des Menschen. Kafkas Erzählung 'In der Strafkolonie' im europäischen Kontext* (Stuttgart, 1986).
73 Letter to Milena, 21 July 1920, in Kafka, *Briefe an Milena*, p. 33.
74 Hartmut Binder, *Kafka in neuer Sicht* (Stuttgart, 1976), pp. 374–95.
75 Marthe Robert, *L'ancien et le nouveau. De Don Quichotte à Franz Kafka* (Paris, 1963), p. 219.
76 Ibid., pp. 283–4.
77 Rainer Stach, *Kafkas erotischer Mythos. Eine ästhetische Konstruktion des Weiblichen* (Frankfurt, 1987).

Chapter 8 Electra, Antigone and Ariadne

1 Marthe Robert, *D'Oedipe à Moïse. Freud et la conscience juive* (Paris, 1974), pp. 95, 99–100.
2 Karl Kraus, 'An einen alten Lehrer', *Die Fackel*, nos 423–5 (May 1916), p. 39.
3 Wendelin Schmidt-Dengler, 'Decadence and Antiquity: The Educational Preconditions of Jung Wien', in *Focus on Vienna 1900: Change and Continuity in Literature, Music, Art and Intellectual History*, ed. Erika Nielsen, Houston German Studies 4 (Munich, 1982), pp. 35ff.
4 Otto Stoessl, 'Ein Wiener Brief' (1897), in *Das junge Wien*, ed. Gotthart Wunberg (Tübingen, 1976), vol. 2, p. 771.
5 Hugo von Hofmannsthal, *Aufzeichnungen*, in *Werke*, ed. Herbert Steiner (Frankfurt, 1973), p. 43.
6 On Schliemann's importance in the history of German culture, cf. Eliza Marian Butler, *The Tyranny of Greece over Germany: A Study of the Influence Exercised by Greek Art and Poetry over Great German Writers of the 18th, 19th and 20th Century* (1935; 2nd edn, Boston, 1958). On the importance of Minoan references see Anton Bammer, 'Wien und Kreta: Jugendstil und minoische Kunst', *Jahreshefte des Österreichischen Archäologischen Institutes* 60, pp. 129–51.
7 Sigmund Freud, *The Complete Letters of Sigmund Freud to Wilhelm Fliess, 1887–1904*, ed. J. M. Masson (Cambridge, Mass., 1985), p. 353.
8 Ibid., p. 391.
9 Ibid., p. 445.
10 Sigmund Freud, *SE*, vol. 21, p. 226; *GW*, vol. 14, p. 519.
11 Paul-Laurent Assoun, 'Logos métapsychologique et archaïque', in Assoun, *L'entendement freudien. Logos et anankè* (Paris, 1984), pp. 146–7.
12 Freud, *SE*, vol. 23, p. 46n; *GW*, vol. 16, pp. 146–7n.
13 Friedrich Nietzsche, *KSA*, vol. 7, p. 45.
14 Secessionist poster reproduced in Carl E. Schorske, *Fin-de-Siècle Vienna* (London, 1979), plate 37, p. 216. The drawing for the poster had been censored and Klimt had had to hide Theseus' nakedness behind some well-placed trees; see the original design, before censorship, in Michael Pabst, *Wiener Grafik um 1900* (Munich, 1984), plate 35, p. 41. The same motif was used for the cover of the special exhibition number of *Ver Sacrum* 1.5–6 (May–June 1898): see Christian M. Nebehay, *Ver Sacrum, 1898–1903* (Munich, 1979), p. 119.

15   Carl E. Schorske, 'Conflit de générations et changement culturel', *Actes de la Recherche en Sciences Sociales*, nos 26–7 (Mar.–Apr. 1979), p. 113.
16   Schorske, *Fin-de-Siècle Vienna*, p. 215n.
17   Louis Séchan and Pierre Lévêque, *Les grandes divinités de la Grèce* (Paris, 1966), pp. 327–8.
18   Pauly Wissowa, 'Gorgon', in *Real-Encyclopädie der classischen Altertumswissenschaft*, vol. 7 (1912).
19   Nietzsche, *CW*, vol. 2, p. 29; *KSA*, vol. 1, p. 270.
20   Paul de Man, *Blindness and Insight: Essays in the Rhetoric of Contemporary Criticism* (3rd edn, Minneapolis, 1985), p. 150.
21   Walter Benjamin, *Das Passagen-Werk*, ed. Rolf Tiedemann (Frankfurt, 1982), p. 72.
22   Freud, *SE*, vol. 18, p. 273; *GW*, vol. 17, p. 47.
23   Werner Hofmann (ed.), *Zauber der Medusa. Europäische Manierismen*, exhibition catalogue, Vienna, 1987; cf. Jean Clair, *Méduse. Contribution à une anthropologie des arts du visuel* (Pairs, 1989), esp. p. 32: 'In times of disturbance, anxiety and confusion [such as the turn of the nineteenth century] it is no longer man who looks on nature and commands her, it is nature, as being radically other than man, who looks on him and turns him to stone.'
24   Charles Baudelaire, 'Madame Bovary par Gustave Flaubert', in *Oeuvres complètes*, ed. Claude Pichois (Paris, 1976), vol. 2, p. 81.
25   Weiner Hofmann, *Gustav Klimt und die Wiener Jahrhundertwende* (Salzburg, 1970), plate 5.
26   Ibid., p. 23.
27   Ludwig Hevesi, *Acht Jahre Sezession* (Vienna, 1906; reprinted Klagenfert, 1984), pp. 81–2.
28   Schorske, *Fin-de-Siècle Vienna*, plate 8.
29   Hugo von Hofmannsthal, *RuA*, vol. 3, p. 452.
30   On this see Michael Worbs, *Nervenkunst. Literatur und Psychoanalyse im Wien der Jahrhundertwende* (Frankfurt, 1983), pp. 259–342. See Ritchie Robertson, '"Ich habe ihm das Beil nicht geben konnen": The Heroine's Failure in Hofmannsthal's *Elektra*', *Orbis Litterarum* 41 (1986), pp. 312–31.
31   Hugo von Hofmannsthal, 'Szenische Vorschriften zu "Elektra" (1903)', *D2*, p. 240.
32   Ibid.
33   Ibid.
34   Ibid., p. 242.
35   Raymond Schwab, *La renaissance orientale* (Paris, 1970).
36   Nietzsche, *CW*, vol. 2, p. 99; *KSA*, vol. 1, p. 333.
37   Walter Jens, *Hofmannsthal und die Griechen* (Tübingen, 1955).
38   Hugo von Hofmannsthal, 'Algernon Charles Swinburne', in *RuA*, vol. 1, p. 146.
39   This parallel between Hofmannsthal and Hölderlin was suggested by Gerhart Baumann in 'Hugo von Hofmannsthal: Elektra', in *Hugo von Hofmannsthal*, ed. Sibylle Bauer, Wege der Forschung 183 (Darmstadt, 1968), p. 301. Nietzsche himself had probably been impressed by this aspect of Hölderlin's interpretation of Greece: see J. P. Stern, *Nietzsche on Tragedy* (Cambridge, 1981), pp. 210ff.
40   Hofmannsthal, 'Ödipus und die Sphinx', in *D2*, p. 381.
41   Friedrich Hölderlin, *Werke und Briefe*, ed. Friedrich Beissner and Jochen Schmidt (Frankfurt, 1969), vol. 2, p. 947.
42   Ibid., p. 940.
43   Antoine Berman, 'Hölderlin ou la traduction comme manifestation', in *Hölderlin vu de France* ed. Bernhard Böschenstein and Jacques Le Rider (Tübingen,

1987). George Steiner has examined the question in *Antigones* (Oxford, 1984), pp. 81–106.

44 Friedrich Hölderlin, 'Anmerkungen zur Antigonä', in Hölderlin, *Werke und Briefe*, p. 791.

45 Ibid., p. 787.

46 Philippe Lacoue-Labarthe, *L'imitation des modernes. Typographie II* (Paris, 1986), pp. 78–83.

47 Hugo von Hofmannsthal/Eberhard von Bodenhausen, *Briefe der Freundschaft*, ed. Dora von Bodenhausen (Dusseldorf, 1953), p. 51.

48 Carl Gustaf Jung, *Versuch einer Darstellung der psychoanalytischen Theorie* (1913).

49 Freud, *SE*, vol. 21, pp. 228–9; *GW*, vol. 16, p. 521.

50 Cf. Hugo von Hofmannsthal, 'Aufzeichnungen zu Reden in Skandinavien' (1916), in *RuA*, vol. 2, pp. 28–42.

51 William H. Rey, *Weltenzweiung und Weltversöhnung in Hofmannsthals griechischen Dramen* (Philadelphia, 1962), p. 81. Critics are still divided over the interpretation of the end of *Elektra*: see Reinhold Schlötterer, 'Elektras Tanz in der Tragödie Hugo von Hofmannsthals', *Hofmannsthal-Blätter*, no. 33 (1986), pp. 47–58.

52 Hofmannsthal, 'Aufzeichnungen'.

53 Rosa Mayreder, *Zur Kritik der Weiblichkeit. Essays* (Jena/Leipzig, 1905), ch. 4: 'Von der Männlichkeit', pp. 102ff.; on Mayreder see Käthe Braun-Prager (ed.), *Rosa Mayreder, Die Krise der Väterlichkeit* (Graz, 1963); Hannah Schnedl-Bubenicek, 'Grenzgängerin der Moderne: Rosa Mayreder', in *Das ewige Klischee. Zum Rollenbild und Selbstverständnis bei Männern und Frauen*, ed. Autorinnengruppe Uni Wien (Vienna/Cologne, 1981), pp. 179–205.

54 Mayreder, *Kritik*, pp. 112–13.

55 Ibid., pp. 117–18. This reflection is still relevant, to judge by the remarks of Robert Stoller: 'The industrial revolution has reduced the importance of man's physical strength; machines work for both sexes. So we now see appearing above the surface man's sense of weakness and his fear of being attacked by his feminine tendencies.' *Sex and Gender* (London, 1968), p. 265.

56 Mayreder, *Kritik*, p. 118.

57 Ibid., p. 129.

58 Ibid., pp. 130ff.

59 Ibid., p. 102.

60 Ibid., p. 150. Mayreder experienced this 'collapse of masculinity' in her own private life. The mental illness of her husband, Karl Mayreder, had as symptom a persecution mania and revolt against 'female tyranny'. Rosa Mayreder, *Tagebücher, 1873–1937*, ed. Harriet Anderson (Frankfurt, 1988), pp. 143 and 226.

61 This point of view seems to constitute an advance objection to the argument of Annelise Maugue in *L'identité masculine en crise au tournant du siècle* (Paris, 1987): 'In the beginning there is the new "New Eve"...' (p. 11). In this study bearing on French culture, Maugue interprets the 'crisis of masculine identity' as a direct consequence of the rise and successful development of the feminist movement. Can the same explanatory schema be applied to the Viennese modernists? It does seem that the Austrian feminist movement around 1900 was one of the least powerful in Europe, though it had some brilliant representatives. See J. Le Rider, *Le cas Otto Weininger* (Paris, 1982), pp. 158–66. Christine Planté, in *La petite soeur de Balzac. Essai sur la femme auteur* (Paris, 1989), reaches a conclusion similar to my own: 'The hate-filled manifestation of the fear of women, masking the fear of change and of oneself, appears at times when social changes give individuals the impression they are facing a vacuum' (p. 106).

62   Ursula Welsch and Michaela Wiesner, *Lou Andreas-Salomé. Vom 'Lebensurgrund' zur Psychoanalyse* (Munich/Vienna, 1988), pp. 134, 157.
63   Mayreder, *Kritik*, p. 158.
64   Ibid., pp. 177–8.
65   *The Freud Journal of Lou Andreas-Salomé*, trans. S. A. Leavey (London, 1965), p. 118.
66   Mayreder, *Kritik*, p. 180.
67   Joan Rivière, 'La feminité en tant que mascarade', *La Psychanalyse*, no. 7 (1964).
68   Rudolph Binion, *Frau Lou: Nietzsche's Wayward Disciple* (Princeton, 1968); analysis along Binion's lines in Michel Matarasso, 'Anthropoanalyse et approche biographique: Lou Andreas-Salomé', *Diogène*, no. 139 (1987), pp. 154–5.
69   Lou Andreas-Salomé, *Fenitschka. Eine Ausschweifung* (1st edn 1898), ed. Ernst Pfeiffer (Frankfurt/Berlin, 1988), p. 81; cf. H. F. Peters, *My Sister, My Wife. Biography of Lou Andreas-Salomé* (London, 1963); Leonie Müller-Loreck, *Die erzählende Dichtung Lou Andreas-Salomés* (Stuttgart, 1976), part 2: 'Die Frau und der Dualismus zwischen Sinnlichkeit und Geist', pp. 73ff.
70   Mayreder, *Kritik*, pp. 229–30.
71   Grete Meisel-Hess, *Weiberhass und Weibverachtung* (Vienna, 1904).
72   Mayreder, *Kritik*, pp. 31ff.; cf. Angelika Schober, 'Nietzsche, le surhumain et l'androgyne', in *Nouvelles lectures de Nietzsche*, ed. Dominique Janicaud, Cahiers L'Âge de l'Homme 1 (Lausanne, 1985), pp. 130–7.
73   *The Freud Journal of Lou Andreas-Salomé*, p. 189.
74   Claudia Böttger, 'Androgynität und Kreativität bei Lou Andreas-Salomé', in *Lou Andreas-Salomé*, ed. Rilke-Gesellschaft (Karlsruhe, 1986), pp. 23–35.
75   Cf. Andreas-Salomé, *Friedrich Nietzsche in seinen Werken* (Vienna, 1894).
76   Mayreder, *Kritik*, p. 297.
77   Nietzsche, *CW*, vol. 10, p. 269; *KSA*, vol. 3, pp. 568–9.
78   Ibid., vol. 8, p. 64; vol. 6, p. 424.
79   Cf. the interesting remarks by Richard Hinton Thomas, *Nietzsche in German Politics and Society, 1890–1918* (2nd edn, La Salle, Ill. 1986), appendix: 'Nietzsche, Women and the Whip', pp. 132–41.
80   Friedrich Nietzsche, Paul Rée and Lou von Salomé, *Die Dokumente ihrer Begegnung*, ed. Ernst Pfeiffer, Karl Schlechta and Ernst Thierbach (Frankfurt, 1971).
81   François Guéry, *Lou Salomé, génie de la vie* (Paris, 1978), pp. 75ff.
82   Paul Bourget, *Essais de psychologie contemporaine*, final expanded edn (Paris, 1901), vol. 1 (1983), p. 12.
83   Letter to Peter Gast, 16 September 1882, in Nietzsche/Rée/Salomé, *Dokumente*.
84   Lou Andreas-Salomé, 'Lebensgebet', in Nietzsche/Rée/Salomé, *Dokumente*, p. 450.
85   Guy de Pourtalès, *Nietzsche en Italie* (Paris, 1929), p. 91. This essay has a trace of the legend that Lou Andreas-Salomé was Jewish – 'a Jewess of Finnish origin' – cf. Matarasso, 'Anthropoanalyse', pp. 144–5.
86   Cf. Charles Andler, 'Sens définitif du mythe d'Ariane-Cosima et de Nietzsche-Dionysos', in *Nietzsche, sa vie et sa pensée*, vol. 2: *Le pessimisme de Nietzsche. La maturité de Nietzsche* (Paris, 1958), pp. 609ff.; discussion of the various possible real-life aliases of the character of Ariadne in Adrian Del Caro, 'Symbolizing Philosophy: Ariadne and the Labyrinth', in *Nietzsche-Studien. Internationales Jahrbuch für die Nietzsche-Forschung* 17 (1988), pp. 125–57; Bernard Pautrat, 'Le fil d'Ariane', in *Versions du soleil. Figures et système de Nietzsche* (Paris, 1972), pp. 314–27.

87   Nietzsche, *CW*, vol. 16, p. 112; *KSA*, vol. 6, p. 348.
88   Nietzsche, *KSA*, vol. 10, p. 433.
89   Nietzsche, *CW*, vol. 16, p. 112; *KSA*, vol. 6, p. 348.
90   Ibid., vol. 4, p. 311; vol. 4, p. 318.
91   Karl Reinhardt, 'Nietzsches Klage der Ariadne', first published in *Die Antike* 11 (1935), pp. 85–109; in *Vermächtnis der Antike* (2nd edn, Göttingen, 1966), pp. 310–33.
92   Nietzsche, *KSA*, vol. 6, pp. 398–401.
93   Ibid., p. 401.
94   Cf. Jacques Derrida, *L'oreille de l'autre. Otobiographies, transferts, traductions*, ed. Claude Levesque and Christie V. McDonald (Montreal, 1982).
95   Del Caro, 'Symbolizing Philosophy', pp. 142ff.
96   Nietzsche, *CW*, vol. 5, p. 43; *KSA*, vol. 5, p. 48.
97   Ibid., p. 263; p. 208.
98   Gilles Deleuze, *Nietzsche* (Paris, 1965), p. 44.
99   Mazzino Montinari, 'Zu Nietzsches Begegnung mit Lou Andreas-Salomé', in *Lou Andreas-Salomé*, ed. Rilke-Gesellschaft, pp. 15–22.
100 Nietzsche, *KSA*, vol. 10, pp. 578–9.
101 Ibid., p. 125.
102 Ibid., vol. 12, p. 402.
103 *The Freud Journal of Lou Andreas-Salomé*, p. 143.
104 Karl Kraus, *Die Fackel*, nos 259–60 (13 July 1908), p. 41; Kraus, *Aphorismen*, ed. Christian Wagenknecht (Frankfurt, 1986), p. 28.
105 Egon Friedell, *Ecce poeta* (Berlin, 1912).
106 Peter Altenberg, 'An Ricarda Huch, 17. 6. 96', in *Leben und Werk in Texten und Bildern*, ed. Hans Christian Kosler (2nd edn, Frankfurt, 1984), p. 100.
107 Kraus, *Die Fackel*, nos 360–2 (7 Nov. 1912), p. 25; *Aphorismen*, p. 272.

Chapter 9   A Triangle of the Times

1   Otto Weininger, *Taschenbuch und Briefe an einen Freund*, ed. Artur Gerber (Leipzig/Vienna, 1919), p. 66; also in an appendix to *GuCh*, p. 626.
2   Éliane Amado Lévy-Valensi, *Les niveaux de l'Être et la connaissance dans leur relation au problème du mal* (Paris, 1962) (chapter 4 of this work is entitled 'Knowledge, Sin and Salvation in Schopenhauer and Lawrence'); Élisabeth de Fontenay, 'La pitié dangereuse', in *Présences de Schopenhauer*, ed. Roger-Pol Droit (Paris, 1989), pp. 83–96.
3   *Parerga et Paralipomena*, in Schopenhauer, *Werke*, ed. Wolfgang von Löhneysen (Darmstadt, 1976), vol. 5, p. 724.
4   Ibid., p. 447.
5   Charles Baudelaire, 'Journaux intimes. Mon coeur mis à nu', in *Oeuvres complètes*, ed. Claude Pichois (Paris, 1975), vol. 1, p. 694.
6   Ibid., p. 706.
7   Ibid., p. 650.
8   Charles Baudelaire, 'Exposition universelle (1855)', in *Oeuvres complètes*, vol. 2, p. 581.
9   Baudelaire, 'Journaux intimes', p. 706.
10 Note by Claude Pichois on p. 1511 of Baudelaire, *Oeuvres complètes*.
11 Lévy-Valensy, *Les niveaux de l'Être*, pp. 626–7.

12   Georg Groddeck, 'Das Zwiegeschlecht des Menschen', in *Psychanalytische Schriften zur Psychosomatik*, ed. Günter Clauser (Wiesbaden, 1966), pp. 258–9.
13   I shall not here repeat my analysis of 'Judaism', chapter 13 of *Sex and Character*: see Jacques Le Rider, *Le cas Otto Weininger. Racines de l'antiféminisme et de l'antisémitisme* (Paris, 1982), pp. 190ff.
14   Roger Lewinter, 'Georg Groddeck: (anti)judaisme et bisexualité', *Nouvelle Revue de Psychanalyse*, no. 7 (1973), p. 200.
15   Sigmund Freud, *SE*, vol. 10, p. 36; *GW*, vol. 7, p. 271.
16   Jean Laplanche and Jean-Bertrand Pontalis, *Vocabulaire de la psychanalyse* (Paris, 1967), p. 75.
17   Freud, *SE*, vol. 10, p. 36n; *GW*, vol. 7, p. 271n.
18   Ibid., vol. 11, p. 95; vol. 8, p. 165.
19   Ibid., footnote.
20   Ibid., vol. 23, p. 91; vol. 16, p. 98.
21   Otto Fenichel, 'Elemente einer psychoanalytischen Theorie des Antisemitismus', in Detlev Claussen, *Vom Judenhass zum Antisemitismus. Materialien einer verleugneten Geschichte* (Darmstadt/Neuwied, 1987), p. 227.
22   Rodolphe Loewenstein, *Psychanalyse de l'antisémitisme* (Paris, 1952), pp. 19–20.
23   Alexander Mitscherlich, 'Die Vorurteilskrankheit. Einleitung zum Thema', *Psyche* 16.5 (1962), pp. 241–5. Fabian Schupper, in his article 'Dynamische Motive des Antisemitismus' in *Jahrbuch der Psychanalyse* 2 (Berne/Stuttgart/Vienna, 1962), pp. 3–24, mentions some interesting variations on the theme. He examines the symbolic meaning of the 'ghetto' as an image of the repressed in the eyes of non-Jews (p. 6). Schupper distinguishes between the old antisemitism (inspired by the revolt against the father) and contemporary antisemitism (inspired by the desire to reunite with the maternal element).
24   Martin Wangh, 'Psychoanalytische Betrachtungen der Dynamik und Genese des Vorurteils, des Antisemitismus und des Nazismus', *Psyche* 16.5 (1962), pp. 273–84.
25   Béla Grunberger, 'Der Antisemit und der Ödipuskomplex', *Psyche* 16.5 (1962), pp. 255–72.
26   Wangh, 'Psychoanalytische Betrachtungen', p. 274.
27   Freud, *SE*, vol. 22, p. 134; *GW*, vol. 15, p. 144.
28   Ibid., vol. 23, p. 105; vol. 16, p. 212.
29   Margarethe Mitscherlich, *Die friedfertige Frau. Eine psychoanalytische Untersuchung zur Aggression der Geschlechter* (Frankfurt, 1985).
30   Jean-François Lyotard, *Heidegger et 'les juifs'* (Paris, 1988), pp. 14–15.
31   Ibid., p. 29.
32   Ibid., p. 43.
33   Ibid., p. 45.
34   Ibid., p. 47.
35   Otto Weininger, *SC*, p. 305; *GuCh*, p. 407. The antisemites habitually used 'Jew' and 'non-Jew' to denote antithetical figures within a manicheistic view of modernity (e.g. Wilhelm Dolles, *Das Jüdische und das Christliche als Geistesrichtung*, 1921); the 'Jew', the evil genius, could get in everywhere, even into the heart of an externally 'Christian' consciousness.
36   Weininger, *SC*, p. 305; *GuCh*, p. 407.
37   Martin Gregor-Dellin, *Richard Wagner. Sein Leben, sein Werk, sein Jahreshundert* (Munich, 1980), p. 34; cf. Friedrich Nietzsche, *CW*, vol. 8, p. 37n; *KSA*, vol. 6, p. 41n; Charles Andler, *Nietzsche, sa vie et sa pensée*, vol. 2: *Le pessisisme esthétique de Nietzsche. La maturité de Nietzsche* (Paris, 1958), appendix 3: 'Richard Wagner est-il israélite?', pp. 622–5.

38 In Gerald Stieg, *Der Brenner und Die Fackel. Ein Beitrag zur Wirkungsgeschichte von Karl Kraus* (Salzburg, 1976), p. 257. The image of Hermann Bahr as a Jew seems to have been quite widespread: Reinhard Farkas, *Hermann Bahr, Dynamik und Dilemma der Moderne* (Vienna, 1989), p. 69, quotes from an attack by the conservative Catholic Karl Muth, who in 1893 declared, 'Bahr is obviously Jewish (Austrian) and has done some of his studying in Paris.'

39 Hermann Bahr, *Wien* (Stuttgart, 1907), p. 69.

40 Sigmund Freud to Arnold Zweig, 18 August 1933, quoted in German in Max Schur, *Freud: Living and Dying* (London, 1972), p. 563. In his *Psychologie des Antisemitismus*, written in 1943–4 and published in Budapest in 1945, the Hungarian psychoanalyst Imre Hermann suggested that the most antisemitic social groups have a concealed resemblance to Jews.

41 Cf. René Major, *De l'élection. Freud face aux idéologies américaine, allemande et soviétique* (Paris, 1986), p. 56.

42 Martin Jay, *The Dialectical Imagination: A History of the Frankfurt School and the Institute of Social Research 1923–1950* (London, 1973), pp. 256–7.

43 Max Horkheimer, *Die Anfänge der bürgerlichen Geschichtsphilosophie* (Stuttgart, 1930).

44 Leo Löwenthal, 'Knut Hamsun. Zur Vorgeschichte der autoritären Ideologie', *Zeitschrift für Sozialforschung* 6 (1937; Paris, 1938), p. 344.

45 Erich Fromm, 'Die socialpsychologische Bedeutung der Mutterrechtstheorie', *Zeitschrift für Sozialforschung* 3 (1934; Paris, 1938), pp. 196ff.

46 Max Horkheimer and Theodor W. Adorno, *Dialektik der Aufklärung* (Frankfurt, 1971), pp. 99–100; in English as *Dialectic of Enlightenment*, trans. John Cumming (London/New York, 1973).

47 Horkheimer and Adorno, *Dialektik*, p. 101.

48 Ibid., pp. 154–5.

49 The expression is from Henri Plard, 'Hannah Arendt et Rahel Levin: illusions et pièges de l'assimilation', in *Hannah Arendt*, special number of *Cahiers du GRIF*, no. 33 (1986), pp. 101–17.

50 Birgit Pelzer, 'Le vent du Nord est mon plus grand ennemi', *Cahiers du GRIF*, no. 33 (1986), p. 134.

51 Hans Mayer, *Aussenseiter* (Frankfurt, 1975), p. 459; cf. Julius Carlebach, 'The Forgotten Connection: Women and Jews in the Conflict between Enlightenment and Romanticism', in *Leo Baeck Institute Year Book* 24 (London, 1979), pp. 107–36.

52 Cf. *Materialien zu Hans Mayers 'Aussenseiter'*, ed. Gert Ueding (Frankfurt, 1978). George Mosse's *Nationalism and Sexuality: Respectability and Abnormal Sexuality in Modern Europe* (New York, 1985) supplies a new collection of arguments and documents in support of Mayer's paralleling of women, Jews and homosexuals.

53 Sander L. Gilman, *Difference and Pathology: Stereotypes of Sexuality, Race and Madness* (Ithaca, 1985).

54 Josef Karniel, *Die Toleranzpolitik Kaiser Josephs II* (Gerlingen, 1985).

55 Quoted in Reinhard Rürup, *Emanzipation und Antisemitismus. Studien zur Juden-frage der bürgerlichen Gesellschaft* (Göttingen, 1975); cf. Christian Wilhelm Dohm, *Über die bürgerlichen Verbesserung der Juden* (Berlin/Stettin, 1781).

56 In Rürup, *Emanzipation*, p. 24.

57 Immanuel Kant, 'Der Streit der Fakultäten', *Allgemeine Anmerkung. Von Religions-sekten*, in *Werke in zehn Bänden*, ed. Wilhelm Weischedel (Darmstadt, 1975), vol. 9, p. 321.

58 Ibid., p. 320n.

59 On the germs of antisemitism in Kant's thought and on Kant's influence on

Weininger see Élisabeth de Fontenoy, 'Sur un soupir de Kant', in *Le racisme, mythes et sciences*, ed. Maurice Olender (Brussels, 1981), pp. 15–29; Jacques Le Rider, 'Nachwort zum Fall Otto Weininger', in *Otto Weininger, Werke und Wirkung*, ed. J. Le Rider and Norbert Leser (Vienna, 1984), pp. 99ff.

60 Wilhelm von Humboldt, 'Gutachten vom 17.7.1809', in *Gesammelte Schriften*, vol. 10 (Berlin, 1903), pp. 97–115; quoted in Rürup, *Emanzipation*, p. 31.

61 Wolfgang Häusler, '"Aus dem Ghetto". Der Aufbruch des österreichischen Judentums in das bürgerliche Zeitalter (1760–1867)', in *Conditio Judaica. Judentum, Antisemitismus und deutschsprächige Literatur vom 18 Jahrhundert bis zum Ersten Weltkrieg*, ed. Hans Otto Horch and Horst Denkler, vol. I (Tübingen, 1988).

62 Ibid., p. 29.

63 Richard Wagner, 'Das Judentum in der Musik', in Wagner, *Mein Denken*, ed. Martin Gregor-Dellin (Munich, 1982), pp. 173–4.

64 Figures from the *Statistiches Jahrbuch der Stadt Wien für das Jahr 1901* (Vienna, 1903); cf. Monika Glettler, *Die Wiener Tschechen um 1900. Strukturanalyse einer nationalen Minderheit in der Grossstadt* (Munich, 1970).

65 Cited in I. A. Hellwing, *Der konfessionelle Antisemitismus im XIX. Jahrhundert in Österreich* (Freiburg/Basle, 1972), p. 55.

66 Peter Leisching, 'Die römisch-katholische Kirche in Cisleithanien', in *Die Konfessionen*, vol. 4 of *Die Habsburgermonarchie 1848–1918*, ed. Adam Wandruszka and Peter Urbanitsch (Vienna, 1985), p. 88.

67 Klaus Lohrmann, 'Die rechtliche Lage der Juden in Wien zwischen 1848 und 1918', *Austriaca*, no. 31 (Dec. 1990), pp. 19–27.

68 On the significance of 'hep' (short for 'Hierosolyma est perdita', Jerusalem is lost), the cry of the German antisemites which goes back as far as the crusade of 1097, see Claussen, *Judenhass*, p. 74.

69 In Hellwing, *Konfessionnelle Antisemitismus*, p. 55; on Karl Lueger see Richard S. Geehr, *Karl Lueger: Mayor of Fin de Siècle Vienna* (Detroit, 1988).

70 See my *Le cas Otto Weininger*, pp. 192, 214ff.

71 Rita Thalmann, 'Alfred Rosenberg: Le mythe du XXe siècle', in *Sexe et race: la différence dans le discours d'exclusion (1870–1933)* (Centre d'Études et de Recherches Germaniques de l'Université de Paris VII, 1986), pp. 110ff.

72 Françoise Derré, *L'oeuvre d'Arthur Schnitzler. Imagerie viennoise et problèmes humains* (Paris, 1966).

73 The inventory of female types is from Barbara Gutt, *Emanzipation bei Arthur Schnitzler* (Berlin, 1978); on the fate of women of lowly estate – servants or governesses – see Elsbeth Dangel, *Wiederholung als Schicksal. Arthur Schnitzlers Roman 'Therese. Chronik eines Frauenlebens'* (Munich, 1985); Eva Tiethen-Vobruba, 'Wiener Vorstadtmädel. Unterschiede zu einem literarischen Klischee', in *Lulu, Lilith, Mona Lisa … Frauenbilder der Jahrhundertwende* (Pfaffenweiler, 1989), pp. 217–45.

74 Dieter Hornig, 'Remarques sur la stratégie narrative d'Arthur Schnitzler (Sous-lieutenant Gustl, Le retour de Casanova, Mademoiselle Else)', in *Arthur Schnitzler, Actes du Colloque des 19–21 octobre 1981*, ed. Christiane Ravy and Gilbert Ravy (Paris, 1983), p. 85.

75 Arthur Schnitzler, 'Leutnant Gustl' (1900), in Schnitzler, *Gesammelte Werke in Einzelausgaben. Das erzählerische Werk*, vol. 2 (Frankfurt, 1977), p. 227.

76 Ibid., p. 222.

77 Ibid., p. 225.

78 Ibid., pp. 208–9. Cf. Istvan Deak, *Beyond Nationalism: A Social and Political*

History of the Habsburg Officer Corps (Oxford, 1990). The Jews were subject to conscription by a decree of Joseph II (1788), and the first Jewish officers had been appointed during the Napoleonic wars. In 1848–9 there were as many Jewish officers in the ranks of the Habsburg armies as in those of the 'revolutionary' army, especially in the Hungarian army of Kossuth. After the introduction of compulsory military service in 1902 there were 59,784 Jews in the Habsburg armies, i.e. 3.9 per cent of the total (while Jews represented 4.5 per cent of the total population of the Danube monarchy). In 1897 178 professional Jewish officers were listed – 1.7 per cent of the total. This proportion was tending to fall, to 109 in 1911 (0.6 per cent). Before 1911 nineteen Jews reached the rank of general, of whom eleven were doctors and one an administrator. The case of Major-General Alexander Ritter von Eiss (born 1832, promoted to general in 1907, eleven years after his retirement) is noteworthy: a militant Zionist, he made a point of attending Zionist meetings in his full-dress uniform. The most famous Jewish general, Baron Samuel Hazai (born 1851), served with the Hungarian *Landwehr*; he became a general in 1910 and served as Hungarian Defence Minister from 1910 to 1907.

79 Wolfgang Nehring, 'Zwischen Identifikation und Distanz. Zur Darstellung der jüdischen Charaktere in Arthur Schnitzlers *Der Weg ins Freie*', in *Akten des VII Internationalen Germanisten-Kongresses Göttingen 1985*, vol. 5: *Auseinandersetzungen um jiddische Sprache und Literatur. Die Assimilationskontroverse*, ed. Walter Roll and Hans Peter Bayerdörfer (Tübingen, 1986), pp. 162–70; Hans Ulrich Lindken, 'Das Judenproblem', in *Arthur Schnitzler. Aspekte und Akzente. Materialien zu Leben und Werk* (Frankfurt/Berne/New York, 1984), pp. 74–118.

80 Hartmut Scheible, *Arthur Schnitzler und die Aufklärung* (Munich, 1972).

81 Arthur Schnitzler, *Der Weg ins Freie*, in Schnitzler, *Gesammelte Werke*, vol. 4 (Frankfurt, 1978), pp. 246.

82 Letter From Lou Andreas-Salomé to Arthur Schnitzler, dated Paris, 15 May 1894 (Schnitzler archive, Marbach am Neckar); quoted in Gutt, *Emanzipation*, pp. 113–14.

83 Cited in Rolf-Peter Janz and Klaus Laermann, *Arthur Schnitzler: Zur Diagnose des Wieners Bürgertums im Fin de siècle* (Stuttgart, 1977), p. 174; cf. Georg Brandes/Arthur Schnitzler, *Briefwechsel*, ed. Kurt Bergel (Berne, 1956), p. 95. Andrea Willi, *Arthur Schnitzlers Roman 'Der Weg ins Freie'. Eine Untersuchung zur Tageskritik und ihren zeitgenossichen Bezugen* (Heidelberg, 1989), has shown that many contemporary critics deplored the work's lack of unity, accusing Schnitzler of having handled too many themes at a time: Jewish–German relations, assimilation, Zionism, relationships between the sexes, female emancipation. Our present investigation shows that these subjects are, in fact, closely bound together. Willi also shows how each critic projected his own personal convictions on to Schnitzler's novel: while Bahr's comments were those of an antisemite, Hugo Bergmann saw *Der Weg ins Freie* as the 'swansong' of assimilation.

84 Schnitzler, *Briefe 1875–1912*, ed. Thérèse Nickl and Heinrich Schnitzler (Frankfurt, 1981), p. 578.

Chapter 10   The Assimilated Jews of Vienna

Epigraph cited in the journal *Pardès*, no. 5 (Paris, 1987), p. 159.

1 Anna Drabek, Wolfgand Häusler, Kurt Schubert et al. (eds), *Das österreichische Judentum. Voraussetzungen und Geschichte* (Vienna/Munich, 1974); overview in

Rita Thalmann, 'La communauté juive de Vienne jusqu'à l'Anschluss', *Austriaca*, no. 26 (1988), pp. 73–82. Several important works have been published since the present chapter was first written: Steven Beller, *Vienna and the Jews, 1867–1938. A Cultural History* (Cambridge, 1989); George E. Berkley, *Vienna and its Jews. The Tragedy of Success, 1880–1980* (Cambridge, Mass., 1988); William O. McCagg Jr., *A History of Habsburg Jews, 1670–1918* (Bloomington, 1989); Robert Wistrich, *The Jews of Vienna in the Age of Franz Joseph* (Oxford, 1989). See also Josef Fraenkel (ed.), *The Jews of Austria* (London, 1967); Hugo Gold, *Geschichte der Juden in Wien* (Tel Aviv, 1966); Michael John and Albert Lichtblau, *Schmelztiegel Wien, einst und jetzt. Zur Geschichte und Gegenwart von Zuwanderung und Minderheiten* (Vienna/Cologne, 1900), excellent chapter on the Jews.

2   Marsha L. Rozenblit, *The Jews of Vienna, 1867–1914. Assimilation and Identity* (Albany, 1983), p. 132.

3   Ivar Oxaal and Walter R. Weitzmann, 'The Jews of Pre-1914 Vienna: An Exploration of Basic Sociological Dimensions', in *Leo Baeck Institute Year Book* 30 (1985), p. 419.

4   Fritz Wittels, *Der Taufjude* (1904); on the influence of this book on Kraus, see Edward Timms, *Karl Kraus, Apocalyptic Satirist: Culture and Catastrophe in Habsburg Vienna* (New Haven/London, 1986), p. 242.

5   Karl Kraus, 'Er ist doch ä Jud', *Die Fackel*, no. 386 (29 Oct. 1913), p. 4.

6   Albert Fuchs, *Geistige Strömungen in Österreich, 1867–1918* (reprint, Vienna, 1978), pp. 36, 282n. Fuchs tells us that on the occasion of the seventieth birthday of Adolf Fischhof the municipal council of Vienna discussed whether some tribute should be paid to him. Karl Lueger, who was not yet antisemitic, approved the motion, but it was rejected by the liberal majority on the council.

7   John W. Boyer, *Political Radicalism in Late Imperial Vienna: The Origins of the Christian-Social Movement, 1848–1897* (Chicago/London, 1981). On the Taaffe government see William A. Jenks, *Austria Under the Iron Ring, 1879–1893* (Charlottesville, 1965).

8   Quoted in Egon Schwarz, 'Melting Pot or Witches' Cauldron? Jews and Antisemites in Vienna at the Turn of the Century', in *Jews and Germans from 1860 to 1933: The Problematic Symbiosis*, ed. David Bronsen (Heidelberg, 1979), p. 237.

9   Ibid. On the three Jellinek brothers – Hermann was a socialist politician, while Moritz made a fortune in Budapest – and on Adolf Jellinek's sons, especially Emil, who invented the Mercedes for the Daimler car company, see Wolfgang Häusler, '"Aus dem Ghetto". Der Aufbruch des österreichischen Judentums in das bürgerliche Zeitalter (1780–1867)', in *Conditio Judaica*, ed. Hans Otto Horch and Horst Denkler, vol. 1 (Tübingen, 1988), pp. 48–50.

10   Dominique Bourel, 'Moritz Güdemann (1835–1918), grand rabbin de Vienne', paper given at the conference 'Les Juifs en Autriche' organized by the Institut Universitaire Martin Buber and the Centre Communautaire Laïc Juif, Brussels, 10–11 Oct. 1987.

11   Walter R. Weitzmann, 'The Politics of the Viennese Jewish Community, 1890–1914', in *Jews, Antisemitism and Culture in Vienna*, ed. Ivar Oxaal, Michael Pollak and Gerhard Botz (London, 1987), pp. 121–51.

12   Jakob Toury, 'Troubled Beginnings: The Emergence of the Österreichisch-Israelitische Union' and 'The Contest of the O. I. Union for the Leadership of Austrian Jewry', in *Leo Baeck Institute Year Book*, no. 30 (1985), pp. 157–75; no. 33 (1988), pp. 179–99.

13   Sigmund Mayer, *Ein jüdischer Kaufmann, 1831–1911. Lebenserinnerungen* (Leipzig, 1911), p. 289.

14   Weitzmann, 'Politics', p. 139.
15   Boyer, *Political Radicalism*, p. 84.
16   Schwarz, 'Melting Pot', p. 240; Robert S. Wistrich, 'The Modernization of
     Viennese Jewry: The Impact of German in a Multi-Ethnic State', in *Toward
     Modernity: The European Jewish Model*, ed. Jakob Katz (New Brunswick/Oxford,
     1987), pp. 43–70. Wistrich shows that Jellinek's opinions were shared by the
     majority of assimilated Viennese Jews, and that Bloch laid emphasis on a
     specifically Austrian identity as opposed to the German or Zionist outlook.
17   G. Wolf, *Die Juden*, vol. 7 of *Die Völker Österreich-Ungarns* (Vienna, 1883).
18   Josef Samuel Bloch, *Der nationale Zwist und die Juden in Österreich* (Vienna,
     1886); Gerald Stourzh, 'Galten die Juden als Nationalität Altösterreichs?', in
     Studia Judaica Austriaca 10: *Prag-Czernowitz-Jerusalem. Der österreichische Staat
     und die Juden vom Zeitalter des Absolutismus bis zum Ende der Monarchie*, ed. Anna
     Drabek, Mordechai Eliav and Gerald Stourzh (Eisenstadt, 1984), pp. 73–116.
19   Julius H. Schoeps, 'Modern Heirs of the Maccabees. The Beginning of the
     Vienna Kadimah', *Leo Baeck Institute Year Book*, no. 27 (1982), pp. 155–70;
     Marsha L. Rozenblit, 'Jewish Student Nationalism at the University of Vienna
     before the First World War', ibid., pp. 171–86; Adolf Gaisbauer, *Davidstern und
     Doppeladler. Zionismus und judischer Nationalismus in Osterreich, 1887–1918*
     (Vienna, 1988); Harald Seewann, *Zirkel und Zionstern, Bilder und Dokumente aus
     der versunkenen Welt des judisch-nationalen Korporationsstudentums. Ein Beitrag zur
     Geschichte des Zionismus auf akademischem Boden*, 2 vols (Graz, 1990).
20   In Albrecht Hirschmüller, *Physiologie und Psychoanalyse im Leben und Werk Josef
     Breuers*, Jahrbuch der Psychoanalyse 4 (Berne, 1978), pp. 282ff.
21   Stefan Zweig, *Die Welt von gestern* (1st edn 1944; Vienna, 1948), pp. 145, 143–4.
22   Ibid., pp. 64–5.
23   Otto Weininger, *SC*, p. 329; *GuCh*, p. 429.
24   Ibid., p. 320; pp. 440–1.
25   Gershom Scholem, *Fidélité et utopie. Essais sur le judaïsme contemporain*
     (French trans., Paris, 1978), p. 93.
26   Marsha Rozenblit, 'The Role of the Gymnasium', in *The Jews of Vienna*, ch. 5.
27   Wolfgang Häusler, in *Das österreichische Judentum*, ed. Drabek et al., p. 112.
28   Oxaal and Weitzmann, 'The Jews of Pre-1914 Vienna'.
29   William J. McGrath, *Dionysian Arts and Populist Politics in Austria* (New Haven/
     London, 1974).
30   Carl E. Schorske, 'Conflit de générations et changement culturel. Réflexions sur
     le cas de Vienne', *Actes de la Recherche en Sciences Sociales*, nos 26–7 (1979),
     pp. 109–16. For a more precise approach to the idea of 'intellectual generation',
     using leading French schools as an example, see Jean-François Sirinelli, *Généra-
     tion intellectuelle, Khâgneux et Normaliens dans l'entre-deux-guerres* (Paris, 1988),
     esp. pp. 642–3. It might be said that for the 'Pernerstorfer circle' and their
     generation the leading high schools of Vienna were the equivalent of the French
     khâgnes which prepare candidates for the prestigious École Normale Supérieure,
     or of the chief English public schools. Sirinelli observes that 'in the years
     leading up to the First World War, some of the Jewish bourgeoisie assiduously
     sought admission to the École Normale Supérieure' (pp. 176–7); he quotes
     Emmanuel Berl to the effect that 'some of the Jewish bourgeoisie made a cult of
     university and academic qualifications.' In that case Vienna would simply be a
     particularly striking example of a tendency visible elsewhere in Europe.
31   On Richard von Kralik and Siegfried Lipiner see Johann Willibald Nagl, Jacob
     Zeidler and Eduard Castle (eds), *Deutsch-österreichische Literaturgeschichte*, vol. 4:
     Von 1890 bis 1918 (Vienna, 1937), pp. 1560–70, 1600–37.

32   Jost Hermand, 'Gralsmotive um die Jahrhundertswende', in *Deutsche Literatur der Jahrhundertwende*, ed. Viktor Žmegač (Königstein, 1981), p. 152.
33   Twenty years later he was to renounce both Vienna and the teaching of philosophy. In *Meine letzten Wünsche für Österreich* (Stuttgart, 1895), a collection of articles from the *Neue Freie Presse* of 2, 3 and 8 December 1894, Brentano was to tell of his disappointments in Vienna after his marriage, which had raised legal and political problems, Brentano being a former Catholic priest.
34   McGrath, *Dionysian Arts*, p. 73.
35   Salomon Wank, 'A Case of Aristocratic Antisemitism in Austria: Count Aerenthal and the Jews, 1878–1907', in *Leo Baeck Institute Year Book* 30 (1985), pp. 435–56.
36   I. A. Hellwing, *Der konfessionelle Antisemitismus im 19. Jahrhundert in Österreich* (Freiburg/Basle, 1972).
37   Freidrich Heer, *Gottes erste Liebe. 2000 Jahre Judentum und Christentum. Genesis des österreichischen Katholiken Adolf Hitler* (Munich/Esslingen, 1967); cf. 'Der Antisemitismus katholischer Kreise', in Peter Leisching, 'Die römisch-katholische Kirche in Cisleithanien', in *Die Konfessionen*, vol. 4 of *Die Habsburgermonarchie, 1848–1919*, ed. Adam Wandruszka and Peter Urbanitsch (Vienna, 1985), pp. 146–52.
38   The standard work on the history of Austrian antisemitism is Peter G. Pulzer, *The Rise of Political Antisemitism in Germany and Austria* (revised edn, London, 1988). See also Victor Conzenius, 'L'antisémitisme autrichien au XIXe et au XXe siècle', in *De l'antijudaïsme antique à l'antisémitisme contemporain*, ed. Valentin Nikiprowetsky (Lille, 1979), pp. 189–208; John Bunzl, 'Zur Geschichte des Antisemitismus in Österreich', in *Antisemitismus in Österreich. Sozialhistorische und soziologische Studien*, ed. John Bunzl and Bernd Marin (Innsbruck, 1983), pp. 9–88.
39   Oxaal and Weitzmann, 'Jews of Pre-1914 Vienna', pp. 400ff.
40   Ibid., pp. 404ff.
41   Ibid., pp. 419ff. Bernard Michel, *Banques et banquiers en Autriche au début du 20e siècle* (Paris, 1976), says, 'Of the key posts in the leading Viennese banks, the ones which governed the market and made history, the Jews held no fewer than 80 per cent' (p. 312). This remains vague. Would the Jewish share of these posts seem as overwhelmingly large if we considered the whole of the banking sector and not just the 'key posts in the leading Viennese banks'?
42   Hans Tietze, *Die Juden Wiens. Geschichte, Wirtschaft, Kultur* (1st edn 1933; reprint Vienna, 1987), p. 233.
43   Hermann Greive, *Geschichte des modernen Antisemitismus in Deutschland* (Darmstadt, 1983), pp. 64ff.
44   Wilhelm Marr, *Der Sieg des Judenthums über das Germanenthum: Vom nicht confessionellen Standpunkt aus betrachtet* (Berne, 1879); *Öffnet die Augen, ihr deutschen Zeitungsleser*, vol. 3 of *Antisemitische Hefte* (Chemnitz, 1880).
45   Ulysse Robert, *Voyage à Vienne* (Paris, 1899), p. 87.
46   On Jakob Wassermann see Daniel Azuelos, 'Judéité et germanité, l'impossible symbiose', *Pardès*, no. 5 (1987), pp. 169–76.
47   Jakob Wassermann, *Mein Weg als Deutscher und als Jude* (1st edn 1921; Berlin, 1987), pp. 107–8.
48   Alex Bein, *Theodor Herzl. Biographie* (Frankfurt/Berlin/Vienna, 1893), pp. 32ff.
49   Heinrich Gomperz (ed.), *Theodor Gomperz: Ein Gelehrtenleben im Bürgertum der Franz-Josefs-Zeit. Auswahl seiner Briefe und Aufzeichnungen 1869–1912*, re-ed. Robert A. Kann (Vienna, 1974).

50   Arthur Schnitzler, *Weg ins Freie*, in *Gesammelte Werke in Einzelausgaben, Das erzählensche Werk*, vol. 4 (Frankfurt, 1978), p. 128.
51   Weininger, *SC*, p. 320; *GuCh*, pp. 416–17.
52   Joseph Roth, *Juden auf Wanderschaft* (Berlin, 1927).
53   Geoffrey F. Field, *Evangelist of Race: The Germanic Vision of Houston Stewart Chamberlain* (New York, 1981).
54   Hermann Cohen, *Deutschtum und Judentum* (Giessen, 1915).
55   Robert Hein, *Studentischer Antisemitismus in Österreich*, österreichischer Verein für Studentengeschichte, Beiträge zur österreichischen Studentengeschichte 10 (Vienna, 1984); cf. Jacques Droz, 'Schönerer et l'antisémitisme autrichien', *Austriaca*, special number on 'Autriche 1867–1938' (June 1988), pp. 9–52; Andrew G. Whiteside, *The Socialism of the Fools: Georg Ritter von Schönerer and Austrian Pan-Germanism* (Berkeley, 1975); Jonny Moser, *Von der emanzipation zur antisemitischen Bewegung. Die Stellung Schönerers und Friedjungs in der Entwicklungsgeschichte der Antisemitismus (1848–1896)*, dissertation (Vienna, 1962).
56   Theodor Billroth, *Über das Lehren und Lernen der medizinischen Wissenschaften* (Vienna, 1975).
57   Hermann Bahr, *Der Antisemitismus. Ein internationales Interview* (1st edn 1894; ed. Hermann Greive, Königstein, 1979); on the development of Bahr's thinking see Donald G. Daviau, 'Hermann Bahr und der Antisemitismus, Zionismus und die Judenfrage', *Literatur und Kritik*, nos 221–2 (Feb.–Mar. 1988), pp. 21–41.
58   This is why the view put forward by Sigurd Paul Scheichl in his 'The Contexts and Nuances of Anti-Jewish Language: Were All the "Antisemites" Antisemites?', in *Jews, Antisemitism and Culture*, ed. Oxaal et al., seems to me dubious. In the interests of historical accuracy generalizations and hasty condemnations have to be avoided, but some of Scheichl's distinctions seem to me rather forced: for example, he sees a difference of degree, or even (he says) of moral quality, between Chamberlain and Weininger on the one hand and Lanz von Liebenfels on the other (p. 92). This may be true, but it does not allow us to say that Chamberlain and Weininger were less antisemitic than Liebenfels. Nor to conclude that 'Antisemitism was thus something quite respectable in Austria around 1900' (p. 104).
59   Hermann Bahr, *Antisemitismus*, p. 15.
60   Hermann Bahr, 'Die Decadence' (1891), in Bahr, *Studien zur Kritik der Moderne* (Frankfurt, 1894), pp. 19–26.
61   Wilfred Daim, *Der Mann, der Hitler die Ideen gab* (reprint, Vienna, 1985).
62   Eduard Gugenberg, 'Ariosophie: Wandlungen und Verkleidungen', *Zeitgeschichte*, nos 9–10 (1984), pp. 303–10.
63   See the chapter on Arthur Trebitsch in Theodor Lessing, *Der jüdischer Selbsthass* (1st edn 1930; Munich, 1984), pp. 101–31, and the article on 'Der jüdische Selbsthass und die Weiberverachtung: Otto Weininger und Arthur Trebitsch', in *Otto Weininger, Werk und Wirkung*, ed. Jacques Le Rider and Norbert Leser (Vienna, 1984), pp. 123–34.
64   Cited in Eberhard Jäckel, *Hitlers Weltanschauung* (3rd edn, Stuttgart, 1986), p. 122.
65   Richard S. Geehr, *Adam Müller-Guttenbrunn and the Aryan Theater of Vienna, 1898–1903: The Approach of Cultural Fascism* (Göppingen, 1973).
66   Quoted in Hugo Gold, *Geschichte der Juden in Wien* (Tel Aviv, 1966), p. 40; cf. John W. Boyer, 'Karl Lueger and the Viennese Jews', in *Leo Baeck Institute Year Book* 26 (1981), pp. 125–41; Richard Geehr (ed.), *'I decide who is a Jew': The Papers of Dr Karl Lueger* (Washington DC, 1982); Monika Glettler, 'Ur-

banisierung und Nationalitätenproblem', in *Wien um 1900. Aufbruch in die Moderne*, ed. Peter Berner, Emil Brix and Wolfgang Mantl (Vienna, 1986), p. 188.

67 Arthur Schnitzler, *Jugend in Wien. Eine Autobiographie*, ed. Therese Nickl and Heinrich Schnitzler (Vienna/Munich, 1968), pp. 328–9.

68 Carl E. Schorske, *Fin-de-Siècle Vienna: Politics and Culture* (London, 1979), p. 299. Schorske's analysis has been continued and deepened by Michael Pollak, *Vienne, 1900. Une identité blessée* (Paris, 1984), see ch. 4: 'De l'identité perdue à l'art pur'.

69 Zweig, *Die Welt von gestern*, pp. 88–9.

70 Michael Pollak, 'Weiningers Antisemitismus: Eine gegen sich selbst gerichtete Verurteilung des intellektuellen Spiels', in *Otto Weininger*, ed. Le Rider and Leser, pp. 109–20.

71 Leon Botstein, *Judentum und Modernität. Essays zur Rolle der Juden in der deutschen und österreichischen Kultur, 1848 bis 1938* (Vienna/Cologne, 1991).

72 Walter R. Weitzmann, 'The Jewish Community's Response to Antisemitism', paper read at Brussels colloquium on the Viennese Jews, 1987.

73 Marsha Rozenblit, 'Organizational Networks and Jewish Identity', in Rozenblit, *The Jews of Vienna*, ch. 7, describes the multiplicity of Viennese Jewish associations.

74 Claudio Magris, *Der habsburgische Mythos in der österreichischen Literatur* (Salzburg, 1966), p. 265.

75 Leo Feld, 'Stefan Zweig', cited in *Die Fackel*, nos 366–7 (11 Jan. 1913), p. 25.

76 Hannah Arendt, 'Juden in der Welt von gestern', in *Die verborgene Tradition* (Frankfurt, 1976), p. 84.

77 Robert Dumont, *Stefan Zweig et la France* (Paris, 1967), p. 55; cf. René Cheval, 'Romain Rolland und Stefan Zweig, eine europäische Freundschaft', in *Österreichische Literatur des 20. Jahrhunderts* ed. Sigurd Paul Scheichl and Gerald Stieg (Innsbruck, 1986), p. 116; Jacques Le Rider, 'Stefan Zweig und Frankreich', *Österreich in Geschichte und Literatur*, no. 1 (1989), pp. 31–42.

78 Dumont, *Stefan Zweig*, p. 79.

79 Quoted in Dumont, *Stefan Zweig*, p. 143. Zweig wrote, for example, 'what in me is German drowns out all other feelings'; and 'all criteria have now changed and every individual now has no more truth than what unites him to his nation.' Cf. Stefan Zweig, *Tagebücher*, ed. Knut Beck (Frankfurt, 1984), e.g. p. 118, enthusiastic remarks on Hindenburg.

80 Bahr, *Der Prophet der Moderne. Tagebücher 1888–1904*, selected and annotated by Reinhard Farkas (Vienna, 1987), p. 56 (dated 28 November 1903).

81 Nathan Birnbaum, *Den Ostjuden ihr Recht* (Vienna, 1915), pp. 24–5.

82 Franz Neubacher, *Freiland, eine liberalsozialistische Utopie* (Vienna, 1987).

83 Leah Hadomi, '*Altneuland*: ein utopischer Roman', in *Juden in der deutschen Literatur. Ein deutsch-israelisches Symposium*, ed. Stéphane Moses and Albrecht Schöne (Frankfurt, 1986), pp. 210–25.

84 Friedrich Stadler, 'Zwei Zentralfiguren im Wiener Fin de siècle: Ernst Mach und Josef Popper-Lynkeus', in *Vom Positivismus zur 'wissenschaftlichen Weltauffassung'. Am Beispiel der Wirkungsgeschichte von Ernst Mach in Österreich von 1895 bis 1934* (Vienna/Munich, 1982), ch. 1. On the life and politics of Popper-Lynkeus see Ingrid Belke, *Die sozialreformerischen Ideen von Josef Popper-Lynkeus (1838–1921), im Zusammenhang mit allgemeinen Reformbestrebungen des Wiener Bürgertums um die Jahrhundertwende* (Tübingen, 1978).

85 Endre Kiss, *Der Tod der k.u.k. Weltordnung in Wien* (Vienna/Cologne/Graz, 1986), pp. 65–75.

86 Josef Popper, *Fürst Bismarck und der Antisemitismus* (1886; Vienna, 1986).
87 Cf. the portrait of Victor Adler in Robert S. Wistrich, *Revolutionary Jews from Marx to Trotsky* (London, 1976), pp. 98–114.
88 Leopold Spira, *Feindbild 'Jud'* (Vienna/Munich, 1981).
89 Robert S. Wistrich, *Socialism and the Jews: The Dilemmas of Assimilation in Germany and Austria-Hungary* (East Brunswick/London/Toronto, 1982).
90 Robert S. Wistrich, 'Austrian Social Democracy and the Problem of Galician Jewry, 1890–1914', in *Leo Baeck Institute Year Book* 26 (1981).
91 Max Zetterbaum, 'Klassengegensätze bei den Juden', *Die Neue Zeit* 1 (1982–3), pp. 37–42.
92 Wistrich, 'Social Democracy, Antisemitism and the Jews of Vienna', in *Jews, Antisemitism and Culture*, ed. Oxaal et al., pp. 117–18.
93 Otto Bauer, *Die Nationalitätenfrage und die Sozialdemocratie* (Vienna, 1907).
94 The expression is from Alain Finkielkraut, *Le Juif imaginaire* (Paris, 1980).

Chapter 11 Sigmund Freud and Theodor Herzl: In the 'New Ghetto'

1 *Juden und Judentum in deutschen Briefen aus drei Jahrhunderten*, ed. Franz Kobler (reprint, Königstein, 1984), p. 364.
2 Sigmund Freud, *SE*, vol. 4, pp. 192–3; *GW*, vols 2–3, pp. 198–9.
3 Sigmund Freud, *Briefe 1873–1939*, ed. Ernst and Lucie Freud (Frankfurt, 1968), p. 412.
4 Marthe Robert, *D'Oedipe à Moïse. Freud et la conscience juive* (Paris, 1974), p. 39. Cf. the overviews in Peter Loewenberg, " 'Sigmund Freud as a Jew": A Study in Ambivalence and Courage', *Journal of the History of Behavioral Sciences* 7 (1971), pp. 363–9; Martin S. Bergmann, 'Moses and the Evolution of Freud's Jewish Identity', *Israel Annals of Psychiatry and Related Disciplines* 14 (1976), pp. 3–26; Justin Miller, 'Interpretation of Freud's Jewishness, 1924–1974', *Journal of the History of the Behavioral Sciences* 17 (1981), pp. 357–74.
5 Freud, *SE*, vol. 4, p. 197; *GW*, vols 2–3, p. 203.
6 This was perhaps also 'the hidden fault of the father': Marie Balmary, *L'homme aux statues. Freud et la faute cachée du père* (Paris, 1979).
7 Some biographers have exaggerated the non-religiousness of Freud's education. See Peter Gay, *A Godless Jew: Freud, Atheism, and the Making of Psychoanalysis* (New Haven/London, 1987), and the review by Willliam J. McGrath, 'Oedipus at Berggasse 19', *New York Review of Books*, 18 August 1988, pp. 5–9.
8 See the Book of Esther in the Old Testament, chapters 3–7.
9 Ernst L. Freud, 'Jugendbriefe Sigmund Freuds', *Neue Rundschau*, no. 80 (1969), p. 684.
10 Freud, *Briefe*, p. 278.
11 Léon Poliakov, 'Freud et Moïse', in *Les Juifs et notre histoire* (Paris, 1973), p. 235.
12 Ibid.
13 Sander L. Gilman, 'Constructing the Image of the Appropriate Therapist: The Struggle of Psychiatry with Psychoanalysis', in *Freud in Exile: Psychoanalysis and its Vicissitudes*, ed. Edward Timms and Naomi Segal (New Haven/London, 1988), pp. 22ff.
14 Guy Rosolato, 'Que contemplait Freud sur l'Acropole?', *Nouvelle Revue de Psychanalyse*, no. 15 (1977); cf. Hans I. Bach, *Jacob Bernays* (Tübingen, 1974).

15   Freud, *SE*, vol. 22, pp. 247–8; *GW*, vol. 16, p. 257.

16   Carl E. Schorske, *Fin-de-Siècle Vienna* (London, 1979), p. 147.

17   Klaus Dethloff (ed.), *Theodor Herzl oder der Moses des Fin de siècle* (Vienna, 1986), pp. 10–11; Peter Loewenberg, 'Theodor Herzl: A Psychoanalytic Study in Charismatic Political Leadership', in *The Psychoanalytic Interpretation of History*, ed. Benjamin B. Volman (New York, 1971), pp. 150–91.

18   Stefan Zweig, *Die Welt von gestern* (1st edn 1944; Vienna, 1948), pp. 30–1.

19   Alex Bein, *Theodor Herzl. Biographie* (Frankfurt/Berlin/Vienna, 1983), pp. 19–20.

20   Sigmund Freud, *An Autobiographical Study*, trans. J. Strachey (London, 1935), pp. 14–15; *GW*, vol. 14, pp. 34–5.

21   Freud, *SE*, vol. 4, p. 209; *GW*, vols 2–3, p. 215.

22   Ibid., p. 213; p. 215.

23   William J. McGrath, 'Student Radicalism in Vienna', *Journal of Contemporary History* 2.3 (1963), pp. 183–201; and McGrath, *Dionysian Art and Populist Politics in Austria* (New Haven/London, 1974).

24   William J. McGrath, *Freud's Discovery of Psychoanalysis: The Politics of Hysteria* (Ithaca/London, 1986), pp. 101–2. Wilhelm W. Hemecker's *Vor Freud. Philosophiegeschichtliche Voraussetzungen der Psychoanalyse* (Munich, 1991) is a very useful study of Freud's formative years.

25   Lucie Gilson, *La psychologie descriptive selon Franz Brentano* (Paris, 1955).

26   See Jacques Le Rider, 'Freud, zwischen Aufklärung und Gegenaufklärung', in *Zwischen Aufklärung und Gegenaufklärung*, ed. Jochen Schmidt (Darmstadt, 1988), pp. 475–96; Le Rider, 'Les intellectuels viennois et Nietzsche. Autour de Sigmund Freud', in *De Sils-Maria à Jerusalem. Nietzsche et le judaïsme. Les intellectuels juifs et Nietzsche*, ed. Dominique Bourel and J. Le Rider (Paris, 1991), pp. 181–200; Paul-Laurent Assoun, *Freud et Nietzsche* (Paris, 1980).

27   McGrath, *Freud's Discovery of Psychoanalysis*, pp. 102ff.

28   Franz Brentano was to pursue his attacks on Nietzsche; cf. 'Nietzsche als Nachahmer Jesu', in Brentano, *Die Lehre Jesu und ihre bleibende Bedeutung*, ed. Alfred Kastil (Leipzig, 1922), pp. 128–32; 'Nietzsche', ch. 31 of Brentano, *Geschichte der Philosophie der Neuzeit*, ed. Klaus Hedwig (Hamburg, 1987), pp. 297–8.

29   Curt Paul Janz, *Nietzsche. Biographie*, vol. 2 (Munich, 1978), pp. 254–8.

30   Richard Frank Krummel, 'Josef Paneth über seine Begegnung mit Nietzsche in der Zarathustra-Zeit', in Nietzsche-Studien, *Internationales Jahrbuch für die Nietzsche-Forschung* 17 (1988), pp. 478–95.

31   Franz Overbeck, from *Erinnerungen an Friedrich Nietzsche*, in Sander L. Gilman, *Begegnungen mit Nietzsche* (Bonn, 1981), document no. 255, p. 473.

32   See the account of the meeting of the Viennese Society for Psychoanalysis, 1 April 1908: *Protokolle der Wiener psychoanalytischen Vereinigung*, ed. Hermann Nunberg and Ernst Federn, vol. 1 (Frankfurt, 1976), p. 238; Aldo Venturelli, 'Nietzsche in der Berggasse 19. Über die erste Nietzsche-Rezeption in Wien', *Nietzsche-Studien* 13 (1984), pp. 448–80.

33   McGrath, *Freud's Discovery of Psychoanalysis*, pp. 107, 109.

34   Carl E. Schorske, 'Politics and parricide in Freud's *Interpretation of Dreams*', in Schorske, *Fin-de-Siècle Vienna*, pp. 181–207.

35   Donald D. Daviau, *Der Mann von übermorgen. Hermann Bahr, 1863–1934* (Vienna, 1984), pp. 53ff.

36   In Bein, *Theodor Herzl*, p. 36.

37   Daviau, *Mann von übermorgen*, p. 52.

38   In Lydia Flem, *La vie quotidienne de Freud et de ses patients* (Paris, 1986), pp. 68–9.

39   Ernest Jones, *LWSF*, vol. 1, p. 183.
40   Ibid., p. 164.
41   Ibid., p. 201.
42   Freud, *Briefe*, pp. 209–10.
43   George Sylvester Viereck, *Glimpses of the Great* (London, 1930), p. 34.
44   Robert, *D'Oedipe à Moïse*, p. 56.
45   Ibid., p. 61.
46   Freud, *SE*, vol. 20, p. 273; cf. Jacquy Chemouni, 'Freud et les associations juives. Contribution à l'étude de sa judéité', *Revue Française de Psychanalyse*, no. 4 (1987), pp. 1207–43.
47   Dennis B. Klein, *Jewish Origins of the Psychoanalytic Movement* (2nd edn, Chicago, 1985), pp. 75–102.
48   Robert, *D'Oedipe à Moïse*, p. 56.
49   Hannah Arendt, 'Aufklärung und Judenfrage', in *Die verborgene Tradition* (Frankfurt, 1976), pp. 108–26.
50   Gay, *A Godless Jew*, p. 124.
51   Jones, *LWSF*, vol. 1, p. 154.
52   Freud, *SE*, vol. 23, p. 51; *GW*, vol. 16, pp. 152–3.
53   Georg Langer, in *Die Erotik der Kabbala* (1923), was perhaps the first to detect a Jewish influence on psychoanalysis. One of the earliest commentators on Freud to take this line was A. A. Roback, *Jewish Influences on Modern Thought* (1929); more recently, David Bakan, *Freud and the Jewish Mystical Tradition* (reprint, Boston, 1975) and Éliane Amado Lévy-Valensi, *Le Moïse de Freud ou la référence occultée* (Monaco, 1984). Ken Frieden, *Freud's Dream of Interpretation* (State University of New York Press, 1990) has reopened the argument over the affinities between the Freudian interpretation of dreams, biblical oneiromancy and the Talmudic commentaries. See also Gerard Haddad, *L'enfant illégitime. Sources talmudiques de la psychanalyse* (2nd augmented edn, Paris, 1990). This tendency to see Judaic sources, or a 'Jewish mind', at work in psychoanalysis is also found in Harold Bloom's *Ruin the Sacred Truths* (Cambridge, Mass., 1989), ch. 6: he cites *Zakhor: Jewish History and Jewish Memory* by Yosef Hayim Yerushalmi (1982) to suggest that 'Freudian memory' is a Jewish memory, and even more that Freudian forgetfulness is a typically Jewish forgetfulness.
54   Estelle Roith, *The Riddle of Freud: Jewish Influences on his Theory of Female Sexuality* (London, 1987).
55   Cited in Gay, *A Godless Jew*, pp. 32–3.
56   Klaus Dethloff, in the introduction to *Theodor Herzl*, lays especial stress on this legalistic turn of mind in Herzl.
57   Johannes Wachter, 'Theodor Herzl: Zionismus und Journalismus', in *Judentum im deutschen Sprachraum*, ed. Karl E. Grozinger (Frankfurt, 1991), pp. 357–70.
58   Bein, *Theodor Herzl*, pp. 83–7.
59   Nike Wagner, 'Theodor Herzl oder des befreite Wien', *Die Zeit*, 5 April 1985 (Hamburg), pp. 73–6.
60   Theodor Herzl, *Tagebücher* (Berlin, 1922), vol. 1, p. 223.
61   Bein, *Theodor Herzl*, p. 103. Steven Beller's monograph, *Herzl* (London, 1991), confirms this approach to Herzl as 'a near-pathological, self-hating version of the Central-European Jew' (p. 1).
62   In Nathaniel Gutman, 'Herzl and Wagner', in *Parsifal*, souvenir programme for the festival of Bayreuth 1981, pp. 24–5.
63   Herzl, *Tagebücher*, for 5 June 1895.
64   Nike Wagner, 'Parsifal et l'antisémitisme juif', *L'Infini*, no. 3 (1983), pp. 22–32.
65   In Leo Goldhammer, 'Theodor Herzl and Sigmund Freud', in *Theodor Herzl*

Jahrbuch 1937, ed. T. Nussenblatt (Vienna, 1937), p. 268; on the subject of Freud and Herzl see also Avner Falk, 'Freud und Herzl', *Midstream*, no. 23 (January 1977), pp. 3–24; Ernst Simon, 'Sigmund Freud, the Jew', in *Leo Baeck Institute Year Book* 2 (London, 1957), pp. 270–305; Jacquy Chemouni, 'Freud et Herzl', in *Freud et le sionisme. Terre psychanalytique, Terre promise* (Paris, 1988), pp. 133–51.

66 Reported by Goldhammer, 'Theodor Herzl'.

67 Freud, *SE*, vol. 4, p. 269; *GW*, vols 2–3, p. 276.

68 Ibid., vol. 4, pp. 441–2; vols 2–3, pp. 443–4.

69 Ibid.

70 Bein, *Theodor Herzl*, pp. 83–7.

71 Didier Anzieu, *L'auto-analyse de Freud et la découverte de la psychanalyse* (2nd edn, Paris, 1975), p. 343.

72 Sigmund Freud, *The Complete Letters of Sigmund Freud to Wilhelm Fliess, 1887–1904*, ed. Jeffrey Moussaieff Masson (Cambridge, Mass., 1985), p. 279.

73 Bein, *Theodor Herzl*, p. 82.

74 Ibid., p. 85n.

75 Arthur Schnitzler, *Briefe 1875–1912*, ed. Therese Nickl and Heinrich Schnitzler (Frankfurt, 1981), p. 237.

76 Theodor Herzl, *Gesammelte zionistische Werke*, vol. 5 (Tel Aviv, 1935), p. 124.

77 Ibid., p. 55.

78 Ibid., p. 89.

79 Schnitzler, *Briefe*, p. 239.

80 Karl Kraus, 'Wiener Kronik' (from *Die Wage*, 15 January 1898), in Kraus, *Frühe Schriften 1892–1900*, ed. J. J. Braakenburg, vol. 2 (Munich, 1979), p. 153; cf. 'Wiener Brief' (from *Breslauer Zeitung*, 16 January 1898), in ibid., pp. 156–7.

81 Daviau, *Mann von übermorgen*, p. 52; see also the study of the novel *Die Rotte Korahs* by Gilbert Ravy, in *Austriaca*, special number 'Autriche 1867–1938' (June 1988), pp. 113–14.

82 Hermann Bahr, 'Das neue Ghetto', *Die Zeit* 14.171 (8 January 1989), reprinted in *Das junge Wien. Österreichishe Literatur- und Kunstkritik, 1887–1902*, ed. Gotthart Wunberg (Tübingen, 1976), p. 812.

83 Anzieu, *L'auto-analyse de Freud*, and 'La bisexualité dans l'auto-analyse de Freud: le rêve "Mon fils, le myope"', *Nouvelle Revue de Psychanalyse*, no. 7 (1973), pp. 179–91; Alexander Grinstein, *On Sigmund Freud's Dreams* (Detroit, 1968), pp. 317–33, Peter Loewenberg, 'A Hidden Zionist Theme in Freud's My Son, the Myops Dream', *Journal of the History of Ideas*, no. 31 (Jan./Mar. 1970), pp. 129–32; David Bakan, *Freud et la tradition mystique juive* (Paris, 1977), pp. 145ff.; Robert, *D'Oedipe à Moïse*, pp. 198–201; Théo Pfrimmer, *Freud, lecteur de la Bible* (Paris, 1982), pp. 120–5; Lydia Flem, 'Freud entre Athènes, Rome et Jérusalem. La géographie d'un regard', *Revue Française de Psychanalyse*, no. 2 (1983), pp. 591–613; Chemouni, 'Freud et Herzl', pp. 193–203.

84 Robert, *D'Oedipe à Moïse*, p. 198.

85 Freud, *The Complete Letters of Sigmund Freud to Wilhelm Fliess, 1887–1904*, ed. Masson, p. 279.

86 Jones, *LWSF*, vol. 3, p. 232.

87 Robert *D'Oedipe à Moïse*, pp. 199–200.

88 Freud, *SE*, vol. 5, p. 443; *GW*, vols 2–3, p. 445.

89 Ibid., p. 444n; p. 447n.

90 Anzieu *L'auto-analyse de Freud*, p. 349.

91   Robert, *D'Oedipe à Moïse*, p. 200.
92   Grinstein, *On Sigmund Freud's Dreams*, p. 322. [Luther's Bible has 'Bei den Wässern'; the Authorized Version has 'rivers', and Coverdale's Psalter, the most familiar to Anglican churchgoers, has 'By the waters'. *Tr.*]
93   Jones, *LWSF*, vol. 3, p. 236.
94   Klein, *Jewish Origins*, p. 72.
95   See article 'B'nai B'rith' in the *Encyclopaedia Judaica*.
96   Freud, *SE*, vol. 5, p. 444; *GW*, vols 2–3, p. 446.
97   Ibid., pp. 443–4; pp. 445–6.
98   Ibid., p. 444; p. 444.
99   Quoted from the Authorized Version.
100   Freud, *The Complete Letters of Sigmund Freud to Wilhelm Fliess*, pp. 326, 336, 403, 408.
101   Jones, *LWSF*, vol. 1, p. 26.
102   In *The Interpretation of Dreams*, Freud speaks of 'my second son, to whom I had given the first name of a great historical figure who had powerfully attracted me in my boyhood, especially since my visit to England'. Freud, *SE*, vol. 5, pp. 447–8; *GW*, vols 2–3, p. 450.
103   Freud, *SE*, vol. 6, pp. 219–20; *GW*, vol. 4, pp. 58–9.
104   Jones, *LWSF*, vol. 1, p. 27.
105   Quoted ibid., p. 195.
106   Letter quoted in McGrath, *Freud's Discovery of Psychoanalysis*, pp. 129–30.
107   Schorske, 'Politics and parricide in Freud's *The Interpretation of Dreams*', in *Fin-de-siècle Vienna*; cf. Flem, 'Freud entre Athènes'.
108   Freud, *SE*, vol. 4, p. 195; *GW*, vols 2–3, p. 200.
109   Ibid., p. 196; p. 202.
110   Ibid., p. 197; p. 202.
111   Ibid., p. 196; p. 202.
112   Freud, *The Complete Letters of Sigmund Freud to Wilhelm Fliess*, p. 449.
113   Freud, *SE*, vol. 13, p. 232; *GW*, vol. 10, p. 195.
114   Ibid., p. 233; p. 198.
115   Conrad Ferdinand Meyer, 'Michelangelo und seine Statuen', in *Sämtliche Werke. Historisch-kritische Ausgabe*, ed. Hans Zeller and Alfred Zäch, vol. 1 (Berne, 1963), p. 331.
116   Heinrich Henel, *The Poetry of Conrad Ferdinand Meyer* (Madison, 1954), pp. 165ff.
117   Jacques Le Rider, 'Freud et la littérature', in *Histoire de la psychanalyse*, ed. Roland Jaccard (Paris, 1982), vol. 1, pp. 42, 49.
118   See e.g. Jones, *LWSF*, vol. 2, p. 411: 'One cannot avoid the pretty obvious conclusion that at this time, and probably before, Freud had identified himself with Moses and was striving to emulate the victory over passions that Michelangelo had depicted in his stupendous achievement.'
119   Leonard Shengold, 'Freud and Joseph', in *Freud and His Self-Analysis*, ed. Karl Kanzer and Jules Glenn (New York, 1979), pp. 67–89.
120   Freud, *SE*, vol. 5, p. 484n; *GW*, vols 2–3, p. 488n.
121   Ibid., pp. 421–5; pp. 425ff.
122   McGrath, *Freud's Discovery of Psychoanalysis*, pp. 47ff.

Chapter 12   Each a Modern Moses

1   Ernest Jones, *LWSF*, vol. 2, p. 226.
2   Ibid.
3   Sigmund Freud/Karl Abraham, *A Psycho-Analytic Dialogue: The Letters of Sigmund Freud and Karl Abraham 1907–26*, ed. H. C. Abraham and E. L. Freud, trans. B. Marsh and H. C. Abraham (London, 1965), p. 34.
4   H. Bloom makes this observation in *Ruin the Sacred Truths* (Cambridge, Mass., 1989), ch. 6; Yosef Hayim Yerushalmi makes the same observation, referring to letters which Freud wrote to Sabina Spielrein at the time he was collaborating with Jung, and afterwards when he broke with Jung, see Yerushalmi, *Freud's Moses: Judaism Terminable and Interminable* (New Haven/London, 1991).
5   Sigmund Freud/Karl Abraham, *Briefe 1907–26*, ed. Hilda C. Abraham and Ernst L. Freud (Frankfurt, 1965), pp. 48–9.
6   Ibid., p. 72.
7   Smiley Blanton, *Diary of My Analysis with Sigmund Freud* (New York, 1971).
8   Sigmund Freud, *Briefe, 1873–1939*, ed. Ernst and Lucie Freud (Frankfurt, 1968), p. 380.
9   Letter in Peter Gay, *A Godless Jew: Freud, Atheism and the Making of Psychoanalysis* (New Haven/London, 1987), p. 148.
10   Freud, *Briefe 1873–1939*, p. 381.
11   Sigmund Freud/Arnold Zweig, *Letters of Sigmund Freud and Arnold Zweig*, ed. E. L. Freud, trans. W. D. Robson-Scott (London, 1970), p. 40.
12   Sarah Kofman, 'Le don artistique et les limites de la psychanalyse', in *L'enfance de l'art. Une interprétation de l'esthétique freudienne* (2nd edn, Paris, 1985), pp. 215–29.
13   Sarah Kofman, *L'énigme de la femme. La femme dans les textes de Freud* (Paris, 1980).
14   Letter of 19 April 1936, in Freud, *Briefe 1873–1939*, p. 443.
15   Sigmund Freud, *SE*, vol. 13, p. xv; *GW*, vol. 14, p. 569.
16   Freud/Abraham, *A Psycho-Analytic Dialogue*, p. 264.
17   Jones, *LWSF*, vol. 3, p. 116.
18   Joseph Wortis, *Fragments of an Analysis With Freud* (New York, 1954), p. 146.
19   In Ernst Simon, 'Sigmund Freud, the Jew', *Leo Baeck Institute Year Book* 2 (London, 1957), pp. 270–305.
20   Jacquy Chemouni, 'Freud et les associations juives. Contributions à l'étude de sa judéité', *Revue Française de Psychanalyse*, no. 4 (1987), pp. 1207–43.
21   Freud, *Briefe 1873–1939*, p. 383.
22   In Gay, *A Godless Jew*, pp. 119–20.
23   Sigmund Freud, 'To the Opening of the Hebrew University', in English in Freud, *GW*, vol. 14, pp. 556–7.
24   Sigmund Freud/Arnold Zweig, *Letters*, p. 40.
25   Ibid., p. 45.
26   Freud, *SE*, vol. 23, p. 55; *GW*, vol. 16, p. 157.
27   Ibid.
28   Ibid., p. 57; pp. 159–60.
29   Marthe Robert, *D'Oedipe à Moise. Freud et la conscience juive* (Paris, 1974), p. 251; Martin Bergmann, 'Moses and the Evolution of Freud's Jewish Identity', *Israel Annals of Psychiatry and Related Disciplines* 14 (1976), pp. 3–26, also in *Judaism and Psychoanalysis*, ed. Mortimer Ostov (New York, 1982); H. P. Blum, 'Freud and the Figure of Moses: The Moses of Freud', *Journal of the American Psychoanalytic Association* 39 (1991), pp. 513–35.

30 Leon Poliakov, 'Freud et Moïse', in *Les Juifs et notre histoire* (Paris, 1973), p. 240. Yerushalmi (*Freud's Moses*, p. 5) recapitulates various sources for the theory that Jewish monotheism originated in Egypt: the historians James Breadsted and W. M. Flinders Petrie, and also Max Weber. Yerushalmi thinks that this theory had even earlier antecedents: Josephus, Strabo, Appian, Celsius, and later John Marsham, John Spencer and John Toland.

31 Friedrich Schiller, 'Die Sendung Moses', in *Sämtliche Werke*, ed. Gerhart Fricke and Herbert Göpfert (Munich, 1976), vol. 4, pp. 783–804.

32 Käte Hamburger, 'Thomas Manns Mose-Erzählung *Das Gesetz* auf dem Hintergrund der Überlieferung und der religionswissenschaftlichen Forschung', in Thomas Mann, *Das Gesetz* (Frankfurt/Berlin, 1964), p. 75.

33 Freud had originally intended to present his work as a 'historical novel'. See his letter to Arnold Zweig of 30 September 1934, in Freud/Zweig, *Letters*.

34 Freud, *Briefe 1873–1939*, p. 455.

35 Goethe, 'Israel in der Wüste', in *Noten und Abhandlungen zu besserem Verständnis des West-östlichen Divans*, Hamburger Ausgabe, ed. Erich Trunz, vol. 2 (Munich, 1972), pp. 207–25.

36 Ibid., p. 637n.

37 Ibid., p. 215.

38 Ibid., p. 224; cf. Norbert Oellers, 'Goethe und Schiller in ihrem Verhältnis zum Judentum', in *Conditio Judaica. Judentum, Antisemitismus und deutschsprachige Literatur vom 18. Jahrhundert bis zum Ersten Weltkrieg*, ed. Hans Otto Horch and Horst Denkler (Tübingen, 1988), pp. 108–30.

39 Freud, *SE*, vol. 23, p. 50; *GW*, vol. 16, p. 151.

40 Friedrich Hölderlin, *Sämtliche Werke und Briefe*, ed. Günter Mieth (Munich, 1970), vol. 2, p. 797.

41 Freud, *SE*, vol. 23, p. 30n; *GW*, vol. 14, p. 151n.

42 Heinrich Heine, 'Das neue israelitische Hospital zu Hamburg', in *Säkularausgabe* (Paris/Berlin, 1979), vol. 2, p. 107.

43 Heinrich Heine, 'Musikalische Saison von 1844, II', in ibid., vol. 11 (1974), p. 257.

44 L. Rosenthal, *Heinrich Heine als Jude* (Frankfurt, 1973).

45 Sander Gilman, 'The Jewish Reader: Freud Reads Heine Reads Freud', in *The Jew's Body* (New York/London, 1991), pp. 50–68; Gilman concludes that 'Heine's text functions for Freud as his own rhetorical double.'

46 Jean Starobinski, 'La salut à la statue', preface to French translation of Josef Popper-Lynkeus, *Fantaisies d'un réaliste*, trans. Cornelius Heim (Paris, 1987), pp. xvi–xvii; cf. Jacques Le Rider, 'La signification de Josef Popper-Lynkeus pour Sigmund Freud', *Austriaca*, no. 21 (1985), pp. 27–34.

47 In Israël Doryon, *Freud et le monothéisme hebreu. L'homme Moïse*, French trans. by Henri Baruk and M. Weisengrun (Paris, 1971), p. 56. There is a facsimile of Freud's letter in *Freudiana from the Collections of the Jewish National and University Library* (Jerusalem, 1973), p. xii.

48 Houston Stewart Chamberlain, *Die Grundlagen des XIX. Jahrhunderts*, Volksausgabe (10th edn, Munich, 1912), p. 495.

49 Houston Stewart Chamberlaim, *Immanuel Kant. Die Persöhnlichkeit als Einführung in das Werk* (1st edn 1905; 2nd edn, 1909), pp. 852–3; *Goethe* (Munich, 1912), p. 692.

50 Jean Favrat, 'La pensée de Paul de Lagarde (1827–1891). Contribution à l'étude de la religion et de la politique dans le nationalisme et le conservatisme allemands au XIXe siècle', thesis for Doctorat d'État, Université de Paris IV, 1976.

51   Paul de Lagarde, *Erklärung hebraïscher Wörter*, Abhandlungen der Königlichen Gesellschaft der Wissenschaft zu Göttingen 26 (1880), pp. 20ff.

52   In Max Schur, *Freud: Living and Dying* (London, 1972), p. 206; cf. chapter 9, note 40 above.

53   Paul Roazen, *La pensée politique et sociale de Freud* (Brussels, 1976), p. 112.

54   Jacques Le Rider, *Le cas Otto Weininger* (Paris, 1982), ch. 4.

55   Jones, *LWSF*, vol. 3, p. 170.

56   Freud, *SE*, vol. 23, pp. 122ff.; *GW*, vol. 16, pp. 197ff.

57   Freud, *SE*, vol. 23, p. 136; *GW*, vol. 16, pp. 245–6. Christoph Schulte, 'An Infidel Jew. Bemerkungen zu Freuds Psychoanalyse der Religion', in *Freuds Gegenwärtigkeit*, ed. Aron Ronald Bodenheimer (Stuttgart, 1991), comments on this passage: 'The hidden point: from the point of view of the psychoanalysis of religion, the Christian antisemite's accusation of deicide is in fact correct, though he does not know why' (p. 328). Schulte also notes that 'Freud, following Nietzsche, considers Saint Paul as the founding figure and shaper of Christian ideology' (p. 338).

58   Freud, *SE*, vol. 23, p. 135; *GW*, vol. 16, pp. 243–4.

59   Ibid., p. 91; pp. 197–8.

60   Ibid., pp. 91–2; p. 198.

61   Ibid., vol. 21, p. 144; vol. 14, p. 105.

62   Sander L. Gilman, 'The Madness of the Jews', in *Difference and Pathology: Stereotypes of Sexuality, Race and Madness* (Ithaca/New York, 1985), ch. 6, pp. 150ff.

63   M. Boudin, 'Sur l'idiotie et l'aliénation mentale des Juifs d'Allemagne', *Bulletin de la Société d'Anthropologie de Paris* (1863), pp. 386–8.

64   Jean-Martin Charcot, *Leçons de mardi à la Salpêtrière* (Paris, 1889), vol. 2, pp. 11–12.

65   Richard von Krafft-Ebing, *Lehrbuch der Psychiatrie auf klinischer Grundlage für practische Ärzte und Studirende*, vol. 1: *Die allgemeine Pathologie und Therapie des Irreseins* (Stuttgart, 1879), p. 139.

66   Jacquy Chemouni, *Freud, la psychanalyse et le judaïsme. Un messianisme sécularisé* (Paris, 1991), pp. 83ff.

67   Martin Engländer, *Die auffallend häufigen Krankheitserscheinungen der jüdischen Rasse* (Vienna, 1902).

68   Cesare Lombroso, *L'antisemitismo e la scienze moderne* (Turin, 1894).

69   Max Nordau, *Zionistische Schriften* (Cologne, 1909), pp. 379ff.

70   Rafael Becker, *Die jüdische Nervosität. Ihre Art, Entstehung und Bekämpfung* (Zurich, 1918); cf. *Die Nervosität bei den Juden. Ein Beitrag zur Rassenpsychologie für Ärzte und gebildete Laien* (Zurich, 1919).

71   Jean-François Lyotard, 'Figure forclose. 1er janvier 1969', *L'écrit du temps*, no. 5 (1984), p. 67.

72   Freud, *SE*, vol. 23, p. 115; *GW*, vol. 16, p. 223.

73   René Major, *De l'élection. Freud face aux idéologies américaine, allemande et soviétique* (Paris, 1986), esp. pp. 37ff., 46, 89.

74   There is a similar remark in Gustav Janouch's 'Conversations with Kafka': ' "Jews and Germans have more than one thing in common," said Kafka in the course of a conversation on the subject of Karel Krakar: "they are retentive, conscientious, hard-working, and cordially detested by everyone else. Jews and Germans are shut out." "Perhaps it is for those very virtues that people hate them," I said. But Kafka shook his head. "Oh no! The reason goes much deeper. In the end it comes down to religion. As regards the Jews that is obvious. As

regards the Germans, it is less clear, because no one has yet destroyed their temple. But it will come."'

75 Jacques Lacan, *Le Séminaire. Livre VII. L'éthique de la psychanalyse* (Paris, 1986), pp. 203ff.

76 Freud, *SE*, vol. 22, pp. 289–93; Heinrich Graf Coudenhove-Kalergi, *Das Wesen des Antisemitismus* (1901), ed. and intro. R. N. Coudenhove-Kalergi (Leipzig/ Vienna, 1929; 2nd edn 1932); cf. Jacquy Chemouni, 'Freud, interprète de l'antisémitisme', *Frénésie: Histoire, Psychiatrie, Psychoanalyse*, no. 4 (1987), pp. 17–36; Hermann Beland, 'Religiose Würzeln des Antisemitismus', *Psyche* 5 (1991), pp. 448–70.

77 Freud, *SE*, vol. 23, p. 286; *GW*, vol. 16, pp. 186ff.

78 Brigitte Stemberger, 'Der Mann Moses in Freuds Gesamtwerk', *Kairos: Zeit-schrift für Religionswissenschaft und Theologie*, nos 3–4 (1974), p. 223. Éliane Amado Lévy-Valensi, *Le Moïse de Freud ou la référence occultée* (Monaco, 1984), suggests that the Zohar was another inspiration for 'Moses the murdered Egyptian'.

79 Marie Moscovici, 'Le roman secret', preface to French trans. of Freud, *L'homme Moïse et le monothéisme* (Paris, 1986), p. 37.

80 Letter of 16 December 1984, in Freud/Zweig, *Letters*, p. 98.

81 Freud, *SE*, vol. 23, p. 66; *GW*, vol. 16, p. 169.

82 Another objection frequently made by detractors of *Moses and Monotheism* is to Freud's hypothesis of 'psycho-Lamarckian heredity', which assumes that psychic characteristics have been passed down among the Jewish people for centuries without substantial alteration. See Michael P. Carroll, '*Moses and Monotheism* Revisited: Freud's Personal Myth?', *American Imago* 44.1 (1987), pp. 15–35. However, Lucille B. Ritvo, *Darwin's Influence on Freud: A Tale of Two Sciences* (New Haven: Yale, 1990), has shown that Freud associated the theory of the passing on of acquired characteristics with Darwin rather than Lamarck.

83 Martin Buber, 'Moses', in *Werke*, vol. 2: *Schriften zur Bibel* (Munich, 1964), p. 11n. Among the first Jewish criticisms of Freud's *Moses* were Trude Weiss-Rosmarin, *The Hebrew Moses: An Answer to Sigmund Freud* (New York, 1939), and Abraham S. Yahuda, 'Sigmund Freud on Moses and His Teaching', in *'Eber-Ve'-Arab* (New York, 1946).

84 Letter of 14 March 1935, in Freud/Zweig, *Letters*, p. 104; Michel de Certeau, 'Freud et l'écriture de l'histoire', *Psychanalystes: Revue du College des Psych-analystes*, no. 19 (1986), p. 6; de Certeau, *Histoire et psychanalyse entre science et fiction* (Paris, 1987).

85 Cf. Jacques Le Rider, 'Les intellectuels viennois et Nietzsche. Autour de Sigmund Freud', in *De Sils-Maria à Jerusalem. Nietzsche et le judaisme. Les intellectuels juifs et Nietzsche*, ed. Dominique Bourel and Jacques Le Rider (Paris, 1991), pp. 197–8.

86 Letter of 12 May 1934, in Freud/Zweig, *Letters*, p. 77.

87 Yerushalmi, *Freud's Moses*, p. 17; the original German text is printed in appendix 1. (The first commentary on this previously unknown Freud text was P. C. Bori, 'Una pagina inedita di Freud. La premessa al romanzo storico su Mose', *Rivista di storia contemporanea*, pp. 1–17.)

88 Ilse Gubrich-Simitis, *Freuds Moses-Studie als Tagtraum*, Die Sigmund-Freud-Vorlesungen 3 (Weinheim, 1991).

89 'Creative Writers and Day-Dreaming', in Freud, *SE*, vol. 9, pp. 141–54; *GW*, vol. 7, pp. 213–23.

90 Here, Gubrich-Simitis is following H. T. Hardin's suggested interpretation of

Freud's early childhood in 'On the Vicissitudes of Freud's Early Mothering. I. Early Environment and Loss', *Psychoanalytic Quarterly* 56 (1988), pp. 628–44; 'II. Alienation from His Biological Mother', *Psychoanalytic Quarterly* 57 (1988), pp. 72–86; 'III. Freiberg, Screen Memories and Loss', ibid., pp. 209–23.

91 Shulamit Volkov, 'Die Erfindung einer Tradition. Zur Entstehung des modernen Judentums in Deutschland', *Historische Zeitschrift* 253.3 (Dec. 1991), pp. 603–28.

92 Stemberger, 'Der Mann Moses', p. 224.

93 Jones, *LWSF*, vol. 3, pp. 210–11, 221.

94 Dennis B. Klein, *Jewish Origins of the Psychoanalytic Movement* (2nd edn, Chicago/London, 1985), p. 160.

95 Freud, *SE*, vol. 23, p. 27n; *GW*, vol. 16, p. 125.

96 Ibid., p. 31; p. 130.

97 Ibid., p. 58; p. 160.

98 Freud, *GW*, vol. 11, p. 163.

99 Ibid., vol. 6, p. 266.

100 Theodor Reik, *Jewish Wit* (New York, 1962), pp. 219ff.; Eliott Oring, *The Jokes of Freud: A Study in Humor and Jewish Identity* (Philadelphia, 1984); Sarah Kofman, *Pourquoi rit-on? Freud et le mot d'esprit* (Paris, 1986); Sander L. Gilman, 'Freud and the Jewish Joke', in Gilman, *Difference and Pathology*, pp. 175ff. Klein, *Jewish Origins*, points out that in 1907 Freud gave a lecture on the *Witz* to B'nai B'rith (p. 161n).

101 Robert, *D'Oedipe à Moise*, p. 275.

102 Ibid., pp. 276ff.

103 Roazen, *Pensée politique et sociale*, p. 113.

104 Freud, *SE*, vol. 23, p. 23; *GW*, vol. 16, p. 121.

105 Eugène Enriquez, *De la horde à l'État. Essai de psychanalyse du lien social* (Paris, 1983), p. 151.

106 Ibid.

107 Karl Abraham, 'Amenhotep IV. (Echnaton)', *Imago: Zeitschrift für Anwendung der Psychanalyse auf die Geisteswissenschaften* 1.4 (1912), pp. 334–60.

108 Estelle Roith, *The Riddle of Freud: Jewish Influences on his Theory of Female Sexuality* (London, 1987), pp. 171–2; cf. Leonard Shengold, 'A Parapraxis of Freud's in relation to Karl Abraham', *American Imago* 29.2 (1972), pp. 123–59.

109 Freud, *SE*, vol. 23, p. 65n; *GW*, vol. 16, p. 168.

110 Robert, *D'Oedipe à Moise*, p. 259ff.

111 Freud, *SE*, vol. 23, p. 190; *GW*, vol. 16, p. 197.

112 Freud, *Briefe, 1873–1939*, p. 459.

113 Jones, *LWSF*, vol. 3, p. 225.

114 See Käte Hamburger, *Der Humor bei Thomas Mann. Zum Joseph-Roman* (Munich, 1965), pp. 231–2 n30.

115 Thomas Mann, 'Joseph und seine Brüder, ein Vortrag' (1942), in *Werke. Das essayistische Werk. Taschenausgabe in acht Bänden*, ed. Hans Burgin, vol. 2: *Schriften und Reden zur Literatur, Kunst und Philosophie* (Frankfurt, 1968), p. 386.

116 Hans Mayer, *Thomas Mann* (Frankfurt, 1980), pp. 217–18.

117 Paul Ladrière, 'Die rationalisierende Funktion der religiösen Ethik in Webers Theorie der Moderne', in *Verabschiedung der (Post)-Moderne?* ed. Jacques Le Rider and Gérard Raulet (Tübingen, 1987), pp. 18–40; cf. Freddy Raphaël, *Judaïsme et capitalisme. Essai sur la controverse entre Max Weber et Werner Sombart* (Paris, 1982).

118 Marianne Krüll, *Freud und sein Vater* (Munich, 1979).

119 Sigmund Freud, 'Anti-Semitism in England' (1938), in *SE*, vol. 23, p. 301.

120 Quoted in Klaus Dethloff (ed.), *Theodor Herzl, oder der Moses des fin de siècle* (Vienna/Cologne, 1986), p. 54.

121 Ibid., p. 245 (extract from *Der Judenstaat*).

122 Theodor Herzl, *Briefe und Tagebücher*, ed. Alex Bein, Hermann Greive, Moshe Scharf and Julius H. Schoeps, vol. 2 (Frankfurt, 1983), p. 242.

123 Amos Elon, *Theodor Herzl. Eine Biographie* (Vienna/Munich, 1979), p. 22; from Reuben Brainin, *Chajej Herzl* ('The Life of Herzl'), vol. 1 (New York, 1919).

124 Elon, *Theodor Herzl*, p. 15.

125 Hans Tietze, *Die Juden Wiens. Geschichte, Wirtschaft, Kultur* (1st edn 1933; reprint Vienna, 1987), p. 264.

126 In Tietze, *Juden Wiens*, p. 266.

127 In Dethloff, *Theodor Herzl*, p. 57.

128 Ibid., p. 245 (from *Der Judenstaat*).

129 Anecdote in Jacob Weinshal, *Hans Herzl* (Tel Aviv, 1945), quoted in Avner Falk, 'Freud and Herzl', *Midstream*, no. 23 (Jan. 1977), pp. 3–24; cf. William J. McGrath, *Freud's Discovery of Psychoanalysis* (Ithaca/London, 1986), pp. 313ff.; Jacquy Chemouni, *Freud et le sionisme* (Paris, 1988), p. 272n.

130 Cf. Sigmund Freud, *The Interpretation of Dreams*, in *GW*, vols 2–3, p. 203.

Chapter 13   Karl Kraus, or the Undiscoverable Jewish Identity

1 Karl Kraus, 'Die demolirte Literatur', in Kraus, *Frühe Schriften, 1892–1900*, ed. Johannes J. Braakenburg (Munich, 1979), vol. 2, pp. 277–97.

2 This error is found in Michel Siegert, 'Karl Kraus et le sionisme', *Cahier de l'Herne Karl Kraus*, no. 28 (1975), pp. 154–9.

3 Karl Kraus, 'Eine Krone für Zion', in *Frühe Schriften*, vol. 2, p. 304.

4 Ibid., p. 306.

5 For a more detailed analysis of Karl Kraus's position, see my article 'Karl Kraus ou l'identité juive déchirée', in *Vienne au tournant du siècle*, ed. François Latraverse and Walter Moser (Montreal/Paris, 1988), pp. 103–51. It will be noticed that when Kraus claims that some degree of antisemitism, if well understood, could advance the social struggle, he is echoing the ideas of Karl Marx in *The Jewish Question* (1844). Cf. Julius Carlebach, *Karl Marx and the Radical Critique of Judaism* (London/Boston, 1978), for an (approving) critique of the idea that Marx suffered from *jüdischer Selbsthass*, developed in particular in Arnold Künzli, *Karl Marx: Eine Psychographie* (Vienna, 1966).

6 Sigurd Paul Scheichl, 'Karl Kraus und die Politik', unpubl. dissertation, University of Innsbruck, 1971; among contributions to the discussion of Karl Kraus's Jewish identity we may mention Wilma Abeles Iggers, *Karl Kraus: A Viennese Critic of the Twentieth Century* (The Hague, 1967), and Klara Pomeranz Carmely, *Das Identitätsproblem jüdischer Autoren im deutschen Sprachraum, von der Jahrhundertwende bis zu Hitler* (Königstein, 1981), pp. 16–43.

7 For such an examination see my 'Karl Kraus ou l'identité juive déchirée', in *Vienne*, ed. Latraverse and Moser.

8 Helmut Arntzen, *Karl Kraus und die Presse* (Munich, 1975), p. 24.

9 Arthur Schnitzler, *Briefe, 1875–1912*, ed. Therese Nickl and Heinrich Schnitzler (Frankfurt, 1981), p. 377.

10 Cf. Sigurd Paul Scheichl, 'Réactions autrichiennes à l'affaire Dreyfus', in *Re-*

lations franco-autrichiennes, 1870–1970, Actes du Colloque de Rouen, 29 Feb. to 2 Mar. 1984, special issue of *Austriaca* (June 1986), pp. 241–59.

11 Wolfgang Bunte, *Peter Rosegger und das Judentum* (Hildesheim/New York, 1977).
12 Brigitte Hamann, *Bertha von Suttner. Ein Leben für den Frieden* (Munich, 1986), pp. 222ff.
13 Jacob Toury, 'Troubled Beginnings: The Emergence of the Österreichisch-Israelitische Union', *Leo Baeck Institute Year Book* 30 (London, 1985), pp. 457–75.
14 Marc Angenot, *La parole pamphlétaire. Typologie des discours modernes* (Paris, 1982), pp. 337ff.
15 Ibid., pp. 339ff.
16 Ibid., pp. 350ff.
17 Werner Kraft, 'Canetti pour et contre Karl Kraus', *Austriaca*, no. 11 (1980), pp. 81–8.
18 Theodor Lessing, *Der jüdische Selbsthass* (1st edn 1930; reprint Munich, 1984), p. 43.
19 *Die Fackel*, nos 890–905 (July 1934), p. 36.
20 Some specialists fundamentally question the validity of the notion of *jüdischer Selbsthass*. Thus Allan Janik in 'Viennese Culture and the Jewish Self-Hatred Hypothesis: A Critique', in *Jews, Antisemitism and Culture in Vienna*, ed. Ivan Oxaal, Michael Pollak and Gerhard Botz (London/New York, 1987), pp. 75–88.
21 Hans Dieter Hellige, 'Rathenau und Harden in der Gesellschaft des Deutschen Kaiserreichs. Eine sozialgeschichtlich-biographische Studie zur Entstehung neokonservativer Positionen bei Unternehmern und Intellektuellen', in Walther Rathenau/Maximilian Harden, *Briefwechsel 1897–1920*, ed. H. D. Hellige (Walther Rathenau Gesamtausgabe 6) (Munich/Heidelberg, 1983); cf. Paul Letourneau, 'Rathenau et la question juive', *Revue d'Allemagne* 13.3 (July–Sept. 1981). Other contributions to the debate over *jüdischer Selbsthass* include Harry Zohn, 'Karl Kraus: "Jüdischer Selbsthasser" oder "Erzjuder"?', *Modern Austrian Literature* 8.1–2 (1975), pp. 1–18; Peter Gay, 'Hermann Levi: A Study in Service and Self Hatred', in *Freud, Jews and Other Germans: Masters and Victims in Modernist Culture* (New York, 1978), pp. 189–230; Sander L. Gilman, *Jewish Self Hatred* (Baltimore, 1987), on Kraus see pp. 233–41; Nike Wagner, 'Incognito ergo sum – Zur jüdischen Frage bei Karl Kraus', *Literatur und Kritik*, nos 219–20 (Nov.–Dec. 1987), pp. 387–99; Kurt Lewin, 'Self-Hatred Among Jews' (1941), in *Resolving Social Conflicts: Selected Papers on Group Dynamics*, ed. Gertrude Weiss (New York, 1948), pp. 186–200; Walter Grab, '"Jüdischer Selbsthass" und jüdische Selbstachtung in der deutschen Literatur und Publizistik 1890–1933', in *Der deutsche Weg der Judenemanzipation, 1789–1938* (Munich/Zurich, 1991), pp. 152–84; Jens Malte Fischer, 'Identifikation mit dem Aggressor? Zur Problematik des jüdischen Selbsthasses um 1900', in *Menora. Jahrbuch für deutsch-jüdische Geschichte* (1992), pp. 23–48.
22 Arnold Zweig, *Caliban oder Politik und Leidenschaft: Versuch über die menschlichen Gruppenleidenschaften, dargetan am Antisemitismus* (Potsdam, 1927), pp. 199ff.
23 Albertø Memmi, *Portrait d'un Juif, II, La libération du Juif* (Paris, 1966), pp. 92ff.
24 Ibid., pp. 94ff. Louis-Albert Revah's *Julien Benda. Un misanthrope juif dans la France de Maurras* (Paris, 1991) has revealed a case of *jüdischer Selbsthass* very similar to Kraus's.
25 Shlomo Avineri, *The Making of Modern Zionism* (London, 1981), pp. 163–78.
26 *Die Fackel*, no. 92 (Jan. 1902), pp. 1ff. The article occupies the entire issue and was reprinted as a pamphlet.
27 Ibid., p. 24.
28 Scheichl, 'Karl Kraus und die Politik', vol. 3, p. 859.

29 Edward Timms, *Karl Kraus, Apocalyptic Satirist: Culture and Catastrophe in Habsburg Vienna* (New Haven/London, 1986), p. 239.

30 'Gebet an die Sonne von Gideon', *Die Fackel*, nos 423–5 (5 May 1916), pp. 58–64.

31 The section on Kraus's Jewishness in Leopold Liegler, *Karl Kraus und sein Werk* (Vienna, 1920), pp. 143ff., makes extensive reference to Weininger and Chamberlain. Martin Buber drew the same parallel in a letter to Werner Kraft of 20 March 1917, see Martin Buber, *Briefwechsel aus sieben Jahrzehnten*, vol. 1: *1897–1918*, ed. Grete Schaeder (Heidelberg, 1972), p. 487.

32 Otto Weininger, *SC*, p. 315; *GuCh*, pp. 421–2.

33 Ibid., p. 317; pp. 426–7.

34 Léon Poliakov, *Le mythe aryen. Essai sur les sources du racisme et des nationalismes* (Paris, 1971).

35 See Hans Mayer, *Aussenseiter* (Frankfurt, 1975), p. 122.

36 Thomas Szasz, *Karl Kraus and the Soul-Doctors* (London, 1977).

37 Gershom Scholem, 'Juifs et Allemands', in *Fidélité et utopie. Essais sur le judaïsme contemporain* (Paris, 1978), pp. 87–8.

38 Otto Weininger, *Über die letzten Dinge* (reprint Munich, 1980), pp. 90–4.

39 *Die Fackel*, no. 290 (11 Nov. 1909), pp. 1–5.

40 *Die Fackel*, nos 413–17 (Dec. 1915), p. 28. In the same issue, pp. 49ff., Kraus printed a violently antisemitic essay on Judaism by Dostoevsky.

41 *Die Fackel*, nos 418–22 (Apr. 1916), pp. 8–9.

42 Ibid., p. 9.

43 *Die Fackel*, nos 457–61 (May 1917), p. 96.

44 Scheichl, 'Kraus und die Politik', pp. 879–83; Emil Sander, *Gesellschaftliche Struktur und literarischer Ausdruck. Über 'Die letzten Tage der Menschheit'* (Königstein, 1979), pp. 165–6.

45 *Die Fackel*, no. 386 (29 Oct. 1913), p. 3.

46 Ibid., pp. 4–5.

47 *Der Brenner* 3 (1912–13), pp. 847–8.

48 Sigurd Paul Scheichl, 'Aspekte des Judentums im *Brenner*', in *Untersuchungen zum 'Brenner'. Festschrift für Ignaz Zangerle* (Salzburg, 1981), pp. 81–2; Gerald Stieg, *Der Brenner und Die Fackel. Ein Beitrag zur Wirkungsgeschichte von Karl Kraus* (Salzburg, 1976), pp. 257–8.

49 Cover of *Ostara: Briefbücherei der Blonden*, no. 101 (1927) ('Lanz Liebenfels und sein Werk, I. Teil: Einführung in die Theorie').

50 *Die Fackel*, nos 890–5 (end of July 1934), pp. 101–2; cf. *Die Dritte Walpurgisnacht* (Munich, 1967), pp. 283–4.

51 *Die Fackel*, nos 847–51 (end of Mar. 1931), pp. 84ff.

52 Ibid., p. 38.

53 Ibid., p. 37.

54 Mayer, *Aussenseiter*, p. 133; Nike Wagner, *Geist und Geschlecht. Karl Kraus und die Erotik der Wiener Moderne* (Frankfurt, 1982); Alfred Pfabigan, 'Frauenverehrung und Frauenverachtung', *Literatur und Kritik*, nos 213–14 (April–May 1987), pp. 123–30.

55 Cf. Alfred Pfabigan, *Karl Kraus und der Sozialismus* (Vienna, 1976), pp. 33–4; Karl Kraus, *Briefe an Sidonie Nádherný von Borutin*, ed. Heinrich Fischer and Michael Lazarus, revised Walter Methlagl and Friedrich Pfäfflin (Munich, 1977), vol. 2: *Sidonie Nádherný in ihren Tagebüchern und Briefen*, pp. 31–2.

56 Robert S. Wistrich, *The Jews of Vienna in the Age of Franz Joseph* (Oxford, 1989), pp. 67–8.

57 *Die Fackel*, no. 150 (23 Dec. 1903), pp. 28–9.

58   Timms, *Karl Kraus*, pp. 188–92.
59   *Die Fackel*, no. 148 (2 Dec. 1903), pp. 28–9.
60   Sander L. Gilman, 'Opera, Homosexuality, and Models of Disease: Richard Strauss's *Salome* in the Context of Images of Disease in the Fin de siècle', in Gilman, *Disease and Representation: Images of Illness from Madness to AIDS* (Ithaca/London, 1988), pp. 155–81.
61   See my 'Karl Kraus ou l'identité juive dechirée', in *Vienne*, ed. Latraverse and Moser, pp. 134–5; Leo Lensing, 'Sexuality and Jewish Identity in Karl Kraus' Literary Polemics Against Heinrich Heine', in *The Jewish Reception of Heinrich Heine*, ed. Mark H. Gelber, *Conditio Judaica*, vol. 1 (Tübingen, 1992).
62   Karl Kraus, 'Heine und die Folgen', *Die Fackel*, nos 329–30 (31 Aug. 1911), pp. 1ff.; cf. Mechtild Borries, *Ein Angriff auf Heinrich Heine. Kritische Betrachtungen zu Karl Kraus* (Cologne/Mainz/Stuttgart, 1971).
63   Kraus, 'Heine und die Folgen'.
64   'Die Feinde Goethe und Heine' and 'Die Freunde Heine und Rothschild', *Die Fackel*, no. 406 (Oct. 1915), pp. 52–89, 90–3.
65   Scheichl, 'Karl Kraus und die Politik', p. 869.
66   *Die Fackel*, nos 360–2 (7 Nov. 1912), pp. 53ff.
67   *Die Fackel*, no 386 (29 Oct. 1903), p. 3.
68   Gilman, *Jewish Self Hatred*.
69   Steven E. Aschheim, *The East European Jew in German and German Jewish Consciousness, 1800–1923* (Madison, Wis. 1982).
70   Theodor Billroth, *Über das Lehren und Lernen der medicinischen Wissenschaften* (Vienna, 1876), p. 153.
71   Eduard Engel, *Sprich deutsch! Ein Buch zur Entwelschung* (1917).
72   Fritz Mauthner, *Beiträge zu einer Kritik der Sprache* (Frankfurt/Berlin, 1982), vol. 1, pp. 169–70; cf. Gershon Weiler, 'Fritz Mauthner: A Study in Jewish Self-Rejection', in *Leo Baeck Institute Year Book* 8 (London, 1963), pp. 136–48.
73   Weininger, *SC*, p. 320; *GuCh*, p. 187.
74   Theodor Herzl, 'Mauschel' (*Die Welt*, 15 Oct. 1897), in *Gesammelte zionistische Werke in fünf Bänden*, vol. 1 (Tel Aviv, 1934), pp. 209–15.
75   Josef Breuer, 'Krankengeschichte (Anna O.)', addressed to Robert Binswanger from the Bellevue Sanatorium in Kreuzlingen, in Albrecht Hirschmüller, *Physiologie und Psychoanalyse im Werk Josef Breuers* (Berne, 1978), pp. 349ff.
76   Richard Wagner, 'Das Judentum in der Musik', in Wagner, *Mein Denken*, ed. Martin Gregor-Dellin (Munich, 1982), pp. 173–90.
77   Ibid., pp. 177ff.
78   In Henry-Louis de La Grange, *Gustav Mahler*, vol. 3 (Paris, 1984), pp. 384ff.
79   Karl Kraus, 'Pro domo et mundo', in *Beim Wort genommen, Werkausgabe*, ed. Heinrich Fischer, vol. 3 (Munich, 1955), p. 294; *Aphorismen*, vol. 8 of *Schriften*, ed. Christian Wagenknecht (Frankfurt, 1986), p. 294.
80   *Die Fackel* 326–8 (1911), p. 44; *Aphorismen*, p. 291.
81   Nike Wagner, *Geist und Geschlecht*, p. 196.
82   Karl Kraus, *Die dritte Walpurgisnacht*, ed. Heinrich Fischer (1st edn 1952; Munich, 1967), p. 139.
83   Franz Kafka, letter of June 1921, to Max Brod, in *Briefe 1902–1924*, see *Gesammelte Werke*, ed. Max Brod (New York/Frankfurt, 1958), pp. 336–7; cf. Hartmut Binder, *Kafka in neuer Sicht* (Stuttgart, 1976), pp. 386ff.

Chapter 14 The 'Cultural Zionism' of Richard Beer-Hofmann

1 Richard Beer-Hofmann, 'Paula. Ein Fragment', in *GW*, pp. 684–5.
2 'Richard Beer-Hofmann. Daten', *Modern Austrian Literature*, no. 2 (1984).
3 Rainer Hank, *Mortifikation und Beschwörung. Zur Veränderung ästhetischer Wahrnehmung in der Moderne am Beispiel des Frühwerkes Richard Beer-Hofmanns* (Frankfurt, 1984), p. 171.
4 Marsha L. Rozenblit, *The Jews of Vienna, 1867–1914: Assimilation and Identity* (Albany, 1984), p. 104.
5 Arthur Schnitzler, *Jugend in Wien. Eine Autobiographie* (Vienna, 1968), pp. 80–1.
6 In Hank, *Mortifikation*, p. 175. Cf. Georg Schroubek, 'Der Ritualmord von Polna. Traditionneller und moderner Wahnglaube', in *Antisemitismus und jüdische Geschichte. Studien zu Ehren von Herbert A. Strauss*, ed. Rainer Erb and Michel Schmidt (Berlin, 1987), pp. 149–71.
7 Hugo von Hofmannsthal/Richard Beer-Hofmann, *Briefwechsel*, ed. Eugene Weber (Frankfurt, 1972), p. vii.
8 Ibid., p. ix.
9 Quoted in Hank, *Mortifikation*, p. 14.
10 Hofmannsthal/Beer-Hofmann, *Briefwechsel*, p. 17.
11 Ibid., p. 7.
12 Eduard Sekler, *Josef Hoffmann. Das architektonische Werk* (Salzburg/Vienna, 1982), pp. 298–9.
13 Werner Vordtriede, 'Gespräche mit Beer-Hofmann', *Neue Rundschau* (1952), p. 131.
14 Letters of 20 July 1894 and 2 April 1900, cf. letter of 10 May 1896, in Hofmannsthal/Beer-Hofmann, *Briefwechsel*, pp. 35, 98, 58–9; Otto Oberhölzer, *Richard Beer-Hofmann. Werk und Weltbild des Dichters* (Berne, 1947), pp. 25–6.
15 Clemens Sokal, 'Junge Novellen', *Neue Revue*, 31 Jan. 1894, in *Das junge Wien. Österreichische Literatur- und Kunstkritik, 1897–1902*, ed. Gotthart Wunberg (Tübingen, 1976), vol. 1, p. 435.
16 Hofmannsthal/Beer-Hofmann, *Briefwechsel*, pp. 24–5.
17 In Hank, *Mortifikation*, p. 32; on the relationship between Lou Andreas-Salomé and Richard Beer-Hofmann see Rudolph Binion, *Frau Lou: Nietzsche's Wayward Disciple* (Princeton, 1968), pp. 190–204; Ursula Welsch and Michaela Wiesner, *Lou Andreas-Salomé. Vom 'Lebensurgrund' zur Psychoanalyse* (Munich/Vienna, 1988), pp. 151–6.
18 Quoted in Alex Bein, *Theodor Herzl. Biographie* (Frankfurt/Vienna, 1983), p. 141.
19 Hank, *Mortifikation*, p. 179.
20 Ibid.
21 Richard Beer-Hofmann, 'Schlaflied für Mirjam', in *GW*, p. 654.
22 Beer-Hofmann, *GW*, p. 611; *TG*, p. 102.
23 Ibid., p. 607; p. 98.
24 Ibid., pp. 613–14; pp. 105–6.
25 Ibid., p. 615; p. 107.
26 Ibid., p. 616; p. 107.
27 Ibid., p. 619; pp. 111–12.
28 Ibid., pp. 621–2; p. 114.
29 Georg Lukács, 'The Moment and Form', in *Soul and Form* (London, 1974), pp.

107–23; cf. Rainer Rochlitz, *Le jeune Lukács* (Paris, 1983), pp. 90–6; Endre Kiss, *Der Tod der k.u.k. Weltordnung in Wien* (Vienna, 1986), pp. 192ff.

30   Pierre Citti, *Contre la décadence. Histoire de l'imagination française dans le roman, 1890–1914* (Paris, 1987), pp. 69ff.

31   Quoted in ibid., p. 72.

32   In ibid., p. 74.

33   In ibid., p. 79.

34   Hugo von Hofmannsthal, *RuA*, vol. 1, pp. 119–290; cf. Ruthard Stäblein, 'Dissociation du sujet et culte du moi. La réception de la décadence barrésienne chez Hugo von Hofmannsthal et Hermann Bahr', in *Vienne au tournant du siècle*, ed. François Latraverse and Walter Moser (Montreal/Paris, 1988), pp. 217–57.

35   Hofmannsthal, *RuAI*, pp. 123ff.

36   Beer-Hofmann, *GW*, pp. 531–2; *TG*, pp. 13–14.

37   Ibid., p. 536; p. 18.

38   Maurice Barrès, 'Le culte du moi. III, Le jardin de Bérénice' (1891), in *L'oeuvre de Maurice Barrès*, ed. Philippe Barrès (Paris, 1965), vol. 1, p. 369.

39   Harry Zohn, '*Ich bin ein Sohn der deutschen Sprache nur.*' *Jüdisches Erbe in der österreichischen Literatur. Darstellungen und Dokumentation* (Vienna/Munich, 1986), p. 41.

40   Beer-Hofmann, *GW*, p. 556; *TG*, p. 40.

41   Ibid., p. 559; p. 43. Cf. the interpretation by Jens Malte Fischer in *Fin de siècle. Kommentar zu einer Epoche* (Munich, 1978), pp. 197–203.

42   Beer-Hofmann, p. 535; *TG*, pp. 16–17.

43   Ibid., p. 566; p. 51.

44   Esther N. Elstun, *Richard Beer-Hofmann: His Life and Work* (Philadelphia, 1983), p. 59.

45   As Hartmut Scheible does in *Literarischer Jugendstil in Wien* (Munich/Zurich, 1984) and in his afterword to 'George's Death', in Beer-Hofmann, *TG*.

46   Gustave Flaubert, *La tentation de saint Antoine* (1849 version) in *Oeuvres*, vol. 1 (Paris, 1961), p. 198.

47   Erwin Rohde, *Psyche. Seelenkult und Unsterblichkeitsglaube der Griechen* (Freiburg/Leipzig, 1890–4; 2nd edn 1898).

48   Beer-Hofmann, *GW*, p. 882.

49   Martin Buber, Preface to ibid., pp. 5ff.

50   This theme is strongly highlighted in Scheible, *Literarischer Jugendstil*, and Hank, *Mortifikation*.

51   Beer-Hofmann, *GW*, pp. 574ff.; *TG*, pp. 61ff.

52   William M. Johnston, *The Austrian Mind: An Intellectual and Social History* (Berkeley, 1972), pp. 223–9.

53   Friedrich Nietzsche, *CW*, vol. 16, p. 88; *KSA*, vol. 6, p. 134.

54   Scheible, afterword to 'George's Death', in Beer-Hofmann, *TG*, p. 125.

55   Beer-Hofmann, *GW*, p. 534; *TG*, pp. 15–16.

56   Cf. Wolfdietrich Rasch, 'Fläche, Welle, Ornament. Zur Deutung der nach-impressionistischen Malerei und des Jugenstils', in Rasch, *Zur deutschen Literatur seit der Jahrhundertwende* (Stuttgart, 1967), pp. 186ff. Hermann Bahr criticized the excessive preciosity of Beer-Hofmann's ornamented style, see Wunberg, *Das junge Wien*, vol. 2, pp. 1038–9.

57   Cf. chapter 7 above, pp. 141–3.

58   Sigmund Freud, 'A Metaphysical Supplement to the Theory of Dreams', in *SE*, vol. 14, p. 223; *GW*, vol. 10, p. 413.

59   *Group Psychology and the Analysis of the Ego*, in *SE*, vol. 18, pp. 75–6; *GW*, vol. 10, pp. 3–161.

60 Janine Chasseguet-Smirgel, 'L'idéal du moi et le groupe', in *Le narcissisme, l'amour de soi*, ed. André Haynal (Paris, 1975), pp. 171–2.

61 Didier Anzieu, 'L'illusion groupale', *Nouvelle Revue de Psychanalyse*, no. 4 (1971).

62 Walter H. Sokel, 'Narzissmus und Judentum. Zum Oeuvre Richard Beer-Hofmanns', in *Zeitgenossenschaft. Zur deutschsprachigen Literatur im 20. Jahrhundert*, ed. Paul Michael Lützeler (Festschrift Egon Schwarz) (Königstein, 1987), pp. 33–47.

63 Olga Schnitzler, *Spiegelbild einer Freundschaft* (Salzburg, 1962), p. 96.

64 Hank, *Mortifikation*, p. 189.

65 Karl Kraus, 'Eine Krone für Zion', in *Frühe Schriften, 1892–1900*, ed. Johannes J. Braakenburg (Munich, 1979), vol. 2, p. 305.

66 See Peter de Mendelssohn's afterword to Thomas Mann, *Frühe Erzählungen*, in *Gesammelte Werke in Einzelbänden*, ed. P. de Mendelssohn (Frankfurt, 1981), p. 684.

67 Thomas Mann, *Wälsungenblut*, in *Gesammelte Werke*, p. 506.

68 Ibid.

69 Erwin Koppen, *Dekadenter Wagnerismus. Studien zur europäischen Literatur des Fin de siècle* (Berlin/New York, 1963), pp. 144ff.

70 Mann, *Wälsungenblut*, p. 521.

71 Erich von Kahler, *Die Verantwortung des Geistes* (Frankfurt, 1952), p. 137.

72 Alfred Werner, *Richard Beer-Hofmann, Sinn und Gehalt. Zum 70. Geburtstag* (Vienna, 1936).

73 Hans Gerhard Neumann, *Richard Beer-Hofmann. Studien und Materialien zur 'Historie von König David'* (Munich, 1972); Antje Kleinewefers, *Das Problem der Erwählung bei Richard Beer-Hofmann* (Hildesheim, 1972); Kathleen Harris, 'Richard Beer-Hofmann: Ein grosser Wiener jüdischer und deutscher Dichter', in *Akten des VII. Internationalen Germanisten-Kongresses* (Göttingen, 1985), vol. 5: *Judische Komponenten in der deutschen Literatur. Die Assimilationskontroverse*, pp. 171–5.

74 Stefan Zweig, *Jeremias. Eine dramatische Dichtung in sieben Bildern* (Leipzig, 1917).

75 Hofmannsthal/Beer-Hofmann, *Briefwechsel*, p. 145.

76 Richard Beer-Hofmann, *Der Graf von Charolais* (1905).

77 Hofmannsthal/Beer-Hofmann, *Briefwechsel*, pp. 148–9.

78 Adam Wandruszka and Peter Urbanitsch (eds), *Die Habsburgermonarchie, 1848–1918*, vol. 3: *Die Völker des Reiches*, part II (Vienna, 1980), p. 928.

79 *Juden im deutschen Kulturbereich. Ein Sammelwerk* (Jüdischer Verlag, Berlin, 3rd edn 1962); Moritz Goldstein, 'Deutsch-Jüdischer Parnass', in *Kunstwart* (1912).

80 Hermann Broch, *SzL*, p. 186. Cf. Ernst Simon, 'Hugo von Hofmannsthal: seine Jüdischen Freunde und seine Stellung zum Judentum', in *Mitteilungsblatt*, no. 38 (Tel Aviv, 14 Oct. 1977), pp. 3–5; Walter Grab, ' "Jüdischer Selbsthass" und jüdische Selbstachtung in der deutschen Literatur und Publizistik 1890–1933', in *Der deutsche Weg der Judenemanzipation, 1789–1938* (Munich/Zurich, 1991), pp. 156ff. Grab particularly notes Hofmannsthal's violently hostile reaction to an essay by his friend and admirer Willy Haas, intended for publication in an anthology called *Juden in der deutschen Literatur*, ed. Gustav Krojanker (Berlin, 1922).

81 Hofmannsthal, *RuA*, vol. 3, p. 41.

82 Gershom Scholem, 'Juden und Deutsche', in *Judaica II* (Frankfurt, 1970), pp. 20–46.

83 Hermann Bahr, *Tagebuch* (Vienna, 1920), pp. 120–1.

84 Robert Musil, *MWQ*, vol. 3, pp. 209–10; *MøE*, p. 844.

85   Arthur Schnitzler, *Briefe 1875–1912*, ed. Therese Nickl and Heinrich Schnitzler (Frankfurt, 1981), p. 380.

86   Martin Buber, 'Die Schaffenden, das Volk und die Bewegung' (1902), in *Die jüdische Bewegung* (Berlin, 1916), cf. Mark H. Gelber, 'The jungjüdische Bewegung. An Unexplored Chapter in German-Jewish Literary and Cultural History', in *Leo Baeck Institute Year Book* 31 (London, 1986), pp. 105–19.

87   Hans Kohn, *Martin Buber. Sein Werk und seine Zeit* (Cologne, 1961), pp. 36–7; Michael Löwy, 'Les Juifs religieux anarchisants', ch. 4 of *Redemption et utopie. Le judaïsme libertaire en Europe centrale* (Paris, 1988), on Buber, pp. 63–75.

88   Scholem, 'Juden und Deutsche', p. 106.

89   Nathan Birnbaum, *Die nationale Wiedergeburt des jüdischen Volkes in seinem Lande als Mittel zur Lösung der Judenfrage. Ein Appell an die Guten und Edlen aller Nationen* (Vienna, 1893); Mathias Acher (pseudonym of Nathan Birnbaum), *Die jüdische Moderne* (Leipzig/Vienna, 1905); reprint of the works of Nathan Birnbaum under the title *Die jüdische Moderne* (Augsburg, 1989). Cf. Joachim Doron, 'Jüdischer Nationalismus bei Nathan Birnbaum (1883–97)', in *Jüdische Integration und Identität in Deutschland und Österreich (1848–1918)*, ed. Walter Grab, Jahrbuch des Instituts für Deutsche Geschichte, Beiheft 6 (Tel Aviv, 1983), pp. 199–230; Robert S. Wistrich, 'The Clash of Ideologies in Jewish Vienna (1880–1918): The Strange Odyssey of Nathan Birnbaum', in *Leo Baeck Institute Year Book* 33 (1988), pp. 201–30.

90   Berthold Feiwel, 'Geleitwort', in *Jüdischer Almanach* (Berlin, 1902), p. 19.

91   Jacques Le Rider, 'Sionisme et antisémitisme: le piège des mots...', in *Karl Kraus et son temps*, ed. Gilbert Krebs and Gerald Stieg, Publications de l'Institut d'Allemand de la Sorbonne Nouvelle 10 (Paris, 1989), pp. 67–83; Mark H. Gelber, 'E. M. Lilien und die jüdische Renaissance', in *Leo Baeck Institute Year Book* 37 (1990), pp. 45–53.

92   Gelber, 'The jungjüdische Bewegung', p. 114.

93   Martin Buber, *Beiträge zur Geschichte des Individuationsproblems*, dissertation, University of Vienna, 1904.

94   Martin Buber, 'Ein Wort über Nietzsche und die Lebenswerte', *Die Kunst im Leben*, no. 2 (Dec. 1900), p. 13.

95   Martin Buber, *Das Problem des Menschen* (Hebrew 1943, in German 1947), in *Werke*, vol. 1; *Schriften zur Philosophie* (Munich/Heidelberg, 1962), p. 384.

96   Gershom Scholem, 'Martin Bubers Auffassung des Judentums', in *Judaica II*, p. 142.

97   Gustav Landauer, 'Martin Buber', *Neue Blätter* 3, special number on Buber (1913), p. 96; quoted in Scholem, 'Martin Bubers Auffassung'. Cf. Buber, 'Das Zion der judischen Frau', in *Die jüdische Bewegung, Erste Folge* (Berlin, 1920), p. 36: 'Jewish woman will heal the fundamental ill of the modern Jew – an excess of nervous life.'

98   Lou Andreas-Salomé, 'Jesus der Jude', *Neue Deutsche Rundschau*, no. 7 (1896), pp. 342–51.

99   Adolf Jellinek, *Studien und Skizzen. Der jüdische Stamm. Ethnographische Studie* (Vienna, 1869), pp. 89–90.

100   Buber, *Die jüdische Bewegung*, p. 42.

101   Paul Mendes-Flohr, 'L'orientalisme fin-de-siècle, les Ostjuden et l'esthétique de l'affirmation juive de soi', *Pardès*, no. 5 (1987), pp. 49–74.

102   Fritz Mauthner, quoted in Scholem, 'Juden und Deutsche', p. 162.

103   Dietmar Goltschnigg, *Mystische Tradition im Roman Robert Musils. Martin Bubers 'Ekstatische Konfessionen' im 'Mann ohne Eigenschaften'* (Heidelberg, 1974).

104   Beer-Hofmann, *GW*, p. 624; *TG*, p. 117.

Conclusion: The (Post)Modern Indeterminacy of Identity

1 Ludwig Wittgenstein, *Culture and Value* (Oxford, 1980), p. 27e.
2 Jacques Bouveresse, 'L'animal cérémoniel: Wittgenstein et l'anthropologie', afterword to Ludwig Wittgenstein, *Remarques sur le rameau d'or de Frazer* (Lausanne, 1982), pp. 67ff.
3 Wittgenstein, *Culture and Value*, p. 6e.
4 Gustav Janouch, *Conversations avec Kafka*, French trans. Bernard Lortholary (Paris, 1978), pp. 231–2.
5 On this point see Bouveresse, 'L'animal cérémoniel', pp. 42–50.
6 Wittgenstein, *Culture and Value*, p. 74e.
7 Cf. Willam W. Bartley III, *Wittgenstein, A Life* (Philadelphia, 1973).
8 Jacques Bouveresse, 'Les derniers jours de l'humanité', *Critique*, nos 339–40 (1975), special number on 'Vienne, debut d'un siècle', pp. 798–800.
9 Allan Janik, 'Wittgenstein and Weininger', in *Essays on Wittgenstein and Weininger* (Amsterdam, 1985); Jacques Le Rider, 'Wittgenstein et Weininger', in *Tradition et rupture. Wittgenstein et la critique du monde moderne* (Brussels, 1990), pp. 43–65.
10 Paul-Laurent Assoun, 'Wittgenstein séduit par Freud; Freud saisi par Wittgenstein', *Le temps de la Reflexion* no. 2 (1981), pp. 355–83; Jacques Bouveresse, 'Wittgenstein face à la psychanalyse', *Austriaca*, no. 21 (1985), pp. 49–62.
11 Bouveresse, 'L'animal cérémoniel', p. 73.
12 Paul Bourget, *Essais de psychologie contemporaine*, vol. 1 (1883; definitive enlarged edition, Paris, 1901), pp. 19–20.
13 Cf. Mazzino Montinari, 'Aufgaben der Nietzsche-Forschung heute: Nietzsches Auseinandersetzung mit der französischen Literatur des 19. Jahrhunderts', *Nietzsche-Studien*, no. 19 (1989), pp. 144ff.
14 Jean-Paul Bier, 'Moderne und Avantgarde aus postmodernistischer Sicht', in *Brochs theoretisches Werk*, ed. Paul Michael Lützeler and Michael Kessler (Frankfurt, 1988), pp. 69–81.
15 Hermann Broch, SzL, p. 176.
16 Ibid., p. 219.
17 Ibid., p. 219–20.
18 Hermann Bahr, *Prophet der Moderne. Tagebücher 1888–1904*, ed. Reinhard Farkas (Vienna, 1987), p. 45. Reinhard Farkas, *Hermann Bahr, Dynamik und Dilemma der Moderne* (Vienna, 1989), pp. 53–4, has shown that for Bahr modernity was actually a twofold movement of decadence (*Dekadenz, Verfall, Entartung*) and regeneration.
19 Carl E. Schorske, *Fin-de-Siècle Vienna: Politics and Culture* (London, 1979), pp. 9, 22.
20 Henri Meschonnic, *Modernité, modernité* (Lagrassse, Aude, 1988), p. 175.
21 E. M. Cioran, 'Sissi ou la vulnérabilité', in *Vienne 1880–1938. L'apocalypse joyeuse*, ed. Jean Clair, catalogue of an exhibition at the Pompidou Centre (Paris, 1986).
22 Jürgen Habermas, 'Theodor W. Adorno: The Primal History of Subjectivity', in *Philosophical-Political Profiles*, trans. F. Lawrence (London, 1983), pp. 99–109; Habermas, 'Ein philosophierender Intellektueller', in *Über Theodor W. Adorno* (Frankfurt, 1968), pp. 35–6; cf. Stefan Nienhaus, *Das Prosagedicht im Wien der Jahrhundertwende. Altenberg, Hofmannsthal, Polgar* (Berlin/New York, 1986), p. 208.

23   Moritz Csaky, 'La pluralité. Pour contribuer à une théorie de l'histoire aus-trienne', *Austriaca*, no. 33 (Dec. 1991), pp. 27–42.
24   Peter Altenberg, *Ausgewählte Werke in zwei Bänden*, ed. Dietrich Simon (Munich, 1979), vol. 1, p. 129.
25   Egon Friedell, *Ecce poeta* (Berlin, 1912), p. 11; on Altenberg's 'transformism' see Josephine M. N. Simpson, *Peter Altenberg: A Neglected Writer of the Viennese Jahrhundertwende* (Frankfurt, 1987), esp. ch. 5.5, 5.6.
26   Thomas Mann, in *Das Altenberg-Buch*, ed. Egon Friedell (Vienna/Leipzig, 1921), p. 75; 'Peter Altenberg', in Thomas Mann, *Autobiographisches*, see *Werke. Das essayistische Werk. Taschenausgabe in acht Bänden*, ed. Hans Bürgin (Frankfurt, 1968), pp. 48–51.
27   Lou Andreas-Salomé, *Lebensrückblick. Grundriss einiger Lebenserinnerungen*, ed. Ernst Pfeiffer, 5th edn (1974), p. 106; cf. Ursula Welsch and Michaela Wiesner, *Lou Andreas-Salomé. Vom 'Lebensurgrund' zur Psychoanalyse* (Munich/Vienna, 1988), p. 157.
28   Egon Friedell, 'Peter Altenberg. Zu seinem 50. Geburtstag. Am 8 März 1909', in *Abschaffung des Genies. Essays bis 1918*, ed. Heribert Illig (Vienna/Munich, 1982), p. 61.
29   Peter Altenberg had converted to Catholicism in 1900 and made no secret of his anti-Zionist opinions.
30   Peter Altenberg, *Pròdrŏmŏs* (Berlin, 1906; 3rd edn, 1912), p. 81.
31   Robert Musil, *MoE*, p. 379.
32   Hermann Broch, 'Nachruf auf Robert Musil', in *SzL*, pp. 98–9.
33   Robert Musil, *GW2*, p. 1462; cf. Marie-Louise Roth, 'Robert Musil zum Prob-lem der Ethik', in *Gedanken und Dichtung. Essays zu Robert Musil* (Sarrebruck, 1987).
34   Friedrich Nietzsche, *CW*, vol. 7, P. 7; *KSA*, vol. 2, p. 18.
35   Ibid., vol. 10, p. 248; vol. 3, p. 551.
36   Musil, *MoE*, part 1. ch. 61, p. 246; *MWQ*, vol. 1, p. 292; cf. Charlotte Dresler-Brumme, *Nietzsches Philosophie in Musils Roman 'Der Mann ohne Eigenschaften'. Eine vergleichende Betrachtung als Beitrag zum Verständnis* (Frankfurt, 1987), pp. 57ff.; Aldo Venturelli, 'Zum Verhältnis Musils zu Nietzsche', in *Robert Musil und das Projekt der Moderne* (Frankfurt, 1988), pp. 27–82; Daniel J. Brooks, 'Aesthetic Nietzscheanism in *MoE*', *Musil-Forum* 15 (1989), pp. 94–112; Jacques Le Rider, 'Musil et Nietzsche', *Europe*, no. 741–2 (1991), pp. 45–9.
37   Niklas Luhmann, 'The Individuality of the Individual: Historical Meanings and Contemporary Problems', in *Reconstructing Individualism: Autonomy, Individuality, and the Self in Western Thought*, ed. Thomas C. Heller, Morton Sosna and David E. Wellbery (Stanford, 1986), pp. 21–2.
38   Nietzsche, *CW*, vol. 16. p. 43; *KSA*, vol. 6, p. 96.
39   Sigmund Freud, *SE*, vol. 19, p. 178; *GW*, vol. 13, p. 400.

Select Bibliography of Works in English

Compiled by Ritchie Robertson

Major Authors

Broch, Hermann, *Hofmannsthal and his Age*, trans. Michael Steinberg (Chicago: University of Chicago Press, 1984).

Freud, Sigmund, *The Pelican Freud Library*, ed. Angela Richards and Albert Dickson (15 vols, Harmondsworth: Penguin, 1974–86).

Freud, Sigmund, *The Standard Edition of the Complete Psychological Works of Sigmund Freud*, ed. and trans. James Strachey and others (London: Hogarth Press, 1953–74).

Herzl, Theodor, *The Complete Diaries of Theodor Herzl*, ed. Raphael Patai, trans. Harry Zohn (5 vols, New York: Yoseloff, 1960).

Herzl, Theodor, *The Jewish State*, trans. Harry Zohn (New York: Herzl Press, 1970).

Hofmannsthal, Hugo von, *Selected Writings*, trans. Mary Hottinger, Tania Stern, James Stern, Michael Hamburger and others (3 vols, London: Routledge and Kegan Paul, 1952–63).

Kraus, Karl, *In These Great Times: A Karl Kraus Reader*, ed. Harry Zohn, trans. Joseph Fabry and others (Manchester: Carcanet, 1984).

Musil, Robert, *The Man Without Qualities*, trans. Eithne Wilkins and Ernst Kaiser (3 vols, London: Secker and Warburg, 1953–60).

Musil, Robert, *Precision and Soul: Essays and Addresses*, ed. and trans. Burton Pike and David S. Luft (Chicago: University of Chicago Press, 1990).

Musil, Robert, *Young Törless*, trans. Eithne Wilkins and Ernst Kaiser (London: Secker and Warburg, 1955).

Schnitzler, Arthur, *My Youth in Vienna*, trans. Catherine Hutter (London: Weidenfeld and Nicolson, 1971).

Schnitzler, Arthur, *The Road to the Open*, trans. Horace Samuel (London: Howard Latimer, 1913).

Schnitzler, Arthur, *Vienna 1900: Games with Love and Death* (Harmondsworth: Penguin, 1973).

Weininger, Otto, *Sex and Character* (London: Heinemann, 1906).

Studies and Biographies

Anderson, Mark, *Kafka's Clothes: Ornament and Aestheticism in the Habsburg Fin de Siècle* (Oxford: Clarendon Press, 1992).

Beller, Steven, *Herzl* (London: Halban, 1991).

Daviau, Donald G., *Hermann Bahr* (Boston: Twayne, 1985).

Elstun, Esther N., *Richard Beer-Hofmann: His Life and Work* (Philadelphia and London: Pennsylvania State University Press, 1983).

Gay, Peter, *Freud: A Life for Our Time* (London: Dent, 1988).

Jones, Ernest, *The Life and Work of Sigmund Freud* (3 vols, London: Hogarth Press, 1953–7).

Jungk, Peter Stephan, *A Life Torn by History: Franz Werfel, 1890–1945* (London: Weidenfeld and Nicolson, 1990).

Luft, David S., *Robert Musil and the Crisis of European Culture, 1880–1942* (Berkeley: University of California Press, 1980).

Lützeler, Paul Michael, *Hermann Broch: A Biography*, trans. Janice Furness (London: Quartet, 1987).

Swales, Martin, *Arthur Schnitzler: A Critical Study* (Oxford: Clarendon Press, 1971).

Thompson, Bruce, *Schnitzler's Vienna: Image of a Society* (London: Routledge, 1990).

Timms, Edward, *Karl Kraus, Apocalyptic Satirist: Culture and Catastrophe in Habsburg Vienna* (New Haven and London: Yale University Press, 1986).

Yates, W. E., *Schnitzler, Hofmannsthal, and the Austrian Theatre* (New Haven and London: Yale University Press, 1992).

General Studies

Anderson, Harriet, *Utopian Feminism: Women's Movements in Fin-de-Siècle Vienna* (New Haven and London: Yale University Press, 1992).

Beller, Steven, *Vienna and the Jews, 1867–1938: A Cultural History* (Cambridge: Cambridge University Press, 1989).

Janik, Allan, and Stephen Toulmin, *Wittgenstein's Vienna* (New York: Simon and Schuster, 1973).

Jelavich, Barbara, *Modern Austria: Empire and Republic, 1815–1986* (Cambridge: Cambridge University Press, 1987).

Johnston, William M., *The Austrian Mind: An Intellectual and Social History* (Berkeley: University of California Press, 1972).

Olsen, Donald J., *The City as a Work of Art: London, Paris, Vienna* (New Haven and London: Yale University Press, 1986).

Pulzer, Peter, *The Rise of Political Anti-Semitism in Germany and Austria*, 2nd edn (London: Halban, 1988).

Rozenblit, Marsha L., *The Jews of Vienna, 1867–1914: Assimilation and Identity* (Albany: State University of New York Press, 1983).

Schorske, Carl L., *Fin-de-Siècle Vienna: Politics and Culture* (Cambridge: Cambridge University Press, 1981).

Wistrich, Robert S., *The Jews of Vienna in the Age of Franz Joseph* (Oxford: Oxford University Press, 1989).

Wistrich, Robert S. (ed.), *Jews and Austrians in the Twentieth Century* (London: Macmillan, 1992).

Index

Index by Mary Madden